THE
LAW OF
SUCCESS

JEREMY P. TARCHER/PENGUIN

a member of

Penguin Group (USA) Inc.

New York

THE
LAW OF
SUCCESS

NAPOLEON HILL

JEREMY P. TARCHER/PENGUIN
Published by the Penguin Group
Penguin Group (USA) Inc., 375 Hudson Street, New York, New York 10014, USA • Penguin Group (Canada), 90 Eglinton Avenue East,
Suite 700, Toronto, Ontario M4P 2Y3, Canada (a division of Pearson Canada Inc.) • Penguin Books Ltd, 80 Strand, London WC2R 0RL,
England • Penguin Ireland, 25 St Stephen's Green, Dublin 2, Ireland (a division of Penguin Books Ltd) • Penguin Group (Australia),
250 Camberwell Road, Camberwell, Victoria 3124, Australia (a division of Pearson Australia Group Pty Ltd) • Penguin Books India Pvt Ltd,
11 Community Centre, Panchsheel Park, New Delhi–110 017, India • Penguin Group (NZ), 67 Apollo Drive,
Rosedale, North Shore 0632, New Zealand (a division of Pearson New Zealand Ltd) • Penguin Books (South Africa) (Pty) Ltd,
24 Sturdee Avenue, Rosebank, Johannesburg 2196, South Africa

Penguin Books Ltd, Registered Offices: 80 Strand, London WC2R 0RL, England

Most Tarcher/Penguin books are available at special quantity discounts for bulk purchase for sales promotions, premiums, fund-raising, and
educational needs. Special books or book excerpts also can be created to fit specific needs. For details, write Penguin Group (USA) Inc.
Special Markets, 375 Hudson Street, New York, NY 10014.

Library of Congress Cataloging-in-Publication Data

Hill, Napoleon, 1883–1970.
The law of success / Napoleon Hill.
p.   cm.
"Napoleon Hill's *The Law of Success* was originally published as an eight-volume set in 1928."
Includes index.
ISBN 978-1-58542-689-8
1. Success in business.   2. Success.   3. Motivation (Psychology).   I. Title.
HF5386.H55   2008   2008042052
650.1—dc22

Printed in the United States of America
13 15 17 19 20 18 16 14

PUBLISHER'S NOTE
Napoleon Hill's *The Law of Success* was originally published as an eight-volume set in 1928. Other than minor adjustments made for clarity or to
meet contemporary typography standards, the publisher has retained the original spellings, usage, and style of the author. The book sometimes
features an antiquated reference or word choice. For purposes of historical accuracy, the publisher has largely left these intact.

Dedicated to

ANDREW CARNEGIE

who suggested the writing of the
course, and to

HENRY FORD

whose astounding achievements
form the foundation for practically
all of the lessons of the course,
and to

EDWIN C. BARNES

a business associate of Thomas A.
Edison, whose close personal friendship over a period of more than fifteen years served to help the author
"carry on" in the face of a great
variety of adversities and much temporary defeat met with in organizing
the course.

Who said it could not be done?
And what great victories has he
to his credit which qualify him to
judge others accurately?

—NAPOLEON HILL

CONTENTS

A PERSONAL STATEMENT
BY THE AUTHOR

Some thirty years ago a young clergyman by the name of Gunsaulus announced in the newspapers of Chicago that he would preach a sermon the following Sunday morning entitled:

"WHAT I WOULD DO IF I HAD A MILLION DOLLARS!"

The announcement caught the eye of Philip D. Armour, the wealthy packing-house king, who decided to hear the sermon.

In his sermon Dr. Gunsaulus pictured a great school of technology where young men and young women could be taught how to succeed in life by developing the ability to THINK in practical rather than in theoretical terms; where they would be taught to "learn by doing." "If I had a million dollars," said the young preacher, "I would start such a school."

After the sermon was over Mr. Armour walked down the aisle to the pulpit, introduced himself, and said, "Young man, I believe you could do all you said you could, and if you will come down to my office tomorrow morning I will give you the million dollars you need."

There is always plenty of capital for those who can create practical plans for using it.

That was the beginning of the Armour Institute of Technology, one of the very practical schools of the country. The school was born in the "imagination" of a young man who never would have been heard of outside of the community in which he preached had it not been for the "imagination," plus the capital, of Philip D. Armour.

Every great railroad, and every outstanding financial institution and every mammoth business enterprise, and every great invention, began in the imagination of some one person.

F. W. Woolworth created the Five and Ten Cent Store Plan in his "imagination" before it became a reality and made him a multimillionaire.

Thomas A. Edison created the talking machine and the moving picture machine and the incandescent electric light bulb and scores of other useful inventions, in his own "imagination," before they became a reality.

During the Chicago fire scores of merchants whose stores went up in smoke stood near the smoldering embers of their former places of business, grieving over their loss. Many of them decided to go away into other cities and start over again. In the group was Marshall Field, who saw, in his own "imagination," the world's greatest retail store, standing on the selfsame spot where his former store had stood, which was then but a ruined mass of smoking timbers. That store became a reality.

Fortunate is the young man or young woman who learns, early in life, to use imagination, and doubly so in this age of greater opportunity.

Imagination is a faculty of the mind which can be cultivated, developed, extended and broadened by use. If this were not true, this course on the Fifteen Laws of Success never would have been created, because it was first conceived in the author's "imagination," from the mere seed of an idea which was sown by a chance remark of the late Andrew Carnegie.

Wherever you are, whoever you are, whatever you may be following as an occupation, there is room for you to make yourself more useful, and in that manner more productive, by developing and using your "imagination."

Success in this world is always a matter of individual effort, yet you will only be deceiving yourself if you believe that you can succeed without the co-operation of other people. Success is a matter of individual effort only to the extent that each person must decide, in his or her own mind, what is wanted. This involves the use of "imagination." From this point on, achieving success is a matter of skillfully and tactfully inducing others to co-operate.

Before you can secure co-operation from others; nay, before you have the right to ask for or expect co-operation from other people, you must first show a willingness to co-operate with them. For this reason the eighth lesson of this course, THE HABIT OF DOING MORE THAN PAID FOR, is one which should have your serious and thoughtful attention. The law upon which this lesson is based, would, of itself, practically insure success to all who practice it in all they do.

In the back pages of this Introduction you will observe a Personal Analysis Chart in which ten well known men have been analyzed for your study and comparison. Observe this chart carefully and note the "danger points" which mean failure to those who do not observe these signals. Of the ten men analyzed eight are known to be successful, while two may be considered failures. Study, carefully, the reason why these two men failed.

Then, study yourself. In the two columns which have been left blank for that purpose, give yourself a rating on each of the Fifteen Laws of Success at the beginning of this course; at the end of the course rate yourself again and observe the improvements you have made.

The purpose of the Law of Success course is to enable you to find out how you may become more capable in your chosen field of work. To this end you will be analyzed and all of your qualities classified so you may organize them and make the best possible use of them.

You may not like the work in which you are now engaged.

There are two ways of getting out of that work. One way is to take but little interest in what you are doing, aiming merely to do enough with which to "get by." Very soon you will find a way out, because the demand for your services will cease.

The other and better way is by making yourself so useful and efficient in what you are now doing that you will attract the favorable attention of those who have the power to promote you into more responsible work that is more to your liking.

It is your privilege to take your choice as to which way you will proceed.

Again you are reminded of the importance of Lesson Nine of this course, through the aid of which you may avail yourself of this "better way" of promoting yourself.

Thousands of people walked over the great Calumet Copper Mine without discovering it. Just one lone man used his "imagination," dug down into the earth a few feet, investigated, and discovered the richest copper deposit on earth.

You and every other person walk, at one time or another, over your "Calumet Mine." Discovery is a matter of investigation and use of "imagination." This course on the Fifteen Laws of Success may lead the way to your "Calumet," and you may be surprised when you discover that you were standing right over this rich mine, in the work in which you are now engaged. In his lecture on "Acres of Diamonds," Russell Conwell tells us that we need not seek opportunity in the distance; that we may find it right where we stand! THIS IS A TRUTH WELL WORTH REMEMBERING!

—NAPOLEON HILL

THE AUTHOR'S ACKNOWLEDGMENT OF HELP RENDERED HIM IN THE WRITING OF THIS COURSE

This course is the result of careful analysis of the life-work of over one hundred men and women who have achieved unusual success in their respective callings.

The author of the course has been more than twenty years in gathering, classifying, testing and organizing the Fifteen Laws upon which the course is based. In his labor he has received valuable assistance either in person or by studying the life-work of the following men:

Henry Ford

Thomas A. Edison

Harvey S. Firestone

John D. Rockefeller

Charles M. Schwab

Woodrow Wilson

Darwin P. Kingsley

Wm. Wrigley, Jr.

A. D. Lasker

E. A. Filene

James J. Hill

Captain George M. Alexander
   (To whom the author was
   formerly an assistant)

Hugh Chalmers

Dr. E. W. Strickler

Edwin C. Barnes

Robert L. Taylor (Fiddling Bob)

George Eastman

Edward Bok

Cyrus H. K. Curtis

George W. Perkins

Henry L. Doherty

George S. Parker

Dr. C. O. Henry

General Rufus A. Ayers

Judge Elbert H. Gary

William Howard Taft

Dr. Elmer Gates

John W. Davis

Samuel Insul

F. W. Woolworth

Judge Daniel T. Wright
   (One of the author's
   law instructors)

Elbert Hubbard

Luther Burbank

O. H. Harriman

John Burroughs

E. H. Harriman

Acknowledgment

E. M. Statler

Andrew Carnegie

John Wanamaker

Marshall Field

Charles P. Steinmetz

Frank Vanderlip

Theodore Roosevelt

Wm. H. French

Dr. Alexander Graham Bell (To whom the author owes credit for most of the Introduction)

Of the men named, perhaps Henry Ford and Andrew Carnegie should be acknowledged as having contributed most toward the building of this course, for the reason that it was Andrew Carnegie who first suggested the writing of the course and Henry Ford whose life-work supplied much of the material out of which the course was developed.

Some of these men are now deceased, but to those who are still living the author wishes to make here grateful acknowledgment of the service they have rendered, without which this course never could have been written.

The author has studied the majority of these men at close range, in person. With many of them he enjoys, or did enjoy before their death, the privilege of close personal friendship which enabled him to gather from their philosophy facts that would not have been available under other conditions.

The author is grateful for having enjoyed the privilege of enlisting the services of the most powerful men on earth, in the building of the Law of Success course. That privilege has been remuneration enough for the work done, if nothing more were ever received for it.

These men have been the back-bone and the foundation and the skeleton of American business, finance, industry and statesmanship.

The Law of Success course epitomizes the philosophy and the rules of procedure which made each of these men a great power in his chosen field of endeavor. It has been the author's intention to present the course in the plainest and most simple terms available, so it could be mastered by very young men and young women, of the high-school age.

With the exception of the psychological law referred to in the Introduction as the "Master Mind," the author lays no claim to having created anything basically new in this course. What he has done, however, has been to organize old truths and known laws into PRACTICAL, USABLE FORM, where they may be properly interpreted and applied by the workaday man whose needs call for a philosophy of simplicity.

In passing upon the merits of the Law of Success Judge Elbert H. Gary said: "Two outstanding features connected with the philosophy impress me most. One is the simplicity with which it has been presented, and the other is the fact that its soundness is so obvious to all that it will be immediately accepted."

The student of this course is warned against passing judgment upon it before having read the entire fifteen lessons. This especially applies to this Introduction, in which it has been necessary to include brief reference to subjects of a more or less technical and scientific nature. The reason for this will be obvious after the student has read the entire fifteen lessons.

The student who takes up this course with an open mind, and sees to it that his or her mind remains "open" until the last lesson shall have been read, will be richly rewarded with a broader and more accurate view of life as a whole.

CONTENTS OF INTRODUCTION: THE MASTER MIND

INTRODUCTION

THE MASTER MIND

"You Can Do It If You Believe You Can!"

This is a course on the fundamentals of Success.

Success is very largely a matter of adjusting one's self to the ever-varying and changing environments of life, in a spirit of harmony and poise. Harmony is based upon understanding of the forces constituting one's environment; therefore, this course is in reality a blueprint that may be followed straight to success, because it helps the student to interpret, understand and make the most of these environmental forces of life.

Before you begin reading the Law of Success lessons you should know something of the history of the course. You should know exactly what the course promises to those who follow it until they have assimilated the laws and principles upon which it is based. You should know its limitations as well as its possibilities as an aid in your fight for a place in the world.

From the viewpoint of entertainment the Law of Success course would be a poor second for most any of the monthly periodicals of the "Snappy Story" variety which may be found upon the news stands of today.

The course has been created for the serious-minded person who devotes at least a portion of his or her time to the business of succeeding in life. The author of the Law of Success course has not intended to compete with those who write purely for the purpose of entertaining.

The author's aim, in preparing this course, has been of a two-fold nature, namely, first—to help the earnest student find out what are his or her weaknesses, and, secondly—to help create a DEFINITE PLAN for bridging those weaknesses.

The most successful men and women on earth have had to correct certain weak spots in their personalities before they began to succeed. The most outstanding of these weaknesses which stand between men and women and success are INTOLERANCE, CUPIDITY, GREED, JEALOUSY, SUSPICION, REVENGE, EGOTISM, CONCEIT, THE TENDENCY TO REAP WHERE THEY HAVE NOT SOWN, and the HABIT OF SPENDING MORE THAN THEY EARN.

All of these common enemies of mankind, and many more not here mentioned, are covered by the Law of Success course in such a manner that any person of reasonable intelligence may master them with but little effort or inconvenience.

You should know, at the very outset, that the Law of Success course has long since passed through the experimental state; that it already has to its credit a record of achievement that is worthy of serious thought and analysis. You should know, also, that the Law of Success course has been examined and endorsed by some of the most practical minds of this generation.

The Law of Success course was first used as a lecture, and was delivered by its author in practically every city and in many of the smaller localities, throughout the United States, over a period of more than seven years. Perhaps you were one of the many hundreds of thousands of people who heard this lecture.

During these lectures the author had assistants located in the audiences for the purpose of interpreting the reaction of those who heard the lecture, and in this manner he learned exactly what effect it had upon people. As a result of this study and analysis many changes were made.

The first big victory was gained for the Law of Success philosophy when it was used by the author as the basis of a course with which 3,000 men and women were trained as a sales army. The majority of these people were without previous experience, of any sort, in the field of selling. Through this training they were enabled to earn more than One Million Dollars ($1,000,000.00) for themselves and paid the author $30,000.00 for his services, covering a period of approximately six months.

The individuals and small groups of salespeople who have found success through the aid of this course are too numerous to be mentioned in this Introduction, but the number is large and the benefits they derived from the course were definite.

The Law of Success philosophy was brought to the attention of the late Don R. Mellett, former publisher of the Canton (Ohio) *Daily News,* who formed a partnership with the author of the course and was preparing to resign as publisher of the Canton *Daily News* and take up the business management of the author's affairs when he was assassinated on July 16, 1926.

Prior to his death Mr. Mellett had made arrangements with Judge Elbert H. Gary, who was then Chairman of the Board of the United States Steel Corporation, to present the Law of Success course to every employee of the Steel Corporation, at a total cost of something like $150,000.00. This plan was halted because of Judge Gary's death, but it proves that the author of the Law of Success has produced an educational plan of an enduring nature. Judge Gary was eminently prepared to judge the value of such a course, and the fact that he analyzed the Law of Success philosophy and was preparing to invest the huge sum of $150,000.00 in it is proof of the soundness of all that is said in behalf of the course.

You will observe, in this General Introduction to the course, a few technical terms which may not be plain to you. Do not allow this to bother you. Make no attempt at first reading to understand these terms. They will be plain to you after you read the remainder of the course. This entire Introduction is intended only as a background for the other fourteen lessons of the course, and you should read it as such. You will not be examined on this Introduction, but you should read it many times, as you will get from it at each reading a thought or an idea which you did not get on previous readings.

In this Introduction you will find a description of a newly discovered law of psychology which is the very foundation stone of all outstanding personal achievements. This law has been referred to by the author as the "Master Mind," meaning a mind that is developed through the harmonious co-operation of two or more people who ally themselves for the purpose of accomplishing any given task.

If you are engaged in the business of selling you may profitably experiment with this law of the "Master Mind" in your daily work. It has been found that a group of six or seven salespeople may use the law so effectively that their sales may be increased to unbelievable proportions.

Life Insurance is supposed to be the hardest thing on earth to sell. This ought not to be true, with an established necessity such as life insurance, but it is. Despite this fact, a small group of men working for the Prudential Life Insurance Company, whose sales are mostly small policies, formed a little friendly group for the purpose of experimenting with the law of the "Master Mind," with the result that every man in the group wrote more insurance during the first three months of the experiment than he had ever written in an entire year before.

What may be accomplished through the aid of this principle, by any small group of intelligent life-insurance salesmen who have learned how to apply the law of the "Master Mind" will stagger the imagination of the most highly optimistic and imaginative person.

No man has a chance to enjoy permanent success until he begins to look in a mirror for the real cause of all his mistakes
—NAPOLEON HILL

The same may be said of other groups of salespeople who are engaged in selling merchandise and other more tangible forms of service than life insurance. Bear this in mind as you read this Introduction to the Law of Success course and it is not unreasonable to expect that this Introduction, alone, may give you sufficient understanding of the law to change the entire course of your life.

It is the personalities back of a business which determine the measure of success the business will enjoy. Modify those personalities so they are more pleasing and more attractive to the patrons of the business and the business will thrive. In any of the great cities of the United States one may purchase merchandise of similar nature and price in scores of stores, yet you will find there is always one outstanding store which does more business than any of the others, and the reason for this is that back of that store is a man, or men, who has attended to the personalities of those who come in contact with the public. People buy personalities as much as merchandise, and it is a question if they are not influenced more by the personalities with which they come in contact than they are by the merchandise.

Life insurance has been reduced to such a scientific basis that the cost of insurance does not vary to any great extent, regardless of the company from which one purchases it, yet out of the hundreds of life insurance companies doing business less than a dozen companies do the bulk of the business of the United States.

Why? Personalities! Ninety-nine people out of every hundred who purchase life insurance policies do not know what is in their policies and, what seems more startling, do not seem to care. What they really purchase is the pleasing personality of some man or woman who knows the value of cultivating such a personality.

Your business in life, or at least the most important part of it, is to achieve success. Success, within the meaning of that term as covered by this course on the Fifteen Laws of Success, is "the attainment of your Definite Chief Aim without violating the rights of other people." Regardless of what your major aim in life may be, you will attain it with much less difficulty after you learn how to cultivate a pleasing personality and after you have learned the delicate art of allying yourself with others in a given undertaking without friction or envy.

One of the greatest problems of life, if not, in fact, the greatest, is that of learning the art of harmonious negotiation with others. This course was created for the purpose of teaching people how to negotiate their way through life with harmony and poise, free from the destructive effects of disagreement and friction which bring millions of people to misery, want and failure every year.

With this statement of the purpose of the course you should be able to approach the lessons with the feeling that a complete transformation is about to take place in your personality.

You cannot enjoy outstanding success in life without power, and *you can never enjoy power without sufficient personality to influence other people to co-operate with you in a spirit of harmony.* This course shows you step by step how to develop such a personality.

Lesson by lesson, the following is a statement of that which you may expect to receive from the Fifteen Laws of Success:

I. A DEFINITE CHIEF AIM will teach you how to save the wasted effort which the majority of people expend in trying to find their life-work. This lesson will show you how to do away forever with aimlessness and fix your heart and hand upon some definite, well conceived purpose as a life-work.

II. SELF-CONFIDENCE will help you master the six basic fears with which every person is cursed—the fear of Poverty, the fear of Ill Health, the fear of Old Age, the fear of Criticism, the fear of Loss of Love of Someone and the fear of Death. It will teach you the difference between egotism and real self-confidence which is based upon definite, usable knowledge.

III. THE HABIT OF SAVING will teach you how to distribute your income systematically so that a definite percentage of it will steadily accumulate, thus forming one of the greatest known sources of personal power. No one may succeed in life without saving money. There is no exception to this rule, and no one may escape it.

IV. INITIATIVE AND LEADERSHIP will show you how to become a leader instead of a follower in your chosen field of endeavor. It will develop in you the instinct for leadership which will cause you gradually to gravitate to the top in all undertakings in which you participate.

V. IMAGINATION will stimulate your mind so that you will conceive new ideas and develop new plans which will help you in attaining the object of your Definite Chief Aim. This lesson will teach you how to "build new houses out of old stones," so to speak. It will show you how to create new ideas out of old, well known concepts, and how to put old ideas to *new uses.* This one lesson, alone, is the equivalent of a very practical course in salesmanship, and it is sure to prove a veritable gold mine of knowledge to the person who is in earnest.

VI. ENTHUSIASM will enable you to "saturate" all with whom you come in contact with interest in you and in your ideas. Enthusiasm is the foundation of a Pleasing Personality, and you must have such a personality in order to influence others to co-operate with you.

VII. SELF-CONTROL is the "balance wheel" with which you control your enthusiasm and direct it where you wish it to carry you. This lesson will teach you, in a most practical manner, to become "the master of your fate, the Captain of your Soul."

VIII. THE HABIT OF DOING MORE THAN PAID FOR is one of the most important lessons of the Law of Success course. It will teach you how to take advantage of the Law of Increasing Returns, which will eventually insure you a return in money far out of proportion to the service you render. No one may become a real leader in any walk of life without practicing the habit of doing more work and better work than that for which he is paid.

IX. PLEASING PERSONALITY is the "fulcrum" on which you must place the "crow-bar" of your efforts, and when so placed, with intelligence, it will enable you to remove mountains of obstacles. This one lesson, alone, has made scores of Master Salesmen. It has developed leaders over night. It will teach you how to transform your personality so that you may adapt yourself to any environment, or to any other personality, in such a manner that you may easily dominate.

X. ACCURATE THOUGHT is one of the important foundation stones of all enduring success. This lesson teaches you how to separate "facts" from mere "information." It teaches you how to organize known facts into two classes: the "important" and the "unimportant." It teaches you how to determine what is an "important" fact. It teaches you how to build definite working plans, in the pursuit of any calling, out of FACTS.

XI. CONCENTRATION teaches you how to focus your attention upon one subject at a time until you have worked out practical plans for mastering that subject. It will teach you how to ally yourself with others in such a manner that you may have the use of their entire knowledge to back you up in your own plans and purposes. It will give you a practical working knowledge of the forces around you, and show you how to harness and use these forces in furthering your own interests.

If you must slander someone don't speak it—but write it—write it in the sand, near the water's edge!

—NAPOLEON HILL

XII. CO-OPERATION will teach you the value of team-work in all you do. In this lesson you will be taught how to apply the law of the "Master Mind" described in this Introduction and in Lesson One of this course. This lesson will show you how to co-ordinate your own efforts with those of others, in such a manner that friction, jealousy, strife, envy and cupidity will be eliminated. You will learn how to make use of all that other people have learned about the work in which you are engaged.

XIII. Profiting by FAILURE will teach you how to make stepping stones out of all of your past and future mistakes and failures. It will teach you the difference between "failure" and "temporary defeat," a difference which is very great and very important. It will teach you how to profit by your own failures and by the failures of other people.

XIV. TOLERANCE will teach you how to avoid the disastrous effects of racial and religious prejudices which mean defeat for millions of people who permit themselves to become entangled in foolish argument over these subjects, thereby poisoning their own minds and closing the door to reason and investigation. This lesson is the twin sister of the one on ACCURATE THOUGHT, for the reason that no one may become an Accurate Thinker without practicing tolerance. Intolerance closes the book of Knowledge and writes on the cover, "Finis! I have learned it all!" Intolerance makes enemies of those who should be friends. It destroys opportunity and fills the mind with doubt, mistrust and prejudice.

XV. Practicing THE GOLDEN RULE will teach you how to make use of this great universal law of human conduct in such a manner that you may easily get harmonious co-operation from any individual or group of individuals. Lack of understanding of the law upon which the Golden Rule philosophy is based is one of the major causes of failure of millions of people who remain in misery, poverty and want all their lives. This lesson has nothing whatsoever to do with religion in any form, nor with sectarianism, nor have any of the other lessons of this course on the Law of Success.

When you have mastered these Fifteen Laws and made them your own, as you may do within a period of from fifteen to thirty weeks, you will be ready to develop sufficient personal power to insure the attainment of your Definite Chief Aim.

The purpose of these Fifteen Laws is to develop or help you organize all the knowledge you have, and all you acquire in the future, so you may turn this knowledge into POWER.

You should read the Law of Success course with a note-book by your side, for you will observe that ideas will begin to "flash" into your mind as you read, as to ways and means of using these laws in advancing your own interests.

You should also begin teaching these laws to those in whom you are most interested, as it is a well known fact that the more one tries to teach a subject the more he learns about that subject. A man who has a family of young boys and girls may so indelibly fix these Fifteen

Laws of Success in their minds that this teaching will change the entire course of their lives. The man with a family should interest his wife in studying this course with him, for reasons which will be plain before you complete reading this Introduction.

POWER is one of the three basic objects of human endeavor.

POWER is of two classes—that which is developed through co-ordination of natural physical laws, and that which is developed by organizing and classifying KNOWLEDGE.

POWER growing out of organized knowledge is the more important because it places in man's possession a tool with which he may transform, redirect and to some extent harness and use the other form of power.

The object of this reading course is to mark the route by which the student may safely travel in gathering such facts as he may wish to weave into his fabric of KNOWLEDGE.

There are two major methods of gathering knowledge, namely, by studying, classifying and assimilating facts which have been organized by other people, and through one's own process of gathering, organizing and classifying facts, generally called "personal experience."

This lesson deals mainly with the ways and means of studying the facts and data gathered and classified by other people.

The state of advancement known as "civilization" is but the measure of knowledge which the race has accumulated. This knowledge is of two classes—mental and physical.

Among the useful knowledge organized by man, he has discovered and catalogued the eighty-odd physical elements of which all material forms in the universe consist.

By study and analysis and accurate measurements man has discovered the "bigness" of the material side of the universe as represented by planets, suns and stars, some of which are known to be over ten million times as large as the little earth on which he lives.

On the other hand, man has discovered the "littleness" of the physical forms which constitute the universe by reducing the eighty-odd physical elements to molecules, atoms, and, finally, to the smallest particle, the electron. An electron cannot be seen; it is but a center of force consisting of a positive or a negative. The electron is the beginning of everything of a physical nature.

Molecules, Atoms and Electrons: To understand both the detail and the perspective of the process through which knowledge is gathered, organized and classified, it seems essential for the student to begin with the smallest and simplest particles of physical matter, because these are the ABC's with which Nature has constructed the entire frame-work of the physical portion of the universe.

The molecule consists of atoms, which are said to be little invisible particles of matter revolving continuously with the speed of lightning, on exactly the same principle that the earth revolves around the sun.

These little particles of matter known as atoms, which revolve in one continuous circuit, in the molecule, are said to be made up of electrons, the smallest particles of physical matter. As already stated, the electron is nothing but two forms of force. The electron is uniform, of but one class, size and nature; thus in a grain of sand or a drop of water the entire principle upon which the whole universe operates is duplicated.

How marvelous! How stupendous! You may gather some slight idea of the magnitude of it all the next time you eat a meal, by remembering that every article of food you eat, the plate on which you eat it, the tableware and the table itself are, in final analysis, but a collection of ELECTRONS.

In the world of physical matter, whether one is looking at the largest star that floats through the heavens or the smallest grain of sand to be found on earth, the object under observation is but an organized collection of molecules, atoms and electrons revolving around one another at inconceivable speed.

Every particle of physical matter is in a continuous state of highly agitated motion. Nothing is ever still, although nearly all physical matter may appear, to the physical eye, to be motionless. There is no "solid" physical matter. The hardest piece of steel is but an organized mass of revolving molecules, atoms and electrons. Moreover, the electrons in a piece of steel are of the same nature, and move at the same rate of speed as the electrons in gold, silver, brass or pewter.

The eighty-odd forms of physical matter appear to be different from one another, and they are different, because they are made up of different combinations of atoms (although the electrons in these atoms are always the same, except that some electrons are positive and some are negative, meaning that some carry a positive charge of electrification while others carry a negative charge).

Through the science of chemistry, matter may be broken up into atoms which are, within themselves, unchangeable. The eighty-odd elements are created through and by reason of combining and changing of

Don't be afraid of a little opposition. Remember that the "Kite" of Success generally rises AGAINST the wind of Adversity—not with it!

the positions of the atoms. To illustrate the modus operandi of chemistry through which this change of atomic position is wrought, in terms of modern science:

"Add four electrons (two positive and two negative) to the hydrogen atom, and you have the element lithium; knock out of the lithium atom (composed of three positive and three negative electrons) one positive and one negative electron, and you have one atom of helium (composed of two positive and two negative electrons)."

Thus it may be seen that the eighty-odd physical elements of the universe differ from one another only in the number of electrons composing their atoms, and the number and arrangement of those atoms in the molecules of each element.

As an illustration, an atom of mercury contains eighty positive charges (electrons) in its nucleus, and eighty negative outlying charges (electrons). If the chemist were to expel two of its positive electrons it would instantly become the metal known as platinum. If the chemist could then go a step further and take from it a negative ("planetary") electron, the mercury atom would then have lost two positive electrons and one negative; that is, one positive charge on the whole; hence it would retain seventy-nine positive charges in the nucleus and seventy-nine outlying negative electrons, thereby becoming GOLD!

The formula through which this electronic change might be produced has been the object of diligent search by the alchemists all down the ages, and by the modern chemists of today.

It is a fact known to every chemist that literally tens of thousands of synthetic substances may be composed out of only four kinds of atoms, viz.: hydrogen, oxygen, nitrogen and carbon.

"Differences in the number of electrons in atoms confer upon them qualitative (chemical) differences, though all atoms of any one element are chemically alike. Differences in the number and spacial arrangement of these atoms (in groups of molecules) constitute both physical and chemical differences in substances, *i.e.,* in compounds. Quite different substances are produced by combinations of precisely the same kinds of atoms, but in different proportions.

"Take from a molecule of certain substances one single atom, and they may be changed from a compound necessary to life and growth into a deadly poison. Phosphorus is an element, and thus contains but one kind of atoms; but some phosphorus is yellow and some is red, varying with the spacial distribution of the atoms in the molecules composing the phosphorus."

It may be stated as a literal truth that the atom is the universal partical with which Nature builds all material forms, from a grain of sand to the largest star that floats through space. The atom is Nature's "building block" out of which she erects an oak tree or a pine, a rock of sandstone or granite, a mouse or an elephant.

Some of the ablest thinkers have reasoned that the earth on which we live, and every material particle on the earth, began with two atoms which attached themselves to each other, and through hundreds of millions of years of flight through space, kept contacting and accumulating other atoms until, step by step, the earth was formed. This, they point out, would account for the various and differing strata of the earth's substances, such as the coal beds, the iron ore deposits, the gold and silver deposits, the copper deposits, etc.

They reason that, as the earth whirled through space, it contacted groups of various kinds of nebulæ, or atoms, which it promptly appropriated, through the law of magnetic attraction. There is much to be seen, in the earth's surface composition, to support this theory, although there may be no positive evidence of its soundness.

These facts concerning the smallest analyzable particles of matter have been briefly referred to as a starting point from which we shall undertake to ascertain how to develop and apply the law of POWER.

It has been noticed that all matter is in a constant state of vibration or motion; that the molecule is made up of rapidly moving particles called atoms, which, in turn, are made up of rapidly moving particles called electrons.

The Vibrating Fluid of Matter: In every particle of matter there is an invisible "fluid" or force which causes the atoms to circle around one another at an inconceivable rate of speed.

This "fluid" is a form of energy which has never been analyzed. Thus far it has baffled the entire scientific world. By many scientists it is believed to be the same energy as that which we call electricity. Others prefer to call it vibration. It is believed by some investigators that the rate of speed with which this force (call it whatever you will) moves determines to a large extent the nature of the outward visible appearance of the physical objects of the universe.

One rate of vibration of this "fluid energy" causes what is known as sound. The human ear can detect only the sound which is produced through from 32,000 to 38,000 vibrations per second.

As the rate of vibrations per second increases above that which we call sound they begin to manifest themselves in the form of heat. Heat begins with about 1,500,000 vibrations per second.

Still higher up the scale vibrations begin to register in the form of light. 3,000,000 vibrations per second create violet light. Above this number vibration sheds ultra-violet rays (which are invisible to the naked eye) and other invisible radiations.

And, still higher up the scale—just how high no one at present seems to know—vibrations create the power with which man THINKS.

It is the belief of the author that the "fluid" portion of all vibration, out of which grow all known forms of energy, is universal in nature; that the "fluid" portion of sound is the same as the "fluid" portion of light, the difference in effect between sound and light being only a difference in rate of vibration, also that the "fluid" portion of thought is exactly the same as that in sound, heat and light, excepting the number of vibrations per second.

Just as there is but one form of physical matter, of which the earth and all the other planets—suns and stars—are composed—the electron—so is there but one form of "fluid" energy, which causes all matter to remain in a constant state of rapid motion.

Air and Ether: The vast space between the suns, moons, stars and other planets of the universe is filled with a form of energy known as ether. It is this author's belief that the "fluid" energy which keeps all particles of matter in motion is the same as the universal "fluid" known as ether which fills all the space of the universe. Within a certain distance of the earth's surface, estimated by some to be about fifty miles, there exists what is called air, which is a gaseous substance composed of oxygen and nitrogen. Air is a conductor of sound vibrations, but a non-conductor of light and the higher vibrations, which are carried by the ether. The ether is a conductor of all vibrations from sound to thought.

Air is a localized substance which performs, in the main, the service of feeding all animal and plant life with oxygen and nitrogen, without which neither could exist. Nitrogen is one of the chief necessities of plant life and oxygen one of the mainstays of animal life. Near the top of very high mountains the air becomes very light, because it contains but little nitrogen, which is the reason why plant life cannot exist there. On the other hand, the "light" air found in high altitudes consists largely of oxygen, which is the chief reason why tubercular patients are sent to high altitudes.

Render more service than that for which you are paid and you will soon be paid for more than you render. The law of "Increasing Returns" takes care of this.

———

12

Even this brief statement concerning molecules, atoms, electrons, air, ether and the like, may be heavy reading to the student, but, as will be seen shortly, this introduction plays an essential part as the foundation of this lesson.

Do not become discouraged if the description of this foundation appears to have none of the thrilling effects of a modern tale of fiction. You are seriously engaged in finding out what are your available powers and how to organize and apply these powers. To complete this discovery successfully you must combine determination, persistency and a well defined DESIRE to gather and organize knowledge.

The late Dr. Alexander Graham Bell, inventor of the long distance telephone and one of the accepted authorities on the subject of vibration, is here introduced in support of this author's theories concerning the subject of vibration:

"Suppose you have the power to make an iron rod vibrate with any desired frequency in a dark room. At first, when vibrating slowly, its movement will be indicated by only one sense, that of touch. As soon as the vibrations increase, a low sound will emanate from it and it will appeal to two senses.

"At about 32,000 vibrations to the second the sound will be loud and shrill, but at 40,000 vibrations it will be silent and the movements of the rod will not be perceived by touch. Its movements will be perceived by no ordinary human sense.

"From this point up to about 1,500,000 vibrations per second, we have no sense that can appreciate any effect of the intervening vibrations. After that stage is reached, movement is indicated first by the sense of temperature and then, when the rod becomes red hot, by the sense of sight. At 3,000,000 it sheds violet light. Above that it sheds ultra-violet rays and other invisible radiations, some of which can be perceived by instruments and employed by us.

"Now it has occurred to me that there must be a great deal to be learned about the effect of those vibrations in the great gap where the ordinary human senses are unable to hear, see or feel the movement. The power to send wireless messages by ether vibrations lies in that gap, but the gap is so great that it seems there must be much more. You must make machines practically to supply new senses, as the wireless instruments do.

"Can it be said, when you think of that great gap, that there are not many forms of vibrations that may give us results as wonderful as, or even more wonderful than, the wireless waves? It seems to me that in this gap lie the vibrations which we have assumed to be given off by our brains and nerve cells when we think. But then, again, they may be higher up, in the scale beyond the vibrations that produce the ultra-violet rays. [AUTHOR'S NOTE: The last sentence suggests the theory held by this author.]

"Do we need a wire to carry these vibrations? Will they not pass through the ether without a wire, just as the wireless waves do? How will they be perceived by the recipient? Will he hear a series of signals or will he find that another man's thoughts have entered into his brain?

"We may indulge in some speculations based on what we know of the wireless waves, which, as I have said, are all we can recognize of a vast series of vibrations which theoretically must exist. If the thought waves are similar to the wireless waves, they must pass from the brain and flow endlessly around the world and the universe. The body and the skull and other solid obstacles would form no obstruction to their passage, as they pass through the ether which surrounds the molecules of every substance, no matter how solid and dense.

"You ask if there would not be constant interference and confusion if other people's thoughts were flowing through our brains and setting up thoughts in them that did not originate with ourselves?

"How do you know that other men's thoughts are not interfering with yours now? I have noticed a good many phenomena of mind disturbances that I have never been able to explain. For instance, there is the inspiration or the discouragement that a speaker feels in addressing an audience. I have experienced this many times in my life and have never been able to define exactly the physical causes of it.

"Many recent scientific discoveries, in my opinion, point to a day not far distant perhaps, when men will read one another's thoughts, when thoughts will be conveyed directly from brain to brain without intervention of speech, writing or any of the present known methods of communication.

"It is not unreasonable to look forward to a time when we shall see without eyes, hear without ears and talk without tongues.

"Briefly, the hypothesis that mind can communicate directly with mind rests on the theory that thought or vital force is a form of electrical disturbance, that it can be taken up by induction and transmitted to a distance either through a wire or simply through the all-pervading ether, as in the case of wireless telegraph waves.

"There are many analogies which suggest that thought is of the nature of an electrical disturbance. A nerve, which is of the same substance as the brain, is an excellent conductor of the electric current. When we first passed an electrical current through the nerves of a dead man we were shocked and amazed to see him sit up and move. The electrified nerves produced contraction of the muscles very much as in life.

"The nerves appear to act upon the muscles very much as the electric current acts upon an electro-magnet. The current magnetizes a bar of iron placed at right angles to it, and the nerves produce, through the intangible current of vital force that flows through them, contraction of the muscular fibers that are arranged at right angles to them.

"It would be possible to cite many reasons why thought and vital force may be regarded as of the same nature as electricity. The electric current is held to be a wave motion of the ether, the hypothetical substance that fills all space and pervades all substances. We believe that there must be ether because without it the electric current could not pass through a vacuum, or sunlight through space. It is reasonable to believe that only a wave motion of a similar character can produce the phenomena of thought and vital force. We may assume that the brain cells act as a battery and that the current produced flows along the nerves.

"But does it end there? Does it not pass out of the body in waves which flow around the world unperceived by our senses, just as the wireless waves passed unperceived before Hertz and others discovered their existence?"

Every Mind Both a Broadcasting and a Receiving Station: This author has proved, times too numerous to enumerate, to his own satisfaction at least, that every human brain is both a broadcasting and a receiving station for vibrations of thought frequency.

If this theory should turn out to be a fact, and methods of reasonable control should be established, imagine the part it would play in the gathering, classifying and organizing of knowledge. The possibility, much less the probability, of such a reality, staggers the mind of man!

Thomas Paine was one of the great minds of the American Revolutionary Period. To him more, perhaps, than to any other one person, we owe both the beginning and the happy ending of the Revolution, for it was his keen mind that both helped in drawing up the Declaration of Independence and in persuading the signers of that document to translate it into terms of reality.

In speaking of the source of his great storehouse of knowledge, Paine thus described it:

"Any person, who has made observations on the state of progress of the human mind, by observing his own, cannot but have observed that there are two distinct classes of what are called Thoughts: those that we produce in ourselves by reflection and the act of thinking, and those that bolt into the mind of their own accord. I have always made it a rule to treat these voluntary visitors with civility, taking care to examine, as well as I was able, if they were worth entertaining; and it is from them I have acquired almost all the knowledge that

15

Every failure is a blessing in disguise, providing it teaches some needed lesson one could not have learned without it. Most so-called Failures are only temporary defeats.

I have. As to the learning that any person gains from school education, it serves only like a small capital, to put him in the way of beginning learning for himself afterwards. Every person of learning is finally his own teacher, the reason for which is, that principles cannot be impressed upon the memory; their place of mental residence is the understanding, and they are never so lasting as when they begin by conception."

In the foregoing words Paine, the great American patriot and philosopher, described an experience which at one time or another is the experience of every person. Who is there so unfortunate as not to have received positive evidence that thoughts and even complete ideas will "pop" into the mind from outside sources?

What means of conveyance is there for such visitors except the ether? Ether fills the boundless space of the universe. It is the medium of conveyance for all known forms of vibration such as sound, light and heat. Why should it not be, also, the medium of conveyance of the vibration of Thought?

Every mind, or brain, is directly connected with every other brain by means of the ether. Every thought released by any brain may be instantly picked up and interpreted by all other brains that are "en rapport" with the sending brain. This author is as sure of this fact as he is that the chemical formula H_2O will produce water. Imagine, if you can, what a part this principle plays in every walk of life.

Nor is the probability of ether being a conveyor of thought from mind to mind the most astounding of its performances. It is the belief of this author that every thought vibration released by any brain is picked up by the ether and kept in motion in circuitous wave lengths corresponding in length to the intensity of the energy used in their release; that these vibrations remain in motion forever; that they are one of the two sources from which thoughts which "pop" into one's mind emanate, the other source being direct and immediate contact through the ether with the brain releasing the thought vibration.

Thus it will be seen that if this theory is a fact the boundless space of the whole universe is now and will continue to become literally a mental library wherein may be found all the thoughts released by mankind.

The author is here laying the foundation for one of the most important hypotheses enumerated in the lesson Self-confidence, a fact which the student should keep in mind as he approaches that lesson.

This is a lesson on Organized Knowledge. Most of the useful knowledge to which the human race has become heir has been preserved and accurately recorded in Nature's Bible. By turning back the pages of this unalterable Bible man has read the story of the terrific struggle through and out of which the present civilization has grown. The pages of this Bible are made up of the physical elements of which this earth and the other planets consist, and of the ether which fills all space.

By turning back the pages written on stone and covered near the surface of this earth on which he lives, man has uncovered the bones, skeletons, footprints and other unmistakable evidence of the history of animal life on this earth, planted there for his enlightenment and guidance by the hand of Mother Nature throughout unbelievable periods of time. The evidence is plain and unmistakable. The great stone pages of Nature's Bible found on this earth and the endless pages of that Bible represented by the ether wherein all past human thought has been recorded, constitute an authentic source of communication between the Creator and man. This Bible was begun before man had reached the thinking stage; indeed, before man had reached the amœba (one-cell animal) stage of development.

This Bible is above and beyond the power of man to alter. Moreover, it tells its story not in the ancient dead languages or hieroglyphics of half savage races, but in universal language which all who have eyes may read. Nature's Bible, from which we have derived all the knowledge that is worth knowing, is one that no man may alter or in any manner tamper with.

The most marvelous discovery yet made by man is that of the recently discovered radio principle, which operates through the aid of ether, an important portion of Nature's Bible. Imagine the ether picking up the ordinary vibration of sound, and transforming that vibration from audio-frequency into radio-frequency, carrying it to a properly attuned receiving station and there transforming it back into its original form of audio-frequency, all in the flash of a second. It should surprise no one that such a force could gather up the vibration of thought and keep that vibration in motion forever.

The established and known fact of instantaneous transmission of sound, through the agency of the ether, by means of the modern radio apparatus, removes the theory of transmission of thought vibration from mind to mind from the possible to the probable.

The Master Mind: We come, now, to the next step in the description of the ways and means by which one may gather, classify and organize useful knowledge, through harmonious alliance of two or more minds, out of which grows a Master Mind.

The term "Master Mind" is abstract, and has no counterpart in the field of known facts, except to a small number of people who have made a careful study of the effect of one mind upon other minds.

This author has searched in vain through all the textbooks and essays available on the subject of the human mind, but nowhere has been found even the slightest reference to the principle here described as the "Master Mind." The term first came to the attention of the author through an interview with Andrew Carnegie, in the manner described in Lesson One.

Chemistry of the Mind: It is this author's belief that the mind is made up of the same universal "fluid" energy as that which constitutes the ether which fills the universe. It is a fact as well known to the layman as to the man of scientific investigation, that some minds clash the moment they come in contact with each other, while other minds show a natural affinity for each other. Between the two extremes of natural antagonism and natural affinity growing out of the meeting or contacting of minds there is a wide range of possibility for varying reactions of mind upon mind.

Some minds are so naturally adapted to each other that "love at first sight" is the inevitable outcome of the contact. Who has not known of such an experience? In other cases minds are so antagonistic that violent mutual dislike shows itself at first meeting. These results occur without a word being spoken, and without the slightest signs of any of the usual causes for love and hate acting as a stimulus.

It is quite probable that the "mind" is made up of a fluid or substance or energy, call it what you will, similar to (if not in fact the same substance as) the ether. When two minds come close enough to each other to form a contact, the mixing of the units of this "mind stuff" (let us call it the electrons of the ether) sets up a chemical reaction and starts vibrations which affect the two individuals pleasantly or unpleasantly.

The effect of the meeting of two minds is obvious to even the most casual observer. Every effect must have a cause! What could be more reasonable than to suspect that the cause of the change in mental attitude between two minds which have just come in close contact is none other than the disturbance of the electrons or units of each mind in the process of rearranging themselves in the new field created by the contact?

For the purpose of establishing this lesson upon a sound foundation we have gone a long way toward success by admitting that the meeting or coming in close contact of two minds sets up in each of those minds a certain noticeable "effect" or state of mind quite different from the one existing immediately prior to the contact. While it is desirable it is not essential to know what is the "cause" of this reaction of mind upon mind. That the reaction takes place, in every instance, is a known fact which gives us a starting point from which we may show what is meant by the term "Master Mind."

To believe in the heroic makes heroes.

—DISRAELI

A Master Mind may be created through the bringing together or blending, in a spirit of perfect harmony, of two or more minds. Out of this harmonious blending the chemistry of the mind creates a third mind which may be appropriated and used by one or all of the individual minds. This Master Mind will remain available as long as the friendly, harmonious alliance between the individual minds exists. It will disintegrate and all evidence of its former existence will disappear the moment the friendly alliance is broken.

This principle of mind chemistry is the basis and cause for practically all the so-called "soul-mate" and "eternal triangle" cases, so many of which unfortunately find their way into the divorce courts and meet with popular ridicule from ignorant and uneducated people who manufacture vulgarity and scandal out of one of the greatest of Nature's laws.

The entire civilized world knows that the first two or three years of association after marriage are often marked by much disagreement, of a more or less petty nature. These are the years of "adjustment." If the marriage survives them it is more than apt to become a permanent alliance. These facts no experienced married person will deny. Again we see the "effect" without understanding the "cause."

While there are other contributing causes, yet, in the main, lack of harmony during these early years of marriage is due to the slowness of the chemistry of the minds in blending harmoniously. Stated differently, the electrons or units of the energy called the mind are often neither extremely friendly nor antagonistic upon first contact; but, through constant association they gradually adapt themselves in harmony, except in rare cases where association has the opposite effect of leading, eventually, to open hostility between these units.

It is a well known fact that after a man and a woman have lived together for ten to fifteen years they become practically indispensable to each other, even though there may not be the slightest evidence of the state of mind called love. Moreover, this association and relationship sexually not only develops a natural affinity between the two minds, but it actually causes the two people to take on a similar facial expression and to resemble each other closely in many other marked ways. Any competent analyst of human nature can easily go into a crowd of strange people and pick out the wife after having been introduced to her husband. The expression of the eyes, the contour of the faces and the tone of the voices of people who have long been associated in marriage, become similar to a marked degree.

So marked is the effect of the chemistry of the human mind that any experienced public speaker may quickly interpret the manner in which his statements are accepted by his audience. Antagonism in the mind of but one person in an audience of one thousand may be readily detected by the speaker who has learned how to "feel" and register the effects of antagonism. Moreover, the public speaker can make these interpretations without observing or in any manner being influenced by the expression on the faces of those in his audience. On account of this fact an audience may cause a speaker to rise to great heights of oratory, or heckle him into failure, without making a sound or denoting a single expression of satisfaction or dissatisfaction through the features of the face.

All "Master Salesmen" know the moment the "psychological time for closing" has arrived; not by what the prospective buyer says, but from the effect of the chemistry of his mind as interpreted or "felt" by the salesman. Words often belie the intentions of those speaking them but a correct interpretation of the chemistry of the mind leaves no loophole for such a possibility. Every able salesman knows that the majority of buyers have the habit of affecting a negative attitude almost to the very climax of a sale.

Every able lawyer has developed a sixth sense whereby he is enabled to "feel" his way through the most artfully selected words of the clever witness who is lying, and correctly interpret that which is in the witness's mind, through the chemistry of the mind. Many lawyers have developed this ability without knowing the real source of it; they possess the technique without the scientific understanding upon which it is based. Many salesmen have done the same thing.

One who is gifted in the art of correctly interpreting the chemistry of the minds of others may, figuratively speaking, walk in at the front door of the mansion of a given mind and leisurely explore the entire building, noting all its details, walking out again with a complete picture of the interior of the building, without the owner of the building so much as knowing that he has entertained a visitor. It will be observed, in the lesson Accurate Thinking, that this principle may be put to a very practical use (having reference to the principle of the chemistry of the mind). The principle is referred to merely as an approach to the major principles of this lesson.

Enough has already been stated to introduce the principle of mind chemistry, and to prove, with the aid of the student's own every-day experiences and casual observations that the moment two minds come within close range of each other a noticeable mental change takes place in both, sometimes registering in the nature of antagonism and at other times registering in the nature of friendliness. Every mind has what might be termed an electric field. The nature of this field varies, depending upon the "mood" of the individual mind back of it, and upon the nature of the chemistry of the mind creating the "field."

It is believed by this author that the normal or natural condition of the chemistry of any individual mind is the result of his physical heredity plus the nature of thoughts which have dominated that mind; that every mind is continuously changing to the extent that the individual's philosophy and general habits of thought change the chemistry of his or her mind. These principles the author BELIEVES to be true. That any individual may voluntarily change the chemistry of his or her mind so that it will either attract or repel all with whom it comes in contact is a KNOWN FACT! Stated in another manner, any person may assume a mental attitude which will attract and please others or repel and antagonize them, and this without the aid of words or facial expression or other form of bodily movement or demeanor.

Go back, now, to the definition of a "Master Mind"—a mind which grows out of the blending and co-ordination of two or more minds, IN A SPIRIT OF PERFECT HARMONY, and you will catch the full significance of the word "harmony" as it is here used. Two minds will not blend nor can they be co-ordinated unless the element of perfect harmony is present, wherein lies the secret of success or failure of practically all business and social partnerships.

Every sales manager and every military commander and every leader in any other walk of life understands the necessity of an "esprit de corps"—a spirit of common understanding and co-operation—in the attainment of success. This mass spirit of harmony of purpose is obtained through discipline, voluntary or forced, of such a nature that the individual minds become blended into a "Master Mind," by which is meant that the chemistry of the individual minds is modified in such a manner that these minds blend and function as one.

The methods through which this blending process takes place are as numerous as the individuals engaged in the various forms of leadership. Every leader has his or her own method of co-ordinating the minds of the followers. One will use force. Another uses persuasion. One will play upon the fear of penalties while another plays upon rewards, in order to reduce the individual minds of a given group of people to where they may be blended into a mass mind. The student will not have to search deeply into history of statesmanship, politics, business or finance, to discover the technique employed by the leaders in these fields in the process of blending the minds of individuals into a mass mind.

If you do not believe in co-operation, look what happens to a wagon that loses a wheel.

The really great leaders of the world, however, have been provided by Nature with a combination of mind chemistry favorable as a nucleus of attraction for other minds. Napoleon was a notable example of a man possessing the magnetic type of mind which had a very decided tendency to attract all minds with which it came in contact. Soldiers followed Napoleon to certain death without flinching, because of the impelling or attracting nature of his personality, and that personality was nothing more nor less than the chemistry of his mind.

No group of minds can be blended into a Master Mind if one of the individuals of that group possesses one of these extremely negative, repellent minds. The negative and positive minds will not blend in the sense here described as a Master Mind. Lack of knowledge of this fact has brought many an otherwise able leader to defeat.

Any able leader who understands this principle of mind chemistry may temporarily blend the minds of practically any group of people, so that it will represent a mass mind, but the composition will disintegrate almost the very moment the leader's presence is removed from the group. The most successful life-insurance sales organizations and other sales forces meet once a week, or more often, for the purpose of—OF WHAT?

FOR THE PURPOSE OF MERGING THE INDIVIDUAL MINDS INTO A MASTER MIND WHICH WILL, FOR A LIMITED NUMBER OF DAYS, SERVE AS A STIMULUS TO THE INDIVIDUAL MINDS!

It may be, and generally is, true that the leaders of these groups do not understand what actually takes place in these meetings, which are usually called "pep meetings." The routine of such meetings is usually given over to talks by the leader and other members of the group, and occasionally from someone outside of the group, meanwhile the minds of the individuals are contacting and recharging one another.

The brain of a human being may be compared to an electric battery in that it will become exhausted or run down, causing the owner of it to feel despondent, discouraged and lacking in "pep." Who is so fortunate as never to have had such a feeling? The human brain, when in this depleted condition, must be recharged, and the manner in which this is done is through contact with a more vital mind or minds. The great leaders understand the necessity of this "recharging" process, and, moreover, they understand how to accomplish this result. THIS KNOWLEDGE IS THE MAIN FEATURE WHICH DISTINGUISHES A LEADER FROM A FOLLOWER!

Fortunate is the person who understands this principle sufficiently well to keep his or her brain vitalized or "recharged" by periodically contacting it with a more vital mind. Sexual contact is one of the most effective of the stimuli through which a mind may be recharged, providing the contact is intelligently made, between man and woman who have genuine affection for each other. Any other sort of sexual relationship is a devitalizer of the mind. Any competent practitioner of Psycho-therapeutics can "recharge" a brain within a few minutes.

Before passing away from the brief reference made to sexual contact as a means of revitalizing a depleted mind it seems appropriate to call attention to the fact that all of the great leaders, in whatever walks of life they have arisen, have been and are people of highly sexed natures. (The word "sex" is not an indecent word. You'll find it in all the dictionaries.)

There is a growing tendency upon the part of the best informed physicians and other health practitioners, to accept the theory that all diseases begin when the brain of the individual is in a depleted or devitalized state. Stated in another way, it is a known fact that a person who has a perfectly vitalized brain is practically, if not entirely, immune from all manner of disease.

Every intelligent health practitioner, of whatever school or type, knows that "Nature" or the mind cures disease in every instance where a cure is effected. Medicines, faith, laying on of hands, chiropractic, osteopathy and all other forms of outside stimulant are nothing more than artificial aids to NATURE, or, to state it correctly, mere methods of setting the chemistry of the mind into motion to the end that it readjusts the cells and tissues of the body, re-vitalizes the brain and otherwise causes the human machine to function normally.

The most orthodox practitioner will admit the truth of this statement.

What, then, may be the possibilities of the future developments in the field of mind chemistry?

Through the principle of harmonious blending of minds perfect health may be enjoyed. Through the aid of this same principle sufficient power may be developed to solve the problem of economic pressure which constantly presses upon every individual.

We may judge the future possibilities of mind chemistry by taking inventory of its past achievements, keeping in mind the fact that these achievements have been largely the result of accidental discovery and of chance groupings of minds. We are approaching the time when the professorate of the universities will teach mind chemistry the same as other subjects are now taught. Meanwhile, study and experimentation in connection with this subject open vistas of possibility for the individual student.

Mind Chemistry and Economic Power: That mind chemistry may be appropriately applied to the workaday affairs of the economic and commercial world is a demonstrable fact.

Through the blending of two or more minds, in a spirit of PERFECT HARMONY, the principle of mind chemistry may be made to develop sufficient power to enable the individuals whose minds have been thus blended to perform seemingly superhuman feats. Power is the force with which man achieves success in any undertaking. Power, in unlimited quantities, may be enjoyed by any group of men, or men and women, who possess the wisdom with which to submerge their own personalities and their own immediate individual interests, through the blending of their minds in a spirit of perfect harmony.

Observe, profitably, the frequency with which the word "harmony" appears throughout this Introduction! There can be no development of a "Master Mind" where this element of PERFECT HARMONY does not exist. The individual units of the mind will not blend with the individual units of another mind UNTIL THE TWO MINDS HAVE BEEN AROUSED AND WARMED, AS IT WERE, WITH A SPIRIT OF PERFECT HARMONY OF PURPOSE. The moment two minds begin to take divergent roads of interest the individual units of each mind separate, and the third element, known as a "MASTER MIND," which grew out of the friendly or harmonious alliance, will disintegrate.

We come, now, to the study of some well known men who have accumulated great power (also great fortunes) through the application of mind chemistry.

Let us begin our study with three men who are known to be men of great achievement in their respective fields of economic, business and professional endeavor.

Their names are Henry Ford, Thomas A. Edison and Harvey S. Firestone.

Of the three Henry Ford is, by far, the most POWERFUL, having reference to economic and financial power. Mr. Ford is the most powerful man now living on earth. Many who have studied Mr. Ford believe him to be the most powerful man who ever lived. As far as is known Mr. Ford is the only man now living, or who ever lived, with sufficient power to outwit the money trust of the United States. Mr. Ford gathers millions of dollars with as great ease as a child fills its bucket with sand when playing on the beach. It has been said, by those who were in position to know, that Mr. Ford, if he needed it, could send out the call for money and gather in a billion dollars (a thousand million dollars) and have it available for use within one week. No one who knows of Ford's achievements doubts this. Those who know him well know that he could do it with no more effort than the average man expends in raising the money with which to pay a month's house rent. He could get this money, if he needed it, through the intelligent application of the principles on which this course is based.

While Mr. Ford's new automobile was in the process of perfection, in 1927, it is said that he received advance orders, with cash payments, for more than 375,000 cars. At an estimated price of $600.00 per car this would amount to $225,000,000.00 which he received before a single car was delivered. Such is the power of confidence in Ford's ability.

Mr. Edison, as everyone knows, is a philosopher, scientist and inventor. He is, perhaps, the keenest Bible student on earth; a student of Nature's Bible, however, and not of the myriads of man-made Bibles. Mr. Edison has such a keen insight into Mother Nature's Bible that he has harnessed and combined, for the good of mankind, more of Nature's laws than any other person now living or who ever lived. It was he who brought together the point of a needle and a piece of revolving wax, in such a way that the vibration of the human voice may be recorded and reproduced through the modern talking machine.

(And it may be Edison who will eventually enable man to pick up and correctly interpret the vibrations of thought which are now recorded in the boundless universe of ether, just as he has enabled man to record and reproduce the spoken word.)

It was Edison who first harnessed the lightning and made it serve as a light for man's use, through the aid of the incandescent electric light bulb.

It was Edison who gave the world the modern moving picture.

These are but a few of his outstanding achievements. These modern "miracles" which he has performed (not by trickery, under the sham pretense of superhuman power, but in the very midst of the bright light of science) transcend all of the so-called "miracles" described in the man-made books of fiction.

Mr. Firestone is the moving spirit in the great Firestone Tire industry, in Akron, Ohio. His industrial achievements are so well known wherever automobiles are used that no special comment on them seems necessary.

All three of these men began their careers, business and professional, without capital and with but little schooling of that type usually referred to as "education."

All three men are now well educated. All three are wealthy. All three are powerful. Now let us inquire into the source of their wealth and power. Thus far we have been dealing only with effect; the true philosopher wishes to understand the *cause* of a given effect.

It is a matter of general knowledge that Mr. Ford, Mr. Edison and Mr. Firestone are close personal friends, and have been so for many years; that in former years they were in the habit of going away to the woods once a year for a period of rest, meditation and recuperation.

But it is not generally known—it is a grave doubt if these three men themselves know it—that there exists between the three men a bond of harmony which has caused their minds to become blended into a "Master Mind" which is the real source of the power of each. This mass mind, growing out of the co-ordination of the individual minds of Ford, Edison and Firestone, has enabled these men to "tune in" on forces (and sources of knowledge) with which most men are to no extent familiar.

If the student doubts either the principle or the effects here described, let him remember that more than half the theory here set forth is a known fact. For example, it is known that these three men have great power. It is known that they are wealthy. It is known that they began without capital and with but little schooling. It is known that they form periodic mind contacts. It is known that they are harmonious and friendly. It is known that their achievements are so outstanding as to make it impossible to compare these achievements with those of other men in their respective fields of activity.

All these "effects" are known to practically every school-boy in the civilized world, therefore there can be no dispute as far as effects are concerned.

Of one fact connected with the *cause* of the achievements of Edison, Ford and Firestone we may be sure, namely, that these achievements were in no way based upon trickery, deceit, the "supernatural" or so-called "revelations" or any other form of unnatural law. These men do not possess a stock of legerdemain. They work with natural laws; laws which, for the most part, are well known to all economists and leaders in the field of science, with the possible exception of the law upon which chemistry of the mind is based. As yet chemistry of the mind is not sufficiently developed to be classed, by scientific men, in their catalogue of known laws.

A "Master Mind" may be created by any group of people who will co-ordinate their minds, in a spirit of perfect harmony. The group may consist of any number from two upward. Best results appear available from the blending of six or seven minds.

It has been suggested that Jesus Christ discovered how to make use of the principle of mind chemistry, and that His seemingly miraculous performances grew out of the power He developed through the blending of the minds of His twelve disciples. It has been pointed out that when one of the disciples (Judas Iscariot) broke faith the "Master Mind" immediately disintegrated and Jesus met with the supreme catastrophe of His life.

When two or more people harmonize their minds and produce the effect known as a "Master Mind," each person in the group becomes vested with the power to contact with and gather knowledge through the "subconscious" minds of all the other members of the group. This power becomes immediately noticeable, having the effect of stimulating the mind to a higher rate of vibration, and otherwise evidencing itself in the form of a more vivid imagination and the consciousness of what appears to be a sixth sense. It is through this sixth sense that new ideas will "flash" into the mind. These ideas take on the nature and form of the subject dominating the mind of the individual. If the entire group has met for the purpose of discussing a given subject, ideas concerning that subject will come pouring into the minds of all present, as if an outside influence were dictating them. The minds of those participating in the "Master Mind" become as magnets, attracting ideas and thought stimuli of the most highly organized and practical nature, from—no one knows where!

The process of mind-blending here described as a "Master Mind" may be likened to the act of one who connects many electric batteries to a single transmission wire, thereby "stepping up" the power flowing over that line. Each battery added increases the power passing over that line by the amount of energy the battery carries. Just so in the case of blending individual minds into a "Master Mind." Each mind, through the principle of mind chemistry, stimulates all the other minds in the group, until the mind energy thus becomes so great that it penetrates to and connects with the universal energy known as ether, which, in turn, touches every atom of the entire universe.

The modern radio apparatus substantiates, to a considerable extent, the theory here expounded. Powerful sending or broadcasting stations must be erected through which the vibration of sound is "stepped up" before it can be picked up by the much higher vibrating energy of the ether and carried in all directions. A "Master Mind" made up of many individual minds, so blended that they produce a strong vibrating energy, constitutes almost an exact counterpart of the radio broadcasting station.

Every public speaker has felt the influence of mind chemistry, for it is a well known fact that as soon as the individual minds of an audience become "en rapport" (attuned to the rate of vibration of the mind of the speaker) with the speaker, there is a noticeable increase of enthusiasm in the speaker's mind, and he often rises to heights of oratory which surprise all, including himself.

Men cease to interest us when we find their limitations. The only sin is limitation. As soon as you once come up to a man's limitations, it is all over with him.

—EMERSON

THE LAW OF SUCCESS

The first five to ten minutes of the average speech are devoted to what is known as "warming up." By this is meant the process through which the minds of the speaker and his audience are becoming blended in a spirit of PERFECT HARMONY.

Every speaker knows what happens when this state of "perfect harmony" fails to materialize upon part of his audience.

The seemingly supernatural phenomena occurring in spiritualistic meetings are the result of the reaction, upon one another, of the minds in the group. These phenomena seldom begin to manifest themselves under ten to twenty minutes after the group is formed, for the reason that this is about the time required for the minds in the group to become harmonized or blended.

The "messages" received by members of a spiritualistic group probably come from one of two sources, or from both, namely:

First: From the vast storehouse of the subconscious mind of some member of the group; or

Second: From the universal storehouse of the ether, in which, it is more than probable, all thought vibration is preserved.

Neither any known natural law nor human reason supports the theory of communication with individuals who have died.

It is a known fact that any individual may explore the store of knowledge in another's mind, through this principle of mind chemistry, and it seems reasonable to suppose that this power may be extended to include contact with whatever vibrations are available in the ether, if there are any.

The theory that all the higher and more refined vibrations, such as those growing out of thought, are preserved in the ether grows out of the known fact that neither matter nor energy (the two known elements of the universe) may be either created or destroyed. It is reasonable to suppose that all vibrations which have been "stepped up" sufficiently to be picked up and absorbed in the ether, will go on forever. The lower vibrations, which do not blend with or otherwise contact the ether, probably live a natural life and die out.

All the so-called geniuses probably gained their reputations because, by mere chance or otherwise, they formed alliances with other minds which enabled them to "step up" their own mind vibrations to where they were enabled to contact the vast Temple of Knowledge recorded and filed in the ether of the universe. All of the great geniuses, as far as this author has been enabled to gather the facts, were highly sexed people. The fact that sexual contact is the greatest known mind stimulant lends color to the theory herein described.

Inquiring further into the source of economic power, as manifested by the achievements of men in the field of business, let us study the case of the Chicago group known as the "Big Six," consisting of Wm. Wrigley, Jr., who owns the chewing gum business bearing his name, and whose individual income is said to be more than Fifteen Million Dollars a year; John R. Thompson, who operates the chain of lunch rooms bearing his name; Mr. Lasker, who owns the Lord & Thomas Advertising Agency; Mr. McCullough, who owns the Parmalee Express Company, the largest transfer business in America; and Mr. Ritchie and Mr. Hertz, who own the Yellow Taxicab business.

A reliable financial reporting company has estimated the yearly income of these six men at upwards of Twenty-five Million Dollars ($25,000,000.00), or an average of more than Four Million Dollars a year per man.

Analysis of the entire group of six men discloses the fact that not one of them had any special educational advantages; that all began without capital or extensive credit; that their financial achievement has been due to their own individual plans, and not to any fortunate turn of the wheel of chance.

Many years ago these six men formed a friendly alliance, meeting at stated periods for the purpose of assisting one another with ideas and suggestions in their various and sundry lines of business endeavor.

With the exception of Hertz and Ritchie none of the six men were in any manner associated in a legal partnership. These meetings were strictly for the purpose of co-operating on the give and take basis of assisting one another with ideas and suggestions, and occasionally by endorsing notes and other securities to assist some member of the group who had met with an emergency making such help necessary.

It is said that each of the individuals belonging to this Big Six group is a millionaire many times over. As a rule there is nothing worthy of special comment on behalf of a man who does nothing more than accumulate a few million dollars. However, there is something connected with the financial success of this particular group of men that is well worth comment, study, analysis and even emulation, and that "something" is the fact that they have learned how to co-ordinate their individual minds by blending them in a spirit of perfect harmony, thereby creating a "Master Mind" that unlocks, to each individual of the group, doors which are closed to most of the human race.

The United States Steel Corporation is one of the strongest and most powerful industrial organizations in the world. The Idea out of which this great industrial giant grew was born

THE LAW OF SUCCESS

in the mind of Elbert H. Gary, a more or less commonplace small-town lawyer who was born and reared in a small Illinois town near Chicago.

Mr. Gary surrounded himself with a group of men whose minds he successfully blended in a spirit of perfect harmony, thereby creating the "Master Mind" which is the moving spirit of the great United States Steel Corporation.

Search where you will, wherever you find an outstanding success in business, finance, industry or in any of the professions, you may be sure that back of the success is some individual who has applied the principle of mind chemistry, out of which a "Master Mind" has been created. These outstanding successes often appear to be the handiwork of but one person, but search closely and the other individuals whose minds have been co-ordinated with his own may be found. Remember that two or more persons may operate the principle of mind chemistry so as to create a "Master Mind."

POWER (man-power) is ORGANIZED KNOWLEDGE, EXPRESSED THROUGH INTELLIGENT EFFORTS!

No effort can be said to be ORGANIZED unless the individuals engaged in the effort co-ordinate their knowledge and energy in a spirit of perfect harmony. Lack of such harmonious co-ordination of effort is the main cause of practically every business failure.

An interesting experiment was conducted by this author, in collaboration with the students of a well known college. Each student was requested to write an essay on "How and Why Henry Ford Became Wealthy."

Each student was required to describe, as a part of his or her essay, what was believed to be the nature of Ford's real assets, of what these assets consisted in detail.

The majority of the students gathered financial statements and inventories of the Ford assets and used these as the basis of their estimates of Ford's wealth.

Included in these "sources of Ford's wealth" were such as cash in banks, raw and finished materials in stock, real estate and buildings, good-will, estimated at from ten to twenty-five per cent of the value of the material assets.

You cannot become a power in your community nor achieve enduring success in any worthy undertaking until you become big enough to blame yourself for your own mistakes and reverses.

One student out of the entire group of several hundred answered as follows:

"Henry Ford's assets consist, in the main, of two items, viz.: (1) Working capital and raw and finished materials; (2) The knowledge, gained from experience, of Henry Ford, himself, and the co-operation of a well trained organization which understands how to apply this knowledge to best advantage from the Ford viewpoint. It is impossible to estimate, with anything approximating correctness, the actual dollars and cents value of either of these two groups of assets, but it is my opinion that their relative values are:

"The organized knowledge of the Ford Organization 75%

The value of cash and physical assets of every nature, including raw and finished

materials . . . . 25%"

This author is of the opinion that this statement was not compiled by the young man whose name was signed to it, without the assistance of some very analytical and experienced mind or minds.

Unquestionably the biggest asset that Henry Ford has is his own brain. Next to this would come the brains of his immediate circle of associates, for it has been through co-ordination of these that the physical assets which he controls were accumulated.

Destroy every plant the Ford Motor Company owns: every piece of machinery; every atom of raw or finished material, every finished automobile, and every dollar on deposit in any bank, and Ford would still be the most powerful man, economically, on earth. The brains which have built the Ford business could duplicate it again in short order. Capital is always available, in unlimited quantities, to such brains as Ford's.

Ford is the most powerful man on earth (economically) because he has the keenest and most practical conception of the principle of ORGANIZED KNOWLEDGE of any man on earth, as far as this author has the means of knowing.

Despite Ford's great power and financial success, it may be that he has blundered often in the application of the principles through which he accumulated this power. There is but little doubt that Ford's methods of mind co-ordination have often been crude; they must needs have been in the earlier days of this experience, before he gained the wisdom of application that would naturally go with maturity of years.

Neither can there be much doubt that Ford's application of the principle of mind chemistry was, at least at the start, the result of a chance alliance with other minds, particularly the mind of Edison. It is more than probable that Mr. Ford's remarkable insight into the laws of nature was first begun as the result of his friendly alliance with his own wife long before he ever met either Mr. Edison or Mr. Firestone. Many a man who never knows the real source of his success is made by his wife, through application of the "Master Mind" principle. Mrs. Ford is a most remarkably intelligent woman, and this author has reason to believe that it was her mind, blended with Mr. Ford's, which gave him his first real start toward power.

It may be mentioned, without in any way depriving Ford of any honor or glory, that in his earlier days of experience he had to combat the powerful enemies of illiteracy and ignorance to a greater extent than did either Edison or Firestone, both of whom were gifted by natural heredity with a most fortunate aptitude for acquiring and applying knowledge. Ford had to hew this talent out of the rough, raw timbers of his hereditary estate.

Within an inconceivably short period of time Ford has mastered three of the most stubborn enemies of mankind and transformed them into assets constituting the very foundation of his success.

These enemies are: Ignorance, illiteracy and poverty!

Any man who can stay the hand of these three savage forces, much less harness and use them to good account, is well worth close study by the less fortunate individuals.

This is an age of INDUSTRIAL POWER in which we are living!

The source of all this POWER is ORGANIZED EFFORT. Not only has the management of industrial enterprises efficiently organized individual workers, but, in many instances, mergers of industry have been effected in such a manner and to the end that these combinations (as in the case of the United States Steel Corporation, for example) have accumulated practically unlimited power.

One may hardly glance at the news of a day's events without seeing a report of some business, industrial or financial merger, bringing under one management enormous resources and thus creating great power.

One day it is a group of banks; another day it is a chain of railroads; the next day it is a combination of steel plants, all merging for the purpose of developing power through highly organized and co-ordinated effort.

Knowledge, general in nature and unorganized, is not POWER; it is only potential power—the material out of which real power may be developed. Any modern library contains an unorganized record of all the knowledge of value to which the present stage of civilization is heir, but this knowledge is not power because it is not organized.

Every form of energy and every species of animal or plant life, to survive, must be organized. The oversized animals whose bones have filled Nature's bone-yard through extinction have left mute but certain evidence that non-organization means annihilation.

From the electron—the smallest particle of matter—to the largest star in the universe: these and every material thing in between these two extremes offer proof positive that one of Nature's first laws is that of ORGANIZATION. Fortunate is the individual who recognizes the importance of this law and makes it his business to familiarize himself with the various ways in which the law may be applied to advantage.

The astute business man has not only recognized the importance of the law of organized effort, but he has made this law the warp and the woof of his POWER.

Without any knowledge, whatsoever, of the principle of mind chemistry, or that such a principle exists, many men have accumulated great power by merely organizing the knowledge they possessed. The majority of all who have discovered the principle of mind chemistry and developed that principle into a "MASTER MIND" have stumbled upon this knowledge by the merest of accident; often failing to recognize the real nature of their discovery or to understand the source of their power.

This author is of the opinion that all living persons who at the present time are consciously making use of the principle of mind chemistry in developing power through the blending of minds, may be counted on the fingers of the two hands, with, perhaps, several fingers left to spare.

If this estimate is even approximately true the student will readily see that there is but slight danger of the field of mind chemistry practice becoming over-crowded.

It is a well known fact that one of the most difficult tasks that any business man must perform is that of inducing those who are associated with him to co-ordinate their efforts in a spirit of harmony. To induce continuous co-operation between a group of workers, in any undertaking, is next to impossible. Only the most efficient leaders can accomplish this highly desired object, but once in a great while such a leader will rise above the horizon in the field of industry, business or finance, and then the world hears of a Henry Ford, Thomas A. Edison, John D. Rockefeller, Sr., E. H. Harriman or James J. Hill.

Never, in the history of the world, has there been such abundant opportunity as there is now for the person who is willing to serve before trying to collect.

Power and success are practically synonomous terms!

One grows out of the other; therefore, any person who has the knowledge and the ability to develop power, through the principle of harmonious co-ordination of effort between individual minds, or in any other manner, may be successful in any reasonable undertaking that is possible of successful termination.

It must not be assumed that a "Master Mind" will immediately spring, mushroom fashion, out of every group of minds which make pretense of co-ordination in a spirit of HARMONY!

Harmony, in the real sense of meaning of the word, is as rare among groups of people as is genuine Christianity among those who proclaim themselves Christians.

Harmony is the nucleus around which the state of mind known as "Master Mind" must be developed. Without this element of harmony there can be no "Master Mind," a truth which cannot be repeated too often.

Woodrow Wilson had in mind the development of a "Master Mind," to be composed of groups of minds representing the civilized nations of the world, in his proposal for establishing the League of Nations. Wilson's conception was the most far-reaching humanitarian idea ever created in the mind of man, because it dealt with a principle which embraces sufficient power to establish a real Brotherhood of Man on earth. The League of Nations, or some similar blending of international minds, in a spirit of harmony, is sure to become a reality.

The time when such unity of minds will take place will be measured largely by the time required for the great universities and NON-SECTARIAN institutions of learning to supplant ignorance and superstition with understanding and wisdom. This time is rapidly approaching.

The Psychology of the Revival Meeting: The old religious orgy known as the "revival" offers a favorable opportunity to study the principle of mind chemistry known as "Master Mind."

It will be observed that music plays no small part in bringing about the harmony essential to the blending of a group of minds in a revival meeting. Without music the revival meeting would be a tame affair.

During revival services the leader of the meeting has no difficulty in creating harmony in the minds of his devotees, but it is a well known fact that this state of harmony lasts no longer than the presence of the leader, after which the "Master Mind" he has temporarily created disintegrates.

By arousing the emotional nature of his followers the revivalist has no difficulty, under the proper stage setting and with the embellishment of the right sort of music, in creating a "Master Mind" which becomes noticeable to all who come in contact with it. The very air becomes charged with a positive, pleasing influence which changes the entire chemistry of all minds present.

The revivalist calls this energy "the Spirit of the Lord."

This author, through experiments conducted with a group of scientific investigators and laymen (who were unaware of the nature of the experiment), has created the same state of mind and the same positive atmosphere without calling it the Spirit of the Lord.

On many occasions this author has witnessed the creation of the same positive atmosphere in a group of men and women engaged in the business of salesmanship, without calling it the Spirit of the Lord.

The author helped conduct a school of salesmanship for Harrison Parker, founder of the Co-operative Society, of Chicago, and, by the use of the same principle of mind chemistry which the revivalist calls the Spirit of the Lord, so transformed the nature of a group of 3,000 men and women (all of whom were without former sales experience) that they sold more than $10,000,000.00 worth of securities in less than nine months, and earned more than $1,000,000 for themselves.

It was found that the average person who joined this school would reach the zenith of his or her selling power within one week, after which it was necessary to revitalize the individual's brain through a group sales meeting. These sales meetings were conducted on very much the same order as are the modern revival meetings of the religionist, with much the same stage equipment, including music and "high-powered" speakers who exhorted the salespeople in very much the same manner as does the modern religious revivalist.

Call it religion, psychology, mind chemistry or anything you please (they are all based upon the same principle), but there is nothing more certain than the fact that wherever a group of minds are brought into contact, in a spirit of PERFECT HARMONY, each mind in the group becomes immediately supplemented and re-enforced by a noticeable energy called a "Master Mind."

For all this writer professes to know this uncharted energy may be the Spirit of the Lord, but it operates just as favorably when called by any other name.

The human brain and nervous system constitute a piece of intricate machinery which but few, if any, understand. When controlled and properly directed this piece of machinery can be made to perform wonders of achievement and if not controlled it will perform wonders fantastic and phantom-like in nature, as may be seen by examining the inmates of any insane asylum.

The human brain has direct connection with a continuous influx of energy from which man derives his power to think. The brain receives this energy, mixes it with the energy created by the food taken into the body, and distributes it to every portion of the body, through the aid of the blood and the nervous system. It thus becomes what we call life.

From what source this outside energy comes no one seems to know; all we know about it is that we must have it or die. It seems reasonable to suppose that this energy is none other than that which we call ether, and that it flows into the body along with the oxygen from the air, as we breathe.

Every normal human body possesses a first-class chemical laboratory and a stock of chemicals sufficient to carry on the business of breaking up, assimilating and properly mixing and compounding the food we take into the body, preparatory to distributing it to wherever it is needed as a body builder.

Ample tests have been made, both with man and beast, to prove that the energy known as the mind plays an important part in this chemical operation of compounding and transforming food into the required substances to build and keep the body in repair.

It is known that worry, excitement or fear will interfere with the digestive process, and in extreme cases stop this process altogether, resulting in illness or death. It is obvious, then, that the mind enters into the chemistry of food digestion and distribution.

It is believed by many eminent authorities, although it may never have been scientifically proved, that the energy known as mind or thought may become contaminated with negative or "unsociable" units to such an extent that the whole nervous system is thrown out of working order, digestion is interfered with and various and sundry forms of disease will manifest themselves. Financial difficulties and unrequited love affairs head the list of causes of such mind disturbances.

A negative environment such as that existing where some member of the family is constantly "nagging," will interfere with the chemistry of the mind to such an extent that the individual will lose ambition and gradually sink into oblivion. It is because of this fact that the old saying that a man's wife may either "make" or "break" him is literally true. In a subsequent lesson a whole chapter on this subject is addressed to the wives of men.

Any high-school student knows that certain food combinations will, if taken into the stomach, result in indigestion, violent pain and even death. Good health depends, in part at least, upon a food combination that "harmonizes." But harmony of food combinations is not sufficient to insure good health; there must be harmony, also, between the units of energy known as the mind.

"Harmony" seems to be one of Nature's laws, without which there can be no such thing as ORGA-NIZED ENERGY, or life in any form whatsoever.

A man is half whipped the minute he begins to feel sorry for himself, or to spin an alibi with which he would explain away his defects.

The health of the body as well as the mind is literally built around, out of and upon the principle of HARMONY! The energy known as life begins to disintegrate and death approaches when the organs of the body stop working in harmony.

The moment harmony ceases at the source of any form of organized energy (power) the units of that energy are thrown into a chaotic state of disorder and the power is rendered neutral or passive.

Harmony is also the nucleus around which the principle of mind chemistry known as a "Master Mind" develops power. Destroy this harmony and you destroy the power growing out of the co-ordinated effort of a group of individual minds.

This truth has been stated, re-stated and presented in every manner which the author could conceive, with unending repetition, for the reason that unless the student grasps this principle and learns to apply it this lesson is useless.

Success in life, no matter what one may call success, is very largely a matter of adaptation to environment in such a manner that there is harmony between the individual and his environment. The palace of a king becomes as a hovel of a peasant if harmony does not abound within its walls. Conversely stated, the hut of a peasant may be made to yield more happiness than that of the mansion of the rich man, if harmony obtains in the former and not in the latter.

Without perfect harmony the science of astronomy would be as useless as the "bones of a saint," because the stars and planets would clash with one another, and all would be in a state of chaos and disorder.

Without the law of harmony an acorn might grow into a heterogeneous tree consisting of the wood of the oak, poplar, maple and what not.

Without the law of harmony the blood might deposit the food which grows finger nails on the scalp where hair is supposed to grow, and thus create a horny growth which might easily be mistaken, by the superstitious, to signify man's relationship to a certain imaginary gentleman with horns, often referred to by the more primitive type.

Without the law of harmony there can be no organization of knowledge, for what, may one ask, is organized knowledge except the harmony of facts and truths and natural laws?

The moment discord begins to creep in at the front door harmony edges out at the back door, so to speak, whether the application is made to a business partnership or the orderly movement of the planets of the heavens.

If the student gathers the impression that the author is laying undue stress upon the importance of HARMONY, let it be remembered that lack of harmony is the first, and often the last and only, cause of FAILURE!

There can be no poetry nor music nor oratory worthy of notice without the presence of harmony.

Good architecture is largely a matter of harmony. Without harmony a house is nothing but a mass of building material, more or less a monstrosity.

Sound business management plants the very sinews of its existence in harmony.

Every well dressed man or woman is a living picture and a moving example of harmony.

With all these workaday illustrations of the important part which harmony plays in the affairs of the world—nay, in the operation of the entire universe—how could any intelligent person leave harmony out of his "Definite Aim" in life? As well have no "definite aim" as to omit harmony as the chief stone of its foundation.

The human body is a complex organization of organs, glands, blood vessels, nerves, brain cells, muscles, etc. The mind energy which stimulates to action and co-ordinates the efforts of the component parts of the body is also a plurality of ever-varying and changing energies. From birth until death there is continuous struggle, often assuming the nature of open combat, between the forces of the mind. For example, the life-long struggle between the motivating forces and desires of the human mind, which takes place between the impulses of right and wrong, is well known to everyone.

Every human being possesses at least two distinct mind powers or personalities, and as many as six distinct personalities have been discovered in one person. One of man's most delicate tasks is that of harmonizing these mind forces so that they may be organized and directed toward the orderly attainment of a given objective. Without this element of harmony no individual can become an accurate thinker.

It is no wonder that leaders in business and industrial enterprises, as well as those in politics and other fields of endeavor, find it so difficult to organize groups of people so they will function in the attainment of a given objective, without friction. Each individual human being possesses forces, within himself, which are hard to harmonize, even when he is placed in the environment most favorable to harmony. If the chemistry of the individual's mind is such that the units of his mind cannot be easily harmonized, think how much more difficult it must be to harmonize a group of minds so they will function as one, in an orderly manner, through what is known as a "Master Mind."

The leader who successfully develops and directs the energies of a "Master Mind" must possess tact, patience, persistence, self-confidence, intimate knowledge of mind chemistry and the ability to adapt himself (in a state of perfect poise and harmony) to quickly changing circumstances, without showing the least sign of annoyance.

How many are there who can measure up to this requirement?

The successful leader must possess the ability to change the color of his mind, chameleon-like, to fit every circumstance that arises in connection with the object of his leadership. Moreover, he must possess the ability to change from one mood to another without showing the slightest signs of anger or lack of self-control. The successful leader must understand the Fifteen Laws of Success and be able to put into practice any combination of these Fifteen Laws whenever occasion demands.

Without this ability no leader can be powerful, and without power no leader can long endure.

The Meaning of Education: There has long been a general misconception of the meaning of the word "educate." The dictionaries have not aided in the elimination of this misunderstanding, because they have defined the word "educate" as an act of imparting knowledge.

The word educate has its roots in the Latin word *educo,* which means to develop FROM WITHIN; to educe; to draw out; to grow through the law of USE.

Nature hates idleness in all its forms. She gives continuous life only to those elements which are in use. Tie up an arm, or any other portion of the body, taking it out of use, and the idle part will soon atrophy and become lifeless. Reverse the order, give an arm more than normal use, such as that engaged in by the blacksmith who wields a heavy hammer all day long, and that arm (developed from within) grows strong.

Power grows out of ORGANIZED KNOWLEDGE, but, mind you, it "grows out of it" through application and use!

A man may become a walking encyclopædia of knowledge without possessing any power of value. This knowledge becomes power only to the extent that it is organized, classified and put into action. Some of the best educated men the world has known possessed much less general knowledge than some who have been known as fools, the difference between the two being that the former put what knowledge they possessed into use while the latter made no such application.

An "educated" person is one who knows how to acquire everything he needs in the attainment of his main purpose in life, without violating the rights of his fellow men. It might be a surprise to many so-called men of "learning" to know that they come nowhere near qualification as men of "education." It might also be a great surprise to many who believe they suffer from lack of "learning" to know that they are well "educated."

The successful lawyer is not necessarily the one who memorizes the greatest number of principles of law. On the contrary, the successful lawyer is the one who knows where to find a principle of law, plus a variety of opinions supporting that principle which fit the immediate needs of a given case.

Seek the counsel of men who will tell you the truth about yourself, even if it hurts you to hear it. Mere commendation will not bring the improvement you need.

In other words, the successful lawyer is he who knows where to find the law he wants when he needs it.

This principle applies, with equal force, to the affairs of industry and business.

Henry Ford had but little elementary schooling, yet he is one of the best "educated" men in the world because he has acquired the ability so to combine natural and economic laws, to say nothing of the minds of men, that he has the power to get anything of a material nature he wants.

Some years ago during the world war Mr. Ford brought suit against the Chicago Tribune, charging that newspaper with libelous publication of statements concerning him, one of which was the statement that Ford was an "ignoramus," an ignorant pacifist, etc.

When the suit came up for trial the attorneys for the Tribune undertook to prove, by Ford himself, that their statement was true; that he was ignorant, and with this object in view they catechized and cross-examined him on all manner of subjects.

One question they asked was:

"How many soldiers did the British send over to subdue the rebellion in the Colonies in 1776?"

With a dry grin on his face Ford nonchalantly replied:

"I do not know just how many, but I have heard that it was a lot more than ever went back."

Loud laughter from Court, jury, court-room spectators, and even from the frustrated lawyer who had asked the question.

This line of interrogation was continued for an hour or more, Ford keeping perfectly calm the meanwhile. Finally, however, he had permitted the "smart Aleck" lawyers to play with him until he was tired of it, and in reply to a question which was particularly obnoxious and insulting, Ford straightened himself up, pointed his finger at the questioning lawyer and replied:

"If I should really wish to answer the foolish question you have just asked, or any of the others you have been asking, let me remind you that I have a row of electric push-buttons hanging over my desk and by placing my finger on the right button I could call in men who could give me the correct answer to all the questions you have asked and to many that you have not the intelligence either to ask or answer. Now, will you kindly tell me why I should bother about filling my mind with a lot of useless details in order to answer every fool question that anyone may ask, when I have able men all about me who can supply me with all the facts I want when I call for them?"

This answer is quoted from memory, but it substantially relates Ford's answer.

There was silence in the court-room. The questioning attorney's under jaw dropped down, his eyes opened widely; the judge leaned forward from the bench and gazed in Mr. Ford's direction; many of the jury awoke and looked around as if they had heard an explosion (which they actually had).

A prominent clergyman who was present in the court-room at the time said, later, that the scene reminded him of that which must have existed when Jesus Christ was on trial before Pontius Pilate, just after He had given His famous reply to Pilate's question, "What is truth?"

In the vernacular of the day, Ford's reply knocked the questioner cold.

Up to the time of that reply the lawyer had been enjoying considerable fun at what he believed to be Ford's expense, by adroitly displaying his (the lawyer's) sample case of general knowledge and comparing it with what he inferred to be Ford's ignorance as to many events and subjects.

But that answer spoiled the lawyer's fun!

It also proved once more (to all who had the intelligence to accept the proof) that true education means mind development; not merely the gathering and classifying of knowledge.

Ford could not, in all probability, have named the capitals of all the States of the United States, but he could have and in fact had gathered the "capital" with which to "turn many wheels" within every State in the Union.

Education—let us not forget this—consists of the power with which to get everything one needs when he needs it, without violating the rights of his fellow men. Ford comes well within that definition, and for the reason which the author has here tried to make plain, by relating the foregoing incident connected with the simple Ford philosophy.

There are many men of "learning" who could easily entangle Ford, theoretically, with a maze of questions none of which he, personally, could answer. But Ford could turn right around and wage a battle in industry or finance that would exterminate those same men, with all of their knowledge and all of their wisdom.

Ford could not go into his chemical laboratory and separate water into its component atoms of hydrogen and oxygen and then re-combine these atoms in their former order, but he knows how to surround himself with chemists who can do this for him if he wants it done. The man who can intelligently use the knowledge possessed by another is as much or more a man of education as the person who merely has the knowledge but does not know what to do with it.

The president of a well known college inherited a large tract of very poor land. This land had no timber of commercial value, no minerals or other valuable appurtenances, therefore it was nothing but a source of expense to him, for he had to pay taxes on it. The State built a highway through the land. An "uneducated" man who was driving his automobile over this road observed that this poor land was on top of a mountain which commanded a wonderful view for many miles in all directions. He (the ignorant one) also observed that the land was covered with a growth of small pines and other saplings. He bought fifty acres of the land for $10.00 an acre. Near the public highway he built a unique log house to which he attached a large dining room. Near the house he put in a gasoline filling station. He built a dozen single-room log houses along the road, these he rented out to tourists at $3.00 a night, each. The dining room, gasoline filling station and log houses brought him a net income of $15,000.00 the first year. The next year he extended his plan by adding fifty more log houses, of three rooms each, which he now rents out as summer country homes to people in a near-by city, at a rental of $150.00 each for the season.

The building material cost him nothing, for it grew on his land in abundance (that same land which the college president believed to be worthless).

Moreover, the unique and unusual appearance of the log bungalows served as an advertisement of the plan, whereas many would have considered it a real calamity had they been compelled to build out of such crude materials.

Less than five miles from the location of these log houses this same man purchased an old worked-out farm of 150 acres, for $25.00 an acre, a price which the seller believed to be extremely high.

By building a dam, one hundred feet in length, the purchaser of this old farm turned a stream of water into a lake that covered fifteen acres of the land, stocked the lake with fish, then sold the farm off in building lots to people who wanted summering places around the lake. The total profit realized from this simple transaction was more than $25,000.00, and the time required for its consummation was one summer.

Yet this man of vision and imagination was not "educated" in the orthodox meaning of that term.

Let us keep in mind the fact that it is through these simple illustrations of the use of organized knowledge that one may become educated and powerful.

In speaking of the transaction here related, the college president who sold the fifty acres of worthless (?) land for $500.00 said:

"Just think of it! That man, whom most of us might call ignorant, mixed his ignorance with fifty acres of worthless land and made the combination yield more yearly than I earn from five years of application of so-called education."

When you lose your sense of humor, get a job running an elevator, because your life will be a series of UPS and DOWNS, anyway.

There is an opportunity, if not scores of them, in every State in America, to make use of the idea here described. From now on make it your business to study the lay of all land you see that is similar to that described in this lesson, and you may find a suitable place for developing a similar money-making enterprise. The idea is particularly adaptable in localities where bathing beaches are few, as people naturally like such conveniences.

The automobile has caused a great system of public highways to be built throughout the United States. On practically every one of these highways there is a suitable spot for a "Cabin City" for tourists which can be turned into a regular money-making mint by the man with the IMAGINATION and SELF-CONFIDENCE to do it.

There are opportunities to make money all around you. This course was designed to help you "see" these opportunities, and to inform you how to make the most of them after you discover them.

Who Can Profit Most by the Law of Success Philosophy?

RAILROAD OFFICIALS who want a better spirit of co-operation between their trainmen and the public they serve.

SALARIED PEOPLE who wish to increase their earning power and market their services to better advantage.

SALESPEOPLE who wish to become masters in their chosen field. The Law of Success philosophy covers every known law of selling, and includes many features not included in any other course.

INDUSTRIAL PLANT MANAGERS who understand the value of greater harmony among their employees.

RAILROAD EMPLOYEES who wish to establish records of efficiency which will lead to more responsible positions, with greater pay.

MERCHANTS who wish to extend their business by adding new customers. The Law of Success philosophy will help any merchant increase his business by teaching him how to make a walking advertisement of every customer who comes into his store.

AUTOMOBILE AGENTS who wish to increase the selling power of their salesmen. A large part of the Law of Success course was developed from the life-work and experience of the greatest automobile salesman living, and it is therefore of unusual help to the Sales Manager who is directing the efforts of Automobile Salesmen.

LIFE INSURANCE AGENTS who wish to add new policy-holders and increase the insurance on present policy-holders. One Life Insurance Salesman, in Ohio, sold a Fifty Thousand Dollar policy to one of the officials of the Central Steel Company, as the result of but one reading of the lesson on "Profiting by Failures." This same salesman has become one of the star men of the New York Life Insurance Company's staff, as the result of his training in the Fifteen Laws of Success.

SCHOOL TEACHERS who wish to advance to the top in their present occupation, or who are looking for an opportunity to enter the more profitable field of business as a life-work.

STUDENTS, both College and High School, who are undecided as to what field of endeavor they wish to enter as a life-work. The Law of Success course covers a complete Personal Analysis service which helps the student of the philosophy to determine the work for which he or she is best fitted.

BANKERS who wish to extend their business through better and more courteous methods of serving their clients.

BANK CLERKS who are ambitious to prepare themselves for executive positions in the field of banking, or in some commercial or industrial field.

PHYSICIANS and DENTISTS who wish to extend their practice without violating the ethics of their profession by direct advertising. A prominent physician has said that the Law of Success course is worth $1,000.00 to any professional man or woman whose professional ethics prevent direct advertising.

PROMOTERS who wish to develop new and heretofore unworked combinations in business or industry. The principle described in this Introduction is said to have made a small fortune for a man who used it as the basis of a real estate promotion.

REAL ESTATE MEN who wish new methods for promoting sales. This Introduction contains a description of an entirely new real-estate promotion plan which is sure to make fortunes for many who will put it to use. This plan may be put into operation in practically every State. Moreover, it may be employed by men who never promoted an enterprise.

FARMERS who wish to discover new methods of marketing their products so as to give them greater net returns, and those who own lands suitable for subdivision promotion under the plan referred to at the end of this Introduction. Thousands of farmers have "gold mines" in the land they own which is not suitable for cultivation, which could be used for recreation and resort purposes, on a highly profitable basis.

STENOGRAPHERS and BOOKKEEPERS who are looking for a practical plan to promote themselves into higher and better paying positions. The Law of Success course is said to be the best course ever written on the subject of marketing personal services.

PRINTERS who want a larger volume of business and more efficient production as the result of better co-operation among their own employees.

DAY LABORERS who have the ambition to advance into more responsible positions, in work that has greater responsibilities and consequently offers more pay.

LAWYERS who wish to extend their clientele through dignified, ethical methods which will bring them to the attention, in a favorable way, of a greater number of people who need legal services.

BUSINESS EXECUTIVES who wish to expand their present business, or who wish to handle their present volume with less expense, as the result of greater co-operation between their employees.

LAUNDRY OWNERS who wish to extend their business by teaching their drivers how to serve more courteously and efficiently.

LIFE INSURANCE GENERAL AGENTS who wish bigger and more efficient sales organizations.

CHAIN STORE MANAGERS who want a greater volume of business as the result of more efficient individual sales efforts.

MARRIED PEOPLE who are unhappy, and therefore unsuccessful, because of lack of harmony and co-operation in the home.

To all described in the foregoing classification the Law of Success philosophy offers both DEFINITE and SPEEDY aid.

Summary of the Introduction

The purpose of this summary is to aid the student in mastering the central idea around which the lesson has been developed. This idea is represented by the term "Master Mind" which has been described in great detail throughout the lesson.

All new ideas, and especially those of an abstract nature, find lodgment in the human mind only after much repetition, a well known truth which accounts for the re-statement, in this summary, of the principle known as the "Master Mind."

A "Master Mind" may be developed by a friendly alliance, in a spirit of harmony of purpose, between two or more minds.

An aim in life is the only fortune worth finding; and it is not to be found in foreign lands, but in the heart itself.
— ROBERT LOUIS STEVENSON

This is an appropriate place at which to explain that out of every alliance of minds, whether in a spirit of harmony or not, there is developed another mind which affects all participating in the alliance. No two or more minds ever met without creating, out of the contact, another mind, but not always is this invisible creation a "Master Mind."

There may be, and altogether too often there is, developed out of the meeting of two or more minds a negative power which is just the opposite to a "Master Mind."

There are certain minds which, as has already been stated throughout this lesson, cannot be made to blend in a spirit of harmony. This principle has its comparable analogy in chemistry, reference to which may enable the student to grasp more clearly the principle here referred to.

For example, the chemical formula H_2O (meaning the combining of two atoms of hydrogen with one atom of oxygen) changes these two elements into water. One atom of hydrogen and one atom of oxygen will not produce water; moreover, they cannot be made to associate themselves in harmony!

There are many known elements which, when combined, are immediately transformed from harmless into deadly poisonous substances. Stated differently, many well known poisonous elements are neutralized and rendered harmless when combined with certain other elements.

Just as the combining of certain elements changes their entire nature, the combining of certain minds changes the nature of those minds, producing either a certain degree of what has been called a "Master Mind," or its opposite, which is highly destructive.

Any man who has found his mother-in-law to be incompatible has experienced the negative application of the principle known as a "Master Mind." For some reason as yet unknown to investigators in the field of mind behavior, the majority of mothers-in-law appear to affect their daughters' husbands in a highly negative manner, the meeting of their minds with those of their sons-in-law creating a highly antagonistic influence instead of a "Master Mind."

This fact is too well known as a truth to make extended comment necessary.

Some minds will not be harmonized and cannot be blended into a "Master Mind," a fact which all leaders of men will do well to remember. It is the leader's responsibility so to group his men that those who have been placed at the most strategic points in his organization are made up of individuals whose minds CAN and WILL BE blended in a spirit of friendliness and harmony.

Ability so to group men is the chief outstanding quality of leadership. In Lesson One of this course the student will discover that this ability was the main source of both the power and fortune accumulated by the late Andrew Carnegie.

Knowing nothing whatsoever of the technical end of the steel business, Carnegie so combined and grouped the men of which his "Master Mind" was composed that he built the most successful steel industry known to the world during his life-time.

Henry Ford's gigantic success may be traced to the successful application of this selfsame principle. With all the self-reliance a man could have, Ford, nevertheless, did not depend upon himself for the knowledge necessary in the successful development of his industries.

Like Carnegie, he surrounded himself with men who supplied the knowledge which he, himself, did not and could not possess.

Moreover, Ford picked men who could and did harmonize in group effort.

The most effective alliances, which have resulted in the creation of the principle known as the "Master Mind," have been those developed out of the blending of the minds of men and women. The reason for this is the fact that the minds of male and female will more readily blend in harmony than will the minds of males. Also, the added stimulus of sexual contact often enters into the development of a "Master Mind" between a man and a woman.

It is a well known fact that the male of the species is keener and more alert for "the chase," let the goal or object of the chase be what it may, when inspired and urged on by a female.

This human trait begins to manifest itself in the male at the age of puberty, and continues throughout his life. The first evidence of it may be observed in athletics, where boys are playing before an audience made up of females.

Remove the women from the audience and the game known as football would soon become a very tame affair. A boy will throw himself into a football game with almost superhuman effort when he knows that the girl of his choice is observing him from the grandstand.

And that same boy will throw himself into the game of accumulating money with the same enthusiasm when inspired and urged on by the woman of his choice; especially if that woman knows how to stimulate his mind with her own, through the law of the "Master Mind."

On the other hand, that same woman may, through a negative application of the law of the "Master Mind" (nagging, jealousy, selfishness, greed, vanity), drag this man down to sure defeat!

The late Elbert Hubbard understood the principle here described so well that when he discovered that the incompatibility between himself and his first wife was dragging him down to sure defeat he ran the gamut of public opinion by divorcing her and marrying the woman who is said to have been the main source of his inspiration.

Not every man would have had the courage to defy public opinion, as Hubbard did, but who is wise enough to say that his action was not for the best interest of all concerned?

A man's chief business in life is to succeed!

The road to success may be, and generally is, obstructed by many influences which must be removed before the goal can be reached. One of the most detrimental of these obstacles is that of unfortunate alliance with minds which do not harmonize. In such cases the alliance must be broken or the end is sure to be defeat and failure.

The man who has mastered the six basic fears, one of which is the Fear of Criticism, will have no hesitancy in taking what may seem to the more convention-bound type of mind to be drastic action when he finds himself circumscribed and bound down by antagonistic alliances, no matter of what nature or with whom they may be.

It is a million times better to meet and face criticism than to be dragged down to failure and oblivion on account of alliances which are not harmonious, whether the alliances be of a business or social nature.

To be perfectly frank, the author is here justifying divorce, when the conditions surrounding marriage are such that harmony cannot prevail. This is not intended to convey the belief that lack of harmony may not be removed through other methods than that of divorce; for there are instances where the cause of antagonism may be removed and harmony established without taking the extreme step of divorce.

If you cannot do great things yourself, remember that you may do small things in a great way.

While it is true that some minds will not blend in a spirit of harmony, and cannot be forced or induced to do so, because of the chemical nature of the individuals' brains, DO NOT BE TOO READY TO CHARGE THE OTHER PARTY TO YOUR ALLIANCE WITH ALL THE RESPONSIBILITY OF LACK OF HARMONY—REMEMBER, *THE TROUBLE MAY BE WITH YOUR OWN BRAIN!*

Remember, also, that a mind which cannot and will not harmonize with one person or persons may harmonize perfectly with other types of minds. Discovery of this truth has resulted in radical changes in methods of employing men. It is no longer customary to discharge a man because he does not fit in the position for which he was originally hired. The discriminating leader endeavors to place such a man in some other position, where, it has been proved more than once, misfits may become valuable men.

The student of this course should be sure that the principle described as the "Master Mind" is thoroughly understood before proceeding with the remaining lessons of the course. The reason for this is the fact that practically the entire course is closely associated with this law of mind operation.

If you are not sure that you understand this law, communicate with the author of the course and secure further explanation by asking such questions as you may wish concerning points in connection with which you believe you need further information.

You cannot spend too much time in serious thought and contemplation in connection with the law of the "Master Mind," for the reason that when you have mastered this law and have learned how to apply it new worlds of opportunity will open to you.

This Introduction, while not really intended as a separate lesson of the Law of Success course, contains sufficient data to enable the student who has an aptitude for selling to become a Master Salesman.

Any sales organization may make effective use of the law of the "Master Mind" by grouping the salesmen in groups of two or more people who will ally themselves in a spirit of friendly co-operation and apply this law as suggested in this lesson.

An agent for a well known make of automobile, who employs twelve salesmen, has grouped his organization in six groups of two men each, with the object of applying the law of the "Master Mind," with the result that all the salesmen have established new high sales records.

This same organization has created what it calls the "One-A-Week Club," meaning that each man belonging to the Club has averaged the sale of one car a week since the Club was organized.

The results of this effort have been surprising to all!

Each man belonging to the Club was provided with a list of 100 prospective purchasers of automobiles. Each salesman sends one postal card a week to each of his 100 prospective purchasers, and makes personal calls on at least ten of these each day.

Each postal card is confined to the description of but one advantage of the automobile the salesman is selling, and asks for a personal interview.

Interviews have increased rapidly, as have, also, sales!

The agent who employs these salesmen has offered an extra cash bonus to each salesman who earns the right to membership in the "One-A-Week Club" by averaging one car a week.

The plan has injected new vitality into the entire organization. Moreover, the results of the plan are showing in the weekly sales record of each salesman.

A similar plan could be adopted very effectively by Life Insurance Agencies. Any enterprising General Agent might easily double or even triple the volume of his business, with the same number of salesmen, through the use of this plan.

Practically no changes whatsoever would need to be made in the method of use of the plan. The Club might be called the "Policy-A-Week Club," meaning that each member pledged himself to sell at least one policy, of an agreed minimum amount, each week.

The student of this course who has mastered the first lesson, and understands how to apply the fundamentals of that lesson (A Definite Chief Aim) will be able to make much more effective use of the plan here described.

It is not suggested or intended that any student shall undertake to apply the principles of this Introduction, until he has mastered at least the next five lessons of the Law of Success course.

The main purpose of this Introduction is to state some of the principles upon which the course is founded. These principles are more accurately described, and the student is taught in a very definite manner how to apply them, in the individual lessons of the course.

The automobile sales organization referred to in this summary meets at luncheon once a week. One hour and a half is devoted to luncheon and to the discussion of ways and means of applying the principles of this course. This gives each man an opportunity to profit by the ideas of all the other members of the organization.

Two tables are set for the luncheon.

NOTICE

Study this chart carefully and compare the ratings of these ten men before grading yourself, in the two columns at the right.

Grade yourself in these two columns, before and after completing the Law of Success course.

THE FIFTEEN LAWS OF SUCCESS	Henry Ford	Benjamin Franklin	George Washington	Theodore Roosevelt	Abraham Lincoln	Woodrow Wilson	William H. Taft	Napoleon Bonaparte	Calvin Coolidge	Jesse James	BEFORE	AFTER
I. Definite Chief Aim - - - - -	100	100	100	100	100	100	100	100	100	0		
II. Self-Confidence - - - - - - -	100	80	90	100	75	80	50	100	60	75		
III. Habit of Saving - - - - - - -	100	100	75	50	20	40	30	40	100	0		
IV. Initiative & Leadership - - -	100	60	100	100	60	90	20	100	25	90		
V. Imagination - - - - - - - - -	90	90	80	80	70	80	65	90	50	60		
VI. Enthusiasm - - - - - - - - - -	75	80	90	100	60	90	50	80	50	80		
VII. Self-Control - - - - - - - - -	100	90	50	75	95	75	80	40	100	50		
VIII. Habit of Doing More Than Paid For -	100	100	100	100	100	100	100	100	100	0		
IX. Pleasing Personality - - - - -	50	90	80	80	80	75	90	100	40	50		
X. Accurate Thinking - - - - -	90	80	75	60	90	80	80	90	70	20		
XI. Concentration - - - - - - - -	100	100	100	100	100	100	100	100	100	75		
XII. Co-operation - - - - - - - -	75	100	100	50	90	40	100	50	60	50		
XIII. Profiting by Failure - - - - -	100	90	75	60	60	60	60	40	40	0		
XIV. Tolerance - - - - - - - - - - -	90	100	80	75	100	70	100	10	75	0		
XV. Practising Golden Rule - - -	100	100	100	100	100	100	100	0	100	0		
GENERAL AVERAGE - - - -	91	90	86	82	81	79	75	70	71	37		

The ten men who have been analyzed, in the above chart, are well known throughout the world. Eight of these are known to be successful, while two are generally considered to have been failures. The failures are Jesse James and Napoleon Bonaparte. They have been analyzed for comparison. Carefully observe where these two men have been graded zero and you will see why they failed. *A grading of zero on any one of the Fifteen Laws of Success is sufficient to cause failure,* even though all other grades are high.

Notice that all the successful men grade 100% on a Definite Chief Aim. This is a prerequisite to success, in all cases, without exception. If you wish to conduct an interesting experiment replace the above ten names with the names of ten people whom you know, five of whom are successful and five of whom are failures, and grade each of them. When you are through, GRADE YOURSELF, taking care to see that you really know what are your weaknesses.

At one table all who have earned the right to membership in the One-A-Week Club are seated. At the other table, which is serviced with tinware instead of china, all who did not earn the right to membership in the Club are seated. These, needless to say, become the object of considerable good-natured chiding from the more fortunate members seated at the other table.

It is possible to make an almost endless variety of adaptations of this plan, both in the field of automobile salesmanship and in other fields of selling.

The justification for its use is that it pays!

It pays not only the leader or manager of the organization, but every member of the sales force as well.

This plan has been briefly described for the purpose of showing the student of this course how to make practical application of the principles outlined in this course.

The final acid test of any theory or rule or principle is that it will ACTUALLY WORK! The law of the "Master Mind" has been proved sound because it WORKS.

If you understand this law you are now ready to proceed with Lesson One, in which you will be further and much more deeply initiated in the application of the principles described in this Introduction.

> *A winner never quits, and a quitter never wins!*

YOUR SIX MOST DANGEROUS ENEMIES

An After-the-Lesson Visit with the Author

The Six Specters are labeled: Fear of Poverty, Fear of Death, Fear of Ill- Health, Fear of the Loss of Love, Fear of Old Age, Fear of Criticism.

Every person on earth is afraid of something. Most fears are inherited. In this essay you may study the six basic fears which do the most damage. Your fears must be mastered before you can win in any worth-while undertaking in life. Find out how many of the six fears are bothering you, but more important than this, determine, also how to conquer these fears.

In this picture you have the opportunity to study your six worst enemies.

These enemies are not beautiful. The artist who drew this picture did not paint the six characters as ugly as they really are. If he had, no one would have believed him.

As you read about these ugly characters analyze yourself and find out which of them does YOU the most damage!

The purpose of this essay is to help the readers of this course throw off these deadly enemies. Observe that the six characters are at your back, where you cannot conveniently see them.

Every human being on this earth is bound down to some extent by one or more of these unseen FEARS. The first step to be taken in killing off these enemies is to find out where and how you acquired them.

They got their grip upon you through two forms of heredity. One is known as physical heredity, to which Darwin devoted so much study. The other is known as social heredity, through which the fears, superstitions and beliefs of men who lived during the dark ages have been passed on from one generation to another.

Let us study, first, the part that physical heredity has played in creating these six BASIC FEARS. Starting at the beginning, we find that Nature has been a cruel builder. From the lowest form of life to the highest, Nature has permitted the stronger to prey upon the weaker forms of animal life.

The fish prey upon the worms and insects, eating them bodily. Birds prey upon the fish. Higher forms of animal life prey upon the birds, and upon one another, all the way up the line to man. And, man preys upon all the other lower forms of animal life, and upon MAN!

The whole story of evolution is one unbroken chain of evidence of cruelty and destruction of the weaker by the stronger. No wonder the weaker forms of animal life have learned to FEAR the stronger. The Fear consciousness is born in every living animal.

———

So much for the FEAR instinct that came to us through physical heredity. Now let us examine social heredity, and find out what part it has played in our make-up. The term "social heredity" has reference to everything that we are taught, everything we learn or gather from observation and experience with other living beings.

Lay aside any prejudices and fixed opinions you may have formed, at least temporarily, and you may know the truth about your Six Worst Enemies, starting with:

The Fear of Poverty! It requires courage to tell the truth about the history of this enemy of mankind, and still greater courage to hear the truth after it has been told. The Fear of Poverty grows out of man's habit of preying upon his fellow men, economically. The animals which have instinct, but no power to THINK, prey upon one another physically. Man, with his superior sense of intuition, and his more powerful weapon of THOUGHT, does not eat his fellow man bodily; he gets more pleasure from eating him FINANCIALLY.

So great an offender is man, in this respect, that nearly every state and nation has been obliged to pass laws, scores of laws, to protect the weak from the strong. Every blue-sky law is indisputable evidence of man's nature to prey upon his weaker brother economically.

The second of the Six Basic Fears with which man is bound down is:

The Fear of Old Age! This Fear grows out of two major causes. First, the thought that Old Age may bring with it POVERTY. Secondly, from false and cruel sectarian teachings which have been so well mixed with fire and brimstone that every human being learned to Fear Old Age because it meant the approach of another and, perhaps, a more horrible world than this.

The third of the Six Basic Fears is:

The Fear of Ill Health: This Fear is born of both physical and social heredity. From birth until death there is eternal warfare within every physical body; warfare between groups of cells, one group being known as the friendly builders of the body, and the other as the destroyers, or "disease germs." The seed of Fear is born in the physical body, to begin with, as the result of Nature's cruel plan of permitting the stronger forms of cell life to prey upon the weaker. Social heredity has played its part through lack of cleanliness and knowledge of sanitation. Also, through the law of suggestion cleverly manipulated by those who profited by ILL HEALTH.

The fourth of the Six Basic Fears is:

The Fear of Loss of Love of Someone: This Fear fills the asylums with the insanely jealous, for jealousy is nothing but a form of insanity. It also fills the divorce courts and causes murders and other forms of cruel punishment. It is a holdover, handed down through social heredity, from the stone age when man preyed upon his fellow man by stealing his mate by physical force. The method, but not the practice, has now changed to some extent. Instead of physical force man now steals his fellow man's mate with pretty colorful ribbons and fast motor cars and bootleg whisky, and sparkling rocks and stately mansions.

Man is improving. He now "entices" where once he "drove."

The fifth of the Six Basic Fears is:

The Fear of Criticism: Just how and where man got this Fear is difficult to determine, but it is certain that he has it. But for this Fear men would not become bald-headed. Bald heads come from tightly fitting hat-bands, which cut off the circulation from the roots of the hair. Women seldom are bald because they wear loose fitting hats. But for Fear of Criticism man would lay aside his hat and keep his hair.

The makers of clothing have not been slow to capitalize this Basic Fear of mankind. Every season the styles change, because the clothes makers know that few people have the courage to wear a garment that is one season out of step with what "They are all wearing." If you doubt this (you gentlemen) start down the street with last year's narrow-brimmed straw hat on, when this year's style calls for the broad brim. Or (you ladies), take a walk down the street on Easter morning with last year's hat on. Observe how uncomfortable you are, thanks to your unseen enemy, the FEAR OF CRITICISM.

The sixth and last of the Six Basic Fears is the most dreaded of them all. It is called:

The Fear of Death! For tens of thousands of years man has been asking the still unanswered questions—"WHENCE?" and "WHITHER?" The more crafty of the race have not been slow to offer the answer to this eternal question, "Where did I come from and where am I going after Death?" "Come into my tent," says one leader, "and you may go to Heaven after Death." Heaven was then pictured as a wonderful city whose streets were lined with gold and studded with precious stones. "Remain out of my tent and you may go straight to hell." Hell was then pictured as a blazing furnace where the poor victim might have the misery of burning forever in brimstone.

No wonder mankind FEARS DEATH!

Take another look at the picture at the beginning of this essay and determine, if you can, which of the Six Basic Fears is doing you the greatest damage. An enemy discovered is an enemy half whipped.

Thanks to the schools and colleges man is slowly discovering these Six Enemies. The most effective tool with which to fight them is ORGANIZED KNOWLEDGE. Ignorance and Fear are twin sisters. They are generally found together.

But for IGNORANCE and SUPERSTITION the Six Basic Fears would disappear from man's nature in one generation. In every public library may be found the remedy for these six enemies of mankind, providing you know what books to read.

Begin by reading *The Science of Power,* by Benjamin Kidd, and you will have broken the strangle hold of most of your Six Basic Fears. Follow this by reading Emerson's essay on Compensation. Then select some good book on auto-suggestion (self-suggestion) and inform yourself on the principle through which your beliefs of today become the realities of tomorrow. *Mind in the Making,* by Robinson, will give you a good start toward understanding your own mind.

Through the principle of social heredity the IGNORANCE and SUPERSTITION of the dark ages have been passed on to you. But, you are living in a modern age. On every hand you may see evidence that every EFFECT has a natural CAUSE. Begin, now, to study effects by their causes and soon you will emancipate your mind from the burden of the Six Basic Fears.

Begin by studying men who have accumulated great wealth, and find out the CAUSE of their achievements. Henry Ford is a good subject to start with. Within the short period of twenty-five years he has whipped POVERTY and made himself the most powerful man on earth. There was no luck or chance or accident back of his achievement. It grew out of his careful observation of certain principles which are as available to you as they were to him.

Henry Ford is not bound down by the Six Basic Fears; make no mistake about this.

If you feel that you are too far away from Ford to study him accurately, then begin by selecting two people whom you know close at hand; one representing your idea of FAILURE and the other corresponding to your idea of SUCCESS. Find out what made one a failure and the other a success. Get the real FACTS. In the process of gathering these facts you will have taught yourself a great lesson on CAUSE and EFFECT.

Nothing ever just "happens." Everything, from the lowest animal form that creeps on the earth or swims in the seas, on up to man, is the EFFECT of Nature's evolutionary process. Evolution is "orderly change." No "miracles" are connected with this orderly change.

Not only do the physical shapes and colors of animals undergo slow, orderly change from one generation to another, but the mind of man is also undergoing constant change. Herein lies your hope for improvement. You have the power to force your mind through a process of rather quick change. In a single month of properly directed self-suggestion you may place your foot upon the neck of every one of your Six Basic Fears. In twelve months of persistent effort you may drive the entire herd into the corner where it will never again do you any serious injury.

You will resemble, tomorrow, the DOMINATING THOUGHTS that you keep alive in your mind today! Plant in your mind the seed of DETERMINATION to whip your Six Basic Fears and the battle will have been half won then and there. Keep this intention in your mind and it will slowly push your Six Worst Enemies out of sight, as they exist nowhere except in your own mind.

One of the most destructive evils is slanderous talk. It breaks human hearts and ruins reputations with a ruthlessness unknown in connection with all other evils.

The man who is powerful FEARS nothing; not even God. The POWERFUL man loves God, but FEARS Him never! Enduring power never grows out of FEAR. Any power that is built upon FEAR is bound to crumble and disintegrate. Understand this great truth and you will never be so unfortunate as to try to raise yourself to power through the FEARS of other people who may owe you temporary allegiance.

Man is of soul and body formed for deeds
Of high resolve; on fancy's boldest wing
To soar unwearied, fearlessly to turn
The keenest pangs to peacefulness, and taste
The joys which mingled sense and spirit yield;

Or he is formed for abjectness and woe,
To grovel on the dunghill of his fears,
To shrink at every sound, to quench the flame
Of natural love in sensualism, to know
That hour as blest when on his worthless days
The frozen hand of death shall set its seal,
Yet fear the cure, though hating the disease.

The one is man that shall hereafter be,
The other, man as vice has made him now.

—SHELLEY

The best rose bush, after all, is not that which has the fewest thorns, but that which bears the finest roses.

—HENRY VAN DYKE

A DEFINITE CHIEF AIM

"You Can Do It If You Believe You Can!"

You are at the beginning of a course of philosophy which, for the first time in the history of the world, has been organized from the known factors which have been used and must always be used by successful people.

Literary style has been completely subordinated for the sake of stating the principles and laws included in this course in such a manner that they may be quickly and easily assimilated by people in every walk of life.

Some of the principles described in the course are familiar to all who will read the course. Others are here stated for the first time. It should be kept in mind, from the first lesson to the last, that the value of the philosophy lies entirely in the thought stimuli it will produce in the mind of the student, and not merely in the lessons themselves.

Stated in another way, this course is intended as a mind stimulant that will cause the student to organize and direct to a DEFINITE end the forces of his or her mind, thus harnessing the stupendous power which most people waste in spasmodic, purposeless thought.

Singleness of purpose is essential for success, no matter what may be one's idea of the definition of success. Yet singleness of purpose is a quality which may, and generally does, call for thought on many allied subjects.

This author traveled a long distance to watch Jack Dempsey train for an oncoming battle. It was observed that he did not rely entirely upon one form of exercise, but resorted to many forms. The punching bag helped him develop one set of muscles, and also trained his eye to be quick. The dumb-bells trained still another set of muscles. Running developed the muscles of his legs and hips. A well balanced food ration supplied the materials needed for building muscle without fat. Proper sleep, relaxation and rest habits provided still other qualities which he must have in order to win.

The student of this course is, or should be, engaged in the business of training for success in the battle of life. To win there are many factors which must have attention. A well organized, alert and energetic mind is produced by various and sundry stimuli, all of which are plainly described in these lessons.

It should be remembered, however, that the mind requires, for its development, a variety of exercise, just as the physical body, to be properly developed, calls for many forms of systematic exercise.

Horses are trained to certain gaits by trainers who hurdle-jump them over handicaps which cause them to develop the desired steps, through habit and repetition. The human mind must be trained in a similar manner, by a variety of thought-inspiring stimuli.

You will observe, before you have gone very far into this philosophy, that the reading of these lessons will superinduce a flow of thoughts covering a wide range of subjects. For this reason the student should read the course with a note-book and pencil at hand, and follow the practice of recording these thoughts or "ideas" as they come into the mind.

By following this suggestion the student will have a collection of ideas, by the time the course has been read two or three times, sufficient to transform his or her entire life-plan.

By following this practice it will be noticed, very soon, that the mind has become like a magnet in that it will attract useful ideas right out of the "thin air," to use the words of a noted scientist who has experimented with this principle for a great number of years.

You will do yourself a great injustice if you undertake this course with even a remote feeling that you do not stand in need of more knowledge than you now possess. In truth, no man knows enough about any worth-while subject to entitle him to feel that he has the last word on that subject.

In the long, hard task of trying to wipe out some of my own ignorance and make way for some of the useful truths of life, I have often seen, in my imagination, the Great Marker who stands at the gateway entrance of life and writes "Poor Fool" on the brow of those who believe they are wise, and "Poor Sinner" on the brow of those who believe they are saints.

Which, translated into workaday language, means that none of us know very much, and by the very nature of our being can never know as much as we need to know in order to live sanely and enjoy life while we live.

Humility is a forerunner of success!

Until we become humble in our own hearts we are not apt to profit greatly by the experiences and thoughts of others.

Sounds like a preachment on morality? Well, what if it does?

Even "preachments," as dry and lacking in interest as they generally are, may be beneficial if they serve to reflect the shadow of our real selves so we may get an approximate idea of our smallness and superficiality.

Success in life is largely predicated upon our knowing men!

The best place to study the man-animal is in your own mind, by taking as accurate an inventory as possible of YOURSELF. When you know yourself thoroughly (if you ever do) you will also know much about others.

To know others, not as they seem to be, but as they really are, study them through:

1. The posture of the body, and the way they walk.
2. The tone of the voice, its quality, pitch, volume.
3. The eyes, whether shifty or direct.
4. The use of words, their trend, nature and quality.

Through these open windows you may literally "walk right into a man's soul" and take a look at the REAL MAN!

Going a step further, if you would know men study them:

When angry

When in love

When money is involved

When eating (alone, and unobserved, as they believe)

When writing

When in trouble

When joyful and triumphant

When downcast and defeated

When facing catastrophe of a hazardous nature

When trying to make a "good impression" on others

When informed of another's misfortune

When informed of another's good fortune

When losing in any sort of a game of sport

When winning at sport

When alone, in a meditative mood.

Before you can know any man, as he really is, you must observe him in all the foregoing moods, and perhaps more, which is practically the equivalent of saying that you have no right to judge others at sight.

Appearances count, there can be no doubt of that, but appearances are often deceiving.

This course has been so designed that the student who masters it may take inventory of himself and of others by other than "snap-judgment" methods. The student who masters this philosophy will be able to look through the outer crust of personal adornment, clothes, so-called culture and the like, and down deep into the heart of all about him.

This is a very broad promise!

It would not have been made if the author of this philosophy had not known, from years of experimentation and analysis, that the promise can be met.

Some who have examined the manuscripts of this course have asked why it was not called a course in Master Salesmanship. The answer is that the word "salesmanship" is commonly associated with the marketing of goods or services, and it would, therefore, narrow down and circumscribe the real nature of the course. It is true that this is a course in Master Salesmanship, providing one takes a deeper-than-the-average view of the meaning of salesmanship.

No person is "Educated" who has not at least a "Speaking Acquaintance" with the Law of Compensation, as it is described by Emerson.

This philosophy is intended to enable those who master it to "sell" their way through life successfully, with the minimum amount of resistance and friction. Such a course, therefore, must help the student organize and make use of much truth which is overlooked by the majority of people who go through life as mediocres.

Not all people are so constituted that they wish to know the truth about all matters vitally affecting life. One of the great surprises the author of this course has met with, in connection with his research activities, is that so few people are willing to hear the truth when it shows up their own weaknesses.

We prefer illusions to realities!

New truths, if accepted at all, are taken with the proverbial grain of salt. Some of us demand more than a mere pinch of salt; we demand enough to pickle new ideas so they become useless.

For these reasons the Introduction to this course, and this lesson as well, cover subjects intended to pave the way for new ideas so those ideas will not be too severe a shock to the mind of the student.

The thought the author wishes to "get across" has been quite plainly stated by the editor of the *American Magazine*, in an editorial which appeared in a recent issue, in the following words:

"On a recent rainy night, Carl Lomen, the reindeer king of Alaska, told me a true story. It has stuck in my crop ever since. And now I am going to pass it along.

"'A certain Greenland Eskimo,' said Lomen, 'was taken on one of the American North Polar expeditions a number of years ago. Later, as a reward for faithful service, he was brought to New York City for a short visit. At all the miracles of sight and sound he was filled with a most amazed wonder. When he returned to his native village he told stories of buildings that rose into the very face of the sky; of street cars, which he described as houses that moved along the trail, with people living in them as they moved; of mammoth bridges, artificial lights, and all the other dazzling concomitants of the metropolis.

"'His people looked at him coldly and walked away. And forthwith throughout the whole village he was dubbed "Sagdluk," meaning "the Liar," and this name he carried in shame to his grave. Long before his death his original name was entirely forgotten.

"'When Knud Rasmussen made his trip from Greenland to Alaska he was accompanied by a Greenland Eskimo named Mitek (Eider Duck). Mitek visited Copenhagen and New York, where he saw many things for the first time and was greatly impressed. Later, upon his return to Greenland, he recalled the tragedy of Sagdluk, and decided that it would not be wise to tell the truth. Instead, he would narrate stories that his people could grasp, and thus save his reputation.

"'So he told them how he and Doctor Rasmussen maintained a kayak on the banks of a great river, the Hudson, and how, each morning, they paddled out for their hunting. Ducks, geese and seals were to be had a-plenty, and they enjoyed the visit immensely.

"'Mitek, in the eyes of his countrymen, is a very honest man. His neighbors treat him with rare respect.'

"The road of the truth-teller has always been rocky. Socrates sipping the hemlock, Christ crucified, Stephen stoned, Bruno burned at the stake, Galileo terrified into retraction of his starry truths—forever could one follow that bloodly trail through the pages of history.

"Something in human nature makes us resent the impact of new ideas."

We hate to be disturbed in the beliefs and prejudices that have been handed down with the family furniture. At maturity too many of us go into hibernation, and live off the fat of ancient fetishes. If a new idea invades our den we rise up snarling from our winter sleep.

The Eskimos, at least, had some excuse. They were unable to visualize the startling pictures drawn by Sagdluk. Their simple lives had been too long circumscribed by the brooding arctic night.

But there is no adequate reason why the average man should ever close his mind to fresh "slants" on life. He does, just the same. Nothing is more tragic—or more common—than mental inertia. For every ten men who are physically lazy there are ten thousand with stagnant minds. And stagnant minds are the breeding places of fear.

An old farmer up in Vermont always used to wind up his prayers with this plea: "Oh, God, give me an open mind!" If more people followed his example they might escape being hamstrung by prejudices. And what a pleasant place to live in the world would be.

Every person should make it his business to gather new ideas from sources other than the environment in which he daily lives and works.

The mind becomes withered, stagnant, narrow and closed unless it searches for new ideas. The farmer should come to the city quite often, and walk among the strange faces and the tall buildings. He will go back to his farm, his mind refreshed, with more courage and greater enthusiasm.

The city man should take a trip to the country every so often and freshen his mind with sights new and different from those associated with his daily labors.

Everyone needs a change of mental environment at regular periods, the same as a change and variety of food are essential. The mind becomes more alert, more elastic and more ready to work with speed and accuracy after it has been bathed in new ideas, outside of one's own field of daily labor.

As a student of this course you will temporarily lay aside the set of ideas with which you perform your daily labors, and enter a field of entirely new (and in some instances, heretofore unheard-of) ideas.

Splendid! You will come out, at the other end of this course, with a new stock of ideas which will make you more efficient, more enthusiastic and more courageous, *no matter in what sort of work you may be engaged.*

Do not be afraid of new ideas! They may mean to you the difference between success and failure.

Some of the ideas introduced in this course will require no further explanation or proof of their soundness because they are familiar to practically everyone. Other ideas here introduced are new, and for that very reason many students of this philosophy may hesitate to accept them as sound.

Every principle described in this course has been thoroughly tested by the author, and the majority of the principles covered have been tested by scores of scientists and others who were quite capable of distinguishing between the merely theoretic and the practical.

For these reasons all principles here covered are known to be workable in the exact manner claimed for them. However, no student of this course is asked to accept any statement made in these lessons without having first satisfied himself or herself, by tests, experiments and analysis, that the statement is sound.

The major evil the student is requested to avoid is that of forming opinions without definite FACTS as the basis, which brings to mind Herbert Spencer's famous admonition, in these words:

"There is a principle which is a bar against all information; which is proof against all argument; and which cannot fail to keep a man in everlasting ignorance. This principle is contempt prior to examination."

It may be well to bear this principle in mind when you come to study the Law of the Master Mind described in these lessons. This law embodies an entirely new principle of mind operation, and, for this reason alone, it will be difficult for many students to accept it as sound until after they have experimented with it.

When the fact is considered, however, that the Law of the Master Mind is believed to be the real basis of most of the achievements of those who are considered geniuses, this Law takes on an aspect which calls for more than "snap-judgment" opinions.

It is believed by many scientific men whose opinions on the subject have been given the author of this philosophy, that the Law of the Master Mind is the basis of

By and Large, there is no such thing as "Something for Nothing." In the long run you get exactly that for which you pay, whether you are buying an automobile or a loaf of bread.

practically all of the more important achievements resulting from group or co-operative effort.

The late Dr. Alexander Graham Bell said he believed the Law of the Master Mind, as it has been described in this philosophy, was not only sound, but that all the higher institutions of learning would soon be teaching that Law as a part of their courses in psychology.

Charles P. Steinmetz said he had experimented with the Law and had arrived at the same conclusion as that stated in these lessons, long before he talked to the author of the Law of Success philosophy about the subject.

Luther Burbank and John Burroughs made similar statements!

Edison was never interrogated on the subject, but other statements of his indicate that he would endorse the Law as being a possibility, if not in fact a reality.

Dr. Elmer Gates endorsed the Law, in a conversation with this author more than fifteen years ago. Dr. Gates is a scientist of the highest order, ranking along with Steinmetz, Edison and Bell.

The author of this philosophy has talked to scores of intelligent business men who, while they were not scientists, admitted they believed in the soundness of the Law of the Master Mind. It is hardly excusable, therefore, for men of less ability to judge such matters, to form opinions as to this Law, without serious, systematic investigation.

Let me lay before you a brief outline of what this lesson is and what it is intended to do for *you!*

Having prepared myself for the practice of law I will offer this introduction as a "statement of my case." The evidence with which to back up my case will be presented in the fifteen lessons of which the course is composed.

The facts out of which this course has been prepared have been gathered through more than twenty-five years of business and professional experience, and my only explanation of the rather free use of the personal pronoun throughout the course is that I am writing from *first-hand experience.*

Before this Reading Course on the Law of Success was published the manuscripts were submitted to two prominent universities with the request that they be read by competent professors with the object of eliminating or correcting any statements that appeared to be unsound, from an economic viewpoint.

This request was complied with and the manuscripts were carefully examined, with the result that not a single change was made with the exception of one or two slight changes in wording.

One of the professors who examined the manuscripts expressed himself, in part, as follows: "It is a tragedy that every boy and girl who enters high school is not efficiently drilled on the fifteen major parts of your Reading Course on the Law of Success. It is regrettable that the great university with which I am connected, and every other university, does not include your course as a part of its curriculum."

Inasmuch as this Reading Course is intended as a map or blueprint that will guide you in the attainment of that coveted goal called "Success," may it not be well here to define success?

Success is the development of the power with which to get whatever one wants in life without interfering with the rights of others.

I would lay particular stress upon the word "power" because it is inseparably related to success. We are living in a world and during an age of intense competition, and the law of the survival of the fittest is everywhere in evidence. Because of these facts all who would enjoy enduring success must go about its attainment through the use of power.

And what is *power*?

Power is *organized* energy or effort. This course is properly called the Law of Success for the reason that it teaches how one may organize *facts* and *knowledge* and the faculties of one's mind into a unit of power.

This course brings you a definite promise, namely:

That through its mastery and application you can get whatever you want, with but two qualifying words—"within reason."

This qualification takes into consideration your education, your wisdom or your lack of it, your physical endurance, your temperament, and all of the other qualities mentioned in the fi-fifteen lessons of this course as being the factors most essential in the attainment of success.

Without a single exception those who have attained unusual success have done so, either consciously or unconsciously, through the aid of all or a portion of the fifteen major factors of which this course is compiled. If you doubt this statement, then master these fifteen lessons so you can go about the analysis with reasonable accuracy and analyze such men as Carnegie, Rockefeller, Hill, Harriman, Ford and others of this type who have accumulated great fortunes of material wealth, and you will see that they understood and applied the principle of *organized effort* which runs, like a golden cord of indisputable evidence, throughout this course.

Nearly twenty years ago I interviewed Mr. Carnegie for the purpose of writing a story about him. During the interview I asked him to what he attributed his *success*. With a merry little twinkle in his eyes he said:

"Young man, before I answer your question will you please define your term 'success'?"

After waiting until he saw that I was somewhat embarrassed by his request he continued: "By success you have reference to my money, have you not?" I assured him that money was the term by which most people measured success, and he then said: "Oh, well—if you wish to know how I got my money—*if that is what you call success*—I will answer your question by saying that we have a master mind here in our business, and that mind is made up of more than a score of men who constitute my personal staff of superintendents and managers and accountants and chemists and other necessary types. No one person in this group is the master mind of which I speak, but the sum total of the minds in the group, co-ordinated, organized and directed to a *definite* end in a spirit of harmonious co-operation is the power that got my money for me. No two minds in the group are exactly alike, but each man in the group does the thing that he is supposed to do and he does it better than any other person in the world could do it."

Then and there the seed out of which this course has been developed was sown in my mind, but that seed did not take root or germinate until later. This interview marked the beginning of years of research which led, finally, to the discovery of the principle of psychology described in the Introduction as the "Master Mind."

I heard all that Mr. Carnegie said, but it took the knowledge gained from many years of subsequent contact with the business world to enable me to assimilate that which he said and clearly grasp and understand the principle back of it, which was nothing more nor less than the principle of *organized effort* upon which this course on the Law of Success is founded.

Carnegie's group of men constituted a "Master Mind" and that mind was so well organized, so well co-ordinated, so powerful, that it could have accumulated millions of dollars for Mr. Carnegie in practically any sort of endeavor of a commercial or industrial nature. The steel business in which that mind was engaged was but an incident in connection with the accumulation of the Carnegie wealth. The same wealth could have been accumulated had the "Master Mind" been directed in the coal business or the banking business or the grocery business, for the reason that back of the mind was *power*—that sort of power which *you* may have when you shall have organized the faculties of your own mind and allied yourself with other well organized minds for the attainment of a *definite chief aim* in life.

If you can run a losing race without blaming your loss on someone else, you have bright prospects of success further down the road in life.

A careful check-up with several of Mr. Carnegie's former business associates, which was made after this course was begun, proves conclusively not only that there is such a law as that which has been called the "Master Mind," but that this law was the chief source of Mr. Carnegie's success.

Perhaps no man was ever associated with Mr. Carnegie who knew him better than did Mr. C. M. Schwab. In the following words Mr. Schwab has very accurately described that "subtle something" in Mr. Carnegie's personality which enabled him to rise to such stupendous heights.

"I never knew a man with so much imagination, lively intelligence and instinctive comprehension. You sensed that he probed your thoughts and took stock of everything that you had ever done or might do. He seemed to catch at your next word before it was spoken. The play of his mind was dazzling and his habit of close observation gave him a store of knowledge about innumerable matters.

"But his outstanding quality, from so rich an endowment, was the power of inspiring other men. Confidence radiated from him. You might be doubtful about something and discuss the matter with Mr. Carnegie. In a flash he would make you see that it was right and then absolutely believe it; or he might settle your doubts by pointing out its weakness. This quality of attracting others, then spurring them on, arose from his own strength.

"The results of his leadership were remarkable. Never before in history of industry, I imagine, was there a man who, without understanding his business in its working details, making no pretense of technical knowledge concerning steel or engineering, was yet able to build up such an enterprise.

"Mr. Carnegie's ability to inspire men rested on something deeper than any faculty of judgment."

In the last sentence Mr. Schwab has conveyed a thought which corroborates the theory of the "Master Mind" to which the author of this course has attributed the chief source of Mr. Carnegie's power.

Mr. Schwab has also confirmed the statement that Mr. Carnegie could have succeeded as well in any other business as he did in the steel business. It is obvious that his success was due to his understanding of his own mind and the minds of other men, and not to mere knowledge of the steel business itself.

This thought is most consoling to those who have not yet attained outstanding success, for it shows that success is solely a matter of correctly applying laws and principles which are available to all; and these laws, let us not forget, are fully described in the Fifteen Lessons of this course.

Mr. Carnegie learned how to apply the law of the "Master Mind." This enabled him to organize the faculties of his own mind and the faculties of other men's minds, and co-ordinate the whole behind a DEFINITE CHIEF AIM.

Every strategist, whether in business or war or industry or other callings, understands the value of *organized,* co-ordinated effort. Every military strategist understands the value of sowing seeds of dissension in the ranks of the opposing forces, because this breaks up the power of co-ordination back of the opposition. During the late world war much was heard about the effects of propaganda, and it seems not an exaggeration to say that the disorganizing forces of propaganda were much more destructive than were all the guns and explosives used in the war.

One of the most important turning-points of the world war came when the allied armies were placed under the direction of the French General, Foch. There are well informed military men who claim that this was the move which spelled doom for the opposing armies.

Any modern railroad bridge is an excellent example of the value of *organized effort,* because it demonstrates quite simply and clearly how thousands of tons of weight may be borne by a comparatively small group of steel bars and beams so arranged that the weight is spread over the entire group.

There was a man who had seven sons who were always quarreling among themselves. One day he called them together and informed them that he wished to demonstrate just what their lack of co-operative effort meant. He had prepared a bundle of seven sticks which he had carefully tied together. One by one he asked his sons to take the bundle and break it. Each son tried, but in vain. Then he cut the strings and handed one of the sticks to each of his sons and asked him to break it over his knee. After the sticks had all been broken, with ease, he said:

"When you boys work together in a spirit of harmony you resemble the bundle of sticks, and no one can defeat you; but when you quarrel among yourselves anyone can defeat you one at a time."

There is a worth-while lesson in this story of the man and his seven quarrelsome sons, and it may be applied to the people of a community, the employees and employers in a given place of employment, or to the state and nation in which we live.

Organized effort may be made a power, but it may also be a dangerous power unless guided with intelligence, which is the chief reason why the fifteenth lesson of this course is devoted largely to describing how to direct the power of organized effort so that it will lead to *success;* that sort of success which is founded upon truth and justice and fairness that lead to ultimate *happiness.*

One of the outstanding tragedies of this age of struggle and money-madness is the fact that so few people are engaged in the effort which they like best. One of the objects of this course is to help each student find his or her particular niche in the world's work, where both material prosperity and *happiness* in abundance may be found. For this purpose a Character Analysis Chart accompanies the Introduction. This chart is designed to help the student take inventory of himself and find out what latent ability and hidden forces lie sleeping within him.

This entire course is intended as a stimulus with which to enable you to see yourself and your hidden forces as they are, and to awaken in you the ambition and the vision and the determination to cause you to go forth and claim that which is rightfully yours.

Less than thirty years ago a man was working in the same shop with Henry Ford, doing practically the same sort of work that he was doing. It has been said that this man was really a more competent workman, in that particular sort of work, than Ford. Today this man is still engaged in the same sort of work, at wages of less than a hundred dollars a week, while Mr. Ford is the world's richest man.

What outstanding difference is there between these two men which has so widely separated them in terms of material wealth? Just this—Ford understood and applied the principle of *organized effort* while the other man did not.

In the little city of Shelby, Ohio, as these lines are being written, for the first time in the history of the world this principle of *organized effort* is being applied for the purpose of bringing about a closer alliance between the churches and the business houses of a community.

The clergymen and business men have formed an alliance, with the result that practically every church in the city is squarely back of every business man, and every business man is squarely back of every church. The effect has been the strengthening of the churches and the business houses to such an extent that it has been said that it would be practically impossible for any individual member of either class to fail in his calling. The others who belong to the alliance will permit no such failures.

Here is an example of what may happen when groups of men form an alliance for the purpose of placing the combined power of the group back of each individual unit. The alliance has brought both material and moral advantages to the city of Shelby such as are enjoyed by but few other cities of its size in America. The plan has worked so effectively and so satisfactorily that a movement is now under way to extend it into other cities throughout America.

A GOOD Encyclopaedia contains most of the known facts of the world, but they are as useless as Sand Dunes until organized and expressed in terms of action.

That you may gain a still more concrete vision of just how this principle of *organized effort* can be made powerful, stop for a moment and allow your imagination to draw a picture of what would likely be the result if every church and every newspaper and every Rotary Club and every Kiwanis Club and every Advertising Club and every Woman's Club and every other civic organization of a similar nature, in your city, or in any other city in the United States, should form an alliance for the purpose of pooling their power and using it for the benefit of all members of these organizations.

The results which might easily be attained by such an alliance stagger the imagination!

There are three outstanding powers in the world of *organized effort*. They are: The churches, the schools and the newspapers. Think what might easily happen if these three great powers and molders of public opinion should ally themselves together for the purpose of bringing about any needed change in human conduct. They could, in a single generation, so modify the present standard of business ethics, for example, that it would practically be business suicide for anyone to try to transact business under any standard except that of the Golden Rule. Such an alliance could be made to produce sufficient influence to change, in a single generation, the business, social and moral tendencies of the entire civilized world. Such an alliance would have sufficient power to *force* upon the minds of the oncoming generations any ideals desired.

Power is *organized effort,* as has already been stated!

Success is based upon power!

That you may have a clear conception of what is meant by the term "organized effort" I have made use of the foregoing illustrations, and for the sake of further emphasis I am going to repeat the statement that the accumulation of great wealth and the attainment of any high station in life such as constitute what we ordinarily call *success*, are based upon the vision to comprehend and the ability to assimilate and apply the major principles of the fifteen lessons of this course.

This course is in complete harmony with the principles of economics and the principles of Applied Psychology. You will observe that those lessons, which depend, for their practical application, upon knowledge of psychology, have been supplemented with sufficient explanation of the psychological principles involved to render the lessons easily understood.

Before the manuscripts for this course went to the publisher they were submitted to some of the foremost bankers and business men of America, that they might be examined, analyzed and criticized by the most practical type of mind. One of the best known bankers in New York City returned the manuscripts with the following comment:

"I hold a master's degree from Yale, but I would willingly exchange all that this degree has brought me in return for what your course on the Law of Success would have brought me had I been afforded the privilege of making it a part of my training while I was studying at Yale.

"My wife and daughter have also read the manuscripts, and my wife has named your course 'the master key-board of life' because she believes that all who understand how to apply it may play a perfect symphony in their respective callings, just as a pianist may play any tune when once the key-board of the piano and the fundamentals of music have been mastered."

No two people on earth are exactly alike, and for this reason no two people would be expected to attain from this course the same viewpoint. Each student should read the course, understand it and then appropriate from its contents whatever he or she needs to develop a well-rounded personality.

This course has been compiled for the purpose of helping the student find out what are his or her natural talents, and for the purpose of helping organize, co-ordinate and put into use the knowledge gained from experience. For more than twenty years I have been gathering, classifying and organizing the material that has gone into the course. During the past fourteen years I have analyzed more than 16,000 men and women, and all of the vital facts gathered from these analyses have been carefully organized and woven into this course. These analyses brought out many interesting facts which have helped to make this course practical and usable. For example, it was discovered that ninety-five per cent of all who were analyzed were failures, and but five per cent were successes. (By the term "failure" is meant that they had failed to find happiness and the ordinary necessities of life without struggle that was almost unbearable.) Perhaps this is about the proportion of successes and failures that might be found if all the people of the world were accurately analyzed. The struggle for a mere existence is terrific among people who have not learned how to organize and direct their natural talents, while the attainment of those necessities, as well as the acquiring of many of the luxuries, is comparatively simple among those who have mastered the principle of *organized effort*.

One of the most startling facts brought to light by those 16,000 analyses was the discovery that the ninety-five per cent who were classed as failures were in that class *because they had no definite chief aim in life,* while the five per cent constituting the successful ones not only had purposes that were *definite,* but they had, also, *definite plans* for the attainment of their purposes.

Another important fact disclosed by these analyses was that the ninety-five per cent constituting the failures were engaged in work which they did not like, while the five per cent constituting the successful ones were doing that which they liked best. It is doubtful whether a person could be a failure while engaged in work which he liked best. Another vital fact learned from the analyses was that all of the five per cent who were succeeding had formed the habit of systematic saving of money, while the ninety-five per cent who were failures saved nothing. This is worthy of serious thought.

One of the chief objects of this course is to aid the student in performing his or her chosen work in such a manner that it will yield the greatest returns in both money and happiness.

A Definite Chief Aim

The key-note of this entire lesson may be found in the word "definite."

It is most appalling to know that ninety-five per cent of the people of the world are drifting aimlessly through life, without the slightest conception of the work for which they are best fitted, and with no conception whatsoever of even the need of such a thing as a *definite* objective toward which to strive.

> *No position in life can be secure, and no achievement can be permanent, unless built upon truth and justice.*

There is a psychological as well as an economic reason for the selection of a *definite chief aim* in life. Let us devote our attention to the psychological side of the question first. It is a well established principle of psychology that a person's acts are always in harmony with the dominating thoughts of his or her mind.

Any *definite chief aim* that is deliberately fixed in the mind and held there, with the determination to realize it, finally saturates the entire subconscious mind until it automatically influences the physical action of the body toward the attainment of that purpose.

Your *definite chief aim* in life should be selected with deliberate care, and after it has been selected it should be written out and placed where you will see it at least once a day, the psychological effect of which is to impress this purpose upon your subconscious mind so strongly that it accepts that purpose as a pattern or blueprint that will eventually dominate your activities in life and lead you, step by step, toward the attainment of the object back of that purpose.

The principle of psychology through which you can impress your *definite chief aim* upon your subconscious mind is called Auto-suggestion, or suggestion which you repeatedly make to yourself. It is a degree of self-hypnotism, but do not be afraid of it on that account, for it was this same principle through the aid of which Napoleon lifted himself from the lowly station of poverty-stricken Corsican to the dictatorship of France. It was through the aid of this same principle that Thomas A. Edison has risen from the lowly beginning of a news butcher to where he is accepted as the leading inventor of the world. It was through the aid of this same principle that Lincoln bridged the mighty chasm between his lowly birth, in a log cabin in the mountains of Kentucky, and the presidency of the greatest nation on earth. It was through the aid of this same principle that Theodore Roosevelt became one of the most aggressive leaders that ever reached the presidency of the United States.

You need have no fear of the principle of Auto-suggestion as long as you are sure that the objective for which you are striving is one that will bring you happiness of an enduring nature. Be sure that your *definite purpose* is constructive; that its attainment will bring hardship and misery to no one; that it will bring you peace and prosperity, then apply, to the limit of your understanding, the principle of self-suggestion for the speedy attainment of this purpose.

On the street corner, just opposite the room in which I am writing, I see a man who stands there all day long and sells peanuts. He is busy every minute. When not actually engaged in making a sale he is roasting and packing the peanuts in little bags. He is one of that great army constituting the ninety-five per cent who have no *definite purpose* in life. He is selling peanuts, not because he likes that work better than anything else he might do, but because he never sat down and thought out a *definite purpose* that would bring him greater returns for his labor. He is selling peanuts because he is a drifter on the sea of life, and one of the tragedies of his work is the fact that the same amount of effort that he puts into it, if directed along other lines, would bring him much greater returns.

Another one of the tragedies of this man's work is the fact that he is unconsciously making use of the principle of self-suggestion, but he is doing it to his own disadvantage. No doubt, if a picture could be made of his thoughts, there would be nothing in that picture except a peanut roaster, some little paper bags and a crowd of people buying peanuts. This man could get out of the peanut business if he had the vision and the ambition first to imagine himself in a more profitable calling, and the perseverance to hold that picture before his mind until it influenced him to take the necessary steps to enter a more profitable calling. He puts sufficient labor into his work to bring him a substantial return if that labor were directed toward the attainment of a *definite purpose* that offered bigger returns.

One of my closest personal friends is one of the best known writers and public speakers of this country. About ten years ago he caught sight of the possibilities of this principle of self-suggestion and began, immediately, to harness it and put it to work. He worked out a plan for its application that proved to be very effective. At that time he was neither a writer nor a speaker.

Each night, just before going to sleep, he would shut his eyes and see, *in his imagination,* a long council table at which he placed (in his imagination) certain well known men whose characteristics he wished to absorb into his own personality. At the end of the table he placed Lincoln, and on either side of the table he placed Napoleon, Washington, Emerson and Elbert Hubbard. He then proceeded to talk to these imaginary figures that he had seated at his imaginary council table, something after this manner:

Mr. Lincoln: I desire to build in my own character those qualities of patience and fairness toward all mankind and the keen sense of humor which were your outstanding characteristics. I need these qualities and I shall not be contented until I have developed them.

Mr. Washington: I desire to build in my own character those qualities of patriotism and self-sacrifice and leadership which were your outstanding characteristics.

Mr. Emerson: I desire to build in my own character those qualities of vision and the ability to interpret the laws of Nature as written in the rocks of prison walls and growing trees and flowing brooks and growing flowers and the faces of little children, which were your outstanding characteristics.

Napoleon: I desire to build in my own character those qualities of self-reliance and the strategic ability to master obstacles and profit by mistakes and develop strength out of defeat, which were your outstanding characteristics.

Mr. Hubbard: I desire to develop the ability to equal and even to excel the ability that you possessed with which to express yourself in clear, concise and forceful language.

Night after night, for many months, this man saw these men seated around that imaginary council table until finally he had imprinted their outstanding characteristics upon his own subconscious mind so clearly that he began to develop a personality which was a composite of their personalities.

The subconscious mind may be likened to a magnet, and when it has been vitalized and thoroughly saturated with any *definite purpose* it has a decided tendency to attract all that is necessary for the fulfillment of that purpose. Like attracts like, and you may see evidence of this law in every blade of grass and every growing tree. The acorn attracts from the soil and the air the necessary materials out of which to grow an oak tree. It never grows a tree that is part oak and part poplar. Every grain of wheat that is planted in the soil attracts the materials out of which to grow a stalk of wheat.

It never makes a mistake and grows both oats and wheat on the same stalk.

And men are subject, also, to this same Law of Attraction. Go into any cheap boarding house district in any city and there you will find people of the same general trend of mind associated together. On the other hand, go into any prosperous community and there you will find people of the same general tendencies associated together. Men who are successful always seek the company of others who are successful, while men who are on the ragged side of life always seek the company of those who are in similar circumstances. "Misery loves company."

Water seeks its level with no finer certainty than man seeks the company of those who occupy his own general status financially and mentally. A professor of Yale University and an illiterate hobo have nothing in common. They would be miserable if thrown together for any great length of time. Oil and water will mix as readily as will men who have nothing in common.

All of which leads up to this statement:

That you will attract to you people who harmonize with your own philosophy of life, whether you wish it or not. This being true, can you not see the importance of vitalizing your mind with a *definite chief aim* that will attract to you people who will be of help to you and not a hindrance? Suppose your *definite chief aim* is far above your present station in life. What of it? It is your privilege—nay, your *DUTY*, to aim high in life. You owe it to yourself and to the community in which you live to set a high standard for yourself.

> *Do not "tell" the world what you can do—"show" it!*

There is much evidence to justify the belief that nothing *within reason* is beyond the possibility of attainment by the man whose *definite chief aim* has been well developed. Some years ago Louis Victor Eytinge was given a life sentence in the Arizona penitentiary. At the time of his imprisonment he was an all-around "bad man," according to his own admissions. In addition to this it was believed that he would die of tuberculosis within a year.

Eytinge had reason to feel discouraged, if anyone ever had. Public feeling against him was intense and he did not have a single friend in the world who came forth and offered him encouragement or help. Then something happened in his own mind that gave him back his health, put the dreaded "white plague" to rout and finally unlocked the prison gates and gave him his freedom.

What was that "something"?

Just this: He made up his mind to whip the white plague and regain his health. That was a very *definite chief aim*. In less than a year from the time the decision was made he had won. Then he extended that *definite chief aim* by making up his mind to gain his freedom. Soon the prison walls melted from around him.

No undesirable environment is strong enough to hold the man or woman who understands how to apply the principle of Auto-suggestion in the creation of a *definite chief aim*. Such a person can throw off the shackles of poverty; destroy the most deadly disease germs; rise from a lowly station in life to power and plenty.

All great leaders base their leadership upon a *definite chief aim*. Followers are willing followers when they know that their leader is a person with a *definite chief aim* who has the courage to back up that purpose with action. Even a balky horse knows when a driver with a *definite chief aim* takes hold of the reins; and yields to that driver. When a man with a *definite chief aim* starts through a crowd everybody stands aside and makes a way for him, but let a man hesitate and show by his actions that he is not sure which way he wants to go and the crowd will step all over his toes and refuse to budge an inch out of his way.

Nowhere is the lack of a *definite chief aim* more noticeable or more detrimental than it is in the relationship between parent and child. Children sense very quickly the wavering attitude of their parents and take advantage of that attitude quite freely. It is the same all through life—men with a *definite chief aim* command respect and attention at all times.

So much for the psychological viewpoint of a *definite purpose*. Let us now turn to the economic side of the question.

If a steamship lost its rudder, in mid-ocean, and began circling around, it would soon exhaust its fuel supply without reaching shore, despite the fact that it would use up enough energy to carry it to shore and back several times.

The man who labors without a *definite purpose* that is backed up by a definite plan for its attainment, resembles the ship that has lost its rudder. Hard labor and good intentions are not sufficient to carry a man through to success, for how may a man be sure that he has attained success unless he has established in his mind some definite object that he wishes?

Every well built house started in the form of a *definite purpose* plus a definite plan in the nature of a set of blueprints. Imagine what would happen if one tried to build a house by the haphazard method, without plans. Workmen would be in each other's way, building material would be piled all over the lot before the foundation was completed, and everybody on the job would have a different notion as to how the house ought to be built. Result, chaos and misunderstandings and cost that would be prohibitive.

Yet had you ever stopped to think that most people finish school, take up employment or enter a trade or profession without the slightest conception of anything that even remotely resembles a *definite purpose* or a definite plan? In view of the fact that science has provided reasonably accurate ways and means of analyzing character and determining the life-work for which people are best fitted, does it not seem a modern tragedy that ninety-five per cent of the adult population of the world is made up of men and women who are failures because they have not found their proper niches in the world's work?

If *success* depends upon power, and if power is *organized effort,* and if the first step in the direction of organization is a *definite purpose,* then one may easily see why such a purpose is essential.

Until a man selects a *definite purpose* in life he dissipates his energies and spreads his thoughts over so many subjects and in so many different directions that they lead not to power, but to indecision and weakness.

With the aid of a small reading glass you can teach yourself a great lesson on the value of *organized effort*. Through the use of such a glass you can focus the sun-rays on a *definite* spot so strongly that they will burn a hole through a plank. Remove the glass (which represents the *definite purpose*) and the same rays of sun may shine on that same plank for a million years without burning it.

A thousand electric dry batteries, when properly organized and connected together with wires, will produce enough power to run a good sized piece of machinery for several hours, but take those same cells singly, disconnected, and not one of them would exert enough energy to turn the machinery over once. The faculties of your mind might properly be likened to those dry cells. When you organize your faculties, according to the plan laid down in the fifteen lessons of this Reading Course on the Law of Success, and direct them toward the attainment of a *definite purpose* in life, you then take advantage of the cooperative or accumulative principle out of which *power* is developed, which is called Organized Effort.

Andrew Carnegie's advice was this: "Place all your eggs in one basket and then watch the basket to see that no one kicks it over." By that advice he meant, of course, that we should not dissipate any of our energies by engaging in side lines. Carnegie was a sound economist and he knew that most men would do well if they so harnessed and directed their energies that some one thing would be done well.

When the plan back of this Reading Course was first born I remember taking the first manuscript to a professor of the University of Texas, and in a spirit of enthusiasm I suggested to him that I had discovered a principle that would be of aid to me in every public speech I delivered thereafter, because I would be better prepared to organize and marshal my thoughts.

He looked at the outline of the fifteen points for a few minutes, then turned to me and said:

"Yes, your discovery is going to help you make better speeches, but that is not all it will do. It will help you become a more effective writer, for I have noticed in your previous writings a tendency to scatter your thoughts. For instance, if you started to describe a beautiful mountain yonder in the distance you would be apt to sidetrack your description by calling attention to a beautiful bed of wild flowers, or a running brook, or a singing bird, detouring here and there, zig-zag fashion, before finally arriving at the proper point from which to view the mountain. In the future you are going to find it much less difficult to describe an object, whether you are speaking or writing, because *your fifteen points represent the very foundation of organization.*"

> *The best compensation for doing things is the ability to do more.*

A man who had no legs once met a man who was blind. To prove conclusively that the lame man was a *man of vision* he proposed to the blind man that they form an alliance that would be of great benefit to both. "You let me climb upon your back," said he to the blind man, "then I will use your legs and you may use my eyes. Between the two of us we will get along more rapidly."

Out of allied effort comes greater power. This is a point that is worthy of much repetition, *because it forms one of the most important parts of the foundation of this Reading Course.* The great fortunes of the world have been accumulated through the use of this principle of allied effort. That which one man can accomplish single handed, during an entire life-time, is but meagre at best, no matter how well organized that man may be, but that which one man may accomplish through the principle of alliance with other men is practically without limitation.

That "master mind" to which Carnegie referred during my interview with him was made up of more than a score of minds. In that group were men of practically every temperament and inclination. Each man was there to play a certain part and he did nothing else. There was perfect understanding and team-work between these men. It was Carnegie's business to keep harmony among them.

And he did it wonderfully well.

If you are familiar with the game of football you know, of course, that the winning team is the one that best co-ordinates the efforts of its players. Team-work is the thing that wins. It is the same in the great game of life.

In your struggle for *success* you should keep constantly in mind the necessity of knowing what it is that you want—of knowing precisely what is your *definite purpose*—and the value of the principle of *organized effort* in the attainment of that which constitutes your *definite purpose*.

In a vague sort of way nearly everyone has a definite purpose—namely, the desire for *money!* But this is not a *definite purpose* within the meaning of the term as it is used in this lesson. Before your purpose could be considered *definite,* even though that purpose were the accumulation of money, you would have to reach a decision as to the precise method through which you intend to accumulate that money. It would be insufficient for you to say that you would make money by going into some sort of business. You would have to decide just what line of business. You would also have to decide just where you would locate. You would also have to decide the business policies under which you would conduct your business.

In answering the question, "What Is Your Definite Purpose In Life," that appears in the questionnaire which I have used for the analysis of more than 16,000 people, many answered about as follows:

"My definite purpose in life is to be of as much service to the world as possible and earn a good living."

That answer is about as *definite* as a frog's conception of the size of the universe is accurate!

The object of this lesson is not to inform you as to what your life-work should be, for indeed this could be done with accuracy only after you had been completely analyzed, but it is intended as a means of impressing upon your mind a clear conception of the value of a *definite purpose* of some nature, and of the value of understanding the principle of *organized effort* as a means of attaining the necessary power with which to materialize your *definite purpose.*

Careful observation of the business philosophy of more than one hundred men and women who have attained outstanding success in their respective callings, disclosed the fact that each was a person of prompt and definite decision.

The habit of working with a *definite chief aim* will breed in you the habit of prompt decision, and this habit will come to your aid in all that you do.

Moreover, the habit of working with a *definite chief aim* will help you to concentrate all your attention on any given task until you have mastered it.

Concentration of effort and the habit of working with a *definite chief aim* are two of the essential factors in success which are always found together. One leads to the other.

The best known successful business men were all men of prompt decision who worked always with one main, outstanding purpose as their chief aim.

Some notable examples are as follows:

Woolworth chose, as his *definite chief aim,* the belting of America with a chain of Five and Ten Cent Stores, and concentrated his mind upon this one task until he "made it and it made him."

Wrigley concentrated his mind on the production and sale of a five-cent package of chewing gum and turned this one idea into millions of dollars.

Edison concentrated upon the work of harmonizing natural laws and made his efforts uncover more useful inventions than any other man who ever lived.

Henry L. Doherty concentrated upon the building and operation of public utility plants and made himself a multi-millionaire.

Ingersoll concentrated on a dollar watch and girdled the earth with "tickers" and made this one idea yield him a fortune.

Statler concentrated on "homelike hotel-service" and made himself wealthy as well as useful to millions of people who use his service.

Edwin C. Barnes concentrated on the sale of Edison Dictating Machines, and retired, while still a young man, with more money than he needs.

Woodrow Wilson concentrated his mind on the White House for twenty-five years, and became its chief tenant, thanks to his knowledge of the value of sticking to a *definite chief aim.*

Lincoln concentrated his mind on freeing the slaves and became our greatest American President while doing it.

Martin W. Littleton heard a speech which filled him with the desire to become a great lawyer, concentrated his mind on that one aim, and is now said to be the most successful lawyer in America, whose fees for a single case seldom fall below $50,000.00.

Rockefeller concentrated on oil and became the richest man of his generation.

Ford concentrated on "flivvers" and made himself the richest and most powerful man who ever lived.

Carnegie concentrated on steel and made his efforts build a great fortune and plastered his name on public libraries throughout America.

Gillette concentrated on a safety razor, gave the entire world a "close shave" and made himself a multi-millionaire.

George Eastman concentrated on the kodak and made the idea yield him a fortune while bringing much pleasure to millions of people.

Russell Conwell concentrated on one simple lecture, "Acres of Diamonds," and made the idea yield more than $6,000,000.

Hearst concentrated on sensational newspapers and made the idea worth millions of dollars.

Helen Keller concentrated on learning to speak, and, despite the fact that she was deaf, dumb and blind, realized her *definite chief aim.*

John H. Patterson concentrated on cash registers and made himself rich and others "careful."

The late Kaiser of Germany concentrated on war and got a big dose of it, let us not forget the fact!

Fleischmann concentrated on the humble little cake of yeast and made things hump themselves all over the world.

Marshall Field concentrated on the world's greatest retail store and lo! it rose before him, a reality.

Philip Armour concentrated on the butchering business and established a great industry, as well as a big fortune.

Millions of people are concentrating, daily, on POVERTY and FAILURE and getting both in over-abundance.

Anyone can "start," but only the thoroughbred will "finish!"

Wright Brothers concentrated on the airplane and mastered the air.

Pullman concentrated on the sleeping car and the idea made him rich and millions of people comfortable in travel.

The Anti-Saloon League concentrated on the Prohibition Amendment and (whether for better or worse) made it a reality.

Thus it will be seen that all who succeed work with some definite, outstanding aim as the object of their labors.

There is some one thing that you can do better than anyone else in the world could do it. Search until you find out what this particular line of endeavor is, make it the object of your *definite chief aim* and then organize all of your forces and attack it with the belief that you are going to win. In your search for the work for which you are best fitted, it will be well if you bear in mind the fact that you will most likely attain the greatest success by finding out what work you like best, for it is a well known fact that a man generally best succeeds in the particular line of endeavor into which he can throw his whole heart and soul.

Let us go back, for the sake of clarity and emphasis, to the psychological principles upon which this lesson is founded, because it will mean a loss that you can ill afford if you fail to grasp the real reason for establishing a *definite chief aim* in your mind. These principles are as follows:

First: Every voluntary movement of the human body is caused, controlled and directed by *thought,* through the operation of the mind.

Second: The presence of any thought or idea in your consciousness tends to produce an associated feeling and to urge you to transform that feeling into appropriate muscular action that is in perfect harmony with the nature of the thought.

For example, if you think of winking your eyelid and there are no counter influences or thoughts in your mind at the time to arrest action, the motor nerve will carry your thought from the seat of government, in your brain, and appropriate or corresponding muscular action takes place immediately.

Stating this principle from another angle: You choose, for example, a *definite purpose* as your lifework and make up your mind that you will carry out that purpose. *From the very moment that you make this choice, this purpose becomes the dominating thought in your consciousness, and you are constantly on the alert for facts, information and knowledge with which to achieve that purpose.* From the time that you plant a *definite purpose* in your mind, your mind begins, both consciously and unconsciously, to gather and store away the material with which you are to accomplish that purpose.

Desire is the factor which determines what your *definite purpose* in life shall be. No one can select your dominating *desire* for you, but once you select it yourself it becomes your *definite chief aim* and occupies the spotlight of your mind until it is satisfied by transformation into reality, unless you permit it to be pushed aside by conflicting desires.

To emphasize the principle that I am here trying to make clear, I believe it not unreasonable to suggest that to be sure of successful achievement, one's *definite chief aim* in life should be backed up with a *burning desire* for its achievement. I have noticed that boys and girls who enter college and pay their way through by working seem to get more out of their schooling than do those whose expenses are paid for them. The secret of this may be found in the fact that those who are willing to work their way through are blessed with a *burning desire* for education, and such a desire, if the object of the desire is within reason, is practically sure of realization.

Science has established, beyond the slightest room for doubt, that through the principle of Auto-suggestion any deeply rooted *desire* saturates the entire body and mind with the nature of the desire and literally transforms the mind into a powerful magnet that will attract the object of the desire, if it be within reason. For the enlightenment of those who might not properly interpret the meaning of this statement I will endeavor to state this principle in another way. For example, merely desiring an automobile will not cause that automobile to come rolling in, but, if there is a *burning desire* for an automobile, that desire will lead to the appropriate action through which an automobile may be paid for.

Merely desiring freedom would never release a man who was confined in prison if it were not sufficiently strong to cause him to do something to entitle himself to freedom.

These are the steps leading from *desire* to fulfillment: First the *burning desire,* then the crystallization of that desire into a *definite purpose,* then sufficient appropriate *action* to achieve that purpose. *Remember that these three steps are always necessary to insure success.*

I once knew a very poor girl who had a *burning desire* for a wealthy husband, and she finally got him, but not without having transformed that desire into the development of a very attractive personality which, in turn, attracted the desired husband.

I once had a *burning desire* to be able to analyze character accurately and that desire was so persistent and so deeply seated that it practically drove me into ten years of research and study of men and women.

George S. Parker makes one of the best fountain pens in the world, and despite the fact that his business is conducted from the little city of Janesville, Wisconsin, he has spread his product all the way around the globe and he has his pen on sale in every civilized country in the world. More than twenty years ago, Mr. Parker's *definite purpose* was established in his mind, and that purpose was to produce the best fountain pen that money could buy. He backed that purpose with a *burning desire* for its realization and if you carry a fountain pen the chances are that you have evidence in your own possession that it has brought him abundant success.

You are a contractor and builder, and, like men who build houses out of mere wood and brick and steel, you must draw up a set of plans after which to shape your *success building*. You are living in a wonderful age, when the materials that go into *success* are plentiful and cheap. You have at your disposal, in the archives of the public libraries, the carefully compiled results of two thousand years of research covering practically every possible line of endeavor in which one would wish to engage. If you would become a preacher you have at hand the entire history of what has been learned by men who have preceded you in this field. If you would become a mechanic you have at hand the entire history of the inventions of machines and the discovery and usages of metals and things metallic in nature. If you would become a lawyer you have at your disposal the entire history of law procedure. Through the Department of Agriculture, at Washington, you have at your disposal all that has been learned about farming and agriculture, where you may use it should you wish to find your life-work in this field.

The world was never so resplendent with *opportunity* as it is today. On every hand there is an ever-increasing demand for the services of the man or the woman who makes a better mouse-trap or performs better stenographic service or preaches a better sermon or digs a better ditch or runs a more accommodating bank.

This lesson will not be completed until you shall have made your choice as to what your *definite chief aim* in life is to be and then recorded a description of that purpose in writing and placed it where you may see it every morning when you arise and every night when you retire.

Procrastination is—but why preach about it? You know that *you* are the hewer of your own wood and the drawer of your own water and the shaper of your own *definite chief aim* in life; therefore, why dwell upon that which you already know?

Every line a man writes, and every act in which he indulges, and every word he utters serves as unescapable evidence of the nature of that which is deeply imbedded in his own heart, a confession that he cannot disavow.

A definite purpose is something that you must create for yourself. No one else will create it for you and it will not create itself. What are you going to do about it? and when? and how?

Start now to analyze your desires and find out what it is that you wish, then make up your mind to get it. Lesson Two will point out to you the next step and show you how to proceed. Nothing is left to chance, in this Reading Course. Every step is marked plainly. Your part is to follow the directions until you arrive at your destination, which is represented by your *definite chief aim*. Make that aim clear and back it up with persistence which does not recognize the word "impossible."

When you come to select your *definite chief aim* just keep in mind the fact that you cannot *aim* too high.

Also keep in mind the never-varying truth that you'll get nowhere if you start nowhere. If your aim in life is vague your achievements will also be vague, and it might well be added, very *meager. Know what you want, when you want it, why you want it and HOW you intend to get it.* This is known to teachers and students of psychology as the WWWH formula—"what, when, why and how."

Read this lesson four times, at intervals of one week apart.

You will see much in the lesson the fourth time you read it that you did not see the first time.

Your success in mastering this course and in making it bring you success will depend very largely, if not entirely, upon how well you follow ALL the instructions it contains.

Do not set up your own rules of study. Follow those laid down in the Course, as they are the result of years of thought and experimentation. If you wish to experiment wait until you master this course in the manner suggested by its author. You will then be in position to experiment more safely. For the present content yourself by being the student. You will, let us hope, become the teacher as well as the student after you have followed the Course until you have mastered it.

If you follow the instructions laid down in this Course for the guidance of its students, you can no more fail than water can run uphill above the level of its source.

Instructions for Applying the Principles of This Lesson

Through the Introduction of this course you became familiar with the principle of psychology known as the "Master Mind."

You are now ready to begin use of this principle as a means of transforming your *definite chief aim* into reality. It must have occurred to you that one might as well have no *definite chief aim* unless one has, also, a very definite and practical plan for making that aim become a reality.

Your first step is to decide what your major aim in life shall be. Your next step is to write out a clear, concise statement of this aim. This should be followed by a statement, in writing, of the plan or plans through which you intend to attain the object of your aim.

Your next and final step will be the forming of an alliance with some person or persons who will co-operate with you in carrying out these plans and transforming your *definite chief aim* into reality.

The purpose of this friendly alliance is to employ the law of the "Master Mind" in support of your plans. The alliance should be made between yourself and those who have your highest and best interests at heart. If you are a married man your wife should be one of the members of this alliance, providing there exists between you a normal state of confidence and sympathy. Other members of this alliance may be your mother, father, brothers or sisters, or some close friend or friends.

If you are a single person your sweetheart, if you have one, should become a member of your alliance. This is no joke—you are now studying one of the most powerful laws of the human mind, and you will serve your own best interests by seriously and earnestly following the rules laid down in this lesson, even though you may not be sure where they will lead you.

Those who join with you in the formation of a friendly alliance for the purpose of aiding you in the creation of a "Master Mind" should sign, with you, your statement of the object of your *definite chief aim*. Every member of your alliance must be fully acquainted with the nature of your object in forming the alliance. Moreover, every member must be in hearty accord with this object, and in full sympathy with you. Each member of your alliance must be supplied with a written copy of your statement of your *definite chief aim*. With this exception, however, *you are explicitly instructed to keep the object of your chief aim to yourself*. The world is full of "Doubting Thomases" and it will do your cause no good to have these rattle-brained people scoffing at you and your ambitions. Remember, what you need is friendly encouragement and help, not derision and doubt.

If you believe in prayer you are instructed to make your *definite chief aim* the object of your prayer at least once every twenty-four hours, and more often if convenient. If you believe there is a God who can and will aid those who are earnestly striving to be of constructive service in the world, surely you feel that you have a right to petition Him for aid in the attainment of what should be the most important thing in life to you.

If those who have been invited to join your friendly alliance believe in prayer, ask them, also, to include the object of this alliance as a part of their daily prayer.

Comes, now, one of the most essential rules which you *must follow*. Arrange with one or all of the members of your friendly alliance to state to you, in the most positive and definite terms at their command, that THEY KNOW YOU CAN AND WILL REALIZE THE

OBJECT OF YOUR DEFINITE CHIEF AIM. This affirmation or statement should be made to you at least once a day; more often if possible.

These steps must be followed persistently, with full faith that they will lead you where you wish to go! It will not suffice to carry out these plans for a few days or a few weeks and then discontinue them. YOU MUST FOLLOW THE DESCRIBED PROCEDURE UNTIL YOU ATTAIN THE OBJECT OF YOUR DEFINITE CHIEF AIM, REGARDLESS OF THE TIME REQUIRED.

From time to time it may become necessary to change the plans you have adopted for the achievement of the object of your *definite chief aim*. Make these changes without hesitation. No human being has sufficient foresight to build plans which need no alteration or change.

If any member of your friendly alliance loses faith in the law known as the "Master Mind," immediately remove that member and replace him or her with some other person.

Andrew Carnegie stated to the author of this course that he had found it necessary to replace some of the members of his "Master Mind." In fact he stated that practically every member of whom his alliance was originally composed had, in time, been removed and replaced with some other person who could adapt himself more loyally and enthusiastically to the spirit and object of the alliance.

You cannot succeed when surrounded by disloyal and unfriendly associates, no matter what may be the object of your *definite chief aim*. Success is built upon loyalty, faith, sincerity, co-operation and the other positive forces with which one must surcharge his environment.

"Yes, he succeeded—but—he almost failed!" So did Robert Fulton and Abraham Lincoln and nearly all the others whom we call successful. No man ever achieved worth-while success who did not, at one time or other, find himself with at least one foot hanging well over the brink of failure.

Many of the students of this course will want to form friendly alliances with those with whom they are associated professionally or in business, with the object of achieving success in their business or profession. In such cases the same rules of procedure which have been here described should be followed. The object of your *definite chief aim* may be one that will benefit you individually, or it may be one that will benefit the business or profession with which you are connected. The law of the "Master Mind" will work the same in either case. If you fail, either temporarily or permanently, in the application of this law *it will be for the reason that some member of your alliance did not enter into the spirit of the alliance with faith, loyalty and sincerity of purpose.*

The last sentence is worthy of a second reading!

The object of your *definite chief aim* should become your "hobby." You should ride this "hobby" continuously; you should sleep with it, eat with it, play with it, work with it, live with it and THINK with it.

Whatever you want you may get if you want it with sufficient intensity, and keep on wanting it, providing the object wanted is one within reason, and you ACTUALLY BELIEVE YOU WILL GET IT! There is a difference, however, between merely "wishing" for something and ACTUALLY BELIEVING you will get it. Lack of understanding of this difference has meant failure to millions of people. The "doers" are the "believers" in all walks of life. Those who BELIEVE they can achieve the object of their *definite chief aim* do not recognize the word impossible. Neither do they acknowledge temporary defeat. They KNOW they are going to succeed, and if one plan fails they quickly replace it with another plan.

Every noteworthy achievement met with some sort of temporary setback before success came. Edison made more than ten thousand experiments before he succeeded in making the first talking machine record the words, "Mary had a little lamb."

If there is one word which should stand out in your mind in connection with this lesson, it is the word PERSISTENCE!

You now have within your possession the pass-key to achievement. You have but to unlock the door to the Temple of Knowledge and walk in. But you must go to the Temple; it will not come to you. If these laws are new to you the "going" will not be easy at first. You will stumble many times, but keep moving! Very soon you will come to the brow of the mountain you have been climbing, and you will behold, in the valleys below, the rich estate of KNOWLEDGE which shall be your reward for your faith and efforts.

Everything has a price. There is no such possibility as "something for nothing." In your experiments with the Law of the Master Mind you are jockeying with Nature, in her highest and noblest form. Nature cannot be tricked or cheated. She will give up to you the object of your struggles only after you have paid her price, which is CONTINUOUS, UNYIELDING, PERSISTENT EFFORT!

What more could be said on this subject?

Neglecting to broaden their view has kept some men doing one thing all their lives.

You have been shown *what to do, when to do it, how to do it* and *why you should do it.* If you will master the next lesson, on Self-confidence, you will then have the faith in yourself to enable you to carry out the instructions laid down for your guidance in this lesson.

Master of human destinies am I!
Fame, love, and fortune on my footsteps wait.
Cities and fields I walk; I penetrate
Deserts and seas remote, and passing by
Hovel and mart and palace—soon or late
I knock, unbidden, once at every gate!
If sleeping, wake—if feasting, rise before
I turn away. It is the hour of fate,
And they who follow me reach every state
Mortals desire, and conquer every foe
Save death; but those who doubt or hesitate,
Condemned to failure, penury, and woe,
Seek me in vain and uselessly implore.
I answer not, and I return no more!

—INGALLS

Amidst all the mysteries by which we are surrounded, nothing is more certain than that we are in the presence of an Infinite and Eternal Energy from which all things proceed.

—HERBERT SPENCER

SELF-CONFIDENCE

"You Can Do It If You Believe You Can!"

Before approaching the fundamental principles upon which this lesson is founded it will be of benefit to you to keep in mind the fact that it is practical—that it brings you the discoveries of more than twenty-five years of research—that it has the approval of the leading scientific men and women of the world who have tested every principle involved.

Skepticism is the deadly enemy of progress and self-development. You might as well lay this book aside and stop right here as to approach this lesson with the feeling that it was written by some long-haired theorist who had never tested the principles upon which the lesson is based.

Surely this is no age for the skeptic, because it is an age in which we have seen more of Nature's laws uncovered and harnessed than had been discovered in all past history of the human race. Within three decades we have witnessed the mastery of the air; we have explored the ocean; we have all but annihilated distances on the earth; we have harnessed the lightning and made it turn the wheels of industry; we have made seven blades of grass grow where but one grew before; we have instantaneous communication between the nations of the world. Truly, this is an age of illumination and unfoldment, but we have as yet barely scratched the surface of knowledge. However, when we shall have unlocked the gate that leads to the secret power which is stored up within us it will bring us knowledge that will make all past discoveries pale into oblivion by comparison.

Thought is the most highly organized form of energy known to man, and this is an age of experimentation and research that is sure to bring us into greater understanding of that mysterious force called thought, which reposes within us. We have already found out enough about the human mind to know that a man may throw off the accumulated effects of a thousand generations of *fear,* through the aid of the principle of *Auto-suggestion.* We have already discovered the fact that *fear* is the chief reason for poverty and failure and misery that takes on a thousand different forms. We have already discovered the fact that the man who masters *fear* may march on to successful achievement in practically any undertaking, despite all efforts to defeat him.

The development of *self-confidence* starts with the elimination of this demon called *fear,* which sits upon a man's shoulder and whispers into his ear, *"You can't do it—you are afraid to try—you are afraid of public opinion—you are afraid that you will fail—you are afraid you have not the ability."*

This *fear* demon is getting into close quarters. Science has found a deadly weapon with which to put it to flight, and this lesson on *self-confidence* has brought you this weapon for use in your battle with the world-old enemy of progress, *fear.*

The Six Basic Fears of Mankind: Every person falls heir to the influence of six basic fears. Under these six fears may be listed the lesser fears. The six basic or major fears are here enumerated and the sources from which they are believed to have grown are described.

The six basic fears are:

a. The fear of Poverty

b. The fear of Old Age

c. The fear of Criticism

d. The fear of Loss of Love of Someone.

e. The fear of Ill Health

f. The fear of Death.

Study the list, then take inventory of your own fears and ascertain under which of the six headings you can classify them.

Every human being who has reached the age of understanding is bound down, to some extent, by one or more of these six basic fears. As the first step in the elimination of these six evils let us examine the sources from whence we inherited them.

Physical and Social Heredity

All that man is, both physically and mentally, he came by through two forms of heredity. One is known as physical heredity and the other is called social heredity.

Through the law of physical heredity man has slowly evolved from the amoeba (a single-cell animal form), through stages of development corresponding to all the known animal forms now on this earth, including those which are known to have existed but which are now extinct.

Every generation through which man has passed has added to his nature something of the traits, habits and physical appearance of that generation. Man's physical inheritance, therefore, is a heterogeneous collection of many habits and physical forms.

There seems little, if any, doubt that while the six basic fears of man could not have been inherited through physical heredity (these six basic fears being mental states of mind and therefore not capable of transmission through physical heredity), it is obvious that through physical heredity a most favorable lodging place for these six fears has been provided.

For example, it is a well known fact that the whole process of physical evolution is based upon death, destruction, pain and cruelty; that the elements of the soil of the earth find transportation, in their upward climb through evolution, based upon the death of one form of life in order that another and higher form may subsist. All vegetation lives by "eating" the elements of the soil and the elements of the air. All forms of animal life live by "eating" some other and weaker form, or some form of vegetation.

The cells of all vegetation have a very high order of intelligence. The cells of all animal life likewise have a very high order of intelligence.

Undoubtedly the animal cells of a fish have learned, out of bitter experience, that the group of animal cells known as a fish hawk are to be greatly feared.

By reason of the fact that many animal forms (including that of most men) live by eating the smaller and weaker animals, the "cell intelligence" of these animals which enter into and become a part of man brings with it the FEAR growing out of their experience in having been eaten alive.

This theory may seem to be far-fetched, and in fact it may not be true, but it is at least a logical theory if it is nothing more. The author makes no particular point of this theory, nor does he insist that it accounts for any of the six basic fears. There is another, and a much better explanation of the source of these fears, which we will proceed to examine, beginning with a description of social heredity.

By far the most important part of man's make-up comes to him through the law of social heredity, this term having reference to the methods by which one generation imposes upon the minds of the generation under its immediate control the superstitions, beliefs, legends and ideas which it, in turn, inherited from the generation preceding.

The term "social heredity" should be understood to mean any and all sources through which a person acquires knowledge, such as schooling of religious and all other natures; reading, word of mouth conversation, story telling and all manner of thought inspiration coming from what is generally accepted as one's "personal experiences."

Through the operation of the law of social heredity anyone having control of the mind of a child may, through intense teaching, plant in that child's mind any idea, whether false or true, in such a manner that the child accepts it as true and it becomes as much a part of the child's personality as any cell or organ of its physical body (and just as hard to change in its nature).

Remember that when you make an appointment with another person you assume the responsibility of punctuality, and that you have not the right to be a single minute late.

It is through the law of social heredity that the religionist plants in the child mind dogmas and creeds and religious ceremonies too numerous to describe, holding those ideas before that mind until the mind accepts them and forever seals them as a part of its irrevocable belief.

The mind of a child which has not come into the age of general understanding, during an average period covering, let us say, the first two years of its life, is plastic, open, clean and free. Any idea planted in such a mind by one in whom the child has confidence takes root and grows, so to speak, in such a manner that it never can be eradicated or wiped out, no matter how opposed to logic or reason that idea may be.

Many religionists claim that they can so deeply implant the tenets of their religion in the mind of a child that there never can be room in that mind for any other religion, either in whole or in part. The claims are not greatly overdrawn.

With this explanation of the manner in which the law of social heredity operates the student will be ready to examine the sources from which man inherits the six basic fears. Moreover, any student (except those who have not yet grown big enough to examine truth that steps upon the "pet corns" of their own superstitions) may check the soundness of the principle of social heredity as it is here applied to the six basic fears, without going outside of his or her own personal experiences.

Fortunately, practically the entire mass of evidence submitted in this lesson is of such a nature that all who sincerely seek the truth may ascertain, for themselves, whether the evidence is sound or not.

For the moment at least, lay aside your prejudices and preconceived ideas (you may always go back and pick them up again, you know) while we study the origin and nature of man's Six Worst Enemies, the six basic fears, beginning with:

The Fear of Poverty: It requires courage to tell the truth about the origin of this fear, and still greater courage, perhaps, to accept the truth after it has been told. The fear of poverty grew out of man's inherited tendency to prey upon his fellow man economically. Nearly all forms of lower animals have instinct but appear not to have the power to reason and think; therefore, they prey upon one another physically. Man, with his superior sense of intuition, thought and reason, does not eat his fellow men bodily; he gets more satisfaction out of eating them FINANCIALLY!

Of all the ages of the world of which we know anything, the age in which we live seems to be the age of money worship. A man is considered less than the dust of the earth unless he can display a fat bank account. Nothing brings man so much suffering and humiliation as does POVERTY. No wonder man FEARS poverty. Through a long line of inherited experiences with the man-animal man has learned, for certain, that this animal cannot always be trusted where matters of money and other evidences of earthly possessions are concerned.

Many marriages have their beginning (and oftentimes their ending) solely on the basis of the wealth possessed by one or both of the contracting parties. It is no wonder that the divorce courts are busy!

"Society" could quite properly be spelled "$ociety," because it is inseparably associated with the dollar mark. So eager is man to possess wealth that he will acquire it in whatever manner he can; through legal methods, if possible, through other methods if necessary.

The fear of poverty is a terrible thing!

A man may commit murder, engage in robbery, rape and all other manner of violation of the rights of others and still regain a high station in the minds of his fellow men, PROVIDING always that he does not lose his wealth. Poverty, therefore, is a crime—an unforgivable sin, as it were.

No wonder man fears it!

Every statute book in the world bears evidence that the fear of poverty is one of the six basic fears of mankind, for in every such book of laws may be found various and sundry laws intended to protect the weak from the strong. To spend time trying to prove either that the fear of poverty is one of man's inherited fears, or that this fear has its origin in man's nature to cheat his fellow man, would be similar to trying to prove that three times two are six. Obviously no man would ever fear poverty if he had any grounds for trusting his fellow men, for there is food and shelter and raiment and luxury of every nature sufficient for the needs of every person on earth, and all these blessings would be enjoyed by every person except for the swinish habit that man has of trying to push all the other "swine" out of the trough, even after he has all and more than he needs.

The second of the six basic fears with which man is bound is:

The Fear of Old Age: In the main this fear grows out of two sources. First, the thought that Old Age may bring with it POVERTY. Secondly, and by far the most common source of origin, from false and cruel sectarian teachings which have been so well mixed with "fire and brimstone" and with "purgatories" and other bogies that human beings have learned to fear Old Age because it meant the approach of another, and possibly a much more HORRIBLE, world than this one which is known to be bad enough.

In the basic fear of Old Age man has two very sound reasons for his apprehension: the one growing out of distrust of his fellow men who may seize whatever worldly goods he may possess, and the other arising from the terrible pictures of the world to come which were deeply planted in his mind, through the law of social heredity, long before he came into possession of that mind.

Is it any wonder that man fears the approach of Old Age?

The third of the six basic fears is:

The Fear of Criticism: Just how man acquired this basic fear it would be hard, if not impossible, definitely to determine, but one thing is certain, he has it in well developed form.

Some believe that this fear made its appearance in the mind of man about the time that politics came into existence. Others believe its source can be traced no further than the first meeting of an organization of females known as a "Woman's Club." Still another school of humorists charges the origin to the contents of the Holy Bible, whose pages abound with some very vitriolic and violent forms of criticism. If the latter claim is correct, and those who believe literally all they find in the Bible are not mistaken, then God is responsible for man's inherent fear of Criticism, because God caused the Bible to be written.

This author, being neither a humorist nor a "prophet," but just an ordinary workaday type of person, is inclined to attribute the basic fear of Criticism to that part of man's inherited nature which prompts him not only to take away his fellow man's goods and wares, but to justify his action by CRITICISM of his fellow man's character.

The fear of Criticism takes on many different forms, the majority of which are petty and trivial in nature, even to the extent of being childish in the extreme.

Bald-headed men, for example, are bald for no other reason than their fear of Criticism. Heads become bald because of the protection of hats with tight fitting bands which cut off the circulation at the roots of the hair. Men wear hats, not because they actually need them for the sake of comfort, but mainly because "everybody's doing it," and the individual falls in line and does it also, lest some other individual CRITICIZE him.

Women seldom have bald heads, or even thin hair, because they wear hats that are loose, the only purpose of which is to make an appearance.

But it must not be imagined that women are free from the fear of Criticism associated with hats. If any woman claims to be superior to man with reference to this fear, ask her to walk down the street wearing a hat that is one or two seasons out of style!

The makers of all manner of clothing have not been slow to capitalize this basic fear of Criticism with which all mankind is cursed. Every season, it will be observed, the "styles" in many articles of wearing apparel change. Who establishes the "styles"? Certainly not the purchaser of clothes, but the manufacturer of clothes. Why does he change the styles so often? Obviously this change is made so that the manufacturer can sell more clothes.

In every soul there has been deposited the seed of a great future, but that seed will never germinate, much less grow to maturity, except through the rendering of useful service.

For the same reason the manufacturers of automobiles (with a few rare and very sensible exceptions) change styles every season.

The manufacturer of clothing knows how the man-animal fears to wear a garment which is one season out of step with "that which they are all wearing now."

Is this not true? Does not your own experience back it up?

We have been describing the manner in which people behave under the influence of the fear of Criticism as applied to the small and petty things of life. Let us now examine human behavior under this fear when it affects people in connection with the more important matters connected with human intercourse. Take, for example, practically any person who has reached the age of "mental maturity" (from thirty-five to forty-five years of age, as a general average), and if you could read his or her mind you would find in that mind a very decided disbelief of and rebellion against most of the fables taught by the majority of the religionists.

Powerful and mighty is the fear of CRITICISM!

The time was, and not so very long ago at that, when the word "infidel" meant ruin to whomsoever it was applied. It is seen, therefore, that man's fear of CRITICISM is not without ample cause for its existence.

The fourth basic fear is that of:

The Fear of Loss of Love of Someone: The source from which this fear originated needs but little description, for it is obvious that it grew out of man's nature to steal his fellow man's mate; or at least to take liberties with her, unknown to her rightful "lord" and master. By nature all men are polygamous, the statement of a truth which will, of course, bring denials from those who are either too old to function in a normal way sexually, or have, from some other cause, lost the contents of certain glands which are responsible for man's tendency toward the plurality of the opposite sex.

There can be but little doubt that jealousy and all other similar forms of more or less mild dementia praecox (insanity) grew out of man's inherited fear of the Loss of Love of Someone.

Of all the "sane fools" studied by this author, that represented by a man who has become jealous of some woman, or that of a woman who has become jealous of some man, is the oddest and strangest. The author, fortunately, never had but one case of personal experience with this form of insanity, but from that experience he learned enough to justify him in stating that the fear of the Loss of Love of Someone is one of the most painful, if not in fact the most painful, of all the six basic fears. And it seems reasonable to add that this fear plays more havoc with the human mind than do any of the other six basic fears, often leading to the more violent forms of permanent insanity.

The fifth basic fear is that of:

The Fear of Ill Health: This fear has its origin, to considerable extent also, in the same sources from which the fears of Poverty and Old Age are derived.

The fear of Ill Health must needs be closely associated with both Poverty and Old Age, because it also leads toward the border line of "terrible worlds" of which man knows not, but of which he has heard some discomforting stories.

The author strongly suspects that those engaged in the business of selling good health methods have had considerable to do with keeping the fear of Ill Health alive in the human mind.

For longer than the record of the human race can be relied upon, the world has known of various and sundry forms of therapy and health purveyors. If a man gains his living from keeping people in good health it seems but natural that he would use every means at his command for persuading people that they needed his services. Thus, in time, it might be that people would inherit a fear of Ill Health.

The sixth and last of the Six Basic Fears is that of:

The Fear of Death! To many this is the worst of all the six basic fears, and the reason why it is so regarded becomes obvious to even the casual student of psychology.

The terrible pangs of fear associated with DEATH may be charged directly to religious fanaticism, the source which is more responsible for it than are all other sources combined.

So-called "heathen" are not as much afraid of DEATH as are the "civilized," especially that portion of the civilized population which has come under the influence of theology.

For hundreds of millions of years man has been asking the still unanswered (and, it may be, the unanswerable) questions, "WHENCE?" and "WHITHER?" "Where did I come from and where am I going after death?"

The more cunning and crafty, as well as the honest but credulous, of the race have not been slow to offer the answer to these questions. In fact the answering of these questions has become one of the so-called "learned" professions, despite the fact that but little learning is required to enter this profession.

Witness, now, the major source of origin of the fear of DEATH!

"Come into my tent, embrace my faith, accept my dogmas (and pay my salary) and I will give you a ticket that will admit you straightway into heaven when you die," says the leader of one form of sectarianism. "Remain out of my tent," says this same leader, "and you will go direct to hell, where you will burn throughout eternity."

While, in fact, the self-appointed leader may not be able to provide safe-conduct into heaven nor, by lack of such provision, allow the unfortunate seeker after truth to descend into hell, the possibility of the latter seems so terrible that it lays hold of the mind and creates that fear of fears, the fear of DEATH!

In truth no man knows, and no man has ever known, what heaven or hell is like, or if such places exist, and this very lack of definite knowledge opens the door of the human mind to the charlatan to enter and control that mind with his stock of legerdemain and various brands of trickery, deceit and fraud.

The truth is this—nothing less and nothing more—That NO MAN KNOWS NOR HAS ANY MAN EVER KNOWN WHERE WE COME FROM AT BIRTH OR WHERE WE GO AT DEATH. Any person claiming otherwise is either deceiving himself or he is a conscious impostor who makes it a business to live without rendering service of value, through play upon the credulity of humanity.

Be it said, in their behalf, however, the majority of those engaged in "selling tickets into heaven" actually believe not only that they know where heaven exists, but that their creeds and formulas will give safe passage to all who embrace them.

This belief may be summed up in one word—CREDULITY!

Religious leaders, generally, make the broad, sweeping claim that the present civilization owes its existence to the work done by the churches. This author, as far as he is personally concerned, is willing to grant their claims to be correct, if, at the same time he be permitted to add that even if this claim be true the theologians haven't a great deal of which to brag.

But, it is not—cannot be—true that civilization has grown out of the efforts of the organized churches and creeds, if by the term "civilization" is meant the uncovering of the natural laws and the many inventions to which the world is the present heir.

If the theologians wish to claim that part of civilization which has to do with man's conduct toward his fellow man they are perfectly welcome to it, as far as this author is concerned; but, on the other hand, if they presume to gobble up the credit for all the scientific discovery of mankind the author begs leave to offer vigorous protest.

It is hardly sufficient to state that social heredity is the method through which man gathers all knowledge that reaches him through the five senses. It is more to the point to state HOW social heredity works, in as many different applications as will give the student a comprehensive understanding of that law.

Let us begin with some of the lower forms of animal life and examine the manner in which they are affected by the law of social heredity.

Shortly after this author began to examine the major sources from which men gather the knowledge which makes them what they are, some thirty-odd years ago, he discovered the nest of a ruffed grouse. The nest was so located that the mother bird could be seen from a considerable distance when she was on the nest. With the aid of a pair of field glasses the bird was closely watched until the young birds were hatched out. It happened that the regular daily observation was made but a few hours after the young birds came out of the shell. Desiring to know what would happen, the author approached the nest. The mother bird remained near by until the intruder was within ten or twelve feet of her, then she disarranged her feathers, stretched one wing over her leg and went hobbling away, making a pretense of being crippled. Being some-

You are fortunate if you have learned the difference between temporary defeat and failure; more fortunate still, if you have learned the truth that the very seed of success is dormant in every defeat that you experience.

what familiar with the tricks of mother birds, the author did not follow, but, instead, went to the nest to take a look at the little ones. Without the slightest signs of fear they turned their eyes toward him, moving their heads first one way and then another. He reached down and picked one of them up. With no signs of fear it stood in the palm of his hand. He laid the bird back in the nest and went away to a safe distance to give the mother bird a chance to return.

The wait was short. Very soon she began cautiously to edge her way back toward the nest until she was within a few feet of it, when she spread her wings and ran as fast as she could, uttering, meanwhile, a series of sounds similar to those of a hen when she has found some morsel of food and wishes to call her brood to partake of it.

She gathered the little birds around and continued to quiver in a highly excited manner, shaking her wings and ruffling her feathers. One could almost hear her words as she gave the little birds their first lesson in self-defense, through the law of SOCIAL HEREDITY:

"You silly little creatures! Do you not know that men are your enemies? Shame on you for allowing that man to pick you up in his hands. It's a wonder he didn't carry you off and eat you alive! The next time you see a man approaching make yourselves scarce. Lie down on the ground, run under leaves, go anywhere to get out of sight, and remain out of sight until the enemy is well on his way."

The little birds stood around and listened to the lecture with intense interest. After the mother bird had quieted down the author again started to approach the nest. When within twenty feet or so of the guarded household the mother bird again started to lead him in the other direction by crumpling up her wing and hobbling along as if she were crippled. He looked at the nest, but the glance was in vain. The little birds were nowhere to be found! They had learned rapidly to avoid their natural enemy, thanks to their natural instinct.

Again the author retreated, awaited until the mother bird had reassembled her household, then came out to visit them, but with similar results. When he approached the spot where he last saw the mother bird not the slightest signs of the little fellows were to be found.

When a small boy the author captured a young crow and made a pet of it. The bird became quite well satisfied with its domestic surroundings and learned to perform many tricks requiring considerable intelligence. After the bird was big enough to fly it was permitted to go wherever it pleased. Sometimes it would be gone for many hours, but it always returned home before dark.

One day some wild crows became involved in a fight with an owl in a field near the house where the pet crow lived. As soon as the pet heard the "caw, caw, caw" of its wild relatives it flew up on top of the house, and with signs of great agitation, walked from one end of the house to the other. Finally it took wing and flew in the direction of the "battle." The author followed to see what would happen. In a few minutes he came up with the pet. It was sitting on the lower branches of a tree and two wild crows were sitting on a limb just above, chattering and walking back and forth, acting very much in the same fashion that angry parents behave toward their off-spring when chastising them.

As the author approached, the two wild crows flew away, one of them circling around the tree a few times, meanwhile letting out a terrible flow of most abusive language, which, no doubt, was directed at its foolish relative who hadn't enough sense to fly while the flying was good.

The pet was called, but it paid no attention. That evening it returned home, but would not come near the house. It sat on a high limb of an apple tree and talked in crow language for about ten minutes, saying, no doubt, that it had decided to go back to the wild life of its fellows, then flew away and did not return until two days later, when it came back and did some more talking in crow language, keeping at a safe distance meanwhile. It then went away and never returned.

Social heredity had robbed the author of a fine pet!

The only consolation he got from the loss of his crow was the thought that it had shown fine sportsmanship by coming back and giving notice of its intention to depart. Many farm hands had left the farm without going to the trouble of this formality.

It is a well known fact that a fox will prey upon all manner of fowl and small animals with the exception of the skunk. No reason need be stated as to why Mr. Skunk enjoys immunity. A fox may tackle a skunk once, but never twice! For this reason a skunk hide, when nailed to a chicken roost, will keep all but the very young and inexperienced foxes at a safe distance.

The odor of a skunk, once experienced, is never to be forgotten. No other smell even remotely resembles it. It is nowhere recorded that any mother fox ever taught her young how to detect and keep away from the familiar smell of a skunk, but all who are informed on "fox lore" know that foxes and skunks never seek lodgment in the same cave.

But one lesson is sufficient to teach the fox all it cares to know about skunks. Through the law of social heredity, operating via the sense of smell, one lesson serves for an entire life-time.

A bullfrog can be caught on a fish-hook by attaching a small piece of red cloth or any other small red object to the hook and dangling it in front of the frog's nose. That is, Mr. Frog may be caught in this manner, provided he is hooked the first time he snaps at the bait, but if he is poorly hooked and makes a get-away, or if he feels the point of the hook when he bites at the bait but is not caught, he will never make the same mistake again. The author spent many hours in stealthy attempt to hook a particularly desirable specimen which had snapped and missed, before learning that but one lesson in social heredity is enough to teach even a humble "croaker" that bits of red flannel are things to be let alone.

The author once owned a very fine male Airedale dog which caused no end of annoyance by his habit of coming home with a young chicken in his mouth. Each time the chicken was taken away from the dog and he was soundly switched, but to no avail; he continued in his liking for fowl.

For the purpose of saving the dog, if possible, and as an experiment with social heredity, this dog was taken to the farm of a neighbor who had a hen and some newly hatched chickens. The hen was placed in the barn and the dog was turned in with her. As soon as everyone was out of sight the dog slowly edged up toward the hen, sniffed the air in her direction a time or two (to make sure she was the kind of meat for which he was looking), then made a dive toward her.

Is it not strange that we fear most that which never happens? That we destroy our initiative by the fear of defeat, when, in reality, defeat is a most useful tonic and should be accepted as such.

Meanwhile Mrs. Hen had been doing some "surveying" on her own account, for she met Mr. Dog more than halfway; moreover, she met him with such a surprise of wings and claws as he had never before experienced. The first round was clearly the hen's. But a nice fat bird, reckoned the dog, was not to slip between his paws so easily; therefore he backed away a short distance, then charged again. This time Mrs. Hen lit upon his back, drove her claws into his skin and made effective use of her sharp bill! Mr. Dog retreated to his corner, looking for all the world as if he were listening for someone to ring the bell and call the fight off until he got his bearings. But Mrs. Hen craved no time for deliberation; she had her adversary on the run and showed that she knew the value of the offensive by keeping him on the run.

One could almost understand her words as she flogged the poor Airedale from one corner to another, keeping up a series of rapid-fire sounds which for all the world resembled the remonstrations of an angry mother who had been called upon to defend her off-spring from an attack by older boys.

The Airedale was a poor soldier! After running around the barn from corner to corner for about two minutes he spread himself on the ground as flat as he could and did his best to protect his eyes with his paws. Mrs. Hen seemed to be making a special attempt to peck out his eyes.

The owner of the hen then stepped in and retrieved her—or, more accurately stating it, he retrieved the dog—which in no way appeared to meet with the dog's disapproval.

The next day a chicken was placed in the cellar where the dog slept. As soon as he saw the bird he tucked his tail between his legs and ran for a corner! He never again attempted to catch a chicken. One lesson in social heredity, via the sense of "touch," was sufficient to teach him that while chicken-chasing may offer some enjoyment, it is also fraught with much hazard.

All these illustrations, with the exception of the first, describe the process of gathering knowledge through direct experience. Observe the marked difference between knowledge gathered by direct experience and that which is gathered through the training of the young by the old, as in the case of the ruffed grouse and her young.

The most impressive lessons are those learned by the young from the old, through highly colored or emotionalized methods of teaching. When the mother grouse spread her wings, stood her feathers on end, shook herself like a man suffering with the palsy and chattered to her young in a highly excited manner, she planted the fear of man in their hearts in a manner which they were never to forget.

The term "social heredity," as used in connection with this lesson, has particular reference to all methods through which a child is taught any idea, dogma, creed, religion or system of ethical conduct, by its parents or those who may have authority over it, before reaching the age at which it may reason and reflect upon such teaching in its own way; estimating the age of such reasoning power at, let us say, seven to twelve years.

There are myriads of forms of *fear*, but none are more deadly than the fear of poverty and old age. We drive our bodies as if they were slaves because we are so afraid of poverty that we wish to hoard money for—*what*—*old age!* This common form of *fear* drives us so hard that we overwork our bodies and bring on the very thing we are struggling to avoid.

What a tragedy to watch a man drive himself when he begins to arrive along about the forty-year mile post of life—the age at which he is just beginning to mature mentally. At forty a man is just entering the age in which he is able to see and understand and assimilate the handwriting of Nature, as it appears in the forests and flowing brooks and faces of men and little children, yet this devil *fear* drives him so hard that he becomes blinded and lost in the entanglement of a maze of conflicting *desires*. The principle of *organized effort* is lost sight of, and instead of laying hold of Nature's forces which are in evidence all around him, and permitting those forces to carry him to the heights of great achievement, he defies them and they become forces of destruction.

Perhaps none of these great forces of Nature are more available for man's unfoldment than is the principle of Auto-suggestion, but ignorance of this force is leading the majority of the human race to apply it so that it acts as a hindrance and not as a help.

Let us here enumerate the facts which show just how this misapplication of a great force of Nature takes place:

Here is a man who meets with some disappointment; a friend proves false, or a neighbor seems indifferent. Forthwith he decides (through self-suggestion) all men are untrustworthy and all neighbors unappreciative. These thoughts so deeply imbed themselves in his subconscious mind that they color his whole attitude toward others. Go back, now, to what was said in Lesson One, about the dominating thoughts of a man's mind attracting people whose thoughts are similar.

Apply the Law of Attraction and you will soon see and understand why the unbeliever attracts other unbelievers.

Reverse the Principle:

Here is a man who sees nothing but the best there is in all whom he meets. If his neighbors seem indifferent he takes no notice of that fact, for he makes it *his business* to fill his mind with dominating thoughts of optimism and good cheer and faith in others. If people speak to him harshly he speaks back in tones of softness. Through the operation of this same eternal Law of Attraction he draws to himself the attention of people whose attitude toward life and whose dominating thoughts harmonize with his own.

Tracing the principle a step further:

Here is a man who has been well schooled and has the ability to render the world some needed service. Somewhere, sometime, he has heard it said that modesty is a great virtue and that to push himself to the front of the stage in the game of life savors of egotism. He quietly slips in at the back door and takes a seat at the rear while other players in the game of life boldly step to the front. He remains in the back row because he *fears* "what *they* will say." Public opinion, or that which he believes to be public opinion, has him pushed to the rear and the world hears but little of him. His schooling counts for naught because he is *afraid* to let the world know that he has had it. He is constantly *suggesting* to *himself* (thus using the great force of Auto-suggestion to his own detriment) that he should remain in the background lest he be criticized, as if criticism would do him any damage or defeat his purpose.

Here is another man who was born of poor parents. Since the first day that he can remember he has seen evidence of poverty. He has heard talk of poverty. He has felt the icy hand of poverty on his shoulders and it has so impressed him that he fixes it in his mind as a curse to which *he must submit.* Quite unconsciously he permits himself to fall victim of the belief "once poor always poor" until that belief becomes the dominating thought of his mind. He resembles a horse that has been harnessed and broken until it forgets that it has the potential power with which to throw off that harness. Auto-suggestion is rapidly relegating him to the back of the stage of life. Finally he becomes a *quitter.* Ambition is gone. Opportunity comes his way no longer, or if it does he has not the vision to see it. *He has accepted his FATE!* It is a well established fact that the faculties of the mind, like the limbs of the body, atrophy and wither away if not used. Self-confidence is no exception. It develops when used but disappears if not used.

> *Your work and mine are peculiarly akin; I am helping the laws of Nature create more perfect specimens of vegetation, while you are using those same laws, through the Law of Success philosophy, to create more perfect specimens of thinkers.*
>
> —LUTHER BURBANK

One of the chief disadvantages of inherited wealth is the fact that it too often leads to inaction and loss of Self-confidence. Some years ago a baby boy was born to Mrs. E. B. McLean, in the city of Washington. His inheritance was said to be around a hundred million dollars. When this baby was taken for an airing in its carriage it was surrounded by nurses and assistant nurses and detectives and other servants whose duty was to see that no harm befell it. As the years passed by this same vigilance was kept up. This child did not have to dress himself; he had servants who did that. Servants watched over him while he slept and while he was at play. He was not permitted to do anything that a servant could do for him. He had grown to the age of ten years. One day he was playing in the yard and noticed that the back gate had been left open. In all of his life he had never been outside of that gate alone, and naturally that was just the thing that he wished to do. During a moment when the servants were not looking he dashed out at the gate, and was run down and killed by an automobile before he reached the middle of the street.

He had used his servants' eyes until his own no longer served him as they might have done had he learned to rely upon them.

Twenty years ago the man whom I served as secretary sent his two sons away to school. One of them went to the University of Virginia and the other to a college in New York. Each month it was a part of my task to make out a check for $100.00 for each of these boys. This was their "pin money," to be spent as they wished. How profitably I remember the way I envied those boys as I made out those checks each month. I often wondered why the hand of fate bore me into the world in poverty. I could look ahead and see how these boys would rise to the high stations in life while I remained a humble clerk.

In due time the boys returned home with their "sheep-skins." Their father was a wealthy man who owned banks and railroads and coal mines and other property of great value. Good positions were waiting for the boys in their father's employ.

But, twenty years of time can play cruel tricks on those who have never had to struggle. Perhaps a better way to state this truth would be that *time gives those who have never had to struggle a chance to play cruel tricks on themselves!* At any rate, these two boys brought home from school other things besides their sheep-skins. They came back with well developed capacities for strong drink—*capacities which they developed because the hundred dollars which each of them received each month made it unnecessary for them to struggle.*

Theirs is a long and sad story, the details of which will not interest you, but you will be interested in their "finis." As this lesson is being written I have on my desk a copy of the newspaper published in the town where these boys lived. Their father has been bankrupted and his costly mansion, where the boys were born, has been placed on the block for sale. One of the boys died of delirium tremens and the other one is in an insane asylum.

Not all rich men's sons turn out so unfortunately, but the fact remains, nevertheless, that inaction leads to atrophy and this, in turn, leads to loss of ambition and Self-confidence, and without these essential qualities a man will be carried through life on the wings of uncertainty, just as a dry leaf may be carried here and there on the bosom of the stray winds.

Far from being a disadvantage, struggle is a decided advantage, because it develops those qualities which would forever lie dormant without it. Many a man has found his place in the world because of having been forced to struggle for existence early in life. Lack of knowledge of the advantages accruing from struggle has prompted many a parent to say, "I had to work hard when I was young, *but I shall see to it that my children have an easy time!*" Poor foolish creatures. An "easy" time usually turns out to be a greater handicap than the average young man or woman can survive. There are worse things in this world than being forced to work in early life. Forced idleness is far worse than forced labor. Being forced to work, and forced to *do your best,* will breed in you temperance and self-control and strength of will and content and a hundred other virtues which the idle will never know.

Not only does lack of the necessity for struggle lead to weakness of ambition and will-power, but, what is more dangerous still, it sets up in a person's mind a state of lethargy that leads to the loss of Self-confidence. The person who has quit struggling because effort is no longer necessary is literally applying the principle of Auto-suggestion in undermining his own power of Self-confidence. Such a person will finally drift into a frame of mind in which he will actually look with more or less contempt upon the person who is forced to carry on.

The human mind, if you will pardon repetition, may be likened to an electric battery. It may be positive or it may be negative. Self-confidence is the quality with which the mind is re-charged and made positive.

Let us apply this line of reasoning to salesmanship and see what part Self-confidence plays in this great field of endeavor. One of the greatest salesmen this country has ever seen was once a clerk in a newspaper office.

It will be worth your while to analyze the method through which he gained his title as "the world's leading salesman."

He was a timid young man with a more or less retiring sort of nature. He was one of those who believe it best to slip in by the back door and take a seat at the rear of the stage of life. One evening he heard a lecture on the subject of this lesson, Self-confidence, and that lecture so impressed him that he left the lecture hall with a firm determination to pull himself out of the rut into which he had drifted.

He went to the Business Manager of the paper and asked for a position as solicitor of advertising and was put to work on a commission basis. Everyone in the office expected to see him fail, as this sort of salesmanship calls for the most positive type of sales ability. He went to his room and made out a list of a certain type of merchants on whom he intended to call. One would think that he would naturally have made up his list of the names of those whom he believed he could sell with the least effort, *but he did nothing of the sort.* He placed on his list only the names of the merchants on whom other advertising solicitors had called without making a sale. His list consisted of only twelve names. Before he made a single call he went out to the city park, took out his list of twelve names, read it over a hundred times, saying to himself as he did so, *"You will purchase advertising space from me before the end of the month."*

Then he began to make his calls. The first day he closed sales with three of the twelve "impossibilities." During the remainder of the week he made sales to two others. By the end of the month he had opened advertising accounts with all but one of the merchants that he had on the list. For the ensuing month he made no sales, for the reason that he made no calls except on this one obstinate merchant. Every morning when the store opened he was on hand to interview this merchant and every morning the merchant said "*No.*" The merchant knew he was not going to buy advertising space, but this young man didn't know it. When the merchant said *No* the young man did not hear it, but kept right on coming. On the last day of the month, after having told this persistent young man *No* for thirty consecutive times, the merchant said:

"Look here, young man, you have wasted a whole month trying to sell me; now, what I would like to know is this—why have you wasted your time?"

"Wasted my time nothing," he retorted; "I have been going to school and you have been my teacher. Now I know all the arguments that a merchant can bring up for not buying, and besides that I have been drilling myself in Self-confidence."

Then the merchant said: "I will make a little confession of my own. I, too, have been going to school, and you have been my teacher. You have taught me a lesson in persistence that is worth money to me, and to show you my appreciation I am going to pay my tuition fee by giving you an order for advertising space."

No man can become a great leader of men unless he has the milk of human kindness in his own heart, and leads by suggestion and kindness, rather than by force.

And that was the way in which the Philadelphia North American's best advertising account was brought in. Likewise, it marked the beginning of a reputation that has made that same young man a millionaire.

He succeeded because he deliberately charged his own mind with sufficient Self-confidence to make that mind an irresistible force. When he sat down to make up that list of twelve names he did something that ninety-nine people out of a hundred would not have done—he selected the names of those whom he believed it would be hard to sell, because he understood that out of the resistance he would meet with in trying to sell them would come strength and Self-confidence. He was one of the very few people who understand that all rivers and *some men* are crooked because of following the line of least resistance.

I am going to digress and here break the line of thought for a moment while recording a word of advice to the wives of men. Remember, these lines are intended only for wives, and husbands are not expected to read that which is here set down.

From having analyzed more than 16,000 people, the majority of whom were married men, I have learned something that may be of value to wives. Let me state my thought in these words:

You have it within your power to send your husband away to his work or his business or his profession each day with a feeling of Self-confidence that will carry him successfully over the rough spots of the day and bring him home again, at night, smiling and happy. One of my acquaintances of former years married a woman who had a set of false teeth. One day his wife dropped her teeth and broke the plate. The husband picked up the pieces and began examining them. He showed such interest in them that his wife said:

"You could make a set of teeth like those if you made up your mind to do it."

This man was a farmer whose ambitions had never carried him beyond the bounds of his little farm until his wife made that remark. She walked over and laid her hand on his shoulder and encouraged him to try his hand at dentistry. She finally coaxed him to make the start, and today he is one of the most prominent and successful dentists in the state of Virginia. I know him well, for he is my father!

No one can foretell the possibilities of achievement available to the man whose wife stands at his back and urges him on to bigger and better endeavor, for it is a well known fact that a woman can arouse a man so that he will perform almost superhuman feats. It is your right and your duty to encourage your husband and urge him on in worthy undertakings until he shall have found his place in the world. You can induce him to put forth greater effort than can any other person in the world. Make him believe that nothing within reason is beyond his power of achievement and you will have rendered him a service that will go a long way toward helping him win in the battle of life.

One of the most successful men in his line in America gives entire credit for his success to his wife. When they were first married she wrote a creed which he signed and placed over his desk. This is a copy of the creed:

I believe in myself. I believe in those who work with me. I believe in my employer. I believe in my friends. I believe in my family. I believe that God will lend me everything I need with which to succeed if I do my best to earn it through faithful and honest service. I believe in prayer and I will never close my eyes in sleep without praying for divine guidance to the end that I will be patient with other people and tolerant with those who do not believe as I do. I believe that success is the result of intelligent effort and does not depend upon luck or sharp practices or double-crossing friends, fellow men or my employer. I believe I will get out of life exactly what I put into it, therefore I will be careful to conduct myself toward others as I would want them to act toward me. I will not slander those whom I do not like. I will not slight my work no matter what I may see others doing. I will render the best service of which I am capable because I have pledged myself to succeed in life and I know that success is always the result of conscientious and efficient effort. Finally, I will forgive those who offend me because I realize that I shall sometimes offend others and I will need their forgiveness.

Signed ....

The woman who wrote this creed was a practical psychologist of the first order. With the influence and guidance of such a woman as a helpmate any man could achieve noteworthy success.

Analyze this creed and you will notice how freely the personal pronoun is used. It starts off with the affirmation of Self-confidence, which is perfectly proper. No man could make this creed his own without developing the positive attitude that would attract to him people who would aid him in his struggle for success.

This would be a splendid creed for every salesman to adopt. It might not hurt your chances for success if *you* adopted it. Mere adoption, however, is not enough. You must *practice* it! Read it over and over until you know it by heart. Then repeat it at least once a day until you have literally transformed it into your mental make-up. Keep a copy of it before you as a daily reminder of your pledge to practice it. By doing so you will be making efficient use of the principle of Auto-suggestion as a means of developing Self-confidence. Never mind what anyone may say about your procedure. Just remember that it is your business to succeed, and this creed, if mastered and applied, will go a long way toward helping you.

You learned in Lesson One that any idea you firmly fix in your subconscious mind, by repeated affirmation, automatically becomes a plan or blueprint which an unseen power uses in directing your efforts toward the attainment of the objective named in the plan.

You have also learned that the principle through which you may fix any idea you choose in your mind is called Auto-suggestion, which simply means a suggestion that you give to your own mind. It was this principle of Auto-suggestion that Emerson had in mind when he wrote:

"Nothing can bring you peace but yourself!"

You might well remember that *Nothing can bring you success but yourself.* Of course you will need the co-operation of others if you aim to attain success of a far-reaching nature, but you will never get that co-operation unless you vitalize your mind with the positive attitude of Self-confidence.

Perhaps you have wondered why a few men advance to highly paid positions while others all around them, who have as much training and who seemingly perform as much work, do not get ahead. Select any two people of these two types that you choose, and study them, and the reason why one advances and the other stands still will be quite obvious to you. You will find that the one who advances *believes in himself.* You will find that he backs this belief with such dynamic, aggressive action that he lets others know that he believes in himself. You will also notice that this Self-confidence is contagious; it is impelling; it is persuasive; it attracts others.

You will also find that the one who does not advance shows clearly, by the look on his face, by the posture of his body, by the lack of briskness in his step, by the uncertainty with which he speaks, that he lacks Self-confidence. No one is going to pay much attention to the person who has no confidence in himself.

If you want a thing done well, call on some busy person to do it. Busy people are generally the most painstaking and thorough in all they do.

He does not attract others because his mind is a negative force that repels rather than attracts.

In no other field of endeavor does Self-confidence or the lack of it play such an important part as in the field of salesmanship, and you do not need to be a character analyst to determine, the moment you meet him, whether a salesman possesses this quality of Self-confidence. If he has it the signs of its influence are written all over him. He inspires you with confidence in him and in the goods he is selling the moment he speaks.

We come, now, to the point at which you are ready to take hold of the principle of Auto-suggestion and make direct use of it in developing yourself into a positive and dynamic and self-reliant person. You are instructed to copy the following formula, sign it and commit it to memory:

Self-Confidence Formula

First: I know that I have the ability to achieve the object of my *definite purpose*, therefore I *demand* of myself persistent, aggressive and continuous action toward its attainment.

Second: I realize that the dominating thoughts of my mind eventually reproduce themselves in outward, bodily action, and gradually transform themselves into physical reality, therefore I will concentrate my mind for thirty minutes daily upon the task of thinking of the person I intend to be, by creating a mental picture of this person and then transforming that picture into reality through practical service.

Third: I know that through the principle of Auto-suggestion, any desire that I persistently hold in my mind will eventually seek expression through some practical means of realizing it, therefore I shall devote ten minutes daily to demanding of myself the development of the factors named in the fifteen lessons of this Reading Course on the Law of Success.

Fourth: I have clearly mapped out and written down a description of my *definite purpose* in life, for the coming five years. I have set a price on my services for each of these five years; a price that I intend to *earn* and *receive,* through strict application of the principle of efficient, satisfactory service which I will render in advance.

Fifth: I fully realize that no wealth or position can long endure unless built upon truth and justice, therefore *I will engage in no transaction which does not benefit all whom it affects.* I will succeed by attracting to me the forces I wish to use, and the co-operation of other people. I will induce others to serve me because I will first serve them. I will eliminate hatred, envy, jealousy, selfishness and cynicism by developing love for all humanity, because I know that a negative attitude toward others can never bring me success. I will cause others to *believe in me* because I will believe in them and in myself.

I will sign my name to this formula, commit it to memory and repeat it aloud once a day with full *faith* that it will gradually influence my entire life so that I will become a successful and happy worker in my chosen field of endeavor.

Signed ....

Before you sign your name to this formula make sure that you intend to carry out its instructions. Back of this formula lies a law that no man can explain. The psychologists refer to this law as Auto-suggestion and let it go at that, but you should bear in mind one point about which there is no uncertainty, and that is the fact that whatever this law is it *actually works!*

Another point to be kept in mind is the fact that, just as electricity will turn the wheels of industry and serve mankind in a million other ways, or snuff out life if wrongly applied, so will this principle of Auto-suggestion lead you up the mountain-side of peace and prosperity, or down into the valley of misery and poverty, according to the application you make of it. If you fill your mind with doubt and unbelief in your ability to achieve, then the principle of Auto-suggestion takes this spirit of unbelief and sets it up in your subconscious mind as your dominating thought and slowly but surely draws you into the whirlpool of *failure*. But, if you fill your mind with radiant Self-confidence, the principle of Auto-suggestion takes this belief and sets it up as your dominating thought and helps you master the obstacles that fall in your way until you reach the mountain-top of *success*.

The Power of Habit

Having, myself, experienced all the difficulties that stand in the road of those who lack the understanding to make practical application of this great principle of Auto-suggestion, let me take you a short way into the principle of habit, through the aid of which you may easily apply the principle of Auto-suggestion in any direction and for any purpose whatsoever.

Habit grows out of environment; out of doing the same thing or thinking the same thoughts or repeating the same words over and over again. Habit may be likened to the groove on a phonograph record, while the human mind may be likened to the needle that fits into that groove. When any habit has been well formed, through repetition of thought or action, the mind has a tendency to attach itself to and follow the course of that habit as closely as the phonograph needle follows the groove in the wax record.

Habit is created by *repeatedly* directing one or more of the five senses of seeing, hearing, smelling, tasting and feeling, in a given direction. It is through this repetition principle that the injurious drug habit is formed. It is through this same principle that the desire for intoxicating drink is formed into a habit.

After habit has been well established it will automatically control and direct our bodily activity, wherein may be found a thought that can be transformed into a powerful factor in the development of *Self-confidence*. The thought is this: *Voluntarily, and by force if necessary, direct your efforts and your thoughts along a desired line until you have formed the habit that will lay hold of you and continue, voluntarily, to direct your efforts along the same line.*

The object in writing out and repeating the Self-confidence formula is to form the habit of making *belief in yourself* the dominating thought of your mind until that thought has been thoroughly imbedded in your subconscious mind, through the principle of *habit*.

You learned to write by repeatedly directing the muscles of your arm and hand over certain outlines known as letters, until finally you formed the habit of tracing these outlines. Now you write with ease and rapidity, without tracing each letter slowly. Writing has become a *habit* with you.

The principle of habit will lay hold of the faculties of your mind just the same as it will influence the physical muscles of your body, as you can easily prove by mastering and applying this lesson on Self-confidence. Any statement that you repeatedly make to yourself, or any *desire* that you deeply plant in your mind through repeated statement, will eventually seek expression through your physical, outward bodily efforts. The principle of habit is the very foundation upon which this lesson on Self-confidence is built, and if you will understand and follow the directions laid down in this lesson you will soon know more about the law of habit, from first-hand knowledge, than could be taught you by a thousand such lessons as this.

You have but little conception of the possibilities which lie sleeping within you, awaiting but the awakening hand of vision to arouse you, and you will never have a better conception of those possibilities unless you develop sufficient Self-confidence to lift you above the commonplace influences of your present environment.

The human mind is a marvelous, mysterious piece of machinery, a fact of which I was reminded a few months ago when I picked up Emerson's *Essays* and re-read his essay on Spiritual Laws. A strange thing happened. I saw in that essay, which I had read scores of times previously, much that I had never noticed before. I saw more in this essay than I had seen during previous readings because the unfoldment of my mind since the last reading had prepared me to interpret more.

The human mind is constantly unfolding, like the petals of a flower, until it reaches the maximum of development. What this maximum is, where it ends, or whether it ends at all or not, are unanswerable questions, but the degree of unfoldment seems to vary according to the nature of the individual and the degree to which he keeps his mind at work. A mind that is forced or coaxed into analytical thought every day seems to keep on unfolding and developing greater powers of interpretation.

Down in Louisville, Kentucky, lives Mr. Lee Cook, a man who has practically no legs and has to wheel himself around on a cart. In spite of the fact that Mr. Cook has been without legs since birth, he is the owner of a great industry and a millionaire through his own efforts. He has proved that a man can get along very well without legs if he has a well developed Self-confidence.

In the city of New York one may see a strong able-bodied and able-headed young man, without legs, rolling himself down Fifth Avenue every afternoon, with cap in hand, begging for a living. His head is perhaps as sound and as able to think as the average.

This young man could duplicate anything that Mr. Cook, of Louisville, has done, if *he thought of himself as Mr. Cook thinks of himself.*

Henry Ford owns more millions of dollars than he will ever need or use. Not so many years ago, he was working as a laborer in a machine shop, with but little schooling and without capital. Scores of other men, some of them with better organized brains than his, worked near him. Ford threw off the poverty consciousness, developed confidence in himself, thought of success and attained it. Those who worked around him could have done as well had they *thought* as he did.

Milo C. Jones, of Wisconsin, was stricken down with paralysis a few years ago. So bad was the stroke that he could not turn himself in bed or move a muscle of his body. His physical body was useless, but there was nothing wrong with his brain, so it began to function in earnest, probably for the first time in its existence. Lying flat on his back in bed, Mr. Jones made that brain create a *definite purpose.* That purpose was prosaic and humble enough in nature, but it was *definite* and it was a *purpose,* something that he had never known before.

His *definite purpose* was to make pork sausage. Calling his family around him he told of his plans and began directing them in carrying the plans into action. With nothing to aid him except a sound mind and plenty of *Self-confidence,* Milo C. Jones spread the name and reputation of "Little Pig Sausage" all over the United States, and accumulated a fortune besides. All this was accomplished after paralysis had made it impossible for him to work with his hands.

Where *thought* prevails power may be found!

Henry Ford has made millions of dollars and is still making millions of dollars each year because *he believed in Henry Ford* and transformed that belief into a *definite purpose* and backed that purpose with a definite plan. The other machinists who worked along with Ford, during the early days of his career, visioned nothing but a weekly pay envelope and that was all they ever got. They demanded nothing out of the ordinary of themselves. If you want to *get more* be sure to *demand* more of yourself. Notice that this demand is to be made on *yourself!*

There comes to mind a well known poem whose author expressed a great psychological truth:

> If you think you are beaten, you are;
>   If you think you dare not, you don't;
> If you like to win, but you think you can't,
>   It is almost certain you won't.
>
> If you think you'll lose you've lost,
>   For out of the world we find
> Success begins with a fellow's will—
>   It's all in the state of mind.
>
> If you think you are outclassed, you are—
>   You've got to think high to rise.
> You've got to be sure of yourself before
>   You can ever win a prize.
>
> Life's battles don't always go
>   To the stronger or faster man;
> But soon or late the man who wins
>   Is the man who thinks he can.

It can do no harm if you commit this poem to memory and use it as a part of your working equipment in the development of Self-confidence.

Somewhere in your make-up there is a "subtle something" which, if it were aroused by the proper outside influence, would carry you to heights of achievement such as you have never before anticipated. Just as a master player can take hold of a violin and cause that instrument to pour forth the most beautiful and entrancing strains of music, so is there some outside influence that can lay hold of your mind and cause you to go forth into the field of your chosen endeavor and play a glorious symphony of *success*. No man knows what hidden forces lie dormant within *you*. You, yourself, do not know your capacity for achievement, and you never will know until you come in contact with that particular stimulus which arouses you to greater action and extends your vision, develops your Self-confidence and moves you with a deeper *desire* to achieve.

It is not unreasonable to expect that some statement, some idea or some stimulating word of this Reading Course on the Law of Success will serve as the needed stimulus that will re-shape your destiny and re-direct your thoughts and energies along a pathway that will lead you, finally, to your coveted goal of life. It is strange, but true, that the most important turning-points of life often come at the most unexpected times and in the most unexpected ways. I have in mind a typical example of how some of the seemingly unimportant experiences of life often turn out to be the most important of all, and I am relating this case because it shows, also, what a man can accomplish when he awakens to a full understanding of the value of Self-confidence. The incident to which I refer happened in the city of Chicago, while I was engaged in the work of character analysis. One day a tramp presented himself at my office and asked for an interview. As I looked up from my work and greeted him he said, "I have come to see the man who wrote this little book," as he removed from his pocket a copy of a book entitled Self-confidence, which I had written many years previously. "It must have been the hand of fate," he continued, "that slipped this book into my pocket yesterday afternoon, because I was about ready to go out there and punch a hole in Lake Michigan. I had about come to the conclusion that everything and everybody, including God, had it in for me until I read this book, and it gave me a new viewpoint and brought me the courage and the hope that sustained me through the night. I made up my mind that if I could see the man who wrote this book he could help me get on my feet again. Now, I am here and I would like to know what you can do for a man like me."

While he was speaking I had been studying him from head to foot, and I am frank to admit that down deep in my heart I did not believe there was anything I could do for him, but I did not wish to tell him so. The glassy stare in his eyes, the lines of discouragement in his face, the posture of his body, the ten days' growth of beard on his face, the nervous manner about this man all conveyed to me the impression that he was hopeless, but I did not have the heart to tell him so, therefore I asked him to sit down and tell me his whole story. I asked him to be perfectly frank and tell me, as nearly as possible, just what had brought him down to the ragged edge of life. I promised him that after I had heard his entire story I would then tell him whether or not I could be of service to him. He related his story, in lengthy detail, the sum and substance of which was this: He had invested his entire fortune in a small manufacturing business. When the world war began in 1914, it was impossible for him to get the raw materials necessary in the operation of his factory, and he therefore failed. The loss of his money broke his heart and so disturbed his mind

> *The only man who makes no mistakes is the man who never does anything. Do not be afraid of mistakes providing you do not make the same one twice.*
> —THEODORE ROOSEVELT

that he left his wife and children and became a tramp. He had actually brooded over his loss until he had reached the point at which he was contemplating suicide.

After he had finished his story, I said to him: "I have listened to you with a great deal of interest, and I wish that there was something which *I* could do to help you, but *there is absolutely nothing.*"

He became as pale as he will be when he is laid away in a coffin, and settled back in his chair and dropped his chin on his chest as much as to say, "That settles it." I waited for a few seconds, then said:

"While there is nothing that I can do for you, there is a man in this building to whom I will introduce you, if you wish, who can help you regain your lost fortune and put you back on your feet again." These words had barely fallen from my lips when he jumped up, grabbed me by the hands and said, "For God's sake lead me to this man."

It was encouraging to note that he had asked this "for God's sake." This indicated that there was still a spark of hope within his breast, so I took him by the arm and led him out into the laboratory where my psychological tests in character analysis were conducted, and stood with him in front of what looked to be a curtain over a door. I pulled the curtain aside and uncovered a tall looking-glass in which he saw himself from head to foot. Pointing my finger at the glass I said:

"There stands the man to whom I promised to introduce you. There is the only man in this world who can put you back on your feet again, and unless you sit down and become acquainted with that man, as you never became acquainted with him before, you might just as well go on over and 'punch a hole' in Lake Michigan, because you will be of no value to yourself or to the world until you know this man better."

He stepped over to the glass, rubbed his hands over his bearded face, studied himself from head to foot for a few moments, then stepped back, dropped his head and began to weep. I knew that the lesson had been driven home, so I led him back to the elevator and sent him away. I never expected to see him again, and I doubted that the lesson would be sufficient to help him regain his place in the world, because he seemed to be too far gone for redemption. He seemed to be not only *down*, but almost *out*.

A few days later I met this man on the street. His transformation had been so complete that I hardly recognized him. He was walking briskly, with his head tilted back. That old, shifting, nervous posture of his body was gone. He was dressed in new clothes from head to foot. He looked prosperous and he felt prosperous. He stopped me and related what had happened to bring about his rapid transformation from a state of abject failure to one of hope and promise.

"I was just on my way to your office," he explained, "to bring you the good news. I went out the very day that I was in your office, a down-and-out tramp, and despite my appearance I sold myself at a salary of $3,000.00 a year. *Think of it, man, three thousand dollars a year!* And my employer advanced me money enough with which to buy some new clothes, as you can see for yourself. He also advanced me some money to send home to my family, and I am once more on the road to success. It seems like a dream when I think that only a few days ago I had lost hope and faith and courage, and was actually contemplating suicide.

"I was coming to tell you that one of these days, when you are least expecting me, I will pay you another visit, and when I do I will be a successful man. I will bring with me a check, signed in blank and made payable to you, and you may fill in the amount because you have saved me from *myself* by introducing me to *myself*—that self which I never knew until you stood me in front of that looking-glass and pointed out the *real* me."

As that man turned and departed in the crowded streets of Chicago I saw, for the first time in my life, what strength and power and possibility lie hidden in the mind of the man who has never discovered the value of *Self-reliance*. Then and there I made up my mind that I, too, would stand in front of that same looking-glass and point an accusing finger at myself for not having discovered the lesson which I had helped another to learn. I did stand before that same looking-glass, and as I did so I then and there fixed in my mind, as my *definite purpose* in life, the determination to help men and women discover the forces that lie sleeping within them. The book you hold in your hands is evidence that my definite purpose is being carried out.

The man whose story I have related is now the president of one of the largest and most successful concerns of its kind in America, with a business that extends from coast to coast and from Canada to Mexico.

A short while after the incident just related, a woman came to my office for personal analysis. She was then a teacher in the Chicago public schools. I gave her an analysis chart and asked her to fill it out. She had been at work on the chart but a few minutes when she came back to my desk, handed back the chart and said, "I do not believe I will fill this out." I asked her why she had decided not to fill out the chart and she replied: "To be perfectly frank with you, one of the questions in this chart put me to thinking and I now know what is wrong with me, therefore I feel it unnecessary to pay you a fee to analyze me." With that the woman went away and I did not hear from her for two years. She went to New York City, became a writer of advertising copy for one of the largest agencies in the country and her income at the time she wrote me was $10,000.00 a year.

This woman sent me a check to cover the cost of my analysis fee, because she felt that the fee had been earned, even though I did not render her the service that I usually render my clients. It is impossible for anyone to foretell what seemingly insignificant incident may lead to an important turning-point in one's career, but there is no denying the fact that these "turning-points" may be more readily recognized by those who have well-rounded-out confidence in themselves.

One of the irreparable losses to the human race lies in the lack of knowledge that there is a definite method through which Self-confidence can be developed in any person of average intelligence. What an immeasurable loss to civilization that young men and women are not taught this known method of developing Self-confidence before they complete their schooling, for no one who lacks faith in himself is really educated in the proper sense of the term.

Oh, what glory and satisfaction would be the happy heritage of the man or woman who could pull aside the curtain of *fear* that hangs over the human race and shuts out the sunlight of understanding that Self-confidence brings, wherever it is in evidence.

Where *fear* controls, noteworthy achievement becomes an impossibility, a fact which brings to mind the definition of *fear,* as stated by a great philosopher:

"Fear is the dungeon of the mind into which it runs and hides and seeks seclusion. Fear brings on superstition and superstition is the dagger with which hypocrisy assassinates the soul."

In front of the typewriter on which I am writing the manuscripts for this Reading Course hangs a sign with the following wording, in big letters:

"Day by day in every way I am becoming more *successful.*"

A skeptic who read that sign asked if I really believed "that stuff" and I replied, "Of course not. All it ever did

> *Love, beauty, joy and worship are forever building, tearing down and rebuilding the foundation of each man's soul.*

for me was to help me get out of the coal mines, where I started as a laborer, and find a place in the world in which I am serving upwards of 100,000 people, in whose minds I am planting the same positive thought that this sign brings out; therefore, why should I believe in it?"

As this man started to leave he said: "Well, perhaps there is something to this sort of philosophy, after all, for I have always been afraid that I would be a failure, and so far my fears have been thoroughly realized."

You are condemning yourself to poverty, misery and failure, or you are driving yourself on toward the heights of great achievement, solely by the thoughts you think. If you *demand* success of yourself and back up this demand with intelligent action you are sure to win. Bear in mind, though, that there is a difference between *demanding* success and just merely wishing for it. You should find out what this difference is, and take advantage of it.

Do you remember what the Bible says (look it up, somewhere in the book of Matthew) about those who have faith as a grain of mustard seed? Go at the task of developing Self-confidence with at least that much faith if not more. Never mind "what *they* will say" because you might as well know that "*they*" will be of little aid to you in your climb up the mountain-side of life toward the object of your *definite purpose*. You have within you all the power you need with which to get whatever you want or need in this world, and about the best way to avail yourself of this power is to *believe in yourself*.

"Know thyself, man; know thyself."

This has been the advice of the philosophers all down the ages. When you *really* know yourself you will know that there is nothing foolish about hanging a sign in front of you that reads like this: "Day by day in every way I am becoming more successful," with due apologies to the Frenchman who made this motto popular. I am not afraid to place this sort of suggestion in front of my desk, and, what is more to the point, I am not afraid to believe that it will influence me so that I will become a more positive and aggressive human being.

More than twenty-five years ago I learned my first lesson in Self-confidence building. One night I was sitting before an open fire-place, listening to a conversation between some older men, on the subject of Capital and Labor. Without invitation I joined in the conversation and said something about employers and employees settling their differences on the Golden Rule basis. My remarks attracted the attention of one of the men, who turned to me, with a look of surprise on his face and said:

"Why, you are a bright boy, and if you would go out and get a schooling you would make your mark in the world."

Those remarks fell on "fertile" ears, even though that was the first time anyone had ever told me that I was bright, or that I might accomplish anything worth while in life. The remark put me to thinking, and the more I allowed my mind to dwell upon that thought the more certain I became that the remark had back of it a possibility.

It might be truthfully stated that whatever service I am rendering the world and whatever good I accomplish, should be credited to that off-hand remark.

Suggestions such as this are often powerful, and none the less so when they are deliberate and self-expressed. Go back, now, to the Self-confidence formula and master it, for it will lead you into the "power-house" of your own mind, where you will tap a force that can be made to carry you to the very top of the Ladder of Success.

Others will believe in you only when you believe in yourself. They will "tune in" on your thoughts and feel toward you just as you feel toward yourself. The law of mental telepathy takes care of this. You are continuously broadcasting what you think of yourself, and if you have no faith in yourself others will pick up the vibrations of your thoughts and mistake them for their own. Once understand the law of mental telepathy and you will know why Self-confidence is the second of the Fifteen Laws of Success.

You should be cautioned, however, to learn the difference between Self-confidence, which is based upon sound knowledge of what you know and what you can do, and egotism, which is only based upon what you *wish* you knew or could do. Learn the difference between these two terms or you will make yourself boresome, ridiculous and annoying to people of culture and understanding. Self-confidence is something which should never be proclaimed or announced except through intelligent performance of constructive deeds.

If you have Self-confidence those around you will discover this fact. Let them make the discovery. They will feel proud of their alertness in having made the discovery, and you will be free from the suspicion of egotism. Opportunity never stalks the person with a highly developed state of egotism, but brick-bats and ugly remarks do. Opportunity forms affinities much more easily and quickly with Self-confidence than it does with egotism. Self-praise is never a proper measure of self-reliance. Bear this in mind and let your Self-confidence speak only through the tongue of constructive service rendered without fuss or flurry.

Self-confidence is the product of knowledge. Know yourself, know how much you know (and how little), why you know it, and how you are going to use it. "Four-flushers" come to grief, therefore, do not pretend to know more than you actually do know. There's no use of pretense, because any educated person will measure you quite accurately after hearing you speak for three minutes. What you really are will speak so loudly that what you "claim" you are will not be heard.

If you heed this warning the last four pages of this one lesson may mark one of the most important turning-points of your life.

Believe in yourself, but do not tell the world what you can do—SHOW IT!

You are now ready for Lesson Three, which will take you the next step up the Ladder of Success.

DISCONTENTMENT

An After-the-Lesson Visit with the Author

The marker stands at the Entrance Gate of Life and writes "Poor Fool" on the brow of the wise man and "Poor Sinner" on the brow of the saint.

The supreme mystery of the universe is life! We come here without our consent, from whence we know not! We go away without our consent, whither, we know not!

We are eternally trying to solve this great riddle of "LIFE," and, for what purpose and to what end?

That we are placed on this earth for a definite reason there can be no doubt by any thinker. May it not be possible that the power which placed us here will know what to do with us when we pass on beyond the Great Divide?

Would it not be a good plan to give the Creator who placed us here on earth, credit for having enough intelligence to know what to do with us after we pass on; or, should we assume the intelligence and the ability to control the future life in our own way?

May it not be possible that we can co-operate with the Creator very intelligently by assuming to control our conduct on this earth to the end that we may be decent to one another and do all the good we can in all the ways we can during this life, leaving the hereafter to one who probably knows, better than we, what is best for us?

The artist has told a powerful story in the picture at the top of this passage.

From birth until death the mind is always reaching out for that which it does not possess.

The little child, playing with its toys on the floor, sees another child with a different sort of toy and immediately tries to lay hands on that toy.

The female child (grown tall) believes the other woman's clothes more becoming than her own and sets out to duplicate them.

The male child (grown tall) sees another man with a bigger collection of railroads or banks or merchandise and says to himself: "How fortunate! How fortunate! How can I separate him from his belongings?"

F. W. Woolworth, the Five and Ten Cent Store king, stood on Fifth Avenue in New York City and gazed upward at the tall Metropolitan Building and said: "How wonderful! I will build one much taller." The crowning achievement of his life was measured by the Woolworth Building. That building stands as a temporary symbol of man's nature to excel the handiwork of other men. A MONUMENT TO THE VANITY OF MAN, WITH BUT LITTLE ELSE TO JUSTIFY ITS EXISTENCE!

The little ragged newsboy on the street stands, with wide-open mouth, and envies the business man as he alights from his automobile at the curb and starts into his office. "How happy I would be," the newsboy says to himself, "if I owned a Lizzie." And, the business man seated at his desk inside, thinks how happy he would be if he could add another million dollars to his already overswollen bank roll.

The grass is always sweeter on the other side of the fence, says the jackass, as he stretches his neck in the attempt to get to it.

Turn a crowd of boys into an apple orchard and they will pass by the nice mellow apples on the ground. The red, juicy ones hanging dangerously high in the top of the tree look much more tempting, and up the tree they will go.

The married man takes a sheepish glance at the daintily dressed ladies on the street and thinks how fortunate he would be if his wife were as pretty as they. Perhaps she is much prettier, but he misses that beauty because—well, because "the grass is always greener on the other side of the fence." Most divorce cases grow out of man's tendency to climb the fence into the other fellow's pastures.

Happiness is always just around the bend; always in sight but just out of reach. Life is never complete, no matter what we have or how much of it we possess. One thing calls for something else to go with it.

Milady buys a pretty hat. She must have a gown to match it. That calls for new shoes and hose and gloves, and other accessories that run into a big bill far beyond her husband's means.

Man longs for a home—just a plain little house setting off in the edge of the woods. He builds it, but it is not complete; he must have shrubbery and flowers and landscaping to go with it. Still it is not complete; he must have a beautiful fence around it, with a graveled driveway.

That calls for a motor car and a garage in which to house it.

All these little touches have been added, but to no avail! The place is now too small. He must have a house with more rooms. The Ford Coupe must be replaced by a Cadillac sedan, so there will be room for company in the cross country tours.

On and on the story goes, ad infinitum!

The young man receives a salary sufficient to keep him and his family fairly comfortable. Then comes a promotion and an advance in salary of a thousand dollars a year. Does he lay the extra thousand dollars away in the savings account and continue living as before? He does nothing of the sort. Immediately he must trade the old car in for a new one. A porch must be added to the house. The wife needs a new wardrobe. The table must be set with better food and more of it. (Pity his poor, groaning stomach.) At the end of the year is he better off with the increase? He is nothing of the sort! The more he gets the more he wants, and the rule applies to the man with millions the same as to the man with but a few thousands.

The young man selects the girl of his choice, believing he cannot live without her. After he gets her he is not sure that he can live with her. If a man remains a bachelor he wonders why he is so stupid as to deprive himself of the joys of married life. If he marries he wonders how she happened to catch him off guard long enough to "harpoon" him.

And the god of Destiny cries out, "O fool, O fool! You are damned if you DO and you are damned if you DON'T."

At every crossroad of Life the imps of Discontentment stand in the shadows of the background, with a grin of mockery on their faces, crying out, "Take the road of your own choice! We will get you in the end!"

At last man becomes disillusioned and begins to learn that Happiness and Contentment are not of this world. Then begins the search for the pass-word that will open the door to him in some world of which he knows not. Surely there must be Happiness on the other side of the Great Divide. In desperation his tired, care-worn heart turns to religion for hope and encouragement.

But, his troubles are not over; they are just starting!

"Come into our tent and accept our creed," says one sect, "and you may go straight to heaven after death." Poor man hesitates, looks and listens. Then he hears the call of another brand of religion whose leader says:

"Stay out of the other camp or you'll go straight to hell! They only sprinkle water on your head, but we push you all the way under, thereby insuring you safe passage into the Land of Promise."

In the midst of sectarian claims and counter-claims poor man becomes undecided. Not knowing whether to turn this way or that, he wonders which brand of religion offers the safest passage-way, until Hope vanishes.

> "Myself when young
>   did eagerly frequent
> Doctor and Saint and heard
>   great argument
> About it and about; but
>   evermore
> Came out by the same door
>   where in I went."

Always seeking but never finding—thus might be described man's struggle for Happiness and Contentment. He tries one religion after another, finally joining the "Big Church" which the world has named the "Damned." His mind becomes an eternal question mark, searching hither and yon for an answer to the questions—"Whence and Whither?"

> "The worldly hope men set
>   their Hearts upon
> Turns Ashes—or it prospers;
>   and anon,
> Like Snow upon the Desert's
>   Dusty Face
> Lighting a little Hour or two—
>   is gone."

Life is an everlasting question-mark!

That which we want most is always in the embryonic distance of the future. Our power to acquire is always a decade or so behind our power to DESIRE!

And, if we catch up with the thing we want we no longer want it!

Fortunate is the young woman who learns this great truth and keeps her lover always guessing, always on the defensive lest he may lose her.

Our favorite author is a hero and a genius until we meet him in person and learn the sad truth that, after all, he is only a man. "How often must we learn this lesson? Men cease to interest us when we find their limitations. The only sin is limitation. As soon as you once come up with a man's limitations, it is all over with him."—EMERSON

How beautiful the mountain yonder in the distance; but, the moment we draw near it we find it to be nothing but a wretched collection of rocks and dirt and trees.

Out of this truth grew the oft-repeated adage "Familiarity breeds contempt."

Beauty and Happiness and Contentment are states of mind. They can never be enjoyed except through vision of the afar. The most beautiful painting of Rembrandt becomes a mere smudge of daubed paint if we come too near it.

Destroy the Hope of unfinished dreams in man's heart and he is finished.

The moment a man ceases to cherish the vision of future achievement he is through. Nature has built man so that his greatest and only lasting Happiness is that which he feels in the pursuit of some yet unattained object. Anticipation is sweeter than realization. That which is at hand does not satisfy. The only enduring satisfaction is that which comes to the person who keeps alive in his heart the HOPE of future achievement. When that hope dies write FINIS across the human heart.

Life's greatest inconsistency is the fact that most of that which we believe is not true. Russel Conwell wrote the most popular lecture ever delivered in the English language. He called it "Acres of Diamonds." The central idea of the lecture was the statement that one need not seek opportunity in the distance; that opportunity may be found in the vicinity of one's birth. Perhaps! but, how many believe it?

Opportunity may be found wherever one really looks for it, and nowhere else! To most men the picking looks better on the other side of the fence. How futile to urge one to try out one's luck in the little home-town when it is man's nature to look for opportunity in some other locality.

Do not worry because the grass looks sweeter on the other side of the fence. Nature intended it so. Thus does she allure us and groom us for the life-long task of GROWTH THROUGH STRUGGLE.

The highest compact we can make with our fellow is: Let there be truth between us two forevermore.

—EMERSON

The only lasting favor which the parent may confer upon the child is that of helping the child to help itself.

THE HABIT OF SAVING

*"Man is a combination of flesh, bone, blood, hair and brain cells.
These are the building materials out of which he shapes, through
the Law of Habit, his own personality."*

To advise one to save money without describing how to save would be somewhat like drawing the picture of a horse and writing under it, "This is a horse." It is obvious to all that the saving of money is one of the essentials for success, but the big question uppermost in the minds of the majority of those who do not save is:

"How can I do it?"

The saving of money is solely a matter of *habit*. For this reason this lesson begins with a brief analysis of the Law of Habit.

It is literally true that man, through the Law of Habit, shapes his own personality. Through repetition, any act indulged in a few times becomes a habit, and the mind appears to be nothing more than a mass of motivating forces growing out of our daily habits.

When once fixed in the mind a habit voluntarily impels one to action. For example, follow a given route to your daily work, or to some other place that you frequently visit, and very soon the habit has been formed and your mind will lead you over that route without thought on your part. Moreover, if you start out with the intention of traveling in another direction, without keeping the thought of the change in routes constantly in mind, you will find yourself following the old route.

Public speakers have found that the telling over and over again of a story, which may be based upon pure fiction, brings into play the Law of Habit, and very soon they forget whether the story is true or not.

Walls of Limitation Built Through Habit

Millions of people go through life in poverty and want because they have made destructive use of the Law of Habit. Not understanding either the Law of Habit or the Law of Attraction through which "like attracts like," those who remain in poverty seldom realize that they are where they are as the result of their own acts.

Fix in your mind the thought that your ability is limited to a given earning capacity and you will never earn more than that, because the law of habit will set up a definite limitation of the amount you can earn, your subconscious mind will accept this limitation, and very soon you will feel yourself "slipping" until finally you will become so hedged in by FEAR OF POVERTY (one of the six basic fears) that opportunity will no longer knock at your door; your doom will be sealed; your fate fixed.

Formation of the Habit of Saving does not mean that you shall limit your earning capacity; it means just the opposite—that you shall apply this law so that it not only conserves that which you earn, in a systematic manner, but it also places you in the way of greater opportunity and gives you the vision, the self-confidence, the imagination, the enthusiasm, the initiative and leadership actually to increase your earning capacity.

Stating this great law in another way, when you thoroughly understand the Law of Habit you may insure yourself success in the great game of money-making by "playing both ends of that game against the middle."

You proceed in this manner:

First, through the law of Definite Chief Aim you set up, in your mind, an accurate, definite description of that which you want, including the amount of money you intend to earn. Your subconscious mind takes over this picture which you have created and uses it as a blueprint, chart or map by which to mold your thoughts and actions into practical plans for attaining the object of your Chief Aim, or purpose. Through the Law of Habit you keep the object of your Definite Chief Aim fixed in your mind (in the manner described in Lesson One) until it becomes firmly and permanently implanted there. This practice will destroy the poverty consciousness and set up, in its place, a prosperity consciousness. You will actually begin to DEMAND prosperity, you will begin to expect it, you will begin to prepare yourself to receive it and to use it wisely, thus paving the way or setting the stage for the development of the Habit of Saving.

Second, having in this manner increased your earning power you will make further use of the Law of Habit by provision, in your written statement of your Definite Chief Aim, for saving a definite proportion of all the money you earn.

Therefore, as your earnings increase, your savings will, likewise, increase in proportion.

By ever urging yourself on and demanding of yourself increased earning power, on the one hand, and by systematically laying aside a definite amount of all your earnings, on the other hand, you will soon reach the point at which you have removed all imaginary limitations from your own mind and you will then be well started on the road toward financial independence.

Nothing could be more practical or more easily accomplished than this!

Reverse the operation of the Law of Habit, by setting up in your mind the Fear of Poverty, and very soon this fear will reduce your earning capacity until you will be barely able to earn sufficient money to take care of your actual necessities.

The publishers of newspapers could create a panic in a week's time by filling their columns with news items concerning the actual business failures of the country, despite the fact that but few businesses, compared to the total number in existence, actually fail.

The so-called "crime waves" are very largely the products of sensational journalism. A single murder case, when exploited by the newspapers of the country, through scare head-lines, is sufficient to start a regular "wave" of similar crimes in various localities. Following the repetition in the daily papers of the Hickman murder story, similar cases began to be reported from other parts of the country.

We are the victims of our habits, no matter who we are or what may be our life-calling. Any idea that is deliberately fixed in the mind, or any idea that is permitted to set itself up in the mind, as the result of suggestion, environment, the influence of associates, etc., is sure to cause us to indulge in acts which conform to the nature of the idea.

Form the habit of thinking and talking of prosperity and abundance, and very soon material evidence of these will begin to manifest itself in the nature of wider opportunity and new and unexpected opportunity.

Like attracts like! If you are in business and have formed the habit of talking and thinking about "business being bad" business will be bad. One pessimist, providing he is permitted to continue his destructive influence long enough, can destroy the work of half a dozen competent men, and he will do it by setting adrift in the minds of his associates the thought of poverty and failure.

> *You are a human magnet and you are constantly attracting to you people whose characters harmonize with your own.*

Don't be this type of man or woman.

One of the most successful bankers in the state of Illinois has this sign hanging in his private office: "WE TALK AND THINK ONLY OF ABUNDANCE HERE. IF YOU HAVE A TALE OF WOE PLEASE KEEP IT, AS WE DO NOT WANT IT."

No business firm wants the services of a pessimist, and those who understand the Law of Attraction and the Law of Habit will no more tolerate the pessimist than they would permit a burglar to roam around their place of business, for the reason that one such person will destroy the usefulness of those around him.

In tens of thousands of homes the general topic of conversation is poverty and want, and that is just what they are getting. They think of poverty, they talk of poverty, they accept poverty as their lot in life. They reason that because their ancestors were poor before them they, also, must remain poor.

The poverty consciousness is formed as the result of the habit of thinking of and fearing poverty. "Lo! the thing I had feared has come upon me."

The Slavery of Debt

Debt is a merciless master, a fatal enemy of the savings habit.

Poverty, alone, is sufficient to kill off ambition, destroy self-confidence and destroy hope, but add to it the burden of debt and all who are victims of these two cruel task-masters are practically doomed to failure.

No man can do his best work, no man can express himself in terms that command respect, no man can either create or carry out a definite purpose in life, with heavy debt hanging over his head. The man who is bound in the slavery of debt is just as helpless as the slave who is bound by ignorance, or by actual chains.

The author has a very close friend whose income is $1,000 a month. His wife loves "society" and tries to make a $20,000 showing on a $12,000 income, with the result that this poor fellow is usually about $8,000 in debt. Every member of his family has the "spending habit," having acquired this from the mother. The children, two girls and one boy, are now of the age when they are thinking of going to college, but this is impossible because of the father's debts. The result is dissension between the father and his children which makes the entire family unhappy and miserable.

It is a terrible thing even to think of going through life like a prisoner in chains, bound down and owned by somebody else on account of debts. The accumulation of debts is a habit. It starts in a small way and grows to enormous proportions slowly, step by step, until finally it takes charge of one's very soul.

Thousands of young men start their married lives with unnecessary debts hanging over their heads and never manage to get out from under the load. After the novelty of marriage begins to wear off (as it usually does) the married couple begin to feel the embarrassment of want, and this feeling grows until it leads, oftentimes, to open dissatisfaction with one another, and eventually to the divorce court.

A man who is bound by the slavery of debt has no time or inclination to set up or work out ideals, with the result that he drifts downward with time until he eventually begins to set up limitations in his own mind, and by these he hedges himself behind prison walls of FEAR and doubt from which he never escapes.

No sacrifice is too great to avoid the misery of debt!

"Think of what you owe yourself and those who are dependent upon you and resolve to be no man's debtor," is the advice of one very successful man whose early chances were destroyed by debt. This man came to himself soon enough to throw off the habit of buying that which he did not need and eventually worked his way out of slavery.

Most men who develop the habit of debt will not be so fortunate as to come to their senses in time to save themselves, because debt is something like quicksand in that it has a tendency to draw its victim deeper and deeper into the mire.

The Fear of Poverty is one of the most destructive of the six basic fears described in Lesson Two. The man who becomes hopelessly in debt is seized with this poverty fear, his ambition and self-confidence become paralyzed, and he sinks gradually into oblivion.

There are two classes of debts, and these are so different in nature that they deserve to be here described, as follows:

1. There are debts incurred for luxuries which become a dead loss.
2. There are debts incurred in the course of professional or business trading which represent service or merchandise that can be converted back into assets.

The first class of debts is the one to be avoided. The second class may be indulged in, providing the one incurring the debts uses judgment and does not go beyond the bounds of reasonable limitation. The moment one buys beyond his limitations he enters the realm of speculation, and speculation swallows more of its victims than it enriches.

Practically all people who live beyond their means are tempted to speculate with the hope that they may recoup, at a single turn of the wheel of fortune, so to speak, their entire indebtedness. The wheel generally stops at the wrong place and, far from finding themselves out of debt, such people as indulge in speculation are bound more closely as slaves of debt.

The Fear of Poverty breaks down the will-power of its victims, and they then find themselves unable to restore their lost fortunes, and, what is still more sad, they lose all ambition to extricate themselves from the slavery of debt.

Hardly a day passes that one may not see an account in the newspapers of at least one suicide as the result of worry over debts. The slavery of debt causes more suicides every year than all other causes combined, which is a slight indication of the cruelty of the poverty fear.

During the war millions of men faced the front-line trenches without flinching, knowing that death might overtake them any moment. Those same men, when facing the Fear of Poverty, often cringe and out of sheer desperation, which paralyzes their reason, sometimes commit suicide.

The person who is free from debt may whip poverty and achieve outstanding financial success, but, if he is bound by debt, such achievement is but a remote possibility, and never a probability.

Fear of Poverty is a negative, destructive state of mind. Moreover, one negative state of mind has a tendency to attract other similar states of mind. For example, the Fear of Poverty may attract the fear of Ill Health, and these two may attract the Fear of Old Age, so that the victim finds himself poverty-stricken, in ill health and actually growing old long before the time when he should begin to show the signs of old age.

Millions of untimely, nameless graves have been filled by this cruel state of mind known as the Fear of Poverty!

Less than a dozen years ago a young man held a responsible position with the City National Bank, of New York City. Through living beyond his income he contracted a large amount of debts which caused him to worry until this destructive habit began to show up in his work and he was dismissed from the bank's service.

He secured another position, at less money, but his creditors embarrassed him so that he decided to resign and go away into another city, where he hoped to escape them until he had accumulated enough money to pay off his indebtedness. Creditors have a way of tracing debtors, so very soon they were close on the heels of this young man, whose employer found out about his indebtedness and dismissed him from his position.

Who told you it couldn't be done? and, what great achievement has he to his credit that entitles him to use the word "impossible" so freely?

He then searched in vain for employment for two months. One cold night he went to the top of one of the tall buildings on Broadway and jumped off. Debt had claimed another victim.

How to Master the Fear of Poverty

To whip the Fear of Poverty one must take two very definite steps, providing one is in debt. First, quit the habit of buying on credit, and follow this by gradually paying off the debts that you have already incurred.

Being free from the worry of indebtedness you are ready to revamp the habits of your mind and re-direct your course toward prosperity. Adopt, as a part of your Definite Chief Aim, the habit of saving a regular proportion of your income, even if this be no more than a penny a day. Very soon this habit will begin to lay hold of your mind and you will actually get joy out of saving.

Any habit may be discontinued by building in its place some other and more desirable habit. The "spending" habit must be replaced by the "saving" habit by all who attain financial independence.

Merely to discontinue an undesirable habit is not enough, as such habits have a tendency to reappear unless the place they formerly occupied in the mind is filled by some other habit of a different nature.

The discontinuance of a habit leaves a "hole" in the mind, and this hole must be filled up with some other form of habit or the old one will return and claim its place.

Throughout this course many psychological formulas, which the student has been requested to memorize and practice, have been described. You will find such a formula in Lesson Two, the object of which is to develop Self-confidence.

These formulas may be assimilated so they become a part of your mental machinery, through the Law of Habit, if you will follow the instructions for their use which accompany each of them.

It is assumed that you are striving to attain financial independence. The accumulation of money is not difficult after you have once mastered the Fear of Poverty and developed in its place the Habit of Saving.

The author of this course would be greatly disappointed to know that any student of the course got the impression from anything in this or any of the other lessons that Success is measured by dollars alone.

However, money does represent an important factor in success, and it must be given its proper value in any philosophy intended to help people in becoming useful, happy and prosperous.

The cold, cruel, relentless truth is that in this age of materialism a man is no more than so many grains of sand, which may be blown helter-skelter by every stray wind of circumstance, unless he is entrenched behind the power of money!

Genius may offer many rewards to those who possess it, but the fact still remains that genius without money with which to give it expression is but an empty, skeleton-like honor.

The man without money is at the mercy of the man who has it!

And this goes, regardless of the amount of ability he may possess, the training he has had or the native genius with which he was gifted by nature.

There is no escape from the fact that people will weigh you very largely in the light of bank balances, no matter who you are or what you can do. The first question that arises, in the minds of most people, when they meet a stranger, is, "How much money has he?" If he has money he is welcomed into homes and business opportunities are thrown his way. All sorts of attention are lavished upon him. He is a prince, and as such is entitled to the best of the land.

But if his shoes are run down at the heels, his clothes are not pressed, his collar is dirty, and he shows plainly the signs of impoverished finances, woe be his lot, for the passing crowd will step on his toes and blow the smoke of disrespect in his face.

These are not pretty statements, but they have one virtue—THEY ARE TRUE!

This tendency to judge people by the money they have, or their power to control money, is not confined to any one class of people. We all have a touch of it, whether we recognize the fact or not.

Thomas A. Edison is one of the best known and most respected inventors in the world, yet it is no misstatement of facts to say that he would have remained a practically unknown, obscure personage had he not followed the habit of conserving his resources and shown his ability to save money.

Henry Ford never would have got to first base with his "horseless carriage" had he not developed, quite early in life, the habit of saving. Moreover, had Mr. Ford not conserved his resources and hedged himself behind their power he would have been "swallowed up" by his competitors or those who covetously desired to take his business away from him, long, long years ago.

Many a man has gone a very long way toward success, only to stumble and fall, never again to rise, because of lack of money in times of emergency. The mortality rate in business each year, due to lack of reserve capital for emergencies, is stupendous. To this one cause are due more of the business failures than to all other causes combined!

Reserve Funds are essential in the successful operation of business!

Likewise, Savings Accounts are essential to success on the part of individuals. Without a savings fund the individual suffers in two ways: first, by inability to seize opportunities that come only to the person with some ready cash, and, second, by embarrassment due to some unexpected emergency calling for cash.

It might be said, also, that the individual suffers in still a third respect by not developing the Habit of Saving, through lack of certain other qualities essential for success which grow out of the practice of the Habit of Saving.

The nickels, dimes and pennies which the average person allows to slip through his fingers would, if systematically saved and properly put to work, eventually bring financial independence.

Through the courtesy of a prominent Building and Loan Association* the following table has been compiled, showing what a monthly saving of $5.00, $10.00, $25.00 or $50.00 will amount to at the end of ten years. These figures are startling when one comes to consider the fact that the average person spends from $5.00 to $50.00 a month for useless merchandise or so-called "entertainment."

The making and saving of money is a science, yet the rules by which money is accumulated are so simple that anyone may follow them. The main prerequisite is a willingness to subordinate the present to the future, by eliminating unnecessary expenditures for luxuries.

* The following figures are reflective of the author's era.

The Amazing Way Your Money Grows

SAVE $5 A MONTH (Only 17 cents a day)

	Amount Saved	Profit	Savings Plus Profits	Withdrawal Value
1st yr.	$ 60.00	$ 4.30	$ 64.30	$ $61.30
2nd yr.	$ 120.00	$ 16.55	$ 136.00	$ 125.00
3rd yr.	$ 180.00	$ 36.30	$ 216.30	$ 191.55
4th yr.	$ 240.00	$ 64.00	$ 304.00	$ 260.20
5th yr.	$ 300.00	$ 101.00	$ 401.00	$ 338.13
6th yr.	$ 360.00	$ 140.00	$ 500.00	$ 414.75
7th yr.	$ 420.00	$ 197.10	$ 617.10	$ 495.43
8th yr.	$ 480.00	$ 257.05	$ 737.05	$ 578.32
9th yr.	$ 540.00	$ 324.95	$ 864.95	$ 687.15
10th yr.	$ 600.00	$ 400.00	$ 1000.00	$ 1000.00

SAVE $10 A MONTH (Only 33 cents a day)

	Amount Saved	Profit	Savings Plus Profits	Withdrawal Value
1st yr.	$ 120.00	$ 8.60	$ 128.60	$ 122.60
2nd yr.	$ 240.00	$ 33.11	$ 273.11	$ 250.00
3rd yr.	$ 360.00	$ 72.60	$ 432.60	$ 383.10
4th yr.	$ 480.00	$ 128.00	$ 608.00	$ 520.40
5th yr.	$ 600.00	$ 202.00	$ 802.00	$ 676.25
6th yr.	$ 720.00	$ 280.00	$ 1000.00	$ 829.50
7th yr.	$ 840.00	$ 394.20	$ 1234.20	$ 990.85
8th yr.	$ 960.00	$ 514.10	$ 1474.10	$ 1156.64
9th yr.	$1080.00	$ 649.90	$ 1729.90	$ 1374.30
10th yr.	$1200.00	$ 800.00	$ 2000.00	$ 2000.00

SAVE $25 A MONTH (Only 83 cents a day)

	Amount Saved	Profit	Savings Plus Profits	Withdrawal Value
1st yr.	$ 300.00	$ 21.50	$ 321.50	$ 306.50
2nd yr.	$ 600.00	$ 82.75	$ 682.75	$ 625.00
3rd yr.	$ 900.00	$ 181.50	$ 1081.50	$ 957.75
4th yr.	$1200.00	$ 320.00	$ 1520.00	$ 1301.00
5th yr.	$1500.00	$ 505.00	$ 2005.00	$ 1690.63
6th yr.	$1800.00	$ 700.00	$ 2500.00	$ 2073.75
7th yr.	$2100.00	$ 985.50	$ 3085.50	$ 2477.13
8th yr.	$2400.00	$ 1285.25	$ 3685.25	$ 2891.60
9th yr.	$2700.00	$ 1624.75	$ 4324.75	$ 3435.75
10th yr.	$3000.00	$ 2000.00	$ 5000.00	$ 5000.00

SAVE $50 A MONTH (Only $1.66 a day)

	Amount Saved	Profit	Savings Plus Profits	Withdrawal Value
1st yr.	$ 600.00	$ 43.00	$ 643.00	$ 613.00
2nd yr.	$1200.00	$ 165.50	$ 1365.50	$ 1250.00
3rd yr.	$1800.00	$ 363.00	$ 2163.00	$ 1915.50
4th yr.	$2400.00	$ 640.00	$ 3040.00	$ 2602.00
5th yr.	$3000.00	$ 1010.00	$ 4010.00	$ 3381.25
6th yr.	$3600.00	$ 1400.00	$ 5000.00	$ 4147.50
7th yr.	$4200.00	$ 1971.00	$ 6171.00	$ 4954.25
8th yr.	$4800.00	$ 2570.50	$ 7370.50	$ 5783.20
9th yr.	$5400.00	$ 3249.50	$ 8649.50	$ 6871.50
10th yr.	$6000.00	$ 4000.00	$ 10,000.00	$ 10,000.00

A young man, who was earning only $20.00 a week as chauffeur for a prominent New York banker, was induced by his employer to keep an accurate account of every cent he spent for one week. The following is an itemized list of his expenses:

Cigarettes	$ .75
Chewing gum	.30
Soda fountain	1.80
Cigars for associates	1.50
Moving picture show	1.00
Shaves, including tips	1.60
Newspaper, daily and Sunday	.22
Shoe shines	.30
	$ 7.47
Board and room	$12.00
Money on hand	.53
	$20.00

These figures tell a tragic story which might as well apply to thousands of other people as to the young man who kept this account. His actual savings out of $20.00 were only 53 cents. He spent $7.47 for items, every one of which could have been greatly reduced, and most of which could have been eliminated entirely. In fact, by shaving himself and shining his own shoes, he could have saved every cent of the $7.47.

Now turn to the table made up by the Building and Loan Association and observe what the saving of $7.47 a week would amount to. Suppose the amount this young man actually saved had been only $25.00 a month; the saving would have increased to the snug sum of $5,000.00 by the end of the first ten years.

Every failure, every adversity, every heartache may be a blessing in disguise providing it softens the animal portion of our nature.

The young man in question was twenty-one years old at the time he kept this expense account. By the time he reached the age of thirty-one years he could have had a substantial amount in the bank, had he saved $25.00 a month, and this saving would have brought him many opportunities that would have led directly to financial independence.

Some who are short-sighted, pseudo-philosophers, are fond of pointing to the fact that no one can become rich merely by saving a few dollars a week. This may be true enough, as far as the reasoning goes (which is not very far) but the other side of the story is that the saving of even a small sum of money places one in position where, oftentimes, this small sum may enable one to take advantage of business opportunities which lead directly and quite rapidly to financial independence.

The foregoing table, showing what a saving of $5.00 a month will amount to at the end of ten years, should be copied and pasted on your mirror, where it will stare you in the face every morning when you get up and every night as you retire, providing you have not already acquired the habit of systematic saving of money. This table should be reproduced, in letters and figures an inch tall, and placed on the walls of every public school throughout the land, where it might serve as a constant reminder to all school children of the value of the savings habit.

Some years ago, before giving serious thought to the value of the savings habit, this author made up an account of the money which had slipped through his fingers. The amount was so alarming that it resulted in the writing of this lesson, and adding the Habit of Saving as one of the Fifteen Laws of Success.

Following is an itemized statement of this account:

$ 4,000.00	inherited, invested in automobile supply business with a friend who lost the entire amount in one year.
3,600.00	extra money earned from sundry writing for magazines and newspapers, all spent uselessly.
30,000.00	earned from training 3,000 salesmen, with the aid of the Law of Success philosophy, invested in a magazine which was not a success because there was no reserve capital back of it.
3,400.00	extra money earned from public addresses, lectures, etc., all of which was spent as it came in.
6,000.00	estimated amount that could have been saved during a period of ten years, out of regular earnings, at the rate of only $50 a month.
$47,000.00	

This amount, had it been saved and invested as received, in Building and Loan Associations, or in some other manner that would have earned compound interest, would have grown into the sum of $94,000.00 at the time this lesson is being written.

The author is not a victim of any of the usual habits of dissipation, such as gambling, drinking and excessive entertaining. It is almost unbelievable that a man whose habits of living are reasonably moderate could spend $47,000.00 within a little over ten years without having anything to show for the money, but it can be done!

A capital reserve of $94,000.00, working at compound interest, is sufficient to give any man all the financial freedom he needs.

I recall one occasion when the president of a large corporation sent me a check for $500.00 for an address I delivered at a banquet given to the employees, and I distinctly recall what went through my mind when I opened the letter and saw the check. I had wanted a new automobile and this check was exactly the amount required for the first payment. I had it spent before it had been in my hands thirty seconds.

Perhaps this is the experience of the majority of people. They think more of how they are going to SPEND what they have than they do about ways and means of SAVING. The idea of saving, and the self-control and self-sacrifice which must accompany it, is always accompanied by thoughts of an unpleasant nature, but oh, how it does thrill one to think of SPENDING.

There is a reason for this, and that reason is the fact that most of us have developed the habit of spending while neglecting the Habit of Saving, and any idea that frequents the human mind but seldom is not as welcome as that which frequents it often.

In truth, the Habit of Saving can be made as fascinating as the habit of spending, but not until it has become a regular, well grounded, systematic habit. We like to do that which is often repeated, which is but another way of stating what the scientists have discovered, that we are victims of our habits.

The habit of saving money requires more force of character than most people have developed, for the reason that saving means self-denial and sacrifice of amusements and pleasures in scores of different ways.

For this very reason one who develops the savings habit acquires, at the same time, many of the other needed habits which lead to success: especially Self-control, Self-confidence, Courage, Poise and Freedom from Fear.

How Much Should One Save?

The first question that will arise is, "How Much Should One Save?" The answer cannot be given in a few words, for the amount one should save depends upon many conditions, some of which may be within one's control and some of which may not be.

Generally speaking, a man who works for a salary should apportion his income about as follows:

Savings Account 20%
Living—Clothes, Food and Shelter 50%
Education 10%
Recreation 10%
Life Insurance 10%
100%

The following, however, indicates the approximate distribution which the average man actually makes of his income:

Savings Account . . . . .NOTHING
Living—Clothes, Food and Shelter 60%
Education 0%
Recreation 35%
Life Insurance .5%
100%

Careful analysis of 178 men who are known to be successful disclosed the fact that all had failed many times before arriving.

Under the item of "recreation" is included, of course, many expenditures that do not really "recreate," such as money spent for alcoholic drinks, dinner parties and other similar items which may actually serve to undermine one's health and destroy character.

An experienced analyst of men has stated that he could tell very accurately, by examining a man's monthly budget, what sort of a life the man is living; moreover, that he will get most of his information from the one item of "recreation." This, then, is an item to be watched as carefully as the greenhouse keeper watches the thermometer which controls the life and death of his plants.

Those who keep budget accounts often include an item called "entertainment," which, in a majority of cases, turns out to be an evil because it depletes the income heavily and when carried to excess depletes, also, the health.

We are living, right now, in an age when the item of "entertainment" is altogether too high in most budget allowances. Tens of thousands of people who earn not more than $50.00 a week are spending as much as one third of their incomes for what they call "entertainment," which comes in a bottle, with a questionable label on it, at anywhere from $6.00 to $12.00 a quart. Not only are these unwise people wasting the money that should go into a savings fund, but, of far greater danger, they are destroying both character and health.

Nothing in this lesson is intended as a preachment on morality, or on any other subject. We are here dealing with cold facts which, to a large extent, constitute the building materials out of which SUCCESS may be created.

However, this is an appropriate place to state some FACTS which have such a direct bearing on the subject of achieving success that they cannot be omitted without weakening this entire course in general and this lesson in particular.

The author of this course is NOT a reformer! Neither is he a preacher on morals, as this field of useful endeavor is quite well covered by others who are able workers. What is here stated, therefore, is intended as a necessary part of a course of philosophy whose purpose is to mark a safe road over which one may travel to honorable achievement.

During the year 1926 the author was in partnership with the late Don R. Mellett, who was, at that time, the publisher of the Canton (Ohio) *Daily News*. Mr. Mellett became interested in the Law of Success philosophy because it offered, as he believed, sound counsel to young men and young women who really wish to get ahead in life. Through the pages of the *Daily News* Mr. Mellett was conducting a fierce battle against the underworld forces of Canton. With the aid of detectives and investigators, some of whom were supplied by the Governor of Ohio, Mr. Mellett and the author gathered accurate data concerning the way most of the people in Canton were living.

In July, 1926, Mr. Mellett was assassinated from ambush, and four men, one of them a former member of the Canton police force, are now serving life sentences in the Ohio State Penitentiary for the crime.

During the investigation into crime conditions in Canton all reports came to the author's office, and the data here described are, therefore, known to be absolutely accurate.

One of the officials of a large industrial plant whose salary was $6,000.00 a year paid a Canton bootlegger an average of $300.00 a month for the liquor (if "stuff" can be called liquor) which he used for "entertaining." His wife participated in these "entertainments" which took place in his own home.

A paying teller in a bank, whose salary was $150.00 a month, was spending an average of $75.00 a month for liquor, and in addition to this unpardonable waste of money, out of a salary which was none too great at most, he was traveling at a pace and with a crowd which meant ruin for him later on.

The superintendent of a large manufacturing plant, whose salary was $5,000.00 a year, and who should have been saving at least $125.00 a month, was actually saving nothing. His bootlegger's bill averaged $150.00 a month.

A policeman whose income was $160.00 a month was spending over $400.00 a month on dinner parties, at a near-by roadhouse. Where he got the difference between his legitimate income and his actual expenditures is a question that reflects no particular credit on the policeman.

A bank official whose income, as near as it could be estimated from his previous years' income tax reports, was about $8,000.00 a year, had a monthly bootlegger's bill of more than $500.00 during the three months that his activities were checked by the Mellett investigators.

A young man who worked in a department store, at a salary of $20.00 a week, was spending an average of $35.00 a week with one bootlegger. The assumption was that he was stealing the difference from his employer. Old Man Trouble awaited this young man, just around the corner, although it is not known by the author whether or not the two have come together as yet.

A salesman for a life insurance company, whose income was not known because he worked on a commission basis, was spending an average of $200.00 a month with one bootlegger. No record of any savings account was found, and the assumption is that he had none. This assumption was later confirmed when the company for which the young man worked had him arrested for embezzlement of its funds. No doubt he was spending the money which he should have turned in to the company. He is now serving a long sentence in the Ohio State Penitentiary.

A young lad who was attending high school was spending large sums for liquor. The actual amount was not obtainable for the reason that he paid cash as he got the liquor, and the bootlegger's records did not, therefore, disclose the actual amount. Later this boy's parents had him locked up "to save him from himself." It was found that he was stealing money from a savings fund kept by his mother, somewhere about the house. He had stolen and spent more than $300.00 of this money when discovered.

This author conducted a Lecture Bureau in forty-one high schools, where he lectured once a month during the entire school season. The principals of these high schools stated that less than two per cent of the students showed any tendency toward saving money, and an examination through the aid of a questionnaire prepared for that purpose disclosed the fact that only five per cent of the students, out of a total of 11,000, of the high-school age, believed that the savings habit was one of the essentials for success.

It is no wonder the rich are becoming richer and the poor are becoming poorer!

Call this a socialistic statement, if you please, but the facts bear out its accuracy. It is not difficult for any man to become rich, in a country of spendthrifts such as this, where millions of people spend every cent that comes into their possession.

Many years ago, before the present wave of mania for spending spread over the country, F. W. Woolworth devised a very simple method of catching the nickels and dimes that millions of people throw away for trash, and his system netted him over ONE HUNDRED MILLION DOLLARS in a few years' time. Woolworth has died, but his system of saving nickels and dimes continues, and his estate is growing bigger and bigger.

Five and Ten Cent Stores are usually painted with a bright red front. That is an appropriate color, for red denotes danger. Every Five and Ten Cent Store is a striking monument that proves, to a nicety, that one of the cardinal faults of this generation is the SPENDING HABIT.

We are all victims of HABIT!

Unfortunately for most of us, we are reared by parents who have no conception whatsoever of the psychology of habit, and, without being aware of their fault, most parents aid and abet their offspring in the development of the spending habit by overindulgence

All salesmen will do well to remember that no one wants anything that someone else is trying to "get rid of."

with spending money, and by lack of training in the Habit of Saving.

The habits of early childhood cling to us all through life.

Fortunate, indeed, is the child whose parents have the foresight and the understanding of the value, as a character builder, of the Habit of Saving, to inculcate this habit in the minds of their children.

It is a training that yields rich rewards.

Give the average man $100.00 that he did not contemplate receiving, and what will he do with it? Why, he will begin to cogitate in his own mind on how he can SPEND the money. Dozens of things that he needs, or THINKS he needs, will flash into his mind, but it is a rather safe bet that it will never occur to him (unless he has acquired the savings habit) to make this $100.00 the beginning of a savings account. Before night comes he will have the

$100.00 spent, or at least he will have decided in his mind how he is going to SPEND IT, thus adding more fuel to the already too bright flame of Habit of Spending.

We are ruled by our habits!

It requires force of character, determination and power of firm DECISION to open a savings account and then add to it a regular, if small, portion of all subsequent income.

There is one rule by which any man may determine, well in advance, whether or not he will ever enjoy the financial freedom and independence which is so universally desired by all men, and this rule has absolutely nothing to do with the amount of one's income.

The rule is that if a man follows the systematic habit of saving a definite proportion of all money he earns or receives in other ways, he is practically sure to place himself in a position of financial independence. If he saves nothing, he IS ABSOLUTELY SURE NEVER TO BE FINANCIALLY INDEPENDENT, no matter how much his income may be.

The one and only exception to this rule is that a man who does not save might possibly inherit such a large sum of money that he could not spend it, or he might inherit it under a trust which would protect it for him, but these eventualities are rather remote; so much so, in fact, that YOU cannot rely upon such a miracle happening to you.

This author enjoys a rather close acquaintance with many hundreds of people throughout the United States and in some foreign countries. For nearly twenty-five years he has been watching many of these acquaintances, and knows, therefore, from actual experience, how they live, why some of them have failed while others have succeeded, and the REASONS FOR BOTH FAILURE AND SUCCESS.

This list of acquaintances covers men who control hundreds of millions of dollars, and actually own many millions which they have acquired. Also men who have had millions of dollars, all of which passed through their fingers and they are now penniless.

For the purpose of showing the student of this philosophy just how the law of habit becomes a sort of pivotal point on which success or failure turns, and exactly why no man can become financially independent without developing the habit of SYSTEMATIC SAVING, the living habits of some of these many acquaintances will be described.

We will begin with a complete history, in his own words, of a man who has made a million dollars in the field of advertising, but who now has nothing to show for his efforts. This story first appeared in the *American Magazine,* and it is here reprinted through the courtesy of the publishers of that publication.

The story is true, in every respect, and it has been included as a part of this lesson because the author of the story, Mr. W. C. Freeman, is willing to have his mistakes made public with the hope that others may avoid them.

"I Have Made a Million Dollars But I Haven't Got a Cent"

While it is embarrassing, yes, humiliating, publicly to confess to an outstanding fault that has made a good deal of a mess of my life today, nevertheless I have decided to make this confession for the good it may do.

I am going to make a clean breast of how I let slip through my fingers all the money I have earned thus far in my life-time, which approximates one million dollars. This amount I made through my work in the field of advertising, except a few thousand dollars I earned up to twenty-five years of age by teaching in country schools and by writing news letters to some country weeklies and daily newspapers.

Maybe one lone million does not seem a lot of money in these days of many millions and even billions; but it is a big sum of money, just the same. If there are any who think to the contrary, let them count a million. I tried to figure out the other night how long it would take to do so. I found I could count an average of one hundred a minute. On this basis it would take me twenty days of eight hours each, plus six hours and forty minutes on the twenty-first day to do the stunt. I doubt very much if you or I were given an assignment to count one million one-dollar bills, upon the promise that all of them would be ours at the end of that time, that we could complete it. It would probably drive us mad—and a lot of use the money would be to us then, wouldn't it?

Let me say at the outset of my story that I do not regret, not for one minute, that I spent ninety per cent of the money I made. To wish any of this ninety per cent back at this time would make me feel that I would have denied much happiness to my family and to many others.

My only regret is that I spent *all* of my money, and more besides. If I had today the ten per cent I could have saved easily, I would have one hundred thousand dollars safely invested, and no debts. If I had this money I would feel really and truly that I was rich; and I mean just this, for I have never had a desire to accumulate money for money's sake.

Those school-teaching and newspaper-correspondence days of mine brought some cares and responsibilities, but they were met optimistically.

I married at the age of twenty-one, with the full approval of parents on both sides, who believed thoroughly in the doctrine preached by Henry Ward Beecher, that "early marriages are virtuous marriages."

Just one month and one day after I was married my father met a tragic death. He was suffocated by coal gas. Having been an educator all his life—and one of the best—he had not accumulated any money.

When he passed out of our family circle it was up to all of us to pull together and get along somehow, which we did.

Apart from the void left in our home by my father's death (my wife and I and my mother and only sister lived together), we had a joyful life, despite the fact that it was a tight squeeze to make ends meet.

My mother, who was exceptionally talented and resourceful (she had taught school with my father until I was born), decided to open our home to a married couple, old friends of the family. They came to live with us and their board helped to pay expenses. My mother was known far and wide for the wonderful meals she served. Later on, two well-to-do women friends of the family were taken into our home; thus increasing our revenue.

My sister helped very substantially by teaching a kindergarten class, which met in the big living-room of our home; my wife contributed her share to the household by taking charge of the sewing and mending.

Those were very happy days. Nobody in the household was extravagant or had any extravagant tendencies except perhaps myself, for I was always inclined to be free with money. I liked to make gifts to the family and to entertain friends.

Think well before you speak because your words may plant the seed of either success or failure in the mind of some other person.

When the first baby came into our home—a boy—we all thought heaven had opened its doors to us. My wife's parents, who took the keenest and deepest interest in our affairs, and who were always ready to lend a helping hand, were equally happy over the coming of their first grandchild. My brother-in-law, much older than my wife, and a bachelor, could not understand at first the joy we all felt; but even he began to strut around like a proud peacock after a while. What a difference a baby makes in a home!

I am injecting these details into my story merely to emphasize how the early days of my life were lived. I had no opportunity to spend much money, and yet I had as much happiness in those days as I have ever had since.

The strange thing about it all is that the experience of those days did not teach me the value of money. If anybody ever had a practical lesson to guide him in his future, I certainly had it.

But let me tell you how this early experience affected me. The birth of my son inspired me to do something that would make more money than I was getting at teaching school and in writing for newspapers. I did not want my wife, mother and sister to feel that they would have to continue indefinitely to do their part in sustaining the household. Why should a fellow, big and strong and healthy as I have always been, and with a reasonable amount of ability, be content to remain a spoke in the wheel? Why shouldn't I be the whole wheel, as far as providing for the family was concerned?

Following my desire to make more money, I took on the selling of books in addition to teaching and writing for newspapers. This earned for me quite a little extra money. Finally, I gave up teaching and concentrated on selling books, and writing for newspapers.

My book-selling took me to Bridgeton, New Jersey. It was here that I got my first real start in making money. I had to be away from home a great deal to do this work, but the sacrifice was worth while. I earned enough money in a few weeks to send more money home than I had contributed to the household in any year from my school-teaching and newspaper correspondence. After combing the territory in the Bridgeton zone, I became interested in a newspaper in that city, the *Morning Star.* It seemed to me that the editor and publisher of this paper needed a helper. I called on him and told him so. He said, "Heavens, young man, how can I hire you? I am not earning enough money to pay for my own living!"

"That's just it," said I. "I believe together we can make the *Star* a success. I'll tell you what I'll do: I'll work for you for one week for one dollar a day. At the end of the week, if I have made good, I'll expect you to pay me three dollars a day for the second week; and then, if I continue to do well, I'll expect you to pay me six dollars a day for the third week, and will continue from then on until the paper makes enough money to pay me fifty dollars a week."

The owner agreed to my proposition. At the end of two months, I was being paid fifty dollars a week, which in those days was considered a big salary. I began to feel that I was well on my way toward making money—but all I wanted it for was to make my family more comfortable. Fifty dollars a week was just four times as much as I had made teaching school.

My job on the *Star* embraced editorial writing (not very brilliant), reporting (just ordinary), the writing and selling of advertisements (fairly successful), proof reading, bill collecting, and so forth. It kept me humping six days a week; but I could stand it, for I was strong and healthy, and, besides, the work was very interesting. I also contributed correspondence to the *New York Sun, Philadelphia Record,* and the Trenton (N. J.) *Times,* which brought me in an average of one hundred and fifty dollars a month, for this was a good news territory.

I learned a lesson on the Star which eventually shaped the course of my life. I found out that there is a great deal more money to be earned by selling advertising for newspapers than in writing for them. Advertising brings grist to the mill.

I put over one advertising stunt on the *Star*—a write-up of the south Jersey oyster indus-try, paid for by the oyster men—that brought in three thousand dollars cash, which the publisher divided with me fifty-fifty. I had never seen so much money at one time in all my life. Think of it! Fifteen hundred dollars—twenty-five per cent more than I had made in two years of school-teaching and odd tasks.

Did I save this money or any part of it? I did not. What was the use? I could do so much with it to make my wife, boy, mother and sister happy that I let it go far easier than I had made it.

But would it not have been a fine thing if I had put this money away for a rainy day?

My work in Bridegton attracted the attention of Sam Hudson, New Jersey correspondent of the *Philadelphia Record,* who was a shining example of that type of newspaper men whose greatest pleasure in life is doing things for others.

Sam told me that it was time for me to get located in a big city. He thought I had it in me to make good. He said he would get me a job in Philadelphia. He did, and I moved with my wife and baby to Germantown. I was given charge of the advertising department of the Germantown (Philadelphia) *Gazette*, a weekly newspaper.

At the start I did not make as much money as I had earned in Bridegton, because I had to give up my newspaper correspondence. The news for this section was covered by other correspondents. But very soon I was making twenty-five per cent more money. The *Gazette* increased its size three times to accommodate its advertising, and each time I received a very substantial increase in salary.

In addition to this, I was given a job to gather social news for the Sunday edition of the *Philadelphia Press*. Bradford Merrill, managing editor of that newspaper, now a very impor-tant New York newspaper executive, assigned me a big territory to cover. This kept me busy every night in the week except Saturdays. I was paid five dollars a column; but I averaged seven columns every Sunday; which made me thirty-five dollars a week extra.

It was more money for me to spend, and I spent it. I did not know anything about budg-eting my expenses. I just let it go as it came. I did not have time, or thought I hadn't, to watch my step in spending.

A year later I was invited to join the advertising staff of the *Philadelphia Press,* a big opportunity for a young man, for I got wonderful training under the management of William L. McLean, now the owner of the Philadelphia *Evening Bulletin.* I still retained my job as gatherer of social news—so my income was just about the same as I had been making in Germantown.

But before long my work attracted the attention of James Elverson, Sr., publisher of the old *Saturday Night* and *Golden Days,* who had just purchased the *Philadelphia Inquirer.* I was offered and accepted the advertising management of this newspaper.

This meant a big increase in my income. And soon afterward there came a happy increase in my family, the birth of a daughter. Then I was able to do what I had longed to do since the birth of my son. I got the family together again under one roof—my wife and two babies, my mother and sister. At last I was able to relieve my mother of any cares or responsibilities, and never again did she have either as long as she lived. She died in her eighty-first year, twenty-five years after my father's death. I shall never forget her last words to me: "Will, you have never caused me a moment's worry since you were born, and I could not have had more than you have given me had I been the Queen of England."

I was making at this time four times more money than my father had made as superintendent of public schools in my home town of Phillipsburg, New Jersey.

All the money, however, passed out of my pockets as easily as water flows through a sieve. Expenses increased with every increase in my income, which is the habit, I suppose, with most people. There was no sane reason, though, for letting my expenses go beyond my income, which I did. I found myself piling up debts, and from this time on I was never out of debt. I did not worry about my debts, though, for I thought I could pay them off at any time. It never occurred to me—not until fully twenty-five years later—that debt eventually would bring upon me not only great anxiety and unhappiness, but that I would lose friends and credit as well.

I am thankful that I was born poor—that I did not come into this world burdened by the whims of wealthy parents, with a bag of gold around my neck.

But I must pat myself on the back for one thing: I was giving full rein to my big fault—spending money as fast as I made it, often faster; but I never shirked my work. I was always trying to find more things to do, and I always found them. I spent very little time with my family. I would go home to dinner every night and romp with the babies until their bedtime, then I would return to the office and often work.

So the years went by. Another daughter arrived. Presently I wanted my daughters to have a pony and cart, and I wanted my son to have a riding horse. Then I thought I needed a team to take me around with the family, driving them to a closed coupé or an open trap. I got them all. Instead of one horse and a carry-all, or perhaps a team, which would have been sufficient for our needs and something we could have afforded, I had to have a stable, with all that goes with it. This outfit cost me nearly one fourth of my annual income.

Then I took up golf. This was in my forty-first year. I went at my play the same as I went at my work—put my whole heart in it. I learned to play pretty well. My son and elder daughter played with me, and they learned to play well, too.

It was necessary that my younger daughter should spend the winter in the South and summers in the Adirondacks; but instead of her mother going with her alone, I felt it would be fine if the son and other daughter went along with them. This arrangement was carried out. They went to Pinehurst, North Carolina, every winter and to expensive resorts in the Adirondacks or in New Hampshire in the summer.

All this took a great deal of money. My son and elder daughter were keen about golf and spent a lot of money on it. I also disbursed quite a little on golf courses around New York. Between the three of us we won 80 prizes, most of which are now in storage. I sat down one day and calculated what these prizes had cost me. I discovered that each trophy had cost me $250.00 or a total of $45,000.00 over a period of fifteen years, an average of $3,000.00 a year. Ridiculous, wasn't it?

I entertained lavishly at my home. Montclair folks thought I was a millionaire. I frequently invited groups of business men to have a day of golf at the club, and then to have dinner with me in the evening. They would have been satisfied with a plain home dinner, but, no, I must serve them an elaborate affair staged by a famous caterer. These dinners never cost less than ten dollars a plate, which did not include the money spent for music while they were dining. I had a negro quartet come to the house. Our dining-room comfortably seated twenty people, and it was filled to capacity many times.

It was all very lovely, and I was glad to be their host. In fact, I was very happy over it. I never stopped to think how rapidly I was piling up debts. The day came when they began to bother me a lot. I had entertained so many guests at the golf club one month, paying for luncheons, cigars, and greens fees, that my bill was four hundred and fifty dollars. This attracted the attention of the directors of the club, who were all good friends of mine and very much interested in my welfare. They made it their business to tell me that I was spending entirely too much money, and they wished for my sake that I could check my expenses.

This gave me a bit of a jolt. It made me think seriously long enough to get rid of my horses and traps—at a big sacrifice, of course. I gave up our home and moved back to the city; but I did not leave any unpaid bills in Montclair. I borrowed the money to pay them. It was always easy for me to get all the money I wanted, despite my well known financial short-comings.

Here are two sidelights on my experience during my "flaring forties."

Besides spending money foolishly and perhaps recklessly, I loaned it with equal abandon. In cleaning out my desk at home before moving to the city I looked over a package of due bills, the total of which was over forty thousand dollars. That was money handed out to just anybody who came along. I tore them all up; but I realized that if I had that money in hand I wouldn't owe a dollar.

One of the prosperous business men I had entertained many times and who in turn had entertained me, said to me: "Billy, I've got to stop going on outings with you. You spend entirely too much money for me. I can't keep up with you."

Think of that coming from a man who was making more money than I was! It should have struck home, but it didn't. I went on spending just the same, and foolishly thinking that I was having a good time, and with no thought of the future. This man is now one of the vice presidents of one of New York's greatest financial institutions, and is reported to be worth many millions of dollars.

I should have taken his advice.

In the fall of 1908, after my disastrous experience of six months in another line of business following my resignation from the Hearst organization, I resumed newspaper work as advertising manager of the *New York Evening Mail*. I had known Henry L. Stoddard, editor and owner, back in the Philadelphia days, when he was political correspondent for the *Press*.

Despite the fact that I was bothered by debts, I did the best work of my life on the *Evening Mail*, and made more money during the five years I was associated with it than I had ever made before. Moreover, Mr. Stoddard gave me the privilege of syndicating advertising talks, which ran in his paper for one thousand consecutive publication days, and earned for me more than fifty-five thousand dollars.

Mr. Stoddard was very generous in many other ways, and frequently paid me special sums of money for doing what he considered unusual things in the way of developing business. During this period, I was so deeply in debt that, in order to keep things moving as smoothly as possible, but without retrenching in the slightest way in my expenses, I borrowed money from Peter to pay Paul and from Paul to pay Peter. That item of fifty-five thousand dollars earned from syndicating advertising talks would have more than paid all my debts and left a nice nest egg besides. But all of it was spent as easily as though I hadn't a care in the world.

In 1915 I went on my own in the advertising business. From that time until the spring of 1922 my fees ran into very big figures. I was still making more money than I ever did, and was spending it just as fast as I made it, until finally my friends got tired of making me loans.

If I had shown the slightest inclination to curb my expenses to the extent of only ten per cent, these wonderful men would have been willing to divide fifty-fifty with me, letting me pay them five per cent of it and saving five per cent. They did not care so much about the return of the money they had loaned me, as that they wanted to see me pull myself together.

The crash in my affairs came five years ago. Two friends who had stood by me loyally became impatient, and told me frankly that I needed a drastic lesson. They gave it to me all right. I was forced into bankruptcy, which nearly broke my heart. I felt that every person I knew was pointing the finger of scorn at me. This was very foolish. While there was comment, it was not at all unfriendly. It was expressive of keen regret that a man who had attained so much prestige in his profession, and had earned so much money, should have allowed himself to get into financial difficulties.

Proud and sensitive to the core I felt the disgrace of bankruptcy so keenly that I decided

Fortunate is the person who has learned that the most certain way to "get" is to first "give" through some sort of useful service.

to go to Florida, where I had once done a special piece of work for a client. It seemed to me to be the coming El Dorado. I figured that maybe I could make sufficient money in a few years so that I could return to New York, not only with a competency but with enough to pay all my debts in full. For a time it looked as though I would realize this ambition; but I was caught in the big

real estate collapse. So here I am back in the old town where I once had big earning power and hundreds of friends and well-wishers.

It has been a strange experience.

One thing is certain: I have learned my lesson at last. I feel sure that opportunities will come my way to redeem myself, and that my earning power will be restored to me. And when that time comes I know that I shall be able to live as well as I ever did, on *forty* per cent of my income. Then I shall divide the remaining sixty per cent into two parts, setting aside thirty per cent to pay my creditors and thirty per cent for insurance and savings.

If I allowed myself to feel depressed over my past, or filled my mind with worries, I would not be capable of carrying on the fight to redeem myself.

Besides, I would be ungrateful to my Maker for having endowed me with wonderful health all my life. Is there any greater blessing?

I would be ungrateful to the memory of my parents, whose splendid training has kept me anchored pretty safely to moral standards. Slipping from moral moorings is infinitely more serious, in the end, than slipping from the thrift standard.

I would lack appreciation of the encouragement and support I have had in generous measure from hundreds of business men and to many good friends who helped me build a fine reputation in my profession.

These memories are the sunshine of my life. And I shall use them to pave the way to my future achievement.

With abundance of health, unfaltering faith, unflagging energy, unceasing optimism, and unbounded confidence that a man can win his fight, even though he commences late in life to realize the kind of fight he must make—is there anything but death to stop him?*

Mr. Freeman's story is the same as that which might be told by thousands of other men who save nothing, with the exception that the amounts of their incomes would vary. The manner of living, the way the money was spent, and why, as told in Mr. Freeman's narrative, show the way the spender's mind works.

Compilation of statistics covering family incomes and expenditures of over 16,000 families of men who have been analyzed by the author disclosed some facts that will be of help to the person who wishes to budget his income and disbursements on a practical working basis that is sound and economical.

The average income runs all the way from $100.00 to $300.00 per month. The budget allowance covering incomes within these two amounts should be about as follows:

A family consisting of two persons, whose income is $100.00 a month, should manage to set aside at least $10 or $12 a month for the savings account. The cost of shelter, or rent, should not exceed $25 or $30 a month. Food costs should average about $25 to $30. Clothing should

* Reprinted by courtesy of *The American Magazine*. Copyright, The Crowell Publishing Company, 1927.

be kept within an expenditure of $15 to $20 a month. Recreation and incidentals should be kept down to about $8 to $10 a month.

A family whose income is $100.00 a month, should that income be increased to $125.00, ought to save at least $20 of the amount.

A family of two persons, whose income is $150.00 a month, should budget their funds about as follows: Savings $25. Shelter or rent $35 to $40. Food $35 to $40. Clothes, $20 to $30. Recreation $10 to $15.

On a salary of $200 a month the budget should be: Savings $50. Shelter or rent $40 to $50. Food $35 to $45. Clothes $30 to $35. Recreation $15 to $20.

A family of two, on a salary or income of $300.00 a month, should apportion the income about thus: Savings $55 to $65. Shelter or rent $45 to $60. Food $45 to $60. Clothes $35 to $45. Recreation and education $50 to $75.

Some might argue that a family of two, making a salary of $300.00 a month, might live just as cheaply as one making but $100 or $125. However, this is not quite correct, because one who has the ability to earn $300.00 a month must as a rule associate with people who make better appearances and more entertainment necessary.

A single man, earning $100.00, $150.00 or $300.00 a month, should save considerably more than a man with a family could save on the same amounts. As a rule, a single man, who has no dependents, and who is not in debt, should live on a budget of $50 a month for room and food, and not to exceed $30 a month for clothes and perhaps $10 for recreation. These amounts might be slightly increased by one who earned from $150.00 to $300.00 a month.

A boy who lives away from home, and whose weekly income is only $20.00 should save $5 of the amount. The remainder should cover cost of food, room and clothes.

A girl, living away from home, on the same income, would require a slightly larger allowance for clothes, as women's wearing apparel is more costly than men's, and it is generally imperative that women watch, more closely than men, their personal appearance.

A family of three will be able to save considerably less than the amounts which can be saved by a family of two. With rare exceptions, however, such as cases where the family is involved in debt which must be absorbed out of the monthly income, any family can save at least five per cent of the gross income.

It is a common practice today for families to purchase automobiles on monthly payments which involve too great an expenditure compared to their income. A man with a Ford income has no business purchasing a Studebaker car. He should curb his desires and content himself with a Ford. Many single men spend their entire incomes, and often go into debt besides, because they maintain automobiles out of keeping with their incomes. This common practice is fatal to success as far as financial independence may be considered a part of success, in thousands of instances.

The instalment plan of buying has become so common, and it is so easy to purchase practically anything one desires, that the tendency to spend out of proportion to one's income is rapidly increasing. This tendency must be curbed by the person who has made up his mind to gain financial independence.

It can be done by anyone who is willing to try.

Another evil, which is both an evil and a blessing, is the fact that this country is so very prosperous that money comes easily, and if not watched it goes still more easily. Since the beginning of the World War there has been a steady demand for practically everything manufactured in the United States, and this condition of prosperity has caused people to lapse into a state of careless, unjustified spending.

There is no virtue in "keeping up with the pace set by neighbors" when this means sacrifice of the habit of saving a regular part of one's income. It is far better, in the long run, to be considered a bit behind the times than it is to go along through youth, into the days of maturity, and finally into old age, without having formed the habit of systematic saving.

It is better to sacrifice during the age of youthfulness, than it is to be compelled to do so during the age of maturity, as all who have not developed the habit of saving generally have to do.

There is nothing quite so humiliating, that carries such great agony and suffering, as poverty in old age, when personal services are no longer marketable, and one must turn to relatives or to charitable institutions for existence.

A budget system should be maintained by every person, both the married and the single, but no budget system will work out if the person trying to keep it lacks the courage to cut expenses on such items as those of entertainment and recreation. If you feel so weak in will-power that you think it necessary to "keep up with the Smiths" with whom you associate socially, and whose income is greater than your own, or who spend all of their income foolishly, then no budget system can be of service to you.

Forming the savings habit means that, to some extent at least, you must seclude yourself from all except a well selected group of friends who enjoy you without elaborate entertaining on your part.

I am thankful for the adversities which have crossed my pathway, for they have taught me tolerance, sympathy, self-control, perseverance and some other virtues I might never have known.

To admit that you lack the courage to trim down your expenditures so that you can save money, even if only a small amount, is the equivalent of admitting at the same time a lack of the sort of character which leads to success.

It has been proved times too numerous to be mentioned, that people who have formed the habit of saving money are always given preference in positions of responsibility; therefore, the saving of money not only adds advantages in the nature of preferred employment and a larger bank account, but it also increases the actual earning capacity. Any business man will prefer to employ a person who saves money regularly, not because of the mere fact that such person saves money, but because of the characteristics possessed by such a person which make him or her more efficient.

Many firms will not employ a man or a woman who does not save money.

It should be a common practice for all business houses to require all employees to save money. This would be a blessing to thousands of people who would not otherwise have the will-power to form the savings habit.

Henry Ford has gone a very long way, perhaps as far as is expedient, to induce his employees not only to save their money, but to spend what they do spend wisely, and to live sanely and economically. The man who induces his employees to form the habit of saving is a practical philanthropist.

Opportunities That Come to Those Who Have Saved Money

A few years ago a young man came to Philadelphia, from the farming district of Pennsylvania, and went to work in a printing plant. One of his fellow workmen owned some shares in a Building and Loan Company, and had formed the habit of saving $5.00 a week, through this Association. This young man was influenced by his associate to open an account with the Building and Loan Company. At the end of three years he had saved $900.00. The printing plant for which he worked got into financial difficulty and was about to fail. He came to the rescue with his $900.00 which he had saved in small amounts, and in return was given a half interest in the business.

By inaugurating a system of close economy he helped the business to pay off its indebtedness, and today he is drawing out of it, as his half of the profits, a little better than $25,000.00 a year.

This opportunity never would have come, or, if it had, he would not have been prepared to embrace it, had he not formed the habit of saving money.

When the Ford automobile was perfected, during the early days of its existence, Henry Ford needed capital to promote the manufacture and sale of his product. He turned to a few friends who had saved up a few thousand dollars, one of whom was Senator Couzens. These friends came to his rescue, put in a few thousand dollars with him, and later drew out millions of dollars in profits.

When Woolworth first started his Five and Ten Cent Store Plan he had no capital, but he turned to a few friends who had saved, by the closest sort of economy and great sacrifice, a few thousand dollars. These friends staked him and later they were paid back hundreds of thousands of dollars in profits.

Van Heusen (of soft-collar fame) conceived the idea of producing a semi-soft collar for men. His idea was sound, but he had not a cent to promote it. He turned to a few friends who had only a few hundred dollars, who gave him a start, and the collar made each of them wealthy.

The men who started the El Producto Cigar business had but little capital, and what they did have was money they had saved from their small earnings as cigar makers. They had a good idea, and knew how to make a good cigar, but the idea would have died "a-bornin'" had they not saved a little money. With their meager savings they launched the cigar, and a few years later they sold out their business to the American Tobacco Company for $8,000,000.00.

Back of practically every great fortune one may find, as its beginning, a well developed habit of saving money.

John D. Rockefeller was an ordinary bookkeeper. He conceived the idea of developing the oil business, which was then not even considered a business. He needed capital, and because he had developed the habit of saving, and had thereby proved that he could conserve the funds of other people, he had no difficulty in borrowing what money he needed.

It may be truthfully stated that the real basis of the Rockefeller fortune is the habit of saving money which Mr. Rockefeller developed, while working as a bookkeeper at a salary of $40.00 a month.

James J. Hill was a poor young man, working as a telegrapher, at a salary of $30.00 a month. He conceived the idea of the Great Northern Railway System, but his idea was out of proportion to his ability to finance. However, he had formed the habit of saving money, and on the meager salary of $30.00 a month had saved enough to enable him to pay his expenses on a trip to Chicago, where he interested capitalists in financing his plan. The fact that he, himself, had saved money on a small salary was considered good evidence that he would be a safe man to trust with other people's money.

Most business men will not trust another man with their money unless he has demonstrated his ability to take care of his own and use it wisely. The test, while it is often embarrassing to those who have not formed the Habit of Saving, is a very practical one.

A young man who worked in a printing plant in the city of Chicago wanted to open a small print shop and go into business for himself. He went to a printing supply house manager and made known his wants, saying he desired credit for a printing press and some type and other small equipment.

The first question asked by the manager was: "Have you saved any money of your own?"

He had! Out of his salary of $30.00 a week he had saved $15.00 a week regularly for nearly four years. He got the credit he wanted. Later on he got more credit, until today he has built up one of the most successful printing plants in the city of Chicago. His name is George B. Williams, and he is well known, as are also the facts here stated, to the author of this course.

Many years after this incident, the author of this course became acquainted with Mr. Williams, and at the end of the war, in 1918, the author went to Mr. Williams and asked for credit amounting to many thousands of dollars, for the purpose of publishing the *Golden Rule* magazine. The first question asked was: "Have you formed the habit of saving money?" Despite the fact that all the money I had saved was lost in the war, the mere fact that I had actually formed the savings habit was the real basis on which I got credit for upward of $30,000.00.

There are opportunities on every corner, but they exist only for those who have ready money, or who can command money because they have formed the Habit of Saving, and developed the other characteristics which go with the formation of the savings habit known by the general term of "character."

Love and Justice are the real arbiters of all disputes. Give them a chance and you will no longer want to defeat a brother sojourner by the wayside of life.

The late J. P. Morgan once said he would rather loan a million dollars to a man of sound character, who had formed the habit of saving money, than he would a thousand dollars to a man without character, who was a spendthrift.

Generally speaking, this is the attitude which the world takes toward all men who save money.

It often happens that a small savings account of no more than two or three hundred dollars is sufficient to start one on the highway to financial independence. A few years ago a young inventor invented a household article which was unique and practical. He was handicapped, as inventors so often are, because he did not have the money to market his invention. Moreover, not having formed the savings habit he found it impossible to borrow money through banking sources.

His room-mate was a young machinist who had saved $200.00. He came to the inventor's aid with this small sum of money, and had enough of the articles manufactured to give them a start. They went out and sold, from house to house, the first supply, then came back and had another supply made up, and so on, until they had accumulated (thanks to the thrift and savings ability of the room-mate) a capital of $1,000.00. With this, plus some credit they secured, they bought the tools for manufacturing their own product.

The young machinist sold his half interest in the business, six years later, for $250,000.00. He never would have handled this much money, during his entire life, had he not formed the habit of saving, which enabled him to come to the rescue of his inventor friend.

This case might be multiplied a thousand times, with but slight variation as to details, as it is fairly descriptive of the beginning of many great fortunes that have been made and are now in the making, in the United States.

It may seem like a sad, cruel fact, but it is a FACT none the less, that if you have no money, and have not developed the habit of saving, you are "out of luck" as far as availing yourself of the opportunity to make money is concerned.

It can do no harm to repeat—in fact it should be repeated over and over again—that the real start of nearly all fortunes, whether great or small, is the formation of the habit of saving money!

Get this basic principle firmly founded in your mind and you will be well on the road toward financial independence!

It is a sad sight to see a man, well along in years, who has sentenced himself to the wearisome treadmill of hard labor all the days of his life because he has neglected forming the habit of saving money, yet there are millions of such men living, in the United States alone, today.

The greatest thing in life is FREEDOM!

There can be no real freedom without a reasonable degree of financial independence. It is a terrible thing to be compelled to be at a certain place, at a certain task (perhaps a task which one does not like) for a certain number of hours every working day of the week, for a whole life-time. In some ways this is the same as being in prison, since one's choice of action is always limited. It is really no better than being in prison with the privilege of a "trusty," and in some ways it is even worse because the man who is imprisoned has escaped the responsibility of providing a place to sleep, something to eat and clothes to wear.

Everything passes at par, temporarily; truth alone remains permanently.

The only hope of escape from this life-long toil which curtails freedom is to form the habit of saving money, and then live up to that habit, no matter how much sacrifice it may require. There is no other way out for millions of people, and unless you are one of the rare exceptions this lesson and all these statements of fact are meant for YOU, and apply to you!

Neither a borrower, nor a lender be:
For loan oft loses both itself and friend,
And borrowing dulls the edge of husbandry.
This above all: to thine own self be true,
And it must follow, as the night the day,
Thou canst not then be false to any man.

—SHAKESPEARE

When you do not know what to do or which way to turn, smile. This will relax your mind and let the sunshine of happiness into your soul.

INITIATIVE AND LEADERSHIP

"You Can Do It If You Believe You Can!"

Before you proceed to the mastery of this lesson your attention is directed to the fact that there is perfect co-ordination of thought running throughout this course. You will observe that the entire fifteen lessons harmonize and blend with each other so that they constitute a perfect chain that has been built, link by link, out of the factors that enter into the development of power through *organized effort.*

You will observe, also, that the same fundamental principles of Applied Psychology form the foundation of each of these fifteen lessons, although different application is made of these principles in each of the lessons.

This lesson, on *Initiative* and *Leadership,* follows the lesson on Self-confidence for the reason that no one could become an efficient leader or take the initiative in any great undertaking without belief in himself.

Initiative and *Leadership* are associated terms in this lesson for the reason that *Leadership* is essential for the attainment of *Success,* and *Initiative* is the very foundation upon which this necessary quality of *Leadership* is built. *Initiative* is as essential to success as a hub is essential to a wagon wheel.

And what is *Initiative?*

It is that exceedingly rare quality that prompts—nay, impels—a person to do that which ought to be done *without being told to do it.* Elbert Hubbard expressed himself on the subject of *Initiative* in these words:

"The world bestows its big prizes, both in money and honors, for one thing, and that is *Initiative*.

"What is initiative? I'll tell you: It is doing the right thing without being told.

"But next to doing the right thing without being told is to do it when you are told once. That is to say, 'Carry the message to Garcia.' Those who can carry a message get high honors, but their pay is not always in proportion.

"Next, there are those who do the right thing only when necessity kicks them from behind, and these get indifference instead of honors, and a pittance for pay.

"This kind spend most of the time polishing a bench with a hard luck story.

"Then, still lower down in the scale than this we have the fellow who will not do the right thing even when someone goes along to show him how and stays to see that he does it; he is always out of a job, and receives the contempt he deserves, unless he has a rich pa, in which case destiny patiently waits around the corner with a stuffed club.

"To which class do *you* belong?"

Inasmuch as you will be expected to take inventory of yourself and determine which of the fifteen factors of this course you need most, after you have completed the fifteenth lesson, it may be well if you begin to get ready for this analysis by answering the question that Elbert Hubbard has asked:

To which class do you belong?

One of the peculiarities of *Leadership* is the fact that it is never found in those who have not acquired the *habit* of taking the initiative. *Leadership* is something that you must invite yourself into; it will never thrust itself upon you. If you will carefully analyze all leaders whom you know you will see that they not only exercised *Initiative,* but they went about their work with a *definite purpose* in mind. You will also see that they possessed that quality described in the third lesson of this course, *Self-confidence*.

These facts are mentioned in this lesson for the reason that it will profit you to observe that successful people make use of *all* the factors covered by the fifteen lessons of the course; and, for the more important reason that it will profit you to understand thoroughly the principle of *organized effort* which this Reading Course is intended to establish in your mind.

This seems an appropriate place to state that this course is not intended as a *short-cut* to success, nor is it intended as a mechanical formula that you may use in noteworthy achievement without effort on your part. The *real* value of the course lies in the *use* that you will make of it, and not in the course itself. The chief purpose of the course is to help you develop in yourself the fifteen qualities covered by the fifteen lessons of the course, and one of the most important of these qualities is *Initiative,* the subject of this lesson.

We will now proceed to apply the principle upon which this lesson is founded by describing, in detail, just how it served successfully to complete a business transaction which most people would call difficult.

In 1916 I needed $25,000.00 with which to create an educational institution, but I had neither this sum nor sufficient collateral with which to borrow it through the usual banking sources. Did I bemoan my fate or think of what I might accomplish if some rich relative or Good Samaritan would come to my rescue by loaning me the necessary capital?

I did nothing of the sort!

I did just what you will be advised, throughout this course, to do. First of all, I made the securing of this capital my *definite chief aim.* Second, I laid out a complete *plan* through which to transform this *aim* into reality. Backed by sufficient Self-confidence and spurred on by *Initiative,* I proceeded to put my plan into action. But, before the "action" stage of the plan had been reached, more than six weeks of constant, persistent study and effort and thought were embodied in it. If a plan is to be sound it must be built of carefully chosen material.

You will here observe the application of the principle of *organized effort,* through the operation of which it is possible for one to ally or associate several interests in such a way that *each of these interests* is greatly strengthened and each supports all the others, just as one link in a chain supports all the other links.

I wanted this $25,000.00 in capital for the purpose of creating a school of Advertising and Salesmanship. Two things were necessary for the organization of such a school. One was the $25,000.00 capital, which I did not have, and the other was the proper course of instruction, which *I did have.* My problem was to *ally myself* with some group of men who needed that which I had, and who would supply the $25,000.00. This alliance had to be made through a plan that would benefit all concerned.

After my plan had been completed, and I was satisfied that it was equitable and sound, I laid it before the owner of a well known and reputable business college which just then was finding competition quite keen and was badly in need of a plan for meeting this competition.

My plan was presented in about these words:

Whereas, you have one of the most reputable business colleges in the city; and,

Whereas, you need some plan with which to meet the stiff competition in your field; and,

Whereas, your good reputation has provided you with all the credit you need; and,

Whereas, I have the plan that will help you meet this competition successfully.

Be it resolved, that we ally ourselves through a plan that will give you that which you need and at the same time supply me with something which I need.

Then I proceeded to unfold my plan, further, in these words:

I have written a very practical course on Advertising and Salesmanship. Having built this course out of my actual experience in training and directing salesmen and my experience in planning and directing many successful advertising campaigns, I have back of it plenty of evidence of its soundness.

The space you occupy and the authority you exercise may be measured with mathematical exactness by the service you render.

If you will use your credit in helping market this course I will place it in your business college, as one of the regular departments of your curriculum and take entire charge of this newly created department. No other business college in the city will be able to meet your competition, for the reason that no other college has such a course as this. The advertising that you do in marketing this course will serve, also, to stimulate the demand for your regular business course. You may charge the entire amount that you spend for this advertising, to my department, and the advertising bill will be paid out of that department, leaving you the accumulative advantage that will accrue to your other departments without cost to you.

Now, I suppose you will want to know where I profit by this transaction, and I will tell you. I want you to enter into a contract with me in which it will be agreed that when the cash receipts from my department equal the amount that you have paid out or contracted to pay out for advertising, my department and my course in Advertising and Salesmanship become my own and I may have the privilege of separating this department from your school and running it under my own name.

The plan was agreeable and the contract was closed. (Please keep in mind that my *definite purpose* was to secure the use of $25,000.00 for which I had no security to offer.)

In a little less than a year the Business College had paid out slightly more than $25,000.00 for advertising and marketing my course and the other expenses incidental to the operation of this newly organized department, while the department had collected and turned back to the College, in tuition fees, a sum equaling the amount the College had spent, and I took the department over, as a going and self-sustaining business, according to the terms of my contract.

As a matter of fact this newly created department not only served to attract students for the other departments of the College, but at the same time the tuition fees collected through this new department were sufficient to place it on a self-sustaining basis before the end of the first year.

Now you can see that while the College did not loan me one penny of actual capital, it nevertheless supplied me with credit which served exactly the same purpose.

I said that my plan was founded upon equity; that it contemplated a benefit to all parties concerned. The benefit accruing to me was the use of the $25,000.00, which resulted in an established and self-sustaining business by the end of the first year. The benefit accruing to the college was the students secured for its regular commercial and business course as a result of the money spent in advertising my department, all advertising having been done under the name of the College.

Today that business college is one of the most successful schools of its kind, and it stands as a monument of sound evidence with which to demonstrate the value of *allied effort*.

This incident has been related, not alone because it shows the value of *initiative* and *leadership,* but for the reason that it leads up to the subject covered by the next lesson of this Reading Course on the Law of Success, which is *imagination.*

There are generally many plans through the operation of which a desired object may be achieved, and it often happens to be true that the obvious and usual methods employed are not the best. The usual method of procedure, in the case related, would have been that of borrowing from a bank. You can see that this method was impractical, in this case, for the reason that no collateral was available.

A great philosopher once said: *"Initiative is the pass-key that opens the door to opportunity."*

I do not recall who this philosopher was, but I know that he was *great* because of the soundness of his statement.

We will now proceed to outline the exact procedure that you must follow if you are to become a person of *initiative* and *leadership.*

First: You must master the habit of *procrastination* and eliminate it from your make-up. This habit of putting off until tomorrow that which you should have done last week or last year or a score of years ago is gnawing at the very vitals of your being, and you can accomplish nothing until you throw it off.

The method through which you eliminate *procrastination* is based upon a well known and scientifically tested principle of psychology which has been referred to in the two preceding lessons of this course as Auto-suggestion.

Copy the following formula and place it conspicuously in your room where you will see it as you retire at night and as you arise in the morning:

Initiative and Leadership

Having chosen a *definite chief aim* as my life-work I now understand it to be my duty to transform this purpose into reality.

Therefore, I will form the habit of taking some *definite* action each day that will carry me one step nearer the attainment of my *definite chief aim.*

I know that *procrastination* is a deadly enemy of all who would become leaders in any undertaking, and I will eliminate this habit from my make-up by:

a. Doing some one definite thing each day, that ought to be done, without anyone telling me to do it.

b. Looking around until I find at least one thing that I can do each day, that I have not been in the habit of doing, and that will be of value to others, without expectation of pay.

c. Telling at least one other person, each day, of the value of practicing this habit of doing something that ought to be done without being told to do it.

I can see that the muscles of the body become strong in proportion to the extent to which they are used, therefore I understand that the *habit of initiative* also becomes fixed in proportion to the extent that it is practiced.

I realize that the place to begin developing the *habit of initiative* is in the small, commonplace things connected with my daily work, therefore I will go at my work each day as if I were doing it solely for the purpose of developing this necessary *habit of initiative.*

I understand that by practicing this *habit* of taking the *initiative* in connection with my daily work I will be not only developing that habit, but I will also be attracting the attention of those who will place greater value on my services as a result of this practice.

Signed ....

Regardless of what you are now doing, every day brings you face to face with a chance to render some service, outside of the course of your regular duties, that will be of value to others. In rendering this additional service, of your own accord, you of course understand that you are not doing so with the object of receiving monetary pay. You are rendering this service because it provides you with ways and means of exercising, developing and making stronger the aggressive spirit of *initiative* which you must possess before you can ever become an outstanding figure in the affairs of your chosen field of life-work.

Those who work for *money* alone, and who receive for their pay nothing but money, are always underpaid, no matter how much they receive. Money is necessary, but the big prizes of life cannot be measured in dollars and cents.

No amount of money could possibly be made to take the place of the happiness and joy and pride that belong to the person who digs a better ditch, or builds a better chicken coop, or sweeps a cleaner floor, or cooks a better meal. Every normal person loves to create something that is better than the average. The joy of *creating* a work of art is a joy that cannot be replaced by money or any other form of material possession.

I have in my employ a young lady who opens, assorts and answers much of my personal mail. She began in my employ more than three years ago. Then her duties were to take dictation when she was asked to do so. Her salary was about the same as that which others receive for similar service. One day I dictated the following motto which I asked her to type-write for me:

Remember that your only limitation is the one that you set up in your own mind.

As she handed the typewritten page back to me she said, "Your motto has given me an idea that is going to be of value to both you and me."

I told her I was glad to have been of service to her. The incident made no particular impression on my mind, but from that day on I could see that it had made a *tremendous* impression on her mind. She began to come back to the office after supper and performed ser-

> "What helped you over the great obstacles of life?" was asked of a highly successful man. "The other obstacles," he replied.

vice that she was neither paid for nor expected to perform. Without anyone telling her to do it she began to bring to my desk letters that she had answered for me. She had studied my style and these letters were attended to as well as I could have done it; in some instances much better. She kept up this habit until my personal secretary resigned. When I began to look for someone to take his place, what was more natural than to turn to this young woman to fill the place. Before I had time to give her the position *she took it on her initiative*. My personal mail began to come to my desk with a new secretary's name attached, and she was that secretary. On her own time, after hours, without additional pay, she had prepared herself for the best position on my staff.

But that is not all. This young lady became so noticeably efficient that she began to attract the attention of others who offered her attractive positions. I have increased her salary many times and she now receives a salary more than four times as large as the amount she received when she first went to work for me as an ordinary stenographer, and, to tell you the truth, I am helpless in the matter, because she has made herself so valuable to me that I cannot get along without her.

That is initiative transformed into practical, understandable terms. I would be remiss in my duties if I failed to direct your attention to an advantage, other than a greatly increased salary, that this young lady's *initiative* has brought her. It has developed in her a spirit of cheerfulness that brings her happiness which most stenographers never know. Her work is not work—it is a great interesting game at which she is playing. Even though she arrives at the office ahead of the regular stenographers and remains there long after they have watched the clock tick off *five o'clock* and *quitting time,* her hours are shorter by far than are those of the other workers. Hours of labor do not drag on the hands of those who are happy at their work.

This brings us to the next step in our description of the exact procedure that you must follow in developing *initiative* and *leadership.*

Second: You of course understand that the only way to get *happiness* is by giving it away, to others. The same applies to the development of *initiative.* You can best develop this essential quality in yourself by making it your business to interest those around you in doing the same. It is a well known fact that a man learns best that which he endeavors to teach others. If a man embraces a certain creed or religious faith, the first thing he does is to go out and try to "sell" it to others. And in exact proportion to the extent to which he impresses others does he impress *himself.*

In the field of salesmanship it is a well known fact that no salesman is successful in selling others until he has first made a good job of selling *himself.* Stated conversely, no salesman can do his best to sell others without sooner or later selling himself that which he is trying to sell to others.

Any statement that a person repeats over and over again for the purpose of inducing others to believe it, he, also, will come to believe, and this holds good whether the statement is false or true.

You can now see the advantage of making it your business to *talk initiative, think initiative, eat initiative, sleep initiative* and *practice initiative.* By so doing you are becoming a person of *initiative* and *leadership,* for it is a well known fact that people will readily, willingly and voluntarily follow the person who shows by his actions that he is a person of *initiative.*

In the place where you work or the community in which you live you come in contact with other people. Make it your business to interest every one of them who will listen to you, in the development of *initiative*. It will not be necessary for you to give your reasons for doing this, nor will it be necessary for you to announce the fact that you are doing it. *Just go ahead and do it.* In your own mind you will understand, of course, that you are doing it because this practice will help you and will, at least, do those whom you influence in the same practice no harm.

If you wish to try an experiment that will prove both interesting and profitable to you, pick out some person of your acquaintance whom you know to be a person who never does anything that he is not expected to do, and begin selling him your idea of *initiative*. Do not stop by merely discussing the subject once; keep it up every time you have a convenient opportunity. Approach the subject from a different angle each time. If you go at this experiment in a tactful and forceful manner you will soon observe a change in the person on whom you are trying the experiment.

And, you will observe something else of more importance still: *You will observe a change in yourself!*

Do not fail to try this experiment.

You cannot talk *initiative* to others without developing a desire to practice it yourself. Through the operation of the principle of Auto-suggestion every statement that you make to others leaves its imprint on your own subconscious mind, and this holds good whether your statements are false or true.

You have often heard the saying: "He who lives by the sword will die by the sword."

Properly interpreted, this simply means that we are constantly attracting to ourselves and weaving into our own characters and personalities those qualities which our influence is helping to create in others. If we help others develop the habit of *initiative,* we, in turn, develop this same habit. If we sow the seeds of hatred and envy and discouragement in others, we, in turn, develop these qualities in ourselves. This principle through which a man comes to resemble in his own nature those whom he most admires is fully brought out in Hawthorne's story, The Great Stone Face, a story that every parent should have his offspring read.

We come, now, to the next step in our description of the exact procedure that you must follow in developing *initiative* and *leadership*.

Third: Before we go further let it be understood what is meant by the term "Leadership," as it is used in connection with this Reading Course on the Law of Success. There are two brands of *leadership,* and one of them is as deadly and destructive as the other is helpful and constructive. The deadly brand, which leads not to *success,* but to *absolute failure,* is the brand adopted by pseudo-leaders who *force* their leadership on unwilling followers. It will not be necessary here to describe this brand or to point out the fields of endeavor in which it is practiced, with the exception of the field of war, and in this field we will mention but one notable example, that of Napoleon.

Napoleon was a *leader;* there can be no doubt about this, but he led his followers and himself to destruction. The details are recorded in the history of France and the French people, where you may study them if you choose.

It is not Napoleon's brand of *leadership* that is recommended in this course, although I will admit that Napoleon possessed all the necessary fundamentals for great leadership, excepting one—he lacked the spirit of helpfulness to others as an objective. His desire for the power that comes through leadership was based solely upon self-aggrandizement. His desire for leadership was built upon personal ambition and not upon the desire to lift the French people to a higher and nobler station in the affairs of nations.

> *Cherish your visions and your dreams as they are the children of your soul; the blue-prints of your ultimate achievements.*

The brand of *leadership* that is recommended through this course of instruction is the brand which leads to self-determination and freedom and self-development and enlightenment and justice. This is the brand that endures. For example, and as a contrast with the brand of *leadership* through which Napoleon raised himself into prominence, consider our own American commoner, Lincoln. The object of his *leadership* was to bring truth and justice and understanding to the people of the United States. Even though he died a martyr to his belief in this brand of *leadership,* his name has been engraved upon the heart of the world in terms of loving kindliness that will never bring aught but good to the world.

Both Lincoln and Napoleon led armies in warfare, but the objects of their *leadership* were as different as night is different from day. If it would give you a better understanding of the principles upon which this Reading Course is based, you could easily be cited to *leadership* of today which resembles both the brand that Napoleon employed and that which Lincoln made the foundation of his life-work, but this is not essential; your own ability to look around and analyze men who take the leading parts in all lines of endeavor is sufficient to enable you to pick out the Lincoln as well as the Napoleon types. Your own judgment will help you decide which type you prefer to emulate.

There can be no doubt in your mind as to the brand of *leadership* that is recommended in this Reading Course, and there should be no question in your mind as to which of the two brands described you will adopt as your brand. We make no recommendations on this subject, however, for the reason that this Reading Course has been prepared as a means of laying before its students the fundamental principles upon which power is developed, and not as a preachment on ethical conduct. We present both the constructive and the destructive possibilities of the principles outlined in this course, that you may become familiar with both, but we leave entirely to your own discretion the choice and application of these principles, believing that your own intelligence will guide you to make a wise selection.

The Penalty of Leadership

In every field of human endeavor, he that is first must perpetually live in the white light of publicity. Whether the leadership be vested in a man or in a manufactured product, emulation and envy are ever at work.

In art, in literature, in music, in industry, the reward and the punishment are always the same. The reward is widespread recognition; the punishment, fierce denial and detraction.

When a man's work becomes a standard for the whole world, it also becomes a target for the shafts of the envious few. If his work be merely mediocre, he will be left severely alone— if he achieve a masterpiece, it will set a million tongues a-wagging.

Jealousy does not protrude its forked tongue at the artist who produces a commonplace painting.

Whatsoever you write, or paint, or play, or sing or build, no one will strive to surpass or slander you, unless your work be stamped with the seal of a genius.

Long, long after a great work or a good work has been done, those who are disappointed or envious continue to cry out that it cannot be done.

Mean voices were raised against the author of the Law of Success before the ink was dry on the first textbooks. Poisoned pens were released against both the author and the philosophy the moment the first edition of the course was printed.

Spiteful little voices in the domain of art were raised against our own Whistler as a mountebank, long after the big world acclaimed him its greatest artistic genius.

Multitudes flocked to Beyreuth to worship at the musical shrine of Wagner, while the little group of those whom he had dethroned and displaced argued angrily that he was no musician at all.

The little world continued to protest that Fulton could never build a steamboat, while the big world flocked to the river banks to see his boat steam by.

Small, narrow voices cried out that Henry Ford would not last another year, but above and beyond the din of their childish prattle Ford went silently about his business and made himself the richest and most powerful man on earth.

The leader is assailed because he is a leader, and the effort to equal him is merely added proof of his leadership.

Failing to equal or to excel, the follower seeks to depreciate and to destroy—but only confirms the superiority of that which he strives to supplant.

There is nothing new in this.

It is as old as the world and as old as the human passions—envy, fear, greed, ambition and the desire to surpass.

And it all avails nothing.

If the leader truly leads, he remains the LEADER!

Master-poet, master-painter, master-workman, each in his turn is assailed, and each holds his laurels through the ages.

That which is good or great makes itself known, no matter how loud the clamor of denial.

A real leader cannot be slandered or damaged by lies of the envious, because all such attempts serve only to turn the spot-light on his ability, and real ability always finds a generous following.

Attempts to destroy real Leadership is love's labor lost, because that which deserves to live, lives!

We come back, now, to the discussion of the third step of the procedure that you must follow in developing *initiative* and *leadership*. This third step takes us back for a review of the principle of *organized effort,* as described in the preceding lessons of this course.

You have already learned that no man can accomplish enduring results of a far-reaching nature without the aid and co-operation of others. You have already learned that when two or more persons ally themselves in any undertaking, in a spirit of harmony and understanding, each person in the alliance thereby multiplies his own powers of achievement. Nowhere is this principle more evidenced than it is in an industry or business in which there is perfect team-work between the employer and the employees. Wherever you find this team-work you find prosperity and goodwill on both sides.

Co-operation is said to be the most important word in the English language. It plays an important part in the affairs of the home, in the relationship of man and wife, parents and children. It plays an important part in the affairs of state. So important is this principle of Co-operation that no leader can become powerful or last long who does not understand and apply it in his *leadership*.

Lack of Co-operation has destroyed more business enterprises than have all other causes combined. In my twenty-five years of active business experience and observation I have witnessed the destruction of all manner of business enterprises because of dissension and lack of application of this principle of Co-operation. In the practice of law I have observed the destruction of homes and divorce cases without end as a result of the lack of Co-operation between man and wife. In the study of the histories of nations it becomes alarmingly obvious that lack of Co-operative effort has been a curse to the human race all back down the ages. Turn back the pages of these histories and study them and you will learn a lesson in Co-operation that will impress itself indelibly upon your mind.

You are paying, and your children and your children's children will continue to pay, for the cost of the most expensive and destructive war the world has ever known, because nations have not yet learned that a part of the world cannot suffer without damage and suffering to the whole world.

This same rule applies, with telling effect, in the conduct of modern business and industry. When an industry becomes disorganized and torn asunder by strikes and other forms of disagreement, both the employers and employees suffer irreparable loss. But, the damage does not stop here; this loss becomes a burden to the public and takes on the form of higher prices and scarcity of the necessities of life.

> *Service, Sacrifice and Self-Control are three words which must be well understood by the person who succeeds in doing something that is of help to the world.*

The people of the United States who rent their homes are feeling the burden, at this very moment, of lack of co-operation between contractors and builders and the workers. So uncertain has the relationship between the contractors and their employees become that the contractors will not undertake a building without adding to the cost an arbitrary sum sufficient to protect them in the event of labor troubles. This additional cost increases rents and places unnecessary burdens upon the backs of millions of people. In this instance the lack of co-operation between a few men places heavy and almost unbearable burdens upon millions of people.

The same evil exists in the operation of our railroads. Lack of harmony and co-operation between the railroad management and the workers has made it necessary for the railroads to increase their freight and passenger rates, and this, in turn, has increased the cost of life's necessities to almost unbearable proportions. Here, again, lack of co-operation between a few leads to hardship for millions of people.

These facts are cited without effort or desire to place the responsibility for this lack of co-operation, since the object of this Reading Course is to help its students get at facts.

It may be truthfully stated that the high cost of living that everywhere manifests itself today has grown out of lack of application of the principle of co-operative *leadership*. Those who wish to decry present systems of government and industrial management may do so, but in the final analysis it becomes obvious to all except those who are not seeking the *truth* that the evils of government and of industry have grown out of lack of *co-operation*.

Nor can it be truthfully said that all the evils of the world are confined to the affairs of state and industry. Take a look at the churches and you will observe the damaging effects of lack of co-operation. No particular church is cited, but analyze any church or group of churches where lack of co-ordination of effort prevails and you will see evidence of disintegration that limits the service those churches could render. For example, take the average town or small city where rivalry has sprung up between the churches and notice what has happened; especially those towns in which the number of churches is far out of proportion to the population.

Through harmonized effort and through co-operation, the churches of the world could wield sufficient influence to render war an impossibility. Through this same principle of co-operative effort the churches and the leaders of business and industry could eliminate rascality and sharp practices, and all this could be brought about speedily.

These possibilities are not mentioned in a spirit of criticism, but only as a means of illustrating the power of co-operation, and to emphasize my belief in the potential power of the churches of the world. So there will be no possibility of misinterpretation of my meaning in the reference that I have here made to the churches I will repeat that which I have so often said in person; namely, that had it not been for the influence of the churches no man would be safe in walking down the street. Men would be at each other's throat like wolves and civilization would still be in the pre-historic age. My complaint is not against the work that the churches have done, but the work that *they could have done* through *leadership* that was based upon the principle of co-ordinated, co-operative effort which would have carried civilization at least a thousand years ahead of where it is today. It is not yet too late for such leadership.

That you may more fully grasp the fundamental principle of co-operative effort you are urged to go to the public library and read The Science of Power, by Benjamin Kidd. Out of scores of volumes by some of the soundest thinkers of the world that I have read during the past fifteen years, no single volume has given me such a full understanding of the possibilities of co-operative effort as has this book. In recommending that you read this book it is not my purpose to endorse the book in its entirety, for it offers some theories with which I am not in accord. If you read it, do so with an open mind and take from it only that which you feel you can use to advantage in achieving the object of your *definite chief aim.* The book will stimulate *thought,* which is the greatest service that any book can render. As a matter of fact the chief object of this Reading Course on the Law of Success is to stimulate deliberate *thought*: particularly that brand of *thought* that is free from bias and prejudice and is seeking *truth* no matter where or how or when it may be found.

During the World War, I was fortunate enough to listen to a great soldier's analysis of how to be a *leader.* This analysis was given to the student-officers of the Second Training Camp at Fort Sheridan, by Major C. A. Bach, a quiet, unassuming army officer acting as an instructor. I have preserved a copy of this address because I believe it to be one of the finest lessons on *leadership* ever recorded.

The wisdom of Major Bach's address is so vital to the business man aspiring to *leadership,* or to the section boss, or to the stenographer, or to the foreman of the shop, or to the president of the works, that I have preserved it as a part of this Reading Course. It is my earnest hope that through the agency of this course this remarkable dissertation on *leadership* will find its way into the hands of every employer and every worker and every ambitious person who aspires to *leadership* in any walk of life. The principles upon which the address is based are as applicable to *leadership* in business and industry and finance as they are in the successful conduct of warfare.

Major Bach spoke as follows:

In a short time each of you men will control the lives of a certain number of other men. You will have in your charge loyal but untrained citizens, who look to you for instruction and guidance. Your word will be their law. Your most casual remark will be remembered. Your mannerisms will be aped. Your clothing, your carriage, your vocabulary, your manner of command will be imitated.

When you join your organization you will find there a willing body of men who ask from you nothing more than the qualities that will command their respect, their loyalty and their obedience.

They are perfectly ready and eager to follow you so long as you can convince them that you have these qualities. When the time comes that they are satisfied you do not possess them you might as well kiss yourself good-bye. Your usefulness in that organization is at an end.

[How remarkably true this is in all manner of *leadership*.]

From the standpoint of society, the world may be divided into leaders and followers. The professions have their leaders, the financial world has its leaders. In all this leadership it is difficult, if not impossible, to separate from the element of pure leadership that selfish element of personal gain or advantage to the individual, without which any leadership would lose its value.

It is in military service only, where men freely sacrifice their lives for a faith, where men are willing to suffer and die for the right or the prevention of a wrong, that we can hope to realize leadership in its most exalted and disinterested sense. Therefore, when I say *leadership,* I mean *military leadership.*

In a few days the great mass of you men will receive commissions as officers. These commissions will not make you leaders; they will merely make you officers. They will place you in a position where you can become leaders if you possess the proper attributes. But you must make good, not so much with the men over you as with the men under you.

Men must and will follow into battle officers who are not leaders, but the driving power behind these men is not enthusiasm but discipline. They go with doubt and trembling that prompts the unspoken question, "What will he do next?" Such men obey the letter of their orders but no more. Of devotion to their commander, of exalted enthusiasm which scorns personal risk, of *self-sacrifice* to insure his personal safety, they know nothing. Their legs carry them forward because their brain and their training tell them they *must* go. Their spirit does not go with them.

> *Make excuses for the shortcomings of others, if you wish, but hold yourself to a strict accountability if you would attain leadership in any undertaking.*

Great results are not achieved by cold, passive, unresponsive soldiers. They don't go very far and they stop as soon as they can. Leadership not only demands but receives the willing, unhesitating, unfaltering obedience and loyalty of other men; and a devotion that will cause them, when the time comes, to follow their uncrowned king to hell and back again, if necessary.

You will ask yourselves: "Of just what, then, does *leadership* consist? What must I do to become a leader? What are the attributes of leadership, and how can I cultivate them?"

Leadership is a composite of a number of qualities. [Just as *success* is a composite of the fifteen factors out of which this Reading Course was built.] Among the most important I would list Self-confidence, Moral Ascendancy, Self-Sacrifice, Paternalism, Fairness, Initiative, Decision, Dignity, Courage.

Self-confidence results, first, from exact knowledge; second, the ability to impart that knowledge; and third, the feeling of superiority over others that naturally follows. All these give the officer poise. To lead, you must *know!* You may bluff all of your men some of the time, but you can't do it all the time. Men will not have confidence in an officer unless he knows his business, and he must know it from the ground up.

The officer should know more about paper work than his first sergeant and company clerk put together; he should know more about messing than his mess sergeant; more about diseases of the horse than his troop farrier. He should be at least as good a shot as any man in his company.

If the officer does not know, and demonstrates the fact that he does not know, it is entirely human for the soldier to say to himself, "To hell with him. He doesn't know as much about this as I do," and calmly disregard the instructions received.

There is no substitute for accurate knowledge!

Become so well informed that men will hunt you up to ask questions; that your brother officers will say to one another, "Ask Smith—he knows."

And not only should each officer know thoroughly the duties of his own grade, but he should study those of the two grades next above him. A two-fold benefit attaches to this. He prepares himself for duties which may fall to his lot any time during battle; he further gains a broader viewpoint which enables him to appreciate the necessity for the issuance of orders and join more intelligently in their execution.

Not only must the officer know but he must be able to put what he knows into grammatical, interesting, forceful English. He must learn to stand on his feet and speak without embarrassment.

I am told that in British training camps student-officers are required to deliver ten minute talks on any subject they choose. That is excellent practice. For to speak clearly one must think clearly, and clear, logical thinking expresses itself in definite, positive orders.

While self-confidence is the result of knowing more than your men, Moral Ascendancy over them is based upon your belief that you are the better man. To gain and maintain this ascendancy you must have self-control, physical vitality and endurance and moral force. You must have yourself so well in hand that, even though in battle you be scared stiff, you will never show fear. For if by so much as a hurried movement or a trembling of the hands, or a change of expression, or a hasty order hastily revoked, you indicate your mental condition it will be reflected in your men in a far greater degree.

In garrison or camp many instances will arise to try your temper and wreck the sweetness of your disposition. If at such times you "fly off the handle" you have no business to be in charge of men. For men in anger say and do things that they almost invariably regret afterward.

An officer should never apologize to his men; also an officer should never be guilty of an act for which his sense of justice tells him he should apologize.

Another element in gaining Moral Ascendency lies in the possession of enough physical vitality and endurance to withstand the hardships to which you and your men are subjected, and a dauntless spirit that enables you not only to accept them cheerfully but to minimize their magnitude.

Make light of your troubles, belittle your trials and you will help vitally to build up within your organization an esprit whose value in time of stress cannot be measured.

Moral force is the third element in gaining Moral Ascendency. To exert moral force you must live clean; you must have sufficient brain power to see the right and the will to do right.

Be an example to your men!

An officer can be a power for good or a power for evil. Don't preach to them—that will be worse than useless. Live the kind of life you would have them lead, and you will be surprised to see the number that will imitate you.

A loud-mouthed, profane captain who is careless of his personal appearance will have a loud-mouthed, profane, dirty company. *Remember what I tell you. Your company will be the reflection of yourself!* If you have a rotten company it will be because you are a rotten captain.

Self-sacrifice is essential to leadership. You will give, give, all the time. You will give of yourself physically, for the longest hours, the hardest work and the greatest responsibility are the lot of the captain. He is the first man up in the morning and the last man in at night. He works while others sleep.

You will give of yourself mentally, in sympathy and appreciation for the troubles of men in your charge. This one's mother has died, and that one has lost all his savings in a bank failure. They may desire help, but more than anything else they desire *sympathy*. Don't make the mistake of turning such men down with the statement that you have troubles of your own, for every time you do that you *knock a stone out of the foundation of your house.*

Your men are your foundation, and your house of *leadership* will tumble about your ears unless it rests securely upon them. Finally, you will give of your own slender financial resources. You will frequently spend your own money to conserve the health and well-being of your men or to assist them when in trouble. Generally you get your money back. Very frequently you must charge it off to profit and loss.

Even so, it is worth the cost.

When I say that paternalism is essential to leadership I use the term in its better sense. I do not now refer to that form of paternalism which robs men of *initiative, self-reliance* and *self-respect*. I refer to the paternalism that manifests itself in a watchful care for the comfort and welfare of those in your charge.

Soldiers are much like children. You must see that they have shelter, food and clothing, the best that your utmost efforts can provide. You must see that they have food to eat before you think of your own; that they have each as good a bed as can be provided before you consider where you will sleep. You must be far more solicitous of their comfort than of your own. You must look after their health. You must conserve their strength by not demanding needless exertion or useless labor.

And by doing all these things you are breathing life into what would be otherwise a mere machine. You are creating a soul in your organization that will make the mass respond to you as though it were one man. And that is esprit.

And when your organization has this esprit you will wake up some morning and discover that the tables have been turned; that instead of your constantly looking out for them they have, without even a hint from you, taken up the task of looking out for you. You will find that a detail is always there to see that your tent, if you have one, is promptly pitched; that the most and the cleanest bedding is brought to your tent; that from some mysterious source two eggs have been added to your supper when no one else has any; that an extra man is helping your men give your horse a supergrooming; that your wishes are anticipated; that every man is "Johnny-on-the-spot." And then you have *arrived!*

You cannot treat all men alike! A punishment that would be dismissed by one man with a shrug of the shoulders is mental anguish for another. A company commander who, for a

> No accurate thinker will judge another person by that which the other person's enemies say about him.

given offense, has a standard punishment that applies to all is either too indolent or too stupid to study the personality of his men. In his case justice is certainly blind.

Study your men as carefully as a surgeon studies a difficult case. And when you are sure of your diagnosis apply the remedy. And remember that you apply the remedy to effect a cure, not merely to see the victim squirm. It may be necessary to cut deep, but when you are satisfied as to your diagnosis don't be diverted from your purpose by any false sympathy for the patient.

Hand in hand with fairness in awarding punishment walks fairness in giving credit. Everybody hates a human hog. When one of your men has accomplished an especially creditable piece of work see that he gets the proper reward. *Turn heaven and earth upside down to get it for him.* Don't try to take it away from him and hog it for yourself. You may do this and get away with it, but you have lost the respect and loyalty of your men. Sooner or later your brother officers will hear of it and shun you like a leper. In war there is glory enough for all. Give the man under you his due. *The man who always takes and never gives is not a leader.* He is a parasite.

There is another kind of fairness—that which will prevent an officer from abusing the privileges of his rank. When you exact respect from soldiers be sure you treat them with equal respect. Build up their manhood and self-respect. Don't try to pull it down.

For an officer to be overbearing and insulting in the treatment of enlisted men is the act of a coward. He ties the man to a tree with the ropes of discipline and then strikes him in the face knowing full well that the man cannot strike back.

Consideration, courtesy and respect from officers toward enlisted men are not incompatible with discipline. They are parts of our discipline. Without initiative and decision no man can expect to lead.

In maneuvers you will frequently see, when an emergency arises, certain men calmly give instant orders which later, on analysis, prove to be, if not exactly the right thing, very nearly the right thing to have done. You will see other men in emergency become badly rattled; their brains refuse to work, or they give a hasty order, revoke it; give another, revoke that; in short, show every indication of being in a blue funk.

Regarding the first man you may say: "That man is a genius. He hasn't had time to reason this thing out. He acts intuitively." Forget it! Genius is merely the capacity for taking infinite pains. The man who was ready is the man who has prepared himself. He has studied beforehand the possible situations that might arise; he has made tentative plans covering such situations. When he is confronted by the emergency he is ready to meet it. He must have sufficient mental alertness to appreciate the problem that confronts him and the power of quick reasoning to determine what changes are necessary in his already formulated plan. He must also have the decision to order the execution and stick to his orders.

Any reasonable order in an emergency is better than no order. The situation is there. Meet it. It is better to do something and do the wrong thing than to hesitate, hunt around for the right thing to do and wind up by doing nothing at all. And, having decided on a line of action, stick to it. Don't vacillate. Men have no confidence in an officer who doesn't know his own mind.

Occasionally you will be called upon to meet a situation which no reasonable human being could anticipate. If you have prepared yourself to meet other emergencies which you could anticipate, the mental training you have thereby gained will enable you to act promptly and with calmness.

You must frequently act without orders from higher authority. Time will not permit you to wait for them. Here again enters the importance of studying the work of officers above you. If you have a comprehensive grasp of the entire situation and can form an idea of the general plan of your superiors, that and your previous emergency training will enable you to determine that the responsibility is yours and to issue the necessary orders without delay.

The element of *personal dignity* is important in military leadership. Be the friend of your men, but do not become their intimate. Your men should stand in awe of you—not *fear!* If your men presume to become familiar it is your fault, and not theirs. Your actions have encouraged them to do so. And, above all things, don't cheapen yourself by courting their friendship or currying their favor. They will despise you for it. If you are worthy of their loyalty and respect and devotion they will surely give all these without asking. If you are not, nothing that you can do will win them.

It is exceedingly difficult for an officer to be dignified while wearing a dirty, spotted uniform and a three days' stubble of whiskers on his face. Such a man lacks self-respect, and self-respect is an essential of dignity.

There may be occasions when your work entails dirty clothes and an unshaved face. Your men all look that way. At such times there is ample reason for your appearance. In fact, it would be a mistake to look too clean—they would think that you were not doing your share. But as soon as this unusual occasion has passed set an example for personal neatness.

And then I would mention *courage*. Moral courage you need as well as mental courage—that kind of moral courage which enables you to adhere without faltering to a determined course of action, which your judgment has indicated is the one best suited to secure the desired results.

You will find many times, especially in action, that, after having issued your orders to do a certain thing, you will be beset by misgivings and doubts; you will see, or think you see, other and better means for accomplishing the object sought. You will be strongly tempted to change your orders. Don't do it until it is clearly manifested that your first orders were radically wrong. For, if you do, you will be again worried by doubts as to the efficacy of your second orders.

Every time you change your orders without obvious reason you weaken your authority and impair the confidence of your men. Have the moral courage to stand by your order and see it through.

Moral courage further demands that you assume the responsibility for your own acts. If your subordinates have loyally carried out your orders and the movement you directed is a failure the failure is *yours*, not theirs. Yours would have been the honor had it been successful. Take the blame if it results in disaster. Don't try to shift it to a subordinate and make him the goat. That is a cowardly act. Furthermore, you will need moral courage to determine the fate of those under you. You will frequently be called upon for recommendations for promotion or demotion of officers and non-commissioned officers in your immediate command.

Keep clearly in mind your *personal integrity* and the duty you owe your country. Do not let yourself be deflected from a strict sense of justice by feelings of personal friendship. If your own brother is your second lieutenant, and you find him unfit to hold his commission, eliminate him. If you don't your lack of moral courage may result in the loss of valuable lives.

There is something wrong about the man whose wife and children do not greet him affectionately on his home-coming.

If, on the other hand, you are called upon for a recommendation concerning a man whom, for personal reasons, you thoroughly dislike, do not fail to do him full justice. Remember that your aim is the general good, not the satisfaction of an individual grudge.

I am taking it for granted that you have physical courage. I need not tell you how necessary that is. Courage is more than bravery. Bravery is fearlessness—the absence of fear. The merest dolt may be brave, because he lacks the mentality to appreciate his danger; he doesn't know enough to be afraid.

Courage, however, is that firmness of spirit, that moral backbone which, while fully appreciating the danger involved, nevertheless goes on with the undertaking. Bravery is physical; courage is mental and moral. You may be cold all over; your hands may tremble;

your legs may quake; your knees be ready to give way—that is fear. If, nevertheless, you go forward; if, in spite of this physical defection you continue to lead your men against the enemy, you have courage. The physical manifestations of fear will pass away. You may never experience them but once. They are the "buck fever" of the hunter who tries to shoot his first deer. You must not give way to them.

A number of years ago, while taking a course in demolitions, the class of which I was a member was handling dynamite. The instructor said, regarding its manipulation: "I must caution you gentlemen to be careful in the use of these explosives. One man has but one accident." And so I would caution you. If you give way to fear that will doubtless beset you in your first action; if you show the white feather; if you let your men go forward while you hunt a shell crater, you will never again have the opportunity of leading those men.

Use judgment in calling on your men for displays of physical courage or bravery. *Don't ask any man to go where you would not go yourself.* If your common sense tells you that the place is too dangerous for you to venture into, then it is too dangerous for him. You know his life is as valuable to him as yours is to you.

Occasionally some of your men must be exposed to danger which you cannot share. A message must be taken across a fire-swept zone. You call for volunteers. If your men know you and know that you are "right" you will never lack volunteers, for they will know your heart is in your work, that you are giving your country the best you have, that you would willingly carry the message yourself if you could. Your example and enthusiasm will have inspired them.

And, lastly, if you aspire to leadership, I would urge you to study men.

Get under their skins and find out what is inside. Some men are quite different from what they appear to be on the surface. Determine the workings of their mind.

Much of General Robert E. Lee's success as a leader may be ascribed to his ability as a *psychologist*. He knew most of his opponents from West Point days; knew the workings of their minds; and he believed that they would do certain things under certain circumstances. In nearly every case he was able to anticipate their movements and block the execution.

You cannot know your opponent in this war in the same way. But you can know your own men. You can study each to determine wherein lies his strength and his weakness; which man can be relied upon to the last gasp and which cannot.

Know your men, know your business, know yourself!

In all literature you will not find a better description of *leadership* than this. Apply it to yourself, or to your business, or to your profession, or to the place where you are employed, and you will observe how well it serves as your guide.

Major Bach's address is one that might well be delivered to every boy and girl who graduates in high school. It might well be delivered to every college graduate. It might well become the book of rules for every man who is placed in a position of leadership over other men, no matter in what calling, business or profession.

In Lesson One you learned the value of a *definite chief aim*. Let it be here emphasized that your aim must be active and not passive. A *definite aim* will never be anything else but a mere wish unless you become a person of initiative and *aggressively* and *persistently* pursue that aim until it has been fulfilled.

You can get nowhere without persistence, a fact which cannot be too often repeated.

The difference between persistence and lack of it is the same as the difference between wishing for a thing and positively determining to get it.

To become a person of initiative you must form the habit of *aggressively* and *persistently* following the object of your *definite chief aim* until you acquire it, whether this requires one year or twenty years. You might as well have no *definite chief aim* as to have such an aim without *continuous* effort to achieve it.

You are not making the most of this course if you do not take some step each day that brings you nearer realization of your *definite chief aim*. Do not fool yourself, or permit yourself to be misled to believe that the object of your *definite chief aim* will materialize if you only wait. The materialization will come through your own determination, backed by your own carefully laid plans and your own initiative in putting those plans into action, or it will not come at all.

One of the major requisites for Leadership is the power of quick and firm DECISION!

Analysis of more than 16,000 people disclosed the fact that Leaders are always men of ready decision, even in matters of small importance, while the follower is NEVER a person of quick decision.

This is worth remembering!

The follower, in whatever walk of life you find him, is a man who seldom knows what he wants. He vacillates, procrastinates, and actually refuses to reach a decision, even in matters of the smallest importance, unless a Leader induces him to do so.

To know that the majority of people cannot and will not reach decisions quickly, if at all, is of great help to the Leader who knows what he wants and has a plan for getting it.

Here it will be observed how closely allied are the two laws covered by Lesson One and this lesson. The Leader not only works with A DEFINITE CHIEF AIM, but he has a very definite plan for attaining the object of that aim. It will be seen, also, that the Law of Self-confidence becomes an important part of the working equipment of the Leader.

The chief reason why the follower does not reach decisions is that he lacks the Self-confidence to do so. Every Leader makes use of the Law of a Definite Purpose, the Law of Self-confidence and the Law of Initiative and Leadership. And if he is an outstanding, successful Leader he makes use, also, of the Laws of Imagination, Enthusiasm, Self-Control, Pleasing Personality, Accurate Thinking, Concentration and Tolerance. Without the combined use of all these Laws no one may become a really great Leader. Omission of a single one of these Laws lessens the power of the Leader proportionately.

A salesman for the LaSalle Extension University called on a real estate dealer, in a small western town, for the purpose of trying to sell the real estate man a course in Salesmanship and Business Management.

When the salesman arrived at the prospective student's office he found the gentleman pecking out a letter by the two-finger method, on an antiquated typewriter. The salesman introduced himself, then proceeded to state his business and describe the course he had come to sell.

The real estate man listened with apparent interest.

After the sales talk had been completed the salesman hesitated, waiting for some signs of "yes" or "no" from his prospective client. Thinking that perhaps he had not made the sales talk quite strong enough, he briefly went over the merits of the course he was selling, a second time. Still there was no response from the prospective student.

The salesman then asked the direct question, "You want this course, do you not?"

In a slow, drawling tone of voice, the real estate man replied:

"Well, I hardly know whether I do or not."

No doubt he was telling the truth, because he was one of the millions of men who find it hard to reach decisions.

Being an able judge of human nature the salesman then arose, put on his hat, placed his literature back in his brief case and made ready to leave. Then he resorted

No man may become an accurate thinker until he learns how to separate mere gossip and information from facts.

to tactics which were somewhat drastic, and took the real estate man by surprise with this startling statement:

"I am going to take it upon myself to say something to you that you will not like, but it may be of help to you.

"Take a look at this office in which you work! The floor is dirty; the walls are dusty; the typewriter you are using looks as if it might be the one Mr. Noah used in the Ark during the big flood; your pants are bagged at the knees; your collar is dirty; your face is unshaved, and you have a look in your eyes that tells me you are defeated.

"Please go ahead and get mad—that's just what I want you to do, because it may shock you into doing some thinking that will be helpful to you and to those who are dependent upon you.

"I can see, in my imagination, the home in which you live. Several little children, none too well dressed, and perhaps none too well fed; a mother whose dress is three seasons out of style, whose eyes carry the same look of defeat that yours do. This little woman whom you married has stuck by you but you have not made good in life as she had hoped, when you were first married, that you would.

"Please remember that I am not now talking to a prospective student, because I would not sell you this course at THIS PARTICULAR MOMENT if you offered to pay cash in advance, because if I did you would not have the initiative to complete it, and we want no failures on our student list.

"The talk I am now giving you will make it impossible, perhaps, for me ever to sell you anything, but it is going to do something for you that has never been done before, providing it makes you think.

"Now, I will tell you in a very few words exactly why you are defeated; why you are pecking out letters on an old typewriter, in an old dirty office, in a little town: IT IS BECAUSE YOU DO NOT HAVE THE POWER TO REACH A DECISION!

"All your life you have been forming the habit of dodging the responsibility of reaching decisions, until you have come, now, to where it is well-nigh impossible for you to do so.

"If you had told me that you wanted the course, or that you did not want it, I could have sympathized with you, because I would have known that lack of funds was what caused you to hesitate, but what did you say? Why, you admitted you did not know whether you wanted it or not.

"If you will think over what I have said I am sure you will acknowledge that it has become a habit with you to dodge the responsibility of reaching clear-cut decisions on practically all matters that affect you."

The real estate man sat glued in his chair, with his under jaw dropped, his eyes bulged in astonishment, but he made no attempt to answer the biting indictment.

The salesman said good-bye and started for the door.

After he had closed the door behind him he again opened it, walked back in, with a smile on his face, took his seat in front of the astonished real estate man, and explained his conduct in this way:

"I do not blame you at all if you feel hurt at my remarks. In fact I sort of hope that you have been offended, but now let me say this, man to man, that I think you have intelligence and I am sure you have ability, but you have fallen into a habit that has whipped you. No man is ever down and out until he is under the sod. You may be temporarily down, but you can get up again, and I am just sportsman enough to give you my hand and offer you a lift, if you will accept my apologies for what I have said.

"You do not belong in this town. You would starve to death in the real estate business in this place, even if you were a Leader in your field. Get yourself a new suit of clothes, even if you have to borrow the money with which to do it, then go over to St. Louis with me and I will introduce you to a real estate man who will give you a chance to earn some money and at the same time teach you some of the important things about this line of work that you can capitalize later on.

"If you haven't enough credit to get the clothes you need I will stand good for you at a store in St. Louis where I have a charge account. I am in earnest and my offer to help you is based upon the highest motive that can actuate a human being. I am successful in my own field, but I have not always been so. I went through just what you are now going through, but, the important thing is that I WENT THROUGH IT, and got it over with, JUST AS YOU ARE GOING TO DO IF YOU WILL FOLLOW MY ADVICE.

"Will you come with me?"

The real estate man started to arise, but his legs wobbled and he sank back into his chair. Despite the fact that he was a great big fellow, with rather pronounced manly qualities, known as the "he-man" type, his emotions got the better of him and he actually wept.

He made a second attempt and got on his feet, shook hands with the salesman, thanked him for his kindness, and said he was going to follow the advice, but he would do so in his own way.

Calling for an application blank he signed for the course on Salesmanship and Business Management, made the first payment in nickels and dimes, and told the salesman he would hear from him again.

Three years later this real estate man had an organization of sixty salesmen, and one of the

THE LAW OF SUCCESS

most successful real estate businesses in the city of St. Louis. The author of this course (who was advertising manager of the LaSalle Extension University at the time this incident happened) has been in this real estate man's office many times and has observed him over a period of more than fifteen years. He is an entirely different man from the person interviewed by the LaSalle salesman over fifteen years ago, and the thing that made him different is the same that will make YOU different: it is the power of DECISION which is so essential to Leadership.

This real estate man is now a Leader in the real estate field. He is directing the efforts of other salesmen and helping them to become more efficient. This one change in his philosophy has turned temporary defeat into success. Every new salesman who goes to work for this man is called into his private office, before he is employed, and told the story of his own transformation, word for word just as it occurred when the LaSalle salesman first met him in his shabby little real estate office.

Some eighteen years ago the author of this course made his first trip to the little town of Lumberport, W. Va. At that time the only means of transportation leading from Clarksburg, the largest near-by center, to Lumberport, was the Baltimore & Ohio Railroad and an interurban electric line which ran within three miles of the town; one could walk the three miles if he chose.

Upon arrival at Clarksburg I found that the only train going to Lumberport in the forenoon had already gone, and not wishing to wait for the later afternoon train I made the trip by trolley, with the intention of walking the three miles. On the way down the rain began to pour, and those three miles had to be navigated on foot, through deep yellow mud. When I arrived at Lumberport my shoes and pants were muddy, and my disposition was none the better for the experience.

The first person I met was V. L. Hornor, who was then cashier of the Lumberport Bank. In a rather loud tone of voice I asked of him, "Why do you not get that trolley line extended from the junction over to Lumberport so your friends can get in and out of town without drowning in mud?"

Mastery of the Fifteen Laws of Success is the equivalent of an insurance policy against failure.
—SAMUEL GOMPERS

"Did you see a river with high banks, at the edge of the town, as you came in?" he asked. I replied that I had seen it. "Well," he continued, "that's the reason we have no street cars running into town. The cost of a bridge would be about $100,000.00, and that is more than the company owning the trolley line is willing to invest. We have been trying for ten years to get them to build a line into town."

"Trying!" I exploded. "How hard have you tried?"

"We have offered them every inducement we could afford, such as free right of way from the junction into the town, and free use of the streets, but that bridge is the stumbling block. They simply will not stand the expense. Claim they cannot afford such an expense for the small amount of revenue they would receive from the three mile extension."

Then the Law of Success philosophy began to come to my rescue!

I asked Mr. Hornor if he would take a walk over to the river with me, that we might look at the spot that was causing so much inconvenience. He said he would be glad to do so.

When we got to the river I began to take inventory of everything in sight. I observed that the Baltimore & Ohio Railroad tracks ran up and down the river banks, on both sides of the river; that the county road crossed the river on a rickety wooden bridge, both approaches to which were over several strands of rail-road track, as the railroad company had its switching yards at that point.

While we were standing there a freight train blocked the crossing and several teams stopped on both sides of the train, waiting for an opportunity to get through. The train kept the road blocked for about twenty-five minutes.

With this combination of circumstances in mind it required but little imagination to see that THREE DIFFERENT PARTIES were or could be interested in the building of the bridge such as would be needed to carry the weight of a street car.

It was obvious that the Baltimore & Ohio Railroad Company would be interested in such a bridge, because that would remove the county road from their switching tracks, and save them a possible accident on the crossing, to say nothing of much loss of time and expense in cutting trains to allow teams to pass.

It was also obvious that the County Commissioners would be interested in the bridge, because it would raise the county road to a better level and make it more serviceable to the public. And, of course the street railway company was interested in the bridge, but IT DID NOT WISH TO PAY THE ENTIRE COST.

All these facts passed through my mind as I stood there and watched the freight train being cut for the traffic to pass through.

A DEFINITE CHIEF AIM took place in my mind. Also, a definite plan for its attainment. The next day I got together a committee of townspeople, consisting of the mayor, councilmen and some leading citizens, and called on the Division Superintendent of the Baltimore & Ohio Railroad Company, at Grafton. We convinced him that it was worth one third of the cost of the bridge to get the county road off his company's tracks. Next we went to the County Commissioners and found them to be quite enthusiastic over the possibility of getting a new bridge by paying for only one third of it. They promised to pay their one third providing we could arrange for the other two thirds.

We then went to the president of the Traction Company that owned the trolley line, at Fairmont, and laid before him an offer to donate all the rights of way and pay for two thirds of the cost of the bridge providing he would begin building the line into town promptly. We found him receptive, also.

Three weeks later a contract had been signed between the Baltimore & Ohio Railroad Company, the Monongahela Valley Traction Company and the County Commissioners of Harrison County, providing for the construction of the bridge, one third of its cost to be paid by each.

Two months later the right of way was being graded and the bridge was under way, and three months after that street cars were running into Lumberport on regular schedule.

This incident meant much to the town of Lumberport, because it provided transportation that enabled people to get in and out of the town without undue effort.

It also meant a great deal to me, because it served to introduce me as one who "got things done." Two very definite advantages resulted from this transaction. The Chief Counsel for the Traction Company gave me a position as his assistant, and later on it was the means of an introduction which led to my appointment as the advertising manager of the LaSalle Extension University.

Lumberport, W. Va., was then, and still is a small town, and Chicago was a large city and located a considerable distance away, but news of Initiative and Leadership has a way of taking on wings and traveling.

Four of the Fifteen Laws of Success were combined in the transaction described, namely: A DEFINITE CHIEF AIM, SELF-CONFIDENCE, IMAGINATION and INITIATIVE and LEADERSHIP. The Law of DOING MORE THAN PAID FOR also entered, somewhat, into the transaction, because I was not offered anything and in fact did not expect pay for what I did.

To be perfectly frank I appointed myself to the job of getting the bridge built more as a sort of challenge to those who said it could not be done than I did with the expectation of getting paid for it. By my attitude I rather intimated to Mr. Hornor that I could get the job done, and he was not slow to snap me up and put me to the test.

It may be helpful to call attention here to the part which IMAGINATION played in this transaction. For ten years the townspeople of Lumberport had been trying to get a street car line built into town. It must not be concluded that the town was without men of ability, because that would be inaccurate. In fact there were many men of ability in the town, but they had been making the mistake which is so commonly made by us all, of trying to solve their problem through one single source, whereas there were actually THREE SOURCES of solution available to them.

$100,000.00 was too much for one company to assume, for the construction of a bridge, but when the cost was distributed between three interested parties the amount to be borne by each was more reasonable.

The question might be asked: "Why did not some of the local townsmen think of this three-way solution?"

In the first place they were so close to their problem that they failed to take a perspective, bird's-eye view of it, which would have suggested the solution. This, also, is a common mistake, and one that is always avoided by great Leaders. In the second place these townspeople had never before co-ordinated their efforts or worked as an organized group with the sole purpose in mind of finding a way to get a street car line built into town. This, also, is another common error made by men in all walks of life—that of failure to work in unison, in a thorough spirit of co-operation.

I, being an outsider, had less difficulty in getting co-operative action than one of their own group might have had. Too often there is a spirit of selfishness in small communities which prompts each individual to think that his ideas should prevail. It is an important part of the Leader's responsibility to induce people to subordinate their own ideas and interests for the good of the whole, and this applies to matters of a civic, business, social, political, financial or industrial nature.

Success, no matter what may be one's conception of that term, is nearly always a question of one's ability to get others to subordinate their own individualities and follow a Leader. The Leader who has the Personality and the Imagination to induce his followers to accept his plans and carry them out faithfully is always an able Leader.

Time is the mighty hand that rocks the eternal cradle of progress and nurses struggling humanity through that period when man needs protection against his own ignorance.

The next lesson, on IMAGINATION, will take you still further into the art of tactful Leadership. In fact Leadership and Imagination are so closely allied and so essential for success that one cannot be successfully applied without the other. Initiative is the moving force that pushes the Leader ahead, but Imagination is the guiding spirit that tells him which way to go.

Imagination enabled the author of this course to analyze the Lumberport bridge problem, break it up into its three component parts, and assemble these parts in a practical working plan. Nearly every problem may be so broken up into parts which are more easily managed, as parts, than they are when assembled as a whole. Perhaps one of the most important advantages of Imagination is that it enables one to separate all problems into their component parts and to reassemble them in more favorable combinations.

It has been said that all battles in warfare are won or lost, not on the firing line, after the battle begins, but back of the lines, through the sound strategy, or the lack of it, used by the generals who plan the battles.

Life is not a goblet to be drained; it is a measure to be filled.

—HADLEY

What is true of warfare is equally true in business, and in most other problems which confront us throughout life. We win or lose according to the nature of the plans we build and carry out, a fact which serves to emphasize the value of the Laws of Initiative and Leadership, Imagination, Self-confidence and a Definite Chief Aim. *With the intelligent use of these four laws one may build plans, for any purpose whatsoever, which cannot be defeated by any person or group of persons who do not employ or understand these laws.*

There is no escape from the truth here stated!

ORGANIZED EFFORT is effort which is directed according to a plan that was conceived with the aid of Imagination, guided by a Definite Chief Aim, and given momentum with Initiative and Self-confidence. These four laws blend into one and become a power in the hands of a Leader. Without their aid effective leadership is impossible.

You are now ready for the lesson on Imagination. Read that lesson with the thought in mind of all that has been here stated and it will take on a deeper meaning.

INTOLERANCE

An After-the-Lesson Visit with the Author

If you must give expression to prejudice and hatred and intolerance, do not speak it, but write it; write it in the sands, near the water's edge.

When the dawn of Intelligence shall spread over the eastern horizon of human progress, and Ignorance and Superstition shall have left their last footprints on the sands of time, it will be recorded in the last chapter of the book of man's crimes that his most grievous sin was that of Intolerance.

The bitterest intolerance grows out of religious, racial and economic prejudices and differences of opinion. How long, O God, until we poor mortals will understand the folly of trying to destroy one another because we are of different religious beliefs and racial tendencies?

Our allotted time on this earth is but a fleeting moment. Like a candle, we are lighted, shine for a moment, and flicker out. Why can we not learn to so live during this brief earthly visit that when the great Caravan called Death draws up and announces this visit completed we will be ready to fold our tents and silently follow out into the great unknown without fear and trembling?

I am hoping that I will find no Jews or Gentiles, Catholics or Protestants, Germans, Englishmen or Frenchmen when I shall have crossed the bar to the other side. I am hoping that I will find there only human Souls, Brothers and Sisters all, unmarked by race, creed or color, for I shall want to be done with intolerance so I may rest in peace throughout eternity.

You will see at the top of the previous page a picture which describes the futility of combat.

The two male deer have engaged in a fight to the finish, each believing that he will be the winner. Off at the side the female awaits the victor, little dreaming that tomorrow the bones of both combatants will be bleaching in the sun.

"Poor foolish animals," someone will say. Perhaps, but not very different from the man family. Man engages his brothers in mortal combat because of competition. The three major forms of competition are sex, economic and religious in nature.

Twenty years ago a great educational institution was doing a thriving business and rendering a worthy service to thousands of students. The two owners of the school married two beautiful and talented young women, who were especially accomplished in the art of piano playing. The two wives became involved in an argument as to which one was the more accomplished in this art. The disagreement was taken up by each of the husbands. They became bitter enemies. Now the bones of that once prosperous school "lie bleaching in the sun."

The two bucks shown in the picture above locked horns over the attention of the doe. The two "man bucks" locked horns over the selfsame impulse.

In one of the great industrial plants two young foremen "locked horns" because one received a promotion which the other believed he should have had. For more than five years the silent undertow of hatred and intolerance showed itself. The men under each of the foremen became inoculated with the spirit of dislike which they saw cropping out in their superiors. Slowly the spirit of retaliation began to spread over the entire plant. The men became divided into little cliques. Production began to fall off. Then came financial difficulty and finally bankruptcy for the company.

Now the bones of a once prosperous business "lie bleaching in the sun," and the two foremen and several thousand others were compelled to start all over again, in another field.

Down in the mountains of West Virginia lived two peaceful families of mountain-folk—the Hatfields and the McCoys. They had been friendly neighbors for three generations. A razorback pig belonging to the McCoy family crawled through the fence into the Hatfield family's corn field. The Hatfields turned their hound loose on the pig. The McCoys retaliated by killing the dog. Then began a feud that has lasted for three generations and cost many lives of the Hatfields and McCoys.

In a fashionable suburb of Philadelphia certain gentlemen of wealth have built their homes. In front of each house the word "INTOLERANCE" is written. One man builds a high steel fence in front of his house. The neighbor next to him, not to be outdone, builds a fence twice as high. Another buys a new motor car and the man next door goes him one better by purchasing two new cars. One remodels his house adding a colonial style porch. The man next door adds a new porch and a Spanish style garage for good measure. The big mansion on top of the hill gives a reception which brings a long line of motor cars filled with people who have nothing in particular in common with the host. Then follows a series of "receptions" all down the "gold-coast" line, each trying to outshine all the others.

The "Mister" (but they don't call him that in fashionable neighborhoods) goes to business in the back seat of a Rolls Royce that is managed by a chauffeur and a footman. Why does he go to business? To make money, of course! Why does he want more money when he already has millions of dollars? So he can keep on out-doing his wealthy neighbors.

Poverty has some advantages—it never drives those who are poverty-stricken to "lock horns" in the attempt to out-poverty their neighbors.

Wherever you see men with their "horns locked" in conflict you may trace the cause of the combat to one of the three causes of intolerance—religious difference of opinion, economic competition or sex competition.

The next time you observe two men engaged in any sort of hostility toward each other, just close your eyes and THINK for a moment and you may see them, in their transformed nature, very much resembling the male deer shown in the picture above. Off at one side you may see the object of the combat—a pile of gold, a religious emblem or a female (or females).

Remember, the purpose of this essay is to tell some of the TRUTH about human nature, with the object of causing its readers to THINK. Its writer seeks no glory or praise, and likely he will receive neither in connection with this particular subject.

Andrew Carnegie and Henry C. Frick did more than any other two men to establish the steel industry. Both made millions of dollars for themselves. Came the day when economic intolerance sprang up between them. To show his contempt for Frick, Carnegie built a tall sky-scraper and named it the "Carnegie Building." Frick retaliated by erecting a much taller building, alongside of the Carnegie Building, naming it the "Frick Building."

These two gentlemen "locked horns" in a fight to the finish, Carnegie lost his mind, and perhaps more, for all we of this world know. What Frick lost is known only to himself and the keeper of the Great Records. In memory their "bones lie bleaching in the sun" of posterity.

The steel men of today are managing things differently. Instead of locking horns they now "interlock directorates," with the result that each is practically a solidified, strong unit of the whole industry. The steel men of today understand the difference between the meaning of the words COMPETITION and CO-OPERATION; a difference which the remainder of us would do well to understand, also.

In England the men who own the mines and those who run the labor unions "locked horns." Had not the cooler heads unlocked those horns the bones of the British empire (including both the owners of industry and the labor unions) should soon have lain "bleaching in the sun." One year of open combat between the unions and the owners of industry, in Great Britain, would have meant annihilation of the British empire. The other nations of the world would have grabbed all the economic machinery now controlled by Britain.

Let the leaders of American industry and unionism not forget!

Fifteen factors enter into the attainment of SUCCESS. One of these is TOLERANCE. The other fourteen are mentioned many times in this series of lessons.

Intolerance binds man's legs with the shackles of IGNORANCE and covers his eyes with the scales of FEAR AND SUPERSTITION. Intolerance closes the book of knowledge and writes on the cover "Open not this book again. The last word has been herein written."

It is not your DUTY to be tolerant; it is your PRIVILEGE!

Remember, as you read this article, that sowing the seed of INTOLERANCE is the sole and exclusive business of some men. All wars and all strikes and all other forms of human suffering bring profit to SOME. If this were not true there would be no wars or strikes or other similar forms of hostility.

In the United States today there is a well organized system of propaganda, the object of which is to stir up strife and hostility between the owners of industries and those who work in those industries. Take another look at the picture at the beginning of this article and you may see what will happen to all who lock horns in labor disagreements, and remember that it is always the bones of the workers (and not those of the leaders of either the unions or the industries) that "lie bleaching in the sun" after the fight is over.

When you feel yourself preparing to "lock horns" with someone remember that it will be more profitable if you LOCK HANDS instead! A warm, hearty handshake leaves no bones bleaching in the sun.

No one has given you an opportunity? Has it ever occurred to you to create opportunity for yourself?

"LOVE is the only bow on life's dark cloud. It is the Morning and the Evening Star. It shines upon the cradle of the babe, and sheds its radiance upon the quiet tomb. It is the mother of Art, inspirer of poet, patriot and philosopher. It is the air and light of every heart, builder of every home, kindler of every fire on every hearth. It was the first to dream of immortality. It fills the world with melody, for Music is the voice of Love. Love is the magician, the enchanter, that changes worthless things to Joy, and makes right royal kings and queens of common clay. It is the perfume of the wondrous flower—the heart—and without that sacred passion, that divine swoon, we are less than beasts; but with it, earth is heaven and we are gods."

—INGERSOLL

Cultivate LOVE for your fellow man and you will no longer want to lock horns with him in futile combat. Love makes every man his brother's keeper.

> Love, indeed, is light from heaven;
> A spark of that immortal fire
> With angels shared, by Allah given,
> To lift from earth our low desire.
> Devotion wafts the mind above,
> But heaven itself descends in love;
> A feeling from the Godhead caught,
> To wean from self each sordid thought;
> A ray of Him who form'd the whole;
> A glory circling round the soul:
>
> —BYRON

I call that man idle who might be better employed.

—SOCRATES

IMAGINATION

"You Can Do It If You Believe You Can!"

Imagination is the workshop of the human mind wherein old ideas and established facts may be reassembled into new combinations and put to new uses. The modern dictionary defines *imagination* as follows:

"The act of constructive intellect in grouping the materials of knowledge or thought into new, original and rational systems; the constructive or creative faculty; embracing poetic, artistic, philosophic, scientific and ethical imagination.

"The picturing power of the mind; the formation of mental images, pictures, or mental representation of objects or ideas, particularly of objects of sense perception and of mathematical reasoning! also the reproduction and combination, usually with more or less irrational or abnormal modification, of the images or ideas of memory or recalled facts of experience."

Imagination has been called the creative power of the soul, but this is somewhat abstract and goes more deeply into the meaning than is necessary from the viewpoint of a student of this course who wishes to use the course only as a means of attaining material or monetary advantages in life.

If you have mastered and thoroughly understood the preceding lessons of this Reading Course you know that the materials out of which you built your *definite chief aim* were assembled and combined in your imagination. You also know that *self-confidence* and *initiative* and *leadership* must be created in your imagination before they can become a reality, for it is in the workshop of your imagination that you will put the principle of Auto-suggestion into operation in creating these necessary qualities.

This lesson on imagination might be called the "hub" of this Reading Course, because every lesson of the course leads to this lesson and makes use of the principle upon which it is based, just as all the telephone wires lead to the exchange office for their source of power. You will never have a *definite purpose* in life, you will never have *self-confidence,* you will never have *initiative* and *leadership* unless you first create these qualities in your *imagination* and see yourself in possession of them.

Just as the oak tree develops from the germ that lies in the acorn, and the bird develops from the germ that lies asleep in the egg, so will your material achievements grow out of the *organized* plans that you create in your *imagination.* First comes the thought; then organization of that thought into ideas and plans; then transformation of those plans into reality. The beginning, as you will observe, is in your *imagination.*

The imagination is both interpretative and creative in nature. It can examine facts, concepts and ideas, and it can create new combinations and plans out of these.

Through its interpretative capacity the imagination has one power not generally attributed to it; namely, the power to register vibrations and thought waves that are put into motion from outside sources, just as the radio-receiving apparatus picks up the vibrations of sound. The principle through which this interpretative capacity of the imagination functions is called telepathy; the communication of thought from one mind to another, at long or short distances, without the aid of physical or mechanical appliances, in the manner explained in the Introduction to this course.

Telepathy is an important factor to a student who is preparing to make effective use of imagination, for the reason that this telepathic capacity of the imagination is constantly picking up thought waves and vibrations of every description. So-called "snap-judgment" and "hunches," which prompt one to form an opinion or decide upon a course of action that is not in harmony with logic and reason, are usually the result of stray thought waves that have registered in the imagination.

The recently developed radio apparatus has enabled us to understand that the elements of the ether are so sensitive and alive that all manner of sound waves are constantly flying here and there with lightning-like speed. You have only to understand the modern radio outfit to understand, also, the principle of telepathy. So well has this principle been established, through psychological research, that we have abundance of proof that two minds which are properly attuned and in harmony with each other may send and receive thought at long distances without the aid of mechanical apparatus of any sort. Rarely have two minds become so well attuned that unbroken chains of thought could be registered in this manner, but there is evidence sufficient to establish the fact that parts of organized thought have been picked up.

That you may understand how closely interwoven are the fifteen factors upon which this Reading Course is based, consider, for example, what happens when a salesman who lacks confidence in himself, and in his goods, walks in to see a prospective buyer. Whether the prospective buyer is conscious of it or not, his imagination immediately "senses" that lack of confidence in the salesman's mind. The salesman's own *thoughts* are actually undermining his efforts. This will explain, from another angle, why *self-confidence* is one of the most important factors entering into the great struggle for success.

The principle of telepathy and the law of attraction, through which like attracts like, explain many a failure. If the mind has a tendency to attract from the ether those thought vibrations which harmonize with the dominating thoughts of a given mind, you can easily understand why a negative mind that dwells upon failure and lacks the vitalizing force of self-confidence would not attract a positive mind that is dominated by thoughts of *success*.

Perhaps these explanations are somewhat abstract to the student who has not made any particular study of the functioning processes of the mind, but it seems necessary to inject them into this lesson as a means of enabling the student to understand and make practical use of the subject of this lesson. The imagination is too often regarded merely as an indefinite, untraceable, indescribable something that does nothing but create fiction. It is this popular disregard of the powers of the imagination that has made necessary these more or less abstract references to one of the most important subjects of this course. Not only is the subject of imagination an important factor in this course; but, it is one of the most interesting subjects, as you will observe when you begin to see how it affects all that you do toward the achievement of your *definite chief aim*.

You will see how important is the subject of *imagination* when you stop to realize that it is the only thing in the world over which you have absolute control. Others may deprive you of your material wealth and cheat you in a thousand ways, but no man can deprive you of the control and use of your *imagination*. Men may deal with you unfairly, as men often do; they may deprive you of your liberty, but *they cannot* take from you the privilege of using your *imagination* as you wish.

The most inspiring poem in all literature was written by Leigh Hunt, while he was a poverty-stricken prisoner in an English prison, where he had been unjustly confined because of his advanced views on politics. This poem is entitled Abou Ben Adhem, and it is here re-printed as a reminder that one of the great things a man may do, in his own imagination, is to forgive those who have dealt unjustly with him:

Abou Ben Adhem (may his tribe increase)
Awoke one night from a deep dream of peace,
And saw within the moonlight of his room,
Making it rich and like a lily in bloom,
An angel writing in a book of gold,
Exceeding peace had made Ben Adhem bold,
And to the presence in the room he said:
"What writest thou?"—the vision raised its head,
And, with a look made of all sweet accord,
Answered, "The names of those who love the Lord."
"And is mine one?" said Abou. "Nay, not so,"
Replied the angel,—Abou spoke more low,
But cheerily still; and said, "I pray thee, then,
Write me as one that loves his fellow men."
The angel wrote, and vanished. The next night
It came again, with a great wakening light,
And showed the names whom love of God had blessed,
And, lo! Ben Adhem's name led all the rest!

Civilization, itself, owes its existence to such men as Leigh Hunt, in whose fertile *imaginations* have been pictured the higher and nobler standards of human relationship. Abou Ben Adhem is a poem that will never die, thanks to this man who pictured in his *imagination* the hope of an ideal that is constructive.

The major trouble with this world today lies in our lack of understanding of the power of *imagination,* for if we understood this great power we could use it as a weapon with which to wipe out poverty and misery and injustice and persecution, and this could be done in a single generation. This is a rather broad statement, and no one understands better than the author of this course how useless such a statement would be if the principle upon which it is founded were not explained in terms of the most practical, workaday nature; therefore, let us proceed to describe what is meant.

To make this description understandable we must accept as a reality the principle of telepathy, through the operation of which every thought we release is registering itself in the minds of other people. We need devote no time to proving that telepathy is a reality, for

The man who slanders his fellowman unwittingly uncovers the real nature of his inner self.

the reason that this lesson on *imagination* cannot be of the slightest value to the student who has not sufficiently informed himself to understand and accept telepathy as an established principle. We will take it for granted that you are one who accepts and understands this principle.

You have often heard of "mob psychology," which is nothing more nor less than some strong, dominating idea that has been created in the mind of one or more persons and registers itself in the minds of other persons, through the principle of telepathy. So strong is the power of mob psychology that two men fighting in the street will often start a "free-for-all" fight in which by-standers will engage each other in battle without even knowing what they are fighting about, or with whom they are fighting.

On armistice day, 1918, we had evidence in abundance to prove the reality of the principle of telepathy, on a scale such as the world had never before witnessed. I remember, distinctly, the impression made on my mind on that eventful day. So strong was this impression that it awakened me at about 3 o'clock in the morning, just as effectively as if someone had aroused me by physical force. As I sat up in bed I knew that something out of the ordinary had happened, and so strange and impelling was the effect of this experience that I got up, dressed myself and went out in the streets of Chicago, where I was met by thousands of others who had felt the touch of the same influence. Everyone was asking: *"What has happened?"*

What had happened was this:

Millions of men had received instructions to cease fighting, and their combined joy set into motion a thought wave that swept the entire world and made itself felt in every normal mind that was capable of registering this thought wave. Perhaps never in the history of the world had so many millions of people *thought of the same thing, in the same manner, at the same time*. For once in the history of the world *everybody* felt something in common, and the effect of this harmonized thought was the world-wide "mob psychology" that we witnessed on armistice day. In connection with this statement it will be helpful if you recall what was said about the method of creating a "Master Mind," through the harmony of thought of two or more persons, in the Introduction to this course.

We will bring the application of this principle a little nearer home by showing how it may be made to make or break the harmonious working relationship of a business or industry. You may not have satisfied yourself that it was the harmony of thought of millions of soldiers that registered in the minds of the people of the world and caused the "mob" psychological condition that was everywhere in evidence on armistice day, but you will need no proof that a disgruntled person always disturbs everyone with whom he comes in contact. It is a well established fact that one such person in a place of employment will disrupt the entire organization. The time is almost at hand when neither the workers nor the employers will tolerate the typical "grouch" inside of a place of employment, for the reason that his state of mind registers itself in the minds of those about him, resulting in distrust, suspicion and lack of harmony. The time is near at hand when the workers in a place of employment will no more tolerate one of their own rank and file who is a typical "grouch" than they would a poisonous snake.

Apply the principle in another way: Place among a group of workers one person whose personality is of the positive, optimistic type, and who makes it his business to sow the seeds of harmony around the place where he works, and his influence will reflect itself in every person who works with him.

If every business is "the extended shadow of one man" as Emerson stated, then it behooves that one man to reflect a shadow of confidence and good cheer and optimism and harmony, that these qualities may, in turn, reflect themselves in all who are connected with the business.

In passing to the next step in our application of the power of *imagination* in the attainment of success we will cite some of the most recent and modern examples of its use in the accumulation of material wealth and the perfection of some of the leading inventions of the world.

In approaching this next step it should be borne in mind that "there is nothing new under the sun." Life on this earth may be likened to a great kaleidoscope before which the scenes and facts and material substances are ever shifting and changing, and all any man can do is to take these facts and substances and re-arrange them in new combinations.

The process through which this is done is called *imagination*.

We have stated that the *imagination* is both interpretative and creative in its nature. It can receive impressions or ideas and out of these it can form new combinations.

As our first illustration of the power of *imagination* in modern business achievement, we will take the case of Clarence Saunders, who organized the Piggly-Wiggly system of self-help grocery stores.

Saunders was a grocery clerk in a small southern retail store. One day he was standing in a line, with a tin tray in his hands, waiting his turn to secure food in a cafeteria. He had never earned more than $20.00 a week before that time, and no one had ever noticed anything about him that indicated unusual ability, but something took place in his mind, as he stood in that line of waiting people, that put his *imagination* to work. With the aid of his *imagination* he lifted that "self-help" idea out of the cafeteria in which he found it (not creating anything new, merely shifting an old idea into a new use) and set it down in a grocery store. In an instant the Piggly-Wiggly chain-store grocery plan had been created and Clarence Saunders, the twenty-dollar-a-week grocery clerk, rapidly became the million-dollar chain-store groceryman of America.

Where, in that transaction, do you see the slightest indication of a performance that you could not duplicate?

Analyze this transaction and measure it by the previous lessons of this course and you will see that Clarence Saunders created a very *definite purpose.* He supported this purpose with sufficient *self-confidence* to cause him to take the *initiative* to transform it into reality. His *imagination* was the workshop in which these three factors, *definite purpose, self-confidence* and *initiative* were brought together and made to supply the momentum for the first step in the organization of the Piggly-Wiggly plan.

Thus are great ideas changed into realities.

When Thomas A. Edison invented the incandescent electric light bulb he merely brought together two old,

> *It will make a big difference to you whether you are a person with a message or a person with a grievance.*

well known principles and associated them in a new combination. Mr. Edison and practically all others who were informed on the subject of electricity, knew that a light could be produced by heating a small wire with electricity, but the difficult problem was to do this without burning the wire in two. In his experimental research Mr. Edison tried out every conceivable sort of wire, hoping to find some substance that would withstand the tremendous heat to which it had to be subjected before a light could be produced.

His invention was half completed, but it was of no practical value until he could find the missing link that would supply the other half. After thousands of tests and much combining of old ideas in his *imagination,* Edison finally found this missing link. In his study of physics he had learned, as all other students of this subject learn, that there can be no combustion without the presence of oxygen. He of course knew that the difficulty with his electric light apparatus was the lack of a method through which to control the heat. When it occurred to him that there could be *no* combustion where there was *no* oxygen he placed the little wire of his electric light apparatus inside of a glass globe, shut out *all* the oxygen, and lo! the mighty incandescent light was a reality.

When the sun goes down tonight you step to the wall, press a button and bring it back again, a performance that would have mystified the people of a few generations ago, and yet there is no mystery back of your act. Thanks to the use of Edison's *imagination,* you have simply brought together two principles both of which were in existence since the beginning of time.

No one who knew him intimately ever accredited Andrew Carnegie with unusual ability, or the power of genius, except in one respect, and that was his ability to select men who *could* and *would* co-operate in a spirit of harmony, in carrying out his wishes. But what additional ability did he need in the accumulation of his millions of dollars?

Any man who understands the principle of *organized effort,* as Carnegie understood it, and knows enough about men to be able to select just those types that are needed in the performance of a given task, could duplicate all that Carnegie accomplished.

Carnegie was a man of *imagination*. He first created a *definite purpose* and then surrounded himself with men who had the training and the vision and the capacity necessary for the transformation of that purpose into reality. Carnegie did not always create his own plans for the attainment of his *definite purpose*. He made it *his* business to know what he wanted, then found the men who could create plans through which to procure it. And that was not only *imagination,* it was genius of the highest order.

But it should be made clear that men of Mr. Carnegie's type are not the only ones who can make profitable use of *imagination*. This great power is as available to the beginner in business as it is to the man who has "arrived."

One morning Charles M. Schwab's private car was backed on the side-track at his Bethlehem Steel plant. As he alighted from his car he was met by a young man stenographer who announced that he had come to make sure that any letters or telegrams Mr. Schwab might wish to write would be taken care of promptly. No one told this young man to be on hand, but he had enough *imagination* to see that his being there would not hurt his chances of advancement. From that day on, this young man was "marked" for promotion. Mr. Schwab singled him out for promotion because he had done that which any of the dozen or so other stenographers in the employ of the Bethlehem Steel Company might have done, but didn't. Today this same man is the president of one of the largest drug concerns in the world and has all of this world's goods and wares that he wants and much more than he needs.

A few years ago I received a letter from a young man who had just finished Business College, and who wanted to secure employment in my office. With his letter he sent a crisp ten-dollar bill that had never been folded. The letter read as follows:

I have just finished a commercial course in a first-class business college and I want a position in your office because I realize how much it would be worth to a young man, just starting out on his business career, to have the privilege of working under the direction of a man like you.

"If the enclosed ten-dollar bill is sufficient to pay for the time you would spend in giving me my first week's instructions I want you to accept it. I will work the first month without pay and you may set my wages after that at whatever I prove to be worth.

"I want this job more than I ever wanted anything in my life and I am willing to make any reasonable sacrifice to get it.   *Very cordially,*

This young man got his chance in my office. His *imagination* gained for him the opportunity that he wanted, and before his first month had expired the president of a life insurance company who heard of this incident offered the young man a private secretaryship at a substantial salary. He is today an official of one of the largest life insurance companies in the world.

Some years ago a young man wrote to Thomas A. Edison for a position. For some reason Mr. Edison did not reply. By no means discouraged on this account the young man made up his mind that he would not only get a reply from Mr. Edison, but what was more important still, he would actually secure the position he sought. He lived a long distance from West Orange, New Jersey, where the Edison industries are located, and he did not have the money with which to pay his railroad fare. But *he did have imagination*. He went to West Orange in a freight car, got his interview, told his story in person and got the job he sought.

Today this same man lives in Bradentown, Florida. He has retired from active business, having made all the money he needs. His name, in case you wish to confirm my statements, is Edwin C. Barnes.

By using his *imagination,* Mr. Barnes saw the advantage of close association with a man like Thomas A. Edison. He saw that such an association would give him the opportunity to study Mr. Edison, and at the same time it would bring him in contact with Mr. Edison's friends, who are among the most influential people of the world.

These are but a few cases in connection with which I have personally observed how men have climbed to high places in the world and accumulated wealth in abundance by making practical use of their *imagination*.

Theodore Roosevelt engraved his name on the tablets of time by one single act during his tenure of office as President of the United States, and after all else that he did while in that office will have been forgotten this one transaction will record him in history as a man of *imagination*.

He started the steam shovels to work on the Panama Canal.

Every President, from Washington on up to Roosevelt, could have started the canal and it would have been completed, but it seemed such a colossal undertaking that it required not only *imagination* but daring courage as well. Roosevelt had both, and the people of the United States have the canal.

> *The reason most people do not like to hear the story of your troubles is that they have a big flock of their own.*

At the age of forty—the age at which the average man begins to think he is too old to start anything new—James J. Hill was still sitting at the telegraph key, at a salary of $30.00 per month. He had no capital. He had no influential friends with capital, but he did have that which is more powerful than either—*imagination*.

In his mind's eye he saw a great railway system that would penetrate the undeveloped northwest and unite the Atlantic and Pacific oceans. So vivid was his *imagination* that he made others see the advantages of such a railway system, and from there on the story is familiar enough to every school-boy. I would emphasize the part of the story that most people never mention—that Hill's Great Northern Railway system became a reality in his own *imagination* first. The railroad was built with steel rails and wooden cross ties, just as other railroads are built, and these things were paid for with capital that was secured in very much the same manner that capital for all railroads is secured, but if you want the real story of James J. Hill's success you must go back to that little country railway station where he worked at $30.00 a month and there pick up the little threads that he wove into a mighty railroad, with materials no more visible than the thoughts which he organized in his *imagination*.

What a mighty power is *imagination*, the workshop of the soul, in which *thoughts* are woven into railroads and skyscrapers and mills and factories and all manner of material wealth.

"I hold it true that thoughts are things;

They're endowed with bodies and breath and wings;

And that we send them forth to fill

The world with good results or ill.

That which we call our secret thought

Speeds forth to earth's remotest spot,

Leaving its blessings or its woes,

Like tracks behind it as it goes.

We build our future, thought by thought,

For good or ill, yet know it not,

Yet so the universe was wrought.

Thought is another name for fate;

Choose, then, thy destiny and wait,

For love brings love and hate brings hate."

If your *imagination* is the mirror of your soul, then you have a perfect right to stand before that mirror and see yourself as you wish to be. You have the right to see reflected in that magic mirror the mansion you intend to own, the factory you intend to manage, the bank of which you intend to be president, the station in life you intend to occupy. *Your imagination* belongs to you! Use it! The more you use it the more efficiently it will serve you.

At the east end of the great Brooklyn Bridge, in New York City, an old man conducts a cobbler shop. When the engineers began driving stakes and marking the foundation place for that great steel structure this man shook his head and said *"It can't be done!"*

Now he looks out from his dingy little shoe-repair shop, shakes his head and asks himself: *"How did they do it?"*

He saw the bridge grow before his very eyes and still he lacks the *imagination* to analyze that which he saw. The engineer who planned the bridge saw it a reality long before a single shovel of dirt had been removed for the foundation stones. The bridge became a reality in his *imagination* because he had trained that *imagination* to weave new combinations out of old ideas.

Through recent experiments in the department of electricity one of our great educational institutions of America has discovered how to put flowers to sleep and wake them up again, with electric "sunlight." This discovery makes possible the growth of vegetables and flowers without the aid of sunshine. In a few more years the city dweller will be raising a crop of vegetables on his back porch, with the aid of a few boxes of dirt and a few electric lights, with some new vegetable maturing every month of the year.

This new discovery, plus a little *imagination,* plus Luther Burbank's discoveries in the field of horticulture, and lo! the city dweller will not only grow vegetables all the year around, within the confines of his back porch, but he will grow bigger vegetables than any which the modern gardener grows in the open sunlight.

In one of the cities on the coast of California all of the land that was suitable for building lots had been developed and put into use. On one side of the city there were some steep hills that could not be used for building purposes, and on the other side the land was unsuitable for buildings because it was so low that the back-water covered it once a day.

A man of *imagination* came to this city. Men of *imagination* usually have keen minds, and this man was no exception. The first day of his arrival he saw the possibilities for making money out of real estate. He secured an option on those hills that were unsuitable for use because of their steepness. He also secured an option on the ground that was unsuitable for use because of the back-water that covered it daily. He secured these options at a very low price because the ground was supposed to be without substantial value.

With the use of a few tons of explosives he turned those steep hills into loose dirt. With the aid of a few tractors and some road scrapers he leveled the ground down and turned it into beautiful building lots, and with the aid of a few mules and carts he dumped the surplus dirt on the low ground and raised it above the water level, thereby turning it into beautiful building lots.

He made a substantial fortune, *for what?*

For removing some dirt from where it was not needed to where it was needed! *For mixing some useless dirt with imagination!*

The people of that little city gave this man credit for being a genius; and he was—the same sort of genius that any one of them could have been had he used his *imagination* as this man used his.

In the field of chemistry it is possible to mix two or more chemical ingredients in such proportions that the mere act of mixing gives each of the ingredients a tremendous amount of energy that it did not possess. It is also possible to mix certain chemical ingredients in such proportions that *all the ingredients of the combination take on an entirely different nature,* as in the case of H_2O, which is a mixture of two parts hydrogen and one part oxygen, creating water.

Chemistry is not the only field in which a combination of various physical materials can be so assembled that each takes on a greater value, or the result is a product entirely foreign in nature to that of its component parts. The man who blew up those useless hills of dirt and stone and removed the surplus from where it was not needed over to the low-land, where it was needed, gave that dirt and stone a value that it did not have before.

A ton of pig-iron is worth but little. Add to that pig-iron carbon, silicon, manganese, sulphur and phosphorus, in the right proportions, and you have transformed it into steel, which is of much greater value. Add still other substances, in the right proportion, including some skilled labor, and that same ton of steel is transformed into watch-springs worth a small fortune. But, in all these transformation processes the one ingredient that is worth most is the one that has no material form—*imagination!*

Here lie great piles of loose brick, lumber, nails and glass. In its present form it is worse than useless for it is a nuisance and an eye-sore. But mix it with the architect's *imagination* and add some skilled labor and lo! it becomes a beautiful mansion worth a king's ransom.

On one of the great highways between New York and Philadelphia stood an old ramshackle, time-worn barn, worth less than fifty dollars. With the aid of a little lumber and some cement, plus *imagination,* this old barn has been turned into a beautiful automobile supply station that earns a small fortune for the man who supplied the *imagination.*

Across the street from my office is a little print-shop that earns coffee and rolls for its owner and his helper, but no more. Less than a dozen blocks away stands one of the most modern printing plants in the world, whose owner spends most of his time traveling and has far more wealth than he will ever use. Twenty-two years ago those two printers were in business together.

The one who owns the big print-shop had the good judgment to ally himself with a man who mixed *imagination* with printing. This man of *imagination* is a writer of advertisements and he keeps the printing plant with which he is associated supplied with more business than it can handle by analyzing its clients' business, creating attractive advertising features and supplying the necessary printed material with which to make these features

I know I am here. I know I had nothing to do with my coming, and I shall have but little, if anything, to do with my going, therefore I will not worry because worries are of no avail.

of service. This plant receives top-notch prices for its printing because the *imagination* mixed with that printing produces a product that most printers cannot supply.

In the city of Chicago the level of a certain boulevard was raised, which spoiled a row of beautiful residences because the side-walk was raised to the level of the second story windows. While the property owners were bemoaning their ill-fortune a man of *imagination* came along, purchased the property for a "song," converted the second stories into business property, and now enjoys a handsome income from his rentals.

As you read these lines please keep in mind all that was stated in the beginning of this lesson; especially the fact that the greatest and most profitable thing you can do with your *imagination* is the act of rearranging old ideas in new combinations.

If you properly use your imagination it will help you convert your failures and mistakes into assets of priceless value; it will lead you to discovery of a truth known only to those who use their *imagination;* namely, that the greatest reverses and misfortunes of life often open the door to golden opportunities.

One of the finest and most highly paid engravers in the United States was formerly a mail-carrier. One day he was fortunate enough to be on a street car that met with an accident and had one of his legs cut off. The street railway company paid him $5,000.00 for his leg. With this money he paid his way through school and became an engraver. The product of his hands, plus his *imagination,* is worth much more than he could earn with his legs, as a mail-carrier. He discovered that he had *imagination* when it became necessary to re-direct his efforts, as a result of the street car accident.

You will never know what is your capacity for achievement until you learn how to mix your efforts with *imagination.* The products of your hands, minus *imagination,* will yield you but a small return, but those selfsame hands, when properly guided by *imagination,* can be made to earn you all the material wealth you can use.

There are two ways in which you can profit by *imagination.* You can develop this faculty in your own mind, or you can ally yourself with those who have already developed it. Andrew Carnegie did both. He not only made use of his own fertile *imagination,* but he gathered around him a group of other men who also possessed this essential quality, for his *definite* purpose in life called for specialists whose *imagination* ran in numerous directions. In that group of men that constituted Mr. Carnegie's "master mind" were men whose *imaginations* were confined to the field of chemistry. He had other men in the group whose *imaginations* were confined to finances. He had still others whose *imaginations* were confined to salesmanship, one of whom was Charles M. Schwab, who is said to have been the most able salesman on Mr. Carnegie's staff.

If you feel that your own *imagination* is inadequate you should form an alliance with someone whose *imagination* is sufficiently developed to supply your deficiency. There are various forms of alliance. For example, there is the alliance of marriage and the alliance of a business partnership and the alliance of friendship and the alliance of employer and employee. Not all men have the capacity to serve their own best interests as employers, and those who haven't this capacity may profit by allying themselves with men of *imagination* who have such capacity.

It is said that Mr. Carnegie made more millionaires of his employees than any other employer in the steel business. Among these was Charles M. Schwab, who displayed evidence of the soundest sort of *imagination* by his good judgment in allying himself with Mr. Carnegie. It is no disgrace to serve in the capacity of employee. To the contrary, it often proves to be the most profitable side of an alliance since not all men are fitted to assume the responsibility of directing other men.

Perhaps there is no field of endeavor in which *imagination* plays such an important part as it does in salesmanship. The master salesman sees the merits of the goods he sells or the service he is rendering, in his own *imagination,* and if he fails to do so he will not make the sale.

A few years ago a sale was made which is said to have been the most far-reaching and important sale of its kind ever made. The object of the sale was not merchandise, but the freedom of a man who was confined in the Ohio penitentiary and the development of a prison reform system that promises a sweeping change in the method of dealing with unfortunate men and women who have become entangled in the meshes of the law.

That you may observe just how *imagination* plays the leading part in salesmanship I will analyze this sale for you, with due apologies for personal references, which cannot be avoided without destroying much of the value of the illustration.

A few years ago I was invited to speak before the inmates of the Ohio penitentiary. When I stepped upon the platform I saw in the audience before me a man whom I had known as a successful business man, more than ten years previously. That man was B——, whose pardon I later secured, and the story of whose release has been spread upon the front page of practically every newspaper in the United States. Perhaps you will recall it.

After I had completed my address I interviewed Mr. B—— and found out that he had been sentenced for forgery, for a period of twenty years. After he had told me his story I said:

"I will have you out of here in less than sixty days!"

With a forced smile he replied: "I admire your spirit but question your judgment. Why, do you know that at least twenty influential men have tried every means at their command to get me released, without success? *It can't be done!*"

I suppose it was that last remark—*It can't be done*—that challenged me to show him that it could be done. I returned to New York City and requested my wife to pack her trunks and get ready for an indefinite stay in the city of Columbus, where the Ohio penitentiary is located.

I had a *definite purpose* in mind! That purpose was to get B—— out of the Ohio penitentiary. Not only did I have in mind securing his release, but I intended to do it in such a way that his release would erase from his breast the scarlet letter of "convict" and at the same time reflect credit upon all who helped to bring about his release.

Not once did I doubt that I would bring about his release, for no salesman can make a sale if he doubts that he can do it. My wife and I returned to Columbus and took up permanent headquarters.

The next day I called on the governor of Ohio and stated the object of my visit in about these words:

"Governor: I have come to ask you to release B—— from the Ohio penitentiary. I have sound reason for asking his release and I hope you will give him his freedom at once, but I have come prepared to stay until he is released, no matter how long that may be.

"During his imprisonment B—— has inaugurated a system of correspondence instruction in the Ohio penitentiary, as you of course know. He has influenced 1729 of the 2518 prisoners of the Ohio penitentiary to take up courses of instruction. He has managed to beg sufficient textbooks and lesson materials with which to keep these men at work on their lessons, and has done this without a penny of expense to the state of Ohio. The warden and the chaplain of the penitentiary tell me that he has carefully observed the prison rules. Surely a man who can influence 1729 men to turn their efforts toward self-betterment cannot be a very bad sort of fellow.

> *If you have been wise and successful I congratulate you; unless you are unable to forget how successful you have been, then I pity you.*

"I have come to ask you to release B—— because I wish to place him at the head of a prison school that will give the 160,000 inmates of the other penitentiaries of the United States a chance to profit by his influence. I am prepared to assume full responsibility for his conduct after his release.

"That is my case, but, before you give me your answer, I want you to know that I am not unmindful of the fact that your enemies will probably criticize you if you release him; in fact if you release him it may cost you many votes if you run for office again."

With his fist clinched and his broad jaw set firmly Governor Vic Donahey of Ohio said:

"If that is what you want with B—— I will release him if it costs me five thousand votes. However, before I sign the pardon I want you to see the Clemency Board and secure its favorable recommendation. I want you also to secure the favorable recommendation of the warden and the chaplain of the Ohio penitentiary. You know a governor is amenable to the Court of Public Opinion, and these gentlemen are the representatives of that Court."

The sale had been made! and the whole transaction had required less than five minutes.

The next day I returned to the governor's office, accompanied by the chaplain of the Ohio penitentiary, and notified the governor that the Clemency Board, the Warden and the Chaplain all joined in recommending the release. Three days later the pardon was signed and B—— walked through the big iron gates, a free man.

I have cited the details to show you that there was nothing difficult about the transaction. The groundwork for the release had all been prepared before I came upon the scene. B—— had done that, by his good conduct and the service he had rendered those 1729 prisoners. When he created the world's first prison correspondence school system he created the key that unlocked the prison doors for himself.

Why, then, had the others who asked for his release failed to secure it?

They failed because they used no *imagination!*

Perhaps they asked the governor for B——'s release on the ground that his parents were prominent people, or on the ground that he was a college graduate and not a bad sort of fellow. *They failed to supply the governor of Ohio with a sufficient motive to justify him in granting a pardon,* for had this not been so he would undoubtedly have released B—— long before I came upon the scene and asked for his release.

Before I went to see the governor I went over all the facts and in my own *imagination* I saw myself in the governor's place and made up my mind what sort of a presentation would appeal most strongly to me if I were in reality in his place.

When I asked for B——'s release I did so in the name of the 160,000 unfortunate men and women inmates of the prisons of the United States who would enjoy the benefits of the correspondence school system that he had created. I said nothing about his prominent parents. I said nothing about my friendship with him during former years. I said nothing about his being a deserving fellow. All these matters might have been used as sound reasons for his release, but they seemed insignificant when compared with the bigger and sounder reason that his release would be of help to 160,000 other people who would feel the influence of his correspondence school system after his release.

When the governor of Ohio came to a decision I doubt not that B—— was of secondary importance as far as his decision was concerned. The governor no doubt saw a possible benefit, not to B—— alone, but to 160,000 other men and women who needed the influence that B—— could supply, if released.

And that was imagination!

It was also salesmanship! In speaking of the incident after it was over, one of the men who had worked diligently for more than a year in trying to secure B——'s freedom, asked:

"How did you do it?"

And I replied: "It was the easiest task I ever performed, because most of the work had been done before I took hold of it. In fact I didn't do it—B—— did it himself."

This man looked at me in bewilderment. He did not see that which I am here trying to make clear; namely, that practically all difficult tasks are easily performed if one approaches them from the right angle. There were two important factors entering B——'s release. The first was the fact that he had supplied the material for a good case before I took it in charge; and the second was the fact that before I called on the governor of Ohio I so completely convinced myself that I had a right to ask for B——'s release that I had no difficulty in presenting my case effectively.

Go back to what was stated in the beginning of this lesson, on the subject of telepathy, and apply it to this case. The governor could tell, long before I had stated my mission, that *I knew I had a good case*. If my brain did not telegraph this thought to his brain, then the look of self-confidence in my eyes and the positive tone of my voice made obvious my belief in the merits of my case.

Again I apologize for these personal references with the explanation that I have used them only because the whole of America was familiar with the B—— case that I have described. I disclaim all credit for the small part I played in the case, for I did nothing except use my *imagination* as an assembly room in which to piece together the factors out of which the sale was made. I did nothing except that which any salesman of *imagination* could have done.

It requires considerable courage to prompt one to use the personal pronoun as freely as it has been used in relating the facts connected with this case, but justification lies in the value of application of the principle of *imagination* to a case with which nearly everybody is familiar.

I cannot recall an incident in my entire life in connection with which the soundness of the fifteen factors that enter into this Reading Course was more clearly manifested than it was in securing the release of B———.

It is but another link in a long chain of evidence that proves to my entire satisfaction the power of *imagination* as a factor in salesmanship. There are endless millions of approaches to every problem, but there is *only one* best approach. Find this one best approach and your problem is easily solved. No matter how much merit your goods may have, there are millions of *wrong* ways in which to offer them. Your *imagination* will assist you in finding the *right* way.

In your search for the *right* way in which to offer your merchandise or your services, remember this peculiar trait of mankind:

Men will grant favors that you request for the benefit of a third person when they would not grant them if requested for your benefit.

Compare this statement with the fact that I asked the governor of Ohio to release B———, not as a favor to me, and not as a favor to B———, but, for the benefit of 160,000 unfortunate inmates of the prisons of America.

Salesmen of *imagination* always offer their wares in such terminology that the advantages of those wares to the prospective purchaser are obvious. It is seldom that any man makes a purchase of merchandise or renders another a favor just to accommodate the salesman. It is a prominent trait of human nature that prompts us all to do that which advances our own interests. This is a cold, indisputable fact, claims of the idealist to the contrary notwithstanding.

To be perfectly plain, *men are selfish!*

To understand the truth is to understand how to present your case, whether you are asking for the release of a man from prison or offering for sale some commodity. In your own *imagination* so plan your presentation of your case that the strongest and most impelling advantages to the buyer are made plain.

This is *imagination!*

A farmer moved to the city, taking with him his well trained shepherd dog. He soon found that the dog was out of place in the city, so he decided to "get rid of him." (Note the words in quotation.) Taking the dog with him he went out into the country and rapped on

> *I never see a person trying to disclose the scarlet letter on another's breast that I do not wonder if he doesn't carry some mark of disgrace which would have ruined him had he been overtaken by justice.*

the door of a farm-house. A man came hobbling to the door, on crutches. The man with the dog greeted the man in the house in these words:

"You wouldn't care to buy a fine shepherd dog, that I wish to get rid of, would you?"

The man on crutches replied, "*No!*" and closed the door.

The man with the dog called at half a dozen other farm-houses, asking the same question, and received the same answer. He made up his mind that no one wanted the dog and returned to the city. That evening he was telling of his misfortune, to a man of *imagination*. The man heard how the owner of the dog had tried in vain to "get rid of him."

"Let me dispose of the dog for you," said the man of *imagination*. The owner was willing. The next morning the man of *imagination* took the dog out into the country and stopped at the first farm-house at which the owner of the dog had called the day before. The same old man hobbled out on crutches and answered the knock at the door.

The man of *imagination* greeted him in this fashion:

"I see you are all crippled with rheumatism. What you need is a fine dog to run errands for you. I have a dog here that has been trained to bring home the cows, drive away wild animals, herd the sheep and perform other useful services. You may have this dog for a hundred dollars."

"All right," said the crippled man, "I'll take him!"

That, too, was *imagination!*

No one wants a dog that someone else wants to "get rid of," but most anyone would like to own a dog that would herd sheep and bring home the cows and perform other useful services.

The dog was the same one that the crippled buyer had refused the day before, but the man who sold the dog was not the man who had tried to "get rid of him." If you use your *imagination* you will know that no one wants anything that someone else is trying to "get rid of."

Remember that which was said about the Law of Attraction through the operation of which "like attracts like." If you look and act the part of a failure you will attract nothing but failures.

Whatever your life-work may be, it calls for the use of *imagination*.

Niagara Falls was nothing but a great mass of roaring water until a man of *imagination* harnessed it and converted the wasted energy into electric current that now turns the wheels of industry. Before this man of *imagination* came along millions of people had seen and heard those roaring falls, but lacked the *imagination* to harness them.

The first Rotary Club of the world was born in the fertile *imagination* of Paul Harris, of Chicago, who saw in this child of his brain an effective means of cultivating prospective clients and the extension of his law practice. The ethics of the legal profession forbid advertising in the usual way, but Paul Harris' *imagination* found a way to extend his law practice without advertising in the usual way.

If the winds of Fortune are temporarily blowing against you, remember that you can harness them and make them carry you toward your *definite purpose,* through the use of your *imagination.* A kite rises against the wind—not with it!

Dr. Frank Crane was a struggling "third-rate" preacher until the starvation wages of the clergy forced him to use his *imagination.* Now he earns upward of a hundred thousand dollars a year for an hour's work a day, writing essays.

Bud Fisher once worked for a mere pittance, but he now earns seventy-five thousand dollars a year by making folks grin, with his Mutt and Jeff comic strip. No art goes into his drawings, therefore he must be selling his *imagination.*

Woolworth was a poorly paid clerk in a retail store—poorly paid, perhaps, because he had not yet found out that he had *imagination.* Before he died he built the tallest office building in the world and girdled the United States with Five and Ten Cent Stores, through the use of his *imagination.*

You will observe, by analyzing these illustrations, that a close study of human nature played an important part in the achievements mentioned. To make profitable use of your *imagination* you must make it give you a keen insight into the motives that cause men to do or refrain from doing a given act. If your *imagination* leads you to understand how quickly people grant your requests when those requests appeal to their self-interest, you can have practically anything you go after.

I saw my wife make a very clever sale to our baby not long ago. The baby was pounding the top of our mahogany library table with a spoon. When my wife reached for the spoon the baby refused to give it up, but being a woman of *imagination* she offered the baby a nice stick of red candy; he dropped the spoon immediately and centered his attention on the more desirable object.

That was *imagination!* It was also salesmanship. She won her point without using force.

I was riding in an automobile with a friend who was driving beyond the speed limit. An officer rode up on a motorcycle and told my friend he was under arrest for speeding. The friend smiled pleasantly at the officer and said: "I'm sorry to have brought you out in all this rain, but I wanted to make the ten o'clock train with my friend here, and I was hitting it up around thirty-five miles an hour."

"No, you were only going twenty-eight miles an hour," replied the officer, "and as long as you are so nice about it I will let you off this time if you will watch yourself hereafter."

And that, too, was *imagination!* Even a traffic cop will listen to reason when approached in the right manner, but woe unto the motorist who tries to bully the cop into believing his speedometer was not registering properly.

There is one form of *imagination* against which I would caution you. It is the brand which prompts some people to *imagine* that they can get something for nothing, or that they can force themselves ahead in the world without observing the rights of others. There are more than 160,000 prisoners in the penal institutions of the United States, practically every one of whom is in prison because he *imagined* he could play the game of life without observing the rights of his fellow men.

There is a man in the Ohio penitentiary who has served more than thirty-five years of time for forgery, and the largest amount he ever got from his misapplication of *imagination* was twelve dollars.

There are a few people who direct their *imaginations* in the vain attempt to work out a way to show what happens when "an immovable body comes in contact with an irresistible force," but these types belong in the psychopathic hospitals.

There is also another form of misapplied *imagination;* namely, that of the young boy or girl who knows more about life than his or her "Dad." But this form is subject to modification with *time.* My own boys have taught me many things that my "Dad" tried, in vain, to teach me when I was their age.

Time and *imagination* (which is often but the product of time) teach us many things, but nothing of more importance than this:

That all men are much alike in many ways.

We all like commendation and many of us like flattery, but it is a debatable question as to whether the indulgence of these tendencies builds character and strength and individuality.

If you would know what your customer is thinking, Mr. Salesman, study yourself and find out what *you* would be thinking if you were in your customer's place.

Study yourself, find out what are the motives which actuate you in the performance of certain deeds and cause you to refrain from performing other deeds, and you will have gone far toward perfecting yourself in the accurate use of *imagination.*

The detective's biggest asset is *imagination*. The first question he asks, when called in to solve a crime is: "*What was the motive?*" If he can find out the motive he can usually find the perpetrator of the crime.

A man who had lost a horse posted a reward of five dollars for its return. Several days later a boy who was supposed to have been "weak-minded" came leading the horse home and claimed the reward. The owner was curious to know how the boy found the horse. "How did you ever think where to look for the horse?" he asked, and the boy replied, "Well, I just thought where I would have gone if I had been a horse and went there, and he had." Not so bad for a "weak-minded" fellow. Some who are not accused of being weak-minded go all the way through life without displaying as much evidence of *imagination* as did this boy.

If you want to know what the other fellow will do, use your *imagination,* put yourself in his place and find out what you would have done. That's *imagination*.

Every person should be somewhat of a dreamer. Every business needs the dreamer. Every industry and every profession needs him. But, the dreamer must be, also, a doer; or else he must form an alliance with someone who can and does translate dreams into reality.

The greatest nation upon the face of this earth was conceived, born and nurtured through the early days of its childhood, as the result of *imagination* in the minds of men who combined dreams with *action!*

Your mind is capable of creating many new and useful combinations of old ideas, but the most important thing it can create is a *definite chief aim* that will give you that which you most desire.

Your *definite chief aim* can be speedily translated into reality after you have fashioned it in the cradle of your *imagination*. If you have faithfully followed the instructions set down for your guidance in Lesson One you are now well on the road toward success, because you know what it is that you want, and you have a plan for getting that which you want.

The battle for the achievement of success is half won when one knows definitely what is wanted. The battle is all over except the "shouting" when one knows what is wanted and has made up his mind to get it, whatever the price may be.

The selection of a *definite chief aim* calls for the use of both *imagination* and decision! The power of decision grows with use. Prompt decision in forcing the *imagination* to create a *definite chief aim* renders more powerful the capacity to reach decisions in other matters.

Adversities and temporary defeat are generally blessings in disguise, for the reason that they force one to use both *imagination* and decision. This is why a man usually makes a better fight when his back is to the wall and he knows there is no retreat. He then reaches the decision to fight instead of running.

The *imagination* is never quite so active as it is when one faces some emergency calling for quick and definite decision and action.

In these moments of emergency men have reached decisions, built plans, used their *imagination* in such a manner that they became known as geniuses. Many a genius has been born out of the necessity for unusual stimulation of the *imagination,* as the result of some trying experience which forced quick thought and prompt decision.

It is a well known fact that the only manner in which an overpampered boy or girl may be made to become useful is by forcing him or her to become self-sustaining. This calls for the exercise of both *imagination* and decision, neither of which would be used except out of necessity.

The Reverend P. W. Welshimer is the pastor of a church in Canton, Ohio, where he has been located for nearly a quarter of a century. Ordinarily pastors do not remain at the head of one church for so great a length of time, and Reverend Welshimer would have been no exception to this rule if he had not mixed *imagination* with his pastoral duties.

Three years constitute the usual time that one pastor may remain in a given pastorate without wearing out his welcome.

The church of which Reverend Welshimer is the leader has a Sunday School of over 5,000 members—the largest membership enjoyed by any church in the United States.

No pastor could have remained at the head of one church for a quarter of a century, with the full consent of his followers, and have built up a Sunday School of this size, without employing the Laws of Initiative and Leadership, a Definite Chief Aim, Self-confidence and Imagination.

The author of this course made it his business to study the methods employed by Reverend Welshimer, and they are here described for the benefit of the students of this philosophy.

It is a well known fact that church factions, jealousy, etc., often lead to disagreements which make a change in leaders essential. Reverend Welshimer has steered around this common obstacle by a unique application of the Law of Imagination. When a new member comes into his church he immediately assigns a DEFINITE task to that member—one that suits the temperament, training and business qualifications of the individual, as nearly as possible—and, to use the minister's own words, he "keeps each member so busy pulling for the church that there is no time left for kicking or disagreeing with other members."

Not a bad policy for application in the field of business, or in any other field. The old saying that "idle hands are the devil's best tools" is more than a mere play upon words, for it is true.

Give any man something to do that he likes to do, and keep him busy doing it, and he will not be apt to degenerate into a disorganizing force. If any member of the Sunday School misses attendance twice in succession a committee from the church calls to find out the reason for the failure to attend. There is a "committee" job for practically every member of the church. In this way Reverend Welshimer delegates to the members, themselves, the responsibility of rounding up the delinquents and keeping them interested in church affairs. He is an organizer of the highest type. His efforts have attracted the attention of business men throughout the country, and times too numerous to be mentioned he has been offered positions, at fancy salaries, by banks, steel plants, business houses, etc., that recognized in him a real Leader.

In the basement of the church Reverend Welshimer operates a first-class printing plant where he publishes, weekly, a very creditable church paper that goes to all the members. The production and distribution of this paper is another source of employment which keeps the church members out of mischief, as practically all of them take some sort of an active interest in it. The paper is devoted exclusively to the affairs of the church as a whole, and those of the individual members. It is read by each member, line by line, because there is always a chance that each member's name may be mentioned in the news locals.

The church has a well trained choir and an orchestra that would be a credit to some of the largest theaters. Here Reverend Welshimer serves the double purpose of supplying entertainment and at the same time keeping the more "temperamental" members who are artists employed so they, also, remain out of mischief, incidentally giving them a chance to do that which they like best.

The late Dr. Harper, who was formerly president of the University of Chicago, was one of the most efficient college presidents of his time. He had a penchant for raising funds in large amounts. It was he who induced John D. Rockefeller to contribute millions of dollars to the support of the University of Chicago.

It may be helpful to the student of this philosophy to study Dr. Harper's technique, because he was a Leader of the highest order. Moreover, I have his own word for it that his leadership was never a matter of chance or accident, but always the result of carefully planned procedure.

The following incident will serve to show just how Dr. Harper made use of *imagination* in raising money in large sums:

He needed an extra million dollars for the construction of a new building. Taking inventory of the wealthy men of Chicago to whom he might turn for this large sum, he decided upon two men, each of whom was a millionaire, and both were bitter enemies.

We cannot sow thistles and reap clover. Nature simply does not run things that way. She goes by cause and effect.

One of these men was, at that time, the head of the Chicago Street Railway system. Choosing the noon hour, when the office force and this man's secretary, in particular, would be apt to be out at lunch, Dr. Harper nonchalantly strolled into the office, and, finding no one on guard at the outer door, walked into the office of his intended "victim," whom he surprised by his appearance unannounced.

"My name is Harper," said the doctor, "and I am president of the University of Chicago. Pardon my intrusion, but I found no one in the outer office (which was no mere accident) so I took the liberty of walking on in.

"I have thought of you and your street railway system many many times. You have built up a wonderful system, and I understand that you have made lots of money for your efforts. I never think of you, however, without its occurring to me that one of these days you will be passing out into the Great Unknown, and after you are gone there will be nothing left as a monument to your name, because others will take over your money, and money has a way of losing its identity very quickly, as soon as it changes hands.

"I have often thought of offering you the opportunity to perpetuate your name by permitting you to build a new Hall out on the University grounds, and naming it after you. I would have offered you this opportunity long ago had it not been for the fact that one of the members of our Board wishes the honor to go to Mr. X—— (the street car head's enemy). Personally, however, I have always favored you and I still favor you, and if I have your permission to do so I am going to try to swing the opposition over to you.

"I have not come to ask for any decision today, however, as I was just passing and thought it a good time to drop in and meet you. Think the matter over and if you wish to talk to me about it again, telephone me at your leisure.

"Good day, sir! I am happy to have had this opportunity of meeting you."

With this he bowed himself out without giving the head of the street car company a chance to say either yes or no. In fact the street car man had very little chance to do any talking. Dr. Harper did the talking. That was as he planned it to be. He went into the office merely to plant the seed, believing that it would germinate and spring into life in due time.

His belief was not without foundation. He had hardly returned to his office at the University when the telephone rang. The street car man was on the other end of the wire. He asked for an appointment with Dr. Harper, which was granted, and the two met in Dr. Harper's office the next morning, and the check for a million dollars was in Dr. Harper's hands an hour later.

Despite the fact that Dr. Harper was a small, rather insignificant-looking man it was said of him that "he had a way about him that enabled him to get everything he went after."

And as to this "way" that he was reputed to have had—what was it?

It was nothing more nor less than his understanding of the power of Imagination. Suppose he had gone to the office of the street car head and asked for an appointment. Sufficient time would have elapsed between the time he called and the time when he would have actually seen his man, to have enabled the latter to anticipate the reason for his call, and also to formulate a good, logical excuse for saying, "No!"

Suppose, again, he had opened his interview with the street car man something like this:

"The University is badly in need of funds and I have come to you to ask your help. You have made lots of money and you owe something to the community in which you have made it. (Which, perhaps, was true.) If you will give us a million dollars we will place your name on a new Hall that we wish to build."

What might have been the result?

In the first place, there would have been no motive suggested that was sufficiently appealing to sway the mind of the street car man. While it may have been true that he "owed something to the community from which he had made a fortune," he probably would not have admitted that fact. In the second place, he would have enjoyed the position of being on the offensive instead of the defensive side of the proposal.

But Dr. Harper, shrewd in the use of Imagination as he was, provided for just such contingencies by the way he stated his case. First, he placed the street car man on the defensive by informing him that it was not certain that he (Dr. Harper) could get the permission of his Board to accept the money and name the Hall after the street car man. In the second place, he intensified the desire of the street car man to have his name on that building because of the thought that his enemy and competitor might get the honor if it got away from him. Moreover (and this was no accident, either), Dr. Harper had made a powerful appeal to one of the most common of all human weaknesses by showing this street car man how to perpetuate his own name.

All of which required a practical application of the Law of Imagination.

Dr. Harper was a Master Salesman. When he asked men for money he always paved the way for success by planting in the mind of the man of whom he asked it a good sound reason why the money should be given; a reason which emphasized some advantage accruing to the man as the result of the gift. Often this would take on the form of a business advantage. Again it would take on the nature of an appeal to that part of man's nature which prompts him to wish to perpetuate his name so it will live after him. But, always, the request for money was carried out according to a plan that had been carefully thought out, embellished and smoothed down with the use of Imagination.

While the Law of Success philosophy was in the embryonic stage, long before it had been organized into a systematic course of instruction and reduced to textbooks, the author was lecturing on this philosophy in a small town in Illinois.

One of the members of the audience was a young life insurance salesman who had but recently taken up that line of work. After hearing what was said on the subject of Imagination he began to apply what he had heard to his own problem of selling life insurance. Something was said, during the lecture, about the value of allied effort, through which men may enjoy greater success by co-operative effort, through a working arrangement under which each "boosts" the interests of the other.

Taking this suggestion as his cue, the young man in question immediately formulated a plan whereby he gained the co-operation of a group of business men who were in no way connected with the insurance business.

Going to the leading grocer in his town he made arrangements with that grocer to give a thousand dollar insurance policy to every customer purchasing no less than fifty dollars' worth of groceries each month. He then made it a part of his business to inform people of this arrangement and brought in many new customers. The groceryman had a large neatly lettered card placed in his store, informing his customers of this offer of free insurance, thus helping himself by offering all his customers an inducement to do ALL their trading in the grocery line with him.

This young life insurance man then went to the leading gasoline filling station owner in the town and made arrangements with him to insure all customers who purchased all their gasoline, oil and other motor supplies from him.

Next he went to the leading restaurant in the town and made a similar arrangement with the owner. Incidentally, this alliance proved to be quite profitable to the restaurant man, who promptly began an advertising campaign in which he stated that his food was so pure, wholesome and good that all who ate at his place regularly would be apt to live much longer, therefore he would insure the life of each regular customer for $1,000.00.

The life insurance salesman then made arrangements with a local builder and real estate man to insure the life of each person buying property from him, for an amount sufficient to pay off the balance due on the property in case the purchaser died before payments were completed.

Charles Chaplin makes a million dollars a year out of a funny, shuffling walk and a pair of baggy trousers, because he does "something different." Take the hint and "individualize" yourself with some distinctive idea.

The young man in question is now the General Agent for one of the largest life insurance companies in the United States, with headquarters in one of the largest cities in Ohio, and his income now averages well above $25,000.00 a year.

The turning-point in his life came when he discovered how he might make practical use of the Law of Imagination.

There is no patent on his plan. It may be duplicated over and over again by other life insurance men who know the value of *imagination*. Just now, if I were engaged in selling life insurance, I think I should make use of this plan by allying myself with a group of automobile distributors in each of several cities, thus enabling them to sell more automobiles and at the same time providing for the sale of a large amount of life insurance, through their efforts.

Financial success is not difficult to achieve after one learns how to make practical use of creative imagination. Someone with sufficient *initiative* and *leadership,* and the necessary *imagination,* will duplicate the fortunes being made each year by the owners of Five and Ten Cent Stores, by developing a system of marketing the same sort of goods now sold in these stores, with the aid of vending machines. This will save a fortune in clerk hire, insure against theft, and cut down the overhead of store operation in many other ways. Such a system can be conducted just as successfully as food can be dispensed with the aid of automatic vending machines.

The seed of the idea has been here sown. It is yours for the taking!

Someone with an inventive turn of the mind is going to make a fortune and at the same time save thousands of lives each year, by perfecting an automatic railroad crossing "control" that will reduce the number of automobile accidents on crossings.

The system, when perfected, will work somewhat after this fashion: A hundred yards or so before reaching the railroad crossing the automobile will cross a platform somewhat on the order of a large scale platform used for weighing heavy objects, and the weight of the automobile will lower a gate and ring a gong. This will force the automobile to slow down. After the lapse of one minute the gate will again rise and the car may continue on its way. Meanwhile, there will have been plenty of time for observation of the track in both directions, to make sure that no trains are approaching.

Imagination, plus some mechanical skill, will give the motorist this much needed safe-guard, and make the man who perfects the system all the money he needs and much more besides.

Some inventor who understands the value of *imagination* and has a working knowledge of the radio principle, may make a fortune by perfecting a burglar alarm system that will signal police headquarters and at the same time switch on lights and ring a gong in the place about to be burglarized, with the aid of apparatus similar to that now used for broadcasting.

Any farmer with enough *imagination* to create a plan, plus the use of a list of all automobile licenses issued in his state, may easily work up a clientele of motorists who will come to his farm and purchase all the vegetables he can produce and all the chickens he can raise, thus saving him the expense of hauling his products to the city. By contracting with each motorist for the season the farmer may accurately estimate the amount of produce he should provide. The advantage to the motorist, accruing under the arrangement, is that he will be sure of direct-from-the-farm produce, at less cost than he could purchase it from local dealers.

The roadside gasoline filling station owner can make effective use of *imagination* by placing a lunch stand near his filling station, and then doing some attractive advertising along the road in each direction, calling attention to his "barbecue," "home-made sandwiches" or whatever else he may wish to specialize on. The lunch stand will cause the motorists to stop, and many of them will purchase gasoline before starting on their way again.

These are simple suggestions, involving no particular amount of complication in connection with their use, yet it is just such uses of *imagination* that bring financial success.

The Piggly-Wiggly self-help store plan, which made millions of dollars for its originator, was a very simple idea which anyone could have adopted, yet considerable *imagination* was required to put the idea to work in a practical sort of way.

The more simple and easily adapted to a need an idea is, the greater is its value, as no one is looking for ideas which are involved with great detail or in any manner complicated.

Imagination is the most important factor entering into the art of selling. The Master Sales-man is always one who makes systematic use of *imagination*. The outstanding merchant re-lies upon *imagination* for the ideas which make his business excel.

Imagination may be used effectively in the sale of even the smallest articles of merchandise, such as ties, shirts, hosiery, etc. Let us proceed to examine just how this may be done.

I walked into one of the best known haberdasheries in the city of Philadelphia, for the purpose of purchasing some shirts and ties.

As I approached the tie counter a young man stepped forward and inquired:

"Is there something you want?"

Now if I had been the man behind the counter I would not have asked that question. He ought to have known, by the fact that I had approached the tie counter, that I wanted to look at ties.

I picked up two or three ties from the counter, examined them briefly, then laid down all but one light blue which somewhat appealed to me. Finally I laid this one down, also, and began to look through the remainder of the assortment.

The young man behind the counter then had a happy idea. Picking up a gaudy-looking yellow tie he wound it around his fingers to show how it would look when tied, and asked:

"Isn't this a beauty?"

Now I hate yellow ties, and the salesman made no particular hit with me by suggesting that a gaudy yellow tie is pretty. If I had been in that salesman's place I would have picked up the blue tie for which I had shown a decided preference, and I would have wound it around my fingers so as to bring out its appearance after being tied. I would have known what my customer wanted by watching the kinds of ties that he picked up and examined. Moreover, I would have known the particular tie that he liked best by the time he held it in his hands. A man will not stand by a counter and fondle a piece of merchan-dise which he does not like. If given the opportunity, any customer will give the alert salesman a clue as to the particular merchandise which should be stressed in an effort to make a sale.

I then moved over to the shirt counter. Here I was met by an elderly gentleman who asked:

"Is there something I can do for you today?"

Well, I thought to myself that if he ever did anything for me it would have to be today, as I might never come back to that particular store again. I told him I wanted to look at shirts, and described the style and color of shirt that I wanted.

The old gentleman made quite a hit with me when he replied by saying:

> *The man who is afraid to give credit to those who help him do a piece of creditable work is so small that Opportunity will pass by without seeing him some day.*

"I am sorry, sir, but they are not wearing that style this season, so we are not showing it."

I said I knew "they" were not wearing the style for which I had asked, and for that very reason, among others, I was going to wear it providing I could find it in stock.

If there is anything which nettles a man—especially that type of man who knows exactly what he wants and describes it the moment he walks into the store—it is to be told that "they are not wearing it this season."

Such a statement is an insult to a man's intelligence, or to what he thinks is his intelligence, and in most cases it is fatal to a sale. If I were selling goods I might think what I pleased about a customer's taste, but I surely would not be so lacking in tact and diplomacy as to tell the customer that I thought he didn't know his business. Rather I would prefer to manage tactfully to show him what I believed to be more appropriate merchandise than that for which he had called, if what he wanted was not in stock.

One of the most famous and highly paid writers in the world has built his fame and fortune on the sole discovery that it is profitable to write about that which people already know and with which they are already in accord. The same rule might as well apply to the sale of merchandise.

The old gentleman finally pulled down some shirt boxes and began laying out shirts which were not even similar to the shirt for which I had asked. I told him that none of these suited, and as I started to walk out he asked if I would like to look at some nice suspenders.

Imagine it! To begin with I do not wear suspenders, and, furthermore, there was nothing about my manner or bearing to indicate that I might like to look at suspenders.

It is proper for a salesman to try to interest a customer in wares for which he makes no inquiry, but judgment should be used and care taken to offer something which the salesman has reason to believe the customer may want.

I walked out of the store without having bought either shirts or ties, and feeling somewhat resentful because I had been so grossly misjudged as to my tastes for colors and styles.

A little further down the street I went into a small, one-man shop which had shirts and ties on display in the window.

Here I was handled differently!

The man behind the counter asked no unnecessary or stereotyped questions. He took one glance at me as I entered the door, sized me up quite accurately and greeted me with a very pleasant "Good morning, sir!"

He then inquired, "Which shall I show you first, shirts or ties?" I said I would look at the shirts first. He then glanced at the style of shirt I was wearing, asked my size, and began laying out shirts of the very type and color for which I was searching, without my saying another word. He laid out six different styles and watched to see which I would pick up first. I looked at each shirt, in turn, and laid them all back on the counter, but the salesman observed that I examined one of the shirts a little more closely than the others, and that I held it a little longer. No sooner had I laid this shirt down than the salesman picked it up and began to explain how it was made. He then went to the tie counter and came back with three very beautiful blue ties, of the very type for which I had been looking, tied each and held it in front of the shirt, calling attention to the perfect harmony between the colors of the ties and the shirt.

Before I had been in the store five minutes I had purchased three shirts and three ties, and was on my way with the package under my arm, feeling that here was a store to which I would return when I needed more shirts and ties.

I learned, afterwards, that the merchant who owns the little shop where I made these purchases pays a monthly rental of $500.00 for the small store, and makes a handsome income from the sale of nothing but shirts, ties and collars. He would have to go out of business, with a fixed charge of $500.00 a month for rent, if it were not for his knowledge of human nature which enables him to make a very high percentage of sales to all who come into his store.

I have often observed women when they were trying on hats, and have wondered why salespeople did not read the prospective buyer's mind by watching her manner of handling the hats.

A woman goes into a store and asks to be shown some hats. The salesperson starts bringing out hats and the prospective buyer starts trying them on. If a hat suits her, even in the slightest sort of way, she will keep it on a few seconds, or a few minutes, but if she does not like it she will pull it right off her head the moment the salesperson takes her hands off the hat.

Finally, when the customer is shown a hat that she likes she will begin to announce that fact, in terms which no well informed salesperson will fail to understand, by arranging her hair under the hat, or pulling it down on her head to just the angle which she likes best, and by looking at the hat from the rear, with the aid of a hand-mirror. The signs of admiration are unmistakable. Finally, the customer will remove the hat from her head, and begin to look at it closely; then she may lay it aside and permit another hat to be tried on her, in which event the clever salesperson will lay aside the hat just removed, and at the opportune time she will bring it back and ask the customer to try it on again.

By careful observation of the customer's likes and dislikes a clever saleswoman may often sell as many as three or four hats to the same customer, at one sitting, by merely watching what appeals to the customer and then concentrating upon the sale of that.

The same rule applies in the sale of other merchandise. The customer will, if closely observed, clearly indicate what is wanted, and, if the clue is followed, very rarely will a customer walk out without buying.

I believe it a conservative estimate when I say that fully seventy-five per cent of the "walk-outs," as the non-purchasing customers are called, are due to lack of tactful showing of merchandise.

Last Fall I went into a hat store to purchase a felt hat. It was a busy Saturday afternoon and I was approached by a young "extra" rush-hour salesman who had not yet learned how to size people up at a glance. For no good reason whatsoever the young man pulled down a brown derby and handed it to me, or rather tried to hand it to me. I thought he was trying to be funny, and refused to take the hat into my hands, saying to him, in an attempt to return his compliment and be funny in turn, "Do you tell bed-time stories also?" He looked at me in surprise, but didn't take the cue which I had offered him.

If I had not observed the young man more closely than he had observed me, and sized him up as an earnest but inexperienced "extra," I would have been highly insulted, for it there is anything I hate it is a derby of any sort, much less a brown derby.

One of the regular salesmen happened to see what was going on, walked over and snatched the brown derby out of the young man's hands, and, with a smile on his face intended as a sort of sop to me, said, "What the hell are you trying to show this gentleman, anyway?"

That spoiled my fun, and the salesman who had immediately recognized me as a gentleman sold me the first hat he brought out.

The customer generally feels complimented when a salesman takes the time to study the customer's personality and lay out merchandise suited to that personality.

I went into one of the largest men's clothing stores in New York City, a few years ago, and asked for a suit, describing exactly what was wanted, but not mentioning price. The young man, who purported to be a salesman, said he did not believe they carried such a suit, but I happened to see exactly what I wanted hanging on a model, and called his attention to the suit. He then made a hit with me by saying, "Oh, that one over there? That's a high-priced suit!"

"Hot heads" go with "cold feet." He who loses his temper is usually a bluffer and when "called" is a quitter.

His reply amused me; it also angered me, so I inquired of the young man what he saw about me which indicated that I did not come in to purchase a high-priced suit? With embarrassment he tried to explain, but his explanations were as bad as the original offense, and I started toward the door, muttering something to myself about "dumb-bells." Before I reached the door I was met by another salesman who had sensed by the way I walked and the expression on my face that I was none too well pleased.

With tact well worth remembering, this salesman engaged me in conversation while I unburdened my woes and then managed to get me to go back with him and look at the suit. Before I left the store I purchased the suit I came in to look at, and two others which I had not intended purchasing.

That was the difference between a salesman and one who drove customers away. Moreover, I later introduced two of my friends to this same salesman and he made sizable sales to each of them.

I was once walking down Michigan Boulevard, in Chicago, when my eye was attracted to a beautiful gray suit in the window of a men's store. I had no notion of buying the suit, but I was curious to know the price, so I opened the door, and, without entering, merely pushed my head inside and asked the first man I saw how much the suit in the window was.

Then followed one of the cleverest bits of sales maneuvering I have ever observed. The salesman knew he could not sell me the suit unless I came into the store, so he said, "Will you not step inside, sir, while I find out the price of the suit?"

Of course he knew the price, all the time, but that was his way of disarming me of the thought that he intended trying to sell me the suit. Of course I had to be as polite as the salesman, so I said, "Certainly," and walked inside.

The salesman said, "Step right this way, sir, and I will get the information for you."

In less than two minutes I found myself standing in front of a case, with my coat off, getting ready to try on a coat like the one I had observed in the window.

After I was in the coat, which happened to fit almost perfectly (which was no accident, thanks to the accurate eyes of an observing salesman) my attention was called to the nice, smooth touch of the material. I rubbed my hand up and down the arm of the coat, as I had seen the salesman do while describing the material, and, sure enough, it was a very fine piece of material. By this time I had again asked the price, and when I was told that the suit was only fifty dollars I was agreeably surprised, because I had been led to believe that it might have been priced much higher. However, when I first saw the suit in the window my guess was that it was priced at about thirty-five dollars, and I doubt that I would have paid that much for it had I not fallen into the hands of a man who knew how to show the suit to best advantage. If the first coat tried on me had been about two sizes too large, or a size too small, I doubt that any sale would have been made, despite the fact that all ready-to-wear suits sold in the better stores are altered to fit the customer.

I bought that suit "on the impulse of the moment," as the psychologist would say, and I am not the only man who buys goods on that same sort of impulse. A single slip on the part of the salesman would have lost him the sale of that suit. If he had replied, "Fifty dollars," when I asked the price I would have said, "Thank you," and have gone my way without looking at the suit.

Later in the season I purchased two more suits from this same salesman, and if I now lived in Chicago the chances are that I would buy still other suits from him, because he always showed me suits that were in keeping with my personality.

The Marshall Field store, in Chicago, gets more for merchandise than does any other store of its kind in the country. Moreover, people knowingly pay more at this store, and feel better satisfied than if they bought the merchandise at another store for less money.

Why is this?

Well, there are many reasons, among them the fact that anything purchased at the Field store which is not entirely satisfactory may be returned and exchanged for other merchandise, or the purchase price may be refunded, just as the customer wishes. An implied guarantee goes with every article sold in the Field store.

Another reason why people will pay more at the Field store is the fact that the merchandise is displayed and shown to better advantage than it is at most other stores. The Field window-displays are truly works of art, no less than if they were created for the sake of art alone, and not merely to sell merchandise. The same is true of the goods displayed in the store. There is harmony and proper grouping of merchandise throughout the Field establishment, and this creates an "atmosphere" that is more—much more—than merely an imaginary one.

Still another reason why the Field store can get more for merchandise than most other merchants is due to the careful selection and supervision of sales-people. One would seldom find a person employed in the Field store whom one would not be willing to accept as a social equal, or as a neighbor. Not a few men have made the acquaintance of girls in the Field store who later became their wives.

Merchandise purchased in the Field store is packed or wrapped more artistically than is common in other stores, which is still another reason why people go out of their way and pay higher prices to trade there.

While we are on the subject of artistic wrapping of merchandise I wish to relate the experience of a friend of mine which will not fail to convey a very definite meaning to those engaged in the business of selling, as it shows how *imagination* may be used even in wrapping merchandise.

This friend had a very fine silver cigarette case which he had carried for years, and of which he was very proud because it was a gift from his wife.

Constant usage had banged the case up rather badly. It had been bent, dented, the hinges warped, etc., until he decided to take it to Caldwell the jeweler, in Philadelphia, to be repaired. He left the case and asked them to send it to his office when it was ready.

About two weeks later a splendid-looking new delivery wagon with the Caldwell name on it drew up in front of his office, and a nice-looking young man in a neat uniform stepped out with a package that was artistically wrapped and tied with a ribbon tape string.

The package happened to be delivered to my friend on his birthday, and, having forgotten about leaving the cigarette case to be repaired, and observing the beauty and size of the package that was handed to him, he naturally imagined that someone had sent him a birthday present.

His secretary and other workers in his office gathered around his desk to watch him open up his "present." He cut the ribbon and removed the outer covering. Under this was a covering of tissue paper, fastened with beautiful gold seals bearing the Caldwell initials and trade-mark. This paper was removed and behold! a most beautiful plush-lined box met his eyes. The box was opened, and, after removing the tissue paper packing, there was a cigarette case which he recognized, after careful examination, as the one he had left to be repaired, but it did not look like the same case, thanks to the *imagination* of the Caldwell manager.

> *E. M. Statler became the most successful hotel man in the world by rendering more service and better service than his guests were asked to pay for.*

Every dent had been carefully straightened out. The hinges had been trued and the case had been polished and cleaned so it shone as it did when it was first purchased.

Simultaneously a prolonged "Oo-o-o-o-o-o-Oh!" of admiration came from the onlookers, including the owner of the cigarette case.

And the bill! Oh, it was a plenty, and yet the price charged for the repair did not seem too high. As a matter of fact everything that entered into the transaction from the packing of the case, with the fine tissue paper cover, the gold seals, the ribbon tape string, the delivery of the package by a neatly uniformed boy, from a well appointed new delivery wagon, was based upon carefully calculated psychology which laid the foundation for a high price for the repair.

People, generally, do not complain of high prices, providing the "service" or embellishment of the merchandise is such as to pave the way for high prices. What people do complain of, and rightly so, is high prices and "sloppy" service.

To me there was a great lesson in this cigarette case incident, and I think there is a lesson in it for any person who makes a business of selling any sort of merchandise.

The goods you are selling may actually be worth all you are asking for them, but if you do not carefully study the subjects of advantageous display and artistic packing you may be accused of overcharging your customers.

On Broad Street, in the city of Philadelphia, there is a fruit shop where those who patronize the store are met at the door by a man in uniform who opens the door for them. He does nothing else but merely open the door, but he does it with a smile (even though it be a carefully studied and rehearsed smile) which makes the customer feel welcome even before he gets inside of the store. This fruit merchant specializes on specially prepared baskets of fruit.

IMAGINATION

Just outside the store is a big blackboard on which are listed the sailing dates of the various ocean liners leaving New York City. This merchant caters to people who wish baskets of fruit delivered on board departing boats on which friends are sailing. If a man's sweetheart, or perhaps his wife or a very dear friend, happens to be sailing on a certain date he naturally wants the basket of fruit he purchases for her to be embellished with frills and "trimmings." Moreover, he is not necessarily looking for something "cheap" or even inexpensive.

All of which the fruit merchant capitalizes! He gets from $10.00 to $25.00 for a basket of fruit which one could purchase just around the corner, not more than a block away, for from $3.00 to $7.50, with the exception that the latter would not be embellished with the seventy-five cents' worth of frills which the former contains.

This merchant's store is a small affair, no larger than the average small fruit-stand store, but he pays a rent of at least $15,000.00 a year for the place and makes more money than half a hundred ordinary fruit stands combined, merely because he knows how to display and deliver his wares so they appeal to the vanity of the buyers. This is but another proof of the value of *imagination*.

The American people—and this means all of them, not merely the so-called rich—are the most extravagant spenders on earth, but they insist on "class" when it comes to appearances such as wrapping and delivery and other embellishments which add no real value to the merchandise they buy. The merchant who understands this, and has learned how to mix IMAGINATION with his merchandise, may reap a rich harvest in return for his knowledge.

And a great many are doing it, too.

The salesman who understands the psychology of proper display, wrapping and delivery of merchandise, and who knows how to show his wares to fit the whims and characteristics of his customers, can make ordinary merchandise bring fancy prices, and what is more important still, he can do so and still retain the patronage of his customers more readily than if he sold the same merchandise without the "studied" appeal and the artistic wrapping and delivery service.

In a "cheap" restaurant, where coffee is served in heavy, thick cups and the silverware is tarnished or dirty, a ham sandwich is only a ham sandwich, and if the restaurant keeper gets fifteen cents for it he is doing well; but just across the street, where the coffee is served in dainty thin cups, on neatly covered tables, by neatly dressed young women, a much smaller ham sandwich will bring a quarter, to say nothing of the cost of the tip to the waitress. The only difference in the sandwiches is merely in appearances; the ham comes from the same butcher and the bread from the same baker, whether purchased from the former or the latter restaurant.

The difference in price is very considerable, but the difference in the merchandise is not a difference of either quality or quantity so much as it is of "atmosphere," or appearances.

People love to buy "appearance" or atmosphere! which is merely a more refined way of saying that which P. T. Barnum said about "one being born every minute."

It is no overstatement of fact to say that a master of sales psychology could go into the average merchant's store, where the stock of goods was worth, let us say, $50,000.00, and at very slight additional expense make the stock bring $60,000.00 to $75,000.00. He would do nothing except coach the salespeople on the proper showing of the merchandise, after having purchased a small amount of more suitable fixtures, perhaps, and re-packed the merchandise in more suitable coverings and boxes.

A man's shirt, packed one to the box, in the right sort of a box, with a piece of ribbon and a sheet of tissue paper added for embellishment, can be made to bring a dollar or a dollar and a half more than the same shirt would bring without the more artistic packing. I know this is true, and I have proved it more times than I can recall, to convince some skeptical merchant who had not studied the effect of "proper displays."

Conversely stated, I have proved, many times, that the finest shirt made cannot be sold for half its value if it is removed from its box and placed on a bargain counter, with inferior looking shirts, both of which examples prove that people do not know what they are buying—that they go more by appearances than they do by actual analysis of the merchandise they purchase.

This is noticeably true in the purchase of automobiles. The American people want, and DEMAND, style in the appearance of automobiles. What is under the hood or in the rear axle they do not know and really do not care, as long as the car looks the part.

Henry Ford required nearly twenty years of experience to learn the truth of the statement just made, and even then, despite all of his analytical ability, he only acknowledged the truth when forced to do so by his competitors. If it were not true that people buy "appearances" more than they buy "reality" Ford never would have created his new automobile. That car is the finest sort of example of a psychologist who appeals to the tendency which people have to purchase "appearance," although, of course, it must be admitted that in this particular example the real value of the car actually exists.

Great achievement is usually born of great sacrifice, and is never the result of selfishness.

I gave a beggar a dime with the suggestion that he invest it in a copy of Elbert Hubbard's Message to Garcia.

LESSON SIX

ENTHUSIASM

"You Can Do It If You Believe You Can!"

Enthusiasm is a state of mind that inspires and arouses one to put *action* into the task at hand. It does more than this—it is contagious, and vitally affects not only the enthusiast, but all with whom he comes in contact.

Enthusiasm bears the same relationship to a human being that steam does to the locomotive—it is the vital moving force that impels *action*. The greatest leaders of men are those who know how to inspire enthusiasm in their followers. Enthusiasm is the most important factor entering into salesmanship. It is, by far, the most vital factor that enters into public speaking.

If you wish to understand the difference between a man who is enthusiastic and one who is not, compare Billy Sunday with the average man of his profession. The finest sermon ever delivered would fall upon deaf ears if it were not backed with enthusiasm by the speaker.

How Enthusiasm Will Affect You

Mix enthusiasm with your work and it will not seem hard or monotonous. Enthusiasm will so energize your entire body that you can get along with less than half the usual amount of sleep and at the same time it will enable you to perform from two to three times as much work as you usually perform in a given period, without fatigue.

For many years I have done most of my writing at night. One night, while I was enthusiastically at work over my typewriter, I looked out of the window of my study, just across the square from the Metropolitan tower, in New York City, and saw what seemed to be the most peculiar reflection of the moon on the tower. It was of a silvery gray shade, such as I had never seen before. Upon closer inspection I found that the reflection was that of the early morning sun and not that of the moon. It was daylight! I had been at work all night, but I was so engrossed in my work that the night had passed as though it were but an hour. I worked at my task all that day and all the following night without stopping, except for a small amount of light food.

Two nights and one day without sleep, and with but little food, without the slightest evidence of fatigue, would not have been possible had I not kept my body energized with *enthusiasm* over the work at hand.

Enthusiasm is not merely a figure of speech; it is a vital force that you can harness and use with profit. Without it you would resemble an electric battery without electricity.

Enthusiasm is the vital force with which you recharge your body and develop a dynamic personality. Some people are blessed with natural *enthusiasm,* while others must acquire it. The procedure through which it may be developed is simple. It begins by the doing of the work or rendering of the service which one likes best. If you should be so situated that you cannot conveniently engage in the work which you like best, for the time being, then you can proceed along another line very effectively by adopting a *definite chief aim* that contemplates your engaging in that particular work at some future time.

Lack of capital and many other circumstances over which you have no immediate control may force you to engage in work which you do not like, but no one can stop you from determining in your own mind what your *definite chief aim* in life shall be, nor can anyone stop you from planning ways and means for translating this aim into reality, nor can anyone stop you from mixing *enthusiasm* with your plans.

Happiness, the final object of all human effort, is a state of mind that can be maintained only through the hope of future achievement. Happiness lies always in the future and never in the past. The happy person is the one who dreams of heights of achievement that are yet unattained. The home you intend to own, the money you intend to earn and place in the bank, the trip you intend to take when you can afford it, the position in life you intend to fill when you have prepared yourself, and the preparation, itself—these are the things that produce happiness. Likewise, these are the materials out of which your *definite chief aim* is formed; these are the things over which you may become *enthusiastic,* no matter what your present station in life may be.

More than twenty years ago I became enthusiastic over an idea. When the idea first took form in my mind I was unprepared to take even the first step toward its transformation into reality. But I nursed it in my mind—I became *enthusiastic* over it as I looked ahead, in my imagination, and saw the time when I would be prepared to make it a reality.

The idea was this: I wanted to become the editor of a magazine, based upon the Golden Rule, through which I could inspire people to keep up courage and deal with one another squarely.

Finally my chance came! and, on armistice day, 1918, I wrote the first editorial for what was to become the material realization of a hope that had lain dormant in my mind for nearly a score of years.

With *enthusiasm* I poured into that editorial the emotions which I had been developing in my heart over a period of more than twenty years. My dream had come true. My editorship of a national magazine had become a reality.

As I have stated, this editorial was written with *enthusiasm*. I took it to a man of my acquaintance and with *enthusiasm* I read it to him. The editorial ended in these words: "At last my twenty-year-old dream is about to come true. It takes money, and a lot of it, to publish a national magazine, and I haven't the slightest idea where I am going to get this essential factor, but this is worrying me not at all because *I know I am going to get it somewhere!*" As I wrote those lines, I mixed *enthusiasm* and faith with them.

I had hardly finished reading this editorial when the man to whom I read it—the first and only person to whom I had shown it—said:

"I can tell you where you are going to get the money, for I am going to supply it."

And he did!

Yes, *enthusiasm* is a vital force; so vital, in fact, that no man who has it highly developed can begin even to approximate his power of achievement.

Before passing to the next step in this lesson, I wish to repeat and to emphasize the fact that you may develop *enthusiasm* over your *definite chief aim* in life, no matter whether you are in position to achieve that purpose at this time or not. You may be a long way from realization of your *definite chief aim,* but if you will kindle the fire of *enthusiasm* in your heart, and keep it burning, before very long the obstacles that now stand in the way of your attainment of that purpose will melt away as if by the force of magic, and you will find yourself in possession of power that you did not know you possessed.

How Your Enthusiasm Will Affect Others

We come, now, to the discussion of one of the most important subjects of this Reading Course, namely, *suggestion.*

In the preceding lessons we have discussed the subject of *Auto-suggestion,* which is self-suggestion. You saw, in Lesson Two, what an important part *Auto-suggestion* played.

Suggestion is the principle through which your words and your acts and even *your state of mind* influence others. That you may comprehend the far-reaching power of *suggestion,* let me refer to the Introduction, in which the principle of telepathy is described. If you now understand and accept the principle of telepathy (the communication of thought from one mind to another without the aid of signs, symbols or sounds) as a reality, you of course understand why *enthusiasm* is contagious, and why it influences all within its radius.

> *One of the most valuable things any man can learn is the art of using the knowledge and experience of others.*

When your own mind is vibrating at a high rate, because it has been stimulated with *enthusiasm,* that vibration registers in the minds of all within its radius, and especially in the minds of those with whom you come in close contact. When a public speaker "senses" the feeling that his audience is "en rapport" with him he merely recognizes the fact that his own *enthusiasm* has influenced the minds of his listeners until their minds are vibrating in harmony with his own.

When the salesman "senses" the fact that the "psychological" moment for closing a sale has arrived, he merely feels the effect of his own *enthusiasm* as it influences the mind of his prospective buyer and places that mind "en rapport" (in harmony) with his own.

The subject of *suggestion* constitutes so vitally an important part of this lesson, and of this entire course, that I will now proceed to describe the three mediums through which it usually operates; namely, what you say, what you do and what you *think!*

When you are *enthusiastic* over the goods you are selling or the services you are offering, or the speech you are delivering, your state of mind becomes obvious to all who hear you, *by the tone of your voice.* Whether you have ever thought of it in this way or not, it is the tone in which you make a statement, more than it is the statement itself, that carries conviction or fails to convince. No mere combination of words can ever take the place of a deep belief in a statement that is expressed with burning *enthusiasm.* Words are but devitalized sounds unless colored with feeling that is born of *enthusiasm.*

Here the printed word fails me, for I can never express with mere type and paper the difference between words that fall from unemotional lips, without the fire of *enthusiasm* back of them, and those which seem to pour forth from a heart that is bursting with eagerness for expression. The difference is there, however.

Thus, *what you say,* and the way in which you say it, conveys a meaning that may be just the opposite to what is intended. This accounts for many a failure by the salesman who presents his arguments in words which seem logical enough, but lack the coloring that can come only from *enthusiasm* that is born of sincerity and belief in the goods he is trying to sell. His words said one thing, but the tone of his voice *suggested* something entirely different; therefore, no sale was made.

That which you *say* is an important factor in the operation of the principle of *suggestion,* but not nearly so important as that which you *do. Your acts will count for more than your words,* and woe unto you if the two fail to harmonize.

If a man preach the Golden Rule as a sound rule of conduct his words will fall upon deaf ears if he does not practice that which he preaches. The most effective sermon that any man can preach on the soundness of the Golden Rule is that which he preaches, by *suggestion,* when he applies this rule in his relationships with his fellow men.

If a salesman of Ford automobiles drives up to his prospective purchaser in a Buick, or some other make of car, all the arguments he can present on behalf of the Ford will be without effect. Once I went into one of the offices of the Dictaphone Company to look at a dictaphone (dictating machine). The salesman in charge presented a logical argument as to the machine's merits, while the stenographer at his side was transcribing letters from a shorthand note-book. His arguments in favor of a dictating machine, as compared with the old method of dictating to a stenographer, did not impress me, because his actions were not in harmony with his words.

Your *thoughts* constitute the most important of the three ways in which you apply the principle of *suggestion,* for the reason that they control the tone of your words and, to some extent at least, your actions. If your *thoughts* and your *actions* and your *words* harmonize, you are bound to influence those with whom you come in contact, more or less toward your way of thinking.

We will now proceed to analyze the subject of *suggestion* and to show you exactly how to apply the principle upon which it operates. As we have already seen, *suggestion* differs from *Auto-suggestion* only in one way—we use it, consciously or unconsciously, when we influence others, while we use *Auto-suggestion* as a means of influencing ourselves.

Before you can influence another person through *suggestion,* that person's mind must be in a state of neutrality; that is, it must be open and receptive to your method of *suggestion.* Right here is where most salesmen fail—they try to make a sale before the mind of the prospective buyer has been rendered receptive or neutralized. This is such a vital point in this lesson that I feel impelled to dwell upon it until there can be no doubt that you understand the principle that I am describing.

When I say that the salesman must neutralize the mind of his prospective purchaser before a sale can be made I mean that the prospective purchaser's mind must be credulous. A state of confidence must have been established and it is obvious that there can be no set rule for either establishing confidence or neutralizing the mind to a state of openness. Here the ingenuity of the salesman must supply that which cannot be set down as a hard and fast rule.

I know a life insurance salesman who sells nothing but large policies, amounting to $100,000.00 and upward. Before this man even approaches the subject of insurance with a prospective client he familiarizes himself with the prospective client's complete history, including his education, his financial status, his eccentricities if he has any, his religious preferences and other data too numerous to be listed. Armed with this information, he manages to secure an introduction under conditions which permit him to know the prospective client in a social as well as a business way. Nothing is said about the sale of life insurance during his first visit, nor his second, and sometimes he does not approach the subject of insurance until he has become very well acquainted with the prospective client.

All this time, however, he is not dissipating his efforts. He is taking advantage of these friendly visits for the purpose of neutralizing his prospective client's mind; that is, he is building up a relationship of confidence so that when the time comes for him to talk life insurance that which he says will fall upon ears that *willingly listen.*

Some years ago I wrote a book entitled How to Sell Your Services. Just before the manuscript went to the publisher, it occurred to me to request some of the well known men of the United States to write letters of endorsement to be published in the book. The printer was then waiting for the manuscript; therefore, I hurriedly wrote a letter to some eight or ten men, in which I briefly outlined exactly what I wanted, but the letter brought back no replies. I had failed to observe two important prerequisites for success—I had written the letter so hurriedly that I had failed to inject the spirit of *enthusiasm* into it, and I had neglected so to word the letter that it had the effect of neutralizing the minds of those to whom it was sent; therefore, I had not paved the way for the application of the principle of *suggestion.*

After I discovered my mistake, I then wrote a letter that was based upon strict application of the principle of *suggestion,* and this letter not only brought back replies from all to whom it was sent, but many of the replies were masterpieces and served, far beyond my fondest hopes, as valuable supplements to the book. For the purpose of comparison, to show you how the principle

A careful inventory of all your past experiences may disclose the startling fact that everything has happened for the best.

of *suggestion* may be used in writing a letter, and what an important part *enthusiasm* plays in giving the written word "flesh," the two letters are here reproduced. It will not be necessary to indicate which letter failed, as that will be quite obvious:

My dear Mr. Ford:

I am just completing a manuscript for a new book entitled How to Sell Your Services. I anticipate the sale of several hundred thousand of these books and I believe those who purchase the book would welcome the opportunity of receiving a message from you as to the best method of marketing personal services.

Would you, therefore, be good enough to give me a few minutes of your time by writing a brief message to be published in my book? This will be a big favor to me personally and I know it would be appreciated by the readers of the book.

Thanking you in advance for any consideration you may care to show me, I am,

Yours very truly,

Hon. Thomas R. Marshall,
Vice-President of the United States,
Washington, D. C.
My dear Mr. Marshall:

Would you care for the opportunity to send a message of encouragement, and possibly a word of advice, to a few hundred thousand of your fellow men who have failed to make their mark in the world as successfully as you have done?

I have about completed a manuscript for a book to be entitled How to Sell Your Services. The main point made in the book is that service rendered is cause *and the pay envelope is* effect; *and that the latter varies in proportion to the efficiency of the former.*

The book would be incomplete without a few words of advice from a few men who, like your-self, have come up from the bottom to enviable positions in the world. Therefore, if you will write me of your views as to the most essential points to be borne in mind by those who are offering personal services for sale I will pass your message on through my book, which will insure its get-ting into hands where it will do a world of good for a class of earnest people who are struggling to find their places in the world's work.

I know you are a busy man, Mr. Marshall, but please bear in mind that by simply calling in your secretary and dictating a brief letter you will be sending forth an important message to possi-bly half a million people. In money this will not be worth to you the two cent stamp that you will place on the letter, but, if estimated from the viewpoint of the good it may do others who are less fortunate than yourself, it may be worth the difference between success and failure to many a worthy person who will read your message, believe in it, and be guided by it.

Very cordially yours,

Now, let us analyze the two letters and find out why one failed in its mission while the other succeeded. This analysis should start with one of the most important fundamentals of salesmanship, namely motive. In the first letter it is obvious that the motive is entirely one of self-interest. The letter states exactly what is wanted, but the wording of it leaves a doubt as to *why* the request is made or whom it is intended to benefit. Study the sentence in the sec-ond paragraph, "This will be a big favor to me personally, etc." Now it may seem to be a peculiar trait, but the truth is that most people will not grant favors just to please others. If I ask you to render a service that will benefit me, without bringing you some corresponding advantage, you will not show much enthusiasm in granting that favor; you may refuse altogether if you have a plausible excuse for refusing. But if I ask you to render a service that will benefit a third person, even though the service must be rendered through me; and if that service is of such a nature that it is likely to reflect credit on you, the chances are that you will render the service willingly.

We see this psychology demonstrated by the man who pitches a dime to the beggar on the street, or perhaps refuses even the dime, but willingly hands over a hundred or a thou-sand dollars to the charity worker who is begging in the name of others.

But the most damaging suggestion of all is contained in the last and most important para-graph of the letter, "Thanking you in advance for *any consideration you may care to show me.*" This sentence strongly suggests that the writer of the letter anticipates a refusal of his request. It clearly indicates lack of *enthusiasm*. It paves the way for a refusal of the request. There is not one single word in the entire letter that places in the mind of a man to whom it is sent a satisfactory reason why he should comply with the request. On the other hand, he can clearly see that the object of the letter is to secure from him a letter of endorsement that will help sell the book. The most important selling argument—in fact, the only selling argument available in connection with this request, has been lost because it was not brought out and established as the real motive for making the request. This argument was but faintly mentioned in the sentence, "I believe those who purchase the book would welcome the opportunity of receiving a message from you as to the best method of marketing personal services."

The opening paragraph of the letter violates an important fundamental of salesmanship because it clearly suggests that the object of the letter is to gain some advantage for its writer, and does not even hint at any corresponding advantage that may accrue to the person to whom it is sent. Instead of neutralizing the mind of the recipient of the letter, as it should do, it has just the opposite effect; it causes him to close his mind against all argument that follows; it puts him in a frame of mind that makes it easy for him to say no. It reminds me of a salesman—or, perhaps I should say, a man who wanted to be a salesman—who once approached me for the purpose of selling me a subscription to the *Saturday Evening Post*. As he held a copy of the magazine in front of me he suggested the answer I should make by this question:

"You wouldn't subscribe for the Post to help me out, would you?"

Of course I said no! He had made it easy for me to say no. There was no *enthusiasm* back of his words, and gloom and discouragement were written all over his face. He needed the commission he would have made on my subscription had I purchased; no doubt about that—but he suggested nothing that appealed to my self-interest motive, therefore he lost a sale. But the loss of this *one sale* was not the sad part of his misfortune; the sad part was that this same attitude was causing him to lose all other sales which he might have made had he changed his approach.

A few weeks later another subscription agent approached me. She was selling a combination of six magazines, one of which was the *Saturday Evening Post*, but how different was her approach. She glanced at my library table, on which she saw several magazines, then at my book shelves, and exclaimed with *enthusiasm:*

"Oh! I see you are a lover of books and magazines."

I *proudly* pleaded guilty to the charge. Observe the word *"proudly,"* for it has an important bearing on this incident. I laid down the manuscript that I was reading when this saleswoman came in, for I could see that she was a woman of intelligence. Just how I came to see this I will leave to your imagination. The important point is that I laid down the manuscript and actually felt myself wanting to hear what she had to say.

With the aid of eleven words, plus a pleasant smile, plus a tone of genuine *enthusiasm,* she had neutralized my mind sufficiently to make me want to hear her. She had performed her most difficult task, with those few words, because I had made up my mind when she was announced that I would keep my manuscript in my hands and thereby convey to her mind, as politely as I could, the fact that I was busy and did not wish to be detained.

Being a student of salesmanship and of *suggestion,* I carefully watched to see what her next move would be. She had a bundle of magazines under her arm and I expected she would unroll it and begin to urge me to purchase, but she didn't. You will recall that I said she was *selling* a combination of six magazines; not merely trying to sell them.

She walked over to my book shelves, pulled out a copy of Emerson's *Essays,* and for the next ten minutes she talked about Emerson's essay on Compensation so interestingly that I lost sight of the roll of magazines that she carried. (She was neutralizing my mind some more.)

> First impressions really do count. Dress to look the part you intend to play in life, but take care not to overdo it.

Incidentally, she gave me a sufficient number of new ideas about Emerson's works to provide material for an excellent editorial.

Then she asked me which magazines I received regularly, and after I told her she smiled as she began to unroll her bundle of magazines and laid them on the table in front of me. She analyzed her magazines one by one, and explained just why I should have each of them. The *Saturday Evening Post* would bring me the cleanest fiction; *Literary Digest* would bring me the news of the world in condensed form, such as a *busy man like myself* would demand; the *American Magazine* would bring me the latest biographies of the men who were leading in business and industry, and so on, until she had covered the entire list.

But I was not responding to her argument as freely as she thought I should have, so she slipped me this gentle *suggestion:*

"A man of your position is bound to be well informed and, if he isn't, it will show up in his own work!"

She spoke the truth! Her remark was both a compliment and a gentle reprimand. She made me feel somewhat sheepish because she had taken inventory of my reading matter—and six of the leading magazines were not on my list. (The six that she was selling.)

Then I began to "slip" by asking her how much the six magazines would cost. She put on the finishing touches of a well presented sales talk by this tactful reply: "The cost? Why, the cost of the entire number is less than you receive for a single page of the typewritten manuscript that you had in your hands when I came in."

Again she spoke the truth. And how did she happen to guess so well what I was getting for my manuscript? The answer is, she didn't guess—*she knew!* She made it a part of her business to draw me out tactfully as to the nature of my work (which in no way made me angry). She became so deeply interested in the manuscript which I had laid down when she came in, that she actually induced me to talk about it. (I am not saying, of course, that this required any great amount of skill or coaxing, for have I not said that *it was my manuscript?*) In my remarks about that manuscript I suspect I *admitted* that I was receiving $250.00 for the fifteen pages; yes, *I am sure I was careless enough to admit that I was being well paid for my work.*

Perhaps she induced me to make the admission. At any rate, the information was valuable to her and she made effective use of it at the psychological moment. For all I know it was a part of her plan to observe carefully all that she saw and heard, with the object of finding out just what my weaknesses were and what I was most interested in discussing. Some salesmen take the time to do this; some do not. She was one of those who did.

Yes, she went away with my order for the six magazines; also my twelve dollars. But that was not all the benefit she derived from tactful *suggestion* plus *enthusiasm;* she got my consent to canvass my office, and before she left she had five other orders from my employees.

At no time during her stay did she leave the impression that I was favoring her by purchasing her magazines. Just to the contrary, she distinctly impressed me with the feeling that she was rendering me a favor. This was tactful suggestion.

Before we get away from this incident, I wish to make an admission—when she drew me into conversation she did it in such a way that I talked with *enthusiasm.* There were two reasons for this. She was one of them; and the other one was the fact that she managed to get me to talk *about my own work!* Of course I am not suggesting that *you* should be meddlesome enough to smile at my carelessness as you read this; or that you should gather from this incident the impression that this tactful saleswoman actually led me to talk of my own work for the purpose of neutralizing my mind so that I would listen to her, when she was ready to talk of her magazines, as patiently as she had listened to me. However, if you should be clever enough to draw a lesson from her method, there is no way for me to stop you from doing so.

As I have stated, when I talked I mixed *enthusiasm* with my conversation. Perhaps I caught the spirit of *enthusiasm* from this clever saleswoman, when she made that opening remark as she came into my study. Yes, I am sure this is where I caught it, and, I am just as sure that her enthusiasm was not a matter of accident. She had trained herself to look for something in her prospective purchaser's office, or his work, or his conversation, over which she could express *enthusiasm*.

Remember, *suggestion* and *enthusiasm* go hand in hand!

I can remember, as though it were yesterday, the feeling that came over me when that would-be salesman pushed that *Saturday Evening Post* in front of me, as he remarked:

"You wouldn't subscribe for the *Post* to help me out, would you?"

His words were chilled, they were lifeless; they lacked *enthusiasm;* they registered an impression in my mind, but that impression was one of coldness. I wanted to see the man go out at the door at which he had come in. Mind you, I am not naturally unsympathetic, but the tone of his voice, the look on his face, his general bearing *suggested* that he was there to ask a favor and not to offer one.

Suggestion is one of the most subtle and powerful principles of psychology. You are making use of it in all that you do and say and think, but, unless you understand the difference between negative suggestion and positive suggestion, you may be using it in such a way that it is bringing you defeat instead of success.

Science has established the fact that through the negative use of suggestion life may be extinguished. Some years ago, in France, a criminal was condemned to death, but before the time for his execution an experiment was performed on him which conclusively proved that through the principle of *suggestion* death could be produced. The criminal was brought to the guillotine and his head was placed under the knife, after he had been blindfolded. A heavy, sharp edged plank was then dropped on his neck, producing a shock similar to that of a sharp edged knife. Warm water was then gently poured on his neck and allowed to trickle slowly down his spine, to imitate the flow of warm blood. In seven minutes the doctors pronounced the man dead. His imagination, through the principle of suggestion, had actually turned the sharp edged plank into a guillotine blade and stopped his heart from beating.

In the little town where I was raised, there lived an old lady who constantly complained that she feared death from cancer. During her childhood she had seen a woman who had cancer and the sight had so impressed itself upon her mind that she began to look for the symptoms of cancer in her own body. She was sure that every little ache and pain was the beginning of her long-looked-for symptom of cancer. I have seen her place her hand on her breast and have heard her exclaim, "Oh, I am sure I have a cancer growing here. I can feel it." When complaining of this imaginary disease, she always placed her hand on her left breast, where she believed the cancer was attacking her.

For more than twenty years she kept this up.

A few weeks ago she died—*with cancer on her left breast!* If suggestion will actually turn the edge of a plank into a guillotine blade and transform healthy body cells into parasites out of which cancer will develop, can you not imagine what it will do in destroying disease germs, if properly directed? *Suggestion* is the law through which mental healers work what appear to be miracles. I have personally witnessed the removal of parasitical growths known as warts, through the aid of suggestion, within forty-eight hours.

You—the reader of this lesson—can be sent to bed with *imaginary* sickness of the worst sort, in two hours' time or less, through the use of *suggestion*. If you should start down the street and three or four people in whom you had confidence should meet you and each exclaim that you look ill you would be ready for a doctor. This brings to mind an experience that I once had with a life insurance salesman. I had made application for a policy, but was undecided as to whether I would take ten or twenty thousand dollars. Meanwhile, the agent had sent me to the life insurance company's doctor to be examined. The following day I was called back for another examination. The second time the examination was more searching, and the doctor carried a worried look on his face. The third day I was called back again, and this time two consulting physicians were there to look me over. They gave me the most searching examination I had ever received or even heard of.

Half the wrecks that strew life's ocean
If some star had been their guide,
Might in safety now be riding,
But they drifted with the Tide.

The next day the agent called on me and addressed me as follows:

"I do not wish to alarm you! but the doctors who examined you do not agree on your analysis. You have not yet decided whether you will take ten or twenty thousand dollars' worth of insurance, and I do not think it fair for me to give you a report on your medical examination until you make this decision, because if I did you might feel that I was urging you to take the larger amount."

Then I spoke up and said: "Well, I have already decided to take the full amount." True enough; I had decided to take the full twenty thousand dollar policy. *I decided the moment the agent planted the suggestion in my mind that perhaps I had some constitutional weakness that would make it hard for me to get as much insurance as I wanted.*

"Very well," said the agent, "now that you have decided I feel it my duty to tell you that two of the doctors believe you have the tubercular germ in your system, while the other two disagree with them." The trick had been turned. Clever suggestion had pushed me over the fence of indecision and we were all satisfied.

Where does *enthusiasm* come in, do you ask? Never mind, it "came in" all right, but if you wish to know who brought it you will have to ask the life insurance agent and his four medical *accomplices,* for I am sure they must have had a hearty laugh at my expense. But the trick was all right. I needed the insurance anyway.

Of course, if you happen to be a life insurance agent you will not grab this idea and work it out on the next prospective client who is slow in making up his mind about taking a policy. Of course you will not!

A few months ago I received one of the most effective pieces of advertising I ever saw. It was a neat little book in which a clever automobile insurance salesman had reprinted press dispatches that he had gathered from all over the country, in which it was shown that sixty-five automobiles had been stolen in a single day. On the back page of the book was this highly *suggestive* statement:

"*Your car may be the next one to go. Is it insured?*"

At the bottom of the page was the salesman's name and address; also his telephone number. Before I had finished reading the first two pages of the book I called the salesman on the telephone and made inquiry about rates. He came right over to see me, and you know the remainder of the story.

Go back, now, to the two letters and let us analyze the second one, which brought the desired replies from all to whom it was sent. Study, carefully, the first paragraph and you will observe that it asks a question which can be answered in but one way. Compare this opening paragraph with that of the first letter, by asking yourself which of the two would have impressed you most favorably. This paragraph is worded as it is for a two-fold purpose; first, it is intended to serve the purpose of neutralizing the mind of the reader so he will read the remainder of the letter in an open-minded attitude; and, second, it asks a question which can be answered in but one way, for the purpose of committing the reader to a viewpoint which harmonizes with the nature of the service that he is to be requested to render in subsequent paragraphs of the letter.

In the second lesson of this course you observed that Andrew Carnegie refused to answer my question, when I asked him to what he attributed his *success,* until he had asked me to define the word *success*. He did this to avoid misunderstanding. The first paragraph of the letter we are analyzing is so worded that it states the object of the letter and at the same time practically forces the reader to accept that object as being sound and reasonable.

Any person who would answer the question asked in this paragraph of the letter under discussion, in the negative, would, by the same answer, convict himself on the charge of selfishness, and no man wants to face himself with a guilty conscience on such a charge. Just as the farmer first plows his ground, then fertilizes it, and perhaps harrows it and prepares it to receive the seed, in order that he may be sure of a crop, so does this paragraph fertilize the mind of the reader and prepare it for the seed which is to be placed there through the subtle *suggestion* that the paragraph contains.

Study, carefully, the second paragraph of the letter and you will observe that it carries a statement of fact which the reader can *neither question nor deny!* It provides him with no reason for argument because it is obviously based upon a sound fundamental. It takes him the second step of the psychological journey that leads straight toward compliance with the request that is carefully clothed and covered up in the third paragraph of the letter, but you will notice that the third paragraph begins by paying the reader a nice little compliment that was not designed to make him angry. "Therefore, if you will write me of your views as to the most essential points to be borne in mind by those who are offering personal services for sale," etc. Study the wording of this sentence, together with the setting in which it has been placed, and you will observe that it hardly appears to be a request at all, and certainly there is nothing about it to suggest that the *writer of the letter is requesting a favor for his personal benefit.* At most, it can be construed merely as a request for a favor for others.

Now study the closing paragraph and notice how tactfully concealed is the suggestion that if the reader should refuse the request he is placing himself in the awkward position of one who does not care enough about those who are less fortunate than himself to spend a two cent stamp and a few minutes of time for their benefit.

From start to finish the letter conveys its strongest impressions by mere *suggestion,* yet this suggestion is so carefully covered that it is not obvious except upon careful analysis of the entire letter.

The whole construction of the letter is such that if the reader lays it aside without complying with the request it makes *he will have to reckon with his own conscience!* This effect is intensified by the last sentence of the last paragraph and especially by the last thirteen words of that sentence, "who will *read your message, believe in it, and be guided by it.*"

This letter brings the reader up with a bang and turns his own conscience into an ally of the writer; it corners him, just as a hunter might corner a rabbit by driving it into a carefully prepared net.

The best evidence that this analysis is correct is the fact that the letter brought replies from every person to whom it was sent, despite the fact that every one of these men was of the type that we speak of as being a man of affairs—the type that is generally supposed to be too busy to answer a letter of this nature. Not only did the letter bring the desired replies, but the men to whom it was sent replied in person, with the exception of the late Theodore Roosevelt, who replied under the signature of a secretary.

Conceit is a fog which envelops a man's real character beyond his own recognition. It weakens his native ability and strengthens all his inconsistencies.

John Wanamaker and Frank A. Vanderlip wrote two of the finest letters I have ever read, each a masterpiece that might well have adorned the pages of a more dignified volume than the one for which the letters were requested. Andrew Carnegie also wrote a letter that was well worth consideration by all who have personal services for sale. William Jennings Bryan wrote a fine letter, as did, also, the late Lord Northcliffe. None of these men wrote merely to please me, for I was unknown to all of them, with the exception of four. *They did not write to please me—they wrote to please themselves and to render a worthy service.* Perhaps the wording of the letter had something to do with this, but, as to that, I make no point other than to state that all of these men whom I have mentioned, and most others of their type, are generally the most willing men to render service for others when they are properly approached.

I wish to take advantage of this appropriate opportunity to state that all of the really big men whom I have had the pleasure of knowing have been the most willing and courteous men of my acquaintance when it came to rendering service that was of benefit to others. Perhaps that was one reason why they were *really* big men.

The human mind is a marvelous piece of machinery!

One of its outstanding characteristics is noticed in the fact that all impressions which reach it, either through outside *suggestion* or Auto-suggestion, are recorded together in groups which harmonize in nature. The negative impressions are stored away, all in one portion of the brain, while the positive impressions are stored in another portion. When one of these impressions (or past experiences) is called into the conscious mind, through the principle of memory, there is a tendency to recall with it all others of a similar nature, just as the raising of one link of a chain brings up other links with it. For example, anything that causes a feeling of doubt to arise in a person's mind is sufficient to call forth all of his experiences which caused him to become doubtful. If a man is asked by a stranger to cash a check, immediately he remembers having cashed checks that were not good, or of having heard of others who did so. Through the law of association all similar emotions, experiences and sense impressions that reach the mind are filed away together, so that the recalling of one has a tendency to bring back to memory all the others.

To arouse a feeling of distrust in a person's mind has a tendency to bring to the surface every doubt-building experience that person ever had. For this reason successful salesmen endeavor to keep away from the discussion of subjects that may arouse the buyer's "chain of doubt impressions" which he has stored away by reason of previous experiences. The successful salesman quickly learns that "knocking" a competitor or a competing article may result in bringing to the buyer's mind certain negative emotions growing out of previous experiences which may make it impossible for the salesman to "neutralize" the buyer's mind.

This principle applies to and controls every sense impression that is lodged in the human mind. Take the feeling of fear, for example; the moment we permit a single emotion that is related to fear to reach the conscious mind, it calls with it all of its unsavory relations. A feeling of courage cannot claim the attention of the conscious mind while a feeling of fear is there. One or the other must dominate. They make poor room-mates because they do not harmonize in nature. Like attracts like. Every thought held in the conscious mind has a tendency to draw to it other thoughts of a similar nature. You see, therefore, that these feelings, thoughts and emotions growing out of past experiences, which claim the attention of the conscious mind, are backed by a regular army of supporting soldiers of a similar nature, that stand ready to aid them in their work.

Deliberately place in your own mind, through the principle of Auto-suggestion, the ambition to succeed through the aid of a *definite chief aim,* and notice how quickly all of your latent or undeveloped ability in the nature of past experiences will become stimulated and aroused to action in your behalf. Plant in a boy's mind, through the principle of *suggestion,* the ambition to become a successful lawyer or doctor or engineer or business man or financier, and if you plant that suggestion deeply enough, and keep it there, by repetition, it will begin to move that boy toward the achievement of the object of that ambition.

If you would plant a *suggestion* "deeply," mix it generously with *enthusiasm;* for enthusiasm is the fertilizer that will insure its rapid growth as well as its permanency.

When that kind-hearted old gentleman planted in my mind the suggestion that I was a "bright boy" and that I could make my mark in the world if I would educate myself, it was not so much *what* he said, as it was the *way in which he said it* that made such a deep and lasting impression on my mind. It was the way in which he gripped my shoulders and the look of confidence in his eyes that drove his suggestion so deeply into my subconscious mind that it never gave me any peace until I commenced taking the steps that led to the fulfillment of the suggestion.

This is a point that I would stress with all the power at my command. *It is not so much what you say as it is the TONE and MANNER in which you say it that makes a lasting impression.*

It naturally follows, therefore, that sincerity of purpose, honesty and earnestness must be placed back of all that one says if one would make a lasting and favorable impression.

Whatever you successfully sell to others you must first sell to *yourself!*

Not long ago I was approached by an agent of the government of Mexico who sought my services as a writer of propaganda for the administration in charge at that time. His approach was about as follows:

"Whereas, Señor has a reputation as an exponent of the Golden Rule philosophy; and whereas, Señor is known throughout the United States as an independent who is not allied with any political faction, now, therefore, would Señor be gracious enough to come to Mexico, study the economic and political affairs of that country, then return to the United States and write a series of articles to appear in the newspapers, recommending to the people of America the immediate recognition of Mexico by the government of the United States, etc."

For this service, I was offered more money than I shall, perhaps, ever possess during my entire life; but I refused the commission, and for a reason that will fail to impress anyone except those who understand the principle which makes it necessary for all who would influence others to remain on good terms with their own conscience.

I could not write convincingly of Mexico's cause for the reason that I did not believe in that cause; therefore, I could not have mixed sufficient *enthusiasm* with my writing to have made it effective, even though I had been willing to prostitute my talent and dip my pen into ink that I knew to be muddy.

I will not endeavor further to explain my philosophy on this incident for the reason that those who are far enough advanced in the study of Auto-suggestion will not need further explanation, while those who are not far enough advanced would not and could not understand.

No man can afford to express, through words or acts, that which is not in harmony with his own belief, and if he does so he must pay by the loss of his ability to influence others.

Please read, aloud, the foregoing paragraph! It is worth emphasizing by repetition, for lack of observation of the principle upon which it is based constitutes the rocks and reefs upon which many a man's *definite chief aim* dashes itself to pieces.

I do not believe that I can afford to try to deceive anyone, about anything, but *I know that I cannot afford to try to deceive myself.* To do so would destroy the power of my pen and render my words ineffective. It is only when I write with the *fire of enthusiasm* burning in my heart that my writing impresses others favorably; and it is only when I speak from a heart that is bursting with belief in my message, that I can move my audience to accept that message.

I would also have you read, aloud, the foregoing paragraph. Yes, I would have you commit it to memory. Even more than this, I would have you write it out and place it where it may serve as a daily reminder of a principle, nay, a *law* as immutable as the law of gravitation, *without which you can never become a power in your chosen life-work.*

There have been times, and many of them, when it *appeared* that if I stood by this principle it would mean starvation!

There have been times when my closest friends and business advisers have strongly urged me to shade my

Is there not food for thought in the fact that no newspaper has ever published any account of "Wild drinking parties" or other similar scandals in connection with the names of Edison, Ford, Rockefeller and most of the other really big fellows?

philosophy for the sake of gaining a needed advantage here and there, but somehow I have managed to cling to it, mainly, I suppose, for the reason that I have preferred peace and harmony in my own heart to the material gain that I might have had by a forced compromise with my conscience.

Strange as it may seem, my deliberations and conclusions on this subject of refusing to strangle my own conscience have seldom been based upon what is commonly called "honesty." That which I have done in the matter of refraining from writing or speaking anything that I did not believe has been solely a question of honor between my conscience and myself. I have tried to express that which my heart dictated because I have aimed to give my words "flesh." It might be said that my motive was based more upon self-interest than it was on a desire to be fair with others, although I have never desired to be unfair with others, so far as I am able to analyze myself.

No man can become a master salesman if he compromises with falsehood. Murder will out, and even though no one ever catches him red-handed in expressing that which he does not believe, his words will fail in the accomplishment of their purpose because he cannot give them "flesh," if they do not come from his heart, and if they are not mixed with genuine, unadulterated *enthusiasm*.

I would also have you read, aloud, the foregoing paragraph, for it embraces a great law that you must *understand and apply* before you can become a person of influence in any undertaking.

In making these requests, for the sake of emphasis, I am not trying to take undue liberties with you. I am giving you full credit for being an adult, a thinker, an intelligent person, yet I know how likely you are to skip over these vital laws without being sufficiently impressed by them to make them a part of your own workaday philosophy. *I know your weakness because I know my own*. It has required the better part of twenty-five years of ups and downs—mostly downs—to impress these basic truths upon my own mind so that they influenced me. I have tried both them and their opposites; therefore, I can speak, not as one who merely *believes* in their soundness, but as one who *knows*.

And what do I mean by "these truths"?

So that you cannot possibly misunderstand my meaning, and so that these words of warning cannot possibly convey an abstract meaning, I will state that by "these truths" I mean this:

You cannot afford to suggest to another person, by word of mouth or by an act of yours, that which you do not believe.

Surely that is plain enough.

And, the reason you cannot afford to do so, is this:

If you compromise with your own conscience, it will not be long before you will have no conscience; for your conscience will fail to guide you, just as an alarm clock will fail to awaken you if you do not heed it.

Surely, that is plain enough, also.

And how do I happen to be an authority on this vital subject, do you ask?

I am an authority because I have experimented with the principle until I know how it works!

"But," you may ask, "how do I know that you are telling the truth?"

The answer is that *you will know only by experimenting for yourself, and by observing others who faithfully apply this principle and those who do not apply it.*

If my evidence needs backing, then consult any man whom you know to be a person who has "tried to get by" without observing this principle, and if he will not or cannot give you the truth you can get it, nevertheless, by analyzing the man.

There is but one thing in the world that gives a man real and enduring power, and that is *character!* *Reputation,* bear in mind, is not *character.* Reputation is that which people are believed to be; character is that which people *are!* If you would be a person of great influence, then be a person of real *character.*

Character is the philosopher's lode-stone through which all who have it may turn the base metals of their life into pure gold. Without *character* you have nothing; you are nothing; and you can be nothing, except a pile of flesh and bone and hair, worth perhaps twenty-five dollars. Character is something that you cannot beg or steal or buy. You can get it only by *building it;* and you can build it by your own *thoughts* and *deeds,* and in no other way.

Through the aid of Auto-suggestion, any person can build a sound character, no matter what his past has been. As a fitting close for this lesson, I wish to emphasize the fact that all who have *character* have *enthusiasm* and personality sufficient to draw to them others who have character.

You will now be instructed as to how you shall proceed in developing *enthusiasm,* in the event that you do not already possess this rare quality.

The instructions will be simple, but you will be unfortunate if you discount their value on that account.

First: Complete the remaining lessons of this course, because other important instructions which are to be co-ordinated with this one will be found in subsequent lessons.

Second: If you have not already done so, write out your *definite chief aim* in clear, simple language, and follow this by writing out the plan through which you intend to transform your *aim* into reality.

Third: Read over the description of your *definite chief aim* each night, just before retiring, and as you read, see yourself (in your imagination) in full possession of the object of your *aim.* Do this with full faith in your ability to transform your *definite chief aim* into reality. *Read aloud, with all the enthusiasm at your command, emphasizing every word. Repeat this reading until the small still voice within you tells you that your purpose will be realized.* Sometimes you will feel the effects of this voice *from within* the first time you read your *definite chief aim;* while at other times, you may have to read it a dozen or fifty times before the assurance comes, but do not stop until you feel it.

If you prefer to do so you may read your *definite chief aim* as a prayer.

The remainder of this lesson is for the person who has not yet learned the power of *faith* and who knows little or nothing of the principle of Auto-suggestion.

To all who are in this class, I would recommend the reading of the seventh and eighth verses of the seventh chapter, and the twentieth verse of the seventeenth chapter of St. Matthew.

One of the greatest powers for good, upon the face of this earth, is faith. To this marvelous power may be traced miracles of the most astounding nature. It offers peace on earth to all who embrace it.

Faith involves a principle that is so far-reaching in its effect that no man can say what are its limitations, or if it has limitations. *Write into the description of your definite chief aim a statement of the qualities that you intend to develop in yourself, and the station in life that you intend to attain, and have faith, as you read this description each night, that you can transform this purpose into reality.* Surely, you cannot miss the suggestion contained in this lesson.

To become successful you must be a person of action. Merely to "know" is not sufficient. It is necessary both to *know* and *do*.

Enthusiasm is the mainspring of the mind which urges one to put knowledge into action.

Billy Sunday is the most successful evangelist this country has ever known. For the purpose of studying his technique and checking up on his psychological methods the author of this course went through three campaigns with Reverend Sunday.

His success is based very largely upon one word—ENTHUSIASM!

By making effective use of the law of suggestion Billy Sunday conveys his own spirit of enthusiasm to the minds of his followers and they become influenced by it. He sells his sermons by the use of exactly the same sort of strategy employed by many Master Salesmen.

Enthusiasm is as essential to a salesman as water is to a duck!

If you think your lot in life has been hard read Up from Slavery *by Booker T. Washington, and you may see how fortunate you have been.*

All successful sales managers understand the psychology of enthusiasm and make use of it, in various ways, as a practical means of helping their men produce more sales.

Practically all sales organizations have get-together meetings at stated times, for the purpose of revitalizing the minds of all members of the sales force, and injecting the spirit of enthusiasm, which can be best done en masse, through group psychology.

Sales meetings might properly be called "revival" meetings, because their purpose is to revive interest and arouse enthusiasm which will enable the salesman to take up the fight with renewed ambition and energy.

During his administration as Sales Manager of the National Cash Register Company, Hugh Chalmers (who later became famous in the motor car industry) faced a most embarrassing situation which threatened to wipe out his position as well as that of thousands of salesmen under his direction.

The company was in financial difficulty. This fact had become known to the salesmen in the field and the effect of it was to cause them to lose their Enthusiasm. Sales began to dwindle until finally the conditions became so alarming that a general meeting of the sales organization was called, to be held at the company's plant in Dayton, Ohio. Salesmen were called in from all over the country.

Mr. Chalmers presided over the meeting. He began by calling on several of his best salesmen to get on their feet and tell what was wrong out in the field that orders had fallen off. One by one they got up, as called, and each man had a most terrible tale of grief to unfold. Business conditions were bad, money was scarce, people were holding off buying until after the Presidential election, etc. As the fifth man began to enumerate the difficulties which had kept him from making his usual quota of sales Mr. Chalmers jumped up on top of a table, held up his hands for silence, and said "STOP! I order this convention to come to a close for ten minutes while I get my shoes shined."

Then turning to a small colored boy who sat near by he ordered the boy to bring his shoe-shine outfit and shine his shoes, right where he stood, on top of the table.

The salesmen in the audience were astounded! Some of them thought that Mr. Chalmers had suddenly lost his mind. They began to whisper among themselves. Meanwhile, the little colored boy shined first one and then the other shoe, taking plenty of time and doing a first-class job.

After the job was finished Mr. Chalmers handed the boy a dime, then went ahead with his speech:

"I want each of you," said he, "to take a good look at this little colored boy. He has the concession for shoe-shining throughout our plant and offices. His predecessor was a white boy, considerably older than himself, and despite the fact that the company subsidized him with a salary of $5.00 a week he could not make a living in this plant, where thousands of people are employed.

"This little colored boy not only makes a good living, without any subsidy from the company, but he is actually saving money out of his earnings each week, working under the same conditions, in the same plant, for the same people.

"Now I wish to ask you a question: Whose fault was it that the white boy did not get more business? Was it his fault, or the fault of his buyers?"

In a mighty roar from the crowd the answer came back:

"IT WAS THE BOY'S FAULT, OF COURSE!"

"Just so," replied Chalmers, "and now I want to tell you this, that you are selling Cash Registers in the same territory, to the same people, with exactly the same business conditions that existed a year ago, yet you are not producing the business that you were then. Now whose fault is that? Is it yours, or the buyer's?"

And again the answer came back with a roar:

"IT IS OUR FAULT, OF COURSE!"

"I am glad that you are frank to acknowledge your faults," Chalmers continued, "and I now wish to tell you what your trouble is: You have heard rumors about this company being in financial trouble and that has killed off your enthusiasm so that you are not making the effort that you formerly made. If you will go back into your territories with a definite promise to send in five orders each during the next thirty days this company will no longer be in financial difficulty, for that additional business will see us clear. Will you do it?"

They said they would, and they did!

That incident has gone down in the history of the National Cash Register Company under the name of Hugh Chalmers' Million Dollar Shoe Shine, for it is said that this turned the tide in the company's affairs and was worth millions of dollars.

Enthusiasm knows no defeat! The Sales Manager who knows how to send out an army of enthusiastic salespeople may set his own price on his services, and what is more important even than this, he can increase the earning capacity of every person under his direction; thus, his enthusiasm benefits not only himself but perhaps hundreds of others.

Enthusiasm is never a matter of chance. There are certain stimuli which produce enthusiasm, the most important of these being as follows:

1. Occupation in work which one loves best.
2. Environment where one comes in contact with others who are enthusiastic and optimistic.
3. Financial success.
4. Complete mastery and application, in one's daily work, of the Fifteen Laws of Success.
5. Good health.
6. Knowledge that one has served others in some helpful manner.
7. Good clothes, appropriate to the needs of one's occupation.

All of these seven sources of stimuli are self-explanatory with the exception of the last. The psychology of clothes is understood by very few people, and for this reason it will be here explained in detail. Clothes constitute the most important part of the embellishment which every person must have in order to feel self-reliant, hopeful and enthusiastic.

The Psychology of Good Clothes

When the good news came from the theater of war, on November the eleventh, 1918, my worldly possessions amounted to but little more than they did the day I came into the world.

The war had destroyed my business and made it necessary for me to make a new start!

My wardrobe consisted of three well worn business suits and two uniforms which I no longer needed.

Knowing all too well that the world forms its first and most lasting impressions of a man by the clothes he wears, I lost no time in visiting my tailor.

Happily, my tailor had known me for many years, therefore he did not judge me entirely by the clothes I wore. If he had I would have been "sunk."

With less than a dollar in change in my pocket, I picked out the cloth for three of the most expensive suits I ever owned, and ordered that they be made up for me at once.

The three suits came to $375.00!

I shall never forget the remark made by the tailor as he took my measure. Glancing first at the three bolts of expensive cloth which I had selected, and then at me, he inquired:

"Dollar-a-year man, eh?"

"No," said I, "if I had been fortunate enough to get on the dollar-a-year payroll I might now have enough money to pay for these suits."

The tailor looked at me with surprise. I don't think he got the joke.

One of the suits was a beautiful dark gray; one was a dark blue; the other was a light blue with a pin stripe.

Fortunately I was in good standing with my tailor, therefore he did not ask when I was going to pay for those expensive suits.

I knew that I could and would pay for them in due time, but could I have convinced him of that? This was

All anyone really requires, as a capital on which to start a successful career, is a sound mind, a healthy body and a genuine desire to be of as much service as possible to as many people as possible.

the thought which was running through my mind, with hope against hope that the question would not be brought up.

I then visited my haberdasher, from whom I purchased three less expensive suits and a complete supply of the best shirts, collars, ties, hosiery and underwear that he carried.

My bill at the haberdasher's amounted to a little over $300.00.

With an air of prosperity I nonchalantly signed the charge ticket and tossed it back to the salesman, with instructions to deliver my purchase the following morning. The feeling of renewed self-reliance and success had begun to come over me, even before I had attired myself in my newly purchased outfit.

I was out of the war and $675.00 in debt, all in less than twenty-four hours.

The following day the first of the three suits ordered from the haberdasher was delivered. I put it on at once, stuffed a new silk handkerchief in the outside pocket of my coat, shoved the $50.00 I had borrowed on my ring down into my pants pocket, and walked down Michigan Boulevard, in Chicago, feeling as rich as Rockefeller.

Every article of clothing I wore, from my underwear out, was of the very best. That it was not paid for was nobody's business except mine and my tailor's and my haberdasher's.

Every morning I dressed myself in an entirely new outfit, and walked down the same street, at precisely the same hour. That hour "happened" to be the time when a certain wealthy publisher usually walked down the same street, on his way to lunch.

I made it my business to speak to him each day, and occasionally I would stop for a minute's chat with him.

After this daily meeting had been going on for about a week I met this publisher one day, but decided I would see if he would let me get by without speaking.

Watching him from under my eyelashes I looked straight ahead, and started to pass him when he stopped and motioned me over to the edge of the sidewalk, placed his hand on my shoulder, looked me over from head to foot, and said: "You look damned prosperous for a man who has just laid aside a uniform. Who makes your clothes?"

"Well," said I, "Wilkie & Sellery made this particular suit."

He then wanted to know what sort of business I was engaged in. That "airy" atmosphere of prosperity which I had been wearing, along with a new and different suit every day, had got the better of his curiosity. (I had hoped that it would.)

Flipping the ashes from my Havana perfecto, I said "Oh, I am preparing the copy for a new magazine that I am going to publish."

"A new magazine, eh?" he queried, "and what are you going to call it?"

"It is to be named *Hill's Golden Rule*."

"Don't forget," said my publisher friend, "that I am in the business of printing and distributing magazines. Perhaps I can serve you, also."

That was the moment for which I had been waiting. I had that very moment, and almost the very spot of ground on which we stood, in mind when I was purchasing those new suits.

But, is it necessary to remind you, that conversation never would have taken place had this publisher observed me walking down that street from day to day, with a "whipped-dog" look on my face, an unpressed suit on my back and a look of poverty in my eyes.

An appearance of prosperity attracts attention always, with no exceptions whatsover. Moreover, a look of prosperity attracts "favorable attention," because the one dominating desire in every human heart is to be prosperous.

My publisher friend invited me to his club for lunch. Before the coffee and cigars had been served he had "talked me out of" the contract for printing and distributing my magazine. I had even "consented" to permit him to supply the capital, without any interest charge.

For the benefit of those who are not familiar with the publishing business may I not offer the information that considerable capital is required for launching a new nationally distributed magazine.

Capital, in such large amounts, is often hard to get, even with the best of security. The capital necessary for launching *Hill's Golden Rule* magazine, which you may have read, was well above $30,000.00, and every cent of it was raised on a "front" created mostly by good clothes. True, there may have been some ability back of those clothes, but many millions of men have ability who never have anything else, and who are never heard of outside of the limited community in which they live. This is a rather sad truth!

To some it may seem an unpardonable extravagance for one who was "broke" to have gone in debt for $675.00 worth of clothes, but the psychology back of that investment more than justified it.

The appearance of prosperity not only made a favorable impression on those to whom I had to look for favors, but of more importance still was the effect that proper attire HAD ON ME.

I not only knew that correct clothes would impress others favorably, but I knew also that good clothes would give me an atmosphere of self-reliance, without which I could not hope to regain my lost fortunes.

I got my first training in the psychology of good clothes from my friend Edwin C. Barnes, who is a close business associate of Thomas A. Edison. Barnes afforded considerable amusement for the Edison staff when, some twenty-odd years ago, he rode into West Orange on a freight train (not being able to raise sufficient money for passenger fare) and announced at the Edison offices that he had come to enter into a partnership with Mr. Edison.

Nearly everybody around the Edison plant laughed at Barnes, except Edison himself. He saw something in the square jaw and determined face of young Barnes which most of the others did not see, despite the fact that the young man looked more like a tramp than he did a future partner of the greatest inventor on earth.

Barnes got his start, sweeping floors in the Edison offices!

That was all he sought—just a chance to get a toehold in the Edison organization. From there on he made history that is well worth emulation by other young men who wish to make places for themselves.

Barnes has now retired from active business, even though he is still a comparatively young man, and spends most of his time at his two beautiful homes in Bradentown, Florida, and Damariscotta, Maine. He is a multimillionaire, prosperous and happy.

I first became acquainted with Barnes during the early days of his association with Edison, before he had "arrived."

In those days he had the largest and most expensive collection of clothes I had ever seen or heard of one man owning. His wardrobe consisted of thirty-one suits; one for each day of the month. He never wore the same suit two days in succession.

Moreover, all his suits were of the most expensive type. (Incidentally, his clothes were made by the same tailors who made those three suits for me.)

He wore socks which cost six dollars per pair.

There is a suitable reward for every virtue and appropriate punishment for every sin a man commits. Both the reward and the punishment are effects over which no man has control, as they come upon him voluntarily.

His shirts and other wearing apparel cost in similar proportion. His cravats were specially made, at a cost of from five to seven dollars and a half each.

One day, in a spirit of fun, I asked him to save some of his old suits which he did not need, for me.

He informed me that he hadn't a single suit which he did not need!

He then gave me a lesson on the psychology of clothes which is well worth remembering. "I do not wear

278

thirty-one suits of clothes," said he, "entirely for the impression they make on other people; I do it mostly for the impression they have on me."

Barnes then told me of the day when he presented himself at the Edison plant, for a position. He said he had to walk around the plant a dozen times before he worked up enough courage to announce himself, because he knew that he looked more like a tramp than he did a desirable employee.

Barnes is said to be the most able salesman ever connected with the great inventor of West Orange. His entire fortune was made through his ability as a salesman, but he has often said that he never could have accomplished the results which have made him both wealthy and famous had it not been for his understanding of the psychology of clothes.

I have met many salesman in my time. During the past ten years I have personally trained and directed the efforts of more than 3,000 salespeople, both men and women, and I have observed that, without a single exception, the star producers were all people who understood and made good use of the psychology of clothes.

I have seen a few well dressed people who made no outstanding records as salesmen, but I have yet to see the first poorly dressed man who became a star producer in the field of selling.

I have studied the psychology of clothes for so long, and I have watched its effect on people in so many different walks of life, that I am fully convinced there is a close connection between clothes and success.

Personally I feel no need of thirty-one suits of clothes, but if my personality demanded a wardrobe of this size I would manage to get it, no matter how much it might cost.

To be well dressed a man should have at least ten suits of clothes. He should have a different suit for each of the seven days of the week, a full dress suit and a Tuxedo, for formal evening occasions, and a cutaway for formal afternoon occasions.

For summer wear he should have an assortment of at least four appropriate light suits, with blue coat and white flannel trousers for informal afternoon and evening occasions. If he plays golf he should have at least one golf suit.

This, of course, is for the man who is a notch or two above the "mediocre" class. The man who is satisfied with mediocrity needs but few clothes.

It may be true, as a well known poet has said, that "clothes do not make the man," but no one can deny the fact that good clothes go a very long way toward giving him a *favorable start*.

A man's bank will generally loan him all the money he wants when he does not need it—when he is prosperous, but never go to your bank for a loan with a shabby-looking suit on your back and a look of poverty in your eyes, for if you do you'll get the gate.

Success attracts success! There is no escape from this great universal law; therefore, if you wish to attract success make sure that you look the part of success, whether your calling is that of day laborer or merchant prince.

For the benefit of the more "dignified" students of this philosophy who may object to resorting to "stunt" stimuli or "trick clothing" as a means of achieving success, it may be profitably explained that practically every successful man on earth has discovered some form of stimulus through which he can and does drive himself on to greater effort.

It may be shocking to members of the Anti-Saloon League, but it is said to be true, nevertheless, that James Whitcomb Riley wrote his best poems when he was under the influence of alcohol. His stimulus was liquor. (The author wishes it distinctly understood that he does not recommend the use of alcoholic or narcotic stimuli, for any purpose whatsoever, as either will eventually destroy both body and mind of all who use them.) Under the influence of alcohol Riley became imaginative, enthusiastic and an entirely different person, according to close personal friends of his.

Edwin Barnes spurred himself into the necessary action to produce outstanding results, with the aid of good clothes.

Some men rise to great heights of achievement as the result of love for some woman. Connect this with the brief suggestion to the subject which was made in the Introduction and you will, if you are a person who knows the ways of men, be able to finish the discussion of this particular phase of enthusiasm stimulus without further comment by the author which might not be appropriate for the younger minds that will assimilate this philosophy.

Underworld characters who are engaged in the dangerous business of highway robbery, burglary, etc., generally "dope" themselves for the occasion of their operations, with cocaine, morphine and other narcotics. Even in this there is a lesson which shows that practically all men need temporary or artificial stimuli to drive them to greater effort than that normally employed in the ordinary pursuits of life.

SUCCESSFUL PEOPLE HAVE DISCOVERED WAYS AND MEANS WHICH THEY BELIEVE BEST SUITED TO THEIR OWN NEEDS, TO PRODUCE STIMULI

WHICH CAUSE THEM TO RISE TO HEIGHTS OF ENDEAVOR ABOVE THE OR-
DINARY.

One of the most successful writers in the world employs an orchestra of beautifully dressed young women who play for him while he writes. Seated in a room that has been artistically decorated to suit his own taste, under lights that have been colored, tinted and softened, these beautiful young ladies, dressed in handsome evening gowns, play his favorite music. To use his own words, "I become drunk with enthusiasm, under the influence of this environment, and rise to heights I never know or feel on other occasions. It is then that I do my work. The thoughts pour in on me as if they were dictated by an unseen and unknown power."

This author gets much of his inspiration from music and art. Once a week he spends at least an hour in an art museum, looking at the works of the masters. On these occasions, again using his own words, "I get enough enthusiasm from one hour's visit in the museum of art to carry me for two days."

Edgar Allan Poe wrote "The Raven" when, it is reported, he was more than half intoxicated. Oscar Wilde wrote his poems under the influence of a form of stimulus which cannot be appropriately mentioned in a course of this nature.

Henry Ford (so it is believed by this author, who admits that this is merely the author's opinion) got his real start as the result of his love for his charming life-companion. It was she who inspired him, gave him faith in himself, and kept him keyed up so that he carried on in the face of adversities which would have killed off a dozen ordinary men.

These incidents are cited as evidence that men of outstanding achievement have, by accident or design, discovered ways and means of stimulating themselves to a high state of enthusiasm.

Associate that which has been here stated with what was said concerning the law of the "Master Mind," in the Introduction, and you will have an entirely new conception of the modus operandi through which that law may be applied. You will also have a somewhat different understanding of the real purpose of "allied effort, in a spirit of perfect harmony," which constitutes the best known method of bringing into use the Law of the Master Mind.

At this point it seems appropriate to call your attention to the manner in which the lessons of this course blend. You will observe that each lesson covers the subject intended to be covered, and in addition to this it

Your employer does not control the sort of service you render. You control that, and it is the thing that makes or breaks you.

281

overlaps and gives the student a better understanding of some other lesson or lessons of the course.

In the light of what has been said in this lesson, for example, the student will better understand the real purpose of the Law of the Master Mind; that purpose being, in the main, a practical method of stimulating the minds of all who participate in the group constituting the Master Mind.

Times too numerous to be here described this author has gone into conference with men whose faces showed the signs of care, who had the appearance of worry written all over them, only to see those same men straighten up their shoulders, tilt their chins at a higher angle, soften their faces with smiles of confidence, and get down to business with that sort of ENTHUSIASM which knows no defeat.

The change took place the moment harmony of purpose was established.

If a man goes about the affairs of life in the same day-in and day-out, prosaic, lackadaisical spirit, devoid of enthusiasm, he is doomed to failure. Nothing can save him until he changes his attitude and learns how to stimulate his mind and body to unusual heights of enthusiasm AT WILL!

The author is unwilling to leave this subject without having stated the principle here described in so many different ways that it is bound to be understood and also respected by the students of this course, who, all will remember, are men and women of all sorts of natures, experiences and degrees of intelligence. For this reason much repetition is essential.

Your business in life, you are reminded once again, is to achieve success!

With the stimulus you will experience from studying this philosophy, and with the aid of the ideas you will gather from it, plus the personal co-operation of the author who will give you an accurate inventory of your outstanding qualities, you should be able to create a DEFINITE PLAN that will lift you to great heights of achievement. However, there is no plan that can produce this desirable result without the aid of some influence that will cause you to arouse yourself, in a spirit of enthusiasm, to where you will exert greater than the ordinary effort which you put into your daily occupation.

You are now ready for the lesson on Self-control!

As you read that lesson you will observe that it has a vital bearing on this lesson, just as this lesson has a direct connection with the preceding lessons on A Definite Chief Aim, Self-confidence, Initiative and Leadership and Imagination.

The next lesson describes the Law which serves as the Balance Wheel of this entire philosophy.

THE SEVEN DEADLY HORSEMEN

An After-the-Lesson Visit with the Author

The "seven horsemen" are labeled, in order shown,—Intolerance, Greed, Revenge, Egotism, Suspicion, Jealously and "?"

The worst enemy that any man has is the one that walks around under his own hat.

If you could see yourself as others see you the enemies that you harbor in your own personality might be discovered and thrown out. The Seven Enemies named in this essay are the commonest which ride millions of men and women to failure without being discovered. Weigh yourself carefully and find out how many of the Seven you are harboring.

You see, in this picture, seven deadly warriors! From birth until death every human being must give battle to these enemies. Your success will be measured very largely by the way you manage your battle against these swift riders.

As you look at this picture you will say, of course, that it is only imagination. True, the picture is imaginary, but the swift riders of destruction are REAL.

If these enemies rode openly, on real horses, they would not be dangerous, because they could be rounded up and put out of commission. But, they ride unseen, in the minds of men. So silently and subtly do they work that most people never recognize their presence.

Take inventory of yourself and find out how many of these seven horsemen you are harboring.

In the foreground you will find the most dangerous and the commonest of the riders. You will be fortunate if you discover this enemy and protect yourself against it. This cruel warrior, INTOLERANCE, has killed more people, destroyed more friendships, brought more misery and suffering into the world and caused more wars than all of the other six horsemen that you see in this picture.

Until you master INTOLERANCE you will never become an accurate thinker. This enemy of mankind closes up the mind and pushes reason and logic and FACTS into the background. If you find yourself hating those whose religious viewpoint is different from your own you may be sure that the most dangerous of the seven deadly horsemen still rides in your brain.

Next, in the picture, you will observe REVENGE and GREED!

These riders travel side by side. Where one is found the other is always close at hand. GREED warps and twists man's brain so that he wants to build a fence around the earth and keep everyone else on the outside of it. This is the enemy that drives man to accumulate millions upon top of millions of dollars which he does not need and can never use. This is the enemy that causes man to twist the screw until he has wrung the last drop of blood from his fellow man.

And, thanks to REVENGE which rides alongside of GREED, the unfortunate person who gives brain-room to these cruel twins is not satisfied to merely take away his fellow man's earthly belongings; he wants to destroy his reputation in the bargain.

"Revenge is a naked sword—
    It has neither hilt nor guard.
Would'st thou wield this brand of the Lord:
    Is thy grasp then firm and hard?
But the closer thy clutch of the blade,
    The deadlier blow thou would'st deal,
Deeper wound in thy hand is made—
    It is thy blood reddens the steel.
And when thou hast dealt the blow—
    When the blade from thy hand has flown—
Instead of the heart of the foe
    Thou may'st find it sheathed in thine own."

If you would know how deadly are ENVY and GREED, study the history of every man who has set out to become RULER OF THIS WORLD!

If you do not wish to undertake so ambitious a program of research, then study the people around you; those who have tried and those who are now trying to "feather their own nests" at the cost of others. GREED and REVENGE stand at the crossroads of life, where they turn aside to failure and misery every person who would take the road that leads to success. It is a part of your business not to permit them to interfere with you when you approach one of these crossroads.

Both individuals and nations rapidly decline where GREED and ENVY ride in the minds of those who dominate. Take a look at Mexico and Spain if you wish to know what happens to the envious and the greedy.

Most important of all, take a look at YOURSELF and make sure that these two deadly enemies are not riding in your brain!

Turn your attention, now, to two more twins of destruction—EGOTISM and SUSPICION. Observe that they, also, ride side by side. There is no hope of success for the person who suffers either from too much self-love or lack of confidence in others.

Someone who likes to manipulate figures has estimated that the largest club in the world is the "IT CAN'T BE DONE CLUB." It is claimed that there are approximately ninety-nine million members of this club in the United States of America alone.

If you have no FAITH in other people you have not the seed of success in you. SUSPICION is a prolific germ. If permitted to get a start it rapidly multiplies itself until it leaves no room for FAITH.

Without faith no man may enjoy enduring success.

Running, like a golden cord of illumination throughout the Bible, is the admonition to have FAITH. Before civilization lost itself in its mad rush for dollars men understood the power of FAITH.

"For verily I say unto you, if ye have faith as a grain of mustard seed, ye shall say unto this mountain, Remove hence to yonder place; and it shall remove; and nothing shall be impossible unto you."

The writer of this passage, which appears in the Bible, understood a great law which but few of today understand. Believe in people if you would have them believe in you. Kill off SUSPICION. If you do not it will kill you off.

If you would have power, cultivate FAITH in mankind!

EGOTISM thrives where SUSPICION exists. Interest yourself in others and you will be too busy to indulge in self-love. Observe those around you who begin every sentence with the personal pronoun, "I," and you will notice that they are suspicious of other people.

The man who can forget himself while engaging in useful service to other people is never cursed with SUSPICION. Study those about you who are both SUSPICIOUS and EGOTISTICAL and see how many of this type you can name who are successful in whatever work they may be engaged in.

And, while making this study of OTHERS, study, also, yourself!

Be sure that you are not bound down by EGOTISM and SUSPICION.

Bringing up the rear of this deadly group of riders you see two horsemen. One is JEALOUSY and the name of the other has been purposely omitted.

Each reader of this article may take inventory of himself and give the seventh rider a name that fits whatever he finds in his own mind.

Some will name this rider DISHONESTY. Others will name it PROCRASTINATION. A few will have the courage to name it UNCONTROLLED SEX DESIRE. As for you, name it whatever you please, but be sure to give it a name.

Perhaps your own imagination will supply an appropriate name as a fellow-traveler for JEALOUSY.

You will be better prepared to give the unnamed rider a name if you know that JEALOUSY is a form of insanity! Facts are sometimes cruel things to face. It is a fact that JEALOUSY is a form of insanity, known to the medical fraternity as "dementia praecox."

> "O jealousy,
> Thou ugliest fiend of hell! thy deadly venom
> Preys on my vitals, turns the healthful hue
> Of my fresh cheek to haggard sallowness,
> And drinks my spirit up!"

You will notice that JEALOUSY rides just back of SUSPICION. Some who read this will say that JEALOUSY and SUSPICION should have ridden side by side, as one often leads to the other in man's mind.

JEALOUSY is the most common form of insanity. It rides in the minds of both men and women; sometimes with a real cause, but more often without any cause whatsoever.

This deadly rider is a great friend of the divorce lawyers!

It also keeps detective agencies busy night and day.

It takes its regular toll of murder. It breaks up homes and makes widows of mothers and orphans of innocent little children. Peace and happiness can never be YOURS as long as this rider remains unharnessed in your brain.

Man and wife may go through life together in poverty and still be very happy, if both are free from this child of insanity known as JEALOUSY. Examine yourself carefully and if you find any evidence of JEALOUSY in your mind begin, at once, to master it.

JEALOUSY rides in many forms.

When it first begins to creep into the brain it manifests itself in something after this fashion:

"I wonder where she is and what she is doing while I am away?"

Or, "I wonder if he does not see another woman when he is away from me?"

When these questions begin to arise in your mind do not call in a detective. Instead, go to the psychopathic hospital and have yourself examined, because more than likely you are suffering from a mild form of insanity.

Get your foot on JEALOUSY'S neck before it gets its clutches on your throat.

After you have read this essay lay it aside and THINK about it.

At first you may say, "This does not apply to me. I have no imaginary horsemen in my brain." And, you may be right—ONE OUT OF EVERY TEN MILLION COULD SAY THIS AND BE RIGHT! The other nine million nine hundred and ninety-nine thousand nine hundred and ninety-nine would be wrong.

Do not fool yourself! You may be in that larger class. The purpose of this article is to get you to see yourself as YOU ARE! If you are suffering failure and poverty and misery in any of their forms you are sure to discover one or more of these deadly riders in your brain.

Make no mistake about it—those who have all they want, including happiness and good health, have driven the seven horsemen out of their brains.

Come back to this essay a month from now, after you have had time to analyze yourself carefully. Read it again and it may bring you face to face with FACTS that will emancipate you from a horde of cruel enemies that now ride within your brain without your knowing it.

No man achieves great success who is unwilling to make personal sacrifices.

SELF-CONTROL

"You Can Do It If You Believe You Can!"

In the preceding lesson you learned of the value of enthusiasm. You also learned how to generate enthusiasm and how to transmit its influence to others, through the principle of *suggestion*.

You come, now, to the study of *self-control,* through which you may direct your *enthusiasm* to constructive ends. Without *self-control* enthusiasm resembles the unharnessed lightning of an electrical storm—it may strike *anywhere;* it may destroy life and property.

Enthusiasm is the vital quality that arouses you to *action,* while *self-control* is the balance wheel that directs your *action* so that it will build up and not tear down.

To be a person who is well "balanced," you must be a person in whom *enthusiasm* and *self-control* are equalized. A survey which I have just completed of the 160,000 adult inmates of the penitentiaries of the United States discloses the startling fact that ninety-two per cent of these unfortunate men and women are in prison because they lacked the necessary *self-control* to direct their energies constructively.

Read the foregoing paragraph again; it is authentic, it is *startling!*

It is a fact that the majority of a man's griefs come about through lack of *self-control.* The holy scriptures are full of admonition in support of *self-control.* They even urge us to love our enemies and to forgive those who injure us. The law of non-resistance runs, like a golden cord, throughout the Bible.

Study the records of those whom the world calls great, and observe that *every one of them possesses this quality of self-control!*

For example, study the characteristics of our own immortal Lincoln. In the midst of his most trying hours he exercised patience, poise and *self-control.* These were some of the qualities which made him the great man that he was. He found disloyalty in some of the members of his cabinet; but, for the reason that this disloyalty was toward him, personally, and because those in whom he found it had qualities which made them valuable to his country, Lincoln exercised *self-control* and disregarded the objectionable qualities.

How many men do you know who have *self-control* to equal this?

In language more forceful than it was polished, Billy Sunday exclaimed from the pulpit: "*There is something as rotten as hell about the man who is always trying to show some other fellow up!*" I wonder if the "devil" didn't yell, "Amen, brother!" when Billy made that statement?

However, *self-control* becomes an important factor in this Reading Course on the Law of Success, not so much because lack of it works hardships on those who become its victims, as for the reason that those who do not exercise it suffer the loss of a great power which they need in their struggle for achievement of their *definite chief aim.*

If you neglect to exercise *self-control,* you are not only likely to injure others, but you are *sure to injure yourself!*

During the early part of my public career I discovered what havoc lack of *self-control* was playing in my life, and this discovery came about through a very commonplace incident. (I believe it not out of place here to digress by making the statement that most of the great truths of life are wrapped up in the ordinary, commonplace events of every-day life.)

This discovery taught me one of the most important lessons I have ever learned. It came about in this way:

One day, in the building in which I had my office, the janitor and I had a misunderstanding. This led to a most violent form of mutual dislike between us. As a means of showing his contempt for me, this janitor would switch off the electric lights of the building when he knew that I was there alone at work in my study. This happened on several occasions until I finally decided to "strike back." My opportunity came one Sunday when I came to my study to prepare an address that I had to deliver the following night. I had hardly seated myself at my desk when off went the lights.

I jumped to my feet and ran toward the basement of the building where I knew I would find the janitor. When I arrived, I found him busily engaged, shoveling coal into the furnace, and whistling as though nothing unusual had happened.

Without ceremony I pitched into him, and for five minutes I hurled adjectives at him which were hotter than the fire that he was feeding. Finally, I ran out of words and had to slow down. Then he straightened himself up, looked back over his shoulder, and in a calm, smooth tone of voice that was full of poise and *self-control,* and with a smile on his face that reached from ear to ear, he said:

"Why, you-all's just a little bit excited this morning, ain't you?"

That remark cut as though it had been a stiletto!

Imagine my feelings as I stood there before an illiterate man who could neither read nor write, but who, despite this handicap, had defeated me in a duel that had been fought on grounds—and with a weapon—of my own choice.

My conscience pointed an accusing finger at me. I knew that not only had I been defeated but, what was worse, I knew that I was the aggressor and that I *was in the wrong,* which only served to intensify my humiliation.

Not only did my conscience point an accusing finger at me, but it placed some very embarrassing thoughts in my mind; it mocked me and it tantalized me. There I stood, a boasted student of advanced psychology, an exponent of the Golden Rule philosophy, having at least a fair acquaintance with the works of Shakespeare, Socrates, Plato, Emerson and the Bible; while facing me stood a man who knew nothing of literature or of philosophy, but who had, despite this lack of knowledge, whipped me in a battle of words.

I turned and went back to my office as rapidly as I could go. There was nothing else for me to do. As I began to think the matter over I saw my mistake, but, true to nature, I was reluctant to do that which I knew must be done to right the wrong. I knew that I would have to apologize to that man before I could place myself at peace in my own heart, much less with him. Finally, I made up my mind to go back down to the basement and suffer this humility which I knew I had to undergo. The decision was not easily reached, nor did I reach it quickly.

I started down, but I walked more slowly than I had when I went down the first trip. I was trying to think how I would make the second approach so as to suffer the least humili-ation possible.

When I got to the basement I called to the janitor to come over to the door. In a calm, kindly tone of voice he asked:

"What do you wish this time?"

I informed him that I had come back to apologize for the wrong I had done, if he would permit me to do so. Again that smile spread all over his face as he said:

> *The man who actually knows just what he wants in life has already gone a long way toward attaining it.*

"For the love of the Lord, you don't have to apologize. Nobody heard you except these four walls and you and me. I ain't going to tell it and I know you ain't going to tell it, so just forget it."

And that remark hurt more than his first one, for he had not only expressed a willingness to forgive me, but he had actually indicated his willingness to help me cover the incident up, so it would not become known and do me an injury.

But I walked over to him and took him by the hand. I shook with more than my hand—I shook with my heart—and as I walked back to my office I felt good for having summoned the courage with which to right the wrong I had done.

This is not the end of the story. *It is only the beginning!* Following this incident, I made a resolution that I would never again place myself in a position in which another man, whether he be an illiterate janitor or a man of letters, could humiliate me because I had lost my *self-control.*

Following that resolution, a remarkable change began to take place in me. My pen began to take on greater power. My spoken words began to carry greater weight. I began to make more friends and fewer enemies among men of my acquaintance. The incident marked one of the most important turning-points of my life. It taught me that no man can control others unless he first controls himself. It gave me a clear conception of the philosophy back of these words, "Whom the gods would destroy, they first make mad." It also gave me a clear conception of the law of non-resistance and helped me interpret many passages of the holy scriptures, bearing on the subject of this law, as I had never before interpreted them.

This incident placed in my hands the pass-key to a storehouse of knowledge that is illuminating and helpful in all that I do, and, later in life, when enemies sought to destroy me, it gave me a powerful weapon of defense that has never failed me.

Lack of *self-control* is the average salesman's most damaging weakness. The prospective buyer says something that the salesman does not wish to hear, and, if he has not this quality of *self-control,* he will "strike back" with a counter remark that is fatal to his sale.

In one of the large department stores of Chicago I witnessed an incident that illustrated the importance of *self-control.* A long line of women were in front of the "complaint" desk, telling their troubles and *the store's faults* to the young woman in charge. Some of the women were angry and unreasonable and some of them made very ugly remarks. The young woman at the desk received the disgruntled women without the slightest sign of resentment at their remarks. With a smile on her face she directed these women to the proper departments with such charming grace and poise that I marveled at her *self-control*.

Standing just back of her was another young woman who was making notations on slips of paper and passing them in front of her, as the women in the line unburdened their troubles. These slips of paper contained the gist of what the women in the line were saying, minus the "vitriolic coloring" and the anger.

The smiling young woman at the desk who was "hearing" the complaints was *stone deaf!* Her assistant supplied her with all the necessary facts, through those slips of paper.

I was so impressed with the plan that I sought the manager of the store and interviewed him. He informed me that he had selected a deaf woman for one of the most trying and important positions in the store for the reason that he had not been able to find any other person with sufficient *self-control* to fill the place.

As I stood and watched that line of angry women, I observed what pleasant effect the smile of the young woman at the desk had upon them. They came before her growling like wolves and went away as meek and quiet as sheep. In fact some of them had "sheepish" looks on their faces as they left, because the young woman's *self-control* had made them ashamed of themselves.

Ever since I witnessed that scene, I have thought of the poise and self-control of that young woman at the desk every time I felt myself becoming irritated at remarks which I did not like, and often I have thought that everybody should have a set of "mental ear muffs" which they could slip over their ears at times. Personally, I have developed the habit of "closing" my ears against much of the idle chatter such as I used to make it my business to resent. Life is too short and there is too much constructive work to be done to justify us in "striking back" at everyone who says that which we do not wish to hear.

In the practice of law I have observed a very clever trick that trial lawyers use when they wish to get a statement of facts from a belligerent witness who answers questions with the proverbial "I do not remember" or "I do not know." When everything else fails, they manage to make such a witness angry; and in this state of mind they cause him to lose his *self-control* and make statements that he would not have made had he kept a "cool" head.

Most of us go through life with our "weather eye" cast skyward in quest of trouble. We usually find that for which we are looking. In my travels I have been a student of men whom I have heard in "Pullman car conversation," and I have observed that practically nine out of every ten have so little *self-control* that they will "invite" themselves into the discussion of almost any subject that may be brought up. But few men are contented to sit in a smoking compartment and listen to a conversation without joining in and "airing" their views.

Once I was traveling from Albany to New York City. On the way down, the "Smoking Car Club" started a conversation about the late Richard Croker, who was then chief of Tammany Hall. The discussion became loud and bitter. Everyone became angry except one old gentleman who was agitating the argument and taking a lively interest in it. He remained calm and seemed to enjoy all the mean things the others said about the "Tiger" of Tammany Hall. Of course, I supposed that he was an enemy of the Tammany Chief, but he *wasn't!*

He was Richard Croker, himself!

This was one of his clever tricks through which he found out what people thought of him and what his enemies' plans were.

Whatever else Richard Croker might have been, he was a man of *self-control*. Perhaps that is one reason why he remained undisputed boss of Tammany Hall as long as he did. *Men who control themselves usually boss the job, no matter what it may be.*

Please read, again, the last sentence of the preceding paragraph, for it carries a subtle suggestion that might be of profit to *you*. This is a commonplace incident, but it is in just such incidents that the great truths of life are hidden—hidden because the settings are ordinary and commonplace.

Not long ago I accompanied my wife on a "bargain-hunting" bee. Our attention was attracted by a crowd of women who were elbowing each other out of the way in front of a petticoat counter at which "bargains" were being offered. One lady who looked to be about forty-five years of age crawled on her hands and knees through the crowd and "bobbed" up in front of a customer who had engaged the attention of the saleswoman ahead of her. In a loud, high-pitched tone of voice she demanded attention. The saleswoman was a diplomat who understood human nature; she also possessed *self-control,* for she smiled sweetly at the intruder and said: "Yes, *Miss;* I will be with you in a moment!"

The intruder calmed herself!

I do not know whether it was the "Yes, *Miss,*" or the sweet tone in which it was said that modified her attitude; but it was one or the other; perhaps it was both. I do know, however, that the saleswoman was rewarded for her *self-control* by the sale of three petticoats, and the happy *"Miss"* went away feeling much younger for the remark.

No man can rise to fame and fortune without carrying others along with him. It simply cannot be done.

Roast turkey is a very popular dish, but overeating of it cost a friend of mine, who is in the printing business, a fifty thousand dollar order. It happened the day after Thanksgiving, when I called at his office for the purpose of introducing him to a prominent Russian who had come to the United States to publish a book. The Russian spoke broken English and it was therefore hard for him to make himself easily understood. During the interview he asked my printer friend a question which was mistaken as a reflection upon his ability as a printer. In an unguarded moment he countered with this remark:

"The trouble with you Bolsheviks is that you look with suspicion on the remainder of the world just because of your own short-sightedness."

My "Bolshevik" friend nudged me on the elbow and whispered:

"The gentleman seems to be sick. We shall call again, when he is feeling better."

But, he never called again. He placed his order with another printer, and I learned afterward that the profit on that order was more than $10,000.00!

Ten thousand dollars seems a high price to pay for a plate of turkey, but that is the price that it cost my printer friend; for he offered me an apology for his conduct on the ground that his turkey dinner had given him indigestion and therefore he had lost his *self-control*.

One of the largest chain store concerns in the world has adopted a unique, though effective, method of employing salespeople who have developed the essential quality of *self-control* which all successful salespeople must possess. This concern has in its employ a very clever woman who visits department stores and other places where salespeople are employed and selects certain ones whom she believes to possess tact and *self-control;* but, to be sure of her judgment, she approaches these salespeople and has them show her their wares. She asks all sorts of questions that are designed to try their patience. If they stand the test, they are offered better positions; if they fail in the test, they have merely allowed a good opportunity to pass by without knowing it.

No doubt all people who refuse or neglect to exercise *self-control* are literally turning opportunity after opportunity away without knowing it. One day I was standing at the glove counter of a large retail store talking to a young man who was employed there. He was telling me that he had been with the store four years, but on account of the "short-sightedness" of the store, his services had not been appreciated and he was looking for another position. In the midst of this conversation a customer walked up to him and asked to see some hats. He paid no attention to the customer's inquiry until he had finished telling me his troubles, despite the fact that the customer was obviously becoming impatient. Finally, he turned to the customer and said: "This isn't the hat department." When the customer inquired as to where he might find that department the young man replied: "Ask the floor-walker over there; he will direct you."

For four years this young man had been standing on top of a fine opportunity but he did not know it. He could have made a friend of every person whom he served in that store and these friends could have made him one of the most valuable men in the store, because they would have come back to trade with him. "Snappy" answers to inquiring customers do not bring them back.

One rainy afternoon an old lady walked into a Pittsburgh department store and wandered around in an aimless sort of way, very much in the manner that people who have no intention of buying often do. Most of the salespeople gave her the "once over" and busied themselves by straightening the stock on their shelves so as to avoid being troubled by her. One of the young men saw her and made it his business to inquire politely if he might serve her. She informed him that she was only waiting for it to stop raining; that she did not wish to make any purchases. The young man assured her that she was welcome, and by engaging her in conversation made her feel that he had meant what he said. When she was ready to go he accompanied her to the street and raised her umbrella for her. She asked for his card and went on her way.

The incident had been forgotten by the young man when, one day, he was called into the office by the head of the firm and shown a letter from a lady who wanted a salesman to go to Scotland and take an order for the furnishings for a mansion.

That lady was Andrew Carnegie's mother; she was also the same woman whom the young man had so courteously escorted to the street many months previously.

In the letter, Mrs. Carnegie specified that this young man was the one whom she desired to be sent to take her order. That order amounted to an enormous sum, and the incident brought the young man an opportunity for advancement that he might never have had except for his courtesy to an old lady who did not look like a "ready sale."

Just as the great fundamental laws of life are wrapped up in the commonest sort of every-day experiences that most of us never notice, so are the *real* opportunities often hidden in the seemingly unimportant transactions of life.

Ask the next ten people whom you meet why they have not accomplished more in their respective lines of endeavor, and at least nine of them will tell you that *opportunity does not seem to come around their way.* Go a step further and analyze each of these nine accurately by observing their actions for one single day, and the chances are that you will find that every one of them is turning away the finest sort of opportunities every hour of the day.

One day I went to visit a friend who was associated with a Commercial School, in the capacity of solicitor. When I asked him how he was getting along he replied: "Rotten! I see a large number of people but I am not making enough sales to give me a good living. In fact my account with the school is overdrawn and I am thinking about changing positions as there is no *opportunity* here."

It happened that I was on my vacation and had ten days' time that I could use as I wished, so I challenged his remark that he had no opportunity by telling him that I could turn his position into $250.00 in a week's time and show him how to make it worth that every week thereafter. He looked at me in amazement and asked me not to joke with him over so serious a matter. When he was finally convinced that I was in earnest he ventured to inquire how I would perform the "miracle."

Then I asked him if he had ever heard of *organized effort,* to which he replied: *"What do you mean by organized effort?"* I informed him that I had reference to the direction of his efforts in such a manner that he would enroll from five to ten students with the same amount of effort that he had been putting into the enrollment of one or of none. He said he was willing to be shown, so I gave him instructions to arrange for me to speak before the employees of one of the local department stores. He made the appointment and I delivered the address. In my talk I outlined a plan through which the employees could not only increase their ability so that they could earn more money in their present positions, but it also offered them an opportunity to prepare themselves for greater responsibilities and better positions. Following my talk, which of course was designed for that purpose, my friend enrolled eight of those employees for night courses in the Commercial School which he represented.

The following night he booked me for a similar address before the employees of a laundry, and following the address he enrolled three more students, two of them *young women who worked over the washing machines at the hardest sort of labor.*

Two days later he booked me for an address before the employees of one of the local banks, and following the address he enrolled four more students, making a total of fifteen students, and the entire time consumed was not more than six hours, including the time required for the delivery of the addresses and the enrollment of the students.

My friend's commission on the transactions was a little over four hundred dollars!

These places of employment were within fifteen minutes' walk of this man's place of business, but he had never thought of looking there for business. Neither had he ever thought of allying himself with a

Fear no man, hate no man, wish no one misfortune, and more than likely you will have plenty of friends.

speaker who could assist him in "group" selling. That man now owns a splendid Commercial School of his own, and I am informed that his net income last year was over $10,000.00.

"No opportunities" come your way? Perhaps they come but you do not see them. Perhaps you will see them in the future as you are preparing yourself, through the aid of this Reading Course on the Law of Success, so that you can recognize an opportunity when you see it. The fifth lesson of this course is on the subject of *imagination,* which was the chief factor that entered into the transaction that I have just related. Imagination, plus a Definite Plan, plus Self-confidence, plus Action, were the main factors that entered into this transaction. You now know how to use all of these, and before you shall have finished this lesson you will understand how to direct these factors through *self-control.*

Now let us examine the scope of meaning of the term *self-control,* as it is used in connection with this course, by describing the general conduct of a person who possesses it. A person with well-developed *self-control* does not indulge in hatred, envy, jealousy, fear, revenge, or any similar destructive emotions. A person with well-developed *self-control* does not go into ecstasies or become ungovernably enthusiastic over anything or anybody.

Greed and selfishness and self-approval beyond the point of accurate self-analysis and appreciation of one's actual merits, indicate lack of *self-control* in one of its most dangerous forms. Self-confidence is one of the important essentials of success, but when this faculty is developed beyond the point of reason it becomes very dangerous.

Self-sacrifice is a commendable quality, but when it is carried to extremes, it, also, becomes one of the dangerous forms of lack of *self-control.*

You owe it to yourself not to permit your emotions to place your happiness in the keeping of another person. Love is essential for happiness, but the person who loves so deeply that his or her happiness is placed entirely in the hands of another, resembles the little lamb who crept into the den of the "nice, gentle little wolf" and begged to be permitted to lie down and go to sleep, or the canary bird that persisted in playing with the cat's whiskers.

A person with well-developed *self-control* will not permit himself to be influenced by the cynic or the pessimist; nor will he permit another person to do his thinking for him.

A person with well-developed *self-control* will stimulate his imagination and his enthusiasm until they have produced *action,* but he will then control that action and not permit it to control him.

A person with well-developed *self-control* will never, under any circumstances, slander another person or seek revenge for any cause whatsoever.

A person with *self-control* will not hate those who do not agree with him; instead, he will endeavor to understand the reason for their disagreement, and profit by it.

We come, now, to a form of lack of *self-control* which causes more grief than all other forms combined; it is the habit of forming opinions before studying the *facts*. We will not analyze this particular form in detail, in this lesson, for the reason that it is fully covered in Lesson Ten, on *accurate thought,* but the subject of *self-control* could not be covered without at least a passing reference to this common evil to which we are all more or less addicted.

No one has any right to form an opinion that is not based either upon that which he believes to be *facts,* or upon a reasonable hypothesis; yet, if you will observe yourself carefully, you will catch yourself forming opinions on nothing more substantial than your desire for a thing to be or not to be.

Another grievous form of lack of *self-control* is the "spending" habit. I have reference, of course, to the habit of spending beyond one's needs. This habit has become so prevalent since the close of the world war that it is alarming. A well known economist has prophesied that three more generations will transform the United States from the richest country in the world to the poorest if the children are not taught the *savings habit,* as a part of their training in both the schools and the homes. On every hand, we see people buying automobiles on the installment plan instead of buying homes. Within the last fifteen years the automobile "fad" has become so popular that literally tens of thousands of people are mortgaging their futures to own cars.

A prominent scientist, who has a keen sense of humor, has prophesied that not only will this habit grow lean bank accounts, but, if persisted in, it will eventually grow babies whose legs will have become transformed into wheels.

This is a speed-mad, money-spending age in which we are living, and the uppermost thought in the minds of most of us is to live faster than our neighbors. Not long ago the general manager of a concern that employs 600 men and women became alarmed over the large number of his employees who were becoming involved with "loan sharks," and decided to put an end to this evil. When he completed his investigation, he found that only nine per cent of his employees had savings accounts, and of the other ninety-one per cent who had no money ahead, seventy-five per cent were in debt in one form or another, some of them being hopelessly involved financially. *Of those who were in debt 210 owned automobiles.*

To do much clear thinking a man must arrange for regular periods of solitude when he can concentrate and indulge his imagination without distraction.
—THOMAS A. EDISON

We are creatures of imitation. We find it hard to resist the temptation to do that which we see others doing. If our neighbor buys a Buick, we must imitate him and if we cannot scrape together enough to make the first payment on a Buick we must, at least, have a Ford. Meanwhile, we take no heed of the morrow. The old-fashioned "rainy-day nest egg" has become obsolete. We live from day to day. We buy our coal by the pound and our flour in five pound sacks, thereby paying a third more for it than it ought to cost, because it is distributed in small quantities.

Of course this warning does not apply to you!

It is intended only for those who are binding themselves in the chains of poverty by spending beyond their earning capacity, and who have not yet heard that there are definite laws which must be observed by all who would attain *success*.

The automobile is one of the modern wonders of the world, but it is more often a luxury than it is a necessity, and tens of thousands of people who are now "stepping on the gas" at a lively pace are going to see some dangerous skidding when their "rainy days" arrive.

It requires considerable *self-control* to use the street cars as a means of transportation when people all around us are driving automobiles, but all who exercise this *self-control* are practically sure to see the day when many who are now driving cars will be either riding the street cars or walking.

It was this modern tendency to spend the entire income which prompted Henry Ford to safe-guard his employees with certain restrictions when he established his famous $5.00 a day minimum wage scale.

Twenty years ago, if a boy wanted a wagon, he fashioned the wheels out of boards and had the pleasure of building it himself. Now, if a boy wants a wagon, he cries for it—*and gets it!*

Lack of *self-control* is being developed in the oncoming generations by their parents who have become victims of the spending habit. Three generations ago, practically any boy could mend his own shoes with the family cobbling outfit. Today the boy takes his shoes to the corner shoe-shop and pays $1.75 for heels and half soles, and this habit is by no means confined to the rich and well-to-do classes.

I repeat—*the spending habit is turning America into a nation of paupers!*

I am safe in assuming that *you* are struggling to attain success, for if you were not you would not be reading this course. Let me remind you, then, that a little savings account will attract many an opportunity to you that would not come your way without it. The size of the account is not so important as is the fact that you have *established the savings habit,* for this habit marks you as a person who exercises an important form of *self-control.*

The modern tendency of those who work for a salary is to spend it all. If a man who receives $3,000.00 a year and manages to get along on it fairly well, receives an increase of $1,000.00 a year, does he continue to live on $3,000.00 and place the increased portion of his income in the savings bank? No, not unless he is one of the few who have developed the savings *habit*. Then, what does he do with this additional $1,000.00? He trades in the old automobile and buys a more expensive one, and at the end of the year he is poorer on a $4,000.00 income than he was the previous year on a $3,000.00 income.

This is a "modern, twentieth century model!" American that I am describing, and you will be lucky if, upon close analysis, you do not find yourself to be one of this class.

Somewhere between the miser who hoards every penny he gets his hands on, in an old sock, and the man who spends every cent he can earn or borrow, there is a "happy medium," and if you enjoy life with reasonable assurance of average freedom and contentment, you must find this half-way point and adopt it as a part of your *self-control* program.

Self-discipline is the most essential factor in the development of personal power, because it enables you to control your appetite and your tendency to spend more than you earn and your habit of "striking back" at those who offend you and the other destructive habits which cause you to dissipate your energies through non-productive effort that takes on forms too numerous to be catalogued in this lesson.

Ask any wise man what he most desires and he will, more than likely, say "more wisdom."

Very early in my public career I was shocked when I learned how many people there are who devote most of their energies to tearing down that which the builders construct. By some queer turn of the wheel of fate one of these destroyers crossed my path by making it his business to try to destroy my reputation. At first, I was inclined to "strike back" at him, but as I sat at my typewriter late one night, a thought came to me which changed my entire attitude toward this man. Removing the sheet of paper that was in my typewriter, I inserted another one on which I stated this thought, in these words:

You have a tremendous advantage over the man who does you an injury: you have it within your power to forgive him, while he has no such advantage over you.

As I finished writing those lines, I made up my mind that I had come to the point at which I had to decide upon a policy that would serve as a guide concerning my attitude toward those who criticize my work or try to destroy my reputation. I reached this decision by reasoning something after this fashion: Two courses of action were open to me. I could waste much of my time and energy in striking back at those who would try to destroy me, or I could devote this energy to furthering my life-work and let the result of that work serve as my sole answer to all who would criticize my efforts or question my motives. I decided upon the latter as being the better policy and adopted it.

"By their deeds you shall know them!"

If your deeds are constructive and you are at peace with yourself, in your own heart, you will not find it necessary to stop and explain your motives, for they will explain themselves.

The world soon forgets its destroyers. It builds its monuments to and bestows its honors upon none but its builders. Keep this fact in mind and you will more easily reconcile yourself to the policy of refusing to waste your energies by "striking back" at those who offend you.

Every person who amounts to anything in this world comes to the point, sooner or later, at which he is forced to settle this question of policy toward his enemies, and if you want proof that it pays to exercise sufficient *self-control* to refrain from dissipating your vital energies by "striking back" then study the records of all who have risen to high stations in life and observe how carefully they curbed this destructive habit.

It is a well known fact that no man ever reached a high station in life without opposition of a violent nature from jealous and envious enemies. The late President Warren G. Harding and ex-President Wilson and John H. Patterson of the National Cash Register Company and scores of others whom I could mention, were victims of this cruel tendency, of a certain type of depraved man, to destroy reputation. But these men wasted no time explaining or "striking back" at their enemies. They exercised *self-control*.

I do not know but that these attacks on men who are in public life, cruel and unjust and untruthful as they often are, serve a good purpose. In my own case, I know that I made a discovery that was of great value to me, as a result of a series of bitter attacks which a contemporary journalist launched against me. I paid no attention to these attacks for four or five years, until finally they became so bold that I decided to override my policy and "strike back" at my antagonist. I sat down at my typewriter and began to write. In all of my experience as a writer I do not believe I ever assembled such a collection of biting adjectives as those which I used on this occasion. The more I wrote, the more angry I became, until I had written all that I could think of on the subject. As the last line was finished, a strange feeling came over me—it was not a feeling of bitterness toward the man who had tried to injure me—it was a feeling of compassion, of sympathy, of forgiveness.

I had unconsciously psycho-analyzed myself by releasing, over the keys of my typewriter, the re-pressed emotions of hate and resentment which I had been unintentionally gathering in my sub-conscious mind over a long period of years.

Now, if I find myself becoming very angry, I sit down at my typewriter and "write it out of my system," then throw away the manuscript, or file it away as an exhibit for my scrap-book to which I can refer back in the years to come—after the evolutionary processes have carried me still higher in the realm of understanding.

Repressed emotions, especially the emotion of hatred, resemble a bomb that has been constructed of high explosives, and unless they are handled with as much understanding of their nature as an expert would handle a bomb, they are as dangerous. A bomb may be rendered harmless by explosion in an open field, or by disintegration in a bath of the proper sort. Also, a feeling of anger or hatred may be rendered harmless by giving expression to it in a manner that harmonizes with the principle of psycho-analysis.

While others may side-track your ambitions not a few times, remember that discouragement most frequently comes from within.

Before *you* can achieve success in the higher and broader sense you must gain such thorough control over yourself that you will be a person of *poise*.

You are the product of at least a million years of evolutionary change. For countless generations preceding you Nature has been tempering and refining the materials that have gone into your make-up. Step by step, she has removed from the generations that have preceded you the animal instincts and baser passions until she has produced, in you, the *finest specimen of animal that lives*. She has endowed you, through this slow evolutionary process, with reason and poise and "balance" sufficient to enable you to control and do with yourself whatever you will.

No other animal has ever been endowed with such *self-control* as you possess. You have been endowed with the power to use the most highly organized form of energy known to man, that of *thought*. It is not improbable that *thought* is the closest connecting link there is between the material, physical things of this world and the world of Divinity.

You have not only the power to *think* but, what is a thousand times more important still, you have the power to *control your thoughts and direct them to do your bidding!*

We are coming, now, to the really important part of this lesson. Read slowly and meditatively! I approach this part of this lesson almost with fear and trembling, for it brings us face to face with a subject which but few men are qualified to discuss with reasonable intelligence.

I repeat, *you have the power to control your thoughts and make them do your bidding!*

Your brain may be likened to a dynamo, in this respect, that it generates or sets into motion the mysterious energy called *thought*. The stimuli that start your brain into action are of two sorts; one is Auto-suggestion and the other is Suggestion. You can select the material out of which your thinking is produced, and that is Auto-suggestion (or self-suggestion). You can permit others to select the material out of which your thinking is produced and that is Suggestion. It is a humiliating fact that most thought is produced by the outside suggestions of others, and it is more humiliating, still, to have to admit that the majority of us accept this suggestion without either examining it or questioning its soundness. We read the daily papers as though every word were based upon fact. We are swayed by the gossip and idle chatter of others as though every word were true.

Thought is the only thing over which you have absolute control, yet, unless you are the proverbial exception, which is about one out of every ten thousand, you permit other people to enter the sacred mansion of your mind and there deposit, through suggestion, their troubles and woes, adversities and falsehoods, just as though you did not have the power to close the door and keep them out.

You have within your control the power to select the material that constitutes the dominating thoughts of your mind, and just as surely as you are reading these lines, those thoughts which dominate your mind will bring you success or failure, according to their nature.

The fact that *thought* is the only thing over which you have absolute control is, within itself, of most profound significance, as it strongly suggests that *thought* is your nearest approach to Divinity, on this earthly plane. This fact also carries another highly impressive suggestion; namely, that *thought* is your most important tool; the one with which you may shape your worldly destiny according to your own liking. Surely, Divine Providence did not make *thought* the sole power over which you have absolute control without associating with that power potentialities which, if understood and developed, would stagger the imagination.

Self-control is solely a matter of *thought-control!*

Please read the foregoing sentence aloud; read it thoughtfully and meditate over it before reading further, because it is, without doubt, the most important single sentence of this entire course.

You are studying this course, presumably because you are earnestly seeking truth and understanding sufficient to enable you to attain some high station in life.

You are searching for the magic key that will unlock the door to the source of power; and yet you have the key in your own hands, and you may make use of it the moment you learn to *control your thoughts.*

Place in your own mind, through the principle of Auto-suggestion, the positive, construc-tive thoughts which harmonize with your *definite chief aim* in life, and that mind will transform those thoughts into physical reality and hand them back to you, as a finished product.

This is thought-control!

When you deliberately choose the thoughts which dominate your mind and firmly refuse admittance to outside suggestion, you are exercising *self-control* in its highest and most efficient form. Man is the only living animal that can do this.

How many millions of years Nature has required in which to produce this animal no one knows, but every intelligent student of psychology knows that the dominating thoughts determine the actions and the nature of the animal.

The process through which one may think accurately is a subject that has been reserved for Lesson Ten, of this course. The point we wish clearly to establish, in this lesson, is that *thought*, whether accurate or inaccurate, is the most highly organized functioning power of your mind; and that *you are but the sum total of your dominating or most prominent thoughts.*

If you would be a master salesman, whether of goods and wares or of personal services, you must exercise sufficient *self-control* to shut out all adverse arguments and suggestions. Most salesmen have so little *self-control* that they hear the prospective purchaser say "no" even before he says it. Not a few salesmen hear this fatal word "no" even before they come into the presence of their prospective purchaser. They have so little *self-control* that they actually *suggest to themselves that their prospective purchaser will say "no" when asked to purchase their wares.*

How different is the man of *self-control!* He not only suggests to himself that his prospec-tive purchaser will say "yes," but if the desired "yes" is not forthcoming, he stays on the job until he breaks down the opposition and forces a "yes." If his prospective purchaser says "no," he does not hear it. If his prospective purchaser says "no"—a second, and a third, and a fourth time—he does not hear it, for he is a man of *self-control* and he permits no sugges-tions to reach his mind except those which he desires to influence him.

The master salesman, whether he be engaged in selling merchandise, or personal services, or sermons, or public addresses, understands how to control his own *thoughts*. Instead of being a person who *accepts, with meek submission, the suggestions of others,* he is a person who persuades others to accept *his suggestions.* By controlling himself and by placing only positive thoughts in his own mind, he thereby becomes a dominating personality, a master salesman.

This, too, is self-control!

A master salesman is one who takes the offensive, and never the defensive side of an argument, if argument arises.

THE LAW OF SUCCESS

Please read the foregoing sentence again!

If you are a master salesman you know that it is necessary for you to keep your prospective purchaser on the defensive, and you also know that it will be fatal to your sale if you permit him to place you on the defensive and keep you there. You may, and of course you will at times, be placed in a position in which you will have to assume the defensive side of the conversation for a time, but it is your business to exercise such perfect poise and *self-control* that you will change places with your prospective purchaser without his noticing that you have done so, by placing him back on the defensive.

> *People like to use their excess energy by "chewing the rag." Wm. Wrigley, Jr., capitalized this human trait by giving them a stick of Spearmint.*

This requires the most consummate skill and *self-control!*

Most salesmen sweep this vital point aside by becoming angry and trying to scare the prospective purchaser into submission, but the master salesman remains calm and serene, and usually comes out the winner.

The word "salesman" has reference to all people who try to persuade or convince others by logical argument or appeal to self-interest. We are all salesmen; or, at least, we should be, no matter what form of service we are rendering or what sort of goods we are offering.

The ability to negotiate with other people without friction and argument is the outstanding quality of all successful people. Observe those nearest you and notice how few there are who understand this art of tactful negotiation. Observe, also, how successful are the few who understand this art, despite the fact that they may have less education than those with whom they negotiate.

It is a knack that can be cultivated.

The art of successful negotiation grows out of patient and painstaking *self-control*. Notice how easily the successful salesman exercises *self-control* when he is handling a customer who is impatient. In his heart such a salesman may be boiling over, but you will see no evidence of it in his face or manner or words.

He has acquired the art of tactful negotiation!

A single frown of disapproval or a single word denoting impatience will often spoil a sale, and no one knows this better than the successful salesman. He makes it his business to control his feelings, and as a reward he sets his own salary mark and chooses his own position.

To watch a person who has acquired the art of successful negotiation is a liberal education, within itself. Watch the public speaker who has acquired this art; notice the firmness of his step as he mounts the platform; observe the firmness of his voice as he begins to speak; study the expression on his face as he sweeps his audience with the mastery of his argument. *He has learned how to negotiate without friction.*

Watch the physician who has acquired this art, as he walks into the sick room and greets his patient with a smile. His bearing, the tone of his voice, the look of assurance on his face, all mark him as one who has acquired the art of successful negotiation, and the patient begins to feel better the moment he enters the sick room.

Watch the foreman of the works who has acquired this art, and observe how his very presence spurs his men to greater effort and inspires them with confidence and enthusiasm.

Watch the lawyer who has acquired this art, and observe how he commands the respect and attention of the court, the jury and his fellow-practitioners. There is something about the tone of his voice, the posture of his body, and the expression on his face which causes his opponent to suffer by comparison. He not only knows his case, but he convinces the court and the jury that he knows, and as his reward he wins his cases and claims big retaining fees.

And all of this is predicated upon *self-control!*

And *self-control* is the result of *thought-control!*

Deliberately place in your own mind the sort of *thoughts* that you desire there, and keep out of your mind those *thoughts* which others place there through *suggestion,* and you will become a person of *self-control.*

This privilege of stimulating your mind with suggestions and thoughts of your own choosing is your prerogative power that Divine Providence gave you, and if you will exercise this holy right there is nothing within the bounds of reason that you cannot attain.

"Losing your temper," and with it your case, or your argument, or your sale, marks you as one who has not yet familiarized himself with the fundamentals upon which *self-control* is based, and the chief one of these fundamentals is the privilege of choosing the *thoughts* that dominate the mind.

A student in one of my classes once asked how one went about controlling one's thoughts when in a state of intense anger, and I replied: *"In exactly the same way that you would change your manner and the tone of your voice if you were in a heated argument with a member of your family and heard the door bell ring, warning you that company was about to visit you. You would control yourself because you would desire to do so."*

If you have ever been in a similar predicament, where you found it necessary to cover up your real feelings and change the expression on your face quickly, you know how easily it can be done, and you also know that it can be done *because one wants to do it!*

Back of all achievement, back of all *self-control,* back of all *thought control,* is that magic something called DESIRE!

It is no misstatement of fact to say that you are limited only by the depth of your *desires!*

When your *desires* are strong enough you will appear to possess superhuman powers to achieve. No one has ever explained this strange phenomenon of the mind, and perhaps no one ever will explain it, but if you doubt that it exists you have but to experiment and be convinced.

If you were in a building that was on fire, and all the doors and windows were locked, the chances are that you would develop sufficient strength with which to break down the average door, because of your intense *desire* to free yourself.

If you *desire* to acquire the art of successful negotiation, as you undoubtedly will when you understand its significance in relation to your achievement of your *definite chief aim,* you will do so, providing your *desire* is intense enough.

Napoleon *desired* to become emperor of France and did rule. Lincoln *desired* to free the slaves, and he accomplished it. The French *desired* that "they shall not pass," at the beginning of the world war, and *they didn't pass!* Edison *desired* to produce light with electricity, and he produced it—although he was many years in doing so. Roosevelt *desired* to unite the Atlantic and Pacific oceans, through the Panama Canal, and he did it. Demosthenes *desired* to become a great public speaker, and despite the handicap of serious impediment of speech, he transformed his desire into reality. Helen Keller *desired* to speak, and despite the fact that she was deaf, dumb and blind, she now speaks. John H. Patterson *desired* to dominate in the production of cash registers, and he did it. Marshall Field *desired* to be the leading merchant of his time, and he did. Shakespeare *desired* to become a great playwright, and, despite the fact that he was only a poor itinerant actor, he made his desire come true. Billy Sunday *desired* to quit playing base-ball and become a master preacher, and he did. James J. Hill *desired* to become an empire builder; and, despite the fact that he was only a poor telegraph operator, he transformed that desire into reality.

Don't say, "It can't be done," or that you are different from these and thousands of others who have achieved noteworthy success in every worthy calling. If you are "different," it is only in this respect: *they desired the object of their achievement with more depth and intensity than you desire yours.*

Plant in your mind the seed of a *desire* that is constructive by making the following your creed and the foundation of your code of ethics:

"I wish to be of service to my fellow men as I journey through life. To do this I have adopted this creed as a guide to be followed in dealing with my fellow-beings:

"To train myself so that never, under any circumstances, will I find fault with any person, no matter how much I may disagree with him or how inferior his work may be, as long as I know he is sincerely trying to do his best.

"To respect my country, my profession and myself. To be honest and fair with my fellow men, as I expect them to be honest and fair with me. To be a loyal citizen of my country. To speak of it with praise, and act always as a worthy custodian of its good name. To be a person whose name carries weight wherever it goes.

"To base my expectations of reward on a solid foundation of service rendered. To be willing to pay the price of success in honest effort. To look upon my work as an opportunity to be seized with joy and made the most of, and not as a painful drudgery to be reluctantly endured.

"To remember that success lies within myself—in my own brain. To expect difficulties and to force my way through them.

"To avoid procrastination in all its forms, and never, under any circumstances, put off until tomorrow any duty that should be performed today.

"Finally, to take a good grip on the joys of life, so I may be courteous to men, faithful to friends, true to God—a fragrance in the path I tread."

The energy which most people dissipate through lack of *self-control* would, if organized and used constructively, bring all the necessities and all the luxuries desired.

The time which many people devote to "gossiping" about others would, if controlled and directed constructively, be sufficient to attain the object of their *definite chief aim* (if they had such an aim).

All successful people grade high on *self-control!* All "failures" grade low, generally zero, on this important law of human conduct.

Study the comparative analysis chart in the Introduction, and observe the *self-control* gradings of Jesse James and Napoleon.

> *It is a peculiar trait of human nature, but it is true, that the most successful men will work harder for the sake of rendering useful service than they will for money alone.*

Study those around you and observe, with profit, that all the successful ones exercise *self-control,* while the "failures" permit their THOUGHTS, WORDS and DEEDS to run wild!

One very common and very destructive form of lack of *self-control* is the habit of talking too much. People of wisdom, who know what they want and are bent on getting it, guard their conversation carefully. There can be no gain from a volume of uninvited, uncontrolled, loosely spoken words.

It is nearly always more profitable to listen than it is to speak. A good listener may, once in a great while, hear something that will add to his stock of knowledge. It requires *self-control* to become a good listener, but the benefits to be gained are worth the effort.

"Taking the conversation away from another person" is a common form of lack of *self-control* which is not only discourteous, but it deprives those who do it of many valuable opportunities to learn from others.

After completing this lesson you should go back to the self-analysis chart, in the Introduction, and re-grade yourself on the Law of Self-control. Perhaps you may wish to reduce your former grading somewhat.

Self-control was one of the marked characteristics of all successful leaders whom I have analyzed, in gathering material for this course. Luther Burbank said that, in his opinion, *self-control* was the most important of the Fifteen Laws of Success. During all his years of patient study and observation of the evolutionary processes of vegetable life he found it necessary to exercise the faculty of *self-control,* despite the fact that he was dealing with inanimate life.

John Burroughs, the naturalist, said practically the same thing; that *self-control* stood near the head of the list, in importance, of the Fifteen Laws of Success.

The man who exercises complete *self-control* cannot be permanently defeated, as Emerson has so well stated in his essay on Compensation, for the reason that obstacles and opposition have a way of melting away when confronted by the determined mind that is guided to a definite end with complete *self-control.*

Every wealthy man whom I have analyzed (referring to those who have become wealthy through their own efforts) showed such positive evidence that *self-control* had been one of his strong points that I reached the conclusion that no man can hope to accumulate great wealth and keep it without exercising this necessary quality.

The saving of money requires the exercise of *self-control* of the highest order, as, I hope, has been made quite clear in the third lesson of this course.

I am indebted to Edward W. Bok for the following rather colorful description of the extent to which he found it necessary to exercise *self-control* before he achieved success and was crowned with fame as one of the great journalists of America:

Why I Believe in Poverty as the Richest Experience That Can Come to a Boy

I make my living trying to edit the *Ladies' Home Journal*. And because the public has been most generous in its acceptance of that periodical, a share of that success has logically come to me. Hence a number of my very good readers cherish an opinion that often I have been tempted to correct, a temptation to which I now yield. My correspondents express the conviction variously, but this extract from a letter is a fair sample:

"It is all very easy for you to preach economy to us when you do not know the necessity for it: To tell us how, as for example in my own case, we must live within my husband's income of eight hundred dollars a year, when you have never known what it is to live on less than thousands. Has it occurred to you, born with the proverbial silver spoon in your mouth, that theoretical writing is pretty cold and futile compared to the actual hand-to-mouth struggle that so many of us live, day by day and year in and year out—an experience that you know not of?"

"An experience that you know not of!"

Now, how far do the facts square with this statement?

Whether or not I was born with the proverbial silver spoon in my mouth, I cannot say. It is true that I was born of well-to-do parents. But when I was six years old my father lost all his means, and faced life at forty-five, in a strange country, without even necessaries. There are men and their wives who know what that means; for a man to try to "come back" at forty-five, and in a strange country!

I had the handicap of not knowing one word of the English language. I went to a public school and learned what I could. And sparse morsels they were! The boys were cruel, as boys are. The teachers were impatient, as tired teachers are.

My father could not find his place in the world. My mother who had always had servants at her beck and call, faced the problems of housekeeping that she had never learned nor been taught. And there was no money.

So, after school hours, my brother and I went home, but not to play. After-school hours meant for us to help a mother who daily grew more frail under the burdens that she could not carry. Not for days, but for years, we two boys got up in the gray cold winter dawn when the beds feel so warm to growing boys, and we sifted the coal ashes of the day-before's fire for a stray lump or two of unburned coal, and with what we had or could find we made the fire and warmed up the room. Then we set the table for the scant breakfast, went to school, and directly after school we washed the dishes, swept and scrubbed the floors. Living in a three-family tenement, each third week meant that we scrubbed the entire three flights of stairs from the third story to the first, as well as the doorsteps and the sidewalk outside. The latter work was the hardest; for we did it on Saturdays, with the boys of the neighborhood looking on none too kindly, so we did it to the echo of the crack of the ball and bat on the adjoining lot!

In the evening when the other boys could sit by the lamp or study their lessons, we two boys went out with a basket and picked up wood and coal in the adjoining lots, or went after the dozen or so pieces of coal left from the ton of coal put in that afternoon by one of the neighbors, with the spot hungrily fixed in mind by one of us during the day, hoping that the man who carried in the coal might not be too careful in picking up the stray lumps!

"An experience that you know not of!" Don't I?

> *Our doubts are traitors, and make us lose the good we oft might win by fearing to attempt.*
> —SHAKESPEARE

At ten years of age I got my first job, washing the windows of a baker's shop at fifty cents a week. In a week or two I was allowed to sell bread and cakes behind the counter after school hours for a dollar a week—handing out freshly baked cakes and warm, delicious-smelling bread, when scarcely a crumb had passed my mouth that day!

Then on Saturday mornings I served a route for a weekly paper, and sold my remaining stock on the street. It meant from sixty to seventy cents for that day's work.

I lived in Brooklyn, New York, and the chief means of transportation to Coney Island at that time was the horse car. Near where we lived the cars would stop to water the horses, the men would jump out and get a drink of water, but the women had no means of quenching their thirst. Seeing this lack I got a pail, filled it with water and a bit of ice, and, with a glass, jumped on each car on Saturday afternoon and all day Sunday, and sold my wares at a cent a glass. And when competition came, as it did very quickly when other boys saw that a Sunday's work meant two or three dollars, I squeezed a lemon or two in my pail, my liquid became "lemonade" and my price two cents a glass, and Sunday meant five dollars to me.

Then, in turn, I became a reporter during the evenings, an office boy day-times, and learned stenography at midnight.

My correspondent says she supports her family of husband and child on eight hundred dollars a year, and says I have never known what that means. I supported a family of three on six dollars and twenty-five cents a week—less than one-half of her yearly income. When my brother and I, combined, brought in eight hundred dollars a year we felt rich!

I have for the first time gone into these details in print so that you may know, at first hand, that the editor of the *Ladies' Home Journal* is not a theorist when he writes or prints articles that seek to preach economy or that reflect a hand-to-hand struggle on a small or an invisible income. There is not a single step, not an inch, on the road of direct poverty that I do not know of or have not experienced. And, having experienced every thought, every feeling and every hardship that come to those who travel that road, I say today that I rejoice with every boy who is going through the same experience.

Nor am I discounting or forgetting one single pang of the keen hardships that such a struggle means. I would not today exchange my years of the keenest hardship that a boy can know or pass through for any single experience that could have come to me. I know what it means to earn—not a dollar, but to earn two cents. I know the value of money as I could have learned it or known it in no other way. I could have been trained for my life-work in no surer way. I could not have arrived at a truer understanding of what it means to face a day without a penny in hand, not a loaf of bread in the cupboard, not a piece of kindling wood for the fire—with nothing to eat, and then be a boy with the hunger of nine and ten, with a mother frail and discouraged!

"An experience that you know not of!" Don't I?

And yet I rejoice in the experience, and I repeat: I envy every boy who is in that condition and going through it. But—and here is the pivot of my strong belief in poverty as an undisguised blessing to a boy—I believe in poverty as a condition to experience, to go through, and then to get out of: not as a condition to stay in. "That's all very well," some will say; "easy enough to say, but how can you get out of it?" No one can definitely tell another that. No one told me. No two persons can find the same way out. Each must find his way for himself. That depends on the boy. I was determined to get out of poverty, because my mother was not born in it, could not stand it and did not belong in it. This gave me the first essential: a purpose. Then I backed up the purpose with effort and willingness to work and to work at anything that came my way, no matter what it was, so long as it meant "the way out." I did not pick and choose; I took what came and did it in the best way

I knew how; and when I didn't like what I was doing I still did it well while I was doing it, but I saw to it that I didn't do it any longer than I had to do it. I used every rung in the ladder as a rung to the one above. It meant effort, but out of the effort and the work came the experience; the upbuilding, the development; the capacity to understand and sympathize; the greatest heritage that can come to a boy. And nothing in the world can give that to a boy, so that it will burn into him, as will poverty.

That is why I believe so strongly in poverty, the greatest blessing in the way of the deepest and fullest experience that can come to a boy. But, as I repeat: always as a condition to work out of, not to stay in.

Before you can develop the habit of perfect *self-control* you must understand the real need for this quality. Also, you must understand the advantages which *self-control* provides those who have learned how to exercise it.

By developing *self-control* you develop, also, other qualities that will add to your personal power. Among other laws which are available to the person who exercises *self-control* is the Law of Retaliation.

You know what "retaliate" means!

In the sense that we are using here it means to "return like for like," and not merely to avenge or to seek revenge, as is commonly meant by the use of this word.

If I do you an injury you retaliate at first opportunity. If I say unjust things about you, you will retaliate in kind, even in greater measure!

On the other hand, if I do you a favor you will reciprocate even in greater measure if possible.

Through the proper use of this law *I can get you to do whatever I wish you to do*. If I wish you to dislike me and to lend your influence toward damaging me, I can accomplish this result by inflicting upon you the sort of treatment that I want you to inflict upon me through retaliation.

If I wish your respect, your friendship and your co-operation I can get these by extending to you my friendship and co-operation.

On these statements I know that we are together. You can compare these statements with your own experience and you will see how beautifully they harmonize.

How often have you heard the remark, "What a wonderful personality that person has." How often have you met people whose personalities you coveted?

The man who attracts you to him through his pleasing personality is merely making use of the Law of Harmonious Attraction, or the Law of Retaliation, both of which, when analyzed, mean that "like attracts like."

If you will study, understand and make intelligent use of the Law of Retaliation you will be an efficient and successful salesman. When you have mastered this simple law and learned how to use it you will have learned all that can be learned about salesmanship.

The first and probably the most important step to be taken in mastering this law is to cultivate complete *self-control*. You must learn to take all sorts of punishment and abuse without retaliating in kind. This *self-control* is a part of the price you must pay for mastery of the Law of Retaliation.

When an angry person starts in to vilify and abuse you, justly or unjustly, just remember that if you retaliate in a like manner you are being drawn down to that person's mental level, therefore *that person is dominating you!*

On the other hand, if you refuse to become angry, if you retain your self-composure and remain calm and serene you retain all your ordinary faculties through which to reason. You take the other fellow by surprise. You retaliate with a weapon with the use of which he is unfamiliar, consequently you easily dominate him.

It is well worth remembering that the customer is the most important factor in any business. If you don't think so, try to get along without him for a while.

Like attracts like! There's no denying this!

Literally speaking, every person with whom you come in contact is a mental looking-glass in which you may see a perfect reflection of your own mental attitude.

As an example of direct application of the Law of Retaliation, let us cite an experience that I recently had with my two small boys, Napoleon Junior and James.

We were on our way to the park to feed the birds and squirrels. Napoleon Junior had bought a bag of peanuts and James had bought a box of "Crackerjack." James took a notion to sample the peanuts. Without asking permission he reached over and made a grab for the bag. He missed and Napoleon Junior "retaliated" with his left fist which landed rather briskly on James' jaw.

I said to James: "Now, see here, son, you didn't go about getting those peanuts in the right manner. Let me show you how to get them." It all happened so quickly that I hadn't the slightest idea when I spoke what I was going to suggest to James, but I sparred for time to analyze the occurrence and work out a better way, if possible, than that adopted by him.

Then I thought of the experiments we had been making in connection with the Law of Retaliation, so I said to James: "Open your box of 'Crackerjack' and offer your little brother some and see what happens." After considerable coaxing I persuaded him to do this. Then a remarkable thing happened—a happening out of which I learned my greatest lesson in sales-manship! *Before Napoleon would touch the "Crackerjack" he insisted on pouring some of his peanuts into James' overcoat pocket.* He "retaliated in kind!" Out of this simple experiment with two small boys I learned more about the art of managing them than I could have learned in any other manner. Incidentally, my boys are beginning to learn how to manipulate this Law of Retaliation which saves them many a physical combat.

None of us have advanced far beyond Napoleon Junior and James as far as the operation and influence of the Law of Retaliation is concerned. We are all just grown-up children and easily influenced through this principle. The habit of "retaliating in kind" is so universally practiced among us that we can properly call this habit the Law of Retaliation. If a person presents us with a gift we never feel satisfied until we have "retaliated" with something as good or better than that which we received. If a person speaks well of us we increase our admiration for that person, and we "retaliate" in return!

Through the principle of retaliation we can actually convert our enemies into loyal friends. If you have an enemy whom you wish to convert into a friend you can prove the truth of this statement if you will forget that dangerous millstone hanging around your neck, which we call "pride" (stubbornness). Make a habit of speaking to this enemy with unusual cordiality. Go out of your way to favor him in every manner possible. He may seem immovable at first, but gradually he will give way to your influence and "retaliate in kind!" The hottest coals of fire ever heaped upon the head of one who has wronged you are the coals of human kindness.

One morning in August, 1863, a young clergyman was called out of bed in a hotel at Lawrence, Kansas. The man who called him was one of Quantrell's guerrillas, and he wanted him to hurry downstairs and be shot. All over the border that morning people were being murdered. A band of raiders had ridden in early to perpetrate the Lawrence massacre.

The guerrilla who called the clergyman was impatient. The latter, when fully awake, was horrified by what he saw going on through his window. As he came downstairs the guerrilla demanded his watch and money, and then wanted to know if he was an abolitionist. The clergyman was trembling. But he decided that if he was to die then and there it would not be with a lie on his lips. So he said that he was, and followed up the admission with a remark that immediately turned the whole affair into another channel.

He and the guerrilla sat down on the porch, while people were being killed through the town, and had a long talk. It lasted until the raiders were ready to leave. When the clergyman's guerrilla mounted to join his confederates he was strictly on the defensive. He handed back the New Englander's valuables, apologized for disturbing him and asked to be thought well of.

That clergyman lived many years after the Lawrence massacre. What did he say to the guerrilla? What was there in his personality that led the latter to sit down and talk? What did they talk about?

"Are you a Yankee abolitionist?" the guerrilla had asked. "Yes, I am," was the reply, "and you know very well that you ought to be ashamed of what you're doing."

This drew the matter directly to a moral issue. It brought the guerrilla up roundly. The clergyman was only a stripling beside this seasoned border ruffian. But he threw a burden of moral proof on to the raider, and in a moment the latter was trying to demonstrate that he might be a better fellow than circumstances would seem to indicate.

After waking this New Englander to kill him on account of his politics, he spent twenty minutes on the witness stand trying to prove an alibi. He went into his personal history at length. He explained matters from the time when he had been a tough little kid who wouldn't say his prayers, and became quite sentimental in recalling how one thing had led to another, and that to something worse, until—well, here he was, and "a mighty bad business to be in, pardner." His last request in riding away was: "Now, pardner, don't think too hard of me, will you?"

The New England clergyman made use of the Law of Retaliation, whether he knew it at that time or not. Imagine what would have happened had he come downstairs with a revolver in his hand and started to meet physical force with physical force!

But he didn't do this! He mastered the guerrilla because he fought him with a force that was unknown to the brigand.

Why is it that when once a man begins to make money the whole world seems to beat a pathway to his door?

Take any person that you know who enjoys financial success and he will tell you that he is being constantly sought, and that opportunities to make money are constantly being urged upon him!

"To him that hath shall be given, but to him that hath not shall be taken away even that which he hath."

This quotation from the Bible used to seem ridiculous to me, yet how true it is when reduced to its concrete meaning.

Yes, "*to him that hath shall be given!*" If he "hath" failure, lack of self-confidence, hatred or lack of *self-control,* to him shall these qualities be given in still greater abundance! But, if he "hath" success, self-confidence, *self-control,* patience, persistence and determination, to him shall these qualities be increased!

Sometimes it may be necessary to meet force with force until we overpower our opponent or adversary, but while he is down is a splendid time to complete the "retaliation" by taking him by the hand and showing him a better way to settle disputes.

Like attracts like! Germany sought to bathe her sword in human blood, in a ruthless escapade of conquest. As a result she has drawn the "retaliation in kind" of most of the civilized world.

It is for you to decide what you want your fellow men to do and *it is for you to get them to do it through the Law of Retaliation!*

"The Divine Economy is automatic and very simple: we receive only that which we give."

How true it is that "we receive only that which we give"! It is not that which we *wish for* that comes back to us, but that *which we give.*

I implore you to make use of this law, not alone for material gain, but, better still, for the attainment of happiness and good-will toward men.

This, after all, is the only real success for which to strive.

Summary

In this lesson we have learned a great principle—probably the most important major principle of psychology! We have learned that our *thoughts* and *actions toward others* resemble an electric magnet which attracts to us the same sort of thought and the same sort of action that we, ourselves, create.

A good hearty laugh is worth ten thousand "groans" and a million "sighs" in any market on earth.

We have learned that "like attracts like," whether in thought or in expression of thought through bodily action. We have learned that the human mind responds, in kind, to whatever thought impressions it receives. We have learned that the human mind resembles mother earth in that it will reproduce a crop of muscular action which corresponds, in kind, to the sensory impressions planted in it. We have learned that kindness begets kindness and unkindness and injustice beget unkindness and injustice.

We have learned that our actions toward others, whether of kindness or unkindness, justice or injustice, come back to us, *even in a larger measure!* We have learned that the human mind responds in kind, to all sensory impressions it receives, therefore we know what we must do to influence any desired action upon the part of another. We have learned that "pride" and "stubbornness" must be brushed away before we can make use of the Law of Retaliation in a constructive way. *We have not learned what the Law of Retaliation is, but we have learned how it works and what it will do;* therefore, it only remains for us to make intelligent use of this great principle.

You are now ready to proceed with Lesson Seven, where you will find other laws which harmonize perfectly with those described in this lesson on Self-control.

It will require the strongest sort of *self-control* to enable the beginner to apply the major law of the next lesson, on the Habit of Doing More Than Paid For, but experience will show that the development of such control is more than justified by the results growing out of such discipline.

If you are successful remember that somewhere, sometime, someone gave you a lift or an idea that started you in the right direction. Remember, also, that you are indebted to life until you help some less fortunate person, just as you were helped.

THE EVOLUTION OF TRANSPORTATION

An After-the-Lesson Visit with the Author

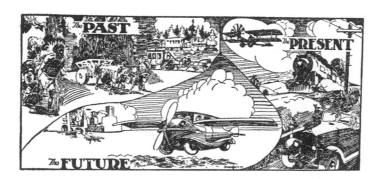

Nothing is permanent except change. Life resembles a great kaleidoscope before which Time is ever shifting, changing and rearranging both the stage setting and the players. New friends are constantly replacing the old. Everything is in a state of flux. In every heart is the seed of both rascality and justice. Every human being is both a criminal and a saint, depending upon the expediency of the moment as to which will assert itself. Honesty and dishonesty are largely matters of individual viewpoint. The weak and the strong, the rich and the poor, the ignorant and the well-informed are exchanging places continuously.

Know YOURSELF and you know the entire human race. There is but one real achievement, and that is the ability to THINK ACCURATELY. We move with the procession, or behind it, but we cannot stand still.

Nothing is permanent except change!

In the picture above you see proof that the law of evolution is working out improvements in the methods of travel. Remember, as you study this picture, that all these changes took place first in the minds of men.

At the extreme left you see the first crude method of transportation. Man was *not satisfied* with this slow process. Those two little words "not satisfied," have been the starting point of all advancement. Think of them as you read this article.

Next, in the picture, you see the history of transportation step by step, as man's brain began to expand. It was a long step forward when man discovered how to hitch a bullock to a wagon and thereby escape the toil of pulling the load. That was practical utility. But, when the stage-coach was ushered into use that was both utility and style. Still man was "not satisfied" and this dissatisfaction created the crude locomotive that you see in the picture.

Now all these methods of travel have been discarded except in certain uncivilized (or uncommercialized) parts of the world. The man drawing the cart, the bullock drawing the cart, the stage-coach and the crude locomotive all belong to ages that have passed.

At the right you see the transportation methods of the present. Compare them with those of the past and you may have a fair idea of the enormous expansion that has taken place in the brain and mind of man. Man now moves about more rapidly than in the past. From the first type of locomotive there has been evolved a powerful machine capable of hauling a hundred cars of freight, compared with the one small, light car that could be drawn with the original. Automobiles that travel at the speed of seventy-five miles an hour are now as common as were the two-wheel carts in ages past. Moreover, they are within the means of all who want them.

And still man's mind was "not satisfied." Travel on the earth was too slow. Turning his eyes upward he watched the birds soaring high in the elements and became "DETERMINED" to excel them. Study, also, the word "determined," for whatever man becomes determined to do man does! Within the brief period of fifteen years man has mastered the air and now travels in the airplane at the rate of a hundred and fifty miles an hour.

Not only has man made the air carry him at amazingly rapid speed, but he has harnessed the ether and made it carry his words all the way around the earth in the fractional part of a second.

———

We have been describing the PAST and the PRESENT!

At the bottom of the picture we may see the next step forward that man will take in methods of travel; a machine that will fly in the air, run on the ground and swim in the water, at the discretion of man.

The purpose of this essay and the picture at the top of the page is to provide food for THOUGHT!

Any influence that causes one to think causes one, also, to grow stronger mentally. Mind stimulants are essential for growth. From the days of the man-drawn cart to the present days of air mastery the only progress that any man has made has been the result of some influence that stimulated his mind to greater than normal action.

The two great major influences that cause the mind of man to grow are the urge of necessity and the urge of desire to create. Some minds develop only after they have undergone failure and defeat and other forms of punishment which arouse them to greater action. Other minds wither away and die under punishment, but grow to unbelievable heights when provided with the opportunity to use their imaginative forces in a creative way.

Study the picture of the evolution of transportation and you will observe one outstanding fact worth remembering, namely, that the whole story has been one of development and advancement that grew out of *necessity*. The entire period described in the picture as "THE PAST" was one wherein the urge was that of necessity.

In the period described in the picture above as "THE PRESENT" the urge has been a combination of both necessity and the desire to create. The period described as "THE FUTURE" will be one in which the strong desire to create will be the sole urge that will drive man's mind on and on to heights as yet undreamed of.

It is a long distance from the days of the man-drawn cart to the present, when man has harnessed the lightning of the clouds and made it turn machinery that will perform as much service in a minute as ten thousand men could perform in a day. But, if the distance has been long the development of man's mind has been correspondingly great, and that development has been sufficient to eventually do the work of the world with machines operated by Nature's forces and not by man's muscles.

The evolutionary changes in the methods of transportation have created other problems for man's mind to solve. The automobile drove man to build better roads and more of them. The automobile and the speedy locomotive, combined, have created dangerous crossings which claim thousands of lives annually. Man's mind must now respond to the urge of "necessity" and meet this emergency.

Keep this essay and remember this prophecy:

Within five years every railroad crossing in the country will be amply protected against automobile accidents, and, the automobile, itself, will manipulate the system that will do the protecting; a system that will be fool-proof and effective; a system that will work whether the driver of the automobile is asleep or awake, drunk or sober.

Come, now, for a brief glimpse at the machinery of the imagination of man, as it works under the stimulant of desire to create.

Some imaginative man; perhaps some fellow who never did anything else of note and who will never do anything worth while again; will create a system of railroad crossing protection that will be operated by the weight of the passing automobile. Within the required distance from the crossing a platform similar to the platform of a large freight scale will cover an entire section of the roadway. As soon as an automobile mounts this platform the weight of the machine will lower a gate, ring a gong and flash a red light in front of the motorist. The gate will rise in one minute, allowing the motorist to pass over the track, thus forcing him to "stop, look and listen."

If you have a highly imaginative mind YOU may be the one who will create this system and collect the royalties from its sale.

To be practical the imaginative mind should be always on the alert for ways and means of diverting waste motion and power into useful channels. Most automobiles are far too heavy in comparison with the load they carry. This weight can be utilized by making it provide the motorist with railroad crossing protection.

Remember, the purpose of this essay is to give you merely the seed of suggestion; not the finished product of an invention ready to set up and render service. The value to you, of this suggestion, lies in the possibility of THOUGHT that you may devote to it, thereby developing and expanding your own mind.

Study yourself and find out to which of the two great major urges to action your mind responds most naturally—the urge of necessity or the desire to create. If you have children, study them and determine to which of these two motives they respond most naturally. Millions of children have had their imagination dwarfed and retarded by parents who removed as much as possible of the urge of necessity. By "making it easy" for your child you may be depriving the world of a genius. Bear in mind the fact that most of the progress that man has made came as the result of bitter, biting NECESSITY!

———

You need no proof that methods of transportation have undergone a continuous process of evolution. So marked has the change been that the old one-lung type of automobile now provokes a laugh wherever it is found on the street.

The law of evolution is always and everywhere at work, changing, tearing down and rebuilding every material element on this earth and throughout the universe. Towns, cities and communities are undergoing constant change. Go back to the place where you lived twenty years ago and you will recognize neither the place nor the people. New faces will have made their appearance. The old faces will have changed. New buildings will have taken the place of the old. Everything will appear differently because everything will be different.

The human mind is also undergoing constant change. If this were not true we would never grow beyond the child-mind age. Every seven years the mind of a normal person becomes noticeably developed and expanded. It is during these periodical changes of the mind that bad habits may be left off and better habits cultivated. Fortunate for the human being that his mind is undergoing a continuous process of orderly change.

The mind that is driven by the urge of necessity, or out of love to create, develops more rapidly than does the mind that is never stimulated to greater action than that which is necessary for existence.

The imaginative faculty of the human mind is the greatest piece of machinery ever created. Out of it has come every man-made machine and every man-made object.

Back of the great industries and railroads and banking houses and commercial enterprises is the all-powerful force of IMAGINATION!

Force your mind to THINK! Proceed by combining old ideas into new plans. Every great invention and every outstanding business or industrial achievement that you can name is, in final analysis, but the application of a combination of plans and ideas that have been used before, in some other manner.

I have yet to find the first man who amounted to very much who had not the courage to assume responsibility for his own mistakes without being accused.

"Back of the beating hammer
   By which the steel is wrought,
Back of the workshop's clamor

The seeker may find the Thought;
The thought that is ever Master
    Of iron and steam and steel,
That rises above disaster
    And tramples it under heel.

"The drudge may fret and tinker
    Or labor with lusty blows,
But back of him stands the Thinker,
    The clear-eyed man who knows;
For into each plow or saber,
    Each piece and part and whole,
Must go the brains of labor,
    Which gives the work a soul.

"Back of the motor's humming,
    Back of the bells that ring,
Back of the hammer's drumming,
    Back of the cranes that swing,
There is the Eye which scans them,
    Watching through stress and strain,
There is the Mind which plans them—
    Back of the brawn, the Brain.

"Might of the roaring boiler,
    Force of the engine's thrust,
Strength of the sweating toiler,
    Greatly in these we trust;
But back of them stands the schemer,
    The Thinker who drives things through,
    Back of the job—the Dreamer
        Who's making the dream come true."

Six months or a year from now come back and read this essay again and you will observe how much more you will get from it than you did at first reading. TIME gives the law of evolution a chance to expand your mind so it can see and understand more.

There are ten weaknesses against which most of us must guard ourselves. One of these is the habit of trying to reap before we have sown, and the other nine are all wrapped up in the one practice of creating alibis to cover every mistake made.

HABIT OF DOING MORE THAN PAID FOR

"You Can Do It If You Believe You Can!"

It may seem to be a departure from the subject of this lesson to start the lesson with a discussion of love, but, if you will reserve your opinion until you have completed the lesson, you may be ready to agree that the subject of love could not have been omitted without impairing the value of the lesson.

The word "love" is here used in an all-embracing sense!

There are many objects, motives and people which arouse one's love-nature. There is some work which we do not like, some that we do like moderately, and, under certain conditions, there may be work that we actually LOVE!

Great artists, for example, generally love their work. The day laborer, on the other hand, usually not only dislikes his work, but may actually hate it.

Work which one does merely for the sake of earning a living is seldom liked. More often it is disliked, or even hated.

When engaged in work which he loves, a man may labor for an unbelievably long period of hours without becoming fatigued. Work that a man dislikes or hates brings on fatigue very quickly.

A man's endurance, therefore, depends very largely on the extent to which he likes, dislikes or loves that which he is doing.

We are here laying the foundation, as you will of course observe, for the statement of one of the most important laws of this philosophy, viz.:

A man is most efficient and will more quickly and easily succeed when engaged in work that he loves, or work that he performs in behalf of some person whom he loves.

Whenever the element of love enters into any task that one performs, the quality of the work becomes immediately improved and the quantity increased, without a corresponding increase in the fatigue caused by the work.

Some years ago a group of socialists, or perhaps they called themselves "co-operators," organized a colony in Louisiana, purchased several hundred acres of farm land, and started to work out an ideal which they believed would give them greater happiness in life and fewer of the worries through a system that provided each person with work at the sort of labor he liked best.

Their idea was to pay no wages to anyone. Each person did the work he liked best, or that for which he might be best equipped, and the products of their combined labors became the property of all. They had their own dairy, their own brick-making plant, their own cattle, poultry, etc. They had their own schools and a printing plant through which they published a paper.

A Swedish gentleman from Minnesota joined the colony, and at his own request he was placed at work in the printing plant. Very soon he complained that he did not like the work, so he was changed and put to work on the farm, operating a tractor. Two days of this was all he could stand, so he again applied for a transfer, and was assigned to the dairy. He could not get along with the cows, so he was once more changed, to the laundry, where he lasted but one day. One by one he tried every job on the works, but liked none of them. It had begun to look as if he did not fit in with the co-operative idea of living, and he was about to withdraw when someone happened to think of one job he had not yet tried—in the brick plant, so he was given a wheelbarrow and put to work wheeling bricks from the kilns and stacking them in piles, in the brick yard. A week's time went by and no complaint was registered by him. When asked if he liked his job he replied, "This ban chust the job I like."

Imagine anyone preferring a job wheeling bricks! However, that job suited the Swede's nature, he worked alone, at a task which called for no thought, and placed upon him no responsibility, which was just what he wanted.

He remained at the job until all the bricks had been wheeled out and stacked, then withdrew from the colony because there was no more brick work to be done. "The nice quiet job ban finished, so I t'ank I ban go back to Minney-so-tie," and back to "Minney-so-tie" he went!

When a man is engaged in work that he loves it is no hardship for him to do more work and better work than that for which he is paid, and for this very reason every man owes it to himself to do his best to find the sort of work he likes best.

I have a perfect right to offer this advice to the students of this philosophy for the reason that I have followed it, myself, without reason to regret having done so.

This seems to be an appropriate place to inject a little personal history concerning both the author and the Law of Success philosophy, the purpose of which is to show that labor performed in a spirit of love for the sake of the labor, itself, never has been and never will be lost.

This entire lesson is devoted to the offering of evidence that it really pays to render more service and better service than one is paid to render. What an empty and useless effort this would be if the author had not, himself, practiced this rule long enough to be able to say just how it works out.

For over a quarter of a century I have been engaged in the labor of love out of which this philosophy has been developed, and I am perfectly sincere when I repeat that which I have stated elsewhere in this course, that I have been amply paid for my labors, by the pleasure I have had as I went along, even if I received nothing more.

My labors on this philosophy made it necessary, many years ago, for me to choose between immediate monetary returns, which I might have enjoyed by directing my efforts along purely commercial lines, and remuneration that comes in later years, and which is represented by both the usual financial standards and other forms of pay which can be measured only in terms of accumulated knowledge that enables one to enjoy the world about him more keenly.

The man who engages in work that he loves best does not always have the support, in his choice, of his closest friends and relatives.

Combating negative suggestions from friends and relatives has required an alarming proportion of my energies, during the years that I have been engaged in research work for the purpose of gathering, organizing, classifying and testing the material which has gone into this course.

These personal references are made solely for the purpose of showing the students of this philosophy that seldom, if ever, can one hope to engage in the work one loves best without meeting with obstacles of some nature. Generally, the chief obstacles in the way of one engaging in the sort of work one loves best is that it may not be the work which brings the greatest remuneration at the start.

To offset this disadvantage, however, the one who engages in the sort of work he loves is generally rewarded with two very decided benefits, namely; first, he usually finds in such work the greatest of all rewards, HAPPINESS, which is priceless, and secondly, his actual reward in money, when averaged over a life-time of effort, is generally much greater, for the

There is no more dangerous person—dangerous to himself and to others—than the person who passes judgment without pretending to know the facts.

reason that labor which is performed in a spirit of love is usually greater in quantity and finer in quality than that which is performed solely for money.

The most embarrassing and, I might without any intention of disrespect say, the most disastrous opposition to my choice of a life-work came from my wife. This, perhaps, will explain why I have made frequent references, in many of the lessons of this course, to the fact that a man's wife may either "make" or "break" him, according to the extent to which she gives or withholds co-operation and encouragement in connection with his chosen work.

My wife's idea was that I should accept a salaried position that would insure a regular monthly income, because I had shown, by the few salaried positions I had held, that I had marketable ability which should command an income of from $6,000.00 to $10,000.00 a year without any very great effort on my part.

In a way I saw my wife's viewpoint and was in sympathy with it, because we had young growing children coming on who needed clothes and education, and a regular salary, even though it were not large, seemed to be a necessity.

Despite this logical argument, however, I chose to override my wife's counsel. Came, then, to her rescue, the combined forces of her family and mine, and collectively they charged me, head-on, with what amounted to a command to right-about-face and settle down on a salary basis.

Studying other people might be all right for a man who had the time to spend in this "unprofitable" manner, they reasoned, but for a young married man with a growing family this seemed hardly the thing to do.

But I remained adamant! I had made my choice and I was determined to stand by it.

The opposition did not yield to my viewpoint, but gradually, of course, it melted away. Meanwhile, the knowledge that my choice had worked at least a temporary hardship on my family, combined with the thought that my dearest friends and relatives were not in harmony with me, greatly increased my labors.

Fortunately, not all of my friends believed my choice unwise!

There were a few friends who not only believed I was following a course that would ultimately bring me out somewhere near the top of the mountain of useful achievement, but, in addition to believing in my plans, they actually went out of their way to encourage me not to be whipped by either adversity or the opposition of relatives.

Of this small group of faithful ones who gave me encouragement at a time when it was badly needed, perhaps one man should have the fullest credit, and this man is Edwin C. Barnes, a business associate of Thomas A. Edison.

Mr. Barnes became interested in my chosen work nearly twenty years ago, and I owe it to him to state here that had it not been for his unwavering faith in the soundness of the Law of Success philosophy I would have yielded to the persuasion of my friends and sought the way of least resistance via the salary route.

This would have saved me much grief and an almost endless amount of criticism, but it would have wrecked the hopes of a life-time, and in the end I would in all probability have lost, also, the finest and most desirable of all things, HAPPINESS! for I have been extremely happy in my work, even during the periods when the remuneration it brought me could be measured by nothing but a mountain of debts which I could not for the moment pay.

Perhaps this may explain, to some extent, why the subject of slavery through debt was so extensively emphasized in Lesson Three, on the Habit of Saving.

We want that lesson to "sink in."

Edwin Barnes not only believed in the soundness of the Law of Success philosophy, but his own financial success had demonstrated, as had also his close business relationship with the greatest inventor on earth, that he had the right to speak with authority on the subject of the laws through which success may be achieved.

I began my work of research with the belief that success could be attained, by anyone with reasonable intelligence and a real desire to succeed, by following certain (then by me unknown) rules of procedure. I wanted to know what these rules were and how they could be applied.

Mr. Barnes believed as I did. Moreover, he was in a position to know that the astounding achievements of his business associate, Mr. Edison, came about entirely through the application of some of the principles which later were tested and included as a part of this philosophy. From his way of thinking it seemed that the accumulation of money, enjoying peace of mind and finding happiness could be brought about by the application of never-varying laws which anyone might master and apply.

That was my belief, also. That belief has now been transformed into not merely a provable, but a PROVED reality, as I hope every student of this course will have reason to understand when the course shall have been mastered.

Please keep in mind that during all these years of research I was not only applying the law covered by this lesson, by DOING MORE THAN PAID FOR, but, I was going much further than this by doing work for which I did not, at the time I was doing it, hope ever to receive pay.

Thus, out of years of chaos, adversity and opposition this philosophy was finally completed and reduced to manuscripts, ready for publication.

For a time nothing happened!

I was resting on my oars, so to speak, before taking the next step toward placing the philosophy in the hands of people who I had reason to believe would welcome it.

"God moves in a mysterious way, His wonders to perform!"

During the earlier years of my experience I thought these words to be empty and meaningless, but I have since modified my belief considerably.

I was invited to deliver an address in Canton, Ohio. My coming had been well advertised and there was reason to expect that I would have a large audience. To the contrary, conflicting meetings being held by two large groups of business men reduced my audience to the lucky number of "thirteen."

It has always been my belief that a man should do his best, regardless of how much he receives for his services, or the number of people he may be serving or the class of people served. I went at my subject as though the hall were filled. Somehow there arose in me a sort of feeling of resentment on account of the way the "wheel of fate" had turned against me, and if I ever made a convincing speech I made it that night.

Down deep in my heart, however, I thought I had failed!

I did not know until the next day that I was making history the night before that was destined to give the Law of Success philosophy its first real impetus.

One of the men who sat in my audience, as one of the "thirteen," was the late Don R. Mellett, who was then the publisher of the Canton *Daily News,* brief reference to whom I made in the Introduction to this course.

After I had finished speaking I slipped out at the back door and returned to my hotel, not wanting to face any of my "thirteen" victims on the way out.

The next day I was invited to Mr. Mellett's office.

Inasmuch as it was he who had taken the initiative by inviting me in to see him I left it to him to do most of the talking. He began in something like this fashion:

"Would you mind telling me your entire life-story, from the days of your early childhood on up to the present?"

I told him I would do so if he could stand the burden of listening to so long a narrative. He said he could, but before I began he cautioned me not to omit the unfavorable side.

"What I wish you to do," said he, "is to mix the fat with the lean and let me take a look at your very soul, not from its most favorable side, but from all sides."

For three hours I talked while Mellett listened!

I omitted nothing. I told him of my struggles, of my mistakes, of my impulses to be dishonest when the tides of fortune swept against me too swiftly, and of my better judgment which prevailed in the end, but only after my conscience and I had engaged in prolonged combat. I told him how I conceived the idea of organizing the Law of Success philosophy, how I had gone about gathering the data that had gone into the philosophy, of the tests I had made which resulted in the elimination of some of the data and the retention of other parts of it.

> *Among the other things you intend to "cut out" in your New Year's resolution, include the word "Impossible!"*

After I had finished Mellett said: "I wish to ask you a very personal question, and I hope you will answer it as frankly as you have told the remainder of your story. Have you accumulated any money from your efforts, and, if not, do you know why you have not?"

"No!" I replied. "I have accumulated nothing but experience and knowledge and a few debts, and the reason, while it may not be sound, is easily explained. The truth is that I have been so busy all these years in trying to eliminate some of my own ignorance so I could intelligently gather and organize the data that have gone into the Law of Success philosophy, that I have had neither the opportunity nor the inclination to turn my efforts to making money."

The serious look on Don Mellett's face, much to my surprise, softened into a smile as he laid his hand on my shoulder and said:

"I knew the answer before you stated it, but I wondered if you knew it. You probably know that you are not the only man who has had to sacrifice immediate monetary remuneration for the sake of gathering knowledge, for in truth your experience has been that of every philosopher from the time of Socrates down to the present."

Those words fell as the sound of music upon my ears!

I had made one of the most embarrassing admissions of my life; I had laid my soul bare, admitting temporary defeat at almost every cross-road which I had passed in my struggles, and I had capped all this off by admitting that an exponent of the Law of Success was, himself, a temporary failure!

How incongruous it seemed! I felt stupid, humiliated and embarrassed as I sat in front of the most searching pair of eyes and the most inquisitive man I had ever met.

The absurdity of it all came over me like a flash—THE PHILOSOPHY OF SUC-CESS CREATED AND BROADCASTED BY A MAN WHO WAS OBVIOUSLY A FAILURE!

This thought struck me so forcibly that I expressed it in words.

"What?" Mellett exclaimed, "a failure?

"Surely you know the difference between failure and temporary defeat," he continued. "No man is a failure who creates a single idea, much less an entire philosophy, that serves to soften the disappointments and minimize the hardships of generations yet unborn."

I wondered what was the object of this interview. My first conjecture was that Mellett wanted some facts on which to base an attack, in his newspaper, on the Law of Success philosophy. Perhaps this thought grew out of some of my previous experiences with newspaper men, a few of whom had been antagonistic toward me. At any rate, I decided at the outset of the interview to give him the facts, without embellishment, come from it what would.

Before I left Mellett's office we had become business partners, with the understanding that he would resign as publisher of the Canton *Daily News* and take over the management of all my affairs, as soon as this could be arranged.

Meanwhile, I began writing a series of Sunday feature-page editorials which were published in the Canton *Daily News,* based upon the Law of Success philosophy.

One of these editorials (the one entitled "Failure," which appears in the back of one of the lessons of this course) came to the attention of Judge Elbert H. Gary, who was at that time the Chairman of the Board of the United States Steel Corporation. This resulted in the opening of communication between Mellett and Judge Gary, which, in turn, led to Judge Gary's offer to purchase the Law of Success course for the use of the employees of the Steel Corporation, in the manner described in the Introduction.

The tides of fortune had begun to turn in my favor!

The seeds of service which I had been sowing over a long period of toilsome years, by DOING MORE THAN PAID FOR, were beginning to germinate at last!

Despite the fact that my partner was assassinated before our plans had much more than started, and Judge Gary died before the Law of Success philosophy could be re-written so it conformed to his requirements, the "love's labor lost" on that fateful night, when I spoke to an audience of thirteen in Canton, Ohio, started a chain of events which now move rapidly without thought or effort on my part.

It is no abuse of confidences to enumerate here a few of the events which show that no labor of love is ever performed at a total loss, and that those who render more service and better service than that for which they are paid sooner or later receive pay for much more than they actually do.

As this lesson is ready to go to the publisher some of the following well known concerns are considering favorably the purchase of the Law of Success course for all their employees, while others have actually arranged for the purchase of the course:

Mr. Daniel Willard, President of the Baltimore & Ohio Railroad Co.

Indian Refining Company

Standard Oil Company

New York Life Insurance Company

The Postal Telegraph Commercial-Cable Company

The Pierce-Arrow Motor Car Company

The Cadillac Motor Car Company

And some fifty other concerns of a similar size.

In addition to this, a newly organized club for boys, similar in nature to the Y. M. C. A., has contracted for the use of the Law of Success course as the basis of its educational program, and estimates that it will distribute more than 100,000 courses of the philosophy within the next two years.

Quite aside from these sources of distribution, the Ralston University Press, of Meriden, Conn., has contracted to publish and distribute the course to individuals throughout the United States, and perhaps in some foreign countries. How many courses they will distribute cannot be accurately estimated, but when one stops to consider the fact that they have a mailing list of approximately 800,000 people who have faith in anything they offer for sale, it seems very reasonable to suppose that their distribution will place tens of thousands of courses in the hands of men and women who are earnestly searching for the knowledge conveyed by the Law of Success philosophy.

Perhaps it is unnecessary, but I wish to explain that my only object in here relating the story of how the Law of Success philosophy has gained the recognition described is to show how the law upon which this lesson is based actually works out in the practical affairs of life.

If I could have made this analysis without the use of the personal pronoun I would have done so.

With this background of history concerning the Law of Success philosophy as a whole, and this lesson in particular, you are better prepared to accept as sound the law on which this lesson is based.

There are more than a score of sound reasons why you should develop the habit of performing more service and *better service* than that for which you are paid, despite the fact that a large majority of the people are not rendering such service.

There are two reasons, however, for rendering such service, which transcend, in importance, all the others; namely,

> *If ye have faith as a grain of mustard seed, ye shall say unto this mountain, Remove hence to yonder place; and it shall remove; and nothing shall be impossible unto you.*

First: By establishing a reputation as being a person who always renders more service and better service than that for which you are paid, you will benefit by comparison with those around you who do not render such service, and the contrast will be so noticeable that *there will be keen competition for your services, no matter what your life-work may be.*

It would be an insult to your intelligence to offer proof of the soundness of this statement, because it is obviously sound. Whether you are preaching sermons, practicing law, writing books, teaching school, or digging ditches, you will become more valuable and you will be able to command greater pay the minute you gain recognition as a person who does more than that for which he is paid.

Second: By far the most important reason why you should render more service than that for which you are paid; a reason that is basic and fundamental in nature; may be described in this way: Suppose that you wished to develop a strong right arm, and suppose that you tried to do so by tying the arm to your side with a rope, thus taking it out of use and giving it a long rest. Would disuse bring strength, or would it bring atrophy and weakness, resulting, finally, in your being compelled to have the arm removed?

You know that if you wished a strong right arm you could develop such an arm *only by giving it the hardest sort of use.* Take a look at the arm of a blacksmith if you wish to know how an arm may be made strong. Out of resistance comes strength. The strongest oak tree of the forest is not the one that is protected from the storm and hidden from the sun, but it is the one that stands in the open, where it is compelled to struggle for its existence against the winds and rains and the scorching sun.

It is through the operation of one of Nature's unvarying laws that struggle and resistance develop strength, and the purpose of this lesson is to show you how to harness this law and so use it that it will aid you in your struggle for success. By performing more service and better service than that for which you are paid, you not only exercise your service-rendering qualities, and thereby develop skill and ability of an extraordinary sort, but you build reputation that is valuable. If you form the habit of rendering such service you will become so adept in your work that you can *command* greater remuneration than those who do not perform such service. You will eventually develop sufficient strength to enable you to remove yourself from any undesirable station in life, and no one can or will desire to stop you.

If you are an employee you can make yourself so valuable, through this habit of performing more service than that for which you are paid, that you can practically set your own wages and no sensible employer will try to stop you. If your employer should be so unfortunate as to try to withhold from you the compensation to which you are entitled, this will not long remain as a handicap because other employers will discover this unusual quality and offer you employment.

The very fact that most people are rendering as little service as they can possibly get by with serves as an advantage to all who are rendering more service than that for which they are paid, because it enables all who do this to profit by comparison. You can "get by" if you render as little service as possible, but that is all you will get; and when work is slack and retrenchment sets in, you will be one of the first to be dismissed.

For more than twenty-five years I have carefully studied men with the object of ascertaining why some achieve noteworthy success while others with just as much ability do not get ahead; and it seems significant that every person whom I have observed applying this principle of rendering more service than that for which he was paid, was holding a better position and receiving more pay than those who merely performed sufficient service to "get by" with.

Personally I never received a promotion in my life that I could not trace directly to recognition that I had gained by rendering more service and better service than that for which I was paid.

I am stressing the importance of making this principle a habit as a means of enabling an employee to promote himself to a higher position, with greater pay, for the reason that this course will be studied by thousands of young men and young women who work for others. However, the principle applies to the employer or to the professional man or woman just the same as to the employee.

Observance of this principle brings a two-fold reward. First, it brings the reward of greater material gain than that enjoyed by those who do not observe it; and, second, it brings that reward of happiness and satisfaction which come only to those who render such service. If you receive no pay except that which comes in your pay envelope, you are underpaid, no matter how much money that envelope contains.

My wife has just returned from the Public Library with a book for me to read. The book is entitled *Observation: Every Man His Own University,* by Russell H. Conwell.

By chance I opened this book at the beginning of the chapter entitled Every Man's University, and, as I read it through, my first impulse was to recommend that *you* go to the Public Library and read the entire book; but, upon second thought, I will not do this; instead, I will recommend that you purchase the book and read it, not once but a hundred times, because it covers the subject of this lesson as though it had been written for that purpose; covers it in a far more impressive manner than I could do it.

The following quotation from the chapter entitled Every Man's University will give you an idea of the golden nugget of truth to be found throughout the book:

"The intellect can be made to look far beyond the range of what men and women ordinarily see, but not all the colleges in the world can alone confer this power—this is the reward of *self-culture;* each must acquire it for himself; and perhaps this is why the power of observing deeply and widely is so much oftener found in those men and those women who have never crossed the threshold of any college but the *University of Hard Knocks.*"

Read that book as a part of this lesson, because it will prepare you to profit by the philosophy and psychology upon which the lesson is built.

We will now analyze the law upon which this entire lesson is founded, namely—

The Law of Increasing Returns!

Let us begin our analysis by showing how Nature employs this law in behalf of the tillers of the soil. The farmer carefully prepares the ground, then sows his wheat and waits while the Law of Increasing Returns brings back the seed he has sown, *plus a manyfold increase.*

But for this Law of Increasing Returns, man would perish, because he could not make the soil produce sufficient food for his existence. There would be no advantage to be gained by sowing a field of wheat if the harvest yield did not return more than was sown.

With this vital "tip" from Nature, which we may gather from the wheat fields, let us proceed to appropriate this Law of Increasing Returns and learn how to apply it to the service we render, to the end that *it may yield returns in excess of and out of proportion to the effort put forth.*

First of all, let us emphasize the fact that there is no trickery or chicanery connected with this Law, although quite a few seem not to have learned this great truth, judging by the number who spend all of their efforts either trying to get something for nothing, or something for less than its true value.

Ultimately, nothing matters very much. The defeat that seems to break your heart today will be but a ripple among the waves of other experiences in the ocean of your life further ahead.

It is to no such end that we recommend the use of the Law of Increasing Returns, for no such end is possible, within the broad meaning of the word *success.*

Another remarkable and noteworthy feature of the Law of Increasing Returns is the fact that it may be used by those who purchase service with as great returns as it can be by those who render service, for proof of which we have but to study the effects of Henry Ford's famous Five-Dollar-a-day minimum wage scale which he inaugurated some years ago.

Those who are familiar with the facts say that Mr. Ford was not playing the part of a philanthropist when he inaugurated this minimum wage scale; but, to the contrary, he was merely taking advantage of a sound business principle which has probably yielded him greater returns, in both dollars and good-will, than any other single policy ever inaugurated at the Ford plant.

By paying more wages than the average, he received more service and better service than the average!

At a single stroke, through the inauguration of that minimum wage policy, Ford attracted the best labor on the market and placed a premium upon the privilege of working in his plant.

I have no authentic figures at hand bearing on the subject, but I have sound reason to conjecture that for every five dollars Ford spent, under this policy, he received at least seven dollars and fifty cents' worth of service. I have, also, sound reason to believe that this policy enabled Ford to reduce the cost of supervision, because employment in his plant became so desirable that no worker would care to run the risk of losing his position by "soldiering" on the job or rendering poor service.

Where other employers were forced to depend upon costly supervision in order to get the service to which they were entitled, and for which they were paying, Ford got the same or better service by the less expensive method of placing a premium upon employment in his plant.

Marshall Field was probably the leading merchant of his time, and the great Field store, in Chicago, stands today as a monument to his ability to apply the Law of Increasing Returns.

A customer purchased an expensive lace waist at the Field store, but did not wear it. Two years later she gave it to her niece as a wedding present. The niece quietly returned the waist to the Field store and exchanged it for other merchandise, despite the fact that it had been out for more than two years and was then out of style.

Not only did the Field store take back the waist, but, what is of more importance it did so *without argument!*

Of course there was no obligation, moral or legal, on the part of the store to accept the return of the waist at that late date, which makes the transaction all the more significant.

The waist was originally priced at fifty dollars, and of course it had to be thrown on the bargain counter and sold for whatever it would bring, but the keen student of human nature will understand that the Field store not only did not lose anything on the waist, but it actually profited by the transaction to an extent that cannot be measured in mere dollars.

The woman who returned the waist knew that she was not entitled to a rebate; therefore, when the store gave her that to which she was not entitled the transaction won her as a permanent customer. But the effect of the transaction did not end here; it only began; for this woman spread the news of the "fair treatment" she had received at the Field store, far and near. It was the talk of the women of her set for many days, and the Field store received more advertising from the transaction than it could have purchased in any other way with ten times the value of the waist.

The success of the Field store was built largely upon Marshall Field's understanding of the Law of Increasing Returns, which prompted him to adopt, as a part of his business policy, the slogan, "The customer is always right."

When you do only that for which you are paid, there is nothing out of the ordinary to *attract favorable comment* about the transaction; but, when you willingly do more than that for which you are paid, your action attracts the favorable attention of all who are affected by the transaction, and goes another step toward establishing a reputation that will eventually set the Law of Increasing Returns to work in your behalf, for this reputation will create a demand for your services, far and wide.

Carol Downes went to work for W. C. Durant, the automobile manufacturer, in a minor position. He is now Mr. Durant's right-hand man, and the president of one of his automobile distributing companies. He promoted himself into this profitable position solely through the aid of the Law of Increasing Returns, which he put into operation by rendering more service and better service than that for which he was paid.

In a recent visit with Mr. Downes I asked him to tell me how he managed to gain promotion so rapidly. In a few brief sentences he told the whole story.

"When I first went to work with Mr. Durant," said he, "I noticed that he always remained at the office long after all the others had gone home for the day, and I made it my business to stay there, also. No one asked me to stay, but I thought someone should be there to give Mr. Durant any assistance he might need. Often he would look around for someone to bring him a letter file, or render some other trivial service, and *always he found me there ready to serve him.* He got into the habit of calling on me; that is about all there is to the story."

> *To love praise, but not worship it, and fear condemnation, but not go down under it, is evidence of a well balanced personality.*

"He got into the habit of calling on me!"

Read that sentence again, for it is full of meaning of the richest sort.

Why did Mr. Durant get into the habit of calling on Mr. Downes? Because *Mr. Downes made it his business to be on hand where he would be seen.* He deliberately placed himself in Mr. Durant's way in order that he might render service that would place the Law of Increasing Returns back of him.

Was he told to do this? *No!*

Was he paid to do it? *Yes!* He was paid by the opportunity it offered for him to bring himself to the attention of the man who had it within his power to promote him.

We are now approaching the most important part of this lesson, because this is an appropriate place at which to suggest that *you* have the same opportunity to make use of the Law of Increasing Returns that Mr. Downes had, and you can go about the application of the Law in exactly the same way that he did, *by being on hand and ready to volunteer your services in the performance of work which others may shirk because they are not paid to do it.*

Stop! Don't say it—don't even think it—if you have the slightest intention of springing that old time-worn phrase entitled, "But *my employer is different.*"

Of course he is different. All men are different in most respects, but they are very much alike in this—they are somewhat *selfish;* in fact they are selfish enough not to want a man such as Carol Downes to cast his lot with their competitor, and this very selfishness may be made to serve you as an asset and not as a liability *if—*

You have the good judgment to make yourself so useful that the person to whom you sell your services cannot get along without you.

One of the most advantageous promotions I ever received came about through an incident which seemed so insignificant that it appeared to be unimportant. One Saturday afternoon, a lawyer, whose office was on the same floor as that of my employer, came in and asked if I knew where he could get a stenographer to do some work which he was compelled to finish that day.

I told him that all of our stenographers had gone to the ball game, and that I would have been gone had he called five minutes later, but that I would be very glad to stay and do his work as I could go to a ball game any day and his work had to be done then.

I did the work for him, and when he asked how much he owed me I replied, "Oh, about a thousand dollars, as long as it is you; if it were for anyone else, I wouldn't charge anything." He smiled, and thanked me.

Little did I think, when I made that remark, that he would ever pay me a thousand dollars for that afternoon's work, but *he did!* Six months later, after I had entirely forgotten the incident, he called on me again, and asked how much salary I was receiving. When I told him he informed me that he was ready to pay me that thousand dollars which I had laughingly said I would charge him for the work I had performed for him and he *did pay it* by giving me a position at a thousand dollars a year increase in salary.

Unconsciously, I had put the Law of Increasing Returns to work in my behalf that afternoon, by giving up the ball game and rendering a service which was obviously rendered out of a desire to be helpful and not for the sake of a monetary consideration.

It was not my duty to give up my Saturday afternoon, but—

It was my privilege!

Furthermore, it was a profitable privilege, because it yielded me a thousand dollars in cash and a much more responsible position than the one I had formerly occupied.

It was Carol Downes' *duty* to be on hand until the usual quitting time, but it was his *privilege* to remain at his post after the other workers had gone, and that privilege properly exercised brought him greater responsibilities and a salary that yields him more in a year than he would have made in a life-time in the position he occupied before he exercised the privilege.

I have been thinking for more than twenty-five years of this *privilege* of performing more service and better service than that for which we are paid, and my thoughts have led me to the conclusion that a single hour devoted each day to rendering service for which we are not paid, can be made to yield bigger returns than we received from the entire remainder of the day during which we are merely performing our *duty*.

(We are still in the neighborhood of the *most important part* of this lesson, therefore, *think* and assimilate as you pass over these pages.)

The Law of Increasing Returns is no invention of mine, nor do I lay claim to the discovery of the principle of rendering more service and better service than

> *The educated man is the man who has learned how to get everything he needs without violating the rights of his fellow men. Education comes from within; you get it by struggle and effort and thought.*

paid for, as a means of utilizing this Law. I merely appropriated them, after many years of careful observation of those forces which enter into the attainment of success, just as *you will appropriate them* after you understand their significance.

You might begin this appropriation process now by trying an experiment which may easily open your eyes and place back of your efforts powers that you did not know you possessed.

Let me caution you, however, not to attempt this experiment in the same spirit in which a certain woman experimented with that Biblical passage which says something to the effect that *if you have faith the size of a grain of mustard, and say to yonder mountain be removed to some other place, it will be removed.* This woman lived near a high mountain that she could see from her front door; therefore, as she retired that night she commanded the mountain to remove itself to some other place.

Next morning she jumped out of bed, rushed to the door and looked out, but lo! the mountain was still there. Then she said:

"Just as I had expected! I knew it would be there."

I am going to ask you to approach this experiment with full *faith* that it will mark one of the most important turning-points of your entire life. I am going to ask you to make the object of this experiment the removal of a mountain that is standing where *your temple of success should stand,* but where it never can stand until you have removed the mountain.

You may never have noticed the mountain to which I refer, but it is standing there in your way just the same, unless you have already discovered and removed it.

"And what is this mountain?" you ask!

It is the feeling that you have been cheated unless you receive material pay for all the service you render.

That feeling may be unconsciously expressing itself and destroying the very foundation of your *temple of success* in scores of ways that you have not observed.

In the very lowly bred type of humanity, this feeling usually seeks outward expression in terms something like this:

"I am not paid to do this and I'll be blankety-blankety-blank if I'll do it!"

You know the type to which reference is made; you have met with it many times, but you have never found a single person of this type who was successful, and you *never will.*

Success must be *attracted* through understanding and application of laws which are as immutable as is the law of gravitation. It cannot be driven into the corner and captured as one would capture a wild steer. For this reason you are requested to enter into the following experiment with the object of familiarizing yourself with one of the most important of these laws; namely, the Law of Increasing Returns.

The experiment:

During the next six months make it your business to render useful service to at least one person every day, for which you *neither expect nor accept monetary pay.*

Go at this experiment with *faith* that it will uncover for your use one of the most powerful laws that enter into the achievement of enduring success, and *you will not be disappointed.*

The rendering of this service may take on any one of more than a score of forms. For example, it may be rendered personally to one or more specific persons; or it may be rendered to your employer, in the nature of work that you perform after hours.

Again, it may be rendered to entire strangers whom you never expect to see again. It matters not to whom you render this service so long as you render it with willingness, and solely for the purpose of benefiting others.

If you carry out this experiment in the proper attitude of mind, you will discover that which all others who have become familiar with the law upon which it is based have discovered; namely, that—

You can no more render service without receiving compensation than you can withhold the rendering of it without suffering the loss of reward.

> *The person who sows a single beautiful thought in the mind of another, renders the world a greater service than that rendered by all the faultfinders combined.*

"Cause and effect, means and ends, seed and fruit, cannot be severed," says Emerson; "for the effect already blooms in the cause, the end pre-exists in the means, the fruit in the seed."

"If you serve an ungrateful master, serve him the more. Put God in your debt. Every stroke shall be repaid. The longer the payment is withholden, the better for you; for compound interest on compound interest is the rate and usage of this exchequer."

"The law of Nature is, Do the thing and you shall have the power; but they who do not the thing have not the power."

"Men suffer all their life long, under the foolish superstition that they can be cheated. But it is as impossible for a man to be cheated by anyone but himself, as for a thing to be, and not to be, at the same time. There is a third silent party to all our bargains. The nature and soul of things takes on itself the guaranty of fulfillment of every contract, so that *honest service cannot come to loss.*"

Before you begin the experiment that you have been requested to undertake, read Emerson's essay on Compensation, for it will go a very long way toward helping you to understand *why* you are making the experiment.

Perhaps you have read Compensation before. Read it again! One of the strange phenomena that you will observe about this essay may be found in the fact that every time you read it you will discover new truths that you did not notice during previous readings.

A few years ago I was invited to deliver the graduation address before the students of an eastern college. During my address I dwelt at length, and with all the emphasis at my command, on the importance of rendering more service and better service than that for which one is paid.

After the address was delivered, the president and the secretary of the college invited me to luncheon. While we were eating, the secretary turned to the president and said:

"I have just found out what this man is doing. He is putting himself ahead in the world by first helping others to get ahead."

In that brief statement he had epitomized the most important part of my philosophy on the subject of success.

It is literally true that you can succeed best and quickest by helping others to succeed.

Some ten years ago, when I was engaged in the advertising business, I built my entire clientele by the application of the fundamentals upon which this lesson is founded. By having my name placed on the follow-up lists of various mail order houses I received their sales literature. When I received a sales letter or a booklet or a folder which I believed I could improve I went right to work on it and made the improvement, then sent it back to the firm that had sent it to me, with a letter stating that this was but a trifling sample of what I could do—that there were plenty of other good ideas where that one came from—and, that I would be glad to render regular service for a monthly fee.

Invariably this brought an order for my services.

On one occasion I remember that the firm was dishonest enough to appropriate my idea and use it without paying me for it, but this turned out to be an advantage to me, in this way: A member of the firm who was familiar with the transaction started another business and as a result of the work I had done for his former associates, for which I was not paid, he engaged me to serve him, on a basis that paid me more than double the amount I would have realized from his original firm.

Thus the Law of Compensation gave back to me, and with compound interest added, that which I had lost by rendering service to those who were dishonest.

If I were looking for a profitable field of employment today, I could find it by again putting into action this plan of re-writing sales literature as a means of creating a market for my services. Perhaps I would find others who would appropriate my ideas without paying for them, but by and large people would not do this for the simple reason that it would be more profitable to them to deal fairly with me and thereby avail themselves of my continued services.

Several years ago I was invited to deliver a lecture before the students of the Palmer School, at Davenport, Iowa. My manager completed arrangements for me to accept the invitation under the regular terms in effect at that time, which were $100.00 for the lecture and my traveling expenses.

When I arrived at Davenport, I found a reception committee awaiting me at the depot and that evening I was given one of the warmest welcomes I had ever received during my public career, up to that time. I met many delightful people from whom I gathered many valuable facts that were of benefit to me; therefore, when I was asked to make out my expense account so the school could give me a check, I told them that I had received my pay, many times over, by that which I had learned while I was there. I refused my fee and returned to my office, in Chicago, feeling well repaid for the trip.

The following morning Dr. Palmer went before the two thousand students of his school and announced what I had said about feeling repaid by what I had learned, and added:

"In the twenty years that I have been conducting this school I have had scores of speakers address the student body, but this is the first time I ever knew a man to refuse his fee because he felt that he had been repaid for his services in other ways. This man is the editor of a national magazine and I advise every one of you to subscribe for that magazine, because such a man as this must have much that each of you will need when you go into the field and offer your services."

By the middle of that week I had received more than $6,000.00 for subscriptions to the magazine of which I was editor, and during the following two years these same two thousand students and their friends sent in more than $50,000.00 for subscriptions.

Tell me, if you can, how or where I could have invested $100.00 as profitably as this, by refusing to accept my $100.00 fee and thereby setting the Law of Increasing Returns to work in my behalf?

We go through two important periods in this life; one is that period during which we are gathering, classifying and organizing knowledge, and the other is that period during which we are struggling for recognition. We must first learn something, which requires more effort than most of us are willing to put into the job; but, after we have learned much that can be of useful service to others, we are still confronted with the problem of convincing them that we can serve them.

One of the most important reasons why we should always be not only ready but *willing* to render service, is the fact that every time we do so, we gain thereby another opportunity to prove to someone that we have ability; we go just one more step toward gaining the necessary recognition that we must all have.

Instead of saying to the world, "Show me the color of your money and I will show you what I can do," reverse the rule and say, "Let me show you the color of my service so that I may take a look at the color of your money if you like my service."

In 1917 a certain woman who was then nearing the fifty-year milepost of life, was working as a stenographer, at fifteen dollars a week. Judging by the salary she must have been none too competent in that work.

Now note this change:

Last year, this same woman cleared a little over $100,000.00 on the lecture platform.

What bridged that mighty chasm between these two earning capacities? you ask, and I answer:

The habit of performing more service and better service than that for which she was paid, thereby taking advantage of the Law of Increasing Returns.

This woman is well known throughout the country, as she is now a prominent lecturer on the subject of Applied Psychology.

Let me show you how she harnessed the Law of Increasing Returns. First, she goes into a city and delivers a series of fifteen free lectures. All may attend who will, without money

> *No man can rise to fame and fortune without carrying others along with him. It simply cannot be done.*

and without price. During the delivery of these fifteen lectures she has the opportunity of "selling herself" to her audience, and at the end of the series she announces the formation of a class for which she charges twenty-five dollars per student.

That's all there is to her plan!

Where she is commanding a small fortune for a year's work there are scores of much more proficient lecturers who are barely getting enough from their work to pay their expenses, simply because they have not yet familiarized themselves with the fundamentals upon which this lesson is based, as she has done.

Now, I would like to have you stop right here and answer this question:

If a fifty-year-old woman, who has no extraordinary qualifications, can harness the Law of Increasing Returns and make it raise her from the position as stenographer at fifteen dollars a week to that of lecturer at over $100,000.00 a year—*why cannot you apply this same law so that it will give you advantages that you do not now possess?*

Never mind what is to come in the remainder of this lesson until you have answered this question and—*answered it AS IT SHOULD BE ANSWERED!*

You are struggling, either meekly or earnestly, to make a place for yourself in the world. Perhaps you are exerting enough effort to bring you success of the highest order, if that effort were coupled with and supported by the Law of Increasing Returns.

For this reason, you owe it to yourself to find out just how you can apply this law to best advantage.

Now go back to that question, again; for I am determined that you shall not pass it by lightly, without giving yourself the benefit of at least trying to answer it.

In other words, there is no mistaking the fact that you are being brought face to face with a question that vitally affects your future, and, if you evade it, the fault will be with you.

You may lay this lesson aside after you have read it, and it is your privilege to do so, without making any attempt to profit by it; but, if you do so, you will never again be able to look at yourself in a mirror without being haunted by the feeling that—

YOU HAVE DELIBERATELY CHEATED YOURSELF!

Perhaps this is telling the truth in an undiplomatic way; but, when you purchased this course on the Law of Success, you did so because you wanted facts, and you are getting them, without the embellishment of apology.

After you have finished this lesson, if you will go back and review the lessons on *Initiative and Leadership* and *Enthusiasm,* you will better understand those lessons.

Those lessons and this one clearly establish the necessity of *taking the initiative, following it with aggressive action* and *doing more than you are paid to do.* If you will *burn* the fundamentals of these three lessons into your consciousness you will be a changed person, and I make this statement regardless of *who you are* or *what your calling may be.*

If this plain language has made you angry, I am glad; for it indicates that you can be moved! Now, if you would profit by the counsel of one who has made many more mistakes than you ever made, and for that reason learned a few of the fundamental truths of life, harness this anger and focus it on *yourself* until it drives you forth to render the service of which you are capable.

If you will do this you can collect a king's ransom as your reward.

Now let us turn our attention to still another important feature of this habit of performing more service and better service than that for which we are paid; namely, the fact that we can develop this habit without asking for permission to do so.

Such service may be rendered through your own initiative, without the consent of any person. You do not have to consult those to whom you render the service, for it is a privilege over which you have entire control.

There are many things you could do that would tend to promote your interests, but most of them require the co-operation or the consent of others. If you render *less* service than that for which you are paid you must do so by leave of the purchaser of the service, or the market for your service will soon cease.

I want you to get the full significance of this right of prerogative, which you have, to render more service and better service than that for which you are paid, for this places squarely *upon your shoulders* the responsibility of rendering such service, and if you fail to do so, you haven't a plausible excuse to offer or an "alibi" upon which to fall back, if you fail in the achievement of your *definite chief aim* in life.

One of the most essential yet the hardest truths that I have had to learn, is that every person should be his own hardest task-master.

We are all fine builders of "alibis" and creators of "excuses" in support of our short-comings.

We are not seeking *facts* and *truths* as they *are,* but, as we wish them to be. We prefer honeyed words of flattery to those of cold, unbiased truth, wherein lies the weakest spot of the man-animal.

Furthermore, we are up in arms against those who dare to uncover the truth for our benefit.

One of the most severe shocks I received in the early part of my public career was the knowledge that men are still being crucified for the high crime of telling the *truth*. I recall an experience I had some ten years ago, with a man who had written a book advertising his business school. He submitted this book to me and paid me to review it and give him my candid opinion of it. I reviewed the book with painstaking care, then did my duty by showing him wherein I believed the book was weak.

Here I learned a great lesson, for that man became so angry that he has never forgiven me for allowing him to look at his book through my eyes. When he asked me to tell him frankly what "criticism" I had to offer of the book, what he really meant was that I should tell him what I saw in the book that I could "compliment."

That's human nature for you!

We court flattery more than we do the *truth*. I know, because I am human.

All of which is in preparation for the "unkindest cut of all" that I am duty-bound to inflict upon you; namely, to suggest that you have not done as well as you might have done for the reason that you have not applied a sufficient amount of truth set out in Lesson Seven, on *Self-control,* to charge yourself with your own mistakes and short-comings.

To do this takes *self-control* and plenty of it.

If you paid some person who had the ability and the *courage* to do it, a hundred dollars to strip you of your vanity and conceit and love for flattery, so that you might see the weakest part of your make-up, the price would be reasonable enough.

We go through life stumbling and falling and struggling to our knees, and struggling and falling some more, making asses of ourselves, and going down, finally, in defeat, largely because we either neglect or *flatly refuse* to learn the *truth* about ourselves.

Since I have come to discover some of my own weaknesses through my work of helping others discover theirs, I blush with shame when I take a retrospective view of life and think how ridiculous I must have seemed in the eyes of those who could see me as I *wouldn't* see myself.

We parade before the enlarged shadows of our own vanity and imagine that those shadows are our real selves, while the few knowing souls with whom we meet stand in the background and look at us with pity or with scorn.

Hold on a minute! I am not through with you yet.

You have paid me to delve into the depths of your real self and give you an introspective inventory of what is there, and I am going to do the job right, as nearly as I can.

350

Not only have you been fooling yourself as to the real cause of your failures of the past, but you have tried to hang these causes on the door of someone else.

When things did not go to suit you, instead of accepting full responsibility for the cause, you have said, "Oh, hang this job!—I don't like the way *'they'* are treating me, so I'm going to *quit!*"

Don't deny it!

Now let me whisper a little secret in your ear—a secret which I have had to gather from grief and heartaches and unnecessary punishment of the hardest sort—

> *All salesmen will profit by remembering that none of us want anything that someone else wishes to "get rid of."*

Instead of "quitting" the job because there were obstacles to master and difficulties to be overcome, you should have faced the facts and then you would have known that life, itself, is just one long series of mastery of difficulties and obstacles.

The measure of a man may be taken very accurately by the extent to which he adapts himself to his environment and makes it his business to accept responsibility for every adversity with which he meets, whether the adversity grows out of a cause within his control or not.

Now, if you feel that I have "panned" you rather severely, have pity on me, O Fellow-Wayfarer, for you surely must know that I have had to punish myself more sorely than I have punished you *before I learned the truth that I am here passing on to you for your use and guidance.*

I have a few enemies—*thank God for them!*—for they have been vulgar and merciless enough to say some things about me that *forced* me to rid myself of some of my most serious short-comings; mainly those which I did not know I possessed. I have profited by the criticism of these enemies without having to pay them for their services in dollars, although I have paid in other ways.

However, it was not until some years ago that I caught sight of some of my most glaring faults which were brought to my attention as I studied Emerson's essay on Compensation, particularly the following part of it:

"Our strength grows out of our weakness.

"Not until we are pricked, and stung, and sorely shot at, awakens the indignation which arms itself with secret forces. *A great man is always willing to be little.* While he sits on the cushion of advantage he goes to sleep. When he is pushed, tormented, defeated, he has a chance to learn something; he has been put on his wits, on his manhood; he has *gained facts;* learned his ignorance; is cured of the insanity of conceit; has got moderation and real skill. The wise man always throws himself on the side of his assailants. It is more his interest than it is theirs to find his weak point. Blame is safer than praise. I hate to be defended in a newspaper. As long as all that is said is said against me, I feel a certain assurance of success. But as soon as honeyed words of praise are spoken of me, I feel as one that lies unprotected before his enemies."

Study this, the philosophy of the immortal Emerson, for it may serve as a modifying force that will temper your metal and prepare you for the battles of life, as carbon tempers the steel.

If you are a very young person, you need to study it all the more, for it often requires the stern realities of many years of experience to prepare one to assimilate and apply this philosophy.

Better that you should understand these great truths as a result of my undiplomatic presentation of them than to be forced to gather them from the less sympathetic sources of cold experience. Experience is a teacher that knows no favorites. When I permit you to profit by the truths I have gathered from the teachings of this cold and unsympathetic teacher called "experience," I am doing my best to show you favoritism, which reminds me, somewhat, of the times when my father used to "do his duty" by me, in the woodshed, always starting with this bit of encouraging philosophy:

"Son, this hurts me worse than it does you."

Thus we approach the close of this lesson without having exhausted the possibilities of the subject; nay, without having more than scratched the surface of it.

There comes to my mind the story of a romance of long ago through which I can leave in your mind the main import of this lesson. This story had its setting in the city of Antioch, in ancient Rome, two thousand years ago, when the great city of Jerusalem and all the land of Judea were under the oppressive heel of Rome.

The star figure of the story was a young Jew by the name of Ben Hur, who was falsely accused of crime and sentenced to hard labor, at the galley's oar. Chained to a bench in the galley, and being forced to tug wearily at the oars, Ben Hur developed a powerful body. Little did his tormentors know that out of his punishment would grow the strength with which he would one day gain his freedom. Perhaps Ben Hur, himself, had no such hopes.

Then came the day of the chariot races: the day that was destined to break the chains that bound Ben Hur to the oars of the galley and give him his freedom.

One span of horses was without a driver. In desperation the owner sought the aid of the young slave because of his mighty arms, and begged him to take the place of the missing driver.

As Ben Hur picked up the reins, a mighty cry went up from the onlookers.

"Look! Look! Those arms!—where did you get them?" they howled, and Ben Hur answered:

"At the galley's oar!"

The race was on. With those mighty arms Ben Hur calmly drove that charging span of horses on to victory; victory that won for him his freedom.

Life, itself, is a great chariot race, and the victory goes only to those who have developed the strength of character and determination and will-power to win.

What matters it that we develop this strength through cruel confinement at the galley's oar, as long as we use it so that it brings us, finally, to victory and freedom.

It is an unvarying law that strength grows out of resistance. If we pity the poor blacksmith who swings a five-pound hammer all day long, we must also admire the wonderful arm that he develops in doing it.

". . . Because of the dual constitution of all things, in labor as in life, there can be no cheating," says Emerson. "The thief steals from himself. The swindler swindles himself. *For the real price of labor is knowledge and virtue, whereof wealth and credit are signs.* The signs, like paper money, may be counterfeited or stolen, but that which they represent; namely, knowledge and virtue, cannot be counterfeited or stolen."

Henry Ford receives fifteen thousand letters a week from people who are begging for a part of his wealth; yet how few of these poor ignorant souls understand that Ford's real wealth is not measured by the dollars he has in the bank, nor the factories he owns, but by the *reputation* he has gained through the rendering of useful service at a reasonable price.

And how did he gain that *reputation?*

Certainly not by rendering as little service as possible and collecting for it *all he could filch from the purchasers.*

The very warp and woof of Ford's business philosophy is this:

"Give the people the best product at the lowest price possible."

When other automobile manufacturers raise their prices, Ford lowers his. When other employers lower wages, Ford increases them. What has happened? This policy has placed the Law of Increasing Returns back of Ford so effectively that he has become the richest and most powerful man in the world.

Oh, you foolish and short-sighted seekers after wealth, who are returning from the daily chase empty-handed,—why do you not take a lesson from men like Ford? Why do you not reverse your philosophy and *give* in order that you may *get?*

I am finishing this lesson on Christmas Eve!

In the room next to my study our children are decorating their Christmas tree, and the rhythm of their voices falls as music upon my ears. They are happy, not alone because they expect to *receive,* but for the deeper reason that they have presents hidden away which they expect to *give*.

From the window of my study, I can see the neighbor's children as they, too, are gleefully engaged in preparing for this wonderful event.

> *There are no lazy men. What may appear to be a lazy man is only an unfortunate person who has not found the work for which he is best suited.*

Throughout the civilized world, millions of people are preparing to celebrate the birth of this Prince of Peace who, more than any other man, set forth the reasons why it is more blessed to give than to receive, and why enduring happiness comes not from *possessing* material wealth, but from rendering service to humanity.

It seems a queer co-incidence that the completion of this particular lesson should have happened on Christmas Eve, yet I am glad that it has, for this has provided me with sufficient justification for reminding you that nowhere in the entire history of civilization could I have found stronger support of the fundamentals of this lesson than may be found in the Sermon on the Mount, in the book of Matthew.

Christianity is one of the greatest and most far-reaching influences in the world today, and I hardly need apologize for reminding you that the tenets of Christ's philosophy are in absolute harmony with the fundamentals upon which this lesson, in the main, is founded.

As I see the happy faces of the children and watch the hurrying crowds of belated Christmas shoppers, all radiant with the splendor of the spirit of *giving,* I cannot help wishing that every eve was Christmas Eve, for then this would be a better world in which the struggle for existence would be reduced to a minimum, and hatred and strife outlawed.

Life is but a short span of years at best. Like a candle we are lighted, flicker for a moment, and then *go out!* If we were placed here for the purpose of laying up treasures for use in a life that lies beyond the dark shadow of Death, may it not be possible that we can best collect these treasures by rendering all the service we can, to all the people we can, in a loving spirit of kindness and sympathy?

I hope you agree with this philosophy.

Here this lesson must end, but it is by no means *completed*. Where I lay down the chain of thought it is now *your duty* to take it up and develop it, in your own way, and to your own benefit.

By the very nature of the subject of this lesson it can never be finished, for it leads into the heart of all human activities. Its purpose is to cause you to take the fundamentals upon which it is based and use them as a stimulus that will cause your mind to unfold, thereby releasing the latent forces that are yours.

This lesson was not written for the purpose of teaching you, but it was intended as a means of causing you to teach yourself one of the great truths of life. It was intended as a source of education, in the true sense of educing, drawing out, developing from within, those forces of mind which are available for your use.

When you deliver the best service of which you are capable, striving each time to excel all your previous efforts, you are making use of the highest form of education. Therefore, when you render more service and better service than that for which you are paid, you, more than anyone else, are profiting by the effort.

It is only through the delivery of such service that mastery in your chosen field of endeavor can be attained. For this reason you should make it a part of your *definite chief aim* to endeavor to surpass all previous records in all that you do. Let this become a part of your daily habits, and follow it with the same regularity with which you eat your meals.

Make it your business to render more service and better service than that for which you are paid, and lo! before you realize what has happened, you will find that THE WORLD IS WILLINGLY PAYING YOU FOR MORE THAN YOU DO!

Compound interest upon compound interest is the rate that you will be paid for such service. Just how this pyramiding of gains takes place is left entirely to you to determine.

Now, what are you going to do with that which you have learned from this lesson? and when? and how? and why? This lesson can be of no value to you unless it moves you to adopt and use the knowledge it has brought you.

Knowledge becomes POWER only through organization and USE! Do not forget this.

You can never become a Leader without doing more than you are paid for, and you cannot become successful without developing leadership in your chosen occupation.

There is always room for the man who can be relied upon to deliver the goods when he said he would.

THE MASTER MIND

An After-the-Lesson Visit with the Author

A Power That Can Bring You Whatever You Want on This Earth

Success is achieved through the application of power.

In the picture at the top of this page you see two forms of POWER!

At the left you see physical power, produced by Nature, with the aid of organized raindrops pouring over Niagara Falls. Man has harnessed this form of power.

At the right you see another, and a much more intensive form of power, produced through the *harmonious* co-ordination of THOUGHT in the minds of men. Observe that the word "harmonious" has been emphasized. In this picture you see a group of men seated at the Directors' Table in a modern business office. The powerful figure rising above the group represents the "Master Mind" which may be created wherever men blend their minds in a spirit of perfect harmony, with some DEFINITE objective in view.

Study this picture! It interprets the greatest POWER known to man.

With the aid of the MIND man has discovered many interesting facts about the earth on which he lives, the air and the ether that fill the endless space about him, and the millions of other planets and heavenly bodies that float through space.

With the aid of a little mechanical contrivance (which his MIND conceived) called a "spectroscope," man has discovered, at a distance of 93,000,000 miles, the nature of the substances of which the sun is made.

We have lived through the stone age, the iron age, the copper age, the religious fanatic age, the scientific research age, the industrial age and we enter, now, the age of THOUGHT.

Out of the spoils of the dark ages through which man has passed he has saved much material that is sound food for THOUGHT. While for more than ten thousand years the battle between IGNORANCE, SUPERSTITION and FEAR on the one side, and INTELLIGENCE on the other, has raged, man has picked up some useful knowledge.

Among other fragments of useful knowledge gathered by man, he has discovered and classified the eighty-three elements of which all physical matter consists. By study and analysis and comparison man has discovered the "bigness" of the material things in the universe as they are represented by the suns and stars, some of them over ten million times as large as the earth on which he lives. On the other hand, man has discovered the "littleness" of things by reducing matter to molecules, atoms, and finally, to the smallest known particle, the electron. An atom is so inconceivably small that a grain of sand contains millions of them.

The molecule is made up of atoms, which are said to be little particles of matter that revolve around each other in one continuous circuit, at lightning speed, very much as the earth and other planets whirl around the sun in an endless circuit.

The atom, in turn, is made up of electrons which are constantly in rapid motion; thus it is said that in every drop of water and every grain of sand the entire principle upon which the whole universe operates, is duplicated.

How marvelous! How stupendous! How do we know these things to be true? Through the aid of the MIND.

You may gather some slight idea of the magnitude of it all the next time you eat a beef-steak, by remembering that the steak on your plate, the plate itself, and the table on which you are eating and the silverware with which you are eating are all, in final analysis, made of exactly the same material, electrons.

In the physical or material world, whether one is looking at the largest star that floats through the heavens or the smallest grain of sand to be found on earth, the object under observation is but an organized collection of molecules, atoms and electrons. (An electron is an inseparable form of power, made up of a positive and a negative pole.)

Man knows much about the physical facts of the universe!

The next great scientific discovery will be the fact, which already exists, that every human brain is both a broadcasting and a receiving station; that every thought vibration released by the brain may be picked up and interpreted by all other brains that are in harmony, or in "tune" with the rate of vibration of the broadcasting brain.

How did man acquire the knowledge that he possesses concerning the physical laws of this earth? How did he learn what has taken place before his time, and during his uncivilized period? He gathered this knowledge by turning back the pages of Nature's Bible and there viewing the unimpeachable evidence of millions of years of struggle among animals of a lower intelligence. By turning back the great stone pages man has uncovered the bones, skeletons, footprints and other unmistakable evidence which Mother Nature has held for his inspection throughout unbelievable periods of time.

Now man is about to turn his attention to another section of Nature's Bible—the one wherein has been written a history of the great mental struggle that has taken place in the realm of THOUGHT. This page is represented by the boundless ether which has picked up and still carries every thought vibration that was ever released from the mind of man.

This great page in Nature's Bible is one that no human being has been able to tamper with. Its records are positive, and soon they may be clearly interpreted. No interpolations by man have been permitted. Of the authenticity of the story written on this page there can be no doubt.

Thanks to EDUCATION (meaning the unfolding, educing, drawing out, developing from within of the human mind) Nature's Bible is now being interpreted. The story of man's long, perilous struggle upward has been written on the pages of this, the greatest of all Bibles.

All who have partly conquered the Six Basic Fears described in another "author's visit" in this series, and who have successfully conquered SUPERSTITION and IGNORANCE, may read the records that have been written in Nature's Bible. To all others this privilege is denied. For this reason there are probably fewer than one thousand people in the entire world at this time who are in even the primary grade as far as the reading of this Bible is concerned.

In the entire world there are probably fewer than one hundred people, today, who know anything about or have ever heard of the chemistry of the mind, through which two or more minds—

—MAY BE BLENDED, IN A SPIRIT OF PERFECT HARMONY, IN SUCH A MANNER THAT THERE IS BORN A THIRD MIND POSSESSING THE SUPER-HUMAN POWER TO READ THE STORY OF THE VIBRATION OF THOUGHT

AS IT HAS BEEN WRITTEN AND NOW EXISTS IN THE IMPERISHABLE RECORDS OF THE ETHER.

The newly-discovered radio principle has shut the mouths of the Doubting Thomases and sent the scientist scurrying into new fields of experimentation. When they emerge from this field of research they will show us that the mind as we understand it today, as compared to the mind of tomorrow, is about the same as comparing the intelligence of a polliwog to that of a professor of biology who has read the entire life-line of animal life, from the amoeba on up to man.

Come for a short visit with a few of the POWERFUL men now living who are making use of power created through the blending, in a spirit of harmony, of two or more minds.

We will begin with three well known men, who are known to be men of great achievement in their respective fields of endeavor. Their names are Henry Ford, Thomas A. Edison and Harvey Firestone.

Of the three Henry Ford is the most POWERFUL, having reference to economic power. Mr. Ford is the most powerful man now living on earth, and is believed to be the most powerful who ever lived. So great is his power that he may have anything of a physical nature that he desires, or its equivalent. Millions of dollars, to him, are but playthings, no harder to acquire than the grains of sand with which the child builds sand-tunnels.

Mr. Edison has such a keen insight into Mother Nature's Bible that he has harnessed and combined for the good of man, more of Nature's laws than any other man who ever lived. It was he who brought together the point of a needle and a piece of wax in such a way that they record and preserve the human voice. It was he who first made the lightning serve to light our houses and streets, through the aid of the incandescent light. It was he who made the camera record and produce all sorts of motion, through the modern moving picture apparatus.

Mr. Firestone's industrial achievement is so well known that it needs no comment. He has made dollars multiply themselves so rapidly that his name has become a by-word wherever automobiles are operated.

All three men began their business and professional careers with no capital and but little schooling of the nature usually referred to as "education."

Perhaps Mr. Ford's beginning was, by far, the most humble of the three. Cursed with poverty, retarded by lack of even the most elementary form of schooling, and handicapped by ignorance in many forms, he has mastered all of these in the inconceivably short period of twenty-five years.

Thus might we briefly describe the achievements of three well known, successful men of POWER!

But, we have been dealing with EFFECT only!

The true philosopher wishes to know something of the cause which produced these desirable EFFECTS.

It is a matter of public knowledge that Mr. Ford, Mr. Edison and Mr. Firestone are close personal friends; that they go away to the woods once a year for a period of recuperation and rest.

But, it is not generally known—it is doubtful if these three men, themselves, even know it—

—THAT THERE EXISTS BETWEEN THE THREE MEN A BOND OF HAR-MONY OUT OF WHICH HAS GROWN A MASTER MIND THAT IS BEING USED BY EACH OF THE THREE. A MIND OF SUPERHUMAN ABILITY, THAT HAS THE CAPACITY TO "TUNE IN" ON FORCES WITH WHICH MOST MEN ARE TO NO EXTENT FAMILIAR.

Let us repeat the statement that out of the blending and harmonizing of two or more minds (twelve or thirteen minds appear to be the most favorable number) may be produced a mind which has the capacity to "tune in" on the vibrations of the ether and pick up, from that source, kindred thoughts, on any subject.

Through the principle of harmony of minds, Ford, Edison and Firestone have created a Master Mind that now supplements the efforts of each of the three, and WHETHER CONSCIOUSLY OR UNCONSCIOUSLY, THIS "MASTER MIND" IS THE CAUSE OF THE SUCCESS OF EACH OF THE THREE.

There is no other answer to their attainment of great power, and their far-reaching success in their respective fields of endeavor, and this is true despite the fact that neither of them may be conscious of the power they have created, or the manner in which they have done so.

In the city of Chicago live six powerful men known as the Big Six. These six men are said to be the most powerful group of men in the middle west. It is said that their combined income totals more than twenty-five million dollars a year.

Every man in the group began in the most humble of circumstances.

Their names are:

Wm. Wrigley, Jr., who owns the Wrigley Chewing Gum business, and whose income is said to be over fifteen million dollars a year. John R. Thompson, who owns the chain of Thompson self-help lunch rooms throughout the country. Mr. Lasker, who owns the Lord & Thomas Advertising Agency. Mr. McCullough, who owns the largest express business in the world. And, Mr. Ritchie and Mr. Hertz, who own the Yellow Taxicab business of the country.

There is nothing startling about a man who does nothing more than become a millionaire, as a rule. However, there is something connected with the financial success of these particular millionaires that is more than startling, for it is well known that there exists between them a bond of friendship out of which has grown the condition of harmony that produces a Master Mind.

These six men, whether by accident or design, have blended their minds in such a way that the mind of each has been supplemented by a superhuman power known as a "Master Mind," and that mind has brought each of them more worldly gain than any person could possibly use to advantage.

The law upon which the principle of a Master Mind operates was discovered by Christ, when he surrounded himself with twelve disciples and created the first Thirteen Club of the world.

Despite the fact that one of the thirteen (Judas) broke the chain of harmony, sufficient seed was sown during the period of harmony that originally existed between these thirteen people, to insure the continuation of THE GREATEST AND MOST FAR-REACHING PHILOSOPHY KNOWN TO THE INHABITANTS OF THIS EARTH.

Many millions of people believe themselves to possess WISDOM. Many of these do possess wisdom, in certain elementary stages, but no man may possess real wisdom without the aid of the power known as a Master Mind, and such a mind cannot be created except through the principle of blending, in harmony, of two or more minds.

Through many years of practical experimentation it has been found that thirteen minds, when blended in a spirit of perfect harmony, produce the most practical results.

Upon this principle, whether consciously or unconsciously, is founded all of the great industrial and commercial successes that are so abundant in this age.

The word "merger" is becoming one of the most popular words in newspaper parlance, because hardly a day goes by that one may not read of some big industrial, commercial, financial or railroad merger. Slowly the world is beginning to learn (in a very few minds only) that through friendly alliance and co-operation great POWER may be developed.

The successful business and industrial and financial enterprises are those managed by leaders who either consciously or unconsciously apply the principle of co-ordinated effort described in this article. If you would be a great leader in any undertaking, surround yourself with other minds that can be blended in a spirit of co-operation so that they act and function as one.

I like to see a man proud of his country, and I like to see him so live that his country is proud of him.

—LINCOLN

If you can grasp this principle and apply it you may have, for your efforts, whatever you want on this earth!

Employers are always on the lookout for a man who does a better job of any sort than is customary, whether it be wrapping a package, writing a letter, or closing a sale.

PLEASING PERSONALITY

"You Can Do It If You Believe You Can!"

What is an *ATTRACTIVE personality?*

Of course the answer is: *A personality that attracts.*

But what *causes* a personality to attract? Let us proceed to find out. *Your* personality is the sum total of your characteristics and appearances which distinguish you from all others. The clothes you wear, the lines in your face, the tone of your voice, the thoughts you think, the character you have developed by those thoughts, all constitute parts of your *personality*.

Whether your *personality* is attractive or not is another matter.

By far the most important part of your *personality* is that which is represented by your character, and is therefore the part that is not visible. The style of your clothes and their appropriateness undoubtedly constitute a very important part of your personality, for it is true that people form first impressions of you from your outward appearance.

Even the manner in which you shake hands forms an important part of your *personality,* and goes a very long way toward attracting or repelling those with whom you shake hands.

This art can be cultivated.

The expression of your eyes also forms an important part of your *personality,* for there are people, and they are more numerous than one might imagine, who can look through your eyes into your heart and see that which is written there by the nature of your most secret thoughts.

The vitality of your body—sometimes called personal magnetism—also constitutes an important part of your *personality*.

Now let us proceed to arrange these outward mediums through which the nature of our *personality* is expressed, so that it will *attract* and not repel.

There is one way in which you can so express the composite of your *personality* that it will *always attract,* even though you may be as homely as the circus "fat woman," and this is by—

Taking a keen heart-interest in the other fellow's "game" in life.

Let me illustrate exactly what is meant, by relating an incident that happened some years ago, from which I was taught a lesson in *master salesmanship*.

One day an old lady called at my office and sent in her card with a message saying that she must see *me personally*. No amount of coaxing by secretaries could induce her to disclose the nature of her visit, therefore I made up my mind that she was some poor old soul who wanted to sell me a book, and remembering that my own mother was a woman, I decided to go out to the reception room and buy her book, whatever it might be.

Please follow every detail thoughtfully; for you, too, may learn a lesson in master salesmanship from this incident.

As I walked down the hall-way from my private office this old lady, who was standing just outside of the railing that led to the main reception room, began to smile.

I had seen many people smile, but never before had I seen one who smiled so sweetly as did this lady. It was one of those contagious smiles, because I caught the spirit of it and began to smile also.

As I reached the railing the old lady extended her hand to shake hands with me. Now, as a rule, I do not become too friendly on first acquaintance when a person calls at my office, for the reason that it is very hard to say "no" if the caller should ask me to do that which I do not wish to do.

However, this dear old lady looked so sweetly innocent and harmless that I extended my hand and *she began to shake it!* whereupon, I discovered that she not only had an attractive smile, but she also had a magnetic hand-shake. She took hold of my hand firmly, but not too firmly, and the very manner in which she went about it telegraphed the thought to my brain that it *was she* who was doing the honors. She made me feel that she was really and truly *glad* to shake my hand, and I believe that she was. I believe that her hand-shake came from the heart as well as from the hand.

I have shaken hands with many thousands of people during my public career, but I do not recall having ever done so with anyone who understood the art of doing it as well as this old lady did. The moment she touched my hand I could feel myself "slipping," and I knew that whatever it was that she had come after she would go away with it, and that I would aid and abet her all I could toward this end.

In other words, that penetrating smile and that warm hand-shake had disarmed me and made me a "willing victim." At a single stroke this old lady had shorn me of that false shell into which I crawl when salesmen come around selling, or *trying to sell,* that which I do not want. To go back to an expression which you found quite frequently in previous lessons of this course, this gentle visitor had "neutralized" my mind and made me want to listen.

Ah, but here is the stumbling point at which most salespeople fall and break their necks, figuratively speaking, for it is as useless to try to sell a man something until you have first made him *want* to listen, as it would be to command the earth to stop rotating.

Note well how this old lady used a smile and a hand-shake as the tools with which to pry open the window that led to my heart; but the most important part of the transaction is yet to be related.

Slowly and deliberately, as if she had all the time there was in the universe (which she did have, as far as I was concerned at that moment) the old lady began to crystallize the first step of her victory into reality by saying:

"I just came here to tell you (what seemed to me to be a long pause) *that I think you are doing the most wonderful work of any man in the world today."*

Every word was emphasized by a gentle, though firm, squeeze of my hand, and *she was looking through my eyes and into my heart as she spoke.*

After I regained consciousness (for it became a standing joke among my assistants at the office that I fainted dead away) I reached down and unlocked the little secret latch that fastened the gate and said:

"Come right in, dear lady,—come right into my private office," and with a gallant bow that would have done credit to the cavaliers of olden times, I bade her come in and "sit awhile."

As she entered my private office, I motioned her to the big easy-chair back of my desk while I took the little hard-seated chair which, under ordinary circumstances, I would have used as a means of discouraging her from taking up too much of my time.

For three-quarters of an hour I listened to one of the most brilliant and charming conversations I have ever heard, and my visitor was doing *all* of the conversing. From the very start she had assumed the initiative and taken the lead, and, up to the end of that first three-quarters of an hour, she found no inclination, on my part, to challenge her right to it.

I repeat, lest you did not get the full import of it, that I was *a willing listener!*

Now comes the part of the story which would make me blush with embarrassment, if it were not for the fact that you and I are separated by the pages of this book; but I must summon the courage with which to tell you the facts because the entire incident would lose its significance if I failed to do this.

As I have stated, my visitor entranced me with brilliant and captivating conversation for three-quarters of an hour. Now, what do you suppose she was talking about all that time?

No! You are wrong.

She was not trying to sell me a book, nor did she once use the personal pronoun "I."

However, she was not only *trying,* but actually *selling* me something, and *that something was myself.*

She had no sooner been seated in that big cushioned chair than she unrolled a package which I had mistaken for a book that she had come to sell me, and sure enough, there was a book in the package—in fact, several of them; for she had a complete year's file of the magazine of which I was then editor (*Hill's Golden Rule*). She turned the pages of those magazines and read places that she had marked here and there, assuring me, in the meanwhile, that *she had always believed the philosophy back of that which she was reading.*

> If you have tried and met with defeat; if you have planned and watched your plans as they were crushed before your eyes; just remember that the greatest men in all history were the products of courage, and courage, you know, is born in the cradle of adversity.

Then, after I was in a state of complete mesmerism, and thoroughly receptive, my visitor tactfully switched the conversation to a subject which, I suspect, she had in mind to discuss with me long before she presented herself at my office; but—*and this is another point at which most salespeople blunder*—had she reversed the order of her conversation and begun where she finished, the chances are that she never would have had the opportunity to sit in that big easy-chair.

During the last three minutes of her visit, she skillfully laid before me the merits of some securities that she was selling. She did not ask me to purchase; but, the way in which she told me of the merits of the securities (plus the way in which she had so impressively told me of the merits of my own "game") had the psychological effect of causing me to want to purchase; and, even though I made no purchase of securities from her, she *made a sale*—because I picked up the telephone and introduced her to a man to whom she later sold more than five times the amount that she had intended selling me.

If that same woman, or another woman, or a man, who had the tact and *personality* that she possessed, should call on me, I would again sit down and listen for three-quarters of an hour.

We are all human; and we are all more or less vain!

We are all alike in this respect—we will listen with intense interest to those who have the tact to talk to us about that which lies closest to our hearts; and then, out of a sense of reciprocity, we will also listen with interest when the speaker finally switches the conversation to the subject which lies closest to his or her heart; and, at the end, we will not only "sign on the dotted line" but we will say, *"What a wonderful personality!"*

In the city of Chicago, some years ago, I was conducting a school of salesmanship for a securities house which employed more than fifteen hundred salespeople. To keep the ranks of that big organization filled, we had to train and employ six hundred new salespeople every week. Of all the thousands of men and women who went through that school, there was but one man who grasped the significance of the principle I am here describing, the first time he heard it analyzed.

This man had never tried to sell securities and frankly admitted, when he entered the salesmanship class, that he was not a salesman. Let's see whether he was or not.

After he had finished his training, one of the "star" salesmen took a notion to play a practical joke on him, believing him to be a credulous person who would believe all that he heard, so this "star" gave him an inside "tip" as to where he would be able to sell some securities without any great effort. This star would make the sale himself, so he said; but the man to whom he referred as being a likely purchaser was an ordinary artist who would purchase with so little urging that he, being a "star," did not wish to waste his time on him.

The newly made salesman was delighted to receive the "tip," and, forthwith, he was on his way to make the sale. As soon as he was out of the office, the "star" gathered the other "stars" around him and told of the joke he was playing; for in reality the artist was a very wealthy man and the "star," himself, had spent nearly a month trying to sell him, but without success. It then developed that all of the "stars" of that particular group had called on this same artist but had failed to interest him.

The newly made salesman was gone about an hour and a half. When he returned he found the "stars" waiting for him with smiles on their faces.

To their surprise, the newly made salesman also wore a broad smile on his face. The "stars" looked at each other inquiringly, for they had expected that this "green" man would not return in a joyful mood.

"Well, did you sell to your man?" inquired the originator of this "joke."

"Certainly," replied the uninitiated one, "and I found that artist to be all you said he was—a perfect gentleman and a very interesting man."

Reaching into his pocket he pulled out an order and a check for $2,000.00.

The "stars" wanted to know how he did it.

"Oh, it wasn't difficult," replied the newly made salesman; "I just walked in and talked to him a few minutes and he brought up the subject of the securities himself, and said he wanted to purchase; therefore, I really did not sell to him—he purchased of his own accord."

When I heard of the transaction, I called the newly made salesman in and asked him to describe, in detail, just how he made the sale, and I will relate it just as he told it.

When he reached the artist's studio, he found him at work on a picture. So engaged in his work was the artist that he did not see the salesman enter; so the salesman walked over to where he could see the picture and stood there looking at it without saying a word.

Finally the artist saw him; then the salesman apologized for the intrusion and began to talk—*about the picture that the artist was painting!*

He knew just enough about art to be able to discuss the merits of the picture with some intelligence; and he was really interested in the subject.

He liked the picture and frankly told the artist so, which, of course, *made the artist very angry!*

For nearly an hour those two men talked of nothing but art; particularly that picture that stood on the artist's easel.

Finally, the artist asked the salesman his name and his business, and the *salesman* (yes, the *master* salesman) replied, "Oh, never mind my business or my name; I am more interested in *you and your art!*"

The artist's face beamed with a smile of joy.

Those words fell as sweet music upon his ears. But, not to be outdone by his polite visitor, he insisted on knowing what mission had brought him to his studio.

Then, with an air of genuine reluctance, this *master salesman*—this real "star"—introduced himself and told his business.

Briefly he described the securities he was selling, and the artist *listened as if he enjoyed every word that was spoken.* After the salesman had finished the artist said:

"Well, well! I have been very foolish. Other salesmen from your firm have been here trying to sell me some of those securities, but they talked nothing but business; in fact, they annoyed me so that I had to ask one of them to leave. Now let me see—what was that fellow's name—oh, yes, it was Mr. Perkins." (Perkins was the "star" who had thought of this clever trick to play on the newly made salesman.) "But you present the matter so differently, and now I see how foolish I have been, and I want you to let me have $2,000.00 worth of those securities."

Think of that—*"You present the matter so differently!"*

And how did this newly made salesman present the matter so differently? Putting the question another way, what did this *master salesman* really sell that artist? Did he sell him securities?

No! he sold him his own picture which he was painting on his own canvas.

The securities were but an incident.

Don't overlook this point. *That master salesman had remembered the story of the old lady who entertained me for three-quarters of an hour by talking about that which was nearest my heart, and it had so impressed him that he made up his mind to study his prospective purchasers and find out what would interest them most, so he could talk about that.*

> *I would rather begin at the bottom and climb to the top than to start at the top and have to remain there.*

This "green," newly made salesman earned $7,900.00 in commissions the first month he was in the field, leading the next highest man by more than double, and the tragedy of it was that not one person out of the entire organization of 1,500 salespeople took the time to find out *how and why* he became the real "star" of the organization, a fact which I believe fully justifies the rather biting reprimand suggested in Lesson Eight to which you may have taken offense.

A Carnegie, or a Rockefeller, or a James J. Hill, or a Marshall Field accumulates a fortune, through the application of the selfsame principles that are available to all the remainder of us; but we envy them their wealth without ever thinking of studying their philosophy and appropriating it to our own use.

We look at a successful man in the hour of his triumph, and wonder how he did it, but we overlook the importance of analyzing his methods and we forget the price he had to pay in careful, well organized preparation which had to be made before he could reap the fruits of his efforts.

Throughout this course on the Law of Success, you will not find a single new principle; every one of them is as old as civilization itself; yet you will find but few people who seem to understand how to apply them.

The salesman who sold those securities to that artist was not only a *master salesman,* but he was a man with an *attractive personality.* He was not much to look at; perhaps that is why the "star" conceived the idea of playing that cruel (?) joke on him; but even a homely person may have a very *attractive personality* in the eyes of those whose handiwork he has praised.

Of course, there are some who will get the wrong conception of the principle I am here trying to make clear, by drawing the conclusion that any sort of cheap flattery will take the place of *genuine heart interest*. I hope that *you* are not one of these. I hope that you are one of those who understand the real psychology upon which this lesson is based, and that you will make it your business to study other people closely enough to find something about them or their work that you *really* admire. Only in this way can you develop a personality that will be irresistibly *attractive*.

Cheap flattery has just the opposite effect to that of constituting an attractive personality. It repels instead of attracting. It is so shallow that even the ignorant easily detect it.

Perhaps you have observed—and if you have not I wish you to do so—that this lesson emphasizes at length the importance of making it your business to take a keen interest in other people and in their work, business or profession. *This emphasis was by no means an accident.*

You will quickly observe that the principles upon which this lesson is based are very closely related to those which constitute the foundation of Lesson Five, on Imagination.

Also, you will observe that this lesson is based upon much the same general principles as those which form the most important part of Lesson Twelve, on Co-operation.

Let us here introduce some very practical suggestions as to how the laws of Imagination, Co-operation and Pleasing Personality may be blended, or co-ordinated to profitable ends, through the creation of usable ideas.

Every thinker knows that "ideas" are the beginning of all successful achievement. The question most often asked, however, is, "How can I learn to create ideas that will earn money?"

In part we will answer this question in this lesson by suggesting some new and novel ideas, any of which might be developed and made very profitable, by almost anyone, in practically any locality.

Idea Number One

The world war has deprived Germany of her enormous trade in toys. Before the war we bought most of our toys from Germany. We are not likely to buy any more toys from German manufacturers in our time, or for a long while afterward.

Toys are in demand, not alone in the United States, but in foreign countries, many of which will not buy toys from Germany. Our only competitor is Japan and her toys are of so poor a quality that her competition means nothing.

But what sort of toys shall I manufacture and where will I get the capital with which to carry on the business, you will ask?

First, go to a local toy dealer and find out just which class of toys sells most rapidly. If you do not feel competent to make improvements on some of the toys now on the market, advertise for an inventor "with an idea for a marketable toy" and you will soon find the mechanical genius who will supply this missing link in your undertaking. Have him make you a working model of just what you want, then go to some small manufacturer, wood-worker, machine shop or the like, and arrange to have your toys manufactured.

You now know just what your toy will cost, so you are ready to go to some big jobber, wholesaler or distributor and arrange for the sale of your entire product.

If you are an able salesman you can finance this whole project on the few dollars required with which to advertise for the inventor. When you find this man you can probably arrange with him to work out a model for you during his spare evening hours, with a promise that you will give him a better job when you are manufacturing your own toys. He will probably give you all the time you want in which to pay him for his labor; or he may do the work in return for an interest in the business.

You can get the manufacturer of your toys to wait for his money until you are paid by the firm to which you sell them; and, if necessary, you can assign to him the invoices for the toys sold and let the money come direct to him.

Of course if you have an unusually pleasing and convincing personality and considerable ability to organize, you will be able to take the working model of your toy to some man of means and, in return for an interest in the business, secure the capital with which to do your own manufacturing.

If you want to know what will sell, watch a crowd of children at play, study their likes and dislikes, find out what will amuse them and you will probably get an idea on which to build your toy. It requires no genius to invent! Common sense is all that is necessary. Simply find out what the people want and then produce it. Produce it well—better than anyone else is doing. Give it a touch of individuality. Make it distinctive.

We spend millions of dollars annually for toys with which to entertain our children. Make your new toy useful as well as interesting. Make it educational if possible. If it entertains and teaches at the same time it will sell readily and live forever. If your toy is in the nature of a

game make it teach the child something about the world in which it lives, geography, arith-
metic, English, physiology, etc. Or, better still, produce a toy that will cause the child to run,

> It is better to be a big man in a small town than to be a small man in a big town, and ever so much easier.

jump or in some other way exercise. Children love to move about and moving about is of benefit to them, especially when stimulated by the play motive.

An indoor baseball game would be a ready seller, especially in the cities. Work out an arrangement for attaching the ball to a string that will be suspended from the ceiling so one child may throw the ball against the wall and then stand back and strike it with a bat as it rebounds. A one-child baseball game, in other words.

Plan Number Two

This will be of interest only to the man or woman who has the self-confidence and the ambition to "run the risk" of making a big income, which, we may add, most people have not.

It is a suggestion that could be put into practical operation by at least forty or fifty people in every large city throughout the United States, and by a smaller number in the smaller cities.

It is intended for the man or woman who can write or will learn to write advertising copy, sales literature, follow-up letters, collection letters and the like, using the ability to write which we will suppose that you possess.

To make practical and profitable use of this suggestion you will need the co-operation of a good advertising agency and from one to five firms or individuals who do enough advertising to warrant their appropriations going through an agency.

You should go to the agency first and make arrangements with it to employ you and pay you seven per cent on the gross expenditures of all accounts which you bring to it; this seven per cent to compensate you for getting the account and for writing the copy and otherwise serving the client in the management of his advertising appropriation. Any reliable agency will gladly give you this amount for all the business you will bring.

Then you go to a firm or individual whose advertising account you wish to handle and say in effect that you wish to go to work *without compensation*. Tell what you can do and what you intend to do for that particular firm that will help it sell more goods. If the firm employs an advertising manager you are to become virtually his assistant *without pay*, on one condition, namely, that the advertising appropriation is to be placed through the agency with which you have the connection. Through this arrangement the firm or individual whose account you thus secure will get the benefit of your personal services, *without cost,* and pay no more for placing its advertising through your agency than it would through any other. If your canvass is convincing and you really take the time to prepare your case, you will get your account without much argument.

You can repeat this transaction until you have as many accounts as you can handle advantageously, which, under ordinary conditions, will be not more than ten or twelve; probably less if one or more of your clients spends upwards of $25,000.00 a year in advertising.

If you are a competent writer of advertising copy and have the ability to create new and profitable ideas for your clients you will be able to hold their business from year to year. You of course understand that you are not to accept more accounts than you can handle individually. You should spend a portion of your time in the place of business of each of your clients; in fact you should have a desk and working equipment right on the grounds, so you can get first-hand information as to your clients' sales problems as well as accurate information as to their goods and wares.

Through this sort of effort you will give the advertising agency a reputation for effective service such as it would get in no other way, and you will please your clients because they will see satisfactory returns from your efforts. As long as you keep the agency and the clients whom you serve satisfied your job is safe and you will make money. A reasonable expectation of returns under this plan would be a gross business of $250,000.00 a year, on which your seven per cent would amount to $17,500.00.

A man or woman of unusual ability could run the figure much higher than this, up to, say, an income of $25,000.00 a year, while the tendency would be, however, to drop down to around $5,000.00 to $7,500.00, which are the figures that the "average" man or woman might reasonably expect to earn.

You can see that the plan has possibilities. It supplies independent work and gives you one hundred per cent of your earning power. It is better than a position as advertising manager, even if the position paid the same money, because it practically places you in a business of your own—one in which your name is constantly developing a survival value.

Plan Number Three

This plan can be put into operation by almost any man or woman of average intelligence, and with but little preparation. Go to any first-class printer and make arrangements with him to handle all the business you bring to him, allowing you a commission of say ten per cent on the gross amount. Then go to the largest users of printed matter and get samples of everything in the way of printing that they use.

Form a partnership or working arrangement with a commercial artist who will go over all this printed matter and wherever suitable or appropriate he will improve the illustrations or make illustrations where none were used before, making a rough pencil sketch which can be pasted to the original printed matter.

Then, if you are not a writer of copy, form a working arrangement with someone who is and get him or her to go over the copy of the printed matter and improve it in every respect possible.

When the work is complete go back to the firm from whom you get the printed matter, taking with you quotations on the work and show what can be done in the way of improvement. Say nothing about your quotations, however, until you have shown how much you could improve the printed matter. You will probably get the entire business of that firm by giving that sort of service in connection with every job of printing it has done.

If you perform your service properly you will soon have all the business that your commercial artist, your copy writer and you can handle. It ought to be good for $5,000.00 a year apiece for you.

Any profits that you earn from the work of others in connection with any of these plans will be a legitimate profit—a profit to which you will be entitled in return for your ability to organize and bring together the necessary talent and ability with which to perform satisfactory service.

If you go into the toy business you will be entitled to a profit on the work of those who make the toys because it will be through your ability that employment for them is available.

It is more than likely that your brains and your ability, when added to that of those who work with you or for you, will greatly increase their earning capacity—even to the extent that they can well afford to see you make a small amount from their efforts *because they will be still earning much more than they could earn without your guidance!*

You are willing to take any of these plans and make a profit out of them, are you not? You see nothing wrong on your part, do you? If you are an employee, working for some other person or firm, may it not be possible that the head of that firm or that individual, with his ability to organize, finance, etc., is increasing your own earning capacity right now?

You want to get out of the employee class and become an employer. We do not blame you for that. Nearly every normal person wants to do the same. The one best first step to take is to serve the firm or individual for whom you are working just as you would wish to be served if you were that individual or the head of that firm.

Who are the big employers of help, today? Are they the rich men's sons who fell heir to employership? Not on your life! They are the men and women who came up from the ranks of the most lowly sort of labor; men and women who have had no greater opportunity than you have. They are in the positions that they hold because their superior ability has enabled them intelligently to direct others. You can acquire that ability if you will try.

Right in the town or city where you live there are people who probably could benefit by knowing you, and who could undoubtedly benefit you in return. In one section of the city lives John Smith who wishes to sell his grocery store and open a moving picture theater. In another section of the city is a man who has a moving picture theater that he would like to trade for a grocery store.

Can you bring them together?

If you can, you will serve both and earn a nice remuneration.

Aspiration is greater than realization, because it keeps us eternally climbing upward toward some unattained goal.

In your town or city are people who want the products raised on the farms in the surrounding community. On those farms are farmers who raise farm products and who want to get them into the hands of those who live in town. If you can find a way of carrying the farm products direct from the farm to the city or town consumer you will enable the farmer to get more for his products and the consumer to get those products for less, and still there will be a margin to pay you for your ingenuity in shortening the route between producer and consumer.

In business there are, broadly speaking, two classes of people—the Producers and the Consumers. The tendency of the times is to find some way of bringing these two together without so many intermediaries. Find a way to shorten the route between producer and consumer and you will have created a plan that will help these two classes and handsomely profit you.

The laborer is worthy of his hire. If you can create such a plan you are entitled to a fair proportion of that which you *save* for the consumer and also a fair proportion of that which you *make* for the producer.

Let us warn you that whatever plan you create as a means of making money you had better see that it slices off a little of the cost to the consumer instead of adding a little to that cost.

The business of bringing producer and consumer together is a profitable business when it is conducted fairly to both, and without a greedy desire to *get all there is in sight!* The American public is wonderfully patient with profiteers who impose upon it, but there is a pivotal point beyond which even the shrewdest of them dare not go.

It may be all right to corner the diamond market and run up enormously high the price of those white rocks which are dug out of the ground in Africa without trouble, but when the prices of food and clothing and other necessities begin to soar skyward there is a chance of someone getting into the bad graces of the American public.

If you crave wealth and are really brave enough to shoulder the burdens which go with it, reverse the usual method of acquiring it by giving your goods and wares to the world at the lowest possible profit you can afford instead of exacting all that you can with safety. Ford has found it profitable to pay his workers, *not as little as he can get them for, but as much as his profits will permit.* He has also found it profitable to reduce the price of his automobile to the consumer while other manufacturers (many of whom have long since failed) continued to increase their price.

There may be some perfectly good plans through the operation of which you could squeeze the consumer and still manage to keep out of jail, but you will enjoy much more peace of mind and in all probability more profits in the long run if your plan, when you complete it, is built along the Ford lines.

You have heard John D. Rockefeller abused considerably, but most of this abuse has been prompted by sheer envy upon the part of those who would like to have his money but who haven't the inclination to earn it. Regardless of your opinion of Rockefeller, do not forget that he began as a humble bookkeeper and that he gradually climbed to the top in the accumulation of money because of his ability to organize and direct other and less able men intelligently. This author can remember when he had to pay twenty-five cents for a gallon of lamp oil and walk two miles through the hot sun and carry it home in a tin can in the bargain. Now, Rockefeller's wagon will deliver it at the back door, in the city or on the farm, at a little over half that sum.

Congratulate yourself when you reach that degree of wisdom which prompts you to see less of the weaknesses of others and more of your own, for you will then be walking in the company of the really great.

Who has a right to begrudge Rockefeller his millions as long as he has reduced the price of a needed commodity. He could just as easily have increased the price of lamp oil to half a dollar, but we seriously doubt that he would be a multi-millionaire today if he had done so.

There are a lot of us who want money, but ninety-nine out of every hundred who start to create a plan through which to get money give all their thought to the scheme through which to get hold of it and *no thought to the service to be given in return for it.*

A Pleasing Personality is one that makes use of Imagination and Co-operation. We have cited the foregoing illustrations of how ideas may be created to show you how to co-ordinate the laws of Imagination, Co-operation and a Pleasing Personality.

Analyze any man who does not have a Pleasing Personality and you will find lacking in that man the faculties of Imagination and Co-operation also.

This brings us to a suitable place at which to introduce one of the greatest lessons on *personality* ever placed on paper. It is also one of the most effective lessons on salesmanship ever written, for the subjects of *attractive personality* and salesmanship must always go hand in hand; they are inseparable.

I have reference to Shakespeare's masterpiece, Mark Antony's speech at the funeral of Caesar. Perhaps you have read this oration, but it is here presented with interpretations in parentheses which may help you to gather a new meaning from it.

The setting for that oration was something like the following:

Caesar is dead, and Brutus, his slayer, is called on to tell the Roman mob, that has gathered at the undertaker's, why he put Caesar out of the way. Picture, in your imagination, a howling mob that was none too friendly to Caesar, and that already believed that Brutus had done a noble deed by murdering him.

Brutus takes the platform and makes a short statement of his reasons for killing Caesar. Confident that he has won the day he takes his seat. His whole demeanor is that of one who believes his word will be accepted without question; it is one of haughtiness.

Mark Antony now takes the platform, knowing that the mob is antagonistic to him because he is a friend of Caesar. In a low, humble tone of voice Antony begins to speak:

Antony: "For Brutus' sake, I am beholding to you."

Fourth Citizen: "What does he say of Brutus?"

Third Citizen: "He says, for Brutus' sake, he finds himself beholding to us all."

Fourth Citizen: "'Twere best he speak no harm of Brutus here."

First Citizen: "This Caesar was a tyrant."

Third Citizen: "Nay, that's certain; we are blest that Rome is rid of him."

Second Citizen: "Peace! Let us hear what Antony can say."

   (Here you will observe, in Antony's opening sentence, his clever method of "neutralizing" the minds of his listeners.)

Antony: "You gentle Romans,—"

    (About as "gentle" as a gang of Bolsheviks in a revolutionary labor meeting.)

All: "Peace, ho! Let us hear him."

    (Had Antony begun his speech by "knocking" Brutus, the history of Rome would have been different.)

Antony: "Friends, Romans, Countrymen, lend me your ears;

    I come to bury Caesar, not to praise him."

    (Allying himself with what he knew to be the state of mind of his listeners.)

    "The evil that men do lives after them;

    The good is oft interred with their bones;

    So let it be with Caesar. The noble Brutus

    Hath told you Caesar was ambitious;

    If it were so, it was a grievous fault;

    And grievously hath Caesar answered it.

    Here, under leave of Brutus and the rest,—

    For Brutus is an honorable man;

    So are they all, all honorable men—Come I to speak at Caesar's funeral.

    He was my friend—faithful, and just to me;

    But Brutus says he was ambitious;

    And Brutus is an honorable man;

    He hath brought many captives home to Rome,

    Whose ransoms did the general coffers fill;

    Did this in Caesar seem ambitious?

    When the poor have cried, Caesar hath wept;

    Ambition should be made of sterner stuff;

    Yet Brutus says he was ambitious;

    And Brutus is an honorable man.

    You all did see that on the Lupercal

    I thrice presented him a kingly crown,

    Which he did thrice refuse. Was this ambition?

    Yet Brutus says he was ambitious;

    And, surely, he is an honorable man.

    I speak not to disprove what Brutus spoke,

But here I am to speak what I do know.

You all did love him once, not without cause;

What cause withholds you then to mourn for him?

O judgment! thou art fled to brutish beasts,

And men have lost their reason. Bear with me,

My heart is in the coffin there with Caesar,

And I must pause till it come back to me."

(At this point Antony paused to give his audience a chance to discuss hurriedly, among themselves, his opening statements. His object in doing this was to observe what effect his words were having, just as a master salesman always encourages his prospective purchaser to talk so he may know what is in his mind.)

First Citizen: "Methinks there is much in his sayings."

Second Citizen: "If thou consider rightly of the matter, Caesar has had great wrong."

Third Citizen: "Has he, masters? I fear there will be worse come in his place."

Fourth Citizen: "Mark'd ye his words? He would not take the crown? Therefore 'tis certain he was not ambitious."

First Citizen: "If it be found so, someone will dear abide it."

Second Citizen: "Poor soul! his eyes are red as fire with weeping."

Third Citizen: "There's not a nobler man in Rome than Antony."

Fourth Citizen: "Now mark him, he begins again to speak."

Antony: "But yesterday the word of Caesar might

Have stood against the world; now lies he there,

And none so poor to do him reverence.

O masters (appealing to their vanity) if I were disposed to stir

Your hearts and minds to mutiny and rage,

I should do Brutus wrong and Cassius wrong,

Who, you all know, are honorable men;"

(Observe how often Antony has repeated the term "honorable." Observe, also, how cleverly he brings in the first suggestion that, perhaps, Brutus and Cassius may not be as honorable as the Roman mob believes them to be. This suggestion is carried in the words "mutiny" and "rage" which he here uses for the first time, after his pause gave him time to observe that the mob was swinging over toward his side of the argument. Observe how carefully he is "feeling" his way and making his words *fit that which he knows to be the frame of mind of his listeners*.)

Antony: "I will not do them wrong; I rather choose

   To wrong the dead, to wrong myself and you,

   Than I will wrong such honorable men."

(Crystallizing his suggestion into hatred of Brutus and Cassius, he then appeals to their curiosity and begins to lay the foundation for his climax—a climax which he knows will win the mob because he is reaching it so cleverly that the mob believes it to be its own conclusion.)

Antony: "But here's a parchment, with the seal of Caesar;

   I found it in his closet; 'tis his will;

   Let but the commons hear this testament,

   Which, pardon me, I do not mean to read—"

(Tightening up on his appeal to their curiosity by making them believe he does not intend to read the will.)

   "And they would go and kiss dead Caesar's wounds

   And dip their napkins in his sacred blood,

   Yea, beg a hair of him for memory,

   And, dying, mention it within their wills,

   Bequeathing it as a rich legacy

   Unto their issue."

(Human nature *always* wants that which is difficult to get, or that of which it is about to be deprived. Observe how craftily Antony has awakened the interest of the mob and made them want to hear the reading of the will, thereby preparing them to hear it with *open minds*. This marks his second step in the process of "neutralizing" their minds.)

All: "The will, the will! We will hear Caesar's will."

Antony: "Have patience, gentle friends, I must not read it;

It is not meet you know how Caesar loved you.

You are not wood, you are not stones, but men;

And, being men, hearing the will of Caesar,

It will inflame you; (Exactly what he wishes to do)

It will make you mad;

'Tis good you know not that you are his heirs,

For if you should, O what will come of it!"

Fourth Citizen: "Read the will; we'll hear it, Antony;

You shall read us the will; Caesar's will."

Antony: "Will you be patient? Will you stay awhile?

I have o'ershot myself to tell you of it;

I fear I wrong the honorable men

Whose daggers have stabb'd Caesar, I do fear it."

("Daggers" and "stabb'd" suggest cruel murder. Observe how cleverly Antony injects this suggestion into his speech, and observe, also, how quickly the mob catches its significance, because, unknown to the mob, Antony has carefully prepared their minds to receive this suggestion.)

Fourth Citizen: "They were traitors, honorable men!"

All: "The will! The testament!"

Second Citizen: "They were villains, murderers; the will!" (Just what Antony would have
    said in the beginning, but he knew it would have a more desirable effect if he planted
    the thought in the minds of the mob and permitted them to say it themselves.)

Antony: "You will compel me then to read the will?

Then make a ring about the corpse of Caesar,

And let me show you him that made the will.

Shall I descend, and will you give me leave?"

(This was the point at which Brutus should have begun to look for a back door through which to make his escape.)

All: "Come down."

Second Citizen: "Descend."

Third Citizen: "Room for Antony, most noble Antony."

Antony: "Nay, press not so upon me, stand far off."

(He knew this command would make them want to draw nearer, which is what he wanted them to do.)

All: "Stand back. Room."

Antony: "If you have tears, prepare to shed them now.

You all do know this mantle; I remember

The first time ever Caesar put it on;

'Twas on a summer's evening, in his tent,

That day he overcame the Nervii;

Look, in this place ran Cassius' dagger through;

See what a rent the envious Casca made;

Through this the well-beloved Brutus stabb'd;

And as he pluck'd his cursed steel away,

Mark how the blood of Caesar followed it,

As rushing out of doors, to be resolved

If Brutus so unkindly knock'd or no;

For Brutus, as you know, was Caesar's angel;

Judge, O you gods, how dearly Caesar loved him!

This was the most unkindest cut of all;

For, when the noble Caesar saw him stab,

Ingratitude, more strong than traitor's arms,

Quite vanquish'd him; then burst his mighty heart;

And, in his mantle muffling up his face,

Even at the base of Pompey's statue,

Which all the while ran blood, great Caesar fell.

O, what a fall was there, my countrymen!

Then I, and you, and all of us fell down

While bloody treason flourish'd over us.

O, now you weep, and I perceive you feel

The dint of pity; these are gracious drops.

Kind soul, why weep you when you but behold

Our Caesar's vesture wounded? Look you here;

Here is himself, marr'd, as you see, with traitors."

384

(Observe how Antony now uses the word "traitors" quite freely, because he knows that it is in harmony with that which is in the minds of the Roman mob.)

First Citizen: "O piteous spectacle!"
Second Citizen: "O woeful day!"
Third Citizen: "O woeful day!"
First Citizen: "O most bloody sight!"
Second Citizen: "We will be revenged."

(Had Brutus been a wise man instead of a braggart he would have been many miles from the scene by this time.)

All: "Revenge! About! Seek! Burn! Fire! Kill! Slay! Let not a traitor live!"

(Here Antony takes the next step toward crystallizing the frenzy of the mob into *action;* but, clever salesman that he is, does not try to *force* this action.)

Antony: "Stay, countrymen."
First Citizen: "Peace there! Hear the noble Antony."
Second Citizen: "We'll hear him, we'll follow him, we'll die with him."

(From these words Antony knows that he has the mob with him. Observe how he takes advantage of this psychological moment—the moment for which all *master salesmen* wait.)

Antony: "Good friends, sweet friends, let me not stir you up to such a sudden flood of
mutiny.
They that have done this deed are honorable.
What private griefs they have, alas, I know not,
That made them do it; they were wise and honorable,
And will, no doubt, with reasons answer you.
I come not, friends, to steal away your hearts:
I am no orator as Brutus is;

But, as you know me all, a plain, blunt man,

That love my friend; and that they know full well

That gave me public leave to speak of him;

For I have neither wit, nor words, nor worth,

Action, nor utterance, nor the power of speech,

To stir men's blood; I only speak right on;

I tell you that which you yourselves do know;

Show you sweet Caesar's wounds, poor, poor, dumb mouths.

And bid them speak for me; but were I Brutus,

And Brutus Antony, there an Antony

Would ruffle up your spirits, and put a tongue

In every wound of Caesar that should move

The stones of Rome to rise and mutiny."

All: "We'll mutiny."

First Citizen: "We'll burn the house of Brutus."

Third Citizen: "Away, then! Come, seek the conspirators."

Antony: "Yet hear me, countrymen; yet hear me speak!"

All: "Peace, ho! Hear Antony. Most noble Antony!"

Antony: "Why, friends, you go to do you know not what;

Wherein hath Caesar thus deserved your love?

Alas, you know not; I must tell you, then;

You have forgot the will I told you of."

(Antony is now ready to play his trump card; he is ready to reach his climax. Observe how well he has marshaled his suggestions, step by step, saving until the last his most important statement; the one on which he relied for *action*. In the great field of salesmanship and in public speaking many a man tries to reach this point too soon; tries to "rush" his audience or his prospective purchaser, and thereby loses his appeal.)

All: "Most true; the will! Let's stay and hear the will."

Antony: "Here is the will, and under Caesar's seal.

To every Roman citizen he gives,

To every several man, seventy-five drachmas."

Second Citizen: "Most noble Caesar! we'll revenge his death."

Third Citizen: "O royal Caesar!"

Antony: "Hear me with patience."

All: "Peace, ho!"

Antony: "Moreover, he hath left you all his walks,

   His private arbors and new planted orchards,

   On this side Tiber; he hath left them you,

   And to your heirs forever; common pleasures,

   To walk abroad and recreate yourself.

   Here was a Caesar! When comes such another?"

First Citizen: "Never, never. Come, away, away!

   We'll burn his body in the holy place,

   And with the brands fire the traitors' houses.

   Take up the body."

Second Citizen: "Go fetch fire."

Third Citizen: "Pluck down benches."

Fourth Citizen: "Pluck down forms, windows, anything."

And that was Brutus' finish!

He lost his case because he lacked the *personality* and the good judgment with which to present his argument *from the viewpoint of the Roman mob,* as Mark Antony did. His whole attitude clearly indicated that he thought pretty well of himself; that he was proud of his deed. We have all seen people, in this day and time, who somewhat resemble Brutus in this respect, but, if we observe closely, we notice that they do not accomplish very much.

Suppose that Mark Antony had mounted the platform in a "strutting" attitude, and had begun his speech in this wise:

"Now *let me* tell you Romans something about this man Brutus—*he is a murderer at heart and*—" he would have gone no further, for the mob would have howled him down.

Clever salesman and practical psychologist that he was, Mark Antony so presented his case that it appeared not to be *his* own idea at all, but that of the Roman mob, itself.

Go back to the lesson on *initiative and leadership* and

The word educate has its roots in the Latin word "educo," which means to educe, to draw out, to develop from within. The best educated man is the one whose mind has been the most highly developed.

read it again, and as you read, compare the psychology of it with that of Mark Antony's speech. Observe how the *"you"* and not *"I"* attitude toward others was emphasized. Observe, if you please, how this same point is emphasized throughout this course, and especially in Lesson Six, on *enthusiasm.*

Shakespeare was, by far, the most able psychologist and writer known to civilization; for that reason, all of his writings are based upon unerring knowledge of the human mind. Throughout this speech, which he placed in the mouth of Mark Antony, you will observe how carefully he assumed the *"you"* attitude; so carefully that the Roman mob was sure that its decision was of its own making.

I must call your attention, however, to the fact that Mark Antony's appeal to the self-interest of the Roman mob was of the crafty type, and was based upon the stealth with which dishonest men often make use of this principle in appealing to the cupidity and avarice of their victims. While Mark Antony displayed evidence of great self-control in being able to assume, at the beginning of his speech, an attitude toward Brutus that was not real, at the same time it is obvious that his entire appeal was based upon his knowledge of how to influence the minds of the Roman mob, through flattery.

The two letters reproduced in Lesson Six, of this course, illustrate, in a very concrete way the value of the *"you"* and the fatality of the *"I"* appeal. Go back and read these letters again and observe how the more successful of the two follows closely the Mark Antony appeal, while the other one is based upon an appeal of just the opposite nature. Whether you are writing a sales letter, or preaching a sermon or writing an advertisement, or a book, you will do well to follow the same principles employed by Mark Antony in his famous speech.

> *I have great wealth that can never be taken away from me; that I can never squander; that cannot be lost by declining stocks or bad investments; I have the wealth of contentment with my lot in life.*

Now let us turn our attention to the study of ways and means through which one may develop a *pleasing personality.*

Let us start with the first essential, which is *character,* for no one may have a *pleasing personality* without the foundation of a sound, positive character. Through the principle of telepathy you "telegraph" the nature of your character to those with whom you come in contact, which is responsible for what you have often called an "intuitive" feeling that the person whom you had just met, but about whom you did not know very much, was not trustworthy.

You may embellish yourself with clothes of the neatest and latest design, and conduct yourself in a most pleasing manner as far as outside appearances go; but if there is greed, and envy, and hatred, and jealousy, and avarice, and selfishness in your heart, you will never *attract* any, except those characters which harmonize with your own. Like attracts like, and you may be sure, therefore, that those who are attracted to you are those whose inward natures parallel your own.

You may embellish yourself with an artificial smile that belies your feelings, and you may practice the art of hand-shaking so that you can imitate, perfectly, the hand-shake of the person who is an adept at this art, but, if these outward manifestations of an *attractive personality* lack that vital factor called *earnestness of purpose* they will repel instead of attract.

How, then, may one build *character?*

The first step in *character* building is rigid *self-discipline:*

In both the first and seventh lessons of this course, you will find the formula through which you may shape your *character* after any pattern that you choose; but I repeat it here, as it is based upon a principle that will bear much repetition, as follows:

First: Select those whose characters were made up of the qualities which you wish to build into your own character, and then proceed, in the manner described in Lesson One, to appropriate these qualities, through the aid of *Auto-suggestion.* Create, in your imagination, a council table and gather your characters around it each night, first having written out a clear, concise statement of the particular qualities that you wish to appropriate from each. Then proceed to affirm or suggest to yourself, in outspoken, audible words, that you are developing the desired qualities in yourself. As you do this close your eyes and see, in your imagination, the figures seated around your imaginary table, in the manner described in Lesson One.

Second: Through the principles described in Lesson Seven, on *Self-control,* control your thoughts and keep your mind vitalized with thoughts of a positive nature. Let the dominating thought of your mind be a picture of the person that you intend to be: the person *that you are deliberately building,* through this procedure. At least a dozen times a day, when you have a few minutes to yourself, shut your eyes and direct your thoughts to the figures which you have selected to sit at your imaginary council table; and feel, with a *faith* that knows *NO LIMITATION,* that you are actually growing to resemble in character those figures of your choice.

Third: Find at least one person each day, and more if possible, in whom you see some good quality that is worthy of praise, and *praise it.* Remember, however, that this praise must not be in the nature of cheap, insincere flattery; it must be genuine. Speak your words of praise with such earnestness that they will impress those to whom you speak; then watch what happens. You will have rendered those whom you praise a decided benefit of great value to them; and, you will have gone just one more step in the direction of developing the habit of looking for and finding the good qualities in others. I cannot overemphasize the far-reaching effects of this habit of praising, openly and enthusiastically, the good qualities in others; for this habit will soon reward you with a feeling of self-respect and manifestation of gratitude from others, that will modify your entire personality. Here, again, the law of attraction enters, and those whom you praise will see, in you, the qualities that you see in them. Your success in the application of this formula will be in exact proportion to your *faith* in its soundness.

I do not merely believe that it is sound—*I know that it is*—and the reason *I know* is that I have used it successfully and I have also taught others how to use it successfully; therefore, I have a right to promise you that you can use it with equal success.

Furthermore, you can, with the aid of this formula, develop an *attractive personality* so speedily that you will surprise all who know you. The development of such a personality is entirely within your own control, a fact which gives you a tremendous advantage and at the same time places upon you the responsibility if you fail or neglect to exercise your privilege.

I now wish to direct your attention to the reason for speaking, aloud, the affirmation that you are developing the desired qualities which you have selected as the materials out of which to develop an *attractive personality*.

This procedure has two desirable effects; namely—

First: It sets into motion the vibration through which the thought back of your words reaches and imbeds itself in your sub-conscious mind, where it takes root and grows until it becomes a great moving force in your outward, physical activities, leading in the direction of transformation of the thought into reality.

Second: It develops in you the ability to speak with force and conviction which will lead, finally, to great ability as a public speaker. No matter what your calling in life may be, you should be able to stand upon your feet and speak convincingly, as this is one of the most effective ways of developing an *attractive personality*.

Put feeling and emotion into your words as you speak, and develop a deep, rich tone of voice. If your voice is inclined to be high pitched, tone it down until it is soft and pleasing.

You can never express an *attractive personality*, to best advantage, through a harsh or shrill voice. You must cultivate your voice until it becomes rhythmical and pleasing to the ear.

Remember that speech is the chief method of expressing your personality, and for this reason it is to your advantage to cultivate a style that is both forceful and pleasing.

I do not recall a single outstanding *attractive personality* that was not made up, in part, of ability to speak with force and conviction. Study the prominent men and women of today, wherever you find them, and observe the significant fact that the more prominent they are the more efficient are they in speaking forcefully.

Study the outstanding figures of the past in politics and statesmanship and observe that the most successful ones were those who were noted for their ability to speak with force and conviction.

In the field of business, industry and finance it seems significant, also, that the most prominent leaders are men and women who are able public speakers.

In fact no one may hope to become a prominent leader in any noteworthy undertaking without developing the ability to speak with forcefulness that carries conviction. While the salesman may never deliver a public address, he will profit, nevertheless, if he develops the ability to do so, because this ability increases his power to talk convincingly in ordinary conversation.

> *Enthusiasm is the mainspring of the soul. Keep it wound up and you will never be without power to get what you actually need.*

Let us now summarize the chief factors which enter into the development of an *attractive personality*, as follows:

First: Form the habit of interesting yourself in other people; and make it your business to find their good qualities and speak of them in terms of praise.

Second: Develop the ability to speak with force and conviction, both in your ordinary conversational tones and before public gatherings, where you must use more volume.

Third: Clothe yourself in a style that is becoming to your physical build and the work in which you are engaged.

Fourth: Develop a positive character, through the aid of the formula outlined in this lesson.

Fifth: Learn how to shake hands so that you express warmth of feeling and enthusiasm through this form of greeting.

Sixth: Attract other people to you by first "attracting yourself" to them.

Seventh: Remember that your only limitation, within reason, is the one which YOU set up in YOUR OWN mind.

These seven points cover the most important factors that enter into the development of an *attractive personality,* but it seems hardly necessary to suggest that such a personality will not develop of its own accord. It *will develop, if you submit yourself to the discipline herein described, with a firm determination to transform yourself into the person that you would like to be.*

As I study this list of seven important factors that enter into the development of an *attractive personality* I feel moved to direct your attention to the second and the fourth as being the *most important.*

If you will cultivate those finer thoughts, and feelings, and actions, out of which a positive character is built, and then learn to express yourself with force and conviction, you will have developed an *attractive personality,* for it will be seen that out of this attainment will come the other qualities here outlined.

There is a great power of *attraction* back of the person who has a positive character, and this power expresses itself through unseen as well as visible sources. The moment you come within speaking distance of such a person, even though not a word is spoken, the influence of the "unseen power within" makes itself felt.

Every "shady" transaction in which you engage, every negative thought that you think, and every destructive act in which you indulge, destroys just so much of that "subtle something" within you that is known as *character.*

"There is full confession in the glances of our eyes; in our smiles; in salutations; in the grasp of the hands. His sin bedaubs him, mars all his good impression. Men know not why they do not trust him, but they do not trust him. His vice glasses his eye, demeans his cheek, pinches the nose, sets the mark of beast on the back of the head, and writes, 'O fool! fool!' on the forehead of a king." (Emerson.)

I would direct your attention, now, to the first of the seven factors that enter into the development of an *attractive personality.* You have observed that all through this lesson I have gone into lengthy detail to show the material advantages of *being agreeable* to other people.

However, the biggest advantage of all lies, not in the possibility of monetary or material gain which this habit offers, but in the beautifying effect that it has upon the character of all who practice it.

Acquire the habit of making yourself agreeable and you profit both materially and mentally; for you will never be as happy in any other way as you will be when you know that you are making others happy.

Remove the chips from your shoulders and quit challenging men to engage you in useless arguments! Remove the smoked glasses through which you see what you believe to be the "blueness" of life and behold the shining sunlight of friendliness in its stead. Throw away your hammer and quit knocking, for surely you must know that the big prizes of life go to the *builders* and not the *destroyers*.

The man who builds a house is an artist; the man who tears it down is a junkman. If you are a person with a *grievance* the world will listen to your vitriolic "ravings," providing it does not "see you coming"; but, if you are a person with a *message* of friendliness and optimism, it will listen because it wishes to do so.

No person with a grievance can be also a person with an attractive personality!

The art of being agreeable—

—Just that one simple trait—

—is the very foundation of all successful salesmanship.

I drive my automobile five miles into the outskirts of the city to purchase gasoline which I could procure within two blocks of my own garage—

Because the man who runs the filling station is an artist; he makes it his business to be agreeable. I go there, not because he has cheaper gasoline, but because I enjoy the vitalizing effect of his *attractive personality!*

I purchase my shoes at the Regal Shoe Store, at Fiftieth Street and Broadway, in New York, not because I cannot find other good shoes at the same price, but for the reason that Mr. Cobb, the manager of that particular Regal Store, has an *attractive personality*. While he is fitting me with shoes, he makes it his business to talk to me on subjects which he *knows to be close to my heart.*

I do my banking at the Harriman National Bank, at Forty-fourth Street and Fifth Avenue, not because there are not scores of other good banks much nearer my place of business; but for the reason that the tellers, and the cashiers, and the lobby detective, and Mr. Harriman, and all of the others, with whom I come in contact, make it their business to *be agreeable*. My account is small but they receive me as though it were large.

I greatly admire John D. Rockefeller, Jr., not because he is the son of one of the world's richest men; but for the better reason that he, too, has acquired the art of *being agreeable.*

In the little city of Lancaster, Pennsylvania, lives M. T. Garvin, a very successful merchant whom I would travel hundreds of miles to visit, not because he is a wealthy merchant, but for the reason that he makes it his business to *be agreeable*. However, I have no doubt that his material success is closely related to this noble art of affability which he has acquired.

I have in my vest pocket a Parker fountain pen, and my wife and children have pens of the same brand, not because there are not other good fountain pens, but for the reason that *I have been attracted to George S. Parker on account of his habit of being agreeable.*

My wife takes the *Ladies' Home Journal,* not because there are not other good magazines of a similar nature, but for the reason that we became attracted to the *Journal* several years ago, while Edward Bok was its editor, because he had acquired the art of *being agreeable.*

O ye struggling pilgrims, who are searching for the rainbow's end; ye drawers of water and hewers of wood, tarry for a moment by the wayside and learn a lesson from the successful men and women who have succeeded because they acquired the art of—*being agreeable!*

You can win, for a time, through ruthlessness and stealth; you can garner in more of this world's goods than you will need, by sheer force and shrewd strategy, without taking the time or going to the trouble of *being agreeable;* but, sooner or later, you will come to that point in life at which you will feel the pangs of remorse and the emptiness of your well filled purse.

I never think of power and position and wealth that was attained by force, without feeling, very deeply, the sentiment expressed by a man whose name I dare not mention, as he stood at the tomb of Napoleon:

"A little while ago I stood by the grave of the old Napoleon—a magnificent tomb of gilt and gold, fit almost for a deity dead—and gazed upon the sarcophagus of rare and nameless marble, where rest at last the ashes of that restless man. I leaned over the balustrade and thought about the career of the greatest soldier of the modern world. I saw him at Toulon. I saw him walking upon the banks of the Seine contemplating suicide. I saw him putting down the mob in the streets of Paris. I saw him at the head of the army in Italy. I saw him crossing the bridge at Lodi with the tri-color in his hand. I saw him in Egypt, in the shadows of the pyramids; I saw him conquer the Alps and mingle the eagles of France with the eagles of the crags. I saw him at Marengo, at Ulm and at Austerlitz. I saw him in

No man has the right to strain the relationship of friendly acquaintance to the breaking point by asking or expecting of a friend that which might prove to be a burden to the friend.

Russia, when the infantry of the snow and the cavalry of the wild blast scattered his legions like winter's withered leaves. I saw him at Leipsic in defeat and disaster—driven by a million bayonets back upon Paris—clutched like a wild beast—banished to Elba. I saw him escape and re-take an empire by the force of his genius. I saw him upon the frightful field of Waterloo, where chance and fate combined to wreck the fortunes of their former king. And I saw him at St. Helena, with his hands crossed behind him, gazing out upon the sad and solemn sea.

"I thought of the widows and orphans he had made, of the tears that had been shed for his glory, and of the only woman who ever loved him, pushed from his heart by the cold hand of ambition. And I said I would rather have been a French peasant and worn wooden shoes; I would rather have lived in a hut with a vine growing over the door, and the grapes growing purple in the amorous kisses of the autumn sun; I would rather have been that poor peasant, with my wife by my side knitting as the day died out of the sky, with my children upon my knees and their arms about me; I would rather have been this man and gone down to the tongueless silence of the dreamless dust, than to have been that imperial personation of force and murder, known as Napoleon the Great."

I leave with you, as a fitting climax for this lesson, the thought of this deathless dissertation on a man who lived by the sword of force and died an ignominious death, an outcast in the eyes of his fellow men; a sore to the memory of civilization; a failure because—

He did not acquire the art of being agreeable! Because he could not or would not subordinate "self" for the good of his followers.

It is pardonable to tell your friends, by tactful suggestion, of your needs, but take care not to ask them outright for assistance if you would retain their friendship.

ACCURATE THOUGHT

"You Can Do It If You Believe You Can!"

This is at one and the same time the most *important,* the most *interesting* and the most difficult to present lesson of this entire course on the Law of Success.

It is important because it deals with a principle which runs through the entire course. It is interesting for the same reason. It is difficult to present for the reason that it will carry the average student far beyond the boundary line of his common experiences and into a realm of *thought* in which he is not accustomed to dwell.

Unless you study this lesson with an open mind, you will miss the very key-stone to the arch of this course, and without this stone you can never complete your Temple of Success.

This lesson will bring you a conception of *thought* which may carry you far above the level to which you have risen by the evolutionary processes to which you have been subjected in the past; and, for this reason, you should not be disappointed if, at first reading, you do not fully understand it. Most of us *disbelieve* that which we cannot understand, and it is with knowledge of this human tendency in mind that I caution you against closing your mind if you do not grasp all that is in this lesson at the first reading.

For thousands of years men made ships of wood, and of nothing else. They used wood because they believed that it was the only substance that would float; but that was because they had not yet advanced far enough in their *thinking* process to understand the truth that steel will float, and that it is far superior to wood for the building of ships. They did not know that anything could float which was lighter than the amount of water is displaced, and until they learned of this great truth they went on making ships of wood.

Until some twenty-five years ago, most men thought that only the birds could fly, but now we know that man can not only equal the flying of the birds, but he can excel it.

Men did not know, until quite recently, that the great open void known as the air is more alive and more sensitive than anything that is on the earth. They did not know that the spoken word would travel through the ether with the speed of a flash of lightning, without the aid of wires. How could they know this when their minds had not been unfolded sufficiently to enable them to grasp it? The purpose of this lesson is to aid *you* in so unfolding and expanding your mind that you will be able to *think* with accuracy, for this unfoldment will open to you a door that leads to all the power you will need in completing your Temple of Success.

All through the preceding lessons of this course you observed that we have dealt with principles which anyone could easily grasp and apply. You will also observe that these principles have been so presented that they lead to *success* as measured by material wealth. This seemed necessary for the reason that to most people the word *success* and the word *money* are synonymous terms. Obviously, the previous lessons of this course were intended for those who look upon worldly things and material wealth as being all that there is to *success*.

Presenting the matter in another way, I was conscious of the fact that the majority of the students of this course would feel disappointed if I pointed out to them a roadway to *success* that leads through other than the doorways of business, and finance, and industry; for it is a matter of common knowledge that most men want success that is spelled $UCCE$$!

Very well—let those who are satisfied with this standard of *success* have it; but some there are who will want to go higher up the ladder, in search of *success* which is measured in other than material standards, and it is for their benefit in particular that this and the subsequent lessons of this course are intended.

Accurate thought involves two fundamentals which all who indulge in it must observe. First, to think accurately you must separate *facts* from mere *information*. There is much "information" available to you that is not based upon facts. Second, you must separate *facts* into two classes; namely, the *important* and the *unimportant,* or, the *relevant* and the *irrelevant*.

Only by so doing can you think clearly.

All *facts* which you can use in the attainment of your *definite chief aim* are important and relevant; all that you cannot use are unimportant and irrelevant. It is mainly the neglect of some to make this distinction which accounts for the chasm which separates so widely people who appear to have equal ability, and who have had equal opportunity. Without going outside of your own circle of acquaintances you can point to one or more persons who have had no greater opportunity than you have had, and who appear to have no more, and perhaps less, ability than you, who are achieving far greater success.

And you wonder why!

Search diligently and you will discover that all such people have acquired the habit of combining and using the *important facts* which affect their line of work. Far from working harder than you, they are perhaps working less and with greater ease. By virtue of their having learned the secret of separating the *important facts* from the *unimportant,* they have provided themselves with a sort of fulcrum and lever with which they can move with their little fingers loads that you cannot budge with the entire weight of your body.

The person who forms the habit of directing his attention to the *important facts* out of which he is constructing his Temple of Success, thereby provides himself with a power which may be likened to a trip-hammer which strikes a ten-ton blow as compared to a tack-hammer which strikes a one-pound blow!

If these similes appear to be elementary you must keep in mind the fact that some of the students of this course have not yet developed the capacity to think in more complicated terms, and to try to force them to do so would be the equivalent of leaving them hopelessly behind.

That you may understand the importance of distinguishing between *facts* and mere *information,* study that type of man who is guided entirely by that which he hears; the type who is influenced by all the "whisperings of the winds of gossip"; that accepts, without analysis, all that he reads in the newspapers and judges others by what their enemies and competitors and contemporaries say about them.

Search your circle of acquaintances and pick out one of this type as an example to keep before your mind while we are on this subject. Observe that this man usually begins his conversation with some such term as this—*"I see by the papers,"* or *"they say."* The *accurate thinker* knows that the newspapers are not always accurate in their reports, and he also knows that what "they say" usually carries more falsehood than truth. If you have not risen above the *"I see by the papers,"* and the *"they say"* class, you have still far to go before you become an *accurate thinker.* Of course, much truth and many *facts* travel in the guise of idle gossip and newspaper reports; but the *accurate thinker* will not accept as such all that he sees and hears.

The great Edison failed ten thousand times before he made the incandescent electric light work. Do not become discouraged and "quit" if you fail once or twice before making your plans work.

This is a point which I feel impelled to emphasize, for the reason that it constitutes the rocks and reefs on which so many people flounder and go down to defeat in a bottomless ocean of false conclusions.

In the realm of legal procedure, there is a principle which is called the law of *evidence;* and the object of this law is to get at the *facts.* Any judge can proceed with justice to all concerned, if he has the *facts* upon which to base his judgment, but he may play havoc with innocent people if he circumvents the law of *evidence* and reaches a conclusion or judgment that is based upon *hearsay information.*

The law of Evidence varies according to the subject and circumstances with which it is used, but you will not go far wrong if, in the absence of that which you know to be *facts,* you form your judgments on the hypothesis that only that part of the evidence before you which furthers your own interests *without working any hardship on others* is based upon *facts.*

This is a crucial and *important* point in this lesson; therefore, I wish to be sure that you do not pass it by lightly. Many a man mistakes, knowingly or otherwise, expediency for *fact;* doing a thing, or refraining from doing it, for the sole reason that his action furthers his own interest without consideration as to whether it interferes with the rights of others.

No matter how regrettable, it is true that most thinking of today, far from being *accurate,* is based upon the sole foundation of expediency. It is amazing to the more advanced student of *accurate thought,* how many people there are who are "honest" when it is profitable to them, but find myriads of facts (?) to justify themselves in following a dishonest course when that course seems to be more profitable or advantageous.

No doubt you know people who are like that.

The *accurate thinker* adopts a standard by which he guides himself, and he follows that standard at all times, whether it works always to his immediate advantage, or carries him, now and then, through the fields of disadvantage (as it undoubtedly will).

The *accurate thinker* deals with *facts,* regardless of how they affect his own interests, for he knows that ultimately this policy will bring him out on top, in full possession of the object of his *definite chief aim* in life. He understands the soundness of the philosophy that the old philosopher, Croesus, had in mind when he said:

"There is a wheel on which the affairs of men revolve, and its mechanism is such that it prevents *any* man from being *always* fortunate."

The *accurate thinker* has but one standard by which he conducts himself, in his intercourse with his fellow men, and that standard is observed by him as faithfully when it brings him temporary disadvantage as it is when it brings him outstanding advantage; for, being an *accurate thinker,* he knows that, by the law of averages, he will more than regain at some future time that which he loses by applying his standard to his own temporary detriment.

You might as well begin to prepare yourself to understand that it requires the staunchest and most unshakable *character* to become an *accurate thinker,* for you can see that this is where the reasoning of this lesson is leading.

There is a certain amount of temporary penalty attached to *accurate thinking;* there is no denying this fact; but, while this is true, it is also true that the compensating *reward,* in the aggregate, is so overwhelmingly greater that you will gladly pay this penalty.

In searching for *facts* it is often necessary to gather them through the sole source of knowledge and experience of others. It then becomes necessary to examine carefully both the evidence submitted and the person from whom the evidence comes; and when the evidence is of such a nature that it affects the interest of the witness who is giving it, there will be reason to scrutinize it all the more carefully, as witnesses who have an interest in the evidence that they are submitting often yield to the temptation to color and pervert it to protect that interest.

If one man slanders another, his remarks should be accepted, if of any weight at all, with at least a grain of the proverbial salt of caution; for it is a common human tendency for men to find nothing but evil in those whom they do not like. The man who has attained to the degree of *accurate thinking* that enables him to speak of his enemy without exaggerating his faults, and minimizing his virtues, is the exception and not the rule.

Some very able men have not yet risen above this vulgar and self-destructive habit of belittling their enemies, competitors and contemporaries. I wish to bring this common tendency to your attention with all possible emphasis, because it is a tendency that is fatal to *accurate thinking*.

Before you can become an *accurate thinker,* you must understand and make allowance for the fact that the moment a man or a woman begins to assume leadership in any walk of life, the slanderers begin to circulate "rumors" and subtle whisperings reflecting upon his or her character.

No matter how fine one's character is or what service he may be engaged in rendering to the world, he cannot escape the notice of those misguided people who delight in *destroying* instead of *building*. Lincoln's political enemies circulated the report that he lived with a colored woman. Washington's political enemies circulated a similar report concerning him.

Since both Lincoln and Washington were southern men, this report was undoubtedly regarded by those who circulated it as being at one and the same time the most fitting and degrading one they could imagine.

But we do not have to go back to our first President to find evidence of this slanderous nature with which men are gifted, for they went a step further, in paying their tributes to the late President Harding, and circulated the report that he had negro blood in his veins.

When Woodrow Wilson came back from Paris with what he believed to be a sound plan for abolishing war and settling international disputes, all except the *accurate thinker* might have been led to believe, by the reports of the *"they say"* chorus, that he was a combination of Nero and Judas Iscariot. The little politicians, and the cheap politicians, and the "interest-paid" politicians, and the plain ignorants who did no thinking of their own, all joined in one mighty chorus for the purpose of destroying the *one and only man in the history of the world who offered a plan for abolishing war.*

The slanderers killed both Harding and Wilson—murdered them with vicious lies. They did the same to Lincoln, only in a somewhat more spectacular manner, by inciting a fanatic to hasten his death with a bullet.

Statesmanship and politics are not the only fields in which the *accurate thinker* must be on guard against the *"they say"* chorus. The moment a man begins to make himself felt in the field of industry or business, this chorus becomes active. If a man makes a better mouse-trap than his neighbor, the world will make a beaten path to his door; no doubt about that; and in the gang that will trail along will be those who come, not to commend, but to condemn and to destroy his reputation. The late John H. Patterson, president of the National Cash Register Company, is a notable example of what may happen to a man who builds a better cash register than that of his neighbor; yet, in the mind of the *accurate thinker,* there is not one scintilla of evidence to support the vicious reports that Mr. Patterson's competitors circulated about him.

As for Wilson and Harding, we may only judge how posterity will view them by observing how it has immortalized the names of Lincoln and Washington. Truth, alone, endures. All else must pass on with Time.

The object of these references is not to eulogize those who stand in no particular need of eulogy; but, it is to direct your attention to the *fact* that *"they say"* evidence is always subject to the closest scrutiny; and all the more so when it is of a negative or destructive nature. No harm can come from accepting, as *fact,* hearsay evidence that is constructive; but its opposite, if accepted at all, should be subjected to the closest inspection possible under the available means of applying the law of evidence.

As an *accurate thinker,* it is both your privilege and your duty to avail yourself of facts, even though you must go out of your way to get them. If you permit yourself to be swayed to and fro by all manner of information that comes to your attention, you will never become an *accurate thinker;* and if you do not *think accurately,* you cannot be sure of attaining the object of your *definite chief aim* in life.

Many a man has gone down to defeat because, due to his prejudice and hatred, he underestimated the virtues of his enemies or competitors. The eyes of the *accurate thinker* see *facts*—not the delusions of prejudice, hate and envy.

> *You are well on the road toward success if you have such a keen conception of life that you never build a plan which contemplates your requesting another person to do that which does not bring that person some corresponding advantage in return for compliance with your request.*

An *accurate thinker* must be something of a good sportsman—in that he is fair enough (with himself at least) to look for virtues as well as faults in other people, for it is not without reason to suppose that all men have some of each of these qualities.

"I do not believe that I can afford to deceive others—*I know I cannot afford to deceive myself!*" This must be the motto of the *accurate thinker.*

With the supposition that these "hints" are sufficient to impress upon your mind the importance of searching for *facts* until you are reasonably sure that you have found them, we will take up the question of organizing, classifying and using these *facts.*

Look, once more, in the circle of your own acquaintances and find a person who appears to accomplish more with less effort than do any of his associates. Study this man and you observe that he is a strategist in that he has learned how to arrange *facts* so that he brings to his aid the Law of Increasing Returns which we described in a previous lesson.

The man who *knows* that he is working with *facts* goes at his task with a feeling of *self-confidence* which enables him to refrain from temporizing, hesitating or waiting to make sure of his ground. He knows in advance what the outcome of his efforts will be; therefore, he moves more rapidly and accomplishes more than does the man who must "feel his way" because he is not sure that he is working with *facts.*

The man who has learned of the advantages of searching for *facts* as the foundation of his thinking has gone a very long way toward the development of *accurate thinking,* but the man who has learned how to separate *facts* into the *important* and the *unimportant* has gone still further. The latter may be compared to the man who uses a trip-hammer, and thereby accomplishes at one blow more than the former, who uses a tack-hammer, can accomplish with ten thousand blows.

Let us analyze, briefly, a few men who have made it their business to deal with the *important* or *relevant facts* pertaining to their life-work.

If it were not for the fact that this course is being adapted to the practical needs of men and women of the present workaday world, we would go back to the great men of the past—Plato, Aristotle, Epictetus, Socrates, Solomon, Moses and Christ—and direct attention to their habit of dealing with *facts*. However, we can find examples nearer our own generation that will serve our purpose to better advantage at this particular point.

Inasmuch as this is an age in which money is looked upon as being the most concrete proof of *success,* let us study a man who has accumulated almost as much of it as has any other man in the history of the world—John D. Rockefeller.

Mr. Rockefeller has one quality that stands out, like a shining star, above all of his other qualities; it is his habit of dealing only with the *relevant facts* pertaining to his life-work. As a very young man (and a very poor young man, at that) Mr. Rockefeller adopted, as his *definite chief aim,* the accumulation of great wealth. It is not my purpose, nor is it of any particular advantage, to enter into Mr. Rockefeller's method of accumulating his fortune other than to observe that his *most pronounced quality* was that of insisting on *facts* as the basis of his business philosophy. Some there are who say that Mr. Rockefeller was not always fair with his competitors. That may or may not be true (as accurate thinkers we will leave the point undisturbed), but no one (not even his competitors) ever accused Mr. Rockefeller of forming "snap-judgments" or of underestimating the strength of his competitors. He not only recognized *facts* that affected his business, wherever and whenever he found them, but *he made it his business to search for them until he was sure he had found them.*

Thomas A. Edison is another example of a man who has attained to greatness through the organization, classification and use of *relevant facts*. Mr. Edison works with natural laws as his chief aids; therefore, he *must* be sure of his *facts* before he can harness those laws. Every time you press a button and switch on an electric light, remember that it was Mr. Edison's capacity for organizing *relevant facts* which made this possible.

Every time you hear a phonograph, remember that Mr. Edison is the man who made it a reality, through his persistent habit of dealing with *relevant facts.*

Every time you see a moving picture, remember that it was born of Mr. Edison's habit of dealing with *important* and *relevant facts.*

In the field of science *relevant facts* are the tools with which men and women work. Mere information, or hearsay evidence, is of no value to Mr. Edison; yet he might have wasted his life working with it, as millions of other people are doing.

Hearsay evidence could never have produced the incandescent electric light, the phonograph or the moving picture, and if it had, the phenomenon would have been an "accident." In this lesson we are trying to prepare the student to avoid "accidents."

The question now arises as to what constitutes an *important* and *relevant fact*.

The answer depends entirely upon what constitutes your *definite chief aim* in life, for an *important* and *relevant fact* is any fact which you can use, without interfering with the rights of others, in the attainment of that purpose.

All other *facts,* as far as you are concerned, are superfluous and of minor importance at most.

However, you can work just as hard in organizing, classifying and using *unimportant* and *irrelevant facts* as you can in dealing with their opposites, but *you will not accomplish as much.*

Up to this point we have been discussing only one factor of *accurate thought,* that which is based upon deductive reasoning. Perhaps this is the point at which some of the students of this course will have to *think* along lines with which they are not familiar, for we come, now, to the discussion of *thought* which does much more than gather, organize and combine *facts*.

Let us call this *creative thought!*

That you may understand why it is called *creative thought* it is necessary briefly to study the process of evolution through which the *thinking man* has been created.

Thinking man has been a long time on the road of evolution, and he has traveled a very long way. In the words of Judge T. Troward (in Bible Mystery and Bible Meaning), "Perfected man is the apex of the Evolutionary Pyramid, and this by a necessary sequence."

Let us trace *thinking man* through the five evolutionary steps through which we believe he has traveled, beginning with the very lowest; namely—

1. The Mineral Period. Here we find life in its lowest form, lying motionless and inert; a mass of mineral substances, with no power to move.
2. Then comes the Vegetable Period. Here we find life in a more active form, with intelligence sufficient to gather food, grow and reproduce, but still unable to move from its fixed moorings.

3. Then comes the Animal Period. Here we find life in a still higher and more intelligent form, with ability to move from place to place.

4. Then comes the Human or Thinking Man Period, where we find life in its highest known form; the highest, because man can *think,* and because *thought* is the highest known form of organized energy. In the realm of *thought* man knows no limitations. He can send his *thoughts* to the stars with the quickness of a flash of lightning. He can gather facts and assemble them in new and varying combinations. He can create hypotheses and translate them into physical reality, through *thought*. He can reason both inductively and deductively.

5. Then comes the Spiritual Period. On this plane the lower forms of life, described in the previously mentioned four periods, converge and become infinitude in nature. At this point *thinking man* has unfolded, expanded and grown until he has projected his thinking ability into *infinite intelligence*. As yet, *thinking man* is but an infant in this fifth period, for he has not learned how to appropriate to his own use this *infinite intelligence* called Spirit. Moreover, with a few rare exceptions, man has not yet recognized *thought* as the connecting link which gives him access to the power of *infinite intelligence*. These exceptions have been such men as Moses, Solomon, Christ, Plato, Aristotle, Socrates, Confucius and a comparatively small number of others of their type. Since their time we have had many who partly uncovered this great *truth;* yet the *truth,* itself, is as available now as it was then.

To make use of *creative thought,* one must work very largely on *faith,* which is the chief reason why more of us do not indulge in this sort of *thought*. The most ignorant of the race can *think* in terms of deductive reasoning, in connection with matters of a purely physical and material nature, but to go a step higher and *think* in terms of *infinite intelligence* is another question. The average man is totally at sea the moment he gets beyond that which he can comprehend with the aid of his five physical senses of seeing, hearing, feeling, smelling and tasting. *Infinite intelligence* works through none of these agencies and we cannot invoke its aid through any of them.

How, then, may one appropriate the power of *infinite intelligence?* is but a natural question.

And the answer is:

Through creative thought!

> *Salesmanship consists very largely in KNOWING and in SHOWING the prospective buyer the real merits of the goods or service you are trying to sell.*

To make clear the exact manner in which this is done I will now call your attention to some of the preceding lessons of this course through which you have been prepared to understand the meaning of *creative thought.*

In the first lesson, and to some extent in practically every other lesson that followed it, up to this one, you have observed the frequent introduction of the term "Auto-suggestion." (Suggestion that you make to yourself.) We now come back to that term again, because Auto-suggestion is the telegraph line, so to speak, over which you may register in your subconscious mind a description or plan of that which you wish to *create* or acquire in physical form.

It is a process you can easily learn to use.

The sub-conscious mind is the intermediary between the conscious *thinking* mind and *infinite intelligence,* and you can invoke the aid of *infinite intelligence* only through the medium of the sub-conscious mind, by giving it clear instructions as to what you want. Here you become familiar with the psychological reason for a *definite chief aim.*

If you have not already seen the importance of creating a *definite chief aim* as the object of your lifework, you will undoubtedly do so before this lesson shall have been mastered.

Knowing, from my own experience as a beginner in the study of this and related subjects, how little I understood such terms as "Sub-conscious Mind" and "Auto-suggestion" and *"Creative Thought,"* I have taken the liberty, throughout this course, of describing these terms through every conceivable simile and illustration, with the object of making their meaning and the method of their application so clear that no student of this course can possibly fail to understand. This accounts for the repetition of terms which you will observe throughout the course, and at the same time serves as an apology to those students who have already advanced far enough to grasp the meaning of much that the beginner will not understand at first reading.

The sub-conscious mind has one outstanding characteristic to which I will now direct your attention; namely, *it records the suggestions which you send it through Auto-suggestion, and invokes the aid of infinite intelligence in translating these suggestions into their natural physical form, through natural means which are in no way out of the ordinary.* It is important that you understand the foregoing sentence, for, if you fail to understand it, you are likely to fail, also, to understand the importance of the very foundation upon which this entire course is built—*that foundation being the principle of infinite intelligence,* which may be reached and appropriated at will through aid of the law of the "Master Mind" described in the Introduction.

Study carefully, thoughtfully and with meditation, the entire preceding paragraph.

The sub-conscious mind has another outstanding characteristic—it accepts and acts upon all suggestions that reach it, whether they are constructive or destructive, and whether they come from the outside or from your own conscious mind.

You can see, therefore, how essential it is for you to observe the law of evidence and carefully follow the principles laid down in the beginning of this lesson, in the selection of that which you will pass on to your sub-conscious mind through Auto-suggestion. You can see why one must search diligently for *facts,* and why one cannot afford to lend a receptive ear to the slanderer and the scandalmonger—for to do so is the equivalent of feeding the sub-conscious mind with food that is poison and ruinous to *creative thought.*

The sub-conscious mind may be likened to the sensitive plate of a camera on which the picture of any object placed before the camera will be recorded. The plate of the camera does not choose the sort of picture to be recorded on it, it records anything which reaches it through the lens. The conscious mind may be likened to the shutter which shuts off the light from the sensitized plate, permitting nothing to reach the plate for record except that which the operator wishes to reach it. The lens of the camera may be likened to Auto-suggestion, for it is the medium which carries the image of the object to be registered, to the sensitized plate of the camera. And *infinite intelligence* may be likened to the one who develops the sensitized plate, after a picture has been recorded on it, thus bringing the picture into physical reality.

The ordinary camera is a splendid instrument with which to compare the whole process of *creative thought.* First comes the selection of the object to be exposed before the camera. This represents one's *definite chief aim* in life. Then comes the actual operation of recording a clear outline of that *purpose,* through the lens of Auto-suggestion, on the sensitized plate of the sub-conscious mind. Here *infinite intelligence* steps in and develops the outline of that *purpose* in a physical form appropriate to the nature of the *purpose.* The part which *you* must play is clear!

You select the picture to be recorded (*definite chief aim*). Then you fix your conscious mind upon this purpose with such intensity that it communicates with the sub-conscious mind, through Auto-suggestion, and registers that picture. You then begin to watch for and to expect manifestations of physical realization of the subject of that picture.

Bear in mind the fact that you do not sit down and wait, nor do you go to bed and sleep, with the expectation of awaking to find that *infinite intelligence* has showered you with the object of your *definite chief aim.* You go right ahead, in the usual way, doing your daily work in accordance with the instructions laid down in Lesson Eight of this course, *with full faith and confidence that natural ways and means for the attainment of the object of your definite purpose will open to you at the proper time and in a suitable manner.*

The way may not open suddenly, from the first step to the last, but it may open one step at a time. Therefore, when you are conscious of an opportunity to take the first step, take it without hesitation, and do the same when the second, and the third, and all subsequent steps,

Any man may become great by doing the common-place things of life in a great spirit, with a genuine desire to be of helpful service to others, regardless of his calling.

essential for the attainment of the object of your *definite chief aim,* are manifested to you.

Infinite intelligence will not build you a home and deliver that home to you, ready to enter; but *infinite intelligence* will open the way and provide the necessary means with which *you* may build your own house.

Infinite intelligence will not command the cashier of your bank to place a definite sum of money to your credit, just because you suggested this to your sub-conscious mind; but *infinite intelligence* will open to you the way in which you may earn or borrow that money and place it to your own credit.

Infinite intelligence will not throw out the present incumbent of the White House and make you President in his place; but *infinite intelligence* would most likely proceed, under the proper circumstances, to influence you to prepare yourself to fill that position with credit and then help you to attain it through the regular method of procedure.

Do not rely upon the performance of miracles for the attainment of the object of your *definite chief aim;* rely upon the power of *infinite intelligence* to guide you, through natural channels, and with the aid of natural laws, for its attainment. Do not expect *infinite intelligence* to bring to you the object of your *definite chief aim;* instead, expect *infinite intelligence* to *direct you toward that object.*

As a beginner, do not expect *infinite intelligence* to move quickly in your behalf; but, as you become more adept in the use of the principle of Auto-suggestion, and as you develop the *faith* and *understanding* required for its quick realization, you can create a *definite chief aim* and witness its immediate translation into physical reality. You did not walk the first time you tried, but now, as an adult (an adept at walking), you walk without effort. You also look down at the little child as it wobbles around, trying to walk, and laugh at its efforts. As a beginner in the use of *creative thought,* you may be compared to the little child who is learning to take its first step.

I have the best of reasons for knowing that this comparison is accurate, but I will not state them. I will let you find out your own reason, in your own way.

Keep in mind, always, the principle of *evolution* through the operation of which everything physical is eternally reaching upward and trying to complete the cycle between *finite* and *infinite* intelligences.

Man, himself, is the highest and most noteworthy example of the working of the principle of evolution. First, we find him down in the minerals of the earth, where there is life but no intelligence. Next, we find him raised, through the growth of vegetation (evolution), to a much higher form of life, where he enjoys sufficient intelligence to feed himself. Next, we find him functioning in the animal period, where he has a comparatively high degree of intelligence, with ability to move around from place to place. Lastly, we find him risen above the lower species of the animal kingdom, to where he functions as a *thinking* entity, with ability to appropriate and use *infinite intelligence*.

Observe that he did not reach this high state all at one bound. He climbed—step by step, perhaps through many reincarnations.

Keep this in mind and you will understand why you cannot reasonably expect *infinite intelligence* to circumvent the natural laws and turn man into the storehouse of *all knowledge* and *all power* until he has prepared himself to use this knowledge and power with higher than finite intelligence.

If you want a fair example of what may happen to a man who suddenly comes into control of power, study some newly-rich or someone who has inherited a fortune. Money-power in the hands of John D. Rockefeller is not only in safe hands, but it is in hands where it is serving mankind throughout the world, blotting out ignorance, destroying contagious disease and serving in a thousand other ways of which the average individual knows nothing.

But place John D. Rockefeller's fortune in the hands of some young lad who has not yet finished high school and you might have another story to tell, the details of which your own imagination and your knowledge of human nature will supply.

I will have more to say on this subject in Lesson Thirteen.

If you have ever done any farming, you understand that certain preparations are necessary before a crop can be produced from the ground. You know, of course, that grain will not grow in the woods, that it requires sunshine and rain for its growth. Likewise, you understand that the farmer must plow the soil and *properly plant the grain*.

After all this has been done, he then waits on *Nature* to do her share of the work; and she does it in due time, without outside help.

This is a perfect simile which illustrates the method through which one may attain the object of one's *definite chief aim*. First comes the preparing of the soil to receive the seed, which is represented by *faith* and *infinite intelligence* and understanding of the principle of Auto-suggestion and the sub-conscious mind through which the seed of a *definite purpose* may be planted. Then comes a period of waiting and working for the realization of the object of that *purpose*. During this period, there must be continuous, intensified *faith,* which serves as the sunshine and the rain, without which the seed will wither and die in the ground. Then comes realization, harvest-time.

And a wonderful harvest *can* be brought forth.

I am fully conscious of the fact that much of that which I am stating will not be understood by the beginner, at the first reading, for I have in mind my own experiences at the start. However, as the evolutionary process carries on its work (and it will do so; make no mistake about this) all the principles described in this and in all other lessons of this course, will become as familiar to you as did the multiplication table after you had mastered it; and, what is of greater importance still, these principles will work with the same unvarying certainty as does the principle of multiplication.

Each lesson of this course has provided you with *definite* instructions to follow. The instructions have been simplified as far as possible, so anyone can understand them. Nothing has been left to the student except to follow the instructions and supply the *faith* in their soundness without which they would be useless.

In this lesson you are dealing with four major factors to which I would again direct your attention with the request that you familiarize yourself with them. They are:

Auto-suggestion, the Sub-conscious Mind, Creative Thought and Infinite Intelligence.

These are the four roadways over which you must travel in your upward climb in quest of knowledge. Observe that *you* control three of these. Observe, also—and this is especially emphasized—that upon the manner in which you traverse these three roadways will depend the *time* and *place* at which they will converge into the fourth, or *infinite intelligence*.

You understand what is meant by the terms Auto-suggestion and Sub-conscious Mind. Let us make sure that you understand, also, what is meant by the term Creative Thought. This means *thought* of a positive, non-destructive, creative nature. The object of Lesson Seven, on Self-control, was to prepare you to understand and successfully apply the principle of Creative Thought. If you have not mastered that lesson you are not ready to make use of Creative Thought in the attainment of your *definite chief aim*.

Let me repeat a simile already used by saying that your sub-conscious mind is the field or the soil in which you sow the seed of your *definite chief aim*. Creative Thought is the

> *Remember that your real wealth can be measured, not by what you have, but, by what you are.*

instrument with which you keep that soil fertilized and conditioned to awaken that seed into growth and maturity. Your sub-conscious mind will not germinate the seed of your *definite chief aim* nor will *infinite intelligence* translate that *purpose* into physical reality if you fill your mind with hatred, and envy, and jealousy, and selfishness and greed. These negative or *destructive thoughts* are the weeds which will choke out the seed of your *definite purpose.*

Creative thought pre-supposes that you will keep your mind in a state of expectancy of attainment of the object of your *definite chief aim;* that you will have full *faith* and confidence in its attainment in due course and in due order.

If this lesson does that which it was intended to do, it will bring you a fuller and deeper realization of the second lesson of this course, on Self-confidence. As you begin to learn how to plant the seed of your *desires* in the fertile soil of your sub-conscious mind, and how to fertilize that seed until it springs into life and action, you will then have reason, indeed, to believe in yourself.

And, after you have reached this point in the process of your evolution, you will have sufficient knowledge of the real source from which you are drawing your power, to give full credit to *infinite intelligence* for all that you had previously credited to your Self-confidence.

Auto-suggestion is a powerful weapon with which one may rise to heights of great achievement, when it is used constructively. Used in a negative manner, however, it may destroy all possibility of success, and if so used continuously it will actually destroy health.

Careful comparison of the experiences of leading physicians and psychiatrists disclosed the startling information that approximately seventy-five per cent of those who are ill are suffering from hypochondria, which is a morbid state of mind causing useless anxiety about one's health.

Stated in plain language, the hypochondriac is a person who believes he or she is suffering with some sort of imaginary disease, and often these unfortunates believe they have every disease of which they ever heard the name.

Hypochondriacal conditions are generally superinduced by auto-intoxication, or poisoning through failure of the intestinal system to throw off the waste matter. The person who suffers with such a toxic condition is not only unable to think with accuracy, but suffers from all sorts of perverted, destructive, illusory thoughts. Many sick people have tonsils removed, or teeth pulled, or the appendix taken out, when their trouble could have been removed with an internal bath and a bottle of Citrate of Magnesia (with due apologies to my friends, the physicians, one of the leading of whom gave me this information).

Hypochondria is the beginning of most cases of insanity!

Dr. Henry R. Rose is authority for the following typical example of the power of Auto-suggestion:

"'If my wife dies I will not believe there is a God.' His wife was ill with pneumonia, and this is the way he greeted me when I reached his home. She had sent for me because the doctor had told her she could not recover. (Most doctors know better than to make a statement such as this in the presence of a patient.) She had called her husband and two sons to her bedside and bidden them good-by. Then she asked that I, her minister, be sent for. I found the husband in the front room sobbing and the sons doing their best to brace her up. When I went into her room she was breathing with difficulty, and the trained nurse told me she was very low.

"I soon found that Mrs. N—— had sent for me to look after her two sons after she was gone. Then I said to her: 'You mustn't give up. YOU ARE NOT GOING TO DIE! You have always been a strong and healthy woman and I do not believe God wants you to die and leave your boys to me or anyone else.'

"I talked to her along this line and then read the 103d Psalm and made a prayer in which I prepared her to get well rather than to enter eternity. I told her to put her faith in God and throw her mind and will against every thought of dying. Then I left her, saying, 'I will come again after the church service, and I will then find you much better.'

"This was on Sunday morning. I called that afternoon. Her husband met me with a smile. He said that the moment I had gone his wife called him and the boys into the room and said: 'Dr. Rose says that I am not going to die; that I am going to get well, and I am.'

"She did get well. But what did it? Two things: Auto-suggestion, superinduced by the suggestion I had given her, and faith on her part. I came just in the nick of time, and so great was her faith in me that I was able to inspire faith in herself. It was that faith that tipped the scales and brought her through the pneumonia. No medicine can cure pneumonia. The physicians admit that. There are cases of pneumonia, perhaps, that nothing can cure. We all sadly agree to that, but there are times, as in this case, when the mind, if worked upon and worked with in just the right way, will turn the tide. While there is life there is hope; but hope must rule supreme and do the good that hope was intended to do.

"Here is another remarkable case showing the power of the human mind when used constructively. A physician asked me to see Mrs. H———. He said there was nothing organically wrong with her, but she just wouldn't eat. Having made up her mind that she could not retain anything on her stomach, she had quit eating, and was slowly starving herself to death. I went to see her and found, first, that she had no religious belief. She had lost her faith in God. I also found that she had no confidence in her power to retain food. My first effort was to restore her faith in the Almighty and to get her to believe that He was with her and would give her power. Then I told her that she could eat anything she wanted. True, her confidence in me was great and my statement impressed her. She began to eat from that day! She was out of her bed in three days, for the first time in weeks. She is a normal, healthy and happy woman today.

"What did it? The same forces as those described in the preceding case; outside suggestion (which she accepted in faith and applied, through self-suggestion) and inward confidence.

"There are times when the mind is sick and it makes the body sick. At such times it needs a stronger mind to heal it by giving it direction and especially by giving it confidence and faith in itself. This is called suggestion. It is transmitting your confidence and power to another, and with such force as to make the other believe as you wish and do as you will. It need not be hypnotism. You can get wonderful results with the patient wide awake and perfectly rational. The patient must believe in you and you must understand the workings of the human mind in order to meet the arguments and questions of the patient. Each one of us can be a healer of this sort and thus help our fellow men.

"It is the duty of every person to read some of the best books on the forces of the human mind and learn what amazing things the mind can do to keep people well and happy. We see the terrible things that wrong thinking does to people, even going to such lengths as to make them positively insane. It is high time we found out the good things the mind can do, not only to cure mental disorders, but physical diseases as well."

You should delve deeper into this subject.

I do not say the mind can cure everything. There is no reliable evidence that certain forms of cancer have been cured by thinking or faith or any mental or religious process. If you would be cured of cancer you must take it at the very beginning and treat it surgically. There is no other way, and it would be criminal to suggest that there is. But the mind can do much with so many types of human indisposition and disease that we ought to rely upon it more often than we do.

Napoleon, during his campaign in Egypt, went among his soldiers who were dying by the hundreds of the black plague. He touched one of them and lifted a second, to inspire the others not to be afraid, for the awful disease seemed to spread as much by the aid of the imagination as in any other way. Goethe tells us that he himself went where there was malignant fever and never contracted it because he put forth his will. These giants among men knew something WE ARE SLOWLY BEGINNING TO FIND OUT—*the power of Auto-suggestion!* This means the influence we have upon ourselves by believing we cannot catch a disease or be sick. There is something about the operation of

We climb to heaven mostly on the ruins of our cherished plans, finding our failures were but friendly guide-posts that led us onward and upward to success.

the automatic or sub-conscious mind by which it rises above disease germs and bids defiance to them when we resolve not to let the thought of them frighten us, or when we go in and out among the sick, even the contagiously sick, without thinking anything about it.

"Imagination will kill a cat," so runs the old adage. It certainly will kill a man, or, on the other hand, it will help him rise to heights of achievement of the most astounding nature, providing he uses it as the basis of self-confidence. There are authentic cases on record of men having actually died because they imagined they were cut by a knife across the jugular vein, when in reality a piece of ice was used and water was allowed to drip so they could hear it and imagine their blood was running out. They had been blindfolded before the experiment was begun. No matter how well you may be when you start for work in the morning, if everyone you meet should say to you, "How ill you look; you should see a doctor," it will not be long before you begin to feel ill, and if this keeps up a few hours you will arrive at home in the evening as limp as a rag and ready for a doctor. Such is the power of the imagination or Auto-suggestion.

The imaginative faculty of the human mind is a marvelous piece of mental machinery, but it may, and usually does, play queer tricks on us unless we keep constantly on guard and control it.

If you allow your imagination to "expect the worst" it will play havoc with you. Young medical students not infrequently become frightened and believe they have every disease on the medical calendar, as the result of medical lectures and class-room discussions of the various diseases.

As has been stated, hypochondria may often be superinduced by toxic poisoning, through improper elimination of the waste matter of the body; also, it may be brought on by false alarm, through improper use of the imagination. In other words, the hypochondrical condition may have as its cause a real physical basis, or it may arise entirely as the result of allowing the imagination to run wild.

Physicians are pretty well agreed upon this point!

Dr. Schofield describes the case of a woman who had a tumor. They placed her on the operating table and gave her anesthetics, when lo! the tumor immediately disappeared, and no operation was necessary. But when she came back to consciousness the tumor returned. The physician then learned that she had been living with a relative who had a real tumor, and that her imagination was so vivid that she had imagined this one upon herself. She was placed on the operating table again, given anesthetics and then she was strapped around the middle so that the tumor could not artificially return. When she revived she was told that a successful operation had been performed but that it would be necessary to wear the bandage for several days. She believed the doctor, and when the bandage was finally removed the tumor did not return. No operation whatever had been performed. She had simply relieved her sub-conscious mind of the thought that she had a tumor and her imagination had nothing to work upon save the idea of health, and, as she had never really been sick, of course she remained normal.

The mind may be cured of imaginary ills in exactly the same manner that it became diseased with those ills, by Auto-suggestion. The best time to work on a faulty imagination is at night, just as you are ready to go to sleep, for then the automatic or sub-conscious mind has everything its own way, and the thoughts or suggestions you give it just as your conscious or "day" mind is about to go off duty will be taken up and worked on during the night.

This may seem impossible, but you can easily test the principle by the following procedure: You wish to get up at seven o'clock tomorrow morning, or at some hour other than your regular time to awaken. Say to yourself, as you are about ready to go to sleep, "I must arise at seven o'clock tomorrow without fail." Repeat this several times, at the same time impressing the fact upon your mind that you must actually arise at the precise moment mentioned. Turn this thought over to your sub-conscious mind with absolute confidence that you will awaken at seven o'clock, and when that hour arrives your sub-conscious mind will awaken you. This test has been successfully made hundreds of times. The sub-conscious mind will awaken you, at any hour you demand, just as if someone came to your bed and tapped you on the shoulder. But you must give the command in no uncertain or indefinite terms.

Likewise, the sub-conscious mind may be given any other sort of orders and it will carry them out as readily as it will awaken you at a given hour. For example, give the command, as you are about to go to sleep each night, for your sub-conscious mind to develop self-confidence, courage, initiative or any other quality, and it will do your bidding.

If the imagination of man can create imaginary ills and send one to bed with those ills, it can also, and just as easily, remove the cause of those ills.

Man is a combination of chemical equivalents the value of which is said to be about twenty-six dollars, with the exception, of course, of that stupendous power called the human mind.

In the aggregate the mind seems to be a complicated machine, but in reality, as far as the manner in which it may be used is concerned, it is the nearest thing to perpetual motion that is known. It works automatically when we are asleep; it works both automatically and in conjunction with the will, or voluntary section, when we are awake.

The mind is deserving of the minutest possible analysis in this lesson because the mind is the energy with which all thinking is done. To learn how to THINK ACCURATELY, the teaching of which is the sole object of this lesson, one must thoroughly understand:

First: That the mind can be controlled, guided and directed to creative, constructive ends.

Second: That the mind can be directed to destructive ends, and, that it may, voluntarily, tear down and destroy unless it is with plan and deliberation controlled and directed constructively.

Third: That the mind has power over every cell of the body, and can be made to cause every cell to do its intended work perfectly, or it may, through neglect or wrong direction, destroy the normal functionary purposes of any or all cells.

Fourth: That all achievement of man is the result of thought, the part which his physical body plays being of secondary importance, and in many instances of no importance whatsoever except as a housing place for the mind.

Fifth: That the greatest of all achievements, whether in literature, art, finance, industry, commerce, transportation, religion, politics or scientific discoveries, are usually the results of ideas conceived in one man's brain but ACTUALLY TRANSFORMED INTO REALITY BY OTHER MEN, through the combined use of their minds and bodies. (Meaning that the conception of an idea is of greater importance than the transformation of that idea into more material form, because relatively few men can conceive useful ideas, while there are hundreds of millions who can develop an idea and give it material form after it has been conceived.)

Sixth: The majority of all thoughts conceived in the minds of men are not ACCURATE, being more in the nature of "opinions" or "snap-judgments."

When Alexander the Great sighed because he had no more worlds (as he believed) that could be conquered he was in a frame of mind similar to that of the present-day

> *When a man really finds himself, at the top of the Ladder of Success, he is never alone, because no man can climb to genuine success without taking others along with him.*

"Alexanders" of science, industry, invention, etc., whose "accurate thoughts" have conquered the air and the sea, explored practically every square mile of the little earth on which we live, and wrested from Nature thousands of "secrets" which, a few generations ago, would have been set down as "miracles" of the most astounding and imponderable sort.

In all this discovery and mastery of mere physical substances is it not strange, indeed, that we have practically neglected and overlooked the most marvelous of all powers, the human mind!

All scientific men who have made a study of the human mind readily agree on this—that the surface has not yet been scratched in the study of the wonderful power which lies dormant in the mind of man, waiting, as the oak tree sleeps in the acorn, to be aroused and put to work. Those who have expressed themselves on the subject are of the opinion that the next great cycle of discovery lies in the realm of the human mind.

The possible nature of these discoveries has been suggested, in many different ways, in practically every lesson of this course, particularly in this and the following lessons of the course.

If these suggestions appear to lead the student of this philosophy into deeper water than he or she is accustomed to, bear in mind the fact that the student has the privilege of stopping at any depth desired, until ready, through thought and study, to go further.

The author of this course has found it necessary to take the lead, and to keep far enough ahead, as it were, to induce the student to go at least a few paces ahead of the normal average range of human thought. It is not expected that any beginner will, at first, try to assimilate and put into use all that has been included in this philosophy. But, if the net result of the course is nothing more than to sow the seed of constructive thought in the mind of the student the author's work will have been completed. Time, plus the student's own desire for knowledge, will do the rest.

This is an appropriate place to state frankly that many of the suggestions passed on through this course would, if literally followed, lead the student far beyond the necessary bounds and present needs of what is ordinarily called business philosophy. Stated differently, this course goes more deeply into the functioning processes of the human mind than is necessary as far as the use of this philosophy as a means of achieving business or financial success is concerned.

418

However, it is presumed that many students of this course will wish to go more deeply into the study of mind power than may be required for purely material achievement, and the author has had in mind these students throughout the labor of organizing and writing this course.

Summary of Principles Involved in Accurate Thinking

We have discovered that the body of man is not singular, but plural—that it consists of billions on top of billions of living, intelligent, individual cells which carry on a very definite, well organized work of building, developing and maintaining the human body.

We have discovered that these cells are directed, in their respective duties, by the subconscious or automatic action of the mind; that the subconscious section of the mind can be, to a very large extent, controlled and directed by the conscious or voluntary section of the mind.

We have found that any idea or thought which is held in the mind, through repetition, has a tendency to direct the physical body to transform such thought or idea into its material equivalent. We have found that any order that is PROPERLY given to the sub-conscious section of the mind (through the law of Auto-suggestion) will be carried out unless it is side-tracked or countermanded by another and stronger order. We have found that the sub-conscious mind does not question the source from which it receives orders, nor the soundness of those orders, but it will proceed to direct the muscular system of the body to carry out any order it receives.

This explains the necessity for guarding closely the environment from which we receive suggestions, and by which we are subtly and quietly influenced at times and in ways of which we do not take cognizance through the conscious mind.

We have found that every movement of the human body is controlled by either the conscious or the sub-conscious section of the mind; that not a muscle can be moved until an order has been sent out by one or the other of these two sections of the mind, for the movement.

When this principle is thoroughly understood we understand, also, the powerful effect of any idea or thought which we create through the faculty of IMAGINATION and hold in the conscious mind until the sub-conscious section of the mind has time to take over that thought and begin the work of transforming it into its material counterpart. When we understand the principle through which any idea is first placed in the conscious mind, and held there until the sub-conscious section of the mind picks it up and appropriates it, we have a practical working knowledge of the Law of Concentration, covered by the next lesson (and, it might be added, we have also a thorough understanding of the reason why the Law of Concentration is necessarily a part of this philosophy).

When we understand this working relationship between the imagination, the conscious mind and the sub-conscious section of the mind, we can see that the very first step in the achievement of any *definite chief aim* is to create a definite picture of that which is desired. This picture is then placed in the conscious mind, through the Law of Concentration, and held there (through the formulas described in the next lesson) until the sub-conscious section of the mind picks it up and translates it into its ultimate and desired form.

Surely this principle has been made clear. It has been stated and restated, over and over, not only for the purpose of thoroughly describing it, but, of greater importance, to IMPRESS UPON THE MIND OF THE STUDENT THE PART IT PLAYS IN ALL HUMAN ACHIEVEMENT.

The Value of Adopting a Chief Aim

This lesson on Accurate Thought not only describes the real purpose of a *definite chief aim,* but it explains in simple terms the principles through which such an aim or purpose may be realized. We first create the objective toward which we are striving, through the imaginative faculty of the mind, then transfer an outline of this objective to paper by writing out a definite statement of it in the nature of a *definite chief aim.* By daily reference to this written statement the idea or thing aimed for is taken up by the conscious mind and handed over to the sub-conscious mind, which, in turn, directs the energies of the body to transform the desire into material form.

Desire

Strong, deeply rooted desire is the starting point of all achievement. Just as the electron is the last unit of matter discernible to the scientist, DESIRE is the seed of all achievement; the starting place, back of which there is nothing, or at least there is nothing of which we have any knowledge.

A *definite chief aim,* which is only another name for DESIRE, would be meaningless unless based upon a deeply seated, strong desire for the object of the *chief aim.* Many people "wish" for many things, but a wish is not the equivalent of a strong DESIRE, and therefore wishes are of little or no value unless they are crystallized into the more definite form of DESIRE.

It is believed by men who have devoted years of research to the subject, that all energy and matter throughout the universe respond to and are controlled by the Law of Attraction which causes elements and forces of a similar nature to gather around certain centers of attraction. It is through the operation of this same universal Law of Attraction that constant, deeply seated, strong DESIRE attracts the physical equivalent or counterpart of the thing desired, or the means of securing it.

Wm. Wrigley, Jr., has amassed a tremendous fortune by concentrating all his efforts on the manufacture and distribution of the "best" package of chewing gum, proving, once more, that the seed of success lies wrapped up in the little things of life.

We have learned, then, if this hypothesis is correct, that all cycles of human achievement work somewhat after this fashion: First, we picture in our conscious minds, through a *definite chief aim* (based upon a strong desire), some objective; we then focus our conscious mind upon this objective, by constant thought of it and belief in its attainment, until the sub-conscious section of the mind takes up the picture or outline of this objective and impels us to take the necessary physical action to transform that picture into reality.

Suggestion and Auto-Suggestion

Through this and other lessons of the Law of Success course the student has learned that sense impressions arising out of one's environment, or from statements or actions of other people, are called suggestions, while sense impressions that we place in our own minds are placed there by self-suggestion, or Auto-suggestion.

All suggestions coming from others, or from environment, influence us only after we have accepted them and passed them on to the sub-conscious mind, through the principle of Auto-suggestion, thus it is seen that suggestion becomes, and must become, Auto-suggestion before it influences the mind of the one receiving it.

Stated in another way, no one may influence another without the consent of the one influenced, as the influencing is done through one's own power of Auto-suggestion.

The conscious mind stands, during the hours when one is awake, as a sentinel, guarding the sub-conscious mind and warding off all suggestions which try to reach it from the outside, until those suggestions have been examined by the conscious mind, passed upon and accepted. This is Nature's way of safe-guarding the human being against intruders who would otherwise take control of any mind desired at will.

It is a wise arrangement.

The Value of Auto-suggestion in Accomplishing the Object of Your Definite Chief Aim

One of the greatest uses to which one may direct the power of Auto-suggestion is that of making it help accomplish the object of one's *definite chief aim* in life.

The procedure through which this may be accomplished is very simple. While the exact formula has been stated in Lesson One, and referred to in many other lessons of the course, the principle upon which it is based will be here, again, described, viz.:

Write out a clear, concise statement of that which you intend to accomplish, as your *definite chief aim,* covering a period of, let us say, the next five years. Make at least two copies of your statement, one to be placed where you can read it several times a day, while you are at work, and the other to be placed in the room where you sleep, where it can be read several times each evening before you go to sleep and just after you arise in the morning.

The suggestive influence of this procedure (impractical though it may seem) will soon impress the object of your *definite chief aim* on your sub-conscious mind and, as if by a stroke of magic, you will begin to observe events taking place which will lead you nearer and nearer the attainment of that object.

From the very day that you reach a definite decision in your own mind as to the precise thing, condition or position in life that you deeply desire, you will observe, if you read books, newspapers and magazines, that important news items and other data bearing on the object of your *definite chief aim* will begin to come to your attention; you will observe, also, that opportunities will begin to come to you that will, if embraced, lead you nearer and nearer the coveted goal of your desire. No one knows better than the author of this course how impossible and impractical this may seem to the person who is not informed on the subject of mind operation; however, this is not an age favorable to the doubter or the skeptic, and the best thing for any person to do is to experiment with this principle until its practicality has been established.

To the present generation it may seem that there are no more worlds to conquer in the field of mechanical invention, but every thinker (even those who are not accurate thinkers) will concede that we are just entering a new era of evolution, experiment and analysis as far as the powers of the human mind are concerned.

The word "impossible" means less now than ever before in the history of the human race. There are some who have actually removed this word from their vocabularies, believing that man can do anything he can imagine and BELIEVE HE CAN DO!

We have learned, for sure, that the universe is made up of two substances: matter and energy. Through patient scientific research we have discovered what we believe to be good evidence that everything that is or ever has been in the way of matter, when analyzed to the finest point, can be traced back to the electron, which is nothing but a form of energy. On the other hand, every material thing that man has created began in the form of energy, through the seed of an idea that was released through the imaginative faculty of the human mind. In other words, the beginning of every material thing is energy and the ending of it is energy.

All matter obeys the command of one form or another of energy. The highest known form of energy is that which functions as the human mind. The human mind, therefore, is the sole directing force of everything man creates, and what he may create with this force in the future, as compared with that which he has created with it in the past, will make his past achievements seem petty and small.

We do not have to wait for future discoveries in connection with the powers of the human mind for evidence that the mind is the greatest force known to mankind. We know, now, that any idea, aim or purpose that is fixed in the mind and held there with a will to achieve or attain its physical or material equivalent, puts into motion powers that cannot be conquered.

Buxton said: "The longer I live the more certain I am that the great difference between men, between the feeble and the powerful, the great and the insignificant, is energy—invincible determination—a purpose once fixed, and then death or victory. That quality will do anything that can be done in this world—and no talents, no circumstances, no opportunities will make a two-legged creature a man without it."

Donald G. Mitchell has well said: "Resolve is what makes a man manifest. Not puny resolve; not crude determinations; not errant purposes—but that strong and indefatigable will which treads down difficulties and danger, as a boy treads down the heaving frostlands of winter, which kindles his eye and brain with proud pulse-beat toward the unattainable. WILL MAKES MEN GIANTS!"

The great Disraeli said: "I have brought myself, by long meditation, to the conviction that a human being with a settled purpose must accomplish it, and that nothing can resist a will which will stake even existence upon its fulfillment."

The most successful physicians are those who mix hope and faith with the medicines they prescribe.

Sir John Simpson said: "A passionate DESIRE and an unwearied will can perform impossibilities, or what may seem to be such to the cold, timid and feeble."

And John Foster adds his testimony when he says: "It is wonderful how even the casualties of life seem to bow to a spirit that will not bow to them, and yield to subserve a design which they may, in their first apparent tendency, threaten to frustrate. When a firm, decisive spirit is recognized, it is curious to see how the space clears around a man and leaves him room and freedom."

Abraham Lincoln said of General Grant: "The great thing about Grant is his cool persistency of purpose. He is not easily excited, and he has got the grip of a bull-dog. When he once gets his teeth in, nothing can shake him off."

It seems appropriate to state here that a strong desire, to be transformed into reality, must be backed with persistency until it is taken over by the sub-conscious mind. It is not enough to feel very deeply the desire for achievement of a *definite chief aim,* for a few hours or a few days, and then forget all about that desire. The desire must be placed in the mind and held there, with PERSISTENCE THAT KNOWS NO DEFEAT, until the automatic or sub-conscious mind takes it over. Up to this point you must stand back of the desire and push it; beyond this point the desire will stand back of you and push you on to achievement.

Persistence may be compared to the dropping of water which finally wears away the hardest stone. When the final chapter of your life shall have been completed it will be found that your persistence, or lack of this sterling quality, played an important part in either your success or your failure.

This author watched the Tunney-Dempsey fight, in Chicago. He also studied the psychology leading up to and surrounding their previous bout. Two things helped Tunney defeat Dempsey, on both occasions, despite the fact that Dempsey is the stronger of the two men, and, as many believe, the better fighter.

And these two things, which spelled Dempsey's doom, were, first, his own lack of self-confidence—the fear that Tunney might defeat him; and, second, Tunney's complete self-reliance and his belief that he would whip Dempsey.

Tunney stepped into the ring, with his chin in the air, an atmosphere of self-assurance and certainty written in his every movement. Dempsey walked in, with a sort of uncertain stride, eying Tunney in a manner that plainly queried, "I wonder what you'll do to me?"

Dempsey was whipped, in his own mind, before he entered the ring. Press agents and propagandists had done the trick, thanks to the superior thinking ability of his opponent, Tunney.

And so the story goes, from the lowest and most brutal of occupations, prize-fighting, on up to the highest and most commendable professions. Success is won by the man who understands how to use his power of thought.

Throughout this course much stress has been laid upon the importance of environment and habit out of which grow the stimuli that put the "wheels" of the human mind into operation. Fortunate is the person who has found how to arouse or stimulate his or her mind so that the powers of that mind will function constructively, as they may be made to do when placed back of any strong, deeply seated desire.

Accurate thinking is thinking that makes intelligent use of all the powers of the human mind, and does not stop with the mere examination, classification and arranging of ideas. Accurate thought creates ideas and it may be made to transform these ideas into their most profitable, constructive form.

The student will perhaps be better prepared to analyze, without a feeling of skepticism and doubt, the principles laid down in this lesson if the fact is kept in mind that the conclusions and hypotheses here enumerated are not solely those of the author. I have had the benefit of close co-operation from some of the leading investigators in the field of mental phenomena, and conclusions reached, as stated in this entire course, are those of many different minds.

In the lesson on Concentration, you will be further instructed in the method of applying the principle of Auto-suggestion. In fact, throughout the course, the principle of gradual unfoldment has been followed, paralleling that of the principle of evolution as nearly as possible. The first lesson laid the foundation for the second, and the second prepared the way for the third, and so on. I have tried to build this course just as Nature builds a man—by a series of steps each of which lifts the student just another step higher and nearer the apex of the pyramid which the course, as a whole, represents.

The purpose in building this course in the manner outlined is one that cannot be described in words, but that purpose will become obvious and clear to you as soon as you shall have mastered the course, for its mastery will open to you a source of knowledge which cannot be imparted by one man to another, but is attainable *only by educing, drawing out and expanding, from within* one's own mind. The reason this knowledge cannot be imparted by one to another is the same as that which makes it impossible for one person to describe colors to a blind person who has never seen colors.

The knowledge of which I write became obvious to me only after I had diligently and faithfully followed the instructions which I have laid down in this course for your guidance and enlightenment; therefore, I speak from experience when I say that there are no illustrations, similes or words with which to describe this knowledge adequately. It can only be imparted from *within*.

With this vague "hint" as to the reward which awaits all who earnestly and intelligently search for the hidden passageway to knowledge to which I refer, we will now discuss that phase of *accurate thought* which will take you as high as you can go—except through the discovery and use of the secret passage-way to which I have alluded.

Thoughts are things!

It is the belief of many that every completed thought starts an unending vibration with which the one who releases it will have to contend at a later time; that man, himself, is but the physical reflection of *thought* that was put into motion by *infinite intelligence.*

"And the Word was made flesh, and dwelt among us, (and we beheld his glory, the glory as of the only begotten of the Father,) full of grace and truth." (St. John i, 13.)

The only hope held out to mankind in the entire Bible is of a reward which may be attained in no way except by *constructive thought.* This is a startling statement, but if you are even an elementary student and interpreter of the Bible you understand that it is a true statement.

If the Bible is plain on any one point above all others, it is on the fact that *thought* is the beginning of all things of a material nature.

At the beginning of every lesson of this course you will observe this motto:

"You can do it if you BELIEVE you can!"

This sentence is based upon a great *truth* which is practically the major premise of the entire Bible teaching. Observe the emphasis which is placed upon the word *BELIEVE.* Back of this word "believe" lies the power with which you can vitalize and give life to the suggestions that you pass on to your sub-conscious mind, through the principle of Auto-suggestion, with the aid of the law of the Master Mind. Do not miss this point. You cannot afford to miss it, as it is the very beginning, the middle and the end of all the power you will ever have.

All thought is creative! However, not all thought is constructive or positive. If you think *thoughts* of misery and poverty and see no way to avoid these conditions, then your *thoughts* will create those very conditions and curse you with them. But reverse the order, and think *thoughts* of a positive, expectant nature and your *thoughts* will create those conditions.

Thought magnetizes your entire personality and *attracts to you* the outward, physical things that harmonize with the nature of your *thoughts*. This has been made

First acquire patience and perseverance, then make up your mind what else you want, and you will be almost sure to get it.

clear in practically every lesson preceding this one, yet it is repeated here, and will be repeated many times more in the lessons that follow. The reason for this constant repetition is that nearly all beginners in the study of mind operation overlook the importance of this fundamental and eternal *truth*.

When you plant a *definite chief aim* in your sub-conscious mind you must fertilize it with full *belief* that *infinite intelligence* will step in and mature that *purpose* into reality in exact accordance with the nature of the purpose. Anything short of such *belief* will bring you disappointment.

When you suggest a *definite chief aim* which embodies some definite desire, in your sub-conscious mind, you must accompany it with such *faith* and *belief* in the ultimate realization of that purpose that you can actually see yourself in possession of the object of the purpose. Conduct yourself in the exact manner in which you would if you were already in possession of the object of your definite purpose, from the moment you suggest it to your sub-conscious mind.

Do not question; do not wonder if the principles of Auto-suggestion will work; do not *doubt,* but *believe!*

Surely this point has been sufficiently emphasized to impress upon your mind its importance. *Positive belief* in the attainment of your *definite purpose* is the very germ with which you fertilize the "egg of your *thought*" and if you fail to give it this fertilization, you might as well expect an unfertilized hen-egg to produce a chicken as to expect the attainment of the object of your *definite chief aim.*

> You never can tell what a thought will do
>   In bringing you hate or love;
> For thoughts are things, and their airy wings
>   Are swifter than a carrier dove.
> They follow the law of the universe,—

Each thought creates its kind,
And they speed o'er the track to bring you back
Whatever went out from your mind.

Thoughts are things! This is a great *truth* which, when you understand it, will bring you as close to the door of that secret passage-way to knowledge, previously mentioned, as is possible for another person to bring you. When you grasp this fundamental *truth* you will soon find that door and open it.

The power to *think* as you wish to *think* is the only power over which you have absolute control.

Please read and study the foregoing sentence until you grasp its meaning. If it is within your power to control your *thoughts* the responsibility then rests upon you as to whether your *thoughts* will be of the positive or the negative type, which brings to mind one of the world's most famous poems:

Out of the night that covers me,
  Black as the pit from pole to pole,
I thank whatever gods may be
  For my unconquerable soul.

In the fell clutch of circumstance
  I have not winced or cried aloud.
Under the bludgeonings of chance
  My head is bloody, but unbowed.

Beyond this place of wrath and tears
  Looms but the horror of the shade,
And yet the menace of the years
  Finds, and shall find, me unafraid.

It matters not how strait the gate,
  How charged with punishments the scroll,
I am the master of my fate,
  I am the captain of my soul.

—HENLEY

Henley did not write this poem until after he had discovered the door to that secret passage-way which I have mentioned.

You are the "master of your fate" and the "captain of your soul," by reason of the fact that you *control your own thoughts,* and, with the aid of your *thoughts,* you may create whatever you desire.

As we approach the close of this lesson, let us pull aside the curtain that hangs over the gateway called *death* and take a look into the Great Beyond. Behold a world peopled with beings who function without the aid of physical bodies. Look closely and, whether for weal or for woe, observe that you look at a world peopled with beings of your own creation, which correspond exactly to the nature of your own *thoughts* as you expressed them before *death.* There they are, the children of your own heart and mind, patterned after the image of your own *thoughts.*

Those which were born of your hatred and envy and jealousy and selfishness and injustice toward your fellow men will not make very desirable neighbors, but you must live with them just the same, for they are your children and you cannot turn them out.

You will be unfortunate, indeed, if you find there no children which were born of love, and justice, and truth, and kindness toward others.

In the light of this allegorical suggestion, the subject of *accurate thought* takes on a new and a much more important aspect, doesn't it?

If there is a possibility that every *thought* you release during this life will step out, in the form of a living being, to greet you after *death,* then you need no further reason for guarding all your *thoughts* more carefully than you would guard the food that you feed your physical body.

I refer to this suggestion as "allegorical" for a reason that you will understand only after you shall have passed through the door of that secret passage-way to knowledge that I have heretofore mentioned.

To ask me how I know these things, before you pass through that door, would be as useless as it would be for a man who has never seen with his physical eyes to ask me what the color red looks like.

I am not urging you to accept this viewpoint. I am not even arguing its soundness. I am merely fulfilling my duty and discharging my responsibility by giving you the suggestion. You must carry it out to a point at which you can accept or reject it, in your own way, and of your own volition.

The term "accurate thought" as used in this lesson refers to *thought* which is of your own creation. Thought that comes to you from others, through either suggestion or direct statement, is not *accurate thought* within the meaning and purpose of this lesson, although it may be thought that is based upon *facts*.

I have now carried you to the apex of the pyramid of this lesson on *accurate thought*. I can take you no further. However, you have not gone the entire distance; you have but *started*. From here on you must be your own guide, but, if you have not wholly missed the great *truth* upon which the lesson is founded, you will not have difficulty in finding your own way.

Let me caution you, however, not to become discouraged if the fundamental *truth* of this lesson does not dawn upon you at first reading. It may require weeks or even months of meditation for you to comprehend fully this *truth,* but it is worth working for.

The principles laid down in the beginning of this lesson you can easily understand and accept, because they are of the most elementary nature. However, as you began to follow the chain of *thought* along toward the close of the lesson, you perhaps found yourself being carried into waters too deep for you to fathom.

Perhaps I can throw one final ray of light on the subject by reminding you that the sound of every voice, and of every note of music, and of every other nature that is being released at the time you are reading these lines is floating through the ether right where you are. To hear these sounds you need but the aid of a modern radio outfit. Without this equipment as a supplement to your own sense of hearing you are powerless to hear these sounds.

Had this same statement been made twenty years ago, you would have believed the one who made it to be insane or a fool. But you now accept the statement without question, because you know it is true.

Thought is a much higher and more perfectly organized form of energy than is mere sound; therefore, it is not beyond the bounds of reason to suppose that every *thought* now being released and every *thought* that has ever been released is also in the ether (or somewhere else) and may be interpreted by those who have the equipment with which to do it.

And, what sort of equipment is necessary? you ask.

That will be answered when you shall have passed through the door that leads to the secret passage-way to knowledge. It cannot be answered before. The passage-way can be reached only through the medium of *your own thoughts*. This is one reason why all the great philosophers of the past admonished man to know himself. "Know thyself" is and has been the cry of the ages. The life of Christ was one uninterrupted promise of hope and possibility based entirely upon the knowledge which all may discover who search within their own beings.

One of the unanswerable mysteries of God's work is the fact that this great discovery is always self-discovery. The *truth* for which man is eternally searching is wrapped up in his own being; therefore, it is fruitless to search far afield in the wilderness of life or in the hearts of other men to find it. To do so brings you no nearer that which you are seeking, but takes you further away from it.

> *Some men die too soon from over-eating, others die from strong drink, while still others just wither up and die because they have nothing else to do.*

And, it may be—who knows but *you?*—that even now, as you finish this lesson, you are nearer the door that leads to the secret passage-way to knowledge than you have ever been before.

With your mastery of this lesson will come a fuller understanding of the principle referred to in the Introduction as the "Master Mind." Surely you now understand the reason for friendly co-operative alliance between two or more people. This alliance "steps up" the minds of those who participate in it, and permits them to contact their thought-power with infinite intelligence.

With this statement the entire Introduction should have a new meaning for you. This lesson has familiarized you with the main reason why you should make use of the law of the Master Mind by showing you the height to which this law may be made to carry all who understand and use it.

By this time you should understand why a few men have risen to great heights of power and fortune, while others all around them remained in poverty and want. If you do not now understand the cause for this, you will by the time you master the remaining lessons of this course.

Do not become discouraged if complete understanding of these principles does not follow your first reading of this lesson. This is the one lesson of the entire course which cannot be fully assimilated by the beginner through one reading. It will give up its rich treasures of knowledge only through thought, reflection and meditation. For this reason you are instructed to read this lesson at least four times, at intervals of one week apart.

You are also instructed to read, again, the Introduction, that you may more accurately and definitely understand the law of the Master Mind and the relationship between this law and the subjects covered by this lesson on *accurate thought*.

The Master Mind is the principle through which you may become an accurate thinker!

Is not this statement both plain and significant?

DISCONTENTMENT

An After-the-Lesson Visit with the Author

The Great Success Lessons That Can Be Learned from Reverses

An all-wise Providence has arranged the affairs of mankind so that every person who comes into the age of reason must bear the cross of FAILURE in one form or another.

You see, in the picture at the top of this page, the heaviest and most cruel of all the crosses, POVERTY!

Hundreds of millions of people living on this earth today find it necessary to struggle under the burden of this cross in order to enjoy the three bare necessities of life, a place to sleep, something to eat and clothes to wear.

Carrying the cross of POVERTY is no joke!

But, it seems significant that the greatest and most successful men and women who ever lived found it necessary to carry this cross before they "arrived."

FAILURE is generally accepted as a curse. But few people ever understand that failure is a curse only when it is accepted as such. But few ever learn the truth that FAILURE is seldom permanent.

Go back over your own experiences for a few years and you will see that your failures generally turned out to be blessings in disguise. Failure teaches men lessons which they would never learn without it. Moreover, it teaches in a language that is universal. Among the great lessons taught by failure is that of HUMILITY.

No man may become great without feeling himself humble and insignificant when compared to the world about him and the stars above him and the harmony with which Nature does her work.

For every rich man's son who becomes a useful, constructive worker in behalf of humanity, there are ninety-nine others rendering useful service who come up through POVERTY and misery. This seems more than a coincidence!

Most people who believe themselves to be failures are not failures at all. Most conditions which people look upon as failure are nothing more than temporary defeat.

If you pity yourself and feel that you are a failure, think how much worse off you would be if you had to change places with others who have real cause for complaint.

In the city of Chicago lives a beautiful young woman. Her eyes are a light blue. Her complexion is extremely fair. She has a sweet charming voice. She is educated and cultured. Three days after graduating in one of the colleges of the East she discovered that she had negro blood in her veins.

The man to whom she was engaged refused to marry her. The negroes do not want her and the whites will not associate with her. During the remainder of her life she must bear the brand of permanent FAILURE.

Remember, this is PERMANENT failure!

As this essay is being written news comes of a beautiful girl baby who was born to an unwed girl and taken into an orphanage, there to be brought up mechanically, without ever knowing the influence of a mother's love. All through life this unfortunate child must bear the brunt of another's mistake which can never be corrected.

How fortunate are YOU, no matter what may be your imaginary failures, that you are not this child.

If you have a strong body and a sound mind you have much for which you ought to be thankful. Millions of people all about you have no such blessings.

Careful analysis of one hundred men and women whom the world has accepted as being "great" shows that they were compelled to undergo hardship and temporary defeat and failure such as YOU probably have never known and never will know.

Woodrow Wilson went to his grave altogether too soon, the victim of cruel slander and disappointment, believing, no doubt, that he was a FAILURE. TIME, the great miracle worker that rights all wrongs and turns failure into success, will place the name of Woodrow Wilson at the top of the page of the really great.

Few now living have the vision to see that out of Wilson's "FAILURE" will come, eventually, such a powerful demand for universal peace that war will be an impossibility.

Lincoln died without knowing that his "FAILURE" gave sound foundation to the greatest nation on this earth.

Columbus died, a prisoner in chains, without ever knowing that his "FAILURE" meant the discovery of the great nation which Lincoln and Wilson helped to preserve, with their "FAILURES."

Do not use the word FAILURE carelessly.

Remember, carrying a burdensome cross temporarily is not FAILURE. If you have the real seed of success within you, a little adversity and temporary defeat will only serve to nuture that seed and cause it to burst forth into maturity.

When Divine Intelligence wants a great man or woman to render some needed service in the world, the fortunate one is tested out through some form of FAILURE. If you are undergoing what you believe to be failure, have patience; you may be passing through your testing time.

No capable executive would select, as his lieutenants, those whom he had not tested for reliability, loyalty, perseverance and other essential qualities.

Responsibility, and all that goes with it in the way of remuneration, always gravitates to the person who will not accept temporary defeat as permanent failure.

"The test of a man is the fight he makes,
   The grit that he daily shows;
The way he stands on his feet and takes
   Fate's numerous bumps and blows,
A coward can smile when there's naught to fear,
   When nothing his progress bars;
But it takes a man to stand up and cheer
   While some other fellow stars.

"It isn't the victory, after all,
   But the fight that a brother makes;

The man who, driven against the wall,
  Still stands up erect and takes
The blows of fate with his head held high:
  Bleeding, and bruised, and pale,
Is the man who'll win in the by and by,
  For he isn't afraid to fail.

"It's the bumps you get, and the jolts you get,
  And the shocks that your courage stands,
The hours of sorrow and vain regret,
  The prize that escapes your hands,
That test your mettle and prove your worth;
  It isn't the blows you deal,
But the blows you take on the good old earth,
  That show if your stuff is real."

Failure often places one in a position where unusual effort must be forthcoming. Many a man has wrung victory from defeat, fighting with his back to the wall, where he could not retreat.

Caesar had long wished to conquer the British. He quietly sailed his soldier-laden ships to the British island, unloaded his troops and supplies, then gave the order to burn all the ships. Calling his soldiers about him he said: "Now it is win or perish. We have no choice."

They won! Men usually win when they make up their minds to do so.

Burn your bridges behind you and observe how well you work when you KNOW THAT YOU HAVE NO RETREAT.

A street car conductor got a leave of absence while he tried out a position in a great mercantile business. "If I do not succeed in holding my new position," he remarked to a friend, "I can always come back to the old job."

At the end of the month he was back, completely cured of all ambition to do anything except work on a street car. Had he resigned instead of asking for a leave of absence he might have made good in the new job.

The Thirteen Club movement, which is now spreading over the entire country, was born as the result of a shocking disappointment experienced by its founder. That shock was sufficient to open the mind to a broader and more comprehensive view of the needs of the age, and this discovery led to the creation of one of the most outstanding influences of this generation.

The Fifteen Laws of Success, upon which this course is based, grew out of twenty years of hardship and poverty and failure such as rarely come to one person in an entire lifetime.

Surely those of you who have followed this series of lessons from the beginning must have read between the lines and back of them a story of struggle which has meant self-discipline and self-discovery such as never would have been known without this hardship.

Study the roadway of life, in the picture at the beginning of this essay, and observe that everyone who travels that road carries a cross. Remember, as you take inventory of your own burdens, that Nature's richest gifts go to those who meet FAILURE without flinching or whining.

Nature's ways are not easily understood. If they were, no one could be tested for great responsibility, with FAILURE!

"When Nature wants to make a man,
And shake a man,
And wake a man;
When Nature wants to make a man
To do the Future's will;
When she tries with all her skill
And she yearns with all her soul
To create him large and whole . . .
With what cunning she prepares him!
How she goads and never spares him!
How she whets him, and she frets him,
And in poverty begets him. . . .
How she often disappoints
How she often anoints,
With what wisdom she will hide him,
Never minding what betide him
Though his genius sob with slighting
And his pride may not forget!

Bids him struggle harder yet.

Makes him lonely

So that only

God's high messages shall reach him,

So that she may surely teach him

What the Hierarchy planned.

Though he may not understand

Gives him passions to command.

How remorselessly she spurs him

With terrific ardor stirs him

When she poignantly prefers him!

Lo, the crisis! Lo, the shout

That must call the leader out.

When the people need salvation

Doth he come to lead the nation. . . .

Then doth Nature show her plan

When the world has found—A MAN!"

There is no FAILURE. That which looks to be failure is usually nothing but temporary defeat. Make sure that you do not accept it as PERMANENT!

There is a sure way to avoid criticism: be nothing and do nothing. Get a job as street sweeper and kill off ambition. The remedy never fails.

CONCENTRATION

"You Can Do It If You Believe You Can!"

This lesson occupies a key-stone position in this course, for the reason that the psychological law upon which it is based is of vital importance to every other lesson of the course.

Let us define the word *concentration,* as it is here used, as follows:

"Concentration is the act of focusing the mind upon a given desire until ways and means for its realization have been worked out and successfully put into operation."

Two important laws enter into the act of *concentrating* the mind on a given *desire*. One is the law of *Auto-suggestion* and the other is the law of *habit*. The former having been fully described in a previous lesson of this course, we will now briefly describe the law of *habit*.

Habit grows out of environment—out of doing the same thing in the same way over and over again—out of repetition—out of thinking the same thoughts over and over—and, when once formed, it resembles a cement block that has hardened in the mold—in that it is hard to break.

Habit is the basis of all memory training, a fact which you may easily demonstrate in remembering the name of a person whom you have just met, by repeating that name over and over until you have fixed it permanently and plainly in your mind.

"The force of education is so great that we may mold the minds and manners of the young into whatever shape we please and give the impressions of such *habits* as shall ever afterwards remain."—Atterbury.

Except on rare occasions when the mind rises above environment, the human mind draws the material out of which *thought* is created, from the surrounding environment, and *habit* crystallizes this thought into a permanent fixture and stores it away in the subconscious mind where it becomes a vital part of our personality which silently influences our actions, forms our prejudices and our biases, and controls our opinions.

A great philosopher had in mind the power of *habit* when he said: "We first endure, then pity, and finally embrace," in speaking of the manner in which honest men come to indulge in crime.

Habit may be likened to the grooves on a phonograph record, while the mind may be likened to the needle point that fits into that groove. When any habit has been well formed (by repetition of thought or action) the mind attaches itself to and follows that habit as closely as the phonograph needle follows the groove in the wax record, no matter what may be the nature of that habit.

We begin to see, therefore, the importance of selecting our environment with the greatest of care, because environment is the mental feeding ground out of which the food that goes into our minds is extracted.

Environment very largely supplies the food and materials out of which we create *thought,* and *habit* crystallizes these into permanency. You of course understand that "environment" is the sum total of sources through which you are influenced by and through the aid of the five senses of seeing, hearing, smelling, tasting and feeling.

"Habit is force which is generally recognized by the average thinking person, but which is commonly viewed in its adverse aspect to the exclusion of its favorable phase. It has been well said that all men are 'the creatures of habit,' and that 'habit is a cable; we weave a thread of it each day and it becomes so strong that we cannot break it.'

"If it be true that habit becomes a cruel tyrant, ruling and compelling men against their will, desire, and inclination—and this is true in many cases—the question naturally arises in the thinking mind whether this mighty force cannot be harnessed and controlled in the service of men, just as have other forces of Nature. If this result can be accomplished, then man may master habit and set it to work, instead of being a slave to it and serving it faithfully though complaining. And the modern psychologists tell us in no uncertain tones that habit may certainly be thus mastered, harnessed and set to work, instead of being allowed to dominate one's actions and character. And thousands of people have applied this new knowledge and have turned the force of habit into new channels, and have compelled it to work their machinery of action, instead of being allowed to run to waste, or else permitted to sweep away the structures that men have erected with care and expense, or to destroy fertile mental fields.

"A habit is a 'mental path' over which our actions have traveled for some time, each passing making the path a little deeper and a little wider. If you have to walk over a field or through a forest, you know how natural it is for you to choose the clearest path in preference to the less worn ones, and greatly in preference to stepping out across the field or through the woods and making a new path. And the line of mental action is precisely the same. It is movement along the lines of least resistance—passage over the well-worn path. Habits are created by repetition and are formed in accordance to a natural law, observable in all animate things and some would say in inanimate things as well. As an instance of the latter, it is pointed out that a piece of paper once folded in a certain way will fold along the same lines the next time. And all users of sewing machines, or other delicate pieces of machinery, know that as a machine or instrument is once 'broken in' so will it tend to run thereafter. The same law is also observable in the case of musical instruments. Clothing or gloves form into creases according to the person using them, and these creases once formed will always be in effect, notwithstanding repeated pressings. Rivers and streams of water cut their courses through the land, and thereafter flow along the habit-course. The law is in operation everywhere.

"These illustrations will help you to form the idea of the nature of habit, and will aid you in forming new mental paths—new mental creases. And—remember this always—the best (and one might say the only) way in which old habits may be removed is to form new habits to counteract and replace the undesirable ones. Form new mental paths over which to travel, and the old ones will soon become less distinct and in time will practically fill up from disuse. Every time you travel over the path of the desirable mental habit, you make the path deeper and wider, and make it so much easier to travel it thereafter. This mental path-making is a very important thing, and I cannot urge upon you too strongly the injunction to start to work making the desirable mental paths over which you wish to travel. Practice, practice, practice—be a good path-maker."

The following are the rules of procedure through which you may form the habits you desire:

First: At the beginning of the formation of a new habit put force and enthusiasm into your expression. Feel what you think. Remember that you are taking the first steps toward making the new mental path; that it is much harder at first than it will be afterwards. Make the path as clear and as deep as you can, at the beginning, so that you can readily see it the next time you wish to follow it.

> *It is a striking coincidence that "American" ends with "I can."*

Second: Keep your attention firmly *concentrated* on the new path-building, and keep your mind away from the old paths, lest you incline toward them. Forget all about the old paths, and concern yourself only with the new ones that you are building to order.

Third: Travel over your newly made paths as often as possible. Make opportunities for doing so, without waiting for them to arise through luck or chance. The oftener you go over the new paths the sooner will they become well worn and easily traveled. Create plans for passing over these new habit-paths, at the very start.

Fourth: Resist the temptation to travel over the older, easier paths that you have been using in the past. Every time you resist a temptation, the stronger do you become, and the easier will it be for you to do so the next time. But every time you yield to the temptation, the easier does it become to yield again, and the more difficult it becomes to resist the next time. You will have a fight on at the start, and this is the critical time. Prove your determination, persistency and will-power now, at the very beginning.

Fifth: Be sure that you have mapped out the right path, as your *definite chief aim,* and then go ahead without fear and without allowing yourself to doubt. "Place your hand upon the plow, and look not backward." Select your goal, then make good, deep, wide mental paths leading straight to it.

As you have already observed, there is a close relationship between *habit* and *Auto-suggestion* (self-suggestion). Through habit, an act repeatedly performed in the same manner has a tendency to become permanent, and eventually we come to perform the act automatically or unconsciously. In playing a piano, for example, the artist can play a familiar piece while his or her conscious mind is on some other subject.

Auto-suggestion is the tool with which we dig a mental path; Concentration is the hand that holds that tool; and Habit is the map or blueprint which the mental path follows. An idea or desire, to be transformed into terms of action or physical reality, must be held in the conscious mind *faithfully* and *persistently* until *habit* begins to give it permanent form.

Let us turn our attention, now, to *environment*.

As we have already seen, we absorb the material for thought from our surrounding environment. The term "environment" covers a very broad field. It consists of the books we read, the people with whom we associate, the community in which we live, the nature of the work in which we are engaged, the country or nation in which we reside, the clothes we wear, the songs we sing, and, most important of all, *the religious and intellectual training we receive prior to the age of fourteen years.*

The purpose of analyzing the subject of *environment* is to show its direct relationship to the personality we are developing, and the importance of so guarding it that its influence will give us the materials out of which we may attain our *definite chief aim* in life.

The mind feeds upon that which we supply it, or that which is forced upon it, through our *environment;* therefore, let us select our environment, as far as possible, with the object of supplying the mind with suitable material out of which to carry on its work of attaining our *definite chief aim.*

If *your* environment is not to your liking, change it!

The first step is to create in your own mind an exact, clear and well rounded out picture of the environment in which you believe you could best attain your *definite chief aim,* and then *concentrate* your mind upon this picture until you transform it into reality.

In Lesson One, of this course, you learned that the first step you must take, in the accomplishment of any *desire,* is to create in your mind a clear, well defined picture of that which you intend to accomplish. This is the first principle to be observed in your plans for the achievement of *success,* and if you fail or neglect to observe it, you cannot succeed, except by chance.

Your daily associates constitute one of the most important and influential parts of your environment, and may work for your progress or your retrogression, according to the nature of those associates. As far as possible, you should select as your most *intimate* daily associates those who are in sympathy with your aims and ideals—especially those represented by your *definite chief aim*—and whose mental attitude inspires you with enthusiasm, self-confidence, determination and ambition.

Remember that every word spoken within your hearing, every sight that reaches your eyes, and every sense impression that you receive through any of the five senses, influences your thought as surely as the sun rises in the east and sets in the west. This being true, can you not see the importance of controlling, as far as possible, the environment in which you live and work? Can you not see the importance of reading books that deal with subjects which are directly related to your *definite chief aim?* Can you not see the importance of talking with people who are in sympathy with your aims, and, who will encourage you and spur you on toward their attainment?

We are living in what we call a "twentieth century civilization." The leading scientists of the world are agreed that Nature has been millions of years in creating, through the process of evolution, our present civilized environment.

How many hundreds of centuries the so-called Indians had lived upon the North American continent, without any appreciable advance toward modern civilization, as we understand it, we have no way of ascertaining. Their environment was the wilderness, and they made no attempt whatsoever to change or improve that environment; the change took place only after new races from afar came over and *forced upon them the environment of progressive civilization in which we are living today.*

Observe what has happened within the short period of *three centuries*. Hunting grounds have been transformed into great cities, and the Indian has taken on education and culture, in many instances, that equal the accomplishment of his white brothers. (In Lesson Fourteen, we discuss the effects of environment from a worldwide viewpoint, and describe, in detail, the principle of *social heredity* which is the chief source through which the effects of environment may be imposed upon the minds of the young.)

The clothes you wear influence you; therefore, they constitute a part of your environment. Soiled or shabby clothes depress you and lower your self-confidence, while clean clothes, of an appropriate style, have just the opposite effect.

It is a well known fact that an observant person can accurately analyze a man by seeing his work-bench, desk or other place of employment. A well organized desk indicates a well organized brain. Show me the merchant's stock of goods and I will tell you whether he has an organized or disorganized brain, as there is a close relationship between one's mental attitude and one's physical environment.

The effects of environment so vitally influence those who work in factories, stores and offices, that employers are gradually realizing the importance of creating an environment that inspires and encourages the workers.

One unusually progressive laundryman, in the city of Chicago, has plainly outdone his competitors, by installing in his work-room a player-piano, in charge of a neatly dressed young woman who keeps it going during the working hours. His laundrywomen are dressed in white uniforms, and there is no evidence about the place that work is drudgery. Through the aid of this pleasant environment, this laundryman turns out more work, earns more profits, and pays better wages than his competitors can pay.

This brings us to an appropriate place at which to describe the method through which *you* may apply the principles directly and indirectly related to the subject of *concentration*.

Let us call this method the—

MAGIC KEY TO SUCCESS!

In presenting you with this "Magic Key" let me first explain that it is no invention or discovery of mine.

It is the same key that is used, in one form or another, by the followers of New Thought and all other sects which are founded upon the positive philosophy of optimism.

This Magic Key constitutes an irresistible power which all who will may use.

The person who receives no pay for his services except that which comes in the pay envelope is underpaid, no matter how much money that envelope may contain.

It will unlock the door to riches!

It will unlock the door to fame!

And, in many instances, it will unlock the door to physical health.

It will unlock the door to education and let you into the storehouse of all your latent ability. It will act as a pass-key to any position in life for which you are fitted.

Through the aid of this Magic Key we have unlocked the secret doors to all of the world's great inventions.

Through its magic powers all of our great geniuses of the past have been developed.

Suppose you are a laborer, in a menial position, and desire a better place in life. The Magic Key will help you attain it! Through its use Carnegie, Rockefeller, Hill, Harriman, Morgan and scores of others of their type have accumulated vast fortunes of material wealth.

It will unlock prison doors and turn human derelicts into useful, trustworthy human beings. It will turn failure into success and misery into happiness.

You ask—"What is this Magic Key?"

And I answer with one word—*concentration!*

Now let me define *concentration* in the sense that it is here used. First, I wish it to be clearly understood that I have no reference to occultism, although I will admit that all the scientists of the world have failed to explain the strange phenomena produced through the aid of *concentration.*

Concentration, in the sense in which it is here used, means the ability, through fixed habit and practice, to keep your mind on one subject until you have thoroughly familiarized yourself with that subject and mastered it. It means the ability to *control your attention and focus it on a given problem until you have solved it.*

It means the ability to throw off the effects of habits which you wish to discard, and the power to build new habits that are more to your liking. It means complete *self-mastery.*

Stating it in another way, *concentration* is the ability to *think* as you wish to think; the ability to control your thoughts and direct them to a *definite* end; and the ability to organize your knowledge into a plan of action that is sound and workable.

You can readily see that in *concentrating* your mind upon your *definite chief aim* in life, you must cover many closely related subjects which blend into each other and complete the main subject upon which you are concentrating.

Ambition and *desire* are the chief factors which enter into the act of successful *concentration*. Without these factors the Magic Key is useless, and the main reason why so few people make use of this key is that most people lack *ambition,* and *desire nothing in particular.*

Desire whatever you may, and if your desire is within reason and if it is strong enough the Magic Key of *concentration* will help you attain it. There are learned men of science who would have us believe that the wonderful power of prayer operates through the principle of *concentration* on the attainment of a *deeply seated desire.*

Nothing was ever created by a human being which was not first created in the imagination, through *desire,* and then transformed into reality through *concentration.*

Now, let us put the Magic Key to a test, through the aid of a definite formula.

First, you must put your foot on the neck of skepticism and doubt! No unbeliever ever enjoyed the benefits of this Magic Key. You must believe in the test that you are about to make.

We will assume that you have thought something about becoming a successful writer, or a powerful public speaker, or a successful business executive, or an able financier. We will take public speaking as the subject of this test, but remember that you must follow instructions to the letter.

Take a plain sheet of paper, ordinary letter size, and write on it the following:

I am going to become a powerful public speaker because this will enable me to render the world useful service that is needed—and because it will yield me a financial return that will provide me with the necessary material things of life.

I will concentrate my mind upon this desire for ten minutes daily, just before retiring at night and just after arising in the morning, for the purpose of determining just how I shall proceed to transform it into reality.

I know that I can become a powerful and magnetic speaker, therefore I will permit nothing to interfere with my doing so.

Signed ....

Sign this pledge, then proceed to do as you have pledged your word that you would do. Keep it up until the desired results have been realized.

Now, when you come to do your *concentrating,* this is the way to go about it: Look ahead one, three, five or even ten years, and see yourself as the most powerful speaker of your time. See, in your imagination, an appropriate income. See yourself in your own home that you have purchased with the proceeds from your efforts as a speaker or lecturer. See yourself in possession of a nice bank account as a reserve for old age. See yourself as a person of influence, due to your great ability as a public speaker. See yourself engaged in a life-calling in which you will not fear the loss of your position.

Paint this picture clearly, through the powers of your imagination, and lo! it will soon become transformed into a beautiful picture of deeply seated *desire.* Use this *desire* as the chief object of your *concentration* and observe what happens.

You now have the secret of the Magic Key!

Do not underestimate the power of the Magic Key because it did not come to you clothed in mysticism, or because it is described in language which all who will may understand. All great truths are simple in final analysis, and easily understood; if they are not they are not *great* truths.

Use this Magic Key with intelligence, and only for the attainment of worthy ends, and it will bring you enduring happiness and success. Forget the mistakes you have made and the failures you have experienced. Quit living in the past, for do you not know that your yesterdays never return? Start all over again, if your previous efforts have not turned out well, and make the next five or ten years tell a story of success that will satisfy your most lofty ambitions.

Make a name for yourself and render the world a great service, through *ambition, desire* and *concentrated effort!*

You can do it if you BELIEVE you can!

Thus endeth the Magic Key.

The presence of any idea or thought in your consciousness tends to produce an "associated" feeling and to urge you to appropriate or corresponding action. Hold a deeply seated *desire* in your consciousness, through the principle of *concentration,* and if you do it with full faith in its realization your act attracts to your aid powers which the entire scientific world has failed to understand or explain with a reasonable hypothesis.

You have a tremendous advantage over the person who slanders you or does you a wilful injustice; you have it within your power to FORGIVE that person.

When you become familiar with the powers of *concentration* you will then understand the reason for choosing a *definite chief aim* as the first step in the attainment of enduring success.

Concentrate your mind upon the attainment of the object of a deeply seated *desire* and very soon you will become a lode-stone that attracts, through the aid of forces which no man can explain, the necessary material counterparts of that *desire,* a statement of fact which paves the way for the description of a principle which constitutes the most important part of this lesson, if not, in fact, the most important part of the entire course, viz.:

When two or more people ally themselves, in a spirit of perfect harmony, for the purpose of attaining a definite end, if that alliance is faithfully observed by all of whom it is composed, the alliance brings, to each of those of whom it is composed, power that is super-human and seemingly irresistible in nature.

Back of the foregoing statement is a law, the nature of which science has not yet determined, and it is this law that I have had in mind in connection with my repeated statements concerning the power of *organized effort* which you will notice throughout this course.

In chemistry we learn that two or more elements may be so compounded that the result is something entirely different in nature, from any of the individual elements. For example, ordinary water, known in chemistry under the formula of H_2O, is a compound consisting of two atoms of hydrogen and one atom of oxygen, *but water is neither hydrogen nor oxygen.* This "marrying" of elements creates *an entirely different substance from that of either of its component parts.*

The same law through which this transformation of physical elements takes place may be responsible for the seemingly superhuman powers resulting from the alliance of two or more people, *in a perfect state of harmony and understanding,* for the attainment of a given end.

This world, and all matter of which the other planets consist, is made up of electrons (an electron being the smallest known analyzable unit of matter, and resembling, in nature, what we call electricity, or a form of energy). On the other hand, *thought,* and that which we call the "mind," is also a form of energy; in fact it is the highest form of energy known. Thought, in other words, is *organized energy,* and it is not improbable that *thought* is exactly the same sort of energy as that which we generate with an electric dynamo, although of a much more highly *organized* form.

Now, if all matter, in final analysis, consists of groups of electrons, which are nothing more than a form of energy which we call electricity, and if the mind is nothing but a form of highly organized electricity, do you not see how it is possible that the laws which affect matter may also govern the mind?

And if combining two or more elements of matter, in the proper proportion and under the right conditions, will produce something entirely different from those original elements (as in the case of H_2O), do you not see how it is possible so to combine the energy of two or more minds that the result will be a sort of composite mind that is totally different from the individual minds of which it consists?

You have undoubtedly noticed the manner in which you are influenced while in the presence of other people. Some people inspire you with optimism and enthusiasm. Their very presence seems to stimulate your own mind to greater action, and, this not only "seems" to be true, but it *is true*. You have noticed that the presence of others had a tendency to lower your vitality and depress you; a tendency which I can assure you was very *real!*

What, do you imagine, could be the cause of these changes that come over us when we come within a certain range of other people, unless it is the change resulting from the blending or combining of their minds with our own, through the operation of a law that is not very well understood, but resembles (if, in fact, it is not the same law) the law through which the combining of two atoms of hydrogen and one atom of oxygen produces water.

I have no scientific basis for this hypothesis, but I have given it many years of serious thought and always I come to the conclusion that it is at least a sound hypothesis, although I have no possible way, as yet, of reducing it to a provable hypothesis.

You need no proof, however, that the presence of some people inspires you, while the presence of others depresses you, as you know this to be a fact. Now it stands to reason that the person who inspires you and arouses your mind to a state of greater activity gives you more power to achieve, while the person whose presence depresses you and lowers your vitality, or causes you to *dissipate* it in useless, disorganized thought, has just the opposite effect on you. You can understand this much without the aid of a hypothesis and without further proof than that which you have experienced time after time.

Come back, now, to the original statement that:

"When two or more people ally themselves, *in a spirit of perfect harmony,* for the purpose of attaining a definite end, if that alliance is *faithfully observed by all of whom it is composed,* the alliance brings, to each of those of whom it is composed, power that is superhuman and seemingly irresistible in nature."

Study, closely, the emphasized part of the foregoing statement, for there you will find the "mental formula" which, if not faithfully observed, destroys the effect of the whole.

One atom of hydrogen combined with one atom of oxygen will not produce water, nor will an alliance in name only, that is not accompanied by *"a spirit of perfect harmony"* (between those forming the alliance), produce *"power that is superhuman and seemingly irresistible in nature."*

I have in mind a family of mountain-folk who, for more than six generations, have lived in the mountainous section of Kentucky. Generation after generation of this family came and went without any noticeable improvement of a mental nature, each generation following in the footsteps of its ancestors. They made their living from the soil, and as far as they knew, or cared, the universe consisted of a little spot of territory known as Letcher County. They married strictly in their own "set," and in their own community.

Finally, one of the members of this family strayed away from the flock, so to speak, and married a well educated and highly cultured woman from the neighbor-state of Virginia. This woman was one of those types of ambitious people who had learned that the universe extended beyond the border line of Letcher County, and covered, at least, the whole of the southern states. She had heard of chemistry, and of botany, and of biology, and of pathology, and of psychology, and of many other subjects that were of importance in the field of education. When her children began to come along to the age of understanding, she talked to them of these subjects; and they, in turn, began to show a keen interest in them.

One of her children is now the president of a great educational institution, where most of these subjects, and many others of equal importance, are taught. Another one of them is a prominent lawyer, while still another is a successful physician.

Her husband (thanks to the influence of her mind) is a well known dental surgeon, and the first of his family, for six generations, to break away from the traditions by which the family had been bound.

The blending of her mind with his *gave him the needed stimulus to spur him on and inspired him with ambition such as he would never have known without her influence.*

For many years I have been studying the biographies of those whom the world calls *great,* and it seems to me more than a mere coincidence that in every instance where the facts were available the person who was really responsible for the *greatness* was in the background, behind the scenes, and seldom heard of by the hero-worshiping public. Not infrequently is this "hidden power" a patient little wife who has inspired her husband and urged him on to great achievement, as was true in the case I have just described.

Henry Ford is one of the modern miracles of this age, and I doubt that this country, or any other, ever produced an industrial genius of his equal. If the *facts* were known (and perhaps they are known) they might trace the cause of Mr. Ford's phenomenal achievements to a woman of whom the public hears but little— *his wife!*

> *Defeat, like a headache, warns us that something has gone wrong. If we are intelligent we look for the cause and profit by the experience.*

We read of Ford's achievements and of his enormous income and imagine him to be blessed with matchless ability; and he is—ability of which the world would never have heard had it not been for the modifying influence of his wife, who has co-operated with him, during all the years of his struggle, *"in a spirit of perfect harmony, for the purpose of attaining a definite end."*

I have in mind another genius who is well known to the entire civilized world, Thomas A. Edison. His inventions are so well known that they need not be named. Every time you press a button and turn on an electric light, or hear a phonograph playing, you should think of Edison, for it was he who perfected both the incandescent light and the modern phonograph. Every time you see a moving picture you should think of Edison, for it was his genius, more than that of any other person, who made this great enterprise possible.

But, as in the case of Henry Ford, back of Mr. Edison stands one of the most remarkable women in America—his wife! No one outside of the Edison family, and perhaps a very few intimate personal friends of theirs, knows to what extent her influence has made Edison's achievements possible. Mrs. Edison once told me that Mr. Edison's outstanding quality, the one which, above all others, was his greatest asset, was that of—

Concentration!

When Mr. Edison starts a line of experiment or research or investigation, he never "lets go" until he either finds that for which he is looking or exhausts every possible effort to do so.

Back of Mr. Edison stand two great powers; one is *concentration* and the other is Mrs. Edison!

Night after night Mr. Edison has worked with such *enthusiasm* that he required but three or four hours of sleep. (Observe what was said about the sustaining effects of *enthusiasm* in Lesson Six of this course.)

Plant a tiny apple seed in the right sort of soil, at the right time of the year, and gradually it will burst forth into a tiny sprig, and then it will expand and grow into an apple tree. That tree does not come from the soil, nor does it come from the elements of the air, but *from both of these sources,* and the man has not yet lived who could explain the law that attracts from the air and the soil the combination of cells of which that apple tree consists.

The tree does not come out of the tiny apple seed, but, *that seed is the beginning of the tree.*

When two or more people ally themselves, *"in a spirit of perfect harmony, for the purpose of attaining a definite end,"* the *end,* itself, or the *desire* back of that end, may be likened to the apple seed, and the blending of the forces of energy of the two or more minds may be likened to the air and the soil out of which come the elements that form the material objects of that *desire.*

The *power* back of the attraction and combination of these forces of the mind can no more be explained than can the power back of the combination of elements out of which an apple tree "grows."

But the all-important thing is that an apple tree will "grow" from a seed thus properly planted, and great *achievement* will follow the systematic blending of two or more minds with a definite object in view.

In Lesson Twelve you will see this principle of allied effort carried to proportions which almost stagger the imagination of all who have not trained themselves to think in terms of *organized thought!*

This course, itself, is a very concrete illustration of the principle underlying that which we have termed *organized effort,* but you will observe that it requires the entire fifteen lessons to complete the description of this principle. Omit a single one of the fifteen lessons and the omission would affect the whole as the removal of one link would affect the whole of a chain.

As I have already stated in many different ways, and for the purpose of emphasis, I now repeat: there is a well founded hypothesis that when one concentrates one's mind upon a given subject, facts of a nature that is closely related to that subject will "pour" in from every conceivable source. The theory is that a deeply seated *desire,* when once planted in the right sort of "mental soil," serves as a center of attraction or magnet that attracts to it everything that harmonizes with the nature of the *desire.*

Dr. Elmer Gates, of Washington, D. C., is perhaps one of the most competent psychologists in the world. He is recognized both in the field of psychology and in other directly and indirectly related fields of science, throughout the world, as being a man of the highest scientific standing.

Come with me, for a moment, and study his methods!

After Dr. Gates has followed a line of investigation as far as possible through the usual channels of research, and has availed himself of all the recorded facts at his command, on a given subject, he then takes a pencil and a tablet and "sits" for further information, by *concentrating his mind on that subject until thoughts related to it begin to FLOW IN UPON HIM.* He writes down these thoughts, as they come (from he knows not where). He told me that many of his most important discoveries came through this method. It was more than twenty years ago that I first talked with Dr. Gates on this subject. Since that time, through the discovery of the radio principle, we have been provided with a reasonable hypothesis through which to explain the results of these "sittings," viz.:

The ether, as we have discovered through the modern radio apparatus, is in a constant state of agitation. Sound waves are floating through the ether at all times, but these waves cannot be detected, beyond a short distance from their source, except by the aid of properly attuned instruments.

Now, it seems reasonable to suppose that *thought,* being the most highly organized form of energy known, is constantly sending waves through the ether, but these waves, like those of sound, can only be detected and correctly interpreted by a properly attuned mind.

There is no doubt that when Dr. Gates sat down in a room and placed himself in a quiet, passive state of mind, the dominating *thoughts* in his mind served as a magnetic force that attracted the related or similar *thought waves* of others as they passed through the ether about him.

Taking the hypothesis just a step further, it has occurred to me many times since the discovery of the modern radio principle, that *every thought that has ever been released in organized form, from the mind of any human being, is still in existence in the form of a wave in the ether, and is constantly passing around and around in a great endless circle;* that the act of *concentrating* one's mind upon a given subject with intensity sends out *thought waves* which reach and blend with those of a related or similar nature, thereby establishing a direct line of communication between the one doing the *concentrating* and the thoughts of a similar nature which have been previously set into motion.

Going still a step further, may it not be possible for one so to attune his mind and harmonize the rate of vibration of *thought* with the rate of vibration of the ether that all knowledge that has been accumulated through the *organized thoughts* of the past is available?

With these hypotheses in mind, go back to Lesson One, of this course, and study Carnegie's description of the "master mind" through which he accumulated his great fortune.

When Carnegie formed an alliance between more than a score of carefully selected minds, he created, by that means of compounding mind power, one of the strongest industrial forces that the world has ever witnessed. With a few notable (and very disastrous)

Is it not strange that the word "Boomerang" has been in the dictionary all these years without its having become generally known that a "Boomerang" is an instrument which comes back and may wound the hand that throws it?

exceptions, the men constituting the "master mind" which Carnegie created thought and *acted as one!*

And, that "master mind" (composed of many individual minds) was *concentrated* upon a single purpose, the nature of which is familiar to everyone who knew Mr. Carnegie; *particularly those who were competing with him in the steel business.*

If you have followed Henry Ford's record, even slightly, you undoubtedly have observed that *concentrated effort* has been one of the outstanding features of his career. Nearly thirty years ago he adopted a policy of standardization as to the general type of automobile that he would build, and he consistently maintained that policy until the change in public demand forced him, in 1927, to change it.

A few years ago, I met the former chief engineer of the Ford plant, and he told me of an incident that happened during the early stages of Mr. Ford's automobile experience which very clearly points to *concentrated effort* as being one of his prominent fundamentals of economic philosophy.

On this occasion the engineers of the Ford plant had gathered in the engineering office for the purpose of discussing a proposed change in the design of the rear axle construction of the Ford automobile. Mr. Ford stood around and listened to the discussion until each man had had his "say," then he walked over to the table, tapped the drawing of the proposed axle with his finger, and said:

"Now listen! the axle we are using does the work for which it was intended, and does it well, and there's going to be no more change in that axle!"

He turned and walked away, and from that day until this the rear axle construction of the Ford automobile has remained substantially the same. It is not improbable that Mr. Ford's success in building and marketing automobiles has been due, very largely, to his policy of consistently *concentrating* his efforts back of one plan, with but one *definite purpose* in mind at a time.

A few years ago I read Edward Bok's book, *The Man from Maine*, which is the biography of his father-in-law, Mr. Cyrus H. K. Curtis, the owner of the *Saturday Evening Post*, the *Ladies' Home Journal*, and several other publications. All through the book I noticed that the outstanding feature of Mr. Curtis' philosophy was that of *concentration* of effort back of a *definite purpose.*

During the early days of his ownership of the *Saturday Evening Post,* when he was pouring money into a losing venture by the hundreds of thousands of dollars, it required *concentrated effort* that was backed by courage such as but few men possess, to enable him to "carry on."

Read *The Man from Maine.* It is a splendid lesson on the subject of *concentration,* and supports, to the smallest detail, the fundamentals upon which this lesson is based.

The *Saturday Evening Post* is now one of the most profitable magazines in the world, but its name would have been long since forgotten had not Mr. Curtis *concentrated* his attention and his fortune on the one *definite purpose* of making it a great magazine.

We have seen what an important part *environment* and *habit* play in connection with the subject of *concentration.* We shall now discuss, briefly, a third subject which is no less related to the subject of *concentration* than are the other two, namely, *memory.*

The principles through which an accurate, unfaltering memory may be trained are few, and comparatively simple; viz.:

1. *Retention:* The receiving of a sense impression through one or more of the five senses, and the recording of this impression, in orderly fashion, in the mind. This process may be likened to the recording of a picture on the sensitized plate of a camera or kodak.

2. *Recall:* The reviving or recalling into the conscious mind of those sense impressions which have been recorded in the sub-conscious mind. This process may be compared to the act of going through a card index and pulling out a card on which information had been previously recorded.

3. *Recognition:* The ability to recognize a sense impression when it is called into the conscious mind, and to identify it as being a duplicate of the original impression, and to associate it with the original source from which it came when it was first recorded. This process enables us to distinguish between "memory" and "imagination."

These are the three principles that enter into the act of remembering. Now let us make application of these principles and determine how to use them effectively, which may be done as follows:

First: When you wish to be sure of your ability to recall a sense impression, such as a name, date or place, be sure to make the impression vivid by *concentrating your attention upon it* to the finest detail. An effective way to do this is to repeat, several times, that which you wish to remember. Just as a photographer must give an "exposure" proper time to record itself on the sensitized plate of the camera, so must we give the sub-conscious mind time to record properly and clearly any sense impression that we wish to be able to recall with readiness.

Second: Associate that which you wish to remember with some other object, name, place or date with which you are quite familiar, and which you can easily recall when you wish, as, for example, the name of your home town, your close friend, the date of your birth, etc., for your mind will then file away the sense impression that you wish to be able to recall, with the one that you can easily recall, so that when bringing forth one into the conscious mind it brings, also, the other one with it.

Third: Repeat that which you wish to remember, a number of times, at the same time *concentrating* your mind upon it, just as you would fix your mind on a certain hour at which you wished to arise in the morning, which, as you know, insures your awakening at that precise hour. The common failing of not being able to remember the names of other people, which most of us have, is due entirely to the fact that we do not properly record the name in the first place. When you are introduced to a person whose name you wish to be able to recall at will, repeat that name four or five times, first making sure that you understood the name correctly. If the name is similar to that of some person whom you know well, associate the two names together, thinking of both as you repeat the name of the one whose name you wish to be able to recall.

If someone gives you a letter to be mailed, look at the letter, then increase its size, in your imagination, and see it hanging over a letter-box. Fix in your mind a letter approximately the size of a door, and associate it with a letter box, and you will observe that the first letter box you pass on the street will cause you to recall that big, odd-looking letter, which you have in your pocket.

Suppose that you were introduced to a lady whose name was Elizabeth Shearer, and you wished to be able to recall her name at will. As you repeat her name associate with it a large pair of scissors, say ten feet in length, and Queen Elizabeth, and you will observe that the recalling of either the large pair of scissors or the name of Queen Elizabeth will help you recall, also, the name of Elizabeth Shearer.

If you wish to be able to remember the name of Lloyd Keith, just repeat the name several times and associate with it the name of Lloyd George and Keith's Theater, either of which you can easily recall at will.

The *law of association* is the most important feature of a well trained memory, yet it is a very simple law. All you have to do to make use of it is to record the name of that which you wish to remember with the name of that which you *can readily* remember, and the recalling of one brings with it the other.

Nearly ten years ago a friend gave me his residence telephone number, in Milwaukee, Wisconsin, and although I did not write it down I remember it today as well as I did the day he gave it to me. This is the way that I recorded it:

The number and exchange were Lakeview 2651.

At the time he gave me the number we were standing at the railroad station, in sight of Lake Michigan; therefore, I used the lake as an associated object with which to file the name of the telephone exchange. It so happened that the telephone number was made up of the age of my brother, who was 26, and my father, who was 51, therefore I associated their names with the number, thus insuring its recall. To recall the telephone exchange and number, therefore, I had only to think of Lake Michigan, my brother and my father.

An acquaintance of mine found himself to be suffering from what is ordinarily called a "wandering mind." He was becoming "absent-minded" and unable to remember. Let him tell you, in his own words which follow, how he overcame this handicap:

"I am fifty years old. For a decade I have been a department manager in a large factory. At first my duties were easy, then the firm had a rapid expansion of business which gave me added responsibilities. Several of the young men in my department developed unusual energy and ability—at least one of them had his eye on my job.

Do you see that "lucky" fellow over there who holds a "soft" position through "pull"? Let me whisper a secret in your ear—Fate is standing in wait for him just around the corner, with a a stuffed club, and it is not stuffed with cotton.

"I had reached the age in life when a man likes to be comfortable and, having been with the company a long time, I felt that I could safely settle back into an easy berth. The effect of this mental attitude was well nigh disastrous to my position.

"About two years ago I noticed that my power of *concentration* was weakening and my duties were becoming irksome. I neglected my correspondence until I looked with dread upon the formidable pile of letters; reports accumulated and subordinates were inconvenienced by the delay. I sat at my desk with my mind wandering elsewhere.

"Other circumstances showed plainly that my mind was not on my work; I forgot to attend an important meeting of the officers of the company. One of the clerks under me caught a bad mistake made in an estimate on a carload of goods, and, of course, saw to it that the manager learned of the incident.

"I was thoroughly alarmed at the situation! and asked for a week's vacation to think things over. I was determined to resign, or find the trouble and remedy it. A few days of earnest introspection at an out-of-the-way mountain resort convinced me that I was suffering from a plain case of mind wandering. I was lacking in *concentration;* my physical and mental activities at the desk had become desultory. I was careless and shiftless and neglectful—all because my mind was not *alertly* on the job. When I had diagnosed my case with satisfaction to myself I next sought the remedy. I needed a complete new set of *working habits,* and I made a resolve to acquire them.

"With paper and pencil I outlined a schedule to cover the working day: first, the morning mail; then, the orders to be filled; dictation; conference with subordinates and miscellaneous duties; ending with a clean desk before I left.

"'*How is habit formed?*' I asked myself mentally. 'By repetition,' came back the answer. 'But I have been doing these things over and over thousands of times,' the other fellow in me protested. 'True, but not in orderly *concentrated* fashion,' replied the echo.

"I returned to the office with mind in leash, but restless, and placed my new working schedule in force at once. I performed the same duties with the same zest and as nearly as possible at the same time every day. When my mind started to slip away I quickly brought it back.

"From a mental stimulus, created by will-power, I progressed in *habit building.* Day after day, I practiced *concentration* of thought. When I found *repetition* becoming comfortable, then I knew that I had won."

Your ability to train your memory, or to develop any desired habit, is a matter, solely, of being able to *fix your attention on a given subject until the outline of that subject has been thoroughly impressed upon the "sensitized plate" of your mind.*

Concentration, itself, is nothing but a matter of control of the *attention!*

You will observe that by reading a line of print with which you are not familiar, and which you have never seen before, and then closing your eyes, you can see that line as plainly as though you were looking at it on the printed page. In reality, you are "looking at it," not on the printed page, but on the sensitized plate of your own mind. If you try this experiment and it does not work the first time it is because you did not *concentrate your attention* on the line closely enough! Repeat the performance a few times and finally you will succeed.

If you wish to memorize poetry, for example, you can do so very quickly by training yourself to fix your *attention* on the lines so closely that you can shut your eyes and see them in your mind as plainly as you see them on the printed page.

So important is this subject of *control of attention* that I feel impelled to emphasize it in such a way that you will not pass it by lightly. I have reserved reference to this important subject until the last, as a climax to this lesson, for the reason that I consider it, by far, the most important part of the lesson.

The astounding results experienced by those who make a practice of "crystal-gazing" are due, entirely, to their ability to *fix attention* upon a given subject for an unbroken period far beyond the ordinary.

Crystal-gazing is nothing but *concentrated attention!*

I have already hinted at that which I will now state as my belief, namely, that it is possible, through the aid of *concentrated attention,* for one so to attune one's mind to the vibration of the ether that all the secrets in the world of unfathomed and uncharted mental phenomena may become as open books which may be read at will.

What a thought this is to ponder over!

I am of the opinion, and not without substantial evidence to support me, that it is possible for one to develop the ability of *fixing the attention* so highly that one may "tune in" and understand that which is in the mind of any person. But this is not all, nor is it the most important part of a hypothesis at which I have arrived after many years of careful research, for I am satisfied that one may just as easily go a step further and "tune in" on the *universal mind* in which all knowledge is stored where it may be appropriated by all who master the art of coming after it.

To a highly orthodox mind these statements may seem very irrational; but, to the student (and, so far, there are but few people in the world who are more than mere students, of an elementary grade, of this subject) who has studied this subject with any appreciable degree of understanding, these hypotheses seem not only possible, but *absolutely probable.*

But put the hypothesis to a test of your own!

You can select no better subject upon which to try an experiment than that which you have selected as your *definite chief aim* in life.

Memorize your *definite chief aim* so you can repeat it without looking at the written page, then make a practice of *fixing your attention on it at least twice a day,* proceeding as follows:

Go into some quiet place where you will not be disturbed; sit down and completely relax your mind and your body; then close your eyes and place your fingers in your ears, thereby excluding the ordinary sound waves and all of the light waves. In that position repeat your *definite chief aim* in life, and as you do so see yourself, in your imagination, in full possession of the object of that aim. If a part of your aim is the accumulation of money, as it undoubtedly is, then see yourself in possession of that money. If a part of the object of your *definite aim* is the ownership of a home, then see a picture of that home, in your imagination, just as you expect to see it in reality. If a part of your *definite aim* is to become a powerful and influential public speaker, then see yourself before an enormous audience, and *feel* yourself playing upon the emotions of that audience as a great violinist would play upon the strings of the violin.

As you approach the end of this lesson, there are two things which you might do, viz.:

First: You might begin, now, to cultivate the ability to *fix attention,* at will, on a given subject, with a feeling that this ability, when fully developed, would bring you the object of your *definite chief aim* in life; or,

Second: You might tilt your nose in the air and with the smile of a cynic say to yourself— "Bosh" and thereby mark yourself a *fool!*

Take your choice!

This lesson was not written as an argument, nor as the subject of a debate. It is your privilege to accept it, in whole or in part, or reject it, just as you please.

But at this place I wish to state, however, that this is not an age of cynicism or doubt. An age that has conquered the air above us and the sea beneath us, that has enabled us to harness the air and turn it into a messenger that will carry the sound of our voice half-way around the earth in the fractional part of a second, certainly is not an age that lends encouragement to the *"doubting Thomases"* or the *"I-don't-believe-it Joneses."*

> *Fish don't bite just for the*
> *wishin',*
> *   Keep a-pullin'!*
> *Change your bait and keep on*
> *fishin';*
> *   Keep a-pullin'!*
> *Luck ain't nailed, to any spot;*
> *Men you envy, like as not,*
> *Envy you your job and lot!*
> *   Keep a-pullin'!*

The human family has passed through the "Stone Age" and the "Iron Age" and the "Steel Age," and unless I have greatly misinterpreted the trend of the times it is now entering the "Mind Power Age," which will eclipse, in stupendous achievement, all the other "ages" combined.

Learn to fix your attention on a given subject, at will, for whatever length of time you choose, and you will have learned the secret passage-way to power and plenty!

This is *concentration!*

You will understand, from this lesson, that the object of forming an alliance between two or more people, and thereby creating a "Master Mind," is to apply the Law of Concentration more effectively than it could be applied through the efforts of but one person.

The principle referred to as the "Master Mind" is nothing more nor less than group concentration of mind power upon the attainment of a definite object or end. Greater power comes through group mind concentration because of the "stepping up" process produced through the reaction of one mind upon another or others.

Persuasion vs. Force

Success, as has been stated in dozens of different ways throughout this course, is very largely a matter of tactful and harmonious negotiation with other people. Generally speaking, the man who understands how to "get people to do things" he wants done may succeed in any calling.

As a fitting climax for this lesson, on the Law of Concentration, we shall describe the principles through which men are influenced; through which cooperation is gained; through which antagonism is eliminated and friendliness developed.

Force sometimes gets what appear to be satisfactory results, but force, alone, never has built and never can build enduring success.

The world war has done more than anything which has happened in the history of the world to show us the futility of force as a means of influencing the human mind. Without going into details or recounting the instances which could be cited, we all know that force was the foundation upon which German philosophy has been built during the past forty years. The doctrine that *might* makes *right* was given a world-wide trial and it failed.

The human body can be imprisoned or controlled by physical force, but it is not so with the human mind. No man on earth can control the mind of a normal, healthy person if that person chooses to exercise his God-given right to control his own mind. The majority of people do not exercise this right. They go through the world, thanks to our faulty educational system, without having discovered the strength which lies dormant in their own minds. Now and then something happens, more in the nature of an accident than anything else, which awakens a person and causes him to discover where his real strength lies and how to use it in the development of industry or one of the professions. Result: a genius is born!

There is a given point at which the human mind stops rising or exploring unless something out of the daily routine happens to "push" it over this obstacle. In some minds this point is very low and in others it is very high. In still others it varies between low and high. The individual who discovers a way to stimulate his mind artificially, arouse it and cause it to go beyond this average stopping point frequently, is sure to be rewarded with fame and fortune if his efforts are of a constructive nature.

The educator who discovers a way to stimulate any mind and cause it to rise above this average stopping point without any bad reactionary effects, will confer a blessing on the human race second to none in the history of the world. We, of course, do not have reference to physical stimulants or narcotics. These will always arouse the mind for a time, but eventually they ruin it entirely. We have reference to a purely mental stimulant, such as that which comes through intense interest, desire, enthusiasm, love, etc., the factors out of which a "Master Mind" may be developed.

The person who makes this discovery will do much toward solving the crime problem. You can do almost anything with a person when you learn how to influence his mind. The mind may be likened to a great field. It is a very fertile field which always produces a crop after the kind of seed which is sown in it. The problem, then, is to learn how to select the right sort of seed and how to sow that seed so that it takes root and grows quickly. We are sowing seed in our minds daily, hourly, nay, every second, but we are doing it promiscuously and more or less unconsciously. We must learn to do it after a carefully prepared *plan,* according to a well laid out design! Haphazardly sown seed in the human mind brings back a haphazard crop! There is no escape from this result.

History is full of notable cases of men who have been transformed from law-abiding, peaceful, constructive citizens to roving, vicious criminals. We also have thousands of cases wherein men of the low, vicious, so-called criminal type have been transformed into constructive, law-abiding citizens. In every one of these cases the transformation of the human being took place in the mind of the man. He created in his own mind, for one reason or another, a picture of what he desired and then proceeded to transform that picture into reality. As a matter of fact, if a picture of any environment, condition or thing be pictured in the human mind and if the mind be focused or concentrated on that picture long enough and persistently enough, and backed up with a *strong desire* for the thing pictured, it is but a short step from the picture to the realization of it in physical or mental form.

The world war brought out many startling tendencies of the human mind which corroborate the work which the psychologist has carried on in his research into the workings of the mind. The following account of a rough, uncouth, unschooled, undisciplined young mountaineer is an excellent case in point:

FOUGHT FOR HIS RELIGION; NOW GREAT WAR HERO

Rotarians Plan to Present Farm to Alvin York,
Unlettered Tennessee Squirrel Hunter

By George W. Dixon

How Alvin Cullom York, an unlettered Tennessee squirrel hunter, became the foremost hero of the American Expeditionary Forces in France, forms a romantic chapter in the history of the world war.

York is a native of Fentress County. He was born and reared among the hardy mountaineers of the Tennessee woods. There is not even a railroad in Fentress County. During his earlier years he was reputed to be a desperate character. He was what was known as a gunman. He was a dead shot with a revolver, and his prowess with the rifle was known far and wide among the plain people of the Tennessee hills.

One day a religious organization pitched its tent in the community in which York and his parents lived. It was a strange sect that came to the mountains looking for converts, but the methods of the evangels of the new cult were full of fire and emotionalism. They denounced the sinner, the vile character and the man who took advantage of his neighbor. They pointed to the religion of the Master as an example that all should follow.

ALVIN GETS RELIGION

Alvin Cullom York startled his neighbors one night by flinging himself down at the mourners' bench. Old men stirred in their seats and women craned their necks, as York wrestled with his sins in the shadows of the Tennessee mountains.

York became an ardent apostle of the new religion. He became an exhorter, a leader in the religious life of the community and, although his marksmanship was as deadly as ever, no one feared him who walked in the path of righteousness.

When the news of the war reached that remote section of Tennessee and the mountaineers were told

There are twelve good reasons for Failure. The first one is the avowed intention of doing no more than one is paid to do, and the person who makes this avowal may see the other eleven by stepping before a looking-glass.

THE LAW OF SUCCESS

that they were going to be "conscripted," York grew sullen and disagreeable. He didn't believe in killing human beings, even in war. His Bible taught him, "Thou shalt not kill." To his mind this was literal and final. He was branded as a "conscientious objector."

The draft officers anticipated trouble. They knew that his mind was made up, and they would have to reach him in some manner other than by threats of punishment.

WAR IN A HOLY CAUSE

They went to York with a Bible and showed him that the war was in a holy cause—the cause of liberty and human freedom. They pointed out that men like himself were called upon by the Higher Powers to make the world free; to protect innocent women and children from violation; to make life worth living for the poor and oppressed; to overcome the "beast" pictured in the Scriptures, and to make the world free for the development of Christian ideals and Christian manhood and womanhood. It was a fight between the hosts of righteousness and the hordes of Satan. The devil was trying to conquer the world through his chosen agents, the Kaiser and his generals.

York's eyes blazed with a fierce light. His big hands closed like a vise. His strong jaws snapped. "The Kaiser," he hissed between his teeth, "the beast! the destroyer of women and children! I'll show him where he belongs if I ever get within gunshot of him!"

He caressed his rifle, kissed his mother good-by and told her he would see her again when the Kaiser had been put out of business.

He went to the training camp and drilled with scrupulous care and strict obedience to orders.

His skill at target practice attracted attention. His comrades were puzzled at his high scores. They had not reckoned that a backwoods squirrel hunter would make fine material for a sniper in the front-line trenches.

York's part in the war is now history. General Pershing has designated him as the foremost individual hero of the war. He won every decoration, including the Congressional Medal, the Croix de Guerre, the Legion of Honor. He faced the Germans without fear of death. He was fighting to vindicate his religion, for the sanctity of the home; the love of women and children; the preservation of the ideals of Christianity and the liberties of the poor and oppressed. Fear was not in his code or his vocabulary. His cool daring electrified more than a million men and set the world to talking about this strange, unlettered hero from the hills of Tennessee.

Here we have a case of a young mountaineer who, had he been approached from just a slightly different angle, undoubtedly would have resisted conscription and, likely as not, would have become so embittered toward his country that he would have become an outlaw, looking for an opportunity to strike back at the first chance.

Those who approached him knew something of the principles through which the human mind works. They knew how to manage young York by first overcoming the resistance that he had worked up in his own mind. This is the very point at which thousands of men, through improper understanding of these principles, are arbitrarily classed as criminals and treated as dangerous, vicious people. Through suggestion these people could have been handled as effectively as young York was handled, and developed into useful, productive human beings.

In your search for ways and means of understanding and manipulating your own mind so you can persuade it to create that which you desire in life, let us remind you that, without a single exception, anything which irritates you and arouses you to anger, hatred, dislike, or cynicism, is destructive and very bad for you.

You can never get the maximum or even a fair average of constructive action out of your mind until you have learned to control it and keep it from becoming stimulated through anger or fear!

These two negatives, anger and fear, are positively destructive to your mind, and as long as you allow them to remain you can be sure of results which are unsatisfactory and away below what you are capable of producing.

In our discussion of environment and habit we learned that the individual mind is amenable to the suggestions of environment; that the minds of the individuals of a crowd blend with one another conforming to the suggestion of the prevailing influence of the leader or dominating figure. Mr. J. A. Fisk gives us an interesting account of the influence of mental suggestion in the revival meeting, which bears out the statement that the crowd mind blends into one, as follows:

Mental Suggestion in the Revival

Modern psychology has firmly established the fact that the greater part of the phenomena of the religious "revival" are *psychical* rather than spiritual in their nature, and *abnormally psychical* at that. The leading authorities recognize the fact that the mental excitement attendant upon the emotional appeals of the "revivalist" must be classified with the phenomena of hypnotic suggestion rather than with that of true religious experience. And those who have made a close study of the subject believe that instead of such excitement tending to elevate the mind and exalt the spirit of the individual, it serves to weaken and degrade the mind and prostitute the spirit by dragging it in the mud of abnormal psychic frenzy and emotional excess. In fact, by some careful observers, familiar with the respective phenomena, the religious "revival" meeting is classed with the public hypnotic "entertainment" as a typical example of psychic intoxication and hysterical excess.

David Starr Jordan, chancellor emeritus of Leland Stanford University, says: "Whisky, cocaine and alcohol bring temporary insanity, and so does a revival of religion." The late Professor William James, of Harvard University, the eminent psychologist, says: "Religious revivalism is more dangerous to the life of society than drunkenness."

It should be unnecessary to state that in this lesson the term "revival" is used in the narrower signification indicating the typical religious emotional excitement known by the term in question, and is not intended to apply to the older and respected religious experience designated by the same term, which was so highly revered among the Puritans, Lutherans and others in the past. A standard reference work speaks of the general subject of the "revival" as follows:

"Revivals occur in all religions. When one takes place a large number of persons who have been comparatively dead or indifferent to spiritual considerations simultaneously or in quick succession become alive to their importance, alter spiritually and morally, and act with exceeding zeal in converting others to their views. A Mohammedan revival takes the form of a return to the strict doctrines of the Koran, and a desire to propagate them by the sword. A Christian minority living in the place is in danger of being massacred by the revivalists. Pentecostal effusion of the Holy Spirit produced a revival within the infant church, followed by numerous conversions from outside. Revivals, though not called by that name, occurred at intervals from apostolic times till the Reformation, the revivalists being sometimes so unsympathetically treated that they left the church and formed sects, while, in other cases, and notably in those of the founders of the monastic orders, they were retained and acted on the church as a whole. The spiritual impulse which led to the Reformation, and the antagonistic one which produced or attended the rise of the Society of Jesus, were both revivalist. It is, however, to sudden increase of spiritual activity within the Protestant churches that the term 'revival' is chiefly confined. The enterprise of the Wesleys and Whitefield in this country and England from 1738 onward was thoroughly revivalist. . . . Since then, various revivals have from time to time occurred, and nearly all denominations aim at their production. The means adopted are prayer for the Holy Spirit, meetings continued night after night, often to a late hour, stirring addresses, chiefly from revivalist lay-men, and after-meetings to deal with those impressed. Ultimately it has been found that some of those appar-ently converted have been steadfast, others have fallen back, while deadness proportioned to the previous excitement temporarily prevails. Sometimes excitable persons at revival meetings utter piercing cries, or even fall prostrate.

Nothing is so contagious as enthusiasm. It is the real alle-gory of the tale of Orpheus. It moves stones, it charms brutes. Enthusiasm is the genius of sincerity and truth accomplishes no victories without it.

—BULWER

"These morbid manifestations are now discouraged, and have in consequence become more rare."

In order to understand the principle of the operation of mental suggestion in the revival meeting, we must first understand something of what is known as *the psychology of the crowd*. Psychologists are aware that the psychology of a crowd, considered as a whole, differs materially from that of the separate individuals composing that crowd. There is a crowd of separate individuals, and a composite crowd in which the emo-tional natures of the units seem to blend and fuse. The change from the first-named crowd to the second arises from the influence of earnest attention, or deep emotional appeals or com-mon interest. When this change occurs the crowd becomes a composite individual, the degree of whose intelligence and emotional control is but little above that of its weakest member. This fact, startling as it may appear to the average reader, is well known and is admitted by the leading psychologists of the day; and many important essays and books have been written thereupon. The predominant characteristics of this "composite-mindedness" of a crowd are the evidences of extreme suggestibility, response to appeals of emotion, vivid imagination, and action arising from imitation—all of which are mental traits universally manifested by primitive man. In short, the crowd manifests *atavism,* or reversion to early racial traits.

Diall, in his Psychology of the Aggregate Mind of an Audience, holds that the mind of an assemblage listening to a powerful speaker undergoes a curious process called "fusion," by which the individuals in the audience, losing their personal traits for the time being, to a greater or less degree, *are reduced, as it were, to a single individual, whose characteristics are those of an impulsive youth of twenty, imbued in general with high ideals, but lacking in reasoning power and will.* Tarde, the French psychologist, advances similar views.

Professor Joseph Jastrow, in his Fact and Fable in Psychology, says:

"In the production of this state of mind a factor as yet unmentioned plays a leading rôle, the power of mental contagion. Error, like truth, flourishes in crowds. At the heart of sympathy each finds a home. . . . No form of contagion is so insidious in its outset, so difficult to check in its advance, so certain to leave germs that may at any moment reveal their pernicious power, as a mental contagion—the contagion of fear, of panic, of fanaticism, of lawlessness, of superstition, of error. . . . In brief, we must add to the many factors which contribute to deception, the recognized lowering of critical ability, of the power of accurate observation, indeed, of rationality, which merely being one of a crowd induces. The conjurer finds it easy to perform to a large audience, because, among other reasons, it is easier to arouse their admiration and sympathy, easier to make them forget themselves and enter into the uncritical spirit of wonderland. It would seem that in some respects the critical tone of an assembly, like the strength of a chain, is that of its weakest member."

Professor Le Bon, in his *The Crowd,* says:

"The sentiments and ideas of all the persons in the gathering take one and the same direction, and their conscious personality vanishes. A collective mind is formed, doubtless transitory, by presenting very clearly marked characteristics. The gathering has become what, in the absence of a better expression, I will call an organized crowd, or, if the term be considered preferable, a psychological crowd. It forms a single being, and is subjected to the law of the mental unity of crowds. . . . The most striking peculiarity presented by a psychological crowd is the following: Whoever be the individuals that compose it, however like or unlike be their mode of life, their occupation, their character, or their intelligence, the fact that they have been transformed into a crowd puts them in possession of a sort of collective mind which makes them feel, think and act in a manner quite different from that in which each individual of them would feel, think and act were he in a state of isolation. There are certain ideas and feelings which do not come into being, or do not transform themselves into acts, except in the case of the individuals forming a crowd. . . . In crowds it is stupidity and not mother wit that is accumulated. In the collective mind the intellectual aptitudes of the individuals, and in consequence their individuality, is weakened. . . . The most careful observations seem to prove that an individual immerged for some length of time in a crowd in action soon finds himself in a special state, which most resembles the state of fascination in which the hypnotized individual finds himself. . . . The conscious personality has entirely vanished, will and discernment are lost. All feelings and thoughts are bent in the direction determined by the hypnotizer. . . . Under the influence of a suggestion he will undertake the accomplishment of certain acts with irresistible impetuosity. This impetuosity is the more irresistible in the case of crowds, from the fact that, the suggestion being the same for all the individuals of the crowd, it gains in strength by reciprocity. Moreover, by the mere fact that he forms part of an organized crowd, a man descends several rungs in the ladder of civilization. Isolated, he may be a cultured individual; in a crowd, he is a barbarian—that is, a creature acting by instinct. He possesses the spontaneity, the violence, the ferocity, and also the enthusiasm and heroism of primitive beings, whom he further tends to resemble by the facility with which he allows himself to be induced to commit acts contrary to his most obvious interests and his best known habits. An individual in a crowd is a grain of sand amid other grains of sand, which the wind stirs up at will."

Professor Davenport, in his Primitive Traits in Religious Revivals, says:

"The mind of the crowd is strangely like that of primitive man. Most of the people in it may be far from primitive in emotion, in thought, in character; nevertheless, the result tends always to be the same. Stimulation immediately begets action. Reason is in abeyance. The cool, rational speaker has little chance beside the skillful emotional orator. The crowd thinks in images, and speech must take this form to be accessible to it. The images are not connected by any natural bond, and they take each other's place like the slides of a magic lantern. It follows from this, of course, that appeals to the imagination have paramount influence. . . . The crowd is united and governed by emotion rather than by reason. Emotion is the natural bond, for men differ much less in this respect than in intellect. It is also true that in a crowd of a thousand men the amount of emotion actually generated and existing is far greater than the sum which might conceivably be obtained by adding together the emotions of the individuals taken by themselves. The explanation of this is that the attention of the crowd is always directed either by the circumstances of the occasion or by the speaker to certain common ideas—as 'salvation' in religious gatherings . . . and every individual in the gathering is stirred with emotion, not only because the idea or the shibboleth stirs him, but also because he is conscious that every other individual in the gathering believes in the idea or the shibboleth, and is stirred by it, too. And this enormously increases the volume of his own emotion and consequently the total volume of emotion in the crowd. As in the case of the primitive mind, imagination has unlocked the floodgates of emotion, which on occasion may become wild enthusiasm or demoniac frenzy."

The student of suggestion will see that not only are the emotional members of a revival audience subject to the effect of the "composite-mindedness" arising from the "psychology of the crowd" and are thereby weakened in resistive power, but that they are also brought under the influence of two other very potent forms of mental suggestion. Added to the powerful suggestion of authority exercised by the revivalist, which is exerted to its fullest

Some men are successful as long as someone else stands back of them and encourages them, and some men are successful in spite of Hell! Take your choice.

along lines very similar to that of the professional hypnotist, is the suggestion of imitation exerted upon each individual by the combined force of the balance of the crowd.

As Durkheim observed in his psychological investigations, the average individual is "intimidated by the mass" of the crowd around him, or before him, and experiences that peculiar psychological influence exerted by the mere number of people as against his individual self. Not only does the suggestible person find it easy to respond to the authoritative suggestions of the preacher and the exhortations of his helpers, but he is also brought under the direct fire of the imitative suggestions of those on all sides who are experiencing emotional activities and who are manifesting them outwardly. Not only does the voice of the shepherd urge forward, but the tinkle of the bellwether's bell is also heard, and the imitative tendency of the flock, which causes one sheep to jump because one ahead of him does so (and so on until the last sheep has jumped), needs but the force of the example of a leader to start into motion the entire flock. This is not an exaggeration—human beings, in times of panic, fright, or deep emotion of any kind, manifest the imitative tendency of the sheep, and the tendency of cattle and horses to "stampede" under imitation.

To the student experienced in the experimental work of the psychological laboratory there is the very closest analogy observed in the respective phenomena of the revival and hypnotic suggestion. In both cases the attention and interest is attracted by the unusual procedure; the element of mystery and awe is induced by words and actions calculated to inspire them; the senses are tired by monotonous talk in an impressive and authoritative tone; and finally the suggestions are projected in a commanding, *suggestive* manner familiar to all students of hypnotic suggestion. The subjects in both cases are prepared for the final suggestions and commands, by previously given minor suggestions, such as: "Stand up," or "Look this way," etc., in the case of the hypnotist; and by: "All those who think so-and-so, stand up," and "All who are willing to become better, stand up," etc., in the case of the revivalist. The impressionable subjects *are thus accustomed to obedience to suggestion by easy stages.* And, finally, the commanding suggestion: "Come right up—*right up—this way—right up—come,* I say, come, *come,* COME!" etc., which takes the impressed ones right off their feet and rushes them to the front, are almost precisely the same in the hypnotic experiment or séance, on the one hand, and the sensational revival, on the other. Every good revivalist would make a good hypnotic operator, and every good hypnotic operator would make a good revivalist if his mind were turned in that direction.

In the revival, the person giving the suggestions has the advantage of breaking down the resistance of his audience by arousing their sentiments and emotions. Tales depicting the influence of mother, home and heaven; songs like "Tell Mother, I'll Be There"; and personal appeals to the revered associations of one's past and early life tend to reduce one to the state of emotional response, and render him most susceptible to strong, repeated suggestions along the same line. Young people and hysterical women are especially susceptible to this form of emotional suggestion. Their feelings are stirred, and the will is influenced by the preaching, the songs, and the personal appeals of the co-workers of the revivalist.

The most sacred sentimental memories are reawakened for the moment and old conditions of mind are reinduced. "Where Is My Wandering Boy Tonight?" brings forth tears to many a one to whom the memory of the mother is sacred, and the preaching that the mother is dwelling in a state of bliss beyond the skies, from which the unconverted child is cut off unless he professes faith, serves to move many to action for the time being. The element of fear is also invoked in the revival—not so much as formerly, it is true, but still to a considerable extent and more subtly. The fear of a sudden death in an unconverted condition is held over the audience, and, "Why not *now*—why not *tonight?*" is asked him, accompanied by the hymn; "Oh, Why Do You Wait, Dear Brother?" As Davenport says:

"It is well known that the employment of symbolic images immensely increases the emotion of an audience. The vocabulary of revivals abounds in them—the cross, the crown, the angel band, hell, heaven. Now vivid imagination and strong feeling and belief are states of mind favorable to suggestion as well as to impulsive action. It is also true that the influence of a crowd largely in sympathy with the ideas suggested is thoroughly coercive or intimidative upon the individual sinner. There is considerable professed conversion which results in the beginning from little more than this form of social pressure, and which may never develop beyond it. Finally, the inhibition of all extraneous ideas is encouraged in revival assemblies both by prayer and speech. There is, therefore, extreme sensitiveness to suggestion. When to these conditions of negative consciousness on the part of an audience there has been added a conductor of the meetings who has a high hypnotic potential, such as Wesley or Finney, or who is only a thoroughly persuasive and magnetic personality, such as Whitefield, there may easily be an influence exerted upon certain individuals of a crowd which closely approaches the abnormal or thoroughly hypnotic. When this point is not reached there is still a great amount of highly acute though normal suggestibility to be reckoned with."

The persons who show signs of being influenced are then "labored with" by either the revivalist or his co-workers. They are urged to surrender their will, and "Leave it all to the Lord." They are told to "Give yourself to God, now, right now, this minute"; or to "Only believe now, and you shall be saved"; or, "Won't you give yourself to Jesus?" etc. They are exhorted and prayed with; arms are placed around their shoulders, and every art of emotional persuasive suggestion is used to make the sinner "give up."

Starbuck in his The Psychology of Religion relates a number of instances of the experiences of converted persons at revivals. One person wrote as follows:

"My will seemed wholly at the mercy of others, particularly of the revivalist M———. There was absolutely no intellectual element. It was pure feeling. There followed a period of ecstasy. I was bent on doing good and was eloquent in appealing to others. The state of moral exaltation did not continue. It was followed by a complete relapse from orthodox religion."

Davenport has the following to say in reply to the claim that the old methods of influencing converts at a revival have passed away with the crude theology of the past:

"I lay particular stress upon this matter here, because, while the employment of irrational fear in revivals has largely passed away, the employment of the hypnotic method has not passed away. There has rather been a recrudescence and a conscious strengthening of it because the old prop of terror is gone. And it cannot be too vigorously emphasized that such a force is not a 'spiritual' force in any high and clear sense at all, but is rather uncanny and psychic and obscure. And the method itself needs to be greatly refined before it can ever be of any spiritual benefit whatever. It is thoroughly primitive and belongs with the animal and instinctive means of fascination. In this bald, crude form, the feline employs it upon the helpless bird and the Indian medicine-man upon the ghost-dance votary. When used, as it has often been, upon little children who are naturally highly suggestible, it has no justification whatever and is mentally and morally injurious in the highest degree. I do not see how violent emotional throes and the use of suggestion in its crude forms can be made serviceable even in the cases of hardened sinners, and certainly with large classes of the population the employment of this means is nothing but psychological malpractice. We guard with intelligent care against quackery in physiological obstetrics. It would be well if a sterner training and prohibition hedged about the spiritual obstetrician, whose function it is to guide the far more delicate process of the new birth."

> *You need have no fear of competition from the person who says, "I'm not paid to do this and I'll not do it." He will never be a dangerous competitor for your job. But watch out for the fellow who remains at his work until it is finished and performs a little more than is expected of him, for he may challenge you at the post and pass you at the grand-stand.*

Some who favor the methods of the revival, but who also recognize the fact that mental suggestion plays a most important part in the phenomena thereof, hold that the objections similar to those here advanced are not valid against the methods of the revival, inasmuch as mental suggestion, as is well known, *may be used for good purposes as well as bad*—for the benefit and uplifting of people as well as in the opposite direction. This being admitted, these good folks argue that mental suggestion in the revival is a legitimate method or "weapon of attack upon the stronghold of the devil." But this argument is found to be defective when examined in its effects and consequences. In the first place, it would seem to identify the emotional, neurotic and hysterical mental states induced by revival methods with the spiritual uplift and moral regeneration which is the accompaniment of true religious experience. It seeks to place the counterfeit on a par with the genuine—the baleful glare of the rays of the psychic moon with the invigorating and animating rays of the spiritual sun. It seeks to raise the hypnotic phase to that of the "spiritual-mindedness" of man. To those who are familiar with the two classes of phenomena, there is a difference as wide as that between the poles existing between them.

As a straw showing how the wind of the best modern religious thought is blowing, we submit the following, from the volume entitled Religion and Miracle, from the pen of Rev. Dr. George A. Gordon, pastor emeritus of the New Old South Church of Boston:

"For this end professional revivalism, with its organizations, its staff of reporters who make the figures suit the hopes of good men, the system of advertisements, and the exclusion or suppression of all sound critical comment, the appeals to emotion and the use of means which have no visible connection with grace and cannot by any possibility lead to glory, is utterly inadequate. The world waits for the vision, the passion, the simplicity and the stern truthfulness of the Hebrew prophet; it awaits the imperial breadth and moral energy of the Christian apostle to the nations; it awaits the teacher who, like Christ, shall carry his doctrine in a great mind and a great character."

While there have undoubtedly been many instances of persons attracted originally by the emotional excitement of the revival, and afterwards leading worthy religious lives in accordance with the higher spiritual nature, still in too many cases the revival has exerted but a temporary effect for good upon the persons yielding to the excitement, and after the stress has passed has resulted in creating an indifference and even an aversion for true religious feeling. The reaction is often equal to the original action. The consequences of "backsliding" are well known in all churches, after a spirited revival. In others there is merely awakened a

> *Until you have learned to be tolerant with those who do not always agree with you—until you have cultivated the habit of saying some kind word of those whom you do not admire—until you have formed the habit of looking for the good instead of the bad there is in others, you will be neither successful nor happy.*

susceptibility to emotional excitement, which causes the individual to undergo repeated stages of "conversion" at each revival, and a subsequent "backsliding" after the influence of the meeting is withdrawn.

Moreover, it is a fact known to psychologists that persons who have given way to the emotional excitement and excesses of the typical revival are rendered afterwards far more suggestible and open to "isms," fads and false religions than before. *The people flocking to the support of the various pseudo-religious adventurers and impostors of the age are generally found to be the same people who were previously the most ardent and excitable converts of the revival.* The ranks of the "Messiahs," "Elijahs" and "Prophets of the Dawn," who have appeared in great numbers in this country and England during the past fifty years, have been recruited almost exclusively from those who have previously "experienced" the revival fervor in the orthodox churches. It is the old story of the training of the hypnotic subject. Especially harmful is this form of emotional intoxication among young people and women. It must be remembered that the period of adolescence is one in which the mental nature of the individual is undergoing great changes. It is a period noted for peculiar development of the emotional nature, the sex nature, and the religious nature. The existing conditions at this period render the psychic debauchery of the revival, séance or hypnotic exhibition particularly harmful. Excessive emotional excitement, coupled with mystery, fear and awe, at this period of life, often results in morbid and abnormal conditions arising in after life. As Davenport well says: "It is no time for the shock of fear or the agony of remorse. The only result of such misguided religious zeal is likely to be a strengthening in many cases of those tendencies, especially in females, toward morbidity and hysteria, toward darkness and doubt."

There are other facts connected with the close relation existing between abnormal religious excitement and the undue arousing of the sexual nature, which are well known to all students of the subject, but which cannot be spoken of here. As a hint, however, the following, from Davenport, will serve its purpose: ". . . At the age of puberty there is an organic process at work which pushes into activity at nearly the same time the sexual and the spiritual. There is no proof, however, of the causation of the latter by the former. But it does appear to be true that the two are closely associated at the point in the physical process where they branch in different directions, *that at that critical period any radical excitation of the one has its influence upon the other.*" A careful consideration of this important statement will serve to explain many things that have sorely perplexed many good people in the past, in connection with revival excitement in a town, camp meetings, etc. This apparent influence of the devil, which so worried our fore-

If you hesitate or turn backward while under fire, you're not a Fighter—you're a "Quitter"; and the Devil, himself, hates the person with a rubber backbone. He smells bad burning.

fathers, is seen to be but the operation of natural psychological and physiological laws. To understand it is to have the remedy at hand."

But what do the authorities say of the revival of the future—the new revival—the real revival? Let Professor Davenport speak for the critics—he is well adapted for the task. He says:

"There will be, I believe, far less use of the revival meeting as a crass coercive instrument for overriding the will and overwhelming the reason of the individual man. The influence of public religious gatherings will be more indirect, more unobtrusive. It will be recognized that hypnotization and forced choices weaken the soul, and there will be no attempt to press to decision in so great a matter under the spell of excitement and contagion and suggestion. . . . The converts may be few. They may be many. They will be measured, not by the capacity of the preacher for administrative hypnotism, but rather by the capacity for unselfish friendship of every Christian man and woman. But of this I think we may be confident—the days of religious effervescence and passional unrestraint are dying. The days of intelligent, undemonstrative and self-sacrificing piety are dawning. To do justly, to love mercy, to walk humbly with God—these remain the cardinal tests of the divine in man. . . . Religious experience is an evolution. We go on from the rudimentary and the primitive to the rational and the spiritual. And, believe Paul, the mature fruit of the Spirit is not the subliminal uprush, the lapse of inhibition, but rational love, joy, peace, long-suffering, kindness, goodness, faithfulness, meekness—self-control."

The Law of Concentration is one of the major principles which must be understood and applied intelligently by all who would successfully experiment with the principle described in this course as the "Master Mind."

The foregoing comments, by leading authorities of the world, will give you a better understanding of the Law of Concentration as it is often used by those who wish to "blend" or "fuse" the minds of a crowd so they will function as a single mind.

You are now ready for the lesson on Co-operation, which will take you further into the methods of applying the psychological laws upon which this philosophy of success is based.

You have failed many times? How fortunate! You ought to know, by now, some of the things NOT to do.

CO-OPERATION

"You Can Do It If You Believe You Can!"

C o-operation is the beginning of all organized effort. As was stated in the first lesson of this course, Andrew Carnegie accumulated a gigantic fortune through the co-operative efforts of a small group of men numbering not more than a score.

You, too, can learn how to use this principle.

There are two forms of Co-operation to which your attention will be directed in this lesson; namely:

First, the Co-operation between people who group themselves together or form alliances for the purpose of attaining a given end, under the principles known as the Law of the Master Mind.

Second, the Co-operation between the conscious and the sub-conscious minds, which forms a reasonable hypothesis of man's ability to contact, communicate with and draw upon *infinite intelligence.*

To one who has not given serious thought to this subject, the foregoing hypothesis may seem unreasonable; but follow the evidence of its soundness, and study the facts upon which the hypothesis is based, and then draw your own conclusions.

Let us begin with a brief review of the physical construction of the body:

"We know that the whole body is traversed by a network of nerves which serve as the channels of communication between the indwelling spiritual ego, which we call mind, and the functions of the external organism.

"*This nervous system is dual.* One system, known as the Sympathetic, is the channel for all those activities which are not consciously directed by our volition, such as the operation of the digestive organs, the repair of the daily wear and tear of the tissues, and the like.

"The other system, known as the Voluntary or Cerebro-spinal system, is the channel through which we receive conscious perception from the physical senses and exercise control over the movements of the body. This system has its center in the brain, while the other has its center in the ganglionic mass at the back of the stomach known as the solar plexus, and sometimes spoken of as the abdominal brain. The cerebro-spinal system is the channel of our volitional or conscious mental action, and the sympathetic system is the channel of that mental action which unconsciously supports the vital functions of the body.

"Thus the cerebro-spinal system is the organ of the conscious mind and the sympathetic is that of the sub-conscious mind.

"But the interaction of conscious and sub-conscious minds requires a similar interaction between the corresponding systems of nerves, and one conspicuous connection by which this is provided is the "vagus" nerve. This nerve passes out of the cerebral region as a portion of the voluntary system, and through it we control the vocal organs; then it passes onward to the thorax, sending out branches to the heart and lungs; and finally, passing through the diaphragm, it loses the outer coating which distinguishes the nerves of the voluntary system and becomes identified with those of the sympathetic system, *so forming a connecting link* between the two and making the man physically a single entity.

"Similarly different areas of the brain indicate their connection with the objective and subjective activities of the mind respectively, and, speaking in a general way, we may assign the frontal portion of the brain to the former, and the posterior portion to the latter, while the intermediate portion partakes of the character of both.

"The intuitional faculty has its correspondence in the upper area of the brain, situated between the frontal and the posterior portions, and, physiologically speaking, it is here that intuitive ideas find entrance. These, at first, are more or less unformed and generalized in character, but are, nevertheless, perceived by the conscious mind; otherwise, we should not be aware of them at all. Then the effort of Nature is to bring these ideas into more definite and usable shape, so the conscious mind lays hold on them and induces a corresponding vibratory current in the voluntary system of nerves, and this in turn induces a similar current in the involuntary system, *thus handing the idea over to the subjective mind*. The vibratory current which had first descended from the apex of the brain to the frontal brain and thus through the voluntary system to the solar plexus is now reversed and ascends from the solar plexus through the sympathetic system to the posterior brain, this return current indicating the action of the subjective mind."

If we were to remove the surface portion of the apex of the brain we should find immediately below it the shining belt of brain substance called the "corpus callosum." *This is the point of union between the subjective and objective,* and, as the current returns from the solar plexus to this point, it is restored to the objective portion of the brain in a fresh form *which it has acquired by the silent alchemy of the subjective mind.* Thus the conception which was at first only vaguely recognized is restored to the objective mind in a definite and workable form, and then the objective mind, acting through the frontal brain—the area of comparison and analysis—proceeds to work upon a clearly perceived idea and to bring out the potentialities that are latent in it.*

The term "subjective mind" is the same as the term "sub-conscious mind," and the term "objective mind" is the same as the term "conscious mind."

Please understand these different terms.

By studying this *dual system* through which the body transmits energy, we discover the exact points at which the two systems are connected, and the manner in which we may transmit a *thought* from the conscious to the sub-conscious mind.

This Co-operative *dual nervous system* is the most important form of co-operation known to man; for it is through the aid of this system that the principle of evolution carries on its work of developing *accurate thought,* as described in Lesson Ten.

When you impress any idea on your sub-conscious mind, through the principle of Auto-suggestion, you do so with the aid of this *dual nervous system:* and when your sub-conscious mind works out a definite plan of any *desire* with which you impress it, the plan is delivered back to your conscious mind through this same *dual nervous system.*

This Co-operative system of nerves literally constitutes a direct line of communication between your ordinary conscious mind and *infinite intelligence.*

Knowing, from my own previous experience as a beginner in the study of this subject, how difficult it is to accept the hypothesis here described, I will illustrate the soundness of the hypothesis in a simple way that you can both understand and demonstrate for yourself.

Before going to sleep at night impress upon your mind the *desire* to arise the next morning at a given hour, say at four A.M., and if your impression is accompanied by a *positive determination* to arise at that hour, your sub-conscious mind will register the impression and awaken you at precisely that time.

---

* Judge T. Troward, in *The Edinburgh Lectures on Mental Science.*

You cannot scare a man who is at peace with God, his fellow men and himself. There is no room for fear in such a man's heart. When fear finds a welcome there is something that needs awakening.

Now the question might well be asked:

"If I can impress my sub-conscious mind with the *desire* to arise at a specified time and it will awaken me at that time, why do I not form the habit of impressing it with other and more important *desires?*"

If you will ask yourself this question, *and insist upon an answer,* you will find yourself very near, if not on the pathway that leads to the secret door to *knowledge,* as described in Lesson Ten.

We will now take up the subject of Co-operation between men who unite, or group themselves together for the purpose of attaining a given end. In the first lesson of this course we referred to this sort of co-operation as *organized effort.*

This course touches some phase of co-operation in practically every lesson. This result was inevitable for the reason that the object of the course is to help the student develop *power,* and power is developed only through *organized effort.*

We are living in an age of co-operative effort. Nearly all successful businesses are conducted under some form of co-operation. The same is true in the field of industry and finance, as well as in the professional field.

Doctors and lawyers have their alliances for mutual aid and protection in the form of Bar Associations and Medical Associations.

The bankers have both local and national Associations for their mutual aid and advancement.

The retail merchants have their Associations for the same purpose.

The automobile owners have grouped themselves into Clubs and Associations.

The printers have their Associations; the plumbers have theirs and the coal dealers have theirs.

Co-operation is the object of all these Associations.

The laboring men have their unions and those who supply the working capital and superintend the efforts of laboring men have their alliances, under various names.

Nations have their co-operative alliances, although they do not appear to have yet discovered the full meaning of "co-operation." The attempt of the late President Wilson to perfect the League of Nations, followed by the efforts of the late President Harding to perfect the same idea under the name of the World Court, indicates the trend of the times in the direction of co-operation.

It is slowly becoming obvious to man that those who most efficiently apply the principle of co-operative effort survive longest, and, that this principle applies from the lowest form of animal life to the highest form of human endeavor.

Mr. Carnegie, and Mr. Rockefeller, and Mr. Ford have taught the business man the value of co-operative effort; that is, they have taught all who cared to observe, the principle through which they accumulated vast fortunes.

Co-operation is the very foundation of all successful leadership. Henry Ford's most tangible asset is the well organized agency force that he has established. This organization not only provides him with an outlet for all the automobiles he can manufacture, but, of greater importance still, it provides him with financial power sufficient to meet any emergency that may arise, a fact which he has already demonstrated on at least one occasion.

As a result of his understanding of the value of the co-operative principle Ford has removed himself from the usual position of dependence upon financial institutions and at the same time provided himself with more commercial power than he can possibly use.

The Federal Reserve Bank System is another example of co-operative effort which practically insures the United States against a money panic.

The chain-store systems constitute another form of commercial co-operation that provides advantage through both the purchasing and the distributing end of the business.

The modern department store, which is the equivalent of a group of small stores operating under one roof, one management and one overhead expense, is another illustration of the advantage of co-operative effort in the commercial field.

In Lesson Fourteen you will observe the possibilities of co-operative effort in its highest form and at the same time you will see the important part that it plays in the development of *power*.

As you have already learned, *power* is *organized effort*. The three most important factors that enter into the process of organizing effort are:

Concentration,
Co-operation and
Co-ordination

How Power Is Developed Through Co-operation

As we have already seen, power is organized effort or energy. Personal power is developed by developing, organizing and co-ordinating the faculties of the mind. This may be accomplished by mastering and applying the fifteen major principles upon which this course is founded. The necessary procedure through which these principles may be mastered is thoroughly described in the fifteenth lesson.

The development of personal power is but the first step to be taken in the development of the potential power that is available through the medium of allied effort, or *co-operation*, which may be called group power.

It is a well known fact that all men who have amassed large fortunes have been known as able "organizers." By this is meant that they possessed the ability to enlist the co-operative efforts of other men who supplied talent and ability which they, themselves, did not possess.

The chief object of this course is so to unfold the principles of *organized* and *co-operative* or allied effort that the student will comprehend their significance and make them the basis of his philosophy.

Take, as an example, any business or profession that you choose and you will observe, by analysis, that it is limited only by lack of application of *organized* and *co-operative* effort. As an illustration, consider the legal profession.

If a law firm consists of but one type of mind it will be greatly handicapped, even though it may be made up of a dozen able men of this particular type. The complicated legal system calls for a greater variety of talent than any one man could possibly provide.

It is evident, therefore, that mere organized effort is not sufficient to insure outstanding success; the organization must consist of individuals each of whom supplies some specialized talent which the other members of the organization do not possess.

A well organized law firm would include talent that was specialized in the preparation of cases; men of vision and imagination who understood how to harmonize the law and the evidence of a case under a sound plan. Men who have such ability are not always possessed of the ability to try a case in court; therefore, men who are proficient in court procedure must be available. Carrying the analysis a step further, it will be seen that there are many different classes of cases which call for men of various types of specialized ability in both the preparation and the trial of these cases. A lawyer who had prepared himself as a specialist in corporation law might be wholly unprepared to handle a case in criminal procedure.

In forming a law partnership, the man who understood the principles of *organized, co-operative effort,* would surround himself with talent that was specialized in every branch of law and legal procedure in which he intended to practice. The man who had no conception of the potential power of these principles would probably select his associates by the usual "hit or miss" method, basing his selections more upon personality or acquaintanceship than consideration of the particular type of legal talent that each possessed.

The subject of *organized effort* has been covered in the preceding lessons of this course, but it is again brought up in connection with this lesson for the purpose of indicating the necessity of forming alliances or organizations consisting of individuals who supply *all of the necessary talent that may be needed for the attainment of the object in mind.*

In nearly all commercial undertakings, there is a need for at least three classes of talent; namely, buyers, salesmen and those who are familiar with finance. It will be readily seen that when these three classes of men *organize* and *co-ordinate* their efforts they avail themselves, through this form of *co-operation,* of *power* which no single individual of the group possesses.

Many a business fails because all of the men back of it are salesmen, or financial men or buyers. By nature, the most able salesmen are optimistic, enthusiastic and emotional; while able financial men, as a rule, are unemotional, deliberate and conservative. Both classes are essential to the success of a commercial enterprise; but either class will prove too much of a load for any business, without the modifying influence of the other class.

It is generally conceded that James J. Hill was the most efficient railroad builder that America ever produced; but it is equally well known that he was not a civil engineer, nor a bridge builder, nor a locomotive engineer, nor a mechanical engineer, nor a chemist, although these highly specialized classes of talent are essential in railroad building. Mr. Hill understood the principles of *organized effort* and *co-operation;* therefore, he surrounded himself with men who possessed all this necessary ability which he lacked.

The modern department store is a splendid example of *organized, co-operative effort.*

Each merchandising department is under the management of one who understands the purchasing and marketing of the goods carried in that department.

Back of all these department managers is a general staff consisting of specialists in buying, selling, financing, and the management of units, or groups, of

A good stock of self-confidence and a new suit of clothes will help you land a position without "pull," but remember that nothing will go so far toward helping you hold it as will push, enthusiasm and determination to do more than that for which you are paid.

485

people. This form of *organized effort* places back of each department both *buying* and *selling* power such as that department could not afford if it were separated from the group and had to be operated under its own overhead, in a separate location.

The United States of America is one of the richest and most *powerful* nations of the world. Upon analysis, it will be seen that this enormous power has grown out of the *co-operative* efforts of the states of the Union.

It was for the purpose of saving this power that the immortal Lincoln made up his mind to erase the Mason and Dixon line. The saving of the Union was of far greater concern to him than was the freedom of the slaves of the South. Had this not been so, the present status of the United States as a power among the nations of the world would be far different from what it is.

It was this same principle of *co-operative* effort that Woodrow Wilson had in mind when he created his plan for a League of Nations. He foresaw the need of such a plan as a medium for preventing war between nations; just as Lincoln foresaw it as a medium for harmonizing the efforts of the people of the United States, thereby preserving the Union.

Thus it is seen that the principle of *organized, co-operative* effort through the aid of which the individual may develop personal power, is the selfsame principle that must be employed in developing group power.

Andrew Carnegie easily dominated the steel business during his active connection with that industry, for the reason that he took advantage of the principle of *organized, co-operative* effort by surrounding himself with highly specialized financial men, chemists, sales managers, buyers of raw materials, transportation experts and others whose services were essential to that industry. He organized this group of *"co-operators"* into what he called a "Master Mind."

Any great university affords an excellent example of the necessity of *organized, co-operative* effort. The professorate is made up of men and women of highly specialized, though vastly different, ability. One department is presided over by experts in literature; another department by expert mathematicians; another department by experts in chemistry; another department by experts in economic philosophy; another department by experts in medicine; another, by experts in law, etc. The university, as a whole, is the equivalent of a group of colleges each of which is directed by experts in its own line, whose efficiency is greatly increased through allied or *co-operative* effort that is directed by a single head.

Analyze *power*, no matter where, or in what form, it may be found, and you will find *organi-*

zation and *co-operation* as the chief factors back of it. You will find these two principles in evidence in the lowest form of vegetation no less than in the highest form of animal, which is man.

Off the coast of Norway is the most famous and irresistible maelstrom in the world. This great whirlpool of ceaseless motion has never been known to give up any victim who was caught in its circling embrace of foaming water.

No less sure of destruction are those unfortunate souls who are caught in the great maelstrom of life toward which all who do not understand the principle of *organized, co-operative* effort are traveling. We are living in a world in which the law of the survival of the fittest is everywhere in evidence. Those who are "fit" are those who have *power*, and power is *organized effort*.

Unfortunate is the person who either through ignorance, or because of egotism, imagines that he can sail this sea of life in the frail bark of independence. Such a person will discover that there are maelstroms more dangerous than any mere whirlpool of unfriendly waters. All natural laws and all of Nature's plans are based upon harmonious, *co-operative* effort, as all who have attained high places in the world have discovered.

Wherever people are engaged in unfriendly combat, no matter what may be its nature, or its cause, one may observe the nearness of one of these maelstroms that awaits the combatants.

Success in life cannot be attained except through peaceful, harmonious, *co-operative* effort. Nor can success be attained single-handed or independently. Even though a man live as a hermit in the wilderness, far from all signs of civilization, he is, nevertheless, *dependent* upon forces outside of himself for an existence. The more he becomes a part of civilization the more *dependent* upon *co-operative* effort he becomes.

Whether a man earns his living by days' work or from the interest on the fortune he has amassed, he will earn it with less opposition through friendly *cooperation* with others. Moreover, the man whose philosophy is based upon *co-operation* instead of *competition* will not only acquire the necessities and the luxuries of life with less effort, but he will enjoy an extra reward in *happiness* such as others will never feel.

Fortunes that are acquired through *co-operative* effort inflict no scars upon the hearts of their owners, which is more than can be said of fortunes that are acquired through conflict and competitive methods that border on extortion.

The accumulation of material wealth, whether the object is that of bare existence or luxury, consumes most of the time that we put into this earthly struggle. If we cannot change

"Quibbling" over salary "to start with" has lost many a man the big opportunity of a life-time. If the position you seek is one that you know you can throw your whole heart into, take it, even if you have to work for nothing until you deliver a good sample of your "goods." Thereafter you will receive pay in proportion to the quality and quantity of the work you perform.

this materialistic tendency of human nature, we can, at least, change the method of pursuing it by adopting *co-operation* as the basis of the pursuit.

Co-operation offers the two–fold reward of providing one with both the necessities and the luxuries of life and the peace of mind which the covetous never know. The avaricious and covetous person may amass a great fortune in material wealth; there is no denying this fact; but he will have sold his soul for a mess of pottage in the bargain.

Let us keep in mind the fact that all success is based upon power, and power grows out of knowledge, that has been organized and expressed in terms of ACTION.

The world pays for but one kind of knowledge, and that is the kind which is expressed in terms of constructive service. In addressing the graduating class of a business college one of the best known bankers in America said:

"You ought to feel proud of your diplomas, because they are evidence that you have been preparing yourselves for *action* in the great field of business.

"One of the advantages of a business college training is that it prepares you for *action!* Not to belittle other methods of education, but to exalt the modern business college method, I am reminded to say that there are some colleges in which the majority of the students are preparing for practically everything else except *action*.

"You came to this business college with but one object in view, and that object is to learn to render service and earn a living. The latest style of clothing has been of little interest to you because you have been preparing yourself for work in which clothes of the latest style will play no important part. You did not come here to learn how to pour tea at an afternoon party nor to become masters at affecting friendliness while inwardly feeling envy for those who wear finer gowns and drive costly motor cars—you came here to learn how to work!"

In the graduating class before which this man spoke were thirteen boys, all of whom were so poor that they had barely enough money with which to pay their way. Some of them were paying their own way by working before and after school hours.

That was twenty-five years ago. Last summer, I met the president of the business college which these boys attended and he gave me the history of each one of them, from the time that they graduated until the time when I talked to him. One of them is the president of one of the big wholesale drug companies, and a wealthy man; one is a successful lawyer; two own large business colleges of their own; one is a professor in the department of economics in one of the largest universities in America; one is the president of one of the large automobile manufacturing companies; two are presidents of banks, and wealthy men; one is the owner of a large department store; one is the vice-president of one of the great railway systems of the country; one is a well established Certified Public Accountant; one is dead; and the thirteenth is compiling this Reading Course on the Law of Success.

Eleven successes out of a class of thirteen boys is not a bad record, thanks to the spirit of *action* developed by that business college training.

It is not the schooling you have had that counts; it is the extent to which you express that which you learned from your schooling through well organized and intelligently directed *action*.

By no means would I belittle higher education, but I would offer hope and encouragement to those who have had no such education, provided they express that which they know, be it ever so little, in intensive *action,* along constructive lines.

One of the greatest Presidents who ever occupied the White House had but little schooling, but he did such a good job of expressing what knowledge he acquired by that little schooling, through properly directed *action,* that his name has been inseparably woven into the history of the United States.

Every city, town and hamlet has its population of those well known characters called "ne'er-do-wells," and if you will analyze these unfortunate people, you will observe that one of their outstanding features is *procrastination.*

Lack of *action* has caused them to slip backward until they got into a "rut," where they will remain unless, through accident, they are forced out into the open road of struggle where unusual *action* will become necessary.

Don't let yourself get into such a condition.

Every office, and every shop, and every bank, and every store, and every other place of employment has its outstanding victims of *procrastination* who are doing the goose-step down the dusty road of *failure* because they have not developed the habit of expressing themselves in *action.*

You can pick out these unfortunates all about you if you will begin to analyze those with whom you come in contact each day. If you will talk to them you will observe that they have built up a false philosophy somewhat of this nature:

"I am doing all I am paid to do, and I am getting by."

Yes, they are "getting by"—but that is all they are getting.

Some years ago, at a time when labor was scarce and wages unusually high, I observed scores of able-bodied men lying about in the parks of Chicago, doing nothing. I became curious to know what sort of an alibi they would offer for their conduct, so I went out one afternoon and interviewed seven of them.

With the aid of a generous supply of cigars and cigarettes and a little loose change I bought myself into the confidence of those whom I interviewed and thereby gained a rather intimate view of their philosophy. All gave exactly the same reason for being there, without employment. They said: "The world will not give me a chance!!!"

The exclamation points are my own.

Think of it—the world would not "give them a chance."

Of course the world wouldn't *give* them a chance.

It never *gives* anyone a chance. A man who wants a chance may create it through *action*, but if he waits for someone to hand it to him on a silver platter he will meet with disappointment.

I fear that this excuse that the world does not *give* a man a chance is quite prevalent, and I strongly suspect that it is one of the commonest causes of poverty and failure.

The seventh man that I interviewed on that well-spent afternoon was an unusually fine looking specimen, physically. He was lying on the ground asleep, with a newspaper over his face. When I lifted the paper from his face, he reached up, took it out of my hands, put it back over his face and went right on sleeping.

Then I used a little strategy by removing the paper from his face and placing it behind me, where he could not get it. He then sat up on the ground and I interviewed him. That fellow was a graduate from two of the great universities of the east, with a master's degree from one, and a Ph.D. from the other.

His story was pathetic.

He had held job after job, but always his employer or his fellow employee "had it in for him." He hadn't been able to make them see the value of his college training. They wouldn't "give him a chance."

Here was a man who might have been at the head of some great business, or the outstanding figure in one of the professions had he not built his house upon the sands of *procrastination* and held to the false belief that the world should pay him for *what he knew!*

Luckily, most college graduates do not build upon such flimsy foundations, because no college on earth can crown with success the man who tries to collect for that which he knows instead of that which he *can do with what he knows*.

The man to whom I have referred was from one of the best known families of Virginia. He traced his ancestry back to the landing of the Mayflower. He threw back his shoulders, pounded himself on the breast with his fist and said: "Just think of it, sir! I am a son of one of the first families of old Virginia!"

My observations lead me to believe that being the son of a "first family" is not always fortunate for either the son or the family. Too often these sons of "first families" try to slide home from third base on their family names. This may be only a peculiar notion of mine, but I have observed that the men and women who are doing the world's work have but little time, and less inclination, to brag about their ancestry.

Not long ago I took a trip back to southwest Virginia, where I was born. It was the first time I had been there in over twenty years. It was a sad sight to compare the sons of some of those who were known as "first families" twenty years ago, with the sons of those who were but plain men who made it their business to express themselves in *action* of the most intensive nature.

The comparison reflected no credit upon the "first family" boys! It is with no feeling of exaltation that I express my gratitude for not having been brought into the world by parents who belonged to the "first family" class. That, of course, was not a matter of choice with me, and if it had been perhaps I, too, would have selected parents of the "first family" type.

Not long ago I was invited to deliver an address in Boston, Mass. After my work was finished, a reception committee volunteered to show me the sights of the city, including a trip to Cambridge, where we visited Harvard University. While there, I observed many sons of "first families"—some of whom were equipped with Packards. Twenty years ago I would have felt proud to be a student at Harvard, with a Packard car, but the illuminating effect of my more mature years has led me to the conclusion that had I had the privilege of going to Harvard I might have done just as well without the aid of a Packard.

I noticed some Harvard boys who had no Packards. They were working as waiters in a restaurant where I

Here's a good joke to play on your employer: Get to your work a little earlier and leave a little later than you are supposed to. Handle his tools as if they belonged to you. Go out of your way to say a kind word about him to your fellow-workers. When there is extra work that needs to be done, volunteer to do it. Do not show surprise when he "gets on to you" and offers you the head of the department or a partnership in the business, for this is the best part of the "joke."

ate, and as far as I could see they were missing nothing of value because they owned no Packards; nor did they seem to be suffering by comparison with those who could boast of the ownership of parents of the "first family" type.

All of which is no reflection upon Harvard University—one of the great universities of the world—nor upon the "first families" who send boys to Harvard. To the contrary, it is intended as a bit of encouragement to those unfortunates who, like myself, have but little and know but little, but express what little they know in terms of constructive, useful *action*.

The psychology of *inaction* is one of the chief reasons why some towns and cities are dying with the dry-rot!

Take the city of X, for example. You'll recognize the city by its description, if you are familiar with this part of the country. Sunday blue-laws have closed up all the restaurants on Sunday. Railroad trains must slow down to twelve miles an hour while passing through the city. "Keep off the grass" signs are prominently displayed in the parks. Unfavorable city ordinances of one sort or another have driven the best industries to other cities. On every hand one may see evidence of restraint. The people of the streets show signs of restraint in their faces, and in their manner, and in their walk.

The mass psychology of the city is negative.

The moment one gets off the train at the depot, this negative atmosphere becomes de-pressingly obvious and makes one want to take the next train out again. The place reminds one of a grave-yard and the people resemble walking ghosts.

They register no signs of *action!*

The bank statements of the banking institutions reflect this negative, *inactive* state of mind. The stores reflect it in their show windows and in the faces of their salespeople. I went into one of the stores to buy a pair of hose. A young woman with bobbed hair who would have been a "flapper" if she hadn't been too lazy, threw out a box of hose on the counter. When I picked up the box, looked the hose over and registered a look of disapproval on my face, she languidly yawned:

"They're the best you can get in this dump!"

"Dump!" She must have been a mind reader, for "dump" was the word that was in my mind before she spoke. The store reminded me of a rubbish dump; the city reminded me of the same. I felt the stuff getting into my own blood. The negative psychology of the people was actually reaching out and gathering me in.

Maine is not the only state that is afflicted with a city such as the one I have described. I could name others, but I might wish to go into politics some day; therefore, I will leave it to you to do your own analyzing and comparing of cities that are alive with *action* and those that are slowly dying with the dry-rot of *inaction*.

I know of some business concerns that are in this same state of *inaction,* but I will omit their names. You probably know some, too.

Many years ago Frank A. Vanderlip, who is one of the best known and most capable bankers in America, went to work for the National City Bank, of New York City.

His salary was above the average from the start, for the reason that he was capable and had a record of successful achievement that made him a valuable man.

He was assigned to a private office that was equipped with a fine mahogany desk and an easy chair. On the top of the desk was an electric push button that led to a secretary's desk outside.

The first day went by without any work coming to his desk. The second, and third, and fourth days went by without any work. No one came in or said anything to him.

By the end of the week he began to feel uneasy. (Men of *action* always feel uneasy when there is no work in sight.)

The following week Mr. Vanderlip went into the president's office and said, "Look here, you are paying me a big salary and giving me nothing to do and it is grating on my nerves!"

The president looked up with a lively twinkle in his keen eyes.

"Now I have been thinking," Mr. Vanderlip continued, "while sitting in there with nothing to do, of a plan for increasing the business of this bank."

The president assured him that both "thinking" and "plans" were valuable, and asked him to continue with his interview.

"I have thought of a plan," Mr. Vanderlip went on, "that will give the bank the benefit of my experience in the bond business. I propose to create a bond department for this bank and advertise it as a feature of our business."

"What! this bank advertise?" queried the president. "Why, we have never advertised since we began business. We have managed to get along without it."

"Well, this is where you are going to begin advertising," said Mr. Vanderlip, "and the first thing you are going to advertise is this new bond department that I have planned."

Mr. Vanderlip won! Men of *action* usually win—that is one of their distinctive features. The National City Bank also won, because that interview was the beginning of one of the most progressive and profitable advertising campaigns ever carried on by any bank, with the result that the National City Bank became one of the most powerful financial institutions of America.

There were other results, also, that are worth naming. Among them the result that Mr. Vanderlip grew with the bank, as men of *action* usually grow in whatever they help to build, until finally he became the president of that great banking house.

In the lesson on *Imagination* you learned how to recombine old ideas into new plans, but no matter how practical your plans may be they will be useless if they are not expressed in *action*. To dream dreams and see visions of the person you would like to be or the station in life you would like to obtain are admirable provided you transform your dreams and visions into reality through intensive *action*.

There are men who dream, but do nothing more. There are others who take the visions of the dreamers and translate them into stone, and marble, and music, and good books, and railroads, and steamships. There are still others who *both dream* and transform these dreams into reality. They are the dreamer-doer types.

There is a psychological as well as an economic reason why you should form the habit of intensive *action*. Your body is made up of billions of tiny cells that are highly sensitive and amenable to the influence of your mind. If your mind is of the lethargic, *inactive* type, the cells of your body become lazy and inactive also. Just as the stagnant water of an inactive pond becomes impure and unhealthful, so will the cells of an inactive body become diseased.

Laziness is nothing but the influence of an inactive mind on the cells of the body. If you doubt this, the next time you feel lazy take a Turkish bath and have yourself well rubbed down, thereby stimulating the cells of your body by artificial means, and see how quickly your laziness disappears. Or, a better way than this, turn your mind toward some game of which you are fond and notice how quickly the cells of your body will respond to your enthusiasm and your lazy feeling will disappear.

Every failure will teach you a lesson that you need to learn if you will keep your eyes and ears open and be willing to be taught. Every adversity is usually a blessing in disguise. Without reverses and temporary defeat, you would never know the sort of metal of which you are made.

The cells of the body respond to the state of mind in exactly the same manner that the people of a city respond to the mass psychology that dominates the city. If a group of leaders engage in sufficient *action* to give a city the reputation of being a "live-wire" city this *action* influences all who live there. The same principle applies to the relationship between the mind and the body. An *active,* dynamic mind keeps the cells of which the physical portions of the body consist, in a constant state of activity.

The artificial conditions under which most inhabitants of our cities live have led to a physical condition known as auto-intoxication, which means self-poisoning through the inactive state of the intestines. Most headaches may be cured in an hour's time by simply cleansing the lower intestines with an enema.

Eight glasses of water a day and a reasonable amount of physical *action* popularly known as "exercise" will take the place of the enema. Try it for a week and then you will not have to be urged to keep it up, for you will feel like a new person, unless the nature of your work is such that you get plenty of physical exercise and drink plenty of water in the regular course of your duties.

On two pages of this book enough sound advice could be recorded to keep the average person healthy and ready for *action* during sixteen of the twenty-four hours of the day, but the advice would be so simple that most people would not follow it.

The amount of work that I perform every day and still keep in good physical condition is a source of wonderment and mystery to those who know me intimately, yet there is no mystery to it, and the system I follow does not cost anything.

Here it is, for your use if you want it:

First: I drink a cup of hot water when I first get up in the morning, before I have breakfast.

Second: My breakfast consists of rolls made of whole wheat and bran, breakfast cereal, fruit, softboiled eggs once in a while, and coffee. For luncheon I eat vegetables (most any kind), whole wheat bread and a glass of buttermilk. Supper, a well cooked steak once or twice a week, vegetables, especially lettuce, and coffee.

Third: I walk an average of ten miles a day: five miles into the country and five miles back, using this period for meditation and thought. Perhaps the thinking is as valuable, as a health builder, as the walk.

Fourth: I lie across a straight bottom chair, flat on my back, with most of my weight resting on the small of my back, with my head and arms relaxed completely, until they almost touch the floor. This gives the nervous energy of my body an opportunity to balance properly and distribute itself, and ten minutes in this position will completely relieve all signs of fatigue, no matter how tired I may be.

Fifth: I take an enema at least once every ten days, and more often if I feel the need of it, using water that is a little below blood temperature, with a tablespoonful of salt in it, chest and knee position.

Sixth: I take a hot shower bath, followed immediately by a cold shower, every day, usually in the morning when I first get up.

These simple things I do for myself. Mother Nature attends to everything else necessary for my health.

I cannot lay too much stress upon the importance of keeping the intestines clean, for it is a well known fact that the city dwellers of today are literally poisoning themselves to death by neglecting to cleanse their intestines with water. You should not wait until you are constipated to take an enema. When you get to the stage of constipation you are practically ill and immediate relief is absolutely essential, but if you will give yourself the proper attention regularly, just as you attend to keeping the outside of your body clean, you will never be bothered with the many troubles which constipation brings.

For more than fifteen years no single week ever passed without my having a headache. Usually I administered a dose of aspirin and got temporary relief. I was suffering with auto-intoxication and did not know it, for the reason that I was not constipated.

When I found out what my trouble was I did two things, both of which I recommend to you; namely, *I quit using aspirin* and I cut down my daily consumption of food nearly one half.

Just a word about aspirin—a word which those who profit by its sale will not like—it affords no permanent cure of headache. All it does might be compared to a lineman that cuts the telegraph wire while the operator is using that wire in a call for aid from the fire department to save the burning building in which he is located. Aspirin cuts or "deadens" the line of nerve communication that runs from the stomach or the intestinal region, where auto-intoxication is pouring poison into the blood, to the brain, where the effect of that poison is registering its call in the form of intense pain.

Cutting the telegraph line over which a call for the fire department is being sent does not put out the fire; nor does it remove the cause to deaden, with the aid of a dose of aspirin, the nerve line over which a headache is registering a call for help.

You cannot be a person of *action* if you permit yourself to go without proper physical attention until auto-intoxication takes your brain and kneads it into an inoperative mass that resembles a ball of putty. Neither can you be a person of *action* if you eat the usual devitalized concoction called "white bread" (which has had all the real food value removed from it) and twice as much meat as your system can digest and properly dispose of.

You cannot be a person of *action* if you run to the pill bottle every time you have, or *imagine* you have, an ache or a pain, or swallow an aspirin tablet every time your intestines call on your brain for a douche bag of water and a spoonful of salt for cleansing purposes.

You cannot be a person of *action* if you *overeat* and *under-exercise.*

You cannot be a person of *action* if you read the patent medicine booklets and begin to imagine yourself ailing with the symptoms described by the clever advertisement writer who has reached your pocket book through the power of *suggestion.*

I have not touched a drug for more than five years, and I have not been either sick or ailing during that time, in spite of the fact that I perform more work each day than most men of my profession. I have *enthusiasm, endurance* and *action* because I eat the sort of simple food that contains the body-building elements that I require, and look after the eliminative processes as carefully as I bathe my body.

If these simple and frank admissions appeal to you as being based upon common sense, take them and put them to the test, and if they serve you as well as they are serving me, both of us will have profited by the courage I had to summon to list them as a part of this lesson.

Usually, when anyone except a physician offers suggestions on the care of the body, he is immediately catalogued as a "long-haired crank," and I will admit that the analysis is often correct. In this instance, I make no stronger recommendations than this:

That you try an enema the next time you have a headache, and if any of the other suggestions appeal to you give them a trial until you are satisfied that they are either sound or unsound.

Before leaving the subject, perhaps I should explain that water which is barely luke-warm should be used for the enema for the reason that this causes the muscles of the intestines to contract, which, in turn, forces the poisonous matter out of the pores of the mucous linings. This exercises those muscles and eventually it will so develop them that they will do their work in the natural way, without the aid of the enema. A warm water enema is very detrimental for the reason that it relaxes the muscles of the intestines, which, in time, causes them to cease functioning altogether, producing what is ordinarily referred to as the "enema habit."

An occasional misfortune is a good thing. It reminds us that no one has absolute independence.

With due apologies to my friends, the physicians and osteopaths and chiropractors and other health builders, I will now invite you back to that part of the subject of this lesson over which there can be no conflict of opinion as to the soundness of my counsel.

There is another enemy which you must conquer before you can become a person of *action,* and that is the *worry habit.*

Worry, and envy, and jealousy, and hatred, and doubt, and fear are all states of mind which are fatal to *action*.

Any of these states of mind will interfere with, and in some instances destroy altogether, the digestive process through which the food is assimilated and prepared for distribution through the body. This interference is purely physical, but the damage does not stop here, because these negative states of mind destroy the most essential factor in the achievement of *success;* namely, *desire* to achieve.

In the first lesson of this course you learned that your *definite chief aim* in life should be supported by a *burning desire* for its realization. You can have no *burning desire* for achievement when you are in a negative state of mind, no matter what the cause of that state of mind may be.

To keep myself in a positive frame of mind I have discovered a very effective "gloom-chaser." That may not be a very dignified way of expressing my meaning, but since the subject of this lesson is *action* and not dignity I will make it serve. The "gloom-chaser" to which I refer is a *hearty laugh.* When I feel "out of sorts" or inclined to argue with somebody over something that is not worthy of discussion, I know that I need my "gloom-chaser," and I proceed to get away where I will disturb no one and have a good hearty laugh. If I can find nothing really funny about which to laugh I simply have a forced laugh. The effect is the same in both cases.

Five minutes of this sort of mental and physical exercise—for it is both—will stimulate *action* that is free from negative tendencies.

Do not take my word for this—try it!

Not long ago I heard a phonograph record entitled, as I recall it, The Laughing Fool, which should be available to all whose dignity forbids them to indulge in a hearty laugh for their health's sake. This record was all that its name implies. It was made by a man and a woman; the man was trying to play a cornet and the woman was laughing at him. She laughed so effectively that she finally made the man laugh, and the suggestion was so pronounced that all who heard it usually joined in and had a good laugh, whether they felt like it or not.

"As a man thinketh in his heart, so is he."

You cannot think *fear* and act courageously. You cannot think hatred and act in a kindly manner toward those with whom you associate. The dominating thoughts of your mind—meaning by this, the strongest and deepest and most frequent of your thoughts—influence the physical *action* of your body.

Every thought put into action by your brain reaches and influences every cell in your body. When you think *fear* your mind telegraphs this thought down to the cells that form the muscles of your legs and tells those muscles to get into *action* and carry you away as rapidly as they can. A man who is afraid runs away because his legs carry him, and they carry him because the *fear* thought in his mind instructed them to do so, even though the instructions were given unconsciously.

In the Introduction to this course you learned how *thought* travels from one mind to another, through the principle of telepathy. In this lesson you should go a step further and learn that *your thoughts* not only register themselves in the minds of other people, through the principle of telepathy, but, *what is a million times more important to you to understand, they register themselves on the cells of your own body* and *affect those cells in a manner that harmonizes with the nature of the thoughts.*

To understand this principle is to understand the soundness of the statement: "As a man thinketh in his heart, so is he."

Action, in the sense that the term is used in this lesson, is of two forms. One is physical and the other is mental. You can be very active with your mind while your body is entirely inactive, except as to the involuntary action of the vital organs. Or you can be very active with both body and mind.

In speaking of men of *action*, either or both of two types may be referred to. One is the care-taker type and the other is the promoter or salesman type. Both of these types are essential in modern business, industry and finance. One is known as a "dynamo" while the other is often referred to as a "balance wheel."

Once in a great while you will find a man who is both a dynamo and a balance wheel, but such well balanced personalities are rare. Most successful business organizations that assume great size are made up of both of these types.

The "balance wheel" who does nothing but compile facts and figures and statistics is just as much a man of *action* as the man who goes upon the platform and sells an idea to a thousand people by the sheer power of his *active* personality. To determine whether a man is a man of *action* or not it is necessary to analyze both his mental and his physical habits.

In the first part of this lesson I said that "the world pays you for what you do and not for what you know." That statement might easily be misconstrued. What the world really pays you for is *what you do* or *what you can get others to do.*

A man who can induce others to co-operate and do effective team-work, or inspire others so that they become more *active*, is no less a man of *action* than the man who renders effective service in a more direct manner.

In the field of industry and business there are men who have the ability so to inspire and direct the efforts of others that all under their direction accomplish more than they could without this directing influence. It is a well known fact that Carnegie so ably directed the efforts of those who constituted his personal staff that he made many wealthy men of those who would never have become wealthy without the directing genius of his brain. The same may be said of practically all great leaders in the field of industry and business—the gain is not all on the side of the leaders. Those under their direction often profit most by their leadership.

It is a common practice for a certain type of man to berate his employers because of their opposite stations in a financial sense. It is usually true that such men would be infinitely worse off without these employers than they are with them.

In the Introduction to this course the value of allied effort was particularly emphasized for the reason that some men have the vision to plan while others have the ability to carry plans into *action* although they do not possess the *imagination* or the vision to create the plans they execute.

It was his understanding of this principle of allied effort that enabled Andrew Carnegie to surround himself with a group of men that was made up of those who could plan and those who could execute. Carnegie had in his group of assistants some of the most efficient salesmen in the world, but if his entire staff had been made up of men who could do nothing but sell he could never have accumulated the fortune that he did. If his entire staff had been made up of salesmen only he would have had *action* in abundance, but *action,* in the sense that it is used in this lesson, must be intelligently guided.

One of the best known law firms in America is made up of two lawyers, one of whom never appears in court. He prepares the firm's cases for trial and the other member of the firm goes to court and tries them. Both are men of intense *action,* but they express it in different ways.

Thousands of people walked over the great Calumet Copper Mine without discovering it. Just one lone man got busy with a pick and found it. You may be standing on your "Calumet Mine" right now, without knowing it, in whatever position you are filling. Dig down and see what is under the surface of your position.

There can be as much *action* in *preparation,* in most undertakings, as in *execution.*

In finding your own place in the world, you should analyze yourself and find out whether you are a "dynamo" or a "balance wheel," and select a *definite chief aim* for yourself that harmonizes with your native ability. If you are in business with others, you should analyze them as well as yourself, and endeavor to see that each person takes the part for which his temperament and native ability best fit him.

Stating it another way, people may be classified under

two headings: one is the promoter and the other is the care-taker. The promoter type makes an able salesman and organizer. The care-taker type makes an excellent conserver of assets after they have been accumulated.

Place the care-taker type in charge of a set of books and he is happy, but place him on the outside selling and he is unhappy and will be a failure at his job. Place the promoter in charge of a set of books and he will be miserable. His nature demands more intense *action*. Action of the passive type will not satisfy his ambitions, and if he is kept at work which does not give him the action his nature demands he will be a failure. It very frequently turns out that men who embezzle funds in their charge are of the promoter type and they would not have yielded to temptation had their efforts been confined to the work for which they are best fitted.

Give a man the sort of work that harmonizes with his nature and the best there is in him will exert itself. One of the outstanding tragedies of the world is the fact that most people never engage in the work for which they are best fitted by nature.

Too often the mistake is made, in the selection of a life-work, of engaging in the work which seems to be the most profitable from a monetary viewpoint, without consideration of native ability. If money alone brought success this procedure would be all right, but *success* in its highest and noblest form calls for peace of mind and enjoyment and happiness which come only to the man who has found the work that he likes best.

The main purpose of this course is to help you analyze yourself and determine what your native ability best fits you to do. You should make this analysis by carefully studying the chart that accompanies the Introduction before you select your *definite chief aim*.

We come, now, to the discussion of the principle through which *action* may be developed. To understand how to become *active* requires understanding of how not to *procrastinate*.

These suggestions will give you the necessary instructions:

First: Form the *habit* of doing each day the most distasteful tasks first. This procedure will be difficult at first, but after you have formed the *habit* you will take pride in pitching into the hardest and most undesirable part of your work first.

Second: Place this sign in front of you where you can see it in your daily work, and put a copy in your bedroom, where it will greet you as you retire and when you arise: *"Do not tell them what you can do; show them!"*

Third: Repeat the following words, aloud, twelve times each night just before you go to sleep: "Tomorrow I will do everything that should be done, when it should be done, and as it should be done. I will perform the most difficult tasks first because this will destroy the habit of procrastination and develop the habit of *action* in its place."

Fourth: Carry out these instructions with faith in their soundness and with belief that they will develop *action,* in body and in mind, sufficient to enable you to realize your *definite chief aim.*

The outstanding feature of this course is the simplicity of the style in which it is written. All great fundamental truths are simple, in final analysis, and whether one is delivering an address or writing a course of instruction, the purpose should be to convey impressions and statements of fact in the clearest and most concise manner possible.

Before closing this lesson, permit me to go back to what was said about the value of a hearty laugh as a healthful stimulant to *action,* and add the statement that singing produces the same effect, and in some instances is far preferable to laughing.

Billy Sunday is one of the most dynamic and *active* preachers in the world, yet it has been said that his sermons would lose much of their effectiveness if it were not for the psychological effect of his song services.

It is a well known fact that the German army was a winning army at the beginning, and long after the beginning of the world war; and it has been said that much of this was due to the fact that the German army was a singing army. Then came the khaki-clad dough-boys from America, and they, too, were singers. Back of their singing was an enduring faith in the cause for which they were fighting. Soon the Germans began to quit singing, and as they did so the tide of war began to turn against them.

If church attendance had nothing else to recommend it, except the psychological effect of the song service, that would be sufficient, for no one can join in the singing of a beautiful hymn without feeling better for it.

For many years I have observed that I could write more effectively after having participated in a song service. Prove my statement to your own satisfaction by going to church next Sunday morning and participating in the song service with all the enthusiasm at your command.

During the war I helped devise ways and means of speeding production in industrial plants that were engaged in manufacturing war supplies. By actual test, in a plant employing 3,000 men and women, the production was increased forty-five per cent in less than thirty days after we had organized the workers into singing groups and installed orchestras and bands that played at ten-minute intervals such stirring songs as "Over There," and "Dixie," and "There'll Be a Hot Time in the Old Town Tonight." The workers caught the rhythm of the music and speeded up their work accordingly.

Properly selected music would stimulate any class of workers to greater *action,* a fact which does not seem to be understood by all who direct the efforts of large numbers of people.

In all my travels I have found but one business firm whose managers made use of music as a stimulant for their workers. This was the Filene Department Store, in Boston, Mass. During the summer months this store provides an orchestra that plays the latest dance music for half an hour before opening time, in the morning. The salespeople use the aisles of the store for dancing and by the time the doors are thrown open they are in an *active* state of mind and body that carries them through the entire day.

Incidentally, I have never seen more courteous or efficient salespeople than those employed by the Filene store. One of the department managers told me that every person in his department performed more service and with less real effort, as a result of the morning music program.

A singing army is a winning army, whether on the field of battle, in warfare, or behind the counters in a department store. There is a book entitled Singing Through Life With God by George Wharton James, which I recommend to all who are interested in the psychology of song.

If I were the manager of an industrial plant in which the work was heavy and monotonous, I would install some sort of musical program that would supply every worker with music. On lower Broadway, in New York City, an ingenious Greek has discovered how to entertain his customers and at the same time speed up the work of his helpers by the use of a phonograph. Every boy in the place keeps time with the music as he draws the cloth across the shoes, and seems to get considerable fun out of his work in doing so. To speed up the work the proprietor has but to speed up the phonograph.

Any form of group effort, where two or more people form a co-operative alliance for the purpose of accomplishing a definite purpose, becomes more powerful than mere individual effort.

A football team may win consistently and continuously, by well co-ordinated team-work, even though the members of the team may be unfriendly and out of harmony in many ways outside of their actual work on the ball ground.

A group of men composing a board of directors may disagree with one another; they may be unfriendly, and

I do not know for sure, but I strongly suspect that the person who performs service that is greater in quantity and better in quality than that for which he is paid, is eventually paid for more than he performs.

in no way in sympathy with one another, and still carry on a business which appears to be very successful.

A man and his wife may live together, accumulate a fair sized or even a great fortune, rear and educate a family, without the bond of harmony which is essential for the development of a Master Mind.

But all of these alliances might be made more powerful and effective if based upon a foundation of perfect harmony, thus permitting the development of a supplemental power known as the Master Mind.

Plain co-operative effort produces power; there can be no doubt about this; but co-operative effort that is based upon complete harmony of purpose develops super-power.

Let every member of any co-operative group set his heart upon the achievement of the same definite end, in a spirit of perfect harmony, and the way has been paved for the development of a Master Mind, providing all members of the group willingly subordinate their own personal interests for the attainment of the objective for which the group is aiming.

The United States of America has become one of the most powerful nations on earth, largely because of the highly organized co-operative effort between the states. It will be helpful to remember that these United States were born as the result of one of the most powerful Master Minds ever created. The members of this Master Mind were the signers of the Declaration of Independence.

The men who signed that document either consciously or unconsciously put into operation the power known as the "Master Mind," and that power was sufficient to enable them to defeat all the soldiers who were sent into the field against them. The men who fought to make the Declaration of Independence endure did not fight for money, alone; they fought for a principle—the principle of freedom, which is the highest known motivating force.

A great leader, whether in business, finance, industry or statesmanship, is one who understands how to create a motivating objective which will be accepted with enthusiasm by every member of his group of followers.

In politics a "live issue" is everything!

By "live issue" is meant some popular objective toward the attainment of which the majority of the voters can be rallied. These "issues" generally are broadcast in the form of snappy slogans, such as "Keep Cool with Coolidge," which suggested to the minds of the voters that to keep Coolidge was the equivalent of keeping prosperity. It worked!

During Lincoln's election campaign the cry was, "Stand back of Lincoln and preserve the Union." It worked.

Woodrow Wilson's campaign managers, during his second campaign, coined the slogan, "He kept us out of war," and it worked.

The degree of power created by the co-operative effort of any group of people is measured, always, by the nature of the motive which the group is laboring to attain. This may be profitably borne in mind by all who organize group effort for any purpose whatsoever. Find a motive around which men may be induced to rally in a highly emotionalized, enthusiastic spirit of perfect harmony and you have found the starting point for the creation of a Master Mind.

It is a well known fact that men will work harder for the attainment of an ideal than they will for mere money. In searching for a "motive" as the basis for developing co-operative group effort it will be profitable to bear this fact in mind.

At the time of the writing of this lesson there is much adverse agitation and general criticism directed against the railroads of the country. Who is back of this agitation this author does not know, but he does know that the very fact that such agitation exists could and should be made the motivating force around which the railroad officials might rally the hundreds of thousands of railroad employees who earn their living by railroading, thereby creating a power that would effectively eliminate this adverse criticism.

The railroads are the very back-bone of the country. Tie up all railroad service and the people of the larger cities would starve before food could reach them. In this fact may be found a motive around which a large majority of the public could be caused to rally in support of any plan for self-protection which the railroad officials might wish to carry out.

The power represented by all of the railroad employees and a majority of the public who patronize the railroads is sufficient to protect the railroads against all manner of adverse legislation and other attempts to depreciate their properties, but the power is only potential until it is organized and placed definitely back of a specific motive.

Man is a queer animal. Give him a sufficiently vitalized motive and the man of but average ability, under ordinary circumstances, will suddenly develop superpower.

What man can and will accomplish to please the woman of his choice (providing the woman knows how to stimulate him to action) has ever been a source of wonderment to students of the human mind.

There are three major motivating forces to which man responds in practically all of his efforts. These are:

1. The motive of self-preservation
2. The motive of sexual contact
3. The motive of financial and social power.

Stated more briefly, the main motives which impel men to action are money, sex and self-preservation. Leaders who are seeking a motivating force out of which to secure action from a following may find it under one or more of these three classifications.

As you have observed, this lesson is very closely related to the Introduction and Lesson One which cover the Law of the Master Mind. It is possible for groups to function co-operatively, without thereby creating a Master Mind, as, for example, where people co-operate merely out of necessity, without the spirit of harmony as the basis of their efforts. This sort of co-operation may produce considerable power, but nothing to compare with that which is possible when every person in an alliance subordinates his or her own individual interests and co-ordinates his or her efforts with those of all other members of the alliance, in perfect harmony.

The extent to which people may be induced to co-operate, in harmony, depends upon the motivating force which impels them to action. Perfect harmony such as is essential for creating a Master Mind can be obtained only when the motivating force of a group is sufficient to cause each member of the group completely to forget his or her own personal interests and work for the good of the group, or for the sake of attaining some idealistic, charitable or philanthropic objective.

The three major motivating forces of mankind have been here stated for the guidance of the Leader who wishes to create plans for securing co-operation from followers who will throw themselves into the carrying out of his plans in a spirit of unselfishness and perfect harmony.

Your position is nothing more than your opportunity to show what sort of ability you have. You will get out of it exactly what you put into it—no more and no less. A "big" position is but the sum total of numerous "little" positions well filled.

Men will not rally to the support of a leader in such a spirit of harmony unless the motive that impels them to do so is one that will induce them to lay aside all thoughts of themselves.

We do well that which we love to do, and fortunate is the Leader who has the good judgment to bear this fact in mind and so lay his plans that all his followers are assigned parts that harmonize with this law.

The leader who gets all there is to be had from his followers does so because he has set up in the mind of each a sufficiently strong motive to get each to subordinate his own interests and work in a perfect spirit of harmony with all other members of the group.

Regardless of who you are, or what your *definite chief aim* may be, if you plan to attain the object of your *chief aim* through the co-operative efforts of others you must set up in the minds of those whose co-operation you seek a motive strong enough to insure their full, undivided, unselfish co-operation, for you will then be placing back of your plans the power of the Law of the Master Mind.

You are now ready to take up Lesson Thirteen, which will teach you how to make working capital out of all mistakes, errors and failures which you have experienced, and also how to profit by the mistakes and failures of others.

The president of one of the great railway systems of the United States said, after reading the next lesson, that "this lesson carries a suggestion which, if heeded and understood, will enable any person to become a master in his chosen life-work."

For reasons which will be plain after you have read the next lesson, it is the author's favorite lesson of this course.

YOUR STANDING ARMY

An After-the-Lesson Visit with the Author

These fifteen soldiers are labeled: Definite Chief Aim, Self-Confidence, Habit of Saving, Imagination, Initiative and Leadership, Enthusiasm, Self-Control, Doing More Than Paid For, Pleasing Personality, Accurate Thought, Concentration, Co-operation, Failure, Tolerance, Golden Rule

Power comes from organized effort. You see in the picture on the previous page the forces which enter into all organized effort. Master these fifteen forces and you may have whatever you want in life. Others will be helpless to defeat your plans. Make these fifteen forces your own and you will be an accurate thinker.

In the picture on the previous page you see the most powerful army on earth! Observe the emphasis on the word POWERFUL.

This army is standing at attention, ready to do the bidding of any person who will command it. It is YOUR army if you will take charge of it.

This army will give you POWER sufficient to mow down all opposition with which you meet. Study the picture carefully, then take inventory of yourself and find out how many of these soldiers you need.

If you are a normal person you long for material success.

Success and POWER are always found together. You cannot be sure of success unless you have power. You cannot have power unless you develop it through fifteen essential qualities.

Each of these fifteen qualities may be likened to the commanding officer of a regiment of soldiers. Develop these qualities in your own mind and you will have POWER.

The most important of the fifteen commanding officers in this army is DEFINITE PURPOSE.

Without the aid of a definite purpose the remainder of the army would be useless to you. Find out, as early in life as possible, what your major purpose in life shall be. Until you do this you are nothing but a drifter, subject to control by every stray wind of circumstance that blows in your direction.

Millions of people go through life without knowing what it is they want.

All have a purpose, but only two out of every hundred have a DEFINITE purpose. Before you decide whether your purpose is DEFINITE or not, look up the meaning of the word in the dictionary.

NOTHING IS IMPOSSIBLE TO THE PERSON WHO KNOWS WHAT IT IS HE WANTS AND MAKES UP HIS MIND TO ACQUIRE IT!

Columbus had a DEFINITE PURPOSE and it became a reality. Lincoln's major DEFINITE PURPOSE was to free the black slaves of the South and he turned that purpose into reality. Roosevelt's major purpose, during his first term of office, was to build the Panama

Canal. He lived to see that purpose realized. Henry Ford's DEFINITE PURPOSE was to build the best popular priced automobile on earth. That purpose, backed persistently, has made him the most powerful man on earth. Burbank's DEFINITE PURPOSE was to improve plant life. Already that purpose has made possible the raising of enough food on ten square miles of land to feed the entire world.

Twenty years ago Edwin C. Barnes formed a DEFINITE PURPOSE in his mind. That purpose was to become the business partner of Thomas A. Edison. At the time his purpose was chosen Mr. Barnes had no qualification entitling him to a partnership with the world's greatest inventor. Despite this handicap he became the partner of the great Edison. Five years ago he retired from active business, with more money than he needs or can use, wealth that he accumulated in partnership with Edison.

NOTHING IS IMPOSSIBLE TO THE MAN WITH A DEFINITE PURPOSE!

Opportunity, capital, co-operation from other men and all other essentials for success gravitate to the man who knows what he wants!

Vitalize your mind with a DEFINITE PURPOSE and immediately your mind becomes a magnet which attracts everything that harmonizes with that purpose.

James J. Hill, the great railroad builder, was a poorly paid telegraph operator. Moreover, he had reached the age of forty and was still ticking away at the telegraph key without any outward appearances of success.

Then something of importance happened! Of importance to Hill and to the people of the United States. He formed the DEFINITE PURPOSE of building a railroad across the great waste desert of the West. Without reputation, without capital, without encouragement from others James J. Hill got the capital and built the greatest of all the railroad systems of the United States.

Woolworth was a poorly paid clerk in a general store. In his mind's eye he saw a chain of novelty stores specializing on five and ten cent sales. That chain of stores became his DEFINITE PURPOSE. He made that purpose come true, and with it more millions than he could use.

Cyrus H. K. Curtis selected, as his DEFINITE PURPOSE, the publishing of the world's greatest magazine. Starting with nothing but the name "Saturday Evening Post," and opposed by friends and advisers who said "It couldn't be done," he transformed that purpose into reality.

Martin W. Littleton is the most highly paid lawyer in the world. It is said that he will accept no retainer under $50,000.00. When he was twelve years old he had never been inside of a school house. He went to hear a lawyer defend a murderer. That speech so impressed him that he grabbed hold of his father's hand and said, "Some day I am going to be the best lawyer in the United States and make speeches like that man."

"Fine chance for an ignorant mountain youth to become a great lawyer," someone might say, but remember that NOTHING IS IMPOSSIBLE TO THE MAN WHO KNOWS WHAT HE WANTS AND MAKES UP HIS MIND TO GET IT.

Study each of the fifteen soldiers shown in command of the army in the picture at the beginning of this essay.

Remember, as you look at the picture, that no one of these soldiers alone is powerful enough to insure success. Remove a single one of them and the entire army would be weakened.

The powerful man is the man who has developed, in his own mind, the entire fifteen qualities represented by the fifteen commanding officers shown in the picture. Before you can have power you must have a DEFINITE PURPOSE; you must have SELF-CONFIDENCE with which to back up that purpose; you must have INITIATIVE and LEADERSHIP with which to exercise your self-confidence; you must have IMAGINATION in creating your definite purpose and in building the plans with which to transform that purpose into reality and put your plans into action. You must mix ENTHUSIASM with your action or it will be insipid and without "kick." You must exercise SELF-CONTROL. You must form the habit of DOING MORE THAN PAID FOR. You must cultivate a PLEASING PERSONALITY. You must acquire the HABIT OF SAVING. You must become an ACCURATE THINKER, remembering, as you develop this quality, that accurate thought is based upon FACTS and not upon hearsay evidence or mere information. You must form the habit of CONCENTRATION by giving your undivided attention to but one task at a time. You must acquire the habit of CO-OPERATION and practice it in all your plans. You must profit by FAILURE, your own and that of others. You must cultivate the habit of TOLERANCE. Last, but by no means the least important, you must make the GOLDEN RULE the foundation of all you do that affects other people.

Keep this picture where you can see it each day and, one by one, call these fifteen soldiers out of the line and study them. Make sure that the counterpart of each is developed in your own mind.

All efficient armies are well disciplined!

The army which you are building in your own mind must, also, be disciplined. It must obey your command at every step.

When you call out of the line the thirteenth soldier, "FAILURE," remember that nothing will go as far toward developing discipline as will failure and temporary defeat. While you are comparing yourself with this soldier determine whether or not you have been profiting by your own failures and temporary defeat.

FAILURE comes to all at one time or another. Make sure, when it comes your way, that you will learn something of value from its visit. Make sure, also, that it would not visit you if there was not room for it in your make-up.

To make progress in this world you must rely solely upon the forces within your own mind for your start. After this start has been made you may turn to others for aid, but the first step must be taken without outside aid.

After you have made this "start," it will surprise you to observe how many willing people you will encounter who will volunteer to assist you.

Success is made up of many facts and factors, chiefly of the fifteen qualities represented by these fifteen soldiers. To enjoy a well balanced and rounded out success one must appropriate as much or as little of each of these fifteen qualities as may be missing in one's own inherited ability.

When you came into this world you were endowed with certain inborn traits, the result of millions of years of evolutionary changes, through thousands of generations of ancestors.

Added to these inborn traits you acquired many other qualities, according to the nature of your environment and the teaching you received during your early childhood. You are the sum total of that which was born in you and that which you have picked up from your experiences, what you have thought and what you have been taught, since birth.

Through the law of chance one in a million people will receive, through inborn heredity and from knowledge acquired after birth, all of the fifteen qualities named in the picture at the beginning of this essay.

All who are not fortunate enough to have thus acquired the essentials for SUCCESS must develop them within themselves.

The first step in this "development" process is to realize what qualities are missing in your naturally acquired equipment. The second step is the strongly planted DESIRE to develop yourself where you are now deficient.

Prayer sometimes works, while at other times it does not work.

It always works when backed with unqualified FAITH. This is a truth which no one will deny, yet, it is a truth which no one can explain. All we know is that prayer works when we BELIEVE it will work. Prayer without FAITH is nothing but an empty collection of words.

A DEFINITE PURPOSE may be transformed into reality only when one BELIEVES it can be done. Perhaps the selfsame law that turns the prayer based upon FAITH into reality transforms, also, a DEFINITE PURPOSE that is founded upon belief into reality.

It can do no harm if you make your DEFINITE PURPOSE in life the object of your daily prayer. And, as you pray remember that prayer based upon FAITH always works.

Develop in your own mind all of the fifteen qualities, from a DEFINITE PURPOSE to the GOLDEN RULE, and you will find the application of FAITH is not difficult.

Take inventory of yourself. Find out how many of the fifteen qualities you now possess. Add to this inventory the missing qualities until you have, in your mind, the entire fifteen. You will then be ready to measure your success in whatever terms you DESIRE.

The qualities represented by the fifteen soldiers shown in this picture are the brick and the mortar and the building material with which you must build your Temple of Success. Master these fifteen qualities and you may play a perfect symphony of success in any undertaking, just as one who has mastered the fundamentals of music may play any piece at sight.

Make these fifteen qualities your own and you will be an EDUCATED person, because you will have the power to get whatever you want in life without violating the rights of others.

> "All worlds are man's, to conquer and to rule
>   This is the glory of his life.
> But this its iron law: first must he school
>   Himself. Here 'gins and ends all strife."

Yesterday is but a dream,

Tomorrow is only a vision.

But today well lived makes

Every yesterday a dream of
    happiness,

And every tomorrow a vision of
    hope.

Look well, therefore, to this day.

          —FROM THE SANSCRIT

FAILURE

"You Can Do It If You Believe You Can!"

Under ordinary circumstances the term "failure" is a negative term. In this lesson, the word will be given a new meaning, because the word has been a very much misused one; and, for that reason, it has brought un-necessary grief and hardship to millions of people.

In the outset, let us distinguish between "failure" and "temporary defeat." Let us see if that which is so often looked upon as "failure" is not, in reality, but "temporary defeat." Moreover, let us see if this temporary defeat is not usually a blessing in disguise, for the reason that it brings us up with a jerk and redirects our energies along different and more desirable lines.

In Lesson Eight of this course, we learned that strength grows out of resistance; and we shall learn, in this lesson, that sound character is usually the handiwork of reverses, and setbacks, and temporary defeat, which the uninformed part of the world calls "failure."

Neither temporary defeat nor adversity amounts to failure in the mind of the person who looks upon it as a teacher that will teach some needed lesson. As a matter of fact, there is a great and lasting lesson in every reverse, and in every defeat; and, usually, it is a lesson that could be learned in no other way than through defeat.

Defeat often talks to us in a "dumb language" that we do not understand. If this were not true, we would not make the same mistakes over and over again without profiting by the lessons that they might teach us. If it were not true, we would observe more closely the mistakes which other people make and profit by them.

The main object of this lesson is to help the student understand and profit by this "dumb language" in which defeat talks to us.

Perhaps I can best help you to interpret the meaning of defeat by taking you back over some of my own experiences covering a period of approximately thirty years. Within this period, I have come to the turning-point, which the uninformed call "failure," seven different times. At each of these seven turning-points I thought I had made a dismal failure; but now I know that what looked to be a failure was nothing more than a kindly, unseen hand, that halted me in my chosen course and with great wisdom forced me to redirect my efforts along more advantageous pathways.

I arrived at this decision, however, only after I had taken a retrospective view of my experiences and had analyzed them in the light of many years of sober and meditative thought.

First Turning-Point

After finishing a course in a business college, I secured a position as stenographer and book-keeper which I held for the ensuing five years. As a result of having practiced the habit of performing more work and better work than that for which I was paid, as described in Lesson Eight of this course, I advanced rapidly until I was assuming responsibilities and receiving a salary far out of proportion to my age. I saved my money; and my bank account amounted to several thousand dollars. My reputation spread rapidly and I found competitive bidders for my services.

To meet these offers from competitors my employer advanced me to the position of General Manager of the mines where I was employed. I was quickly getting on top of the world, and *I knew it!*

Ah! but that was the sad part of my fate—*I knew it!*

Then the kindly hand of Fate reached out and gave me a gentle nudge. My employer lost his fortune and I lost my position. This was my first real defeat; and, even though it came about as a result of causes beyond my control, I should have learned a lesson from it; which, of course, I did, but not until many years later.

Second Turning-Point

My next position was that of Sales Manager for a large lumber manufacturing concern in the South. I knew nothing about lumber, and but little about sales management; but I had learned that it was beneficial to render more service than that for which I was paid; and I had also learned that it paid to take the initiative and find out what ought to be done without someone telling me to do it. A good sized bank account, plus a record of steady advancement in my previous position, gave me all the self-confidence I needed, with some to spare, perhaps.

My advancement was rapid, my salary having been increased twice during the first year. I did so well in the management of sales that my employer took me into partnership with him. We began to make money and I began to see myself *on top of the world again!*

To stand "on top of the world" gives one a wonderful sensation; but it is a very dangerous place to stand, unless one stands very firmly, because the fall is so long and hard if one should stumble.

I was succeeding by leaps and bounds!

Up to that time it had never occurred to me that *success* could be measured in terms other than money and authority. Perhaps this was due to the fact that I had more money than I needed and more authority than I could manage safely at that age.

Not only was I "succeeding," from my viewpoint of success, but I knew I was engaged in the one and only business suited to my temperament. Nothing could have induced me to change into another line of endeavor. That is—nothing except that which happened, which *forced* me to change.

The unseen hand of Fate allowed me to strut around under the influence of my own vanity until I had commenced to feel my importance. In the light of my more sober years, I now wonder if the Unseen Hand does not purposely permit us foolish human beings to parade ourselves before our own mirrors of vanity until we come to see how vulgarly we are acting and become ashamed of ourselves. At any rate, I seemed to have a clear track ahead of me; there was plenty of coal in the bunker; there was water in the tank; my hand was on the throttle—I opened it wide and sped along at a rapid pace.

Alas! Fate awaited me just around the corner, with a stuffed club that was not stuffed with cotton. Of course I did not see the impending crash until it came. Mine was a sad story, but not unlike that which many another might tell if he would be frank with himself.

Like a stroke of lightning out of a clear sky, the 1907 panic swept down upon me; and, overnight, it rendered me an enduring service by destroying my business and relieving me of every dollar that I possessed.

This was my first serious *defeat!* I mistook it, then, for failure; but it was not, and before I complete this lesson I will tell you why it was not.

Third Turning-Point

It required the 1907 panic, and the defeat that it brought me, to divert and redirect my efforts from the lumber business to the study of law. Nothing on earth, except defeat, could have brought about this result; thus, the third turning-point of my life was ushered in on the wings of that which most people would call "failure," which reminds me to state again that every defeat teaches a needed lesson to those who are ready and willing to be taught.

When I entered law school, it was with the firm belief that I would emerge doubly prepared to catch up with the end of the rainbow and claim my pot of gold; for I still had no other conception of success except that of *money* and power.

One of the greatest leaders who ever lived stated the secret of his leadership in six words, as follows: "Kindness is more powerful than compulsion."

I attended law school at night and worked as an automobile salesman during the day. My sales experience in the lumber business was turned to good advantage. I prospered rapidly, doing so well (still featuring the habit of performing more service and better service than that for which I was paid) that the opportunity came to enter the automobile manufacturing business. I saw the need for trained automobile mechanics, therefore I opened an educational department in the manufacturing plant and began to train ordinary machinists in automobile assembling and repair work. The school prospered, paying me over a thousand dollars a month in net profits.

Again I was beginning to near the end of the rainbow. Again I knew I had at last found my niche in the world's work; that nothing could swerve me from my course or divert my attention from the automobile business.

My banker knew that I was prospering, therefore he loaned me money with which to expand. A peculiar trait of bankers—a trait which may be more or less developed in the remainder of us also—is that they will loan us money without any hesitation when we are *prosperous!*

My banker loaned me money until I was hopelessly in his debt, then he took over my business as calmly as if it had belonged to him, which it did!

From the station of a man of affairs who enjoyed an income of more than a thousand dollars a month, I was suddenly reduced to poverty.

Now, twenty years later, I thank the hand of Fate for this forced change; but at that time I looked upon the change as nothing but *failure.*

The rainbow's end had disappeared, and with it the proverbial pot of gold which is supposed to be found at its end. It was many years afterwards that I learned the truth that this temporary *defeat* was probably the greatest single blessing that ever came my way, because it forced me out of a business that in no way helped me to develop knowledge of self or of others, and directed my efforts into a channel which brought me a rich experience of which I was in need.

For the first time in life I began to ask myself if it were not possible for one to find something of value other than money and power at the rainbow's end. This temporary questioning attitude did not amount to open rebellion, mind you, nor did I follow it far enough to get the answer. It merely came as a fleeting thought, as do so many other thoughts to which we pay no attention, and passed out of my mind. Had I known as much then as I now know about the Law of Compensation, and had I been able to interpret experiences as I can now interpret them, I would have recognized that event as a gentle nudge from the hand of Fate.

After putting up the hardest fight of my life, up to that time, I accepted my temporary defeat as *failure* and thus was ushered in my next and fourth turning-point, which gave me an opportunity to put into use the knowledge of law that I had acquired.

Fourth Turning-Point

Because I was my wife's husband and her people had influence I secured the appointment as assistant to the chief counsel for one of the largest coal companies in the world. My salary was greatly out of proportion to those usually paid to beginners, and still further out of proportion to what I was worth; but pull was pull, and I was there just the same. It happened that what I lacked in legal skill I more than made up through the application of the principle of performing more service than that for which I was paid, and by taking the initiative and doing that which should have been done without being told to do it.

I was holding my position without difficulty. I practically had a soft berth for life had I cared to keep it.

Without consultation with my friends, and without warning, I resigned!

This was the first turning-point that was of my own selection. It was not forced upon me. I saw the old man Fate coming and beat him to the door. When pressed for a reason for resigning, I gave what seemed to me to be a very sound one, but I had trouble convincing the family circle that I had acted wisely.

I quit that position because the work was too easy and I was performing it with too little effort. I saw myself drifting into the habit of inertia. I felt myself becoming accustomed to taking life easily and I knew that the next step would be retrogression. I had so many friends at court that there was no particular impelling urge that made it necessary for me to keep moving. I was among friends and relatives, and I had a position that I could keep as long as I wished it, without exerting myself. I received an income that provided me with all the necessities and some of the luxuries, including a motor car and enough gasoline to keep it running.

What more did I need?

"Nothing!" I was beginning to say to myself.

This was the attitude toward which I felt myself slipping. It was an attitude which, for some reason that is still unknown to me, startled me so sharply that I made what many believed to be an irrational move by resigning. However ignorant I might have been in other matters at the time, I have felt thankful ever since for having had sense enough to realize that strength and growth come only through continuous effort and *struggle,* that disuse brings atrophy and decay.

This move proved to be the next most important turning-point of my life, although it was followed by ten years of effort which brought almost every conceivable grief that the human heart can experience. I quit my job in the legal field, where I was getting along well, living among friends and relatives, where I had what they believed to be an unusually bright and promising future ahead of me. I am frank to admit that it has been an ever-increasing source of wonderment to me as to why and how I gathered the courage to make the move that I did. As far as I am able to interpret the event, I arrived at my decision to resign more because of a "hunch," or a sort of "prompting" which I then did not understand, than by logical reasoning.

I selected Chicago as my new field of endeavor. I did this because I believed Chicago to be a place where one might find out if one had those sterner qualities which are so essential for survival in a world of keen competition. I made up my mind that if I could gain recognition, in any honorable sort of work, in Chicago, it would prove that I had the sort of material in my make-up that might be developed into real ability. That was a queer process of reasoning; at least it was an unusual process for me to indulge in at that time, which reminds me to state that we human beings often take unto ourselves credit for intelligence to which we are not entitled. I fear we too often assume credit for wisdom and for results that accrue from causes over which we have absolutely no control.

While I do not mean to convey the impression that I believe all of our acts to be controlled by causes beyond our power to direct, yet I strongly urge you to study and correctly interpret those causes which mark the most vital turning-points of your life; the points at which your efforts are diverted—from the old into new channels—in spite of all that you can do. *At least refrain from accepting any defeat as failure until you shall have had time to analyze the final result.*

My first position in Chicago was that of advertising manager of a large correspondence school. I knew but little about advertising, but my previous experience as a salesman, plus the advantage gained by rendering more service than that for which I was paid, enabled me to make an unusual showing.

The first year I earned $5,200.00.

I was "coming back" by leaps and bounds. Gradually the rainbow's end began to circle around me, and I saw, once more, the shining pot of gold almost within my reach. History is full of evidence that a feast usually precedes a famine. I was enjoying a feast but did not anticipate the famine that was to follow. I was getting along so well that I thoroughly approved of myself.

Self-approval is a dangerous state of mind.

This is a great truth which many people do not learn until the softening hand of Time has rested upon their shoulders for the better part of a life-time. Some never do learn it, and those who do are those who finally begin to understand the "dumb language" of defeat.

> *Remember this, when things go against you, that of all the expressions you carry in your face the light of joy shines farthest out to sea.*

I am convinced that one has but few, if any, more dangerous enemies to combat than that of self-approval. Personally I fear it more than defeat.

This brings me to my fifth turning-point, which was also of my own choice.

Fifth Turning-Point

I had made such a good record as advertising manager of the correspondence school that the president of the school induced me to resign my position and go into the candy manufacturing business with him. We organized the Betsy Ross Candy Company and I became its first president, thus beginning the next most important turning-point of my life.

The business grew rapidly until we had a chain of stores in eighteen different cities. Again I saw my rainbow's end almost within my reach. I knew that I had at last found the business in which I wished to remain for life. The candy business was profitable and, because I looked upon money as being the only evidence of success, I naturally believed I was about to corner success.

Everything went smoothly until my business associate and a third man, whom we had taken into the business, took a notion to gain control of my interest in the business without paying for it.

Their plan was successful, in a way, but I balked more stiffly than they had anticipated I would; therefore, for the purpose of "gentle persuasion," they had me arrested on a false charge and then offered to withdraw the charge on condition that I turn over to them my interest in the business.

I had commenced to learn, for the first time, that there was much cruelty, and injustice, and dishonesty in the hearts of men.

When the time for a preliminary hearing came, the complaining witnesses were nowhere to be found. But I had them brought and forced them to go on the witness stand and tell their stories, which resulted in my vindication, and a damage suit against the perpetrators of the injustice.

This incident brought about an irreparable breach between my business associates and myself, which finally cost me my interest in the business, but that was but slight when compared to that which it cost my associates; for they are still paying, and no doubt will continue to pay as long as they live.

My damage suit was brought under what is known as a "tort" action, through which damages were claimed for malicious damage to character. In Illinois, where the action was brought, judgment under a tort action gives the one in favor of whom the judgment is rendered the right to have the person against whom it is obtained placed in jail until the amount of the judgment has been paid.

In due time I got a heavy judgment against my former business associates. *I could then have had both of them placed behind the bars.*

For the first time in my life I was brought face to face with the opportunity to strike back at my enemies in a manner that would hurt. I had in my possession a weapon with "teeth" in it—a weapon placed there by the enemies, themselves.

The feeling that swept over me was a queer one!

Would I have my enemies jailed, or would I take advantage of this opportunity to extend them mercy, thereby proving myself to be made of a different type of material.

Then and there was laid, in my heart, the foundation upon which the Fifteenth Lesson of this course is built, for I made up my mind to permit my enemies to go free—as free as they could be made by my having extended them mercy and forgiveness.

But long before my decision had been reached the hand of Fate had commenced to deal roughly with these misguided fellow men who had tried, in vain, to destroy me. Time, the master worker, to which we must all submit sooner or later, had already been at work on my former business associates, and it had dealt with them less mercifully than I had done. One of them was later sentenced to a long term in the penitentiary, for another crime that he had committed against some other person, and the other one had, meanwhile, been reduced to pauperism.

We can circumvent the laws which men place upon statute books, but the Law of Compensation never!

The judgment which I obtained against these men stands on the records of the Superior Court, of Chicago, as silent evidence of vindication of my character; but it serves me in a more important way than that—it serves as a reminder that I could forgive enemies who had tried to destroy me, and for this reason, instead of destroying my character, I suspect that the incident served to strengthen it.

Being arrested seemed, at the time, a terrible disgrace, even though the charge was false. I did not relish the experience, and I would not wish to go through a similar experience again, but I am bound to admit that it was worth all the grief it cost me, because it gave me the opportunity to find out that revenge was not a part of my make-up.

Here I would direct your attention to a close analysis of the events described in this lesson, for if you observe carefully you can see how this entire course of study has been evolved out of these experiences. Each temporary defeat left its mark upon my heart and provided some part of the material of which this course has been built.

We would cease to fear or to run away from trying experiences if we observed, from the biographies of men of destiny, that nearly every one of them was sorely tried and run through the mill of merciless experience before he "arrived." This leads me to wonder if the hand of Fate does not test "the metal of which we are made" in various and sundry ways before placing great responsibilities upon our shoulders.

Before approaching the next turning-point of my life, may I not call your attention to the significant fact that each turning-point carried me nearer and nearer my rainbow's end, and brought me some useful knowledge which became, later, a permanent part of my philosophy of life.

Sixth Turning-Point

We come, now, to the turning-point which probably brought me nearer the rainbow's end than any of the others had, because it placed me in a position where I found it necessary to bring into use all the knowledge I had acquired up to that time, concerning practically every subject with which I was acquainted, and gave me opportunity for self-expression and development such as rarely comes to a man so early in life. This turning-point came shortly after my dreams of success in the candy business had been shattered, when I turned my efforts to teaching Advertising and Salesmanship as a department of one of the colleges of the Middle West.

Some wise philosopher has said that we never learn very much about a given subject until we commence teaching it to others. My first experience as a teacher proved this to be true. My school prospered from the very beginning. I had a resident class and also a correspondence school through which I was teaching students in nearly every English-speaking country. Despite the ravages of war, the school was growing rapidly and I again saw the end of the rainbow within sight.

Then came the second military draft which practically destroyed my school, as it caught most of those who were enrolled as students. At one stroke I charged off more than $75,000.00 in tuition fees and at the same time contributed my own service to my country.

Once more I was penniless!

Unfortunate is the person who has never had the thrill of being penniless at one time or another; for, as Edward Bok has truthfully stated, poverty is the richest experience that can come to a man; an experience which, however, he advises one to get away from as quickly as possible.

Again I was forced to redirect my efforts, but, before I proceed to describe the next and last important turning-point, I wish to call your attention to the fact that no single event described up to this point is, within itself, of any practical significance. The six turning-points that I have briefly described meant nothing to me, taken singly, and they will mean nothing to you if analyzed singly. But take these events collectively and they form a very significant foundation for the next turning-point, and constitute reliable evidence that we human beings are constantly undergoing evolutionary changes as a result of the experiences of life with which we meet, even though no single experience may seem to convey a definite, usable lesson.

It is far better to be associated with a few who are right than with the mob which is wrong, because right is always the winner in the end.

I feel impelled to dwell at length on the point which I am here trying to make clear, because I have now reached the point in my career at which men go down in permanent defeat or rise, with renewed energies, to heights of attainment of stupendous proportions, according to the manner in which they interpret their past experiences and use those experiences as the basis of working plans. If my story stopped here it would be of no value to you, but there is another and a more significant chapter yet to be written, covering the seventh and most important of all the turning-points of my life.

It must have been obvious to you, all through my description of the six turning-points already outlined, that I had not really found my place in the world. It must have been obvious to you that most, if not all, of my temporary defeats were due mainly to the fact that I had not yet discovered the work into which I could throw my heart and soul. Finding the work for which one is best fitted and which one likes best is very much like finding the one person whom one loves best; there is no rule by which to make the search, but when the right niche is contacted one immediately recognizes it.

Seventh Turning-Point

Before I finish I will describe the collective lessons that I learned from each of the seven turning-points of my life, but first let me describe the seventh and last of these turning-points. To do so, I must go back to that eventful day—*November Eleven, Nineteen Hundred and Eighteen!*

That was armistice day, as everyone knows. The war had left me without a penny, as I have already stated, but I was happy to know that the slaughter had ceased and reason was about to reclaim civilization once more.

As I stood in front of my office window and looked out at the howling mob that was celebrating the end of the war, my mind went back into my yesterdays, especially to that eventful day when that kind old gentleman laid his hand on my shoulder and told me that if I would acquire an education I could make my mark in the world. I had been acquiring that education without knowing it. Over a period of more than twenty years I had been going to school in the University of Hard Knocks, as you must have observed from my description of the various turning-points of my life. As I stood in front of that window my entire past, with its bitter and its sweet, its ups and its downs, passed before me in review.

The time had come for another turning-point!

I sat down to my typewriter and, to my astonishment, my hands began to play a regular tune upon the key-board. I had never written so rapidly or so easily before. I did not plan or think about that which I was writing—*I just wrote that which came into my mind!*

Unconsciously, I was laying the foundation for the most important turning-point of my life; for, when I had finished, I had prepared a document through which I financed a national magazine that gave me contact with people throughout the English-speaking world. So greatly did that document influence my own career, and the lives of tens of thousands of other people, that I believe it will be of interest to the students of this course; therefore, I am reproducing it, just as it appeared in *Hill's Golden Rule* magazine, where it was first published, as follows:

"A Personal Visit with Your Editor"

I am writing on Monday, November eleventh, 1918. Today will go down in history as the greatest holiday.

On the street, just outside of my office window, the surging crowds of people are celebrating the downfall of an influence that has menaced civilization for the past four years.

The war is over!

Soon our boys will be coming back home from the battlefields of France.

The lord and master of Brute Force is nothing but a shadowy ghost of the past!

Two thousand years ago the Son of man was an outcast, with no place of abode. Now the situation has been reversed and the devil has no place to lay his head.

Let each of us take unto himself the great lesson that this world war has taught; namely, only that which is based upon justice and mercy toward all—the weak and the strong, the rich and the poor, alike—can survive. All else must pass on.

Out of this war will come a new idealism—an idealism that will be based upon the Golden Rule philosophy; an idealism that will guide us, not to see how much we can "do our fellow man for"; but how much we can do for him that will ameliorate his hardships and make him happier as he tarries by the wayside of life.

Emerson embodied this idealism in his great essay, the Law of Compensation. Another great Philosopher embodied it in these words, "Whatsoever a man soweth, that shall he also reap."

The time for practicing the Golden Rule philosophy is upon us. In business as well as in social relationships he who neglects or refuses to use this philosophy as the basis of his dealings will but hasten the time of his failure.

And, while I am intoxicated with the glorious news of the war's ending, is it not fitting that I should attempt to do something to help preserve for the generations yet to come, one of the great lessons to be learned from William Hohenzollern's effort to rule the earth by *force?*

I can best do this by going back twenty-two years for my beginning. Come with me, won't you?

It was a bleak November morning, probably not far from the eleventh of the month, that I got my first job as a laborer in the coal mine regions of Virginia, at wages of a dollar a day.

A dollar a day was a big sum in those days; especially to a boy of my age. Of this, I paid fifty cents a day for my board and room.

Shortly after I began work, the miners became dissatisfied and commenced talking about striking. I listened eagerly to all that was said. I was especially interested in the organizer who had organized the union. He was one of the smoothest speakers I had ever heard, and his words fascinated me. He said one thing, in particular, that I have never forgotten; and, if I knew where to find him, I would look him up today and thank him warmly for saying it. The philosophy which I gathered from his words has had a most profound and enduring influence upon me.

Perhaps you will say that most labor agitators are not very sound philosophers; and I would agree with you if you said so. Maybe this one was not a sound philosopher, but surely the philosophy he expounded on this occasion was sound.

Standing on a dry goods box, in the corner of an old shop where he was holding a meeting, he said:

"Men, we are talking about striking. Before you vote I wish to call your attention to something that will benefit you if you will heed what I say.

"You want more money for your work; and I wish to see you get it, because I believe you deserve it.

"May I not tell you how to get more money and still retain the good-will of the owner of this mine?

"We can call a strike and probably force them to pay more money, but we cannot force them to do this and like it. Before we call a strike, let us be fair with the owner of the mine and with ourselves; let us go to the owner and ask him if he will divide the profits of his mine with us fairly.

> *No one is living aright unless he so lives that whoever meets him goes away more confident and joyous for the contact.*
> —LILIAN WHITING

"If he says 'yes,' as he probably will, then let us ask him how much he made last month and, if he will divide among us a fair proportion of any additional profits he may make if we all jump in and help him earn more next month.

"He, being human, like each of us, will no doubt say—'Why, certainly boys; go to it and I'll divide with you.' It is but natural that he would say that, boys.

"After he agrees to the plan, as I believe he will if we make him see that we are in earnest, I want every one of you to come to work with a smile on your face for the next thirty days. I want to hear you whistling a tune as you go into the mines. I want you to go at your work with the feeling that you are one of the partners in this business.

"Without hurting yourself you can do almost twice as much work as you are doing; and if you do more work, you are sure to help the owner of this mine make more money. And if he makes more money he will be glad to divide a part of it with you. He will do this for sound business reasons if not out of a spirit of fair play.

"He will retaliate as surely as there is a God above us. If he doesn't, I'll be personally responsible to you, and if you say so I'll help blow this mine into smithereens!

"That's how much I think of the plan, boys! Are you with me?"

They were, to the man!

Those words sank into my heart as though they had been burned there with a red-hot iron.

The following month every man in the mines received a bonus of twenty per cent of his month's earnings. Every month thereafter each man received a bright red envelope with his part of the extra earnings in it. On the outside of the envelope were these printed words:

Your part of the profits from the work which you did that you were not paid to do.

I have gone through some pretty tough experiences since those days of twenty-odd years ago, but I have always come out on top—a little wiser, a little happier, and a little better prepared to be of service to my fellow men, owing to my having applied the principle of performing more work than I was actually paid to perform.

It may be of interest to you to know that the last position I held in the coal business was that of Assistant to the Chief Counsel for one of the largest companies in the world. It is a considerable jump from the position of common laborer in the coal mines to that of Assistant to the Chief Counsel of one of the largest companies—a jump that I never could have made without the aid of this principle of performing more work than I was paid to perform.

I wish I had the space in which to tell you of the scores of times that this idea of performing more work than I was paid to perform has helped me over rough spots.

Many have been the times that I have placed an employer so deeply in my debt, through the aid of this principle, that I got whatever I asked for, without hesitation or quibbling; without complaint or hard feelings; and, what is more important, without the feeling that I was taking unfair advantage of my employer.

I believe most earnestly that anything a man acquires from his fellow man without the full consent of the one from whom it is acquired, will eventually burn a hole in his pocket, or blister the palms of his hands, to say nothing of gnawing at his conscience until his heart aches with regret.

As I said in the beginning, I am writing on the morning of the eleventh of November, while the crowds are celebrating the great victory of *right* over *wrong!*

Therefore, it is but natural that I should turn to the silence of my heart for some thought to pass on to the world today—some thought that will help keep alive in the minds of Americans the spirit of idealism for which they have fought and in which they entered the world war.

I find nothing more appropriate than the philosophy which I have related, because I earnestly believe it was the arrogant disregard of this philosophy that brought Germany— the Kaiser and his people—to grief. To get this philosophy into the hearts of those who need it I shall publish a magazine to be called *Hill's Golden Rule.*

It takes money to publish national magazines, and I haven't very much of it at this writing; but before another month shall have passed, through the aid of the philosophy that I have tried to emphasize here, I shall find someone who will supply the necessary money and make it possible for me to pass on to the world the simple philosophy that lifted me out of the dirty coal mines and gave me a place where I can be of service to humanity. The philosophy which will raise you, my dear reader, whoever you may be and whatever you may be doing, into whatever position in life you may make up your mind to attain.

Every person has, or ought to have, the inherent desire to own something of monetary value. In at least a vague sort of way, every person who works for others (and this includes practically all of us) looks forward to the time when he will have some sort of a business or a profession of his own.

The best way to realize that ambition is to perform more work than one is paid to perform. You can get along with but little schooling; you can get along with but little capital; you can overcome almost any obstacle with which you are confronted, if you are honestly and earnestly willing to do the best work of which you are capable, regardless of the amount of money you receive for it. . . .

(*Note:* It is the afternoon of November the twenty-first, just ten days since I wrote the fore-going editorial. I have just read it to George B. Williams, of Chicago, a man who came up from the bottom through the aid of the philosophy of which I have written, and he *has made the publication of* Hill's Golden Rule *magazine possible.*)

It was in this somewhat dramatic manner that a desire which had lain dormant in my mind for nearly twenty years became translated into reality. During all that time I had wanted to become the editor of a newspaper. Back more than thirty years ago, when I was a very small boy, I used to "kick" the press for my father when he was publishing a small weekly news-paper, and I grew to love the smell of printer's ink.

Perhaps this desire was subconsciously gaining momentum all those years of preparation, while I was going through the experiences outlined in the turning-points of my life, until it had finally to burst forth in terms of action; or it may be that there was another plan, over which I had no control, that urged me on and on, never giving me any rest in any other line of work, until I began the publication of my first magazine. That point can be passed for the moment. The important thing to which I would direct your attention is the fact that I found my proper niche in the world's work and I was very happy over it.

Strangely enough, I entered upon this work with never a thought of looking for either the end of the rainbow or the proverbial pot of gold which is supposed to be found at its end. For the first time in my life, I seemed to realize, beyond room for doubt, that there was something else to be sought in life that was worth more than gold; therefore, I went at my editorial work with but one main thought in mind—and I pause while you ponder over this thought—

And that thought was to render the world the best service of which I was capable, whether my efforts brought me a penny in return or not!

> *To give pleasure to a single heart by a single kind act is better than a thousand head-bowings in prayer.*
>
> —SAADI

The publication of *Hill's Golden Rule* magazine brought me in contact with the thinking class of people all over the country. It gave me my big chance to be heard. The message of optimism and good-will among men that it carried became so popular that I was invited to go on a country-wide speaking tour during the early part of 1920, during which I had the privilege of meeting and talking with some of the most progressive thinkers of this generation. Contact with these people went a very long way toward giving me the courage to keep on doing the good work that I had started. This tour was a liberal education, within itself, because it brought me in exceedingly close contact with people in practically all walks of life, and gave me a chance to see that the United States of America was a pretty large country.

Comes, now, a description of the climax of the seventh turning-point of my life.

During my speaking tour I was sitting in a restaurant in Dallas, Texas, watching the hardest downpour of rain that I have ever seen. The water was pouring down over the plate-glass window in two great streams, and playing backward and forward from one of these streams to the other were little streams, making what resembled a great ladder of water.

As I looked at this unusual scene, the thought "flashed into my mind" that I would have a splendid lecture if I organized all that I had learned from the seven turning-points of my life and all I had learned from studying the lives of successful men, and offered it under the title of the "Magic Ladder to Success."

On the back of an envelope I outlined the fifteen points out of which this lecture was built, and later I worked these points into a lecture that was literally built from the temporary defeats described in the seven turning-points of my life.

All that I lay claim to knowing that is of value is represented by these fifteen points; and the material out of which this knowledge was gathered is nothing more or less than the knowledge that was *forced* upon me through experiences which have undoubtedly been classed, by some, as *failures!*

The reading course, of which this lesson is a part, is but the sum total of that which I gathered through these "failures." If this course proves to be of value to you, as I hope it will, you may give the credit to those "failures" described in this lesson.

Perhaps you will wish to know what material, monetary benefits I have gained from these turning-points, for you probably realize that we are living in an age in which life is an irksome struggle for existence and none too pleasant for those who are cursed with poverty.

All right! I'll be frank with you.

To begin with, the estimated income from the sale of this course is all that I need, and this, despite the fact that I have insisted that my publishers apply the Ford philosophy and sell the course at a popular price that is within the reach of all who want it.

In addition to the income from the sale of the course (which, please bear in mind, is but the sale of knowledge I have gathered through "failure"), I am now engaged in writing a series of illustrated editorials that is to be syndicated and published in the newspapers of the country. These editorials are based upon these same fifteen points as outlined in this course.

The estimated net income from the sale of the editorials is more than enough to care for my needs.

In addition to this I am now engaged in collaboration with a group of scientists, psychologists and business men, in writing a postgraduate course which will soon be available to all students who have mastered this more elementary course, covering not only the fifteen laws here outlined, from a more advanced viewpoint, but including still other laws which have but recently been discovered.

I have mentioned these facts only because I know what a common thing it is for all of us to measure success in terms of dollars, and to refuse, as unsound, all philosophy that does not foot up a good bank balance.

Practically all the past years of my life I have been poor—exceedingly poor—as far as bank balances were concerned. This condition has been, very largely, a matter of choice with me, because I have been putting the best of my time into the toilsome job of throwing off some of my ignorance and gathering in some of the knowledge of life of which I felt myself in need.

From the experiences described in these seven turning-points of my life, I have gathered a few golden threads of knowledge that I could have gained in no other way than through *defeat!*

My own experiences have led me to believe that the "dumb language" of *defeat* is the plainest and most effective language in the world, once one begins to understand it. I am almost tempted to say that I believe it to be the universal language in which Nature cries out to us when we will listen to no other language.

I am glad that I have experienced much defeat!

It has had the effect of tempering me with the courage to undertake tasks that I would never have begun had I been surrounded by protecting influences.

Defeat is a destructive force only when it is accepted as failure! When accepted as teaching some needed lesson it is always a blessing.

If we could read the secret history of our enemies, we should find in each man's life sorrow and suffering enough to disarm all hostility.

—LONGFELLOW

I used to hate my enemies!

That was before I learned how well they were serving me by keeping me everlastingly on the alert lest some weak spot in my character provide an opening through which they might damage me.

In view of what I have learned of the value of enemies, if I had none I would feel it my duty to create a few. They would discover my defects and point them out to me, whereas my friends, if they saw my weaknesses at all, would say nothing about them.

Of all Joaquin Miller's poems none expressed a nobler thought than did this one:

"All honor to him who shall win a prize,"
    The world has cried for a thousand years;
But to him who tries, and who fails, and dies,
    I give great honor, and glory, and tears.

Give glory and honor and pitiful tears
    To all who fail in their deeds sublime;
Their ghosts are many in the van of years,
    They were born with Time, in advance of Time.

Oh, great is the hero who wins a name;
    But greater many, and many a time,
Some pale-faced fellow who dies in shame
    And lets God finish the thought sublime.

And great is the man with a sword undrawn,
    And good is the man who refrains from wine;
But the man who fails and yet still fights on,
    Lo, he is the twin-brother of mine.

There can be no failure for the man who "still fights on." A man has never failed until he accepts temporary defeat as failure. There is a wide difference between temporary defeat and failure; a difference I have tried to emphasize throughout this lesson.

In her poem entitled When Nature Wants a Man, Angela Morgan expressed a great truth in support of the theory set out in this lesson, that adversity and defeat are generally blessings in disguise.

When Nature wants to drill a man,
And thrill a man,
And skill a man.
When Nature wants to mold a man

To play the noblest part;
When she yearns with all her heart
To create so great and bold a man
That all the world shall praise—
Watch her method, watch her ways!
How she ruthlessly perfects
Whom she royally elects;
How she hammers him and hurts him,
And with mighty blows converts him
Into trial shapes of clay which only Nature understands—
While his tortured heart is crying and he lifts beseeching hands!—
How she bends, but never breaks,
When his good she undertakes. . . .
How she uses whom she chooses
And with every purpose fuses him,
By every art induces him
To try his splendor out—
Nature knows what she's about.

When Nature wants to take a man,
And shake a man,
And wake a man;
When Nature wants to make a man
To do the Future's will;
When she tries with all her skill
And she yearns with all her soul
To create him large and whole . . .
With what cunning she prepares him!
How she goads and never spares him,
How she whets him, and she frets him,
And in poverty begets him . . .
How she often disappoints
Whom she sacredly anoints,
With what wisdom she will hide him,

Never minding what betide him
Though his genius sob with slighting and his pride may not forget!
Bids him struggle harder yet.
Makes him lonely
So that only
God's high messages shall reach him,
So that she may surely teach him
What the Hierarchy planned.
Though he may not understand,
Gives him passions to command.
How remorselessly she spurs him
With terrific ardor stirs him
When she poignantly prefers him!

When Nature wants to name a man
And fame a man
And tame a man;
When Nature wants to shame a man
To do his heavenly best . . .
When she tries the highest test
That she reckoning may bring—
When she wants a god or king!
How she reins him and restrains him
So his body scarce contains him
While she fires him
And inspires him!
Keeps him yearning, ever burning for a tantalizing goal—
Lures and lacerates his soul.
Sets a challenge for his spirit,
Draws it higher when he's near it—
Makes a jungle, that he clear it;
Makes a desert that he fear it
And subdue it if he can—
So doth Nature make a man.

Then, to test his spirit's wrath

Hurls a mountain in his path—

Puts a bitter choice before him

And relentlessly stands o'er him.

"Climb, or perish!" so she says. . . .

Watch her purpose, watch her ways!

Nature's plan is wondrous kind

Could we understand her mind . . .

Fools are they who call her blind.

When his feet are torn and bleeding

Yet his spirit mounts unheeding,

All his higher powers speeding,

Blazing newer paths and fine;

When the force that is divine

Leaps to challenge every failure and his ardor still is sweet

And love and hope are burning in the presence of defeat . . .

Lo, the crisis! Lo, the shout

That must call the leader out.

When the people need salvation

Doth he come to lead the nation. . . .

Then doth Nature show her plan

When the world has found—a MAN!*

I am convinced that failure is Nature's plan through which she hurdle-jumps men of destiny and prepares them to do their work. Failure is Nature's great crucible in which she burns the dross from the human heart and so purifies the metal of the man that it can stand the test of hard usage.

I have found evidence to support this theory in the study of the records of scores of great men, from Socrates and Christ on down the centuries to the well known men of achievement of our modern times. The success of each man seemed to be in almost exact ratio to the extent of the obstacles and difficulties he had to surmount.

No man ever arose from the knock-out blow of defeat without being stronger and wiser

* From "Forward, March!" The John Lane Company.

for the experience. Defeat talks to us in a language all its own; a language to which we must listen whether we like it or not.

Of course one must have considerable courage to look upon defeat as a blessing in disguise; but the attainment of any position in life, that is worth having, requires a lot of "sand," which brings to mind a poem that harmonizes with the philosophy of this lesson.

I observed a locomotive in the railroad yards one day,
It was waiting in the roundhouse where the locomotives stay;
It was panting for the journey, it was coaled and fully manned,
And it had a box the fireman was filling full of sand.

It appears that locomotives cannot always get a grip
On their slender iron pavement, 'cause the wheels are apt to slip;
And when they reach a slippery spot, their tactics they command,
And to get a grip upon the rail, they sprinkle it with sand.

It's about the way with travel along life's slippery track—
If your load is rather heavy, you're always slipping back;
So, if a common locomotive you completely understand,
You'll provide yourself in starting with a good supply of sand.

If your track is steep and hilly and you have a heavy grade,
If those who've gone before you have the rails quite slippery made,
If you ever reach the summit of the upper tableland,
You'll find you'll have to do it with a liberal use of sand.

If you strike some frigid weather and discover to your cost,
That you're liable to slip upon a heavy coat of frost,
Then some prompt decided action will be called into demand,
And you'll slip 'way to the bottom if you haven't any sand.

You can get to any station that is on life's schedule seen,
If there's fire beneath the boiler of ambition's strong machine,
And you'll reach a place called Flushtown at a rate of speed that's grand,
If for all the slippery places you've a good supply of sand.

> 'Tis the human touch in this
> world that counts,
> The touch of your hand and
> mine,
> Which means far more to the
> fainting heart,
> Than shelter and bread and
> wine;
> For shelter is gone when the
> night is o'er,
> And bread lasts only a day,
> But the touch of the hand and
> the sound of the voice,
> Sing on in the soul alway.
> —SPENCER M. TREE

It can do you no harm if you memorize the poems quoted in this lesson and make the philosophy upon which they are based a part of your own.

As I near the end of this lesson on Failure, there comes to mind a bit of philosophy taken from the works of the great Shakespeare, which I wish to challenge because I believe it to be unsound. It is stated in the following quotation:

> There is a tide in the affairs of men
> Which, taken at the flood, leads on to fortune;
> Omitted, all the voyage of their life
> Is bound in shallows, and in miseries.
> On such a full sea are we now afloat;
> And we must take the current when it serves,
> Or lose our ventures.

Fear and admission of failure are the ties which cause us to be "bound in shallows, and in miseries." We can break these ties and throw them off. Nay, we can turn them to advantage and make them serve as a tow-line with which to pull ourselves ashore if we observe and profit by the lessons they teach.

> Who ne'er has suffered, he has lived but half,
> Who never failed, he never strove or sought,
> Who never wept is stranger to a laugh,
> And he who never doubted never thought.

As I near the end of this, my favorite lesson of this course, I close my eyes for a moment and see before me a great army of men and women whose faces show the lines of care and despair.

Some are in rags, having reached the last stage of that long, long trail which men call *failure!*

Others are in better circumstances, but the fear of starvation shows plainly on their faces; the smile of courage has left their lips; and they, too, seem to have given up the battle.

The scene shifts!

I look again and I am carried backward into the history of man's struggle for a place in the sun, and there I see, also, the "failures" of the past—failures that have meant more to the human race than all the so-called successes recorded in the history of the world.

I see the homely face of Socrates as he stood at the very end of that trail called failure, waiting, with upturned eyes, through those moments which must have seemed like an eternity, just before he drank the cup of hemlock that was forced upon him by his tormentors.

I see, also, Christopher Columbus, a prisoner in chains, which was the tribute paid him for his sacrifice in having set sail on an unknown and uncharted sea, to discover an unknown continent.

I see, also, the face of Thomas Paine, the man whom the English sought to capture and put to death as the real instigator of the American Revolution. I see him lying in a filthy prison, in France, as he waited calmly, under the shadow of the guillotine, for the death which he expected would be meted out to him for his part in behalf of humanity.

And I see, also, the face of the Man of Galilee, as he suffered on the cross of Calvary—the reward he received for his efforts in behalf of suffering humanity.

"Failures," all!

Oh, to be such a failure. Oh, to go down in history, as these men did, as one who was brave enough to place humanity above the *individual* and principle above pecuniary gain.

On such "failures" rest the hopes of the world.

> Oh, men, who are labeled "failures"—up, rise up! again and do!
> Somewhere in the world of action is room; there is room for you.
> No failure was e'er recorded, in the annals of truthful men,
> Except of the craven-hearted who fails, nor attempts again.
> The glory is in the doing, and not in the trophy won;
> The walls that are laid in darkness may laugh to the kiss of the sun.
> Oh, weary and worn and stricken, oh, child of fate's cruel gales!
> I sing—that it haply may cheer him—I sing to the man who fails.

Be thankful for the defeat which men call failure, because if you can survive it and keep on trying it gives you a chance to prove your ability to rise to the heights of achievement in your chosen field of endeavor.

No one has the right to brand you as a failure except yourself.

If, in a moment of despair, you should feel inclined to brand yourself as a failure, just remember those words of the wealthy philosopher, Croesus, who was advisor to Cyrus, king of the Persians:

"I am reminded, O king, and take this lesson to heart, that there is a wheel on which the affairs of men revolve and its mechanism is such that it prevents *any* man from being *always* fortunate."

What a wonderful lesson is wrapped up in those words—a lesson of hope and courage and promise.

Who of us has not seen "off" days, when everything seemed to go wrong? These are the days when we see only the flat side of the great wheel of life.

Let us remember that the wheel is always turning. If it brings us sorrow today, it will bring us joy tomorrow. Life is a cycle of varying events—fortunes and misfortunes.

We cannot stop this wheel of fate from turning, but we can modify the misfortune it brings us by remembering that good fortune will follow, just as surely as night follows day, if we but keep faith with ourselves and earnestly and honestly do our best.

> *Strive not to banish pain and doubt,*
> *In pleasure's noisy din;*
> *The peace thou seekest from without,*
> *Is only found within.*
>
> —CARY

In his greatest hours of trial the immortal Lincoln was heard, often, to say: *"And this, too, will soon pass."*

If you are smarting from the effects of some temporary defeat which you find it hard to forget, let me recommend this stimulating little poem, by Walter Malone.

OPPORTUNITY

They do me wrong who say I come no more
    When once I knock and fail to find you in;
For every day I stand outside your door,
    And bid you wake, and rise to fight and win.
Wail not for precious chances passed away;
    Weep not for golden ages on the wane;

Each night I burn the records of the day;
    At sunrise every soul is born again.
Laugh like a boy at splendors that have sped,
    To vanished joys be blind and deaf and dumb;
My judgments seal the dead past with its dead,
    But never bind a moment yet to come.

Though deep in mire wring not your hands and weep,
    I lend my arm to all who say, "I can!"
No shamefaced outcast ever sank so deep
    But yet might rise and be again a man!
Dost thou behold thy lost youth all aghast?
    Dost reel from righteous retribution's blow?
Then turn from blotted archives of the past
    And find the future's pages white as snow.
Art thou a mourner? Rouse thee from thy spell;
    Art thou a sinner? Sin may be forgiven;
Each morning gives thee wings to flee from hell,
    Each night a star to guide thy feet to heaven.

There are souls in this world which have the gift of finding joy everywhere, and of leaving it behind them everywhere they go.

——FABER

TOLERANCE

"You Can Do It If You Believe You Can!"

There are two significant features about *intolerance,* and your attention is directed to
these at the beginning of this lesson.

These features are:

First: Intolerance is a form of ignorance which must be mastered before any form of enduring success may be attained. It is the chief cause of all wars. It makes enemies in business
and in the professions. It disintegrates the organized forces of society in a thousand forms,
and stands, like a mighty giant, as a barrier to the abolition of war. It dethrones reason and
substitutes mob psychology in its place.

Second: Intolerance is the chief disintegrating force in the organized religions of the world,
where it plays havoc with the greatest power for good there is on this earth; by breaking up
that power into small sects and denominations which spend as much effort opposing each
other as they do in destroying the evils of the world.

But this indictment against *intolerance* is general. Let's see how it affects you, the individual.
It is, of course, obvious that anything which impedes the progress of civilization stands, also,
as a barrier to each individual; and, stating it conversely, anything that beclouds the mind of
the individual and retards his mental, moral and spiritual development, retards, also, the
progress of civilization.

All of which is an abstract statement of a great truth; and, inasmuch as abstract statements
are neither interesting nor highly informative, let us proceed to illustrate more concretely
the damaging effects of *intolerance.*

I will begin this illustration by describing an incident which I have mentioned quite freely in practically every public address that I have delivered within the past five years; but, inasmuch as the cold printed page has a modifying effect which makes possible the misinterpretation of the incident here described, I believe it necessary to caution you not to read back of the lines a meaning which I had no intention of placing there. You will do yourself an injustice if you either neglect or intentionally refuse to study this illustration in the exact words and with the exact meaning which I have intended those words to convey—a meaning as clear as I know how to make the English language convey it.

As you read of this incident, place yourself in my position and see if you, also, have not had a parallel experience, and, if so, what lesson did it teach you?

One day I was introduced to a young man of unusually fine appearance. His clear eye, his warm hand-clasp, the tone of his voice and the splendid taste with which he was groomed marked him as a young man of the highest intellectual type. He was of the typical young American college student type, and as I ran my eyes over him, hurriedly studying his personality, as one will naturally do under such circumstances, I observed a Knights of Columbus pin on his vest.

Instantly, I released his hand as if it were a piece of ice!

This was done so quickly that it surprised both him and me. As I excused myself and started to walk away, I glanced down at the Masonic pin that I wore on my own vest, then took another look at his Knights of Columbus pin, and wondered why a couple of trinkets such as these could dig such a deep chasm between men who knew nothing of each other.

All the remainder of that day I kept thinking of the incident, because it bothered me. I had always taken considerable pride in the thought that I was tolerant with all men; but here was a spontaneous outburst of *intolerance* which proved that down in my sub-conscious mind existed a complex that was influencing me toward narrow-mindedness.

This discovery so shocked me that I began a systematic process of psycho-analysis through which I searched into the very depths of my soul for the cause of my rudeness.

I asked myself over and over again:

"Why did you abruptly release that young man's hand and turn away from him, when you knew nothing about him?"

Of course the answer led me, always, back to that Knights of Columbus pin that he wore. But that was not a real answer and therefore it did not satisfy me.

Then I began to do some research work in the field of religion. I began to study both Catholicism and Protestantism until I had traced both back to their beginning, a line of procedure which I must confess brought me more understanding of the problems of life than I had gathered from all other sources. For one thing it disclosed the fact that Catholicism and Protestantism differ more in *form* than they do in *effect;* that both are founded on exactly the same *cause,* which is Christianity.

But this was by no means all, nor was it the most important of my discoveries, for my research led, of necessity, in many directions, and forced me into the field of biology where I learned much that I needed to know about life in general and the human being in particular. My research led, also, to the study of Darwin's hypothesis of evolution, as outlined in his Origin of Species, and this, in turn, led to a much wider analysis of the subject of psychology than that which I had previously made.

As I began to reach out in this direction and that, for knowledge, my mind began to unfold and broaden with such alarming rapidity that I practically found it necessary to—

Wipe the slate of what I believed to be my previously gathered knowledge, and to unlearn much that I had previously believed to be truth.

Comprehend the meaning of that which I have just stated!

Imagine yourself suddenly discovering that most of your philosophy of life had been built of bias and prejudice, making it necessary for you to acknowledge that, far from being a finished scholar, *you were barely qualified to become an intelligent student!*

That was exactly the position in which I found myself, with respect to many of what I believed to be sound fundamentals of life; but of all the discoveries to which this research led, none was more important than that of the relative importance of *physical* and *social* heredity, for it was this discovery that disclosed the *cause* for my action when I turned away from a man whom I did not know, on the occasion that I have described.

It was this discovery that disclosed to me *how* and *where* I acquired my views of religion, of politics, of economics and many other equally important subjects, and I both regret and rejoice to state that *I found most of my views on these subjects without support by even a reasonable hypothesis,* much less sound *facts* or reason.

I then recalled a conversation between the late Senator Robert L. Taylor and myself, in which we were discussing the subject of politics. It was a friendly discussion, as we were of the same political faith, but the Senator asked me a question for which I never forgave him until I began the research to which I have referred.

"I see that you are a very staunch Democrat," said he, "and I wonder if you know *why* you are?"

I thought of the question for a few seconds, then blurted out this reply:

> *Hearts, like doors, can ope with*
> *ease,*
> *To very, very little keys;*
> *And don't forget that they are*
> *these:*
> *"I thank you, sir," and "If you*
> *please."*

"I am a Democrat because my father was one, of course!"

With a broad grin on his face the Senator then nailed me with this rejoinder:

"Just as I thought! Now wouldn't you be in a bad fix if your father had been a horse-thief?"

It was many years later, after I began the research work herein described, that I understood the real meaning of Senator Taylor's joke. Too often we hold opinions that are based upon no sounder foundation than that of what someone else believes.

That you may have a detailed illustration of the far-reaching effects of one of the important principles uncovered by the incident to which I have referred, and—

That you may learn how and where you acquired your philosophy of life, in general;

That you may trace your prejudices and your biases to their original source;

That you may discover, as I discovered, how largely you are the result of the training you received before you reached the age of fifteen years—

I will now quote the full text of a plan which I submitted to Mr. Edward Bok's Committee, The American Peace Award, for the abolition of war. This plan covers not only the most important of the principles to which I refer, but, as you will observe, it shows how the principle of *organized effort,* as outlined in Lesson One of this course, may be applied to one of the most important of the world's problems, and at the same time gives you a more comprehensive idea of how to apply this principle in the *attainment* of your *definite chief aim.*

How to Abolish War

The Background

Before offering this plan for the prevention of war, it seems necessary to sketch briefly a background that will clearly describe the principle which constitutes the warp and the woof of the plan.

The causes of war may be properly omitted for the reason that they have but little, if any, relation to the principle through which war may be prevented.

The beginning of this sketch deals with two important factors which constitute the chief controlling forces of civilization. One is *physical heredity* and the other is *social heredity*.

The size and form of the body, the texture of the skin, the color of the eyes, and the functioning power of the vital organs are all the result of physical heredity; they are static and fixed and cannot be changed, for they are the result of a million years of evolution; but by far the most important part of what we are is the result of social heredity, and came to us from the effects of our environment and early training.

Our conception of religion, politics, economics, philosophy and other subjects of a similar nature, including war, is entirely the result of those dominating forces of our environment and training.

The Catholic is a Catholic because of his early training, and the Protestant is a Protestant for the same reason; but this is hardly stating the truth with sufficient emphasis, for it might be properly said that the Catholic is a Catholic and the Protestant is a Protestant *because he cannot help it!* With but few exceptions the religion of the adult is the result of his religious training during the years between four and fourteen when his religion was *forced* upon him by his parents or those who had control of his schooling.

A prominent clergyman indicated how well he understood the principle of social heredity when he said: "Give me the control of the child until it is twelve years old and you can teach it any religion you may please after that time, for I will have planted my own religion so deeply in its mind that no power on earth could undo my work."

The outstanding and most prominent of man's beliefs are those which were forced upon him, or which he absorbed of his own volition, under *highly emotionalized* conditions, when his mind was receptive. Under such conditions the evangelist can plant the idea of religion more deeply and permanently during an hour's revival service than he could through years of training under ordinary conditions, when the mind was not in an emotionalized state.

The people of the United States have immortalized Washington and Lincoln because they were the leaders of the nation during times when the minds of the people were highly emotionalized, as the result of calamities which shook the very foundation of our country and vitally affected the interests of all the people. Through the principle of social heredity, operating through the schools (American history), and through other forms of impressive teaching, the immortality of Washington and Lincoln is planted in the minds of the young and in that way kept alive.

The three great *organized forces* through which social heredity operates are:

The *schools*, the *churches* and the *public press*.

Any ideal that has the active co-operation of these three forces may, *during the brief period of one generation, be forced upon the minds of the young so effectively that they cannot resist it.*

In 1914 the world awoke one morning to find itself aflame with warfare on a scale previously unheard of, and the outstanding feature of importance of that world-wide calamity was the highly organized German armies. For more than three years these armies gained ground so rapidly that world domination by Germany seemed certain. The German military machine operated with efficiency such as had never before been demonstrated in warfare. With "kultur" as her avowed ideal, modern Germany swept the opposing armies before her as though they were leaderless, despite the fact that the allied forces outnumbered her own on every front.

The capacity for sacrifice in the German soldiers, in support of the ideal of "kultur," was the outstanding surprise of the war; and that capacity was largely the result of the work of two men. Through the German educational system, which they controlled, the psychology which carried the world into war in 1914 was created in the definite form of "kultur." These men were Adalbert Falk, Prussian Minister of Education until 1879, and the German Emperor William II.

The agency through which these men produced this result was *social heredity:* the imposing of an ideal on the minds of the young, under highly emotionalized conditions.

"Kultur," as a national ideal, was fixed in the minds of the young of Germany, beginning first in the elementary schools and extending on up through the high schools and universities. *The teachers and professors were forced to implant the ideal of "kultur" in the minds of the students,* and out of this teaching, in a single generation, grew the capacity for sacrifice of the individual for the interest of the nation which surprised the modern world.

As Benjamin Kidd so well stated the case: "The aim of the state of Germany was everywhere to orientate public opinion through the heads of both its spiritual and temporal departments, through the bureaucracy, through the officers of the army, through the State direction of the press; and, last of all, through the State direction of the entire trade and industry of the nation, so as to bring the idealism of the whole people to a conception of and to a support of the national policy of modern Germany."

Germany controlled the press, the clergy and the schools; therefore, is it any wonder that she grew an army of soldiers, during one generation, which represented to a man her ideal of "kultur"? Is it any wonder that the German soldiers faced certain death with fearless impunity, when one stops to consider the fact that they had been taught, from early childhood, that this sacrifice was a rare privilege?

Turn, now, from this brief description of the modus operandi through which Germany prepared her people for war, to another strange phenomenon, Japan. No western nation, with the exception of Germany, has so clearly manifested its understanding of the far-reaching influence of social heredity, as has Japan. Within a single generation Japan has advanced from her standing as

It takes but a second to administer a rebuke, but it may take a life-time for the one who has been rebuked to forget it.

a fourth-rate nation to the ranks of nations that are the recognized powers of the civilized world. Study Japan and you will find that she forces upon the minds of her young, through exactly the same agencies employed by Germany, the ideal of subordination of individual rights for the sake of accumulation of power by the nation.

In all of her controversies with China, competent observers have seen that back of the apparent causes of the controversies was Japan's stealthy attempt to control the minds of the young by controlling the schools. *If Japan could control the minds of the young of China, she could dominate that gigantic nation within one generation.*

If you would study the effect of social heredity as it is being used for the development of a national ideal by still another nation of the West, observe what has been going on in Russia since the ascendency to power of the soviet government of Russia which is now patterning the minds of the young to conform with a national ideal, *the nature of which it requires no master analyst to interpret.* That ideal, when fully developed during the maturity of the present generation, will represent exactly that which the soviet government wishes it to represent.

Of all the flood of propaganda concerning the soviet government of Russia that has been poured into this country through the tens of thousands of columns of newspaper space devoted to it since the close of the war, the following brief dispatch is by far the most significant:

RUSS REDS ORDER BOOKS. Contracts being let in Germany for 20,000,000 volumes. Educational propaganda is aimed chiefly at children.

(By George Witts)

Special Cable to the *Chicago Daily News* Foreign Service. Berlin, Germany, November 9th, 1920.

Contracts for printing 20,000,000 books *in the Russian language,* chiefly for children, are being placed in Germany on behalf of the soviet government by Grschebin, a well known Petrograd publisher and a friend of Maxim Gorky. Grschebin first went to England, but was received with indifference when he broached the subject to the British government. *The Germans, however, not only welcomed him eagerly but submitted prices so low that they could not possibly be underbidden in any other country.* The Ullsteins, Berlin newspaper and book publishers, have agreed to print several million of the books at less than cost.

This shows what is going on over there.

Far from being shocked by this significant press dispatch, the majority of the newspapers of America did not publish it, and those that did give it space placed it in an obscure part of the paper, in small type. Its real significance will become more apparent some twenty-odd years from now, when the soviet government of Russia will have grown an army of soldiers who will support, to the man, *whatever national ideal the soviet government sets up.*

The possibility of war exists as a stern reality today solely because the principle of social heredity has not only been used as a sanctioning force in support of war, but it has actually been used as a chief agency through which the minds of men have been deliberately prepared for war. For evidence with which to support this statement, examine any national or world history and *observe how tactfully and effectively war has been glorified and so described that it not only did not shock the mind of the student, but it actually established a plausible justification of war.*

Go into the public squares of our cities and observe the monuments that have been erected to the leaders of war. Observe the posture of these statues as they stand as living symbols to glorify men who did nothing more than lead armies on escapades of destruction. Notice how well these statues of warriors, mounted on charging steeds, serve as agencies through which to stimulate the minds of the young and prepare them for the acceptance of war, not only as a pardonable act, but as a distinctly desirable source of attainment of glory, fame and honor. At the time of this writing some well meaning ladies are having the image of Confederate Soldiers carved in the deathless granite on the face of Stone Mountain, in Georgia, in figures a hundred feet tall, thus seeking to perpetuate the memory of a lost "cause" that never was a "cause" and therefore the sooner forgotten, the better.

If these references to far-away Russia, Japan and Germany seem unimpressive and abstract, then let us study the principle of social heredity as it is now functioning on a highly developed scale here in the United States; for it may be expecting too much of the average of our race to suppose that they will be interested in that which is taking place outside of the spot of ground that is bounded on the north by Canada, on the east by the Atlantic, on the west by the Pacific and on the south by Mexico.

We, too, are setting up in the minds of our young a national ideal, and this ideal is being so effectively developed, through the principle of social heredity, that it has already become the dominating ideal of the nation.

This ideal is the desire for wealth!

The first question we ask about a new acquaintance is not, "Who are you?" but, "What have you?" And the next question we ask is, *"How can we get that which you have?"*

Our ideal is not measured in terms of warfare, but in terms of finance and industry and business. Our Patrick Henrys and our George Washingtons and our Abraham Lincolns of a few generations ago are now represented by the able leaders who manage our steel mills and our coal mines and our timber lands and our banking institutions and our railroads.

We may deny this indictment if we choose, but the facts do not support the denial.

The outstanding problem of the American people today is the spirit of unrest upon the part of the masses who find the struggle for existence becoming harder and harder because the most competent brains of the country are engaged in the highly competitive attempt to accumulate wealth and to control the wealth-producing machinery of the nation.

It is not necessary to dwell at length upon this description of our dominating ideal, or to offer evidence in support of its existence, for the reason that its existence is obvious and as well understood by the most ignorant as it is by those who make a pretense of thinking accurately.

So deeply seated has this mad desire for money become that we are perfectly willing for the other nations of the world to cut themselves to pieces in warfare so long as they do not interfere with our scramble for wealth; nor is this the saddest part of the indictment that we might render against ourselves, for we are not only *willing* for other nations to engage in warfare, but there is considerable reason to believe that those of us who profit by the sale of war supplies actually encourage this warfare among other nations.

The Plan

War grows out of the desire of the individual to gain advantage at the expense of his fellow men, and the smoldering embers of this desire are fanned into a flame through the grouping of these individuals who place the interests of the group above those of other groups.

War cannot be stopped suddenly!

It can be eliminated only by education, through the aid of the principle of subordination of the individual interests to the broader interests of the human race as a whole.

Man's tendencies and activities, as we have already stated, grow out of two great forces. One is *physical* heredity, and the other is *social* heredity. Through physical heredity, man inherits those early tendencies to destroy his fellow man out of self-protection. This practice is a hold-over from the age when the struggle for existence was so great that only the physically strong could survive.

> *Unfortunate, indeed, is the man who becomes so used to evil that it no longer appears to be horrible.*

Gradually men began to learn that the individual could survive under more favorable circumstances by allying himself with others, and out of that discovery grew our modern society, through which groups of people have formed states, and these groups, in turn, have formed nations. There is but little tendency toward warfare between the individuals of a particular group or nation, for they have learned, through the principle of *social* heredity, that they can best survive by subordinating the interest of the individual to that of the group.

Now, the problem is to extend this principle of grouping so that *the nations of the world will subordinate their individual interests to those of the human race as a whole.*

This can be brought about only through the principle of *social* heredity. *By forcing upon the minds of the young of all races the fact that war is horrible and does not serve either the interest of the individual engaging in it or the group to which the individual belongs.*

The question then arises, "How can this be done?" Before we answer this question, let us again define the term *"social heredity"* and find out what its possibilities are.

Social heredity is the principle through which the young of the race absorb from their environment, and particularly from their earlier training by parents, teachers and religious leaders, *the beliefs and tendencies of the adults who dominate them.*

Any plan to abolish war, to be successful, depends upon the successful co-ordination of effort between *all the churches and schools of the world for the avowed purpose of so fertilizing the minds of the young with the idea of abolishing war that the very word "war" will strike terror in their hearts.*

THERE IS NO OTHER WAY OF ABOLISHING WAR!

The next question that arises, "How can the churches and schools of the world be organized with this high ideal as an objective?" The answer is that not all of them can be induced to enter into such an alliance, at one time; but a sufficient number of the more influential ones can be induced, and this, in time, will lead or *force* the remainder into the alliance, as rapidly as public opinion begins to *demand* it.

Then comes the question, "Who has sufficient influence to call a conference of the most powerful religious and educational leaders?" The answer is:

The President and Congress of the United States.

Such an undertaking would *command* the support of the press on a scale heretofore un-heard of, and through this source alone the propaganda would begin to reach and fertilize the minds of the people in every civilized country in the world, in preparation for the adoption of the plan in the churches and schools throughout the world.

The plan for the abolition of war might be likened to a great dramatic play, with these as the chief factors:

STAGE SETTING: At the Capitol of the United States.

STAR ACTORS: The President and members of Congress.

MINOR ACTORS: The leading clergymen of all denominations, and the leading educators, all on the stage by invitation and at the expense of the United States government.

PRESS ROOM: Representatives of the news-gathering agencies of the world.

STAGE EQUIPMENT: A radio broadcasting outfit that would distribute the entire proceedings half-way round the earth.

TITLE OF THE PLAY: "Thou shalt not kill!"

OBJECT OF THE PLAY: The creation of a World Court, to be made up of representatives of all races, whose duty it would be to hear evidence and adjudicate the cases arising out of disagreement between nations.

Other factors would enter into this great world drama, but they would be of minor importance. The main issues and the most essential factors are here enumerated.

One other question remains, "Who will start the machinery of the United States government into action to call this conference?" and the answer is:

Public opinion, through the aid of an able organizer and leader, who will organize and direct the efforts of a Golden Rule Society, the object of which will be to move the President and Congress into action.

No League of Nations and no mere agreement between nations can abolish war as long as there is the slightest evidence of sanction of war in the hearts of the people. Universal peace between nations will grow out of a movement that will be begun and carried on, at first, by a comparatively small number of thinkers. Gradually this number will grow until it will be composed of the leading educators, clergymen and publicists of the world, and these, in turn, will so deeply and permanently establish *peace* as a world ideal that it will become a reality.

This desirable end may be attained in a single generation under the right sort of leadership; but, more likely, it will not be attained for many generations to come, for the reason that those who have the ability to assume this leadership are too busy in their pursuit of worldly wealth to make the necessary sacrifice for the good of generations yet unborn.

War can be eliminated, not by appeal to reason, but by appeal to the emotional side of humanity. This appeal must be made by *organizing and highly emotionalizing the people of the different nations of the world in support of a universal plan for peace, and this plan must be forced upon the minds of the oncoming generations with the same diligent care that we now force upon the minds of our young the ideal of our respective religions.*

It is not stating the possibilities too strongly to say that the churches of the world could establish universal peace as an international ideal within one generation if they would but *direct toward that end one-half of the effort which they now employ in opposing one another.*

We would still be within the bounds of conservatism if we stated that the Christian churches, alone, have sufficient influence to establish universal peace as a world-wide ideal, within three generations, if the various sects would combine their forces for the purpose.

That which the leading churches of all religions, the leading schools and the public press of the world could accomplish in forcing the ideal of universal peace upon *both the adult and the child mind of the world* within a single generation, staggers the imagination.

If the organized religions of the world, as they now exist, will not subordinate their individual interests and purposes to that of establishing universal peace, then the remedy lies in establishing a universal church of the world that will function through all races and whose creed will be based entirely upon the one purpose of implanting in the minds of the young the ideal of world-wide peace.

Such a church would gradually attract a following from the rank and file of all other churches.

And if the educational institutions of the world will not co-operate in fostering this high ideal of universal peace, then the remedy lies in the creation of an entirely new educational system that will implant in the minds of the young the ideal of universal peace.

And if the public press of the world will not co-operate in setting up the ideal of universal peace, then the remedy lies in the creation of an independent press that will utilize both the printed page and the forces of the air for the purpose of creating mass support of this high ideal.

In brief, if the present *organized forces* of the world will not lend their support to establishing universal peace, as an international ideal, then new organizations must be created which will do so.

The majority of the people of the world want peace, wherein lies the possibility of its attainment!

At first thought, it seems too much to expect that the organized churches of the world can be induced to pool their power and subordinate their individual interests to those of civilization as a whole.

But this seemingly insurmountable obstacle is, in reality, no obstacle at all, for the reason that whatever support this plan borrows from the churches it gives back to them, a thousandfold, through the increased power the church attains.

Let us see just what advantages the church realizes by participation in this plan to establish *universal peace* as a world ideal. First of all, it will be clearly seen that no individual church loses any of its advantages by allying itself with other denominations in establishing this world ideal. The alliance in no way changes or interferes with the creed of any church. Every church entering the alliance will come out of it with all the power and advantages that it possessed before it went in, plus the

Greatly begin! though thou have time,
But for a line, be that sublime—
Not failure, but low aim is crime.

additional advantage of greater influence which the church, as a whole, will enjoy by reason of having served as the leading factor in forcing upon civilization the greatest single benefit it has enjoyed in the history of the world.

If the church gained no other advantages from the alliance, this one would be sufficient to compensate it. But *the important advantage that the church will have gained by this alliance is the discovery that it has sufficient power to force its ideals upon the world when it places its combined support back of the undertaking.*

By this alliance the church will have grasped the far-reaching significance of the principle of *organized effort* through the aid of which it might easily have dominated the world and imposed its ideals upon civilization.

The church is by far the greatest potential power in the world today, but its power is merely potential and will remain so until it makes use of the principle of allied or *organized* effort; that is to say, until *all denominations formulate a working agreement under which the combined strength of organized religion will be used as a means of forcing a higher ideal upon the minds of the young.*

The reason that the church is the greatest potential power in the world is the fact that its power grows out of man's emotions. *Emotion rules the world, and the church is the only organization which rests solely upon the power of emotion. The church is the only organized factor of society which has the power to harness and direct the emotional forces of civilization, for the reason that the emotions are controlled by FAITH and not by reason! And the church is the only great organized body in which faith of the world is centered.*

The church stands today as so many disconnected units of power, and it is not overstating the possibilities to say that when these units shall have been connected, *through allied effort,* the combined power of that alliance *will rule the world and there is no opposing power on earth that can defeat it!*

It is in no discouraging spirit that this statement is followed by another which may seem still more radical; namely:

The task of bringing about this alliance of the churches in support of the world ideal of universal peace must rest upon the female members of the church, for the reason that the abolition of war promises advantages that may be prolonged into the future and that may accrue only to the unborn generations.

In Schopenhauer's bitter arraignment of woman, he unconsciously stated a truth upon which the hope of civilization rests, when he declared that *the race is always to her more than the individual.* In terms that are uncompromising, Schopenhauer charges woman with being the natural enemy of man because of this inborn trait *of placing the interests of the race above those of the individual.*

It seems a reasonable prophecy to suggest that civilization passed into a new era, beginning with the world war, in which woman is destined to take into her own hands the raising of the ethical standards of the world. This is a hopeful sign, because it is woman's nature to subordinate the interests of the present to those of the future. It is woman's nature to implant, in the mind of the young, ideals that will accrue to the benefit of generations yet unborn, while man is motivated generally by expediency of the present.

In Schopenhauer's vicious attack upon woman, he has stated a great truth concerning her nature: a truth which might well be utilized by all who engage in the worthy work of establishing *universal peace as a world ideal.*

The women's clubs of the world are destined to play a part in world affairs other than that of gaining suffrage for women.

LET CIVILIZATION REMEMBER THIS!

Those who do not want peace are the ones who profit by war. In numbers, this class constitutes but a fragment of the power of the world, and could be swept aside as though it did not exist, if the multitude who do not want war were organized with the high ideal of universal peace as their objective.

In closing, it seems appropriate to apologize for the unfinished state of this essay, but it may be pardonable to suggest that the bricks and the mortar, and the foundation stones, and all the other necessary materials for the construction of the *temple of universal peace* have been here assembled, where they might be re-arranged and transformed into this high ideal as a world reality.

Let us now proceed to apply the principle of *social heredity* to the subject of business economy, and ascertain whether or not it can be made of practical benefit in the attainment of material wealth.

If I were a banker I would procure a list of all the births in the families within a given distance of my place of business, and every child would receive an appropriate letter, congratulating it on its arrival in the world at such an opportune time, in such a favorable community; and from that time on it would receive from my bank a birthday reminder of an appropriate nature. When it arrived at the story-book age, it would receive from my bank an interesting story book in which the advantages of saving would be told in story form. If the child were a girl, it would receive doll "cut-out" books, with the name of my bank on the back of each doll, as a birthday gift. If it were a boy, it would receive baseball bats. One of the most important floors (or even a whole, near-by building) of my banking house would be set aside as a children's play-room; and it would be equipped with merry-go-rounds, sliding-boards, see-saws, scooters, games and sand piles, with a competent supervisor in charge to give the kiddies a good time. I would let that play-room become the popular habitat of the children of the community, where mothers might leave their youngsters in safety while shopping or visiting.

I would entertain those youngsters so royally that when they grew up and became bank depositors, whose accounts were worth while, they would be inseparably bound to my bank; and, meanwhile, I would, in no way, be lessening my chances of making depositors of the fathers and mothers of those children.

If I were the owner of a business school, I would begin cultivating the boys and girls of my community from the time they reached the fifth grade, on up through high school, so that by the time they were through high school and ready to choose a vocation, I would have the name of my business school well fixed in their minds.

If I were a grocer, or a department store owner, or a druggist, I would cultivate the children, thereby attracting both them and their parents to my place of business; for it is a well known fact that there is no shorter route to the heart of a parent than that which leads through interest manifested in the offspring. If I were a department store owner, and used whole pages of newspaper space, as most of them do, I would run a comic strip at the bottom of each page, illustrating it with scenes in my play-room, and in this way induce the children to read my advertisements.

Singleness of purpose is one of the chief essentials for success in life, no matter what may be one's aim.

—JOHN D. ROCKEFELLER, JR.

If I were a preacher, I would equip the basement of my church with a children's play-room that would attract the children of the community every day in the week; and, if my study were near by, I would go into that play-room and enjoy the fun with the little fellows, thereby gaining the inspiration with which to preach better sermons while at the same time raising parishioners for tomorrow. I can think of no more effective method than this of rendering a service that would be in harmony with Christianity, and which would, at the same time, make my church a popular place of abode for the young folks.

If I were a national advertiser, or the owner of a mail order house, I would find appropriate ways and means of establishing a point of contact with the children of the country; for, let me repeat, there is no better way of influencing the parent than that of "capturing" the child.

If I were a barber, I would have a room equipped exclusively for children, for this would bring me the patronage of both the children and their parents.

In the outskirts of every city there is an opportunity for a flourishing business for someone who will operate a restaurant and serve meals of the better "home-cooked" quality, and cater to families who wish to take the children and dine out occasionally. I would have the place equipped with well stocked fishing ponds, and ponies, and all sorts of animals and birds in which children are interested, if I were operating it, and induce the children to come out regularly and spend the entire day. Why speak of gold mines when opportunities such as this are abundant?

These are but a few of the ways in which the principle of *social heredity* might be used to advantage in business.

Attract the children and you attract the parents!

If nations can build soldiers of war to order, by bending the minds of their young in the direction of war, business men can build customers to order through the same principle.

We come, now, to another important feature of this lesson through which we may see, from another angle, how power may be accumulated by co-operative, *organized effort.*

In the plan for the abolition of war, you observed how co-ordination of effort between three of the great organized powers of the world (the schools, churches and the public press) might serve to force universal peace.

We learned many lessons of value from the world war, outrageous and destructive as it was, but none of greater importance than that of the effect of *organized effort*. You will recall that the tide of war began to break in favor of the allied armies just after all armed forces were placed under the direction of General Foch, which brought about complete coordination of effort in the allied ranks.

Never before, in the history of the world, had so much power been concentrated in one group of men as that which was created through the *organized effort* of the allied armies. We come, now, to one of the most outstanding and significant facts to be found in the analysis of these allied armies, namely, that they were made up of the most cosmopolitan group of soldiers ever assembled on this earth.

Catholics and Protestants, Jews and Gentiles, blacks and whites, yellows and tans, and every race on earth were represented in those armies. If they had any differences on account of race or creed, they laid them aside and subordinated them to the *cause* for which they were fighting. Under the stress of war, that great mass of humanity was reduced to a common level where they fought shoulder to shoulder, side by side, without asking any questions as to each other's racial tendencies or religious beliefs.

If they could lay aside *intolerance* long enough to fight for their lives over there, why can we not do the same while we fight for a higher standard of ethics in business and finance and industry over here?

Is it only when civilized people are fighting for their lives that they have the foresight to lay aside *intolerance* and co-operate in the furtherance of a common end?

If it were advantageous to the allied armies to think and act as one thoroughly co-ordinated body, would it be less advantageous for the people of a city or a community or an industry to do so?

If all the churches and schools and newspapers and clubs and civic organizations of your city allied themselves for the furtherance of a common cause, do you not see how such an alliance would create sufficient power to insure the success of that cause?

Bring the illustration still nearer your own individual interests by an imaginary alliance between all of the employers and all of the employees of your city, for the purpose of reducing friction and misunderstandings, thereby enabling them to render better service at a lower cost to the public and greater profit to themselves.

> *If a man has built a sound character it makes but little difference what people say about him, because he will win in the end.*
>
> —NAPOLEON HILL, SR.

We learned from the world war that we cannot destory a part without weakening the whole; that when one nation or group of people is reduced to poverty and want, the remainder of the world suffers, also. Stated conversely, we learned from the world war that *co-operation* and *tolerance* are the very foundation of enduring success.

Surely the more thoughtful and observant individuals will not fail to profit (as individuals) by these great lessons which we learned from the world war.

I am not unmindful of the fact that *you* are probably studying this course for the purpose of profiting, in every way possible, from a purely personal viewpoint, by the principles upon which it is founded. For this very reason, I have endeavored to outline the application of these principles to as wide a scope of subjects as possible.

In this lesson, you have had opportunity to observe the application of the principles underlying the subjects of *organized effort, tolerance* and *social heredity* to an extent which must have given you much food for thought, and which must have given your *imagination* much room for profitable exercise.

I have endeavored to show you how these principles may be employed both in the furtherance of your own individual interests, in whatever calling you may be engaged, and for the benefit of civilization as a whole.

Whether your calling is that of preaching sermons, selling goods or personal services, practicing law, directing the efforts of others, or working as a day laborer, it seems not too much to hope that you will find in this lesson a stimulus to thought which may lead you to higher achievements. If, perchance, you are a writer of advertisements you will surely find in this lesson sufficient food for thought to add more power to your pen. If you have personal services for sale, it is not unreasonable to expect that this lesson will suggest ways and means of marketing those services to greater advantage.

In uncovering for you the source from which *intolerance* is usually developed, this lesson has led you, also, to the study of other thought-provoking subjects which might easily mark the most profitable turning-point of your life. Books and lessons, in themselves, are of but little value; their real value, if any, lies not in their printed pages, but *in the possible action which they may arouse in the reader.*

For example, when my proof-reader had finished reading the manuscript of this lesson, she informed me that it had so impressed her and her husband that they intended to go into the advertising business and supply banks with an advertising service that would reach the parents through the children. She believes the plan is worth $10,000.00 a year to her.

Frankly, her plan so appealed to me that I would estimate its value at a minimum of more than three times the amount she mentioned, and I doubt not that it could be made to yield five times that amount, if it were properly organized and marketed by an able salesman.

Nor is that all that this lesson has accomplished before passing from the manuscript stage. A prominent business college owner, to whom I showed the manuscript, has already begun to put into effect the suggestion which referred to the use of *social heredity* as a means of "cultivating" students; and he is sanguine enough to believe that a plan, similar to the one he intends using, could be sold to the majority of the 1500 business colleges in the United States and Canada, on a basis that would yield the promoter of the plan a yearly income greater than the salary received by the President of the United States.

And, as this lesson is being completed, I am in receipt of a letter from Dr. Charles F. Crouch, of Atlanta, Georgia, in which he informs me that a group of prominent business men in Atlanta have just organized the Golden Rule Club, the main object of which is to put into operation, on a nation-wide scale, the plan for the abolition of war, as outlined in this lesson. (A copy of that portion of this lesson dealing with the subject of abolition of war was sent to Dr. Crouch several weeks before the completion of the lesson.)

These three events, happening one after the other, within a period of a few weeks, have strengthened my belief that this is the most important lesson of the entire fifteen, but its value to *you* will depend entirely upon the extent to which it stimulates you to *think* and to *act* as you would not have done without its influence.

The chief object of this course and, particularly, of this lesson is to *educate,* more than it is to *inform*—meaning by the word "educate" to educe, to draw out! to develop from within; *to cause you to use the power that lies sleeping within you, awaiting the awakening hand of some appropriate stimulus to arouse you to action.*

In conclusion, may I leave with you my personal sentiments on tolerance, in the following essay which I wrote, in the hour of my most trying experience, when an enemy was trying to ruin my reputation and destroy the results of a life-time of honest effort to do some good in the world.

TOLERANCE!

When the dawn of Intelligence shall have spread its wings over the eastern horizon of progress, and Ignorance and Superstition shall have left their last footprints on the sands of Time, it will be recorded in the book of man's crimes and mistakes that his most grievous sin was that of Intolerance!

The bitterest Intolerance grows out of racial and religious differences of opinion, as the result of early childhood training. How long, O Master of Human Destinies, until we poor mortals will understand the folly of trying to destroy one another because of dogmas and creeds and other superficial matters over which we do not agree?

Our allotted time on this earth is but a fleeting moment, at most!

Like a candle, we are lighted, shine for a moment and flicker out! Why can we not so live during this short earthly sojourn that when the Great Caravan called Death draws up and announces this visit about finished we will be ready to fold our tents, and, like the Arabs of the Desert, silently follow the Caravan out into the Darkness of the Unknown without fear and trembling?

I am hoping that I will find no Jews or Gentiles, Catholics or Protestants, Germans or Englishmen, Frenchmen or Russians, Blacks or Whites, Reds or Yellows, when I shall have crossed the Bar to the Other Side.

I am hoping I will find there only human Souls, Brothers and Sisters all, unmarked by race, creed or color, for I shall want to be done with Intolerance so I may lie down and rest an æon or two, undisturbed by the strife, ignorance, superstition and petty misunderstandings which mark with chaos and grief this earthly existence.

No man could possibly read the Law of Success philosophy, even once, without becoming, thereby, better prepared to succeed in any calling.

—ELBERT H. GARY

THE GOLDEN RULE

"You Can Do It If You Believe You Can!"

With this lesson we approach the apex of the pyramid of this course on the Law of Success.

This lesson is the Guiding Star that will enable you to use profitably and *constructively* the knowledge assembled in the preceding lessons.

There is more power wrapped up in the preceding lessons of this course than most men could trust themselves with; therefore, this lesson is a governor that will, if observed and applied, enable you to steer your ship of knowledge over the rocks and reefs of failure that usually beset the pathway of all who come suddenly into possession of power.

For more than twenty-five years I have been observing the manner in which men behave themselves when in possession of power, and I have been forced to the conclusion that the man who attains it in any other than by the slow, step-by-step process, is constantly in danger of destroying himself and all whom he influences.

It must have become obvious to you, long before this, that this entire course leads to the attainment of *power* of proportions which may be made to perform the seemingly "impossible." Happily, it becomes apparent that this *power* can only be attained by the observance of many fundamental principles all of which converge in this lesson, which is based upon a law that both equals and transcends in importance every other law outlined in the preceding lessons.

Likewise, it becomes apparent to the thoughtful student that this *power* can endure only by faithful observance of the law upon which this lesson is based, wherein lies the "safety-valve" that protects the careless student from the dangers of his own follies; and protects, also, those whom he might endanger if he tried to circumvent the injunction laid down in this lesson.

To "prank" with the power that may be attained from the knowledge wrapped up in the preceding lessons of this course, without a full understanding and strict observance of the law laid down in this lesson, is the equivalent of "pranking" with a power which may destroy as well as create.

I am speaking, now, not of that which I suspect to be true, but, of that which *I KNOW TO BE TRUE!* The truth upon which this entire course, and this lesson in particular, is founded, is no invention of mine. I lay no claim to it except that of having observed its unvarying application in the every-day walks of life over a period of more than twenty-five years of struggle; and, of having appropriated as much of it as, in the light of my human frailties and weaknesses, I could make use of.

If you demand *positive* proof of the soundness of the laws upon which this course in general, and this lesson in particular, is founded, I must plead inability to offer it except through one witness, and that is *yourself.*

You may have *positive* proof only by testing and applying these laws for yourself.

If you demand more substantial and authoritative evidence than my own, then I am privileged to refer you to the teachings and philosophy of Christ, Plato, Socrates, Epictetus, Confucius, Emerson and two of the more modern philosophers, James and Münsterberg, from whose works I have appropriated all that constitutes the more important fundamentals of this lesson, with the exception of that which I have gathered from my own limited experience.

For more than four thousand years men have been preaching the Golden Rule as a suitable rule of conduct among men, but unfortunately the world has accepted the letter while totally missing the spirit of this Universal Injunction. We have accepted the Golden Rule philosophy merely as a sound rule of ethical conduct but we have failed to understand the law upon which it is based.

I have heard the Golden Rule quoted scores of times, but I do not recall having ever heard an explanation of the law upon which it is based, and not until recent years did I understand that law, from which I am led to believe that those who quoted it did not understand it.

The Golden Rule means, substantially, to do unto others as you would wish them to do unto you if your positions were reversed.

But why? What is the *real* reason for this kindly consideration of others?

The real reason is this:

There is an eternal law through the operation of which we reap that which we sow. When you select the rule of conduct by which you guide yourself in your transactions with others, you will be fair and just, very likely, if you know that you are setting into motion, by that selection, a *power* that will run its course for weal or woe in the lives of others, returning, finally, to help or to hinder you, according to its nature.

"Whatsoever a man soweth that shall he also reap"!

It is your privilege to deal unjustly with others, but, if you understand the law upon which the Golden Rule is based, you must know that your unjust dealings will "come home to roost."

If you fully understood the principles described in Lesson Ten, on *accurate thought,* it will be quite easy for you to understand the law upon which the Golden Rule is based. You cannot pervert or change the course of this law, *but you can adapt yourself to its nature and thereby use it as an irresistible power that will carry you to heights of achievement which could not be attained without its aid.*

This law does not stop by merely flinging back upon you your *acts* of injustice and unkindness toward others; it goes further than this—much further—and returns to you the results of every *thought* that you release.

Therefore, not alone is it advisable to "do unto others as you wish them to do unto you," but to avail yourself fully of the benefits of this great Universal Law you must "think of others as you wish them to think of you."

The law upon which the Golden Rule is based begins affecting you, either for good or evil, the moment you release a *thought*. It has amounted almost to a world-wide tragedy that people have not generally understood this law. Despite the simplicity of the law it is practically all there is to be learned that is of enduring value to man, for it is the medium through which we become the masters of our own destiny.

Understand this law and you understand *all* that the Bible has to unfold to you, for the Bible presents one unbroken chain of evidence in support of the fact that man is the maker of his own destiny; and, that his *thoughts* and *acts* are the tools with which he does the *making*.

During ages of less enlightenment and tolerance than that of the present, some of the greatest thinkers the world has ever produced have paid with their lives for daring to uncover this Universal Law so that it might be understood by all. In the light of the past history of the world, it is an encouraging bit of evidence, in support of the fact that men are gradually throwing off the veil of ignorance and intolerance, to note that I stand in no danger of bodily harm for writing that which would have cost me my life a few centuries ago.

While this course deals with the highest laws of the universe, which man is capable of interpreting, the aim, nevertheless, has been to show how these laws may be used in the practical affairs of life. With this object of practical application in mind, let us now proceed to analyze the effect of the Golden Rule through the following incident.

The Power of Prayer

"No," said the lawyer, "I shan't press your claim against that man; you can get someone else to take the case, or you can withdraw it; just as you please."

Every man takes care that his neighbor does not cheat him. But a day comes when he begins to care that he does not cheat his neighbor. Then all goes well. He has changed his market cart into a chariot of the sun.

"Think there isn't any money in it?"

"There probably would be some little money in it, but it would come from the sale of the little house that the man occupies and calls his home! But I don't want to meddle with the matter, anyhow."

"Got frightened out of it, eh?"

"Not at all."

"I suppose likely the fellow begged hard to be let off?"

"Well, yes, he did."

"And you caved in, likely?"

"Yes."

"What in creation did you do?"

"I believe I shed a few tears."

"And the old fellow begged you hard, you say?"

"No, I didn't say so; he didn't speak a word to me."

"Well, may I respectfully inquire whom he did address in your hearing?"

"God Almighty."

"Ah, he took to praying, did he?"

"Not for my benefit, in the least. You see, I found the little house easily enough and knocked on the outer door, which stood ajar; but nobody heard me, so I stepped into the little hall and saw through the crack of a door a cozy sitting-room, and there on the bed, with her silver head high on the pillows, was an old lady who looked for all the world just like my mother did the last time I ever saw her on earth. Well, I was on the point of knocking, when she said: 'Come, father, now begin; I'm all ready.' And down on his knees by her side went an old, white-haired man, still older than his wife, I should judge, and I couldn't have knocked then, for the life of me. Well, he began. First, he reminded God they were still His submissive children, mother and he, and no matter what He saw fit to bring upon them they shouldn't rebel at His will. Of course 'twas going to be very hard for them to go out homeless in their old age, especially with poor mother so sick and help-less, and, oh! how different it all might have been if only one of the boys had been spared. Then his voice kind of broke, and a white hand stole from under the coverlid and moved softly over his snowy hair. Then he went on to repeat that nothing could be so sharp again as the parting with those three sons—unless mother and he should be separated.

"But, at last, he fell to comforting himself with the fact that the dear Lord knew that it was through no fault of his own that mother and he were threatened with the loss of their dear little home, which meant beggary and the alms-house—a place they prayed to be de-livered from entering if it should be consistent with God's will. And then he quoted a mul-titude of promises concerning the safety of those who put their trust in the Lord. In fact, it was the most thrilling plea to which I ever listened. And at last, he prayed for God's blessing on those who were about to demand justice."

The lawyer then continued, more lowly than ever: "And I—believe—I'd rather go to the poor-house myself tonight than to stain my heart and hands with the blood of such a pros-ecution as that."

"Little afraid to defeat the old man's prayer, eh?"

"Bless your soul, man, you couldn't defeat it!" said the lawyer. "I tell you he left it all sub-ject to the will of God; but he claimed that we were told to make known our desires unto God; but of all the pleadings I ever heard that beat all. You see, I was taught that kind of thing myself in my childhood. Anyway, why was I sent to hear that prayer? I am sure I don't know, but I hand the case over."

"I wish," said the client, twisting uneasily, "you hadn't told me about the old man's prayer."
"Why so?"

"Well, because I want the money the place would bring; but I was taught the Bible straight enough when I was a youngster and I'd hate to run counter to what you tell about. I wish you hadn't heard a word about it, and, another time, I wouldn't listen to petitions not intended for my ears."

The lawyer smiled.

"My dear fellow," he said, "you're wrong again. It was intended for my ears, and yours, too; and God Almighty intended it. My old mother used to sing about God's moving in a mysterious way, as I remember it."

"Well, my mother used to sing it, too," said the claimant, as he twisted the claim-papers in his fingers. "You can call in the morning, if you like, and tell 'mother' and 'him' the claim has been met."

"In a mysterious way," added the lawyer, smiling.

Neither this lesson nor the course of which it is a part is based upon an appeal to maudlin sentiment, but there can be no escape from the truth that *success*, in its highest and noblest form, brings one, finally, to view all human relationships with a feeling of deep emotion such as that which this lawyer felt when he overheard the old man's prayer.

It may be an old-fashioned idea, but somehow I can't get away from the belief that *no man can attain success in its highest form without the aid of earnest prayer!*

Prayer is the key with which one may open the secret doorway referred to in Lesson Ten. In this age of mundane affairs, when the uppermost thought of the majority of people is centered upon the accumulation of wealth, or the struggle for a mere existence, it is both easy and natural for us to overlook the power of earnest prayer.

I am not saying that you should resort to prayer as a means of solving your daily problems which press for immediate attention; no, I am not going that far in a course of instruction which will be studied largely by those who are seeking in it the road to *success* that is measured in dollars; but, may I not modestly suggest to *you* that you, at least, give *prayer* a trial after *everything else fails* to bring you a *satisfying success?*

Thirty men, red-eyed and disheveled, lined up before the judge of the San Francisco police court. It was the regular morning company of drunks and disorderlies. Some were old and hardened; others hung their heads in shame. Just as the momentary disorder attending the bringing in of the prisoners quieted down, a strange thing happened. A strong, clear voice from below began singing:

> "Last night I lay a–sleeping,
>   There came a dream so fair."

"Last night!" It had been for them all a nightmare or a drunken stupor. The song was such a contrast to the horrible fact that no one could fail of a sudden shock at the thought the song suggested.

"I stood in old Jerusalem,
    Beside the Temple there,"

the song went on. The judge had paused. He made a quiet inquiry. A former member of a famous opera company known all over the country was awaiting trial for forgery. It was he who was singing in his cell.

Meantime the song went on, and every man in the line showed emotion. One or two dropped on their knees; one boy at the end of the line, after a desperate effort at self-control, leaned against the wall, buried his face against his folded arms, and sobbed, "Oh, mother, mother."

The sobs, cutting to the very heart the men who heard, and the song, still welling its way through the court-room, blended in the hush. At length one man protested. "Judge," said he, "have we got to submit to this? We're here to take our punishment, but this—" He, too, began to sob.

It was impossible to proceed with the business of the court; yet the court gave no order to stop the song. The police sergeant, after an effort to keep the men in line, stepped back and waited with the rest. The song moved on to its climax:

"Jerusalem, Jerusalem!
    Sing, for the night is o'er!
Hosanna, in the highest!
    Hosanna, for evermore!"

In an ecstasy of melody the last words rang out, and then there was silence. The judge looked into the faces of the men before him. There was not one who was not touched by the song; not one in whom some better impulse was not stirred. He did not call the cases singly—a kind word of advice, and he dismissed them all. No man was fined or sentenced to the work-house that morning. The song had done more good than *punishment* could possibly have accomplished.

You have read the story of a Golden Rule lawyer and a Golden Rule judge. In these two

*A trifling kindness here and
there,
Is but a simple, small affair;
Yet if your life has sown this
free,
Wide shall your happy harvest
be.*

commonplace incidents of every-day life you have observed how the Golden Rule works when *applied*.

A passive attitude toward the Golden Rule will bring no results; it is not enough merely to *believe* in the philosophy, while, at the same time, failing to *apply* it in your relationships with others. If you want results you must take an *active* attitude toward the Golden Rule. A mere passive attitude, represented by belief in its soundness, will avail you nothing.

Nor will it avail you anything to proclaim to the world your belief in the Golden Rule while your actions are not in harmony with your proclamation. Conversely stated, it will avail you nothing to appear to practice the Golden Rule, while, at heart, you are willing and eager to use this universal law of right conduct as a cloak to cover up a covetous and selfish nature. Murder will out. Even the most ignorant person will "sense" you for what you are.

"Human character does evermore publish itself. It will not be concealed. It hates darkness—it rushes into light. . . . I heard an experienced counselor say that he never feared the effect upon a jury of a lawyer who does not believe in his heart that his client ought to have a verdict. If he does not believe it, his unbelief will appear to the jury, despite all his protestations, and will become their unbelief. This is that law whereby a work of art, of whatever kind, sets us in the same state of mind wherein the artist was when he made it. That which we do not believe we cannot *adequately say,* though we may repeat the words ever so often. It was this conviction which Swedenborg expressed when he described a group of persons in the spiritual world endeavoring in vain to articulate a proposition which they did not believe; but they could not, though they twisted and folded their lips even to indignation.

"A man passes for what he is worth. What he is engraves itself on his face, on his form, on his fortunes, in letters of light which all men may read but himself. . . . If you would not be known to do anything, never do it. A man may play the fool in the drifts of a desert, but every grain of sand shall seem to see."—Emerson

It is the law upon which the Golden Rule philosophy is based to which Emerson has reference in the foregoing quotation. It was this same law that he had in mind when he wrote the following:

"Every violation of truth is not only a sort of suicide in the liar, but is a stab at the health of human society. On the most profitable lie the course of events presently lays a destructive tax; whilst frankness proves to be the best tactics, for it invites frankness, puts the parties on a convenient footing and makes their business a friendship. Trust men and they will be true to you; treat them greatly and they will show themselves great, though they make an exception in your favor to all their rules of trade."

The Golden Rule philosophy is based upon a law which no man can circumvent. This law is the same law that is described in Lesson Ten, on Accurate Thought, through the operation of which one's thoughts are transformed into reality corresponding exactly to the nature of the thoughts.

"Once grant the creative power of our thought and there is an end of struggling for our own way, and an end of gaining it *at some one else's expense;* for, since by the terms of the hypothesis we can create what we like, the simplest way of getting what we want is, not to snatch it from somebody else, but to make it for ourselves; and, since there is no limit to thought there can be no need for straining, and for everyone to have his own way in *this manner,* would be to banish all strife, want, sickness, and sorrow from the earth."

"Now, it is precisely on this assumption of the creative power of our thought that the whole Bible rests. If not, what is the meaning of being saved by Faith? Faith is essentially thought; and, therefore, every call to have faith in God is a call to trust in the power of our own thought about God. 'According to your faith be it unto you,' says the Old Testament. The entire book is nothing but one continuous statement of the creative power of Thought.

"The Law of Man's Individuality is, therefore, the Law of Liberty, and equally it is the Gospel of peace; for when we truly understand the law of our own individuality, we see that the same law finds its expression in everyone else; and, consequently, we shall reverence *the law in others* exactly in proportion as we value it in ourselves. To do this is to follow the Golden Rule of doing to others what we would they should do unto us; and because we know that the Law of Liberty in ourselves must include the free use of our creative power, there is no longer any inducement to infringe the rights of others, for we can satisfy all our desires by the exercise of our knowledge of the law.

"As this comes to be understood, co-operation will take the place of competition, with the result of removing all ground for enmity, whether between individuals, classes, or nations. . . ."

(The foregoing quotation is from *Bible Mystery and Bible Meaning* by the late Judge T. Troward, published by Robert McBride & Company, New York City. Judge Troward was the author of several interesting volumes, among them The Edinburgh Lectures, which is recommended to all students of this course.)

If you wish to know what happens to a man when he totally disregards the law upon which the Golden Rule philosophy is based, pick out any man in your community whom you know to live for the single dominating purpose of accumulating wealth, and who has no conscientious scruples as to how he accumulates that wealth. Study this man and you will observe that there is no warmth to his soul; there is no kindness to his words; there is no welcome to his face. He has become a slave to the desire for wealth; he is too busy to enjoy life and too selfish to wish to help others enjoy it. He walks, and talks, and breathes, but he is nothing but a human automaton. Yet there are many who envy such a man and wish that they might occupy his position, foolishly believing him to be a *success*.

There can never be *success* without happiness, and no man can be happy without dispensing happiness to others. Moreover, the dispensation must be voluntary and with no other object in view than that of spreading sunshine into the hearts of those whose hearts are heavy-laden with burdens.

George D. Herron had in mind the law upon which the Golden Rule philosophy is based when he said:

"We have talked much of the brotherhood to come; but brotherhood has always been the fact of our life, long before it became a modern and inspired sentiment. Only we have been brothers in slavery and torment, brothers in ignorance and its perdition, brothers in disease, and war, and want, brothers in prostitution and hypocrisy. What happens to one of us sooner or later happens to all; we have always been unescapably involved in common destiny. The world constantly tends to the level of the downmost man in it; and that downmost man is the world's real ruler, hugging it close to his bosom, dragging it down to his death. You do not think so, but it is true, and it ought to be true. For if there were some way by which some of us could get free, apart from others, if there were some way by which some of us could have heaven while others had hell, if there were some way by which part of the world could escape some form of the blight and peril and misery of disinherited labor, then indeed would our world be lost and damned; but since men have never been able to separate themselves from one another's woes and wrongs, since history is fairly stricken with the lesson that we cannot escape brotherhood of some kind, since the whole of life is teaching us that we are hourly choosing between brotherhood in suffering and brotherhood in good, it remains for us to choose the brotherhood of a co-operative world, with all its fruits thereof—the fruits of *love* and *liberty*."

> *No idle person is ever safe, whether he be rich or poor, white or black, educated or illiterate.*
>
> —BOOKER T. WASHINGTON

The world war ushered us into an age of co-operative effort in which the law of "live and let live" stands out like a shining star to guide us in our relationships with each other. This great universal call for co-operative effort is taking on many forms, not the least important of which are the Rotary Clubs, the Kiwanis Clubs, the Lions Clubs and the many other luncheon clubs which bring men together in a spirit of friendly intercourse, for these clubs mark the beginning of an age of friendly competition in business. The next step will be a closer alliance of all such clubs in an out-and-out spirit of friendly co-operation.

The attempt by Woodrow Wilson and his contemporaries to establish the League of Nations, followed by the efforts of Warren G. Harding to give footing to the same cause under the name of the World Court, marked the first attempt in the history of the world to make the Golden Rule effective as a common meeting ground for the nations of the world.

There is no escape from the fact that the world has awakened to the truth in George D. Herron's statement that "we are hourly choosing between brotherhood in suffering and brotherhood in good." The world war has taught us—nay, forced upon us—the truth that a part of the world cannot suffer without injury to the whole world. These facts are called to your attention, not in the nature of a preachment on morality, but for the purpose of directing your attention to the underlying law through which these changes are being brought about. For more than four thousand years the world has been thinking about the Golden Rule philosophy, and that *thought* is now becoming transformed into realization of the benefits that accrue to those who apply it.

Still mindful of the fact that the student of this course is interested in a material success that can be measured by bank balances, it seems appropriate to suggest here that all who will may profit by shaping their business philosophy to conform with this sweeping change toward co-operation which is taking place all over the world.

If you can grasp the significance of the tremendous change that has come over the world since the close of the world war, and if you can interpret the meaning of all the luncheon clubs and other similar gatherings which bring men and women together in a spirit of friendly co-operation, surely your imagination will suggest to you the fact that this is an opportune time to profit by adopting this spirit of friendly co-operation as the basis of your own business or professional philosophy.

Stated conversely, it must be obvious to all who make any pretense of thinking accurately, that the time is at hand when failure to adopt the Golden Rule as the foundation of one's business or professional philosophy is the equivalent of economic suicide.

———

Perhaps you have wondered why the subject of *honesty* has not been mentioned in this course, as a prerequisite to *success,* and, if so, the answer will be found in this lesson. The Golden Rule philosophy, when rightly understood and applied, makes dishonesty impossible. It does more than this—it makes impossible all the other destructive qualities such as selfishness, greed, envy, bigotry, hatred and malice.

When you apply the Golden Rule, you become, at one and the same time, both the judge and the judged—the accused and the accuser. This places one in a position in which *honesty* begins in one's own heart, toward one's self, and extends to all others with equal effect. *Honesty* based upon the Golden Rule is not the brand of honesty which recognizes nothing but the question of expediency.

It is no credit to be honest, when honesty is obviously the most *profitable* policy, lest one lose a good customer or a valuable client or be sent to jail for trickery. But when honesty means either a temporary or a permanent material loss, then it becomes an *honor* of the highest degree to all who practice it. Such honesty has its appropriate reward in the accumulated power of character and reputation enjoyed by all who deserve it.

Those who understand and apply the Golden Rule philosophy are always scrupulously honest, not alone out of their desire to be just with others, but because of their desire to be just with themselves. They understand the eternal law upon which the Golden Rule is based, and they know that through the operation of this law *every thought they release and every act in which they indulge has its counterpart in some fact or circumstance with which they will later be confronted.*

Golden Rule philosophers are honest because they understand the truth that honesty adds to their own character that "vital something" which gives it life and power. Those who understand the law through which the Golden Rule operates would poison their own drinking water as quickly as they would indulge in acts of injustice to others, for they know that such injustice starts a chain of causation that will not only bring them physical suffering, but will destroy their characters, stain for ill their reputations and render impossible the attainment of enduring success.

The law through which the Golden Rule philosophy operates is none other than the law through which the principle of Auto-suggestion operates. This statement gives you a suggestion from which you should be able to make a deduction of a far-reaching nature and of inestimable value.

Test your progress in the mastery of this course by analyzing the foregoing statement and determining, before you read on, what suggestion it offers you.

Of what possible benefit could it be to you to know that when you do unto others as if you were the others, which is the sum and substance of the Golden Rule, you are putting into motion a chain of causation through the aid of a law which affects the others according to the nature of your act, *and at the same time planting in your character, through your sub-conscious mind, the effects of that act?*

This question practically suggests its own answer, but as I am determined to cause you to think this vital subject out for yourself I will put the question in still another form, viz.:

If all your acts toward others, and even your thoughts of others, are registered in your sub-conscious mind, through the principle of Auto-suggestion, thereby building your own character in exact duplicate of your *thoughts* and *acts,* can you not see how important it is to guard those acts and thoughts?

We are now in the very heart of the real reason for doing unto others as we would have them do unto us, for it is obvious that whatever we do unto others we do unto ourselves.

Stated in another way, every *act* and every *thought* you release modifies your own character in exact conformity with the nature of the act or thought, and your character is a sort of center of magnetic attraction which attracts to you the people and conditions that harmonize with it.

You cannot indulge in an act toward another person without having first created the nature of that act in your own *thought, and you cannot release a thought without planting the sum and substance and nature of it in your own sub-conscious mind, there to become a part and parcel of your own character.*

> *There is no defeat except from within. There is really no insurmountable barrier save your own inherent weakness of purpose.*
>
> —EMERSON

Grasp this simple principle and you will understand why you cannot afford to hate or envy another person. You will also understand why you cannot afford to strike back, in kind, at those who do you an injustice. Likewise, you will understand the injunction, "Return good for evil."

Understand the law upon which the Golden Rule injunction is based and you will understand, also, the law that eternally binds all mankind in a single bond of fellowship and renders it impossible for you to injure another person, by *thought* or *deed,* without injuring yourself; and, likewise, adds to your own character the results of every kind *thought* and *deed* in which you indulge.

Understand this law and you will then know, beyond room for the slightest doubt, that you are constantly punishing yourself for every wrong you commit and rewarding yourself for every act of constructive conduct in which you indulge.

It seems almost an act of Providence that the greatest wrong and the most severe injustice ever done me by one of my fellow men was done just as I began this lesson. (Some of the students of this course will know what it is to which I refer.)

This injustice has worked a temporary hardship on me, but that is of little consequence compared to the advantage it has given me by providing a timely opportunity for me to test the soundness of the entire premise upon which this lesson is founded.

The injustice to which I refer left two courses of action open to me. I could have claimed relief by "striking back" at my antagonist, through both civil court action and criminal libel proceedings, or I could have stood upon my right to forgive him. One course of action would have brought me a substantial sum of money and whatever joy and satisfaction there may be in defeating and *punishing* an enemy. The other course of action would have brought me self-respect which is enjoyed by those who have successfully met the test and discovered that they have evolved to the point at which they can repeat the Lord's Prayer and *mean it!*

I chose the latter course. I did so, despite the recommendations of close personal friends to "strike back," and despite the offer of a prominent lawyer to do my "striking" for me *without cost.*

But the lawyer offered to do the impossible, for the reason that no man can "strike back" at another *without cost.* Not always is the cost of a monetary nature, for there are other things with which one may pay that are dearer than money.

It would be as hopeless to try to make one who was not familiar with the law upon which the Golden Rule is based understand why I refused to strike back at this enemy as it would to try to describe the law of gravitation to an ape. If you understand this law you understand, also, why I chose to *forgive* my enemy.

In the Lord's Prayer we are admonished to forgive our enemies, but that admonition will fall on deaf ears except where the listener understands the law upon which it is based. That law is none other than the law upon which the Golden Rule is based. It is the law that forms the foundation of this entire lesson, and through which we must inevitably reap that which we sow. There is no escape from the operation of this law, nor is there any cause to try to avoid its consequences if we refrain from putting into motion *thoughts* and *acts* that are destructive.

That we may more concretely describe the law upon which this lesson is based, let us embody the law in a code of ethics such as one who wishes to follow literally the injunction of the Golden Rule might appropriately adopt, as follows.

My Code of Ethics

I. I believe in the Golden Rule as the basis of all human conduct; therefore, I will never do to another person that which I would not be willing for that person to do to me if our positions were reversed.

II. I will be honest, even to the slightest detail, in all my transactions with others, not alone because of my desire to be fair with them, but because of my desire to impress the idea of honesty on my own sub-conscious mind, thereby weaving this essential quality into my own character.

III. I will forgive those who are unjust toward me, with no thought as to whether they deserve it or not, because I understand the law through which forgiveness of others strengthens my own character and wipes out the effects of my own transgressions, in my sub-conscious mind.

IV. I will be just, generous and fair with others always, even though I know that these acts will go unnoticed and unrewarded, in the ordinary terms of reward, because I understand and intend to apply the law through the aid of which one's own character is but the sum total of one's own *acts* and *deeds*.

V. Whatever time I may have to devote to the discovery and exposure of the weaknesses and faults of others I will devote, more profitably, to the discovery and *correction* of my own.

VI. I will slander no person, no matter how much I may believe another person may deserve it, because I wish to plant no destructive suggestions in my own sub-conscious mind.

VII. I recognize the power of Thought as being an inlet leading into my brain from the universal ocean of life; therefore, I will set no destructive thoughts afloat upon that ocean lest they pollute the minds of others.

VIII. I will conquer the common human tendency toward hatred, and envy, and selfishness, and jealousy, and malice, and pessimism, and doubt, and fear; for I believe these to be the seed from which the world harvests most of its troubles.

IX. When my mind is not occupied with thoughts that tend toward the attainment of my *definite chief aim* in life, I will voluntarily keep it filled with thoughts of courage, and self-confidence, and good-will toward others, and faith, and kindness, and loyalty, and love for truth, and justice, for I believe these to be the seed from which the world reaps its harvest of progressive growth.

X. I understand that a mere passive belief in the soundness of the Golden Rule philosophy is of no value whatsoever, either to myself or to others; therefore, I will *actively* put into operation this universal rule for good in all my transactions with others.

XI. I understand the law through the operation of which my own character is developed from my own *acts* and *thoughts;* therefore, I will guard with care all that goes into its development.

XII. Realizing that enduring happiness comes only through helping others find it; that no act of kindness is without its reward, even though it may never be directly repaid, I will do my best to assist others when and where the opportunity appears.

You have noticed frequent reference to Emerson throughout this course. Every student of the course should own a copy of Emerson's *Essays,* and the essay on Compensation should be read and studied at least every three months. Observe, as you read this essay, that it deals with the same law as that upon which the Golden Rule is based.

There are people who believe that the Golden Rule philosophy is nothing more than a theory, and that it is in no way connected with an immutable law. They have arrived at this conclusion because of personal experience wherein they rendered service to others without enjoying the benefits of direct reciprocation.

How many are there who have not rendered service to others that was neither reciprocated nor appreciated? I am sure that I have had such an experience, not once, but many times, and I am equally sure that I will have similar experiences in the future, nor will I discontinue rendering service to others merely because *they* neither reciprocate nor appreciate my efforts.

And here is the reason:

When I render service to another, or indulge in an act of kindness, I store away in my sub-conscious mind the effect of my efforts, which may be likened to the "charging" of an electric battery. By and by, if I indulge in a sufficient number of such acts I will have developed a positive, dynamic character that will *attract* to me people who harmonize with or resemble my own character.

Those whom I *attract* to me will reciprocate the acts of kindness and the service that I have rendered others,

> *You have not fulfilled every duty unless you have fulfilled that of being pleasant.*
> —CHARLES BUXTON

thus the Law of Compensation will have balanced the scales of justice for me, bringing back from one source the results of service that I rendered through an entirely different source.

You have often heard it said that a salesman's first sale should be to himself, which means that unless he first convinces himself of the merits of his wares he will not be able to convince others. Here, again, enters this same Law of Attraction, for it is a well known fact that *enthusiasm* is contagious, and when a salesman shows great *enthusiasm* over his wares he will arouse a corresponding interest in the minds of others.

You can comprehend this law quite easily by regarding yourself as a sort of human magnet that attracts those whose characters harmonize with your own. In thus regarding yourself as a magnet that attracts to you all who harmonize with your dominating characteristics and repels all who do not so harmonize, you should keep in mind, also, the fact that *you are the builder of that magnet;* also, that you may change its nature so that it will correspond to any ideal that you may wish to set up and follow.

And, most important of all, you should keep in mind the fact that this entire process of change takes place through *thought!*

Your character is but the sum total of your *thoughts* and *deeds!* This truth has been stated in many different ways throughout this course.

Because of this great truth it is impossible for you to render any useful service or indulge in any act of kindness toward others without benefiting thereby. Moreover, it is just as impossible for you to indulge in any destructive *act* or *thought* without paying the penalty in the loss of a corresponding amount of your own power.

Positive thought develops a dynamic personality. *Negative thought* develops a personality of an opposite nature. In many of the preceding lessons of this course, and in this one, definite instructions are given as to the exact method of developing personality through *positive thought*. These instructions are particularly detailed in Lesson Two, on *Self-confidence*. In that lesson you have a very definite formula to follow. All of the formulas provided in this course are for the purpose of helping you *consciously* to direct the power of *thought* in the development of a personality that will attract to you those who will be of help in the attainment of your *definite chief aim.*

You need no proof that your hostile or unkind *acts* toward others bring back the effects of retaliation. Moreover, this retaliation is usually definite and immediate. Likewise, you need no proof that you can accomplish more by dealing with others in such a way that they will want to co-operate with you. If you mastered the seventh lesson, on Self-control, you now understand how to induce others to act toward you as you wish them to act—*through your own attitude toward them.*

The law of "an eye for an eye and a tooth for a tooth" is based upon the selfsame law as that upon which the Golden Rule operates. This is nothing more than the law of retaliation with which all of us are familiar. Even the most selfish person will respond to this law, *because he cannot help it!* If I speak ill of you, even though I tell the truth, you will not think kindly of me. Furthermore, you will most likely retaliate in kind. But, if I speak of your virtues you will think kindly of me, and when the opportunity appears you will reciprocate in kind in the majority of instances.

Through the operation of this law of attraction the uninformed are constantly attracting trouble and grief and hatred and opposition from others by their *unguarded words* and *destructive acts.*

Do unto others as you would have them do unto you!

We have heard that injunction expressed thousands of times, yet how many of us understand the law upon which it is based? To make this injunction somewhat clearer it might be well to state it more in detail, about as follows:

Do unto others as you would have them do unto you, *bearing in mind the fact that human nature has a tendency to retaliate in kind.*

Confucius must have had in mind the law of retaliation when he stated the Golden Rule philosophy in about this way:

Do not unto others that which you would not have them do unto you.

And he might well have added an explanation to the effect that the reason for his injunction was based upon the common tendency of man to retaliate in kind.

Those who do not understand the law upon which the Golden Rule is based are inclined to argue that it will not work, for the reason that men are inclined toward the principle of exacting "an eye for an eye and a tooth for a tooth," which is nothing more nor less than the law of retaliation. If they would go a step further in their reasoning they would understand that they are looking at the *negative* effects of this law, and that the selfsame law is capable of producing *positive* effects as well.

In other words, if you would not have your own eye plucked out, then insure against this misfortune by refraining from plucking out the other fellow's eye. Go a step further and render the other fellow an act of kindly, helpful service, and *through the operation of this same law of retaliation* he will render you a similar service.

And, if he should fail to reciprocate your kindness—what then?

You have profited, nevertheless, because of the effect of your act on *your own sub-conscious mind!*

Thus by indulging in acts of kindness and applying, always, the Golden Rule philosophy, you are sure of benefit from one source and at the same time you have a pretty fair chance of profiting from another source.

It might happen that you would base all of your acts toward others on the Golden Rule without enjoying any direct reciprocation for a long period of time, and it might so happen that those to whom you rendered those acts of kindness would never reciprocate, but meantime you have been adding vitality to your own character and sooner or later this *positive character* which you have been building will begin to assert itself and you will discover that you have been receiving compound interest on compound interest in return for those acts of kindness which appeared to have been wasted on those who neither appreciated nor reciprocated them.

Remember that your *reputation* is made by others, but your *character* is made by *you!*

You want your reputation to be a favorable one, but you cannot be sure that it will be for the reason that it is something that exists outside of your own control, in the minds of others. It is what others believe you to be. With your character it is different. Your character is that which *you are,* as the results of your *thoughts* and *deeds.* You control it. You can make it weak, good or bad. When you are satisfied and know in your mind that your character is above reproach you need not worry about your reputation, for it is as impossible for your character to be destroyed or damaged by anyone except yourself as it is to destroy matter or energy.

It was this truth that Emerson had in mind when he said: "A political victory, a rise of rents, the recovery of your sick or the return of your absent friend, or some other quite external event raises your spirits, and you think your days are prepared for you. *Do not believe it.* It can never be so. *Nothing can bring you peace but yourself. Nothing can bring you peace but the triumph of principles.*"

One reason for being just toward others is the fact that such action may cause them to reciprocate, in kind, but a better reason is the fact that kindness and justice toward others develop *positive character* in all who indulge in these acts.

You may withhold from me the reward to which I am entitled for rendering you helpful service, but no one can deprive me of the benefit I will derive from the rendering of that service in so far as it adds to my own *character.*

We are living in a great industrial age. Everywhere we see the evolutionary forces working great changes in the method and manner of living, and rearranging the relationships between men, in the ordinary pursuit of life, liberty and a living.

This is an age of organized effort. On every hand we see evidence that organization is the basis of all financial success, and while other factors than that of organization enter into the attainment of success, this factor is still one of major importance.

This industrial age has created two comparatively new terms. One is called "capital" and the other "labor." Capital and labor constitute the main wheels in the machinery of organized effort. These two great forces enjoy success in exact ratio to the extent that both understand and apply the Golden Rule philosophy. Despite this fact, however, harmony between these two forces does not always prevail, thanks to the destroyers of confidence who make a living by sowing the seed of dissension and stirring up strife between employers and employees.

During the past fifteen years I have devoted considerable time to the study of the causes of disagreement between employers and employees. Also, I have gathered much information on this subject from other men who, likewise, have been studying this problem.

There is but one solution which will, if understood by all concerned, bring harmony out of chaos and establish a perfect working relationship between capital and labor. The remedy is no invention of mine. It is based upon a great universal law of Nature. This remedy has been well stated by one of the great men of this generation, in the following words:

"The question we propose to consider is exciting deep interest at the present time, but no more than its importance demands. It is one of the hopeful signs of the times that these subjects of vital interest to human happiness are constantly coming up for a hearing, are engaging the attention of the wisest men, and stirring the minds of all classes of people. The wide prevalence of this movement shows that a new life is beating in the heart of humanity, operating upon their faculties like the warm breath of spring upon the frozen ground and the dormant germs of the plant. It will make a great stir, it will break up many frozen and dead forms, it will produce great and, in some cases, it may be, destructive changes, but it announces the blossoming of new hopes, and the coming of new harvests for the supply of human wants and the means of greater happiness. There is great need of wisdom to guide the new forces coming into action. Every man is under the most solemn obligation to do his part in forming a correct public opinion and giving wise direction to popular will.

"The only solution for the problems of labor, of want, of abundance, of suffering and sorrow can only be found by regarding them from a moral and spiritual point of view. They must be seen and examined in a light that is not of themselves. *The true relations of labor and capital can never be discovered by human selfishness.* They must be viewed from a higher purpose than wages or the accumulation of wealth. They must be regarded from their bearing upon the purposes for which man was created. It is from this point of view I propose to consider the subject before us.

"Capital and labor are essential to each other. Their interests are so bound together that they cannot be separated. In civilized and enlightened communities they are mutually dependent. If there is any difference, capital is more dependent upon labor than labor upon capital. Life can be sustained without capital. Animals, with a few exceptions, have no property, and take no anxious thought for the morrow, and our Lord commends them to our notice as examples worthy of imitation. 'Behold the fowls of the air,' He says, 'for they sow not, neither do they reap nor gather into barns, yet your heavenly Father feedeth them.' The savages live without capital. Indeed, the great mass of human beings live by their labor from day to day, from hand to mouth. But no man can live upon his wealth. He cannot eat his gold and silver; he cannot clothe himself with deeds and certificates of stock. Capital can do nothing without labor, *and its only value consists in its power to purchase labor or its results.* It is itself the product of labor. It has no occasion, therefore, to assume an importance that does not belong to it. Absolutely dependent, however, as it is upon labor for its value, it is an essential factor in human progress.

"The moment man begins to rise from a savage and comparatively independent state to a civilized and dependent one, capital becomes necessary. Men come into more intimate relations with one another. Instead of each one doing everything, men begin to devote themselves to special employments, and to depend upon others to provide many things for them while they engage in some special occupation. In this way labor becomes diversified. One man works in iron, another in wood; one manufactures cloth, another makes it into garments; some raise food to feed those who build houses and manufacture implements of husbandry. This necessitates a system of exchanges, and to facilitate exchanges roads must be made, and men must be employed to make them. As population increases and necessities multiply, the business of exchange becomes enlarged, until we have immense manufactories, railroads girding the earth with iron bands, steamships plowing every sea, and a multitude of men who cannot raise bread or make a garment, or do anything directly for the supply of their own wants.

"Now, we can see how we become more dependent upon others as our wants are multiplied and civilization advances. Each one works in his special employment, does better work, because he can devote his whole thought and time to a form of use for which he is specially fitted, and contributes more largely to the public good. While he is working for others, all others are working for him. Every member of the community is working for the whole body, and the whole body for every member. This is the law of perfect life, a law which rules everywhere in the material body. Every man who is engaged in any employment useful to body or mind is a philanthropist, a public benefactor, whether he raises corn on the prairie, cotton in Texas or India, mines coal in the chambers of the earth, or feeds it to engines in the hold of a steamship. If selfishness did not pervert and blast human motives, all men and women would be fulfilling the law of charity while engaged in their daily employment.

"To carry on this vast system of exchanges, to place the forest and the farm, the factory and the mine side by side, and deliver the products of all climes at every door, requires immense capital. One man cannot work his farm or factory, and build a railroad or a line of steamships. As raindrops acting singly cannot drive a mill or supply steam for an engine, but, collected in a vast reservoir, become the resistless power of Niagara, or the force which drives the engine and steamship like mighty shuttles from mountain to seacoast and from shore to shore, so a few dollars in a multitude of pockets are powerless to provide the means for these vast operations, but combined they move the world.

"Capital is a friend of labor and essential to its economical exercise and just reward. It can be, and often is, a terrible enemy, when employed for selfish purposes alone; but the great mass of it is more friendly to human happiness than is generally supposed. It cannot be employed without in some way, either directly or indirectly, helping the laborer. We think of the evils we suffer, but allow the good we enjoy to pass unnoticed. We think of the evils that larger means would relieve and the comforts they would provide, but overlook the blessings we enjoy that would have been impossible without large accumulations of capital. It is the part of wisdom to form a just estimate of the good we receive as well as the evils we suffer.

"It is a common saying at the present time, that the rich are growing richer and the poor poorer; but when all man's possessions are taken into the account there are good reasons for doubting this assertion. It is true that the rich are growing richer. It is also true that the condition of the laborer is constantly improving. *The common laborer has conveniences and comforts which princes could not command a century ago.* He is better clothed, has a greater variety and abundance of food, lives in a more comfortable dwelling, and has many more conveniences for the conduct of domestic affairs and the prosecution of labor than money could purchase but a few years ago. An emperor could not travel with the ease, the comfort, and the swiftness that the common laborer can today. He may think that he stands alone, with no one to help. But, in truth, he has an immense retinue of servants constantly waiting upon him, ready and anxious to do his bidding. It requires a vast army of men and an immense outlay of capital to provide a common dinner, such as every man and woman, with few exceptions, has enjoyed today.

"Think of the vast combination of means and men and forces necessary to provide even a frugal meal. The Chinaman raises your tea, the Brazilian your coffee, the East Indian your spices, the Cuban your sugar, the farmer upon the western prairies your bread and possibly your beef, the gardener your vegetables, the dairyman your butter and milk; the miner has dug from the hills the coal with which your food was cooked and your house was warmed, the cabinet-maker has provided you with chairs and tables, the cutler with knives and forks, the potter with dishes, the Irishman has made your table-cloth, the butcher has dressed your meat, the miller your flour.

"But these various articles of food, and the means of preparing and serving them, were produced at immense distances from you and from one another. Oceans had to be traversed, hills leveled, valleys filled, and mountains tunneled, ships must be built, railways constructed, and a vast army of men instructed and employed in every mechanical art before the materials for your dinner could be prepared and served. There must also be men to collect these materials, to buy and sell and distribute them. Everyone stands in his own place and does his own work, and receives his wages. But he is none the less working for you, and serving you as truly and effectively as he would be if he were in your special employment and received his wages from your hand. In the light of these facts, which everyone must acknowledge, we may be able to see more clearly the truth, that every man and woman who does useful work is a public benefactor, and the thought of it and the purpose of it will ennoble the labor and the laborer. We are all bound together by common ties. The rich and the poor, the learned and the ignorant, the strong and the weak, are woven together in one social and civic web. Harm to one is harm to all; help to one is help to all.

"You see what a vast army of servants it requires to provide your dinner. Do you not see that it demands a corresponding amount of capital to provide and keep this complicated machinery in motion? And do you not see that every man, woman and child is enjoying the benefit of it? How could we get our coal, our meat, our flour, our tea and coffee, sugar and rice? The laborer cannot build ships and sail them and support himself while doing it. *The farmer cannot leave his farm and take his produce to the market. The miner cannot mine and transport his coal.* The farmer in Kansas may be burning corn today to cook his food and warm his dwelling, and the miner may be hungry for the bread which the corn would supply, because they cannot exchange the fruits of their labor. Every acre of land, every forest and mine has been increased in value by railways and steamboats, and the comforts of life and the means of social and intellectual culture have been carried to the most inaccessible places.

"But the benefits of capital are not limited to supplying present wants and comforts. It opens new avenues for labor. It diversifies it and gives a wider field to everyone to do the kind of work for which he is best fitted by natural taste and genius. The number of employments created by railways, steamships, telegraph, and manufactories by machinery can hardly be estimated. Capital is also largely invested in supplying the means of intellectual and spiritual culture. Books are multiplied at constantly diminishing prices, and the best thought of the world, by means of our great publishing houses, is made accessible to the humblest workman. There is no better example of the benefits the common laborer derives from capital than the daily newspaper. For two or three cents the history of the world for twenty-four hours is brought to every door. The laborer, while riding to or from his work in a comfortable car, can visit all parts of the known world and get a truer idea of the events of the day than he could if he were bodily present. A battle in China or Africa, an earthquake in Spain, a dynamite explosion in London, a debate in Congress, the movements of men in public and private life for the suppression of vice, for enlightening the ignorant, helping the needy, and improving the people generally; are spread before him in a small compass, and bring him into contact and on equality, in regard to the world's history, with kings and queens, with saints and sages, and people in every condition in life. *Do you ever think,* while reading the morning paper, how many men have been running on your errands, collecting intelligence for you from all parts of the earth, and putting it into a form convenient for your use? It required the investment of millions of money and the employment of thousands of men to produce that paper and leave it at your door. And what did all this service cost you? A few cents.

"These are examples of the benefits which everyone derives from capital, benefits which could not be obtained without vast expenditures of money; benefits which come to us without our care and lay their blessings at our feet. Capital cannot be invested in any useful production without blessing a multitude of people. It sets the machinery of life in motion, it multiplies employment; it places the product of all climes at every door, it draws the people of all nations together; brings mind in contact with mind, and gives to every man and woman a large and valuable share of the product. These are facts which it would be well for everyone, however poor he may be, to consider.

"If capital is such a blessing to labor; if it can only be brought into use by labor, and derives all its value from it, how can there be any conflict between them? There could be none if both the capitalist and laborer acted from humane and Christian principles. But they do not. They are governed by inhuman and unchristian principles. Each party seeks to get the largest returns for the least service. Capital desires larger profits, labor higher wages. The interests of the capitalist and the laborer come into direct collision. In this warfare capital has great advantages, and has been prompt to take them. It has demanded and taken the lion's share of the profits. It has despised the servant that enriched it. It has regarded the laborer as a menial, a slave, whose rights and happiness it was not bound to respect. It influences legislators to enact laws in its favor, subsidizes governments and wields its power for its own advantage. Capital has been a lord and labor a servant. While the servant remained docile and obedient, content with such compensation as its lord chose to give, there was no conflict. But labor is rising from a servile, submissive, and hopeless condition. It has acquired strength and intelligence; has gained the idea that it has rights that ought to be respected, and begins to assert and combine to support them.

"Each party in this warfare regards the subject from its own selfish interests. The capitalist supposes that gain to labor is loss to him, and that he must look to his own interests first; that the cheaper the labor the larger his gains. Consequently it is for his interest to keep the price as low as possible. On the contrary, the laborer thinks that he loses what the capitalist gains, and, consequently, that it is for his interest to get as large wages as possible. From these opposite points of view their interests appear to be directly hostile. What one party gains the other loses; hence the conflict. Both are acting from selfish motives, and, consequently, must be wrong. Both parties see only half of the truth, and, mistaking that for the whole of it, they fall into a mistake ruinous to both. Each one stands on his own ground, and regards the subject wholly from his point of view and in the misleading light of his own selfishness. Passion inflames the mind and blinds the understanding; and when passion is aroused men will sacrifice their own interests to injure others, and both will suffer loss. They will wage continual warfare against each other; they will resort to all devices, and take advantage of every necessity to win a victory. Capital tries to starve the laborer into submission, like a beleaguered city; and hunger and want are most powerful weapons. Labor sullenly resists, and tries to destroy the value of capital by rendering it unproductive. If necessity or interest compels a truce, it is a sullen one, and maintained with the purpose of renewing hostilities as soon as there is any prospect of success. Thus laborers and capitalists confront each other like two armed hosts, ready at any time to renew the conflict. *It will be renewed, without doubt, and continued with varying success until both parties discover that they are mistaken, that their interests are mutual, and can only be secured to the fullest extent by co-operation and giving to each the reward it deserves.* The capitalist and the laborer must clasp hands across the bottomless pit into which so much wealth and work has been cast.

"How this reconciliation is to be effected is a question that is occupying the minds of many wise and good men on both sides at the present time. Wise and impartial legislation will, no doubt, be an important agent in restraining blind passion and protecting all classes from insatiable greed; and it is the duty of every man to use his best endeavors to secure such legislation both in state and national governments. Organizations of laborers for protecting their own rights and securing a better reward for their labor, will have a great influence. That influence will continue to increase as their temper becomes normal and firm, and their demands are based *on justice and humanity.* Violence and threats will effect no good. Dynamite, whether in the form of explosives or the more destructive force of fierce and reckless passion, will heal no wounds nor subdue any hostile feeling. Arbitration is, doubtless, the wisest and most practicable means now available to bring about amicable relations between these hostile parties and secure justice to both. Giving the laborer a share in the profits of the business has worked well in some cases, but it is attended with great practical difficulties which require more wisdom, self-control and genuine regard for the common interests of both parties than often can be found. Many devices may have a partial and temporary effect. But no permanent progress can be made in settling this conflict without restraining and finally removing its cause.

"Its real central cause is an inordinate love of self and the world, and that cause will continue to operate as long as it exists. It may be restrained and moderated, but it will assert itself when occasion offers. Every wise man must, therefore, seek to remove the cause, and as far as he can do it he will control effects. Purify the fountain, and you make the whole stream pure and wholesome.

"There is a principle of universal influence that must underlie and guide every successful effort to bring these two great factors of human good which now confront each other with hostile purpose, into harmony. It is no invention or discovery of mine. It embodies a higher than human wisdom. It is not difficult to understand or apply. The child can comprehend it and act according to it. It is universal in its application, and wholly useful in its effects. It will lighten the burdens of labor and increase its rewards. It will give security to capital and make it more productive. It is simply the Golden Rule, embodied in these words: '*Therefore all things whatsoever ye would that men should do to you, do ye even so to them: for this is the law and the prophets.*'

"Before proceeding to apply this principle to the case in hand, let me call your special attention to it. It is a very remarkable law of human life which seems to have been generally overlooked by statesmen, philosophers and religious teachers. This rule embodies the whole of religion; it comprises all the precepts, commandments, and means of the future triumphs of good over evil, of truth over error, and the peace and happiness of men, foretold in the glorious visions of the prophets. Mark the words. It does not merely say that it is a wise rule; that it accords with the principles of the Divine order revealed in the law and the prophets. *It embodies them all; it 'IS the law and the prophets.'* It comprises love to God. It says we should regard Him as we desire to have Him regard us; that we should do to Him as we wish to have Him do to us. If we desire to have Him love us with all His heart, with all His soul, with all His mind, and with all His strength, we must love Him in the same manner. If we desire to have our neighbor love us as he loves himself, we must love him as we love ourself. Here, then, is the universal and Divine law of human service and fellowship. It is not a precept of human wisdom; it has its origin in the Divine nature, and its embodiment in human nature. Now, let us apply it to the conflict between labor and capital.

"You are a capitalist. Your money is invested in manufactures, in land, in mines, in merchandise, railways, and ships, or you loan it to others on interest. You employ, directly or indirectly, men to use your capital. You cannot come to a just conclusion concerning your rights and duties and privileges by looking wholly at your own gains. The glitter of the silver and gold will exercise so potent a spell over your mind that it will blind you to everything else. You can see no interest but your own. The laborer is not known or regarded as a man who has any interests you are bound to regard. You see him only as your slave, your tool, your means of adding to your wealth. In this light he is a friend so far as he serves you, an enemy so far as he does not. But change your point of view. Put yourself in his place; put him in your place. How would you like to have him treat you if you were in his place? Perhaps you have been there. In all probability you have, for the capitalist today was the laborer yesterday, and the laborer today will be the employer tomorrow. You know from lively and painful experience how you would like to be treated. Would you like to be regarded as a mere tool? As a means of enriching another? Would you like to have your wages kept down to the bare necessities of life? Would you like to be regarded with indifference and treated with brutality? Would you like to have your blood, your strength, your soul coined into dollars for the benefit of another? These questions are easy to answer. Everyone knows that he would rejoice to be treated kindly, to have his interests regarded, his rights recognized and protected. Everyone knows that such regard awakens a response in his own heart. Kindness begets kindness; respect awakens respect. Put yourself in his place. Imagine that you are dealing with yourself, and you will have no difficulty in deciding whether you should give the screw another turn, that you may wring a penny more from the muscles of the worker, or relax its pressure, and, if possible, add something to his wages, and give him respect for his service. Do to him as you would have him do to you in changed conditions.

"You are a laborer. You receive a certain sum for a day's work. Put yourself in the place of your employer. How would you like to have the men you employed work for you? Would you think it right that they should regard you as their enemy? Would you think it honest in them to slight their work, *to do as little and to get as much as possible?* If you had a large contract which must be completed at a fixed time or you would suffer great loss, would you like to have your workmen take advantage of your necessity to compel an increase of their wages? Would you think it right and wise in them to interfere with you in the management of your business? To dictate whom you should employ, and on what terms you should employ them? Would you not rather have them do honest work in a kind and good spirit? Would you not be much more disposed to look to their interests, to lighten their labor, to increase their wages when you could afford to do so, and look after the welfare of their families, when you found that they regarded yours? I know that it would be so. It is true that men are selfish, and that some men are so mean and contracted in spirit that they cannot see any interest but their own; whose hearts, not made of flesh but of silver and gold, are so hard that they are not touched by any human feeling, and care not how much others suffer if they can make a cent by it. But they are the exception, not the rule. We are influenced by the regard and devotion of others to our interests. The laborer who knows that his employer feels kindly toward him, desires to treat him justly and to regard his good, will do better work and more of it, and will be disposed to look to his employer's interests as well as his own.

"I am well aware that many will think this Divine and humane law of doing to others as we would have them do to us, is impracticable in this selfish and worldly age. If both parties would be governed by it, everyone can see how happy would be the results. But, it will be said, they will not. The laborer will not work unless compelled by want. He will take advantage of every necessity. As soon as he gains a little independence of his employer he becomes proud, arrogant and hostile. The employer will seize upon every means to keep the workmen dependent upon him, and to make as much out of them as possible. Every inch of ground which labor yields capital will occupy and intrench itself in it, and from its vantage bring the laborer into greater dependence and more abject submission. But this is a mistake. The history of the world testifies that when the minds of men are not embittered by intense hostility and their feelings outraged by cruel wrongs, they are ready to listen to calm, disinterested and judicious counsel. A man who employed a large number of laborers in mining coal told me that he had never known an instance to fail of a calm and candid response when he had appealed to honorable motives, as a man to man, both of whom acknowledged a common humanity. There is a recent and most notable instance in this city of the happy effect of calm, disinterested and judicious counsel in settling difficulties between employers and workmen that were disastrous to both.

"When the mind is inflamed by passion men will not listen to reason. They become blind to their own interests and regardless of the interests of others. *Difficulties are never settled while passion rages. They are never settled by conflict. One party may be subdued by power; but the sense of wrong will remain; the fire of passion will slumber ready to break out again on the first occasion.* But let the laborer or the capitalist feel assured that the other party has no wish to take any advantage, that there is a sincere desire and determination on both sides to be just and pay due regard to their common interests, and all the conflict between them would cease, as the wild waves of the ocean sink to calm when the winds are at rest. The laborer and the capitalist have a mutual and common interest. Neither can permanently prosper without the prosperity of the other. They are parts of one body. If labor is the arm, capital is the blood. Devitalize or waste the blood, and the arm loses its power. Destroy the arm, and the blood is useless. Let each care for the other, and both are benefited. *Let each take the Golden Rule as a guide,* and all cause of hostility will be removed, all conflict will cease, and they will go hand in hand to do their work and reap their just reward."

If you have mastered the fundamentals upon which this lesson is based, you understand why it is that no public speaker can move his audience or convince men of his argument unless he, himself, believes that which he is saying.

You also understand why no salesman can convince his prospective purchaser unless he has first convinced himself of the merits of his goods.

Throughout this entire course one particular principle has been emphasized for the purpose of illustrating the truth that every personality is the sum total of the individual's *thoughts* and *acts*—that we come to resemble the nature of our dominating *thoughts*.

Thought is the only power that can systematically organize, accumulate and assemble facts and materials according to a definite plan. A flowing river can assemble dirt and build land, and a storm can gather and assemble sticks into a shapeless mass of debris, but neither storms nor river can *think;* therefore, the materials which they assemble are not assembled in organized, definite form.

Man, alone, has the power to transform his *thoughts* into physical reality; man, alone, can dream and make his dreams come true.

Man has the power to create ideals and rise to their attainment.

How did it happen that man is the only creature on earth that knows how to use the power of *thought?* It "happened" because man is the apex of the pyramid of evolution, the product of millions of years of struggle during which man has risen above the other creatures of the earth *as the result of his own thoughts and their effects upon himself.*

Just when, where and how the first rays of *thought* began to flow into man's brain no one knows, but we all know that *thought* is the power which distinguishes man from all other creatures; likewise, we all know that *thought* is the power that has enabled man to lift himself above all other creatures.

No one knows the limitations of the power of *thought,* or whether or not it has any limitations. Whatever man *believes* he can do he eventually does. But a few generations back the more imaginative writers dared to write of the "horseless carriage," and lo! it became a reality and is now a common vehicle. Through the evolutionary power of *thought* the hopes and ambitions of one generation become a reality in the next.

The power of *thought* has been given the dominating position throughout this course, for the reason that it belongs in that position. Man's dominating position in the world is the direct result of *thought,* and it must be this power that you, as an individual, will use in the attainment of *success,* no matter what may be your idea of what represents *success.*

You have now arrived at the point at which you should take inventory of yourself for the purpose of ascertaining what qualities you need to give you a well balanced and rounded out personality.

Fifteen major factors entered into the building of this course. Analyze yourself carefully, with the assistance of one or more other persons if you feel that you need it, for the purpose of ascertaining in which of the fifteen factors of this course you are the weakest, and then concentrate your efforts upon those particular lessons until you have fully developed those factors which they represent.

INDECISION

An After-the-Lesson Visit with the Author

TIME!

Procrastination robs you of opportunity. It is a significant fact that no great leader was ever known to procrastinate. You are fortunate if AMBITION drives you into action, never permitting you to falter or turn back, once you have rendered a DECISION to go forward. Second by second, as the clock ticks off the distance TIME is running a race with YOU. Delay means defeat, because no man may ever make up a second of lost TIME. TIME is a master worker which heals the wounds of failure and disappointment and rights all wrongs and turns all mistakes into capital, but, it favors only those who kill off procrastination and remain in ACTION when decisions are to made.

Life is a great checker-board. The player opposite you is TIME.

If you hesitate you will be wiped off the board. If you keep moving you may win. The only real capital is TIME, but it is capital only when used.

You may be shocked if you keep accurate account of the TIME you waste in a single day. Take a look at the picture above if you wish to know the fate of all who play carelessly with TIME.

The picture at top of this page tells a true story of one of the chief causes of FAILURE! One of the players is "TIME" and the other is Mr. Average Man; let us call him YOU.

Move by move Time has wiped off Mr. Average Man's men until he is finally cornered, where Time will get him, no matter which way he moves. INDECISION has driven him into the corner.

Ask any well informed salesman and he will tell you that indecision is the outstanding weakness of the majority of people. Every salesman is familiar with that time-worn alibi, "I will think it over," which is the last trench-line of defense of those who have not the courage to say either yes or no. Like the player in the picture on the previous page, they cannot decide which way to move. Meanwhile, Time forces them into a corner where they can't move.

The great leaders of the world were men and women of quick decision.

General Grant had but little to commend him as an able General except the quality of firm decision, but this was sufficient to offset all of his weaknesses. The whole story of his military success may be gathered from his reply to his critics when he said "We will fight it out along these lines if it takes all summer."

When Napoleon reached a decision to move his armies in a given direction, he permitted nothing to cause him to change that decision. If his line of march brought his soldiers to a ditch, dug by his opponents to stop him, he would give the order to charge the ditch until it had been filled with dead men and horses sufficient to bridge it.

The suspense of indecision drives millions of people to failure. A condemned man once said that the thought of his approaching execution was not so terrifying, once he had reached the decision in his own mind to accept the inevitable.

Lack of decision is the chief stumbling block of all revival meeting workers. Their entire work is to get men and women to reach a decision in their own minds to accept a given religious tenet. Billy Sunday once said, "Indecision is the devil's favorite tool."

Andrew Carnegie visualized a great steel industry, but that industry would not be what it is today had he not reached a decision in his own mind to transform his vision into reality.

James J. Hill saw, in his mind's eye, a great transcontinental railway system, but that railroad never would have become a reality had he not reached a decision to start the project.

Imagination, alone, is not enough to insure success.

Millions of people have imagination and build plans that would easily bring them both fame and fortune, but those plans never reach the DECISION stage.

Samuel Insul was an ordinary stenographer, in the employ of Thomas A. Edison. Through the aid of his imagination he saw the great commercial possibilities of electricity. But, he did more than see the possibilities—he reached a decision to transform the mere possibilities into realities, and today he is a multimillionaire electric light plant operator.

Demosthenes was a poor Greek lad who had a strong desire to be a great public speaker. Nothing unusual about that; others have "desired" this and similar ability without living to see their desires realized. But, Demosthenes added DECISION to DESIRE, and, despite the fact that he was a stammerer he mastered this handicap and made himself one of the great orators of the world.

Martin W. Littleton was a poor lad who never saw the inside of a school house until he was past twelve years of age. His father took him to hear a great lawyer defend a murderer, in one of the southern cities. The speech made such a profound impression on the lad's mind that he grabbed his father by the hand and said, "Father, one of these days I am going to become the ablest lawyer in America."

That was a DEFINITE DECISION!

Today Martin W. Littleton accepts no fee under $50,000.00, and it is said that he is kept busy all the time. He became an able lawyer because he reached a DECISION to do so.

Edwin C. Barnes reached a DECISION in his own mind to become the partner of Thomas A. Edison. Handicapped by lack of schooling, without money to pay his railroad fare, and with no influential friends to introduce him to Mr. Edison, young Barnes made his way to East Orange on a freight car and so thoroughly sold himself to Mr. Edison that he got his opportunity which led to a partnership. Today, just twenty years since that decision was reached, Mr. Barnes lives at Bradenton, Florida, retired, with all the money he needs.

Men of decision usually get all that they go after!

Well within the memory of this writer a little group of men met at Westerville, Ohio, and organized what they called the Anti-Saloon League. Saloon men treated them as a joke. People, generally, made fun of them. But, they had reached a decision.

That decision was so pronounced that it finally drove the powerful saloon men into the corner.

William Wrigley, Jr., reached a decision to devote his entire business career to the manufacture and sale of a five-cent package of chewing gum. He has made that decision bring him financial returns running into millions of dollars a year.

Henry Ford reached a decision to manufacture and sell a popular priced automobile that would be within the means of all who wished to own it. That decision has made Ford the most powerful man on earth and brought travel opportunity to millions of people.

All these men had two outstanding qualities: A DEFINITE PURPOSE and a firm DECISION to transform that purpose into reality.

The man of DECISION gets that which he goes after, no matter how long it takes, or how difficult the task. An able salesman wanted to meet a Cleveland banker. The banker would not see him. One morning this salesman waited near the banker's house until he saw him get into his automobile and start down town. Watching his opportunity, the salesman drove his own automobile into the banker's, causing slight damage to the automobile. Alighting from his own car, he handed the banker his card, expressed regret on account of the damage done, but promised the banker a new car exactly like the one that had been damaged. That afternoon a new car was delivered to the banker, and out of that transaction grew a friendship that terminated, finally, in a business partnership which still exists.

The man of DECISION cannot be stopped!

The man of INDECISION cannot be started! Take your own choice.

> Behind him lay the gray Azores,
> Behind the Gates of Hercules;
> Before him not the ghosts of shores;
> Before him only shoreless seas.
> The good mate said: "Now must we pray,
> For lo! the very stars are gone.
> Brave Adm'r'l, speak; what shall I say?"
> "Why, say: 'Sail on and on!'"

When Columbus began his famous voyage he made one of the most far-reaching DECISIONS in the history of mankind. Had he not remained firm on that decision the freedom of America, as we know it today, would never have been known.

Take notice of those about you and observe this significant fact—THAT THE SUC-CESSFUL MEN AND WOMEN ARE THOSE WHO REACH DECISIONS

QUICKLY AND THEN STAND FIRMLY BY THOSE DECISIONS AFTER THEY ARE MADE.

If you are one of those who make up their minds today and change them again tomorrow you are doomed to failure. If you are not sure which way to move it is better to shut your eyes and move in the dark than to remain still and make no move at all.

The world will forgive you if you make mistakes, but it will never forgive you if you make no DECISIONS, because it will never hear of you outside of the community in which you live.

No matter who you are or what may be your lifework, you are playing checkers with TIME! It is always your next move. Move with quick DECISION and Time will favor you. Stand still and Time will wipe you off the board.

You cannot always make the right move, but, if you make enough moves you may take advantage of the law of averages and pile up a creditable score before the great game of LIFE is ended.

INDEX

ABOUT THE AUTHOR

Napoleon Hill was born in 1883 in Wise County, Virginia. He worked as a secretary, a "mountain reporter" for a local newspaper, the manager of a coal mine and a lumber yard, and attended law school, before he began working as a journalist for *Bob Taylor's Magazine*—a job that led to his meeting steel magnate Andrew Carnegie, which changed the course of his life. Carnegie believed success could be distilled into principles that any person could follow, and urged Hill to interview the greatest industrialists of the era in order to discover these principles. Hill took on the challenge, which lasted twenty years and formed the building block for *Think and Grow Rich*. This wealth-building classic and all-time bestseller of its kind has sold more than 15 million copies worldwide. Hill devoted the remainder of his life to discovering and refining the principles of success. After a long and rich career as an author, magazine publisher, lecturer, and consultant to business leaders, the motivational pioneer died in 1970 in South Carolina.

Look for these favorites from

TARCHER SUCCESS CLASSICS

The Prosperity Bible
featuring classics by Napoleon Hill, Benjamin Franklin,
Wallace D. Wattles, Florence Scovel Schinn, and others
978-1-58542-614-0

Think and Grow Rich
Revised and Updated for the 21st Century
by Napoleon Hill
978-1-58542-433-7

Think and Grow Rich Deluxe Edition
by Napoleon Hill
978-1-58542-659-1

Your Magic Power to Be Rich!
by Napoleon Hill
978-1-58542-555-6

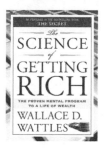

The Science of Getting Rich
by Wallace D. Wattles
978-1-58542-601-0

The Master Key System
by Charles F. Hannel
978-1-58542-627-0

The Secret of the Ages
by Robert Collier
978-1-58542-629-4

In Tune with the Infinite
by Ralph Waldo Trine
978-1-58542-663-8

Acres of Diamonds
by Russell H. Conwell
978-1-58542-690-4

A Message to Garcia and Other Classic Success Writings
by Elbert Hubbard
978-1-58542-691-1

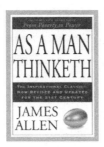

As a Man Thinketh
Revised and Updated for the 21st Century
by James Allen
978-1-58542-638-6

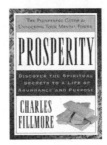

Prosperity
by Charles Fillmore
978-1-58542-674-4

TARCHER
PENGUIN

www.penguin.com